AFTERLIVES OF LETTERS

Studies of the Weatherhead East Asian Institute, Columbia University

STUDIES OF THE WEATHERHEAD EAST ASIAN INSTITUTE,
COLUMBIA UNIVERSITY

The Studies of the Weatherhead East Asian Institute of Columbia University were inaugurated in 1962 to bring to a wider public the results of significant new research on modern and contemporary East Asia.

For a list of books in the series, see page 413.

Afterlives of Letters

The Transnational Origins of Modern Literature in China, Japan, and Korea

Satoru Hashimoto

Columbia University Press   New York

Columbia University Press wishes to express its appreciation for assistance given by the Chiang Ching-kuo Foundation for International Scholarly Exchange and Council for Cultural Affairs in the publication of this book.

Columbia University Press
Publishers Since 1893
New York   Chichester, West Sussex
cup.columbia.edu
Copyright © 2023 Columbia University Press
All rights reserved

Library of Congress Cataloging-in-Publication Data
Names: Hashimoto, Satoru, 1980– author.
Title: Afterlives of letters : the transnational origins of modern literature in China, Japan, and Korea / Satoru Hashimoto.
Description: New York : Columbia University Press, [2023] | Series: Studies of the Weatherhead East Asian Institute, Columbia University | Includes bibliographical references and index.
Identifiers: LCCN 2023006776 (print) | LCCN 2023006777 (ebook) | ISBN 9780231211529 (hardback) | ISBN 9780231211536 (trade paperback) | ISBN 9780231558952 (ebook)
Subjects: LCSH: East Asian literature—19th century—History and criticism. | East Asian literature—20th century—History and criticism. | LCGFT: Literary criticism.
Classification: LCC PL493 .H37 2023 (print) | LCC PL493 (ebook) | DDC 895.09—dc23/eng/20230425
LC record available at https://lccn.loc.gov/2023006776
LC ebook record available at https://lccn.loc.gov/2023006777

Cover image: © Shutterstock

To my friends, past and present

Contents

Acknowledgments ix
Conventions xiii

Introduction 1

PART ONE A Multilayered Contact Space in Turn-of-the-Century East Asia 23

CHAPTER ONE
Literature's Search for Itself: Liang Qichao and Meiji Political Fiction 37

CHAPTER TWO
Literature and Life in Exile: Sin Ch'aeho's Engagement with Liang Qichao's Work 69

PART TWO Reforming Language and Redefining "Literature" 99

CHAPTER THREE
Parody and Repetition: Rereading the Works of Lu Xun, Mori Ōgai, and Yi Kwangsu 111

CHAPTER FOUR
History as Rewriting: The Historical Fiction of Lu Xun,
Mori Ōgai, and Yi Kwangsu   162

PART THREE Japan's Imperial Mimicry and Its Critique   197

CHAPTER FIVE
Archaeology of Resistance: Zhou Zuoren's Cultural Criticism
in Wartime East Asia   209

CHAPTER SIX
Transnational Allegory: Intertextualizing Lu Xun in Late
Colonial Korean, Taiwanese, and Manchukuo Literatures   238

Conclusion   284

Notes   291
Bibliography   347
Index   383

Acknowledgments

This book is a product of a journey that has spanned more than a decade and a half, meandered through East Asia, North America, and Europe, straddled multiple boundaries between nations, languages, and ideologies, and kept transforming my world. Along this journey, identical words assumed disparate resonances, idioms revealed unfathomable depths of connotation, and what can be said in one place turned out to have little chance to be said in another—to the point that at times I almost lost my way. But I have been enormously fortunate on the way to have met friends, teachers, and colleagues who have shared with me their unflagging passion for tackling complex questions of human culture, carved out spaces for intellectual freedom against all odds, and helped me make sense of this world. I am grateful for their support and encouragement, without which this book would not have been born.

My gratitude goes to David Wang. The high bar he sets for scholarly rigor and breadth and the unrelenting moral support he has given me over the years are inspirations and encouragements to which this book owes its existence. I am thankful for Karen Thornber. It is her work and championship of scholarly diversity that have enabled this book to have its comparative scope. I thank David Damrosch for the many hours of conversation I had with him, which have helped shape the methodology in this book. I am indebted to Leo Lee. This book stands on the ground he broke with his trailblazing spirit of intellectual creativity and capaciousness. I am grateful for Takahiro Nakajima. His work on Chinese philosophy is an *origin* of this project in the exact sense of the term that it explores.

I thank my colleagues Leo Lisi, Paola Marrati, Yi-Ping Ong, and Lisa Siraganian in the Department of Comparative Thought and Literature at Johns Hopkins University for their support and encouragement of this project. At the University of Maryland, College Park, I was fortunate to have such supportive colleagues as Mercédès Baillargeon, Lauretta Clough, Fatemeh Keshavarz, Michele Mason, Bob Ramsey, Andy Schonebaum, Lindsay Yotsukura, and Minglang Zhou. My postdoc year at the University of Chicago had an enriching impact on this work thanks to my conversations with Michael Bourdaghs, Kyeong-Hee Choi, and Ashton Lazarus. Research for this book was made possible by the financial support of the Chiang Ching-kuo Foundation, the College of Arts and Sciences at the University of Maryland (College Park), Academia Sinica, and the Fulbright Program, as well as, at Harvard University, the Graduate School of Arts and Sciences, the Fairbank Center for Chinese Studies, the Reischauer Institute for Japanese Studies, the Asia Center, and the Harvard-Yenching Institute.

The publication of this book is supported by the Helen Tartar First Book Subvention Award of the American Comparative Literature Association.

Many colleagues have offered me opportunities to present on various portions of this project, provided invaluable feedback, guided me to relevant sources, and given me inspirations that helped form my thinking. I would like to thank especially Young-Seo Baik, Richard Calichman, Kang-i Sun Chang, Wen-Hsun Chang, Jingling Chen, Letty Chen, Yu-yu Cheng, Lik-kwan Cheung, Pang-yuan Chi, Kuei-fen Chiu, Bunkun Chou, Tarryn Li-Min Chun, Wendong Cui, Wiebke Denecke, Will Fleming, Josh Fogel, Inhye Han, Will Hedberg, Xiang He, Siao-chen Hu, Ying-che Huang, Ted Huters, Hoduk Hwang, Misato Ido, Myŏngsin Im, Masato Ishida, Tsuyoshi Ishii, Qingming Ke, Hang Kim, John Kim, Faye Kleeman, Chia Cian Ko, Yasuo Kobayashi, Wook-Yon Lee, Jie Li, Wenching Li, Shaoyang Lin, Olga Lomová, Chun-yu Lu, Xiaolu Ma, Adhira Mangalagiri, Mark McConaghy, Tobie Meyer-Fong, Yasushi Ōki, Shaw-Yu Pan, Hsiao-yen Peng, Michael Puett, Marta Puxan, Ying Qian, Andy

Rodekohr, Carlos Rojas, Haun Saussy, Shuang Shen, Mi-Ryong Shim, Masahisa Suzuki, Yasunari Takada, Xiaofei Tian, Jing Tsu, Atsuko Ueda, Tadashi Uchino, Sebastian Veg, Ban Wang, Pu Wang, Lindsay Waters, Lawrence Wang-chi Wong, Miya Qiong Xie, Noriyasu Yamashita, Longxi Zhang, and Xudong Zhang. It has been a great pleasure to work with my editor, Christine Dunbar, and the staff of Columbia University Press, as well as Ariana King at the Weatherhead East Asian Institute, on the production of this book. I also thank the anonymous reviewers who provided helpful comments on the manuscript.

For their kindness and support, I thank my late father, Shu Hashimoto, and my mother, Setsuko Hashimoto. I was fortunate that I could show my father at least the stack of manuscript pages that have become this book before he passed away last year. My children Sophia and Sage have always kept shaking up my biases—a real source of critical thinking on which my intellectual life depends. And finally, to my friend and wife, Yunju Eum, thank you. The debt I owe you is simply beyond measure.

Portions of chapter 1 appeared in Satoru Hashimoto, "Civilization in Transformation: Liang Qichao's Theory and Practice of Translation, 1890s–1920s," in *Translation and Modernization in East Asia in the Nineteenth and Early Twentieth Centuries*, ed. Lawrence Wang-Chi Wong (Hong Kong: The Chinese University of Hong Kong Press, 2018). An earlier version of the section on Yi Kwangsu in chapter 3 appeared, in Japanese, in Satoru Hashimoto, "Kindaisei to 'jō' no seijigaku: I Gwansu *Mujō* ni okeru chōsō no jikansei," in *Tōyō bunka kenkyūjo kiyō* 170 (2016). Portions of the section on Lu Xun in chapter 4 appeared in "World of Letters: Lu Xun, Benjamin, and *Daodejing*," *Journal of World Literature* 1, no. 1 (2016). Material in the sections on Kim Saryang and Long Yingzong in chapter 6 appeared, in Chinese, in "Kuazu yuyan: Jin Shiliang, Long Yingzong zhimin houqi chuangzuo yu Lu Xun zuopin de huwenxing tansuo," *Wenxue* 2 (2014). These early writings have been revised and reprinted with permission.

Conventions

Chinese words are transliterated in *hanyu pinyin,* Japanese words in the Hepburn system, and Korean words in a modified McCune-Reischauer system.

For the sake of consistency, I adopt the standardized *fanti* script for Chinese characters in Chinese words. *Hangul* is used for Korean proper nouns, with the exception of words for which the context calls for *hanja* transcription. The same Chinese characters can take different forms depending on linguistic, periodical, and other cultural contexts. I use forms that are appropriate for the contexts in question, but for the purpose of simplicity, I adopt the standardized *fanti* script in occasional cases where the same word is discussed across multiple contexts (such as "文學" as it appears in Chinese, Japanese, and Korean).

AFTERLIVES OF LETTERS

Introduction

THE ANACHRONISM OF MODERN LITERATURE

In 1925, Lu Xun 鲁迅 (1881–1936), arguably the most important founding figure of modern Chinese literature, wrote a prose poem titled "Si hou 死後" (After Death).[1] The speaker of the poem finds himself dead by the roadside in a dream and realizes that his worst fear about death has come true: his motor nerves have been destroyed, but his perception still works. He hears a crowd gathering and chatting around his corpse and becomes curious about what they have to say, despite his lifetime policy of ignoring criticism from others. His skin itches as an ant crawls along his spine and flies land on his face, licking his nose and lips as if "looking for material to argue about." He almost passes out from anger when he hears the flies leaving with the comment: "What a pity!" After a while, someone arrives with a police officer, puts a straw mat over his body, and nails it into a coffin, making him realize that he is "a complete failure." He then says to himself, "Unfortunately, I have long had no pen and paper; even if I had, I could not write; and even if I wrote, I could not find a place to publish it. So I can only let it go." While still irritated by a creased corner of his shirt sticking into his back, the speaker finally begins to feel calmer in the coffin and consoles himself that he will get used to it or perish before long. As he tries to meditate quietly, however, a voice suddenly greets him: "Hello, are you dead?" The familiar voice, he remembers, belongs to the messenger boy of an antiquarian bookshop whom he has not seen for more than two decades. To the embarrassed speaker, the boy nonchalantly announces the delivery of a vintage Jiajing-period black-edged edition of the Ming-dynasty print of the Gongyang commentary on the *Spring and Autumn Annals*. The speaker is upset at the absurdity of having to deal with something like a Ming-dynasty print in his situation and tries to calm himself by shutting his eyes, letting the boy disappear. He feels in the end as if tears were welling up in his eyes amid the pleasure of dying "like a shadow," without satisfying the hopes of either his friends or enemies. "But no tears came after all. Only did I see as if a flash sparked before my eyes. At that point, I sat up."[2] So the poem ends.

Afterlives of Letters is a study of how literature in its modern, aesthetic sense emerged in late nineteenth- and early twentieth-century China, Japan, and Korea in a transregional cultural context. I begin my inquiry with this eerie prose poem because of its ironic perspective, which reveals a fundamental anachronism inherent in the genre of modern literature. This book argues that modern literature came into being in East Asia through writerly attempts at reconstructing the present's historical relationship to the past across the radical cultural transformations caused by modernization. My argument elucidates writers' anachronistic engagement with the classical cultures that are being made obsolete by modernization, rather than their progressive departure from them, as a hitherto underexplored textual dynamic integral to the beginnings of modern literature in the region, thereby seeking to renew our understanding of modern East Asian literatures.

In "After Death," Lu Xun revisits in a dream narrative the theme of the "loner" and the "crowd" that underlies many of his works.[3] An embodiment of the spirit of modernity, the loner is the one awake to the present reality in the "iron house" of old culture in which the crowd remains dormant and is about to suffocate; he dares to write and publish his works in order to wake a few shallow sleepers even at the cost of their painless deaths from suffocation, in the hope of breaking down the ailing culture to start a novel construction.[4] The young Lu Xun had encapsulated this fighting spirit in the voice of Zarathustra in the epigraph to his seminal essay "Moluo shili shuo 摩羅詩力說" (On the Power of Mara Poetry, 1907):

求古源盡者將求方來之泉，將求新源。嗟我昆弟，新生之作，新泉之湧於淵深，其非遠矣。

Whoever has become wise about ancient origins will surely, in the end, seek new wells of the future and new origins [*neuen Ursprüngen*].

Yes my brothers, it will not be overly long and *new peoples* will originate and new wells will roar down into new depths.[5]

The old wells of Chinese culture have dried up, but the supine people do not raise their voices. In this essay, Lu Xun envisions the advent of a new literature in China by taking examples of poets of resistance from a broader world—from Byron, the "Satanic" poet whose self-sacrificial devotion to the Greek War of Independence he particularly admired, to Shelley, Pushkin, Adam Mickiewicz of Poland, and Sándor Petőfi of Hungary. He demands that a hero-poet emerge in China on their heels to smash the "desolation" of a falling culture and single-handedly wake the people up to the world's present exigencies with the power of his "voice of the heart" (*xinsheng* 心聲).[6] This sublime, history-making figure epitomizes the Nietzschean desire to break away from the past to take present action: "As he who acts is . . . always without a conscience, so is he also always without knowledge; he forgets most things so as to do one thing, he is unjust towards what lies behind him, and he recognizes the rights only of that which is now to come into being and no other rights whatever."[7] The modern writer will forget what came before him, no matter how "unjust" it may be; he does so for the sole sake of "that which is now to come into being," in search of "new wells of the future and new origins," and, ultimately, the birth of "new peoples."

But in "After Death," the loner is dead. With his motor nerves defunct, he can no longer act or write; his helpless corpse is at the mercy of the crowd's gossiping and opining, symbolized by the flies' nosy hunt for "material to argue about." It is stowed away in a crude coffin, irritated by crawling ants and a creased shirt without a proper place to rest; no tomb is erected to commemorate his legacy, leaving it to the stubborn normalcy gatekept by the police. He can only say to himself, "Unfortunately, I have long had no pen and paper; even if I had, I could not write; and even if I wrote, I could not find a place to publish it." He can "only let it go." The precarious remaining of the loner's body can be read as a metaphor for the fate of his works, speaking to the problematic of writing in general, which Derrida famously characterized as "the carrier of death," in the sense that it indicates the absence of a live speaker.[8] Just as the loner is estranged from his dead body, so too does he lack control over how his writing is received, read, or understood. The "remaining" of the text "is not drawn into any circular trajectory, any proper trajectory between its beginning [*origine*] and its end."[9] The Nietzschean chasing of newness compounds the insecurity of the circulation and signification of writing, for it defies the established "literature" that tames such uncertainty to demarcate a proper trajectory of textual dissemination.

Modern literature, by virtue of its very newness, intensifies the text's intrinsic inability to determine its course of circulation and thus fails to provide itself with a well-defined realm of existence. "After Death" illustrates this irony with the uncanny image of the abrupt delivery of an antique book into the speaker's coffin. Conjured up is a palimpsestic literary past going back centuries, which constitutes the "worldliness" of the delivered text.[10] *The Spring and Autumn Annals*, or the *Chunqiu* 春秋, the chronicle of the ancient state of Lu covering the years from 722 to 481 BCE, became one of the five classics in the Confucian canon in the Western Han dynasty (202 BCE–8 CE) and produced three schools of commentary. The Gongyang school lost its authority and became obsolete amid the polemics between the old-text and new-text Confucians in the Eastern Han dynasty (25–220 CE), but through the bustling print culture in the Jiajing period (1522–1566) of the Ming dynasty (1368–1644), its commentary made it to the eighteenth century, when it was reinvigorated by the Changzhou school of thought, laying the groundwork for its late Qing revival as an intellectual foundation of the Hundred Days' Reform, the failed court-initiated modernization measures spearheaded by Kang Youwei 康有為 (1858–1927) in 1898.[11] This textual provenance culminates in a copy that ended up in a Republican-era secondhand bookshop. But has modern writing not rendered this sort of literary past outdated? Has it not created a novel literary domain safe from puzzling returns of such a past?[12]

"After Death" allegorizes the insecurity of anachronism that inheres in the origin of modern literature, where the creation of newness in the present is always already threatened by the returning past. What haunts the present is not a past "invented" as a tradition to serve the modern or revived as an accepted modern literary form or taste, but a past that is being made defunct by modernization, becoming so incommensurable with the present that the latter has difficulty reckoning with it.[13] Just as the speaker's corpse is irritated by the ants, flies, and creased shirt in the coffin, so is modern literature disturbed by the past that comes back to infiltrate its desired proper domain. The speaker's "failure" does not bespeak a state of lack relative to a complete model but a structural condition of modern literature that is inextricable from the lingering afterlives of past cultures. *Afterlives of Letters* attends to this anachronistic structure and examines writerly practices of reconstituting the present's relationship to the past, which had become bafflingly confused because of modernity's incessant search for newness, as a dynamic essential to the emergence of modern literature in East Asia.

RUPTURE, CONTINUITY, AND ANACHRONISM

Scholars have avidly tried to determine the origins of modern literature in East Asia. Their discussions, as if to mirror the ambivalence of the term "origin" itself, have predominantly been concerned with a twofold task. On the one hand, they have attempted to identify and characterize works, authors, journals, media, or movements that embody literary modernity and thus grasp the rupture they created from previous literatures. Assuming such a rupture, they have sought on the other hand to establish some historical continuity that would have existed between premodern and modern.

The former approach considers modern literature in an overall framework of modernization that the region underwent beginning in the nineteenth century. It often focuses on the diverse processes of the birth of "national literature" along with "national language" as an institution of the nation state, whose establishment constituted a hallmark of East Asian modernization. The provenance of this approach rests in the discourses put forward by late nineteenth- to early twentieth-century writers and critics themselves in their attempts at demarcating a clear-cut domain for modern literature as distinct from past literatures. Like Lu Xun, many intellectuals deemed certain aspects of their cultural pasts to be outdated and thus to be overcome in order to embrace modern civilization and regarded modern literature to be an essential component of that process.[14] This discourse registers modern literature as a realm of modern culture delineated against the cultural past and continues to inform many of the histories, anthologies, and criticisms of the region's national literatures.[15]

This conception of origin has been formulated in an influential way in Karatani Kōjin's *Origins of Modern Japanese Literature*.[16] Karatani has singled out certain motifs, including "landscape," "interiority," and "the child," as the defining characteristics of modern literature and used them as criteria to distinguish it from literatures before, and attributed the new literature thus defined to a national literature. In terms of "origins," therefore, Karatani has articulated the emergence, at a certain point in history, of something that did not exist before in Japan and that can be defined by a set of concepts.[17]

The attempts at defining rupture have gone hand in hand with those at establishing continuity across it. The latter effort has been pursued particularly in the genre of nation-based "literary history," which began to be written almost contemporaneously with the emergence of modern literature in East Asia. It was at that time that literary histories covering broad genres from low to high were written; that China, Japan, and Korea as nations were considered to have such histories individually; and that their literatures were compared to those of other nations in the world.[18] Ultimately driven by the need to restore identity to a literature considered cut off from its past, those histories created narratives to put the nation's literature in a coherent historical perspective from ancient to modern times, turning the literary past into a national tradition construed as the nation's "public property" freed from appropriation by privileged elites.[19] To be sure, owing to the strained projection of a modern notion onto the past, national literary histories are burdened by the contrived relationships among the terms "national," "literary," and "history"; nevertheless, they continue to lay the dominant groundwork for writing complete histories capable of positioning modern literature vis-à-vis classical literature going back to antiquity.[20]

Whereas the ideas of rupture and continuity in a national context have shaped the usual understanding of the origin of modern literature in East Asia, *Afterlives of Letters* dwells on the contested boundaries between classical and modern cultures in a transregional context. It focuses on writers' engagement with the past against which modernity was conceived: a cultural past deemed outdated with respect to the values and norms of modern culture. It explores the relationship between the classical and the modern, which became so convoluted by the incessant pursuit of the exigencies of the here and now that a simple recovery of continuity could not resolve it—the tangled relationship in which, to refer to De Man's formulation, "modernity... appears as the horizon of a historical process that has to remain a gamble."[21] It then considers how modern literature emerged *between* classical and modern cultures, in anachronistic attempts at reconstructing the present's relationship with the cultural past. I characterize those attempts as "anachronistic" in contradistinction to the interplays of rupture and continuity, so as to indicate that they were out of place in the orthodox chronology of cultural modernization in which those interplays take place. As we will see later in this introduction, that cultural past was quintessentially attributed to the traditions of classical letters in East Asia that had developed through transregional cultural exchanges mediated especially by classical Chinese writing. *Afterlives of Letters* therefore examines the emergence of modern literature in China, Japan, and Korea through writers' engagement with this transregional cultural past and elucidates its origins—which are, *contra* Karatani, anachronistic and transnational at the same time.[22]

WHAT *IS* MODERN LITERATURE IN EAST ASIA?

The formation of modern literature in East Asia was prompted by the fundamental desire for severance from the past and affirmation of the here and now as the absolute topos for creativity. It radically destabilized the culturally accepted ideas of what could be taken seriously as literature and opened them up to redefinition, self-transformation, and even deconstruction. This led East Asian writers to look beyond the established cultural boundaries and grasp "literature" through examples gleaned from the world at large.[23]

The idea of literature as an open concept thus constituted through examples, rather than an institution whose function in society is culturally determined, can be traced back to Europe in the eighteenth century.[24] The modern concept of literature was then translated into East Asian languages as 文學 (Chn. *wenxue*; Jpn. *bungaku*; Kor. *munhak*) beginning in the mid–nineteenth century.²⁵ Conceptually, therefore, modern literature was introduced from the West into East Asia and took root as part of modern culture writ large, which was to be separated from past cultures where literature had meant something different. So understood, the "modern" of modern literature contrasts with the premodern or implies a rupture from the past. Modern literature can hence be conceptualized as a particular case in the totality of the global process of cultural modernization in which the region became engulfed in earnest in the nineteenth century. This conceptual-historical understanding tends to focus on the transculturations of Western literatures that claim authoritative positions in modern culture—or sometimes those of Japanese literature in the cases of China and Korea—in considering how modern literature came into being in the region. These approaches address important dynamics but only partially capture the conceptual openness of literature in its modern sense. This book illuminates the missing half of the picture: the afterlives of the cultural past that modernization renders out of date. Through this revisionary approach, it lays bare the origins of modern literature in their irreducible anachronism, so that it wrests modern literature from the cultural confines of modernization and does full justice to its semantic openness—an openness that is coterminous with the open horizons of the modern world.

My approach, which is underpinned by a methodological bracketing of the conceptual discourse of modern literature, is thus directly called for by the latter's open construct as a concept, or its intrinsic resistance to being grasped as a case in a given totality. "Literature" in its modern sense, or what I call "modern literature" in this book, is a branch of an *aesthetic* endeavor that includes other genres such as painting, sculpture, poetry, and music. That literature is an "aesthetic" endeavor means that the literariness of a text is determined by—here we can use Kant's terminology—the reflecting power of judgment; that is, whether a text is or is not literature is judged without a universal principle (or rule, law) given in advance. Instead, the judgment is made merely based on the particularities of the given text in such a way that the latter becomes an example of a universal principle yet to be found.²⁶ Characterizing literature in this modern aesthetic sense, Eagleton has claimed that "there is no 'essence' of literature whatsoever."²⁷ Frye has pointed out that such a principle is not found even in the object itself, as he has contended with regard to art in general: "Thus the question of whether a thing 'is' a work of art or not is one which cannot be settled by appealing to something in the nature of the thing itself."[28] Literariness thus cannot be reduced to a single semantic feature such as "lack of practical purpose" or "fictionality"; as Wellek has noted, "At least one result should emerge: a literary work of art is not a simple object but rather a highly complex organization of a stratified character with multiple meanings and relationships."[29] In fact, literature in this modern sense can be said to be independent of any external underpinning, as Foucault maintained in his oft-quoted articulation: "literature ... becomes merely a manifestation of a language which has no other law than that of affirming—in opposition to all other forms of discourse—its own precipitous existence."[30]

Modern East Asian intellectuals frequently grappled with the question: What is literature? And their eager ventures to define literature for the new era, which I will survey in the introduction to part II, themselves bespeak modern literature as a concept in the making. An iconic case is the Japanese writer Natsume Sōseki 夏目漱石 (1867–1916), who undertook to "fundamentally create, for myself, the concept of what literature is."[31] Convinced that "trying to understand what literature is by reading books of literature would be no different from washing blood with blood," Sōseki "shut away all books of literature deep in the trunk" and wrote what culminated in the monumental *Theory of Literature*, or *Bungaku ron* 文学論 (1907).[32] Yet he later called it "the corpse of a failure" and declared, "my *Theory of Literature* is ... something like the ruins of an unfinished urban district that was knocked down by an earthquake even before its construction was finished."[33] His perception of its intrinsic failure, as much as its content, makes this work a quintessential discourse of modern literature.

When a text is read as literature in its modern sense, there is no objectively delineated notion of what literature is behind that judgment. This conceptual openness gives literature its crucial critical function to "[allow] one to *say everything* [*tout dire*]" in potential defiance of the laws or prohibitions inherent in other forms of discourse, including the sanctioned institution or practice of "literature" itself.[34] This self-reflexive working of modern literature informs a chief thread of my discussion throughout this book that pertains to the politics of giving voice to those who lack a medium to represent themselves in the existing order of discourse. Absent an objective concept, judgment of what is and is not legitimately accepted as literature becomes dependent on the overall context.[35] "It is convention, social acceptance, and the work of criticism in the broadest sense that determines where it [an object, or a text] belongs," Frye has claimed.[36] In this sense, Cavell has contemplated aesthetic judgment as a function of ordinary language and argued that "what a work of art means cannot be *said*."[37] In modern literature, the social process of constructing a culture that takes some texts seriously as literature and excludes others coincides with a counter-process of criticizing, displacing, and replacing the already constructed realm of literature, driven by the imperative to "say everything." At the hinge of these dialectic movements is the practice of engaging with existing literature to engender a new mode of representation that puts the very meaning of literature at stake—a practice that I will repeatedly turn to in this study. This dialectic process is helpfully elucidated by Adorno's formulation: "The concept of art is located in a historically changing constellation of moments; it refuses definition.... The definition of what art is is always indicated by what it once was; but that definition is only legitimized by what art has become, and it is open to what it wants to, and perhaps can, become."[38] A work grapples with previous examples of literature only by self-reflexively exploring possible new forms of its manifestation in the present condition and testing the limits of what can be accepted as literature. Each time a work is created, it puts what counts as literature into question in the face of the sociopolitical reality. Modern literature as a medium thus engages deeply with the sociopolitical situation not because it is defined by an external historical process—such as that of "modernization" conceived of extraliterarily—but because it constitutes an intrinsic process of self-transformation ("a historically changing constellation of moments") driven by the exigencies of the present reality and free from the authority of extrinsic definitions. A work's newness, by altering the constellation, gives that constellation an afterlife. *Afterlives of Letters* explores how such moments of self-transformation emerged in East Asian works against the backdrop of the demand for modernization—moments that indicate the origins of modern literature.

WHY "EAST ASIA"?

To undertake this task, I adopt in this book a comparative method with a regional focus, primarily engaging modern and premodern Chinese-, Japanese-, and Korean-language materials. This approach is uniquely functional in shedding light on the tangled relationship between the cultural past and the modern works I examine. Late nineteenth- to early twentieth-century writers in China, Japan, and Korea sought to produce novel literature in the contexts where they had tacit knowledge, something like what Eliot called "historical sense,"[39] with regard to what was culturally accepted as literature, or what it was like to read and write refined letters. This literary culture or "habitus,"[40] to borrow from Bourdieu, was not completely divided by national boundaries, and many of its aspects were shared across nations. For it was the product of sedimented traditions that had accumulated through centuries of transregional cultural contacts.

Since Chinese script and writing circulated from the Central Plain to the Korean peninsula and to the Japanese archipelago, China had served as the "reference culture" in relation to which Korea and Japan developed their literatures in various forms of classical Chinese and their respective vernacular writings.[41] A major shift in this process that is particularly relevant to this study occurred with the popularization of vernacular fiction in the Ming and the Qing (1644–1911) dynasties in China. This new genre was quickly and avidly received in Korea and Japan and inspired writers in these countries to produce their own versions of vernacular fiction, adding an important layer to their literary traditions. The accumulations of these traditions formed literary cultures in late nineteenth- to early twentieth-century China, Japan, and Korea that were distinct yet echoed each other across the region.

Those transnationally interrelated cultures still exerted significant power before the hegemony shifted to nationalized modern cultures, and East Asian writers made those surviving cultures their main target in their incipient efforts to create fresh literature. In so doing, they identified the cultural past to overcome by attributing it especially to the tradition of classical Chinese letters, which had long served as the primary medium for the region's transnational cultural exchanges and symbolized the culture that had wielded the most power and distinction, and subsumed it under the progressivist discourse of modernization. This discursive operation enabled the writers to conceive of past literatures as that which modern literature was no longer, or that out of which literature was to evolve into a modern form commensurate with its Western counterparts. It firmly registered literature in an overall project of cultural modernization aimed at the creation of national culture, and thus prompted the discussions on a complete redefinition of literature.

This discourse is exemplified in the Korean writer Yi Kwangsu's 이광수 (1892–1950) essay "Munhak iran hao? 文學이란 何오?" (What Is Literature?). In this celebrated 1916 work of criticism, Yi first and foremost proclaims a redefinition of literature by virtue of translation; as he writes, "What is called *'munhak'* [文學] today signifies what the Westerners mean by it—that is, the term *'munhak'* is a translation of the Western term 'Literatur' or 'literature.' Therefore, the term *'munhak'* does not mean what people have long understood by it, but designates the *'munhak'* signified by the Western term."[42] This redefinition is bolstered by the affirmation of a general historical process in which "new Western culture is gradually intruding" on his nation. He suggests that "Koreans should bathe their whole bodies in this new civilization after casting off their old clothes and washing off their old dirt. With an emancipated spirit, then, they should embark on building a new spiritual civilization."[43] He then ascribes the "old clothes" and "old dirt" to be removed—the cultural past to be left behind—to the tradition of Korean culture that has developed through close contact with Chinese culture:

> Our ancestors, without hearts or guts, were so foolish that they became slaves of Chinese thought and eradicated their own culture. Having all grown up under the influence of Chinese morality and culture, today's Koreans are only Koreans in name and indeed are but a type of Chinese in substance. What a pity it is that they still revere Chinese script and writing [*hanja hanmun* 漢字漢文] and cannot extricate themselves from Chinese thought![44]

In this provocative contention, Korea's cultural past embedded in the transregional exchange of letters, symbolized quite bluntly by "Chinese script and writing," is designated as the opposite of the modern culture that it ought to build to achieve national independence, and modern literature is conceived of as an integral part of this program. To the extent that cultural modernization is politically urgent, literature is to be redefined completely, becoming "modern literature" as a distinct entity. So much so that Yi draws a striking conclusion: "To sum up, it should be said that Korean literature does not have a past but only has a future," and he envisions modern Korean literature as a creation on a *tabula rasa*: "From now on, many geniuses should appear and develop the trackless field of literature in Korea."[45]

The all-powerful discourse of cultural modernization, on which Yi draws heavily here, can be traced back most archetypically to the Japanese thinker Fukuzawa Yukichi's 福澤諭吉 (1835–1901) seminal treatise "Datsu a ron 脱亜論" (On Leaving Asia Behind, 1885) in the East Asian context.

> Though Japan finds its territories on the easternmost edge of Asia [*ajia* 亜細亜], the spirit of its nation has already broken away from the obstinacy of Asia and transitioned into the civilization of the West. Now, unfortunate are its two neighbors, one called China and the other Korea.... As Japan, China, and Korea face each other, China and Korea resemble one another more than Japan does these two, which do not know how to reform individuals or countries ... and cling to old ways and customs just as they have always done since hundreds and thousands of years ago. On this stage of action where civilization makes daily progress, they broach Confucianism on the matter of education and attribute the principles of school education to [the old Confucian virtues of] humanity, righteousness, ritual, and wisdom [*jin gi rei chi* 仁義禮智].[46]

The geopolitical distinction Fukuzawa postulates between Japan, on the one hand, and China and Korea, on the other, metaphorizes the periodical separation between the modern and the premodern. The latter terms, the backward Other of "civilization," are symbolized by Confucianism, a kernel of the tradition of Chinese letters, which since its introduction into Japan has formed a fecund and dynamic intellectual tradition in that country. Fukuzawa himself, whose father was a Sinologist, said he had been "educated entirely in Confucianism" in his youth.[47] Yet this cultural past is now ascribed to "Asia" and represented as stagnant and ahistorical. It is against this forged representation that Japan identifies its new self as a member of the Western-originated modern civilization and conceives of its progress as tantamount to "leaving Asia behind." This Orientalist notion of "Asia," underlying the self-other distinction—be it demarcated between or within nations—that structures the East Asian discourse of modernization, has political implications, just as it does in European Orientalism.[48] Indeed, Fukuzawa insisted that Japan, having broken with its "bad old friends," should "deal with China and Korea just as the Westerners do them," foreshadowing Japan's eventual imperialist foray into those countries.[49]

The discourse of cultural modernization, which I will further consider when outlining the processes of language reform later in the introduction to part II, is as much about demarcating the present as about representing the past. The cultural past that Yi and Fukuzawa targeted through this representation is exactly the kind of history that Hegel insisted should "remain buried in the obscurity of a voiceless past." Alluding to the findings of the historical linguistics of his time about the affinity between Sanskrit and the European languages, Hegel suggested that such intermediary, transregional cultural connections—surpassing national particularity yet falling short of world-historical universality—should "lie outside history proper [and] in fact preceded it."[50] It was by reducing transregional cultural interplays, among other things, to a silenced past that History was founded as a modern concept consisting of nations' self-conscious struggles for recognition on the world-historical stage. National history in this modern sense began to be written in East Asia in the late nineteenth to early twentieth centuries and constituted a discursive foundation for the "literary history" produced independently for each nation.[51]

Afterlives of Letters first and foremost tries to revisit modern literature at its origins in its sheer conceptual openness, and in order to do so, it methodologically brackets out the discourse of cultural modernization, which treats modern literature as a mere instance in its conceptual framework. This approach is made possible by the transregional comparative method in this book, which brings back to our reading of modern texts precisely the sort of cultural past that modernization relegates to something passé, ahistorical, or irrelevant against which the modern is to recognize itself. Revisited from this perspective, the works I will examine reveal textual moments at which they engage with the cultural past to engender a new mode of representation that interrogates the culturally demarcated realm of literature so as to convey voices that have eluded it. These moments allow me to offer a revisionary understanding of modern literature in East Asia as emerging from attempts at resolving rather than reinforcing the incommensurability between the past and the present, as resting *between* cultures seen as incompatible rather than registered in a particular (modern) culture. Modern literature came into being in the midst of the entangled relationships between the past that is unhistoricized and epistemologically irreducible to the modern on the one hand and the present that is inexplicable by the premodern episteme on the other.

Thus recovering the afterlives of the past as structurally constitutive of the modern, this study uncovers a regional structure of modern literature grounded on the *longue durée* of East Asian letters that has until now rarely been recognized. In this sense, it seeks to enter a dialogue, in the context of the West, with studies like Auerbach's and Curtius's magna opera and, outside the West, with research by scholars including Karen Thornber, Sheldon Pollock, and Ronit Ricci, to consider a midscale formation of world literature.[52] Like these predecessors *Afterlives of Letters* takes its transregional comparative method not as an affirmation of a regional identity in lieu of a national one but as a practice of critique, here meant especially to redeem the original forces of self-reflexive critique attributable to literature in modern times.

Afterlives of Letters thus explores an intersection of area studies and comparative literature. It provides a critique of the perception of area studies as confined to particularity, providing individual data in support of a disciplinary concept, theory, or idea of putative universal validity, typically devised based on cases from the West. It is long past time to leave behind this legacy notion, which is rooted in the historical provenance of area studies in the Cold War–era United States as a strategic program to design "curricula organized by area rather than by discipline."[53] *Afterlives of Letters* also seeks to expand the scope of comparative literature, which has for much of its history focused on relationships among Western literatures or on relationships between a non-Western national literature and Western literatures, while often regarding Asia as a space where commonalities are so general as to be undeserving of comparison.⁵⁴ This book makes the case that rigorous attention to relationships among non-Western literatures, particularly those written in non-Western languages, will contribute new insights to our understanding of literature and comparison at large. Hence, the longstanding philological prowess of area studies needs to advance historically grounded inquiries where it intersects with other disciplines such as comparative literature; as Jing Tsu has contended, "the once limiting, naturalizing linguistic mandate of area studies moves to center stage as a valuable source of pluralism . . . opening the way to a deeper historical engagement across a broad interdisciplinary base."⁵⁵ Like many modern values and institutions, "literature" in its modern sense is an open-ended, *universal* endeavor whose meaning is transformed by diverse examples emerging from distinct historical experiences. By probing how modern literatures originated within historically shaped literary cultures in East Asia, this book ultimately aspires to advance a collaborative movement toward "universalizing" our conception of modern literature and, based on it, a remapping of world literature.⁵⁶

OVERVIEW

The works I examine in this book constitute examples that display the emergence of literature in its modern sense in the shifting cross-cultural contexts where the present's relationship to the past was persistently called into question. Each of those examples provides and transforms the meaning of modern literature without possessing the authority to normalize it or the power to initiate a linear or teleological development of it. In what follows, I explore the diverse and interrelated manifestations of modern literature by contextualizing my textual analyses within three phases of the changing cultural circumstances of transregional East Asia in the late nineteenth to early twentieth centuries.

In part I, I examine works produced in the context of the region's shared literary cultures that gained renewed relevance amid the opening of modern international relations. An important corollary of this study resides in the reassessment of turn-of-the-century East Asian works that are often considered transitional, no longer "premodern" but not yet properly "modern," as forming quintessential origins of modern literature.

While palpably indebted to classical literatures, the works considered in part I display textual moments at which the culturally assigned function of literature is brought into question as they respond to the modern exigencies of representing the nation. Part I opens with a brief historical account of how turn-of-the-century literary cultures in China, Japan, and Korea began to interact with each other as communication and diplomacy were modernized and how those cultures, thanks especially to the shared classical Chinese writing and canons, informed transregional personal and textual exchanges, constituting a multilayered contact space where modern literature came into being.

Prominent cases of such textual exchanges were catalyzed by the Chinese reformist Liang Qichao's 梁啟超 (1873–1929) translational, editorial, and literary work. Chapter 1 focuses on the Chinese translation of a celebrated Japanese political novel in which Liang was involved, as well as Liang's own work of political fiction. Turn-of-the-century East Asian political novels exhibit a striking anachronism: they rely heavily on classical literature's affective function to convey moral values for the markedly modern purpose of telling a story of nation-building and eventually effecting political reforms. My analysis follows the course of this process to the point where it undergoes protracted suspension and reaches an anomic moment where the received function of literature proves bankrupt, prompting literature to interrogate the very cultural context in which it gains its virtue *as* literature.

Liang Qichao's writings were avidly read, translated, and adapted by Korean intellectuals in the first decade of the twentieth century. Among them was Sin Ch'aeho 신채호 (1880–1936), whose literary works are the focus of chapter 2. Best known as a pioneer of national history in Korea, Sin grappled with an aporia of East Asian modernity *par excellence*: he had to produce valuable writing—namely, Korean national history—by drawing on sources that owe their existence to obsolete cultural norms, which he deemed fraught with a Sinocentric bias and detrimental to Korean subjectivity. I locate a vital inspiration for his tackling of this task in his 1908 Korean translation of Liang's fictionalization of the history of Italian nation-building and examine his literary biography of the legendary Koguryŏ general Ŭlji mundŏk, which amounts to a hermeneutic battle to read a Korean national story in Sinocentric documents. I analyze how this attempt ultimately exposes extant text's intrinsic semantic

Introduction 17

indeterminacy and performatively frees it from the conventional practice of literary reading. Sin's historiographical endeavor encapsulates the affirmation of the afterlives of classical culture as a fertile terrain for seeking novel modes of literary representation whose value is yet to be culturally established.

The works I examine in part I represent efforts to reuse and renovate classical literary forms to meet present cultural demands. Almost contemporaneously with these efforts, intellectuals made parallel yet often competing attempts at modernizing and nationalizing literary culture itself, especially through language reform. Part II opens with an overview of language reform and the related discourses for redefining literature, outlining the cultural sea change in late nineteenth- to early twentieth-century East Asia at whose forefront the authors I focus on in this part found themselves: Lu Xun, Mori Ōgai 森鷗外 (1862–1922), and Yi Kwangsu.

Chapter 3 rereads representative fictional works by these three authors that have been canonized as the foundational texts of modern Chinese, Japanese, and Korean literatures, respectively. My intervention consists in analyzing the critical relationships that those works create to the cultural past, adding to scholarship that has tended to characterize them by virtue of the linguistic, formal, or thematic ruptures they caused in national literary traditions. I conceptualize these relationships in terms of "parody" broadly defined and contend that these works' parodic engagement with various aspects of past culture produced new modes of representation to convey voices that had eluded existing "literature." Whereas the significance of a parody is elucidated in a continuum of cultural history where a new work inscribes difference, some of the references to previous texts that I consider call into question such continuity itself. I thus supplement my inquiry by attending to textual moments in which repetition, without differences that can be capitalized on, engenders radical newness.

This leads us to chapter 4, which examines a body of works by Lu Xun, Mori Ōgai, and Yi Kwangsu in the genre of historical fiction. Previous studies have struggled to bring out the significance of these modern writers' treatment of premodern subject matter in idiosyncratic forms that conspicuously and even self-consciously renounced the effort to forge an organic synthesis of the past and the present, going so far as to undermine the coherence of the narrative point of view or to leave narratological excesses unattended. Serving as an imaginative sandbox in which to build a story to reckon with the meaning of the present in history, historical fiction constitutes a generic allegory of modern literature in East Asia produced at the juncture of profound cultural changes through which the past became powerless to position the present in its episteme, while posing a forceful resistance to present norms and values.

In the *grand récit* of East Asian modernization, understood as a shift of geopolitical power from the premodern Sinocentric to the modern Eurocentric orders, Japan's quick ascendency to international power constitutes a hallmark. Yet the country's subsequent imperialization exposed the irony that, while appropriating the Western-originated rhetoric of the civilizing mission, it evoked the region's shared culture—especially the legacies of classical Chinese letters—to discursively bolster its imperialist rule, suggesting a case of the return of the repressed that is symptomatic of East Asian modernization conceived as a severance from the cultural past. I call this oft-neglected aspect of Japanese imperialism "imperial mimicry." In part III, I explore how modern literature, as it emerged as a creative practice of overcoming just such a severance, served in semicolonial China and colonial Korea, Taiwan, and Manchukuo during the Second Sino-Japanese War (1937–1945) as a structural critique of Japanese imperialism in an alternative to orthodox cultural nationalism and modernization.

Chapter 5 considers the Chinese writer Zhou Zuoren 周作人 (1885–1967) with a focus on his wartime essays, which are underappreciated largely because of his scandalous collaboration with the Japanese occupation authorities, in conjunction with his earlier cultural criticism. Zhou finds the sources of modern Chinese literature in its inextricable relationship with the literary pasts that are not immediately compatible with modern cultural values, and at the same stroke he locates modern creativity in the afterlives of multilayered, border-crossing traditions that are irreducible to cultural nationalism. Zhou suggests that it is through such cultural creativity that both China and Japan are able to aspire to a universalism of "human life" that acknowledges every ordinary people's right to self-affirmation and happiness—a universalism that defies appropriation by a particular civilization. I read Zhou's criticism as the practice of an archaeology of resistance to Japanese imperialism in the context of a transnational cultural history of East Asia.

In chapter 6, I examine the intertextualization of Lu Xun's works in late colonial writings by Kim Saryang 김사량 (1914–1950), Long Yingzong 龍瑛宗 (1911–1999), and Gu Ding 古丁 (1914–c. 1964), who were active respectively in colonial Korea, Taiwan, and Manchukuo. These writers, to different degrees and in different manners, adapted to the literary fields sanctioned by the Japanese cultural authorities and attained prominent recognition in them. Yet the intertextuality in their writings, especially their references to Lu Xun's works, provides a window onto the dialogic workings of their language, and hence their resistance to imperial cultural intervention. Through late colonial intertextualizations, Lu Xun's writings emerge as a transnational allegory that points to the historical significance of modern literature in East Asia beyond national or imperial appropriation.

The relationship between the cultural past and present is hard to grasp with a ready-made concept in East Asian modernity, and it is through the efforts to reckon with that perplexing relationship that the pursuit of modern literature, an indispensable discursive practice in search of freedom in modern society, emerged in the region. In the twenty-first century, when the legitimacy of the status quo of modern civilization has once again been called into serious question, the past civilizations of East Asia, together with those of other regions, must contribute philosophical resources to our common pursuit of moral community. These efforts, if they are not to be reduced to toxic antimodern fundamentalism or reinforce things as they are, must engender a new mode of representation that can challenge cultural norms. And in this sense, we are called on to revisit the original moments of modern literature at this historical juncture.

The task is to envision a radical future, just as Lu Xun indicated with the ambivalence of the phrase "I sat up," "*zuoqilai le* 坐起來了" at the end of "After Death." The movement of the speaker on the constative level indicates either his restoration to life in the dream or his awakening from the dream. But this irreducible ambiguity, by shaking up the represented distinction between life and death and between reality and dream, points to the speaker's resurrection into a new world that calls for a new mode of representation. "After Death" ultimately envisions new literature as emerging right in the middle of the inexorable cycles of the new and the old, allegorizing the modern practice of literature that I explore in what follows. But we must start in the midst of these cycles. Our study begins with the failure of the court-based reform campaign that Kang Youwei, who is credited with the late Qing revival of the Gongyang commentary, spearheaded in 1898, which prompted his eminent disciple Liang Qichao to go into exile.

PART I

A Multilayered Contact Space in Turn-of-the-Century East Asia

In late 1898, the Chinese reformist Liang Qichao was on a Japanese military vessel bound for Hiroshima. Just a few months earlier, he had joined the political reform campaigns in the Qing court led by his mentor Kang Youwei. Their venture, known as the Hundred Days' Reform, had ended in failure as the court's conservative factions gathered around the Empress Dowager Cixi (1835–1908) had swiftly cracked down on it, capturing and executing many of their allies. In imminent danger, Liang had sought refuge at the Japanese Consulate in Tianjin and obtained safe passage out of the country. On the ship, the captain reportedly offered the disgraced reformist a copy of a Japanese novel called *Kajin no kigū* 佳人之奇遇 (Chance Meetings with Beautiful Women, 1885–1897, published in eight installments; hereafter referred to as *Chance Meetings*). This political novel written by Shiba Shirō 柴四朗 (1853–1922) had been hugely popular in Japan when its first volumes appeared about a decade before.[1] It is said to have so inspired Liang that he began translating it into Chinese while he was still on board.[2] Shortly after he settled in Yokohama, he put together the translation in collaboration with his compatriots in Japan and serialized it in *Qing yi bao* 清議報 (China Discussion), the widely circulated journal he edited. Following the rendition of *Chance Meetings*, Liang's prolific translational, editorial, and literary work in exile catalyzed a burst of textual circulation in late nineteenth- to early twentieth-century East Asia. The popular journals he ran carried numerous translations and adaptations of Japanese materials on an array of subjects, from law to economics, politics, and history; his writings were avidly read, translated, and adapted in Korea, especially in the first decade of the twentieth century.[3]

Liang traveled to Japan amid a sea change in the region's geopolitical order. Following its humiliating defeat in the First Sino-Japanese War (1894–1895), China lost its long-held authority as the civilizational center of the region, while Japan colonized Taiwan and gained unprecedented regional power. Korea consequently severed its historic tributary relationship with China, only to invite competing interventions from Japan and Russia. As a result of its victory in the Russo-Japanese War (1904–1905), Japan increased its political influence in Korea, eventually forcing it to surrender diplomatic sovereignty in 1905 and colonizing it in 1910. The modernized and imperialized Japan rose to a new regional power, attracting numerous intellectuals and students from across Asia.[4]

Liang's publication in Japan played a significant part, as Joshua Fogel has put it, in the "introduction of modern Western civilization to China" as well as to Korea.[5] This process of mediation, however, was fundamentally shaped by cultural-historical conditions in turn-of-the-century East Asia—the precise conditions that derived from the traditions of tightly interrelated East Asian cultures and reputedly enabled Liang to quickly begin translating a Japanese novel into Chinese even before his ship had crossed the narrow waters of the Yellow Sea. Liang's works illustrate the textual circulation in the region that was not only propelled by the world-historical forces of modernization or the dissemination of "modern Western civilization" but was also informed by the surviving powers of the regional literary cultures, which modernization was quickly rendering out of date. His works bespeak a paradoxical structure in which the spread of ideas following the modern civilizational hierarchy—positing the West at the center, Japan on a periphery, and China and Korea on more distant peripheries—hinged on the legacies of the classical civilizational order that was being replaced by it. The cultural exchanges in turn-of-the-century East Asia were defined by the competing forces of progress and the afterlives of classical letters.

AWASH WITH MODERN CIVILIZATION

The Hundred Days' Reforms came on the heels of China's already decades-long endeavor to introduce modern civilization from the West through the Self-Strengthening Movement.[6] The devastating results of the two Opium Wars (1839–1842, 1856–1860) and the ensuing signing of unequal treaties with Western powers drove the Qing court to intensify its efforts to transform the declining empire into a viable modern state. The 1861 inception of the Zongli yamen 總理衙門, the imperial bureau in charge of foreign affairs that commissioned the seminal publication of *Wanguo gongfa* 萬國公法 (Elements of International Law) in 1864, laid the institutional groundwork for China's entry into the modern international order.[7] The official measures to modernize the country involved as much development in military, mining, transportation, and other areas of science and engineering as the training of interpreters and the systematic translation of Western materials. In order to accelerate the introduction of up-to-date knowledge from the West and enhance diplomatic and commercial agencies, the government founded the Tongwen guan 同文館 (School of Common Languages) in Beijing in 1862 and the Guangfang yanguan 廣方言館 (School of Broad Languages) in Shanghai the following year.[8] In 1872, it began dispatching officially selected students to the United States and Europe to further facilitate communication with the West. These nascent endeavors entered a new phase as Kang Youwei's court-based reform movement gained traction.

The Tokugawa shogunate (1603–1867) in the meantime was also grappling with the arrival of Western powers on Japan's shores.[9] The government had been dealing with a growing number of foreign ships on the coasts since the late eighteenth century, when four American warships under the command of Commodore Perry, called the "Black Ships," reached Uraga at the entrance of Edo Bay in 1853. In the following year, coerced by the display of overwhelming force, the shogunate agreed to sign the Japan-U.S. Treaty of Peace and Amity and open treaty ports in Shimoda and Hakodate to U.S. vessels, and this led to the conclusion of treaties of commerce with other Western powers in 1858.

Having opened its doors to the modern world, the shogunate promoted "foreign learning" (*yōgaku* 洋学) and established a dedicated in-house bureau called Bansho shirabesho 蕃書調所 (Research Institute for Barbarian Books) in 1856. Formally called Yōgakusho 洋学所 (Institute for Foreign Learning, est. 1855) and renamed Yōsho shirabesho 洋書調所 (Research Institute for Foreign Books) in 1862, this bureau was put in charge of translating, studying, and teaching Western books in an array of modern science and engineering fields as well as training interpreters and translators to assume responsible posts in diplomacy and commerce.[10] Beginning in 1860, the shogunate sent official observation envoys almost yearly to the United States and Europe, while powerful feudal domains also clandestinely dispatched students to the West.[11] These late Edo measures of modernization prepared the Meiji Restoration in 1868, at which point the shogunate ceded power to the forces gathered under the authority of the emperor, furthering the nation-building efforts.

The Korean coast was also threatened by Western ships beginning in the early nineteenth century.[12] Though the Chosŏn court was initially able to drive away Western powers through armed skirmishes, it was pressured into trade and diplomacy negotiations with the young Meiji government, which menaced the shores of Kanghwa Island just west of Seoul in 1875. The Chosŏn government was pressed to sign the Korea-Japan Treaty of Amity in 1876, followed by the Korea-U.S. Amity and Trade Treaty concluded in 1882; similar unequal treaties were ratified with Britain and Germany in the same year. Thus forced to open the country to international relations, the court sought modern knowledge from its neighbors, dispatching delegates consisting of diplomats, literati, and students to Japan (four delegations of *susinsa* 修信使 from 1876 to 1882; an observation envoy *chosa sich'aldan* 朝士視察團 in 1881) and to China (*yŏngsŏnsa* 領選使 in 1881). The first diplomatic mission to the United States, which included a few accompanying students, was sent in 1883. The court founded the T'ongni kimu amun 統理機務衙門 in 1880 to modernize the administration of foreign affairs, while investing in education in Western languages and scholarship in an effort to train native officials to run a modern state. It inaugurated the school of English, named Tongmun hak 同文學, in 1883 and expanded it into the first royal institution of modern education, the Yukyŏng gongwŏn 育英公院, in 1886.[13]

As they wrestled with the West's military, political, and economic power, China, Japan, and Korea became integrated into the modern international order and the global market. In order to survive and excel in that competitive field, they modernized the interfaces with the outside world, from diplomacy to transportation, translation, and education. This historical watershed set the stage for East Asian writers to engage with world literature at large. An estimation based on A Ying's catalogue of late Qing fiction designates 628 pieces as translations as opposed to 479 as original works.[14] A study by Tarumoto Teruo lists 1,135 translations among the total of 2,372 works of fiction published in China between 1840 and 1911.[15] Guo Tingli identifies as many as 2,569 works of fiction translated between the 1870s and 1919.[16] An overwhelming majority of the late Qing translations were of European, American, and Russian works.[17] As for Japan, a 2001 catalogue enumerates approximately 4,500 items of translated literature published during the Meiji era (1868–1912), among which Western works predominate.[18] The scope of literary translation in modern Korea broadened significantly with the launch of *T'aesŏ munye sinbo* 泰西文藝新報 (New Journal of European Literature), a short-lived journal published from 1918 to 1919 dedicated to the translation and criticism of European literatures, and continued to grow through the 1920s and 1930s. It is estimated that between 1895 and 1919, a total of about 300 translated works of fiction, poems, plays, and essays were published, a majority of which were Korean renderings of Western works.[19]

CHINA, JAPAN, AND KOREA OPEN TO ONE ANOTHER

The often-overlooked flip side of the opening of East Asian trade ports to the world was revivified communication within the region; modernization reinvigorated and gave new significance to the region's centuries-old cultural contacts. Well before the Sino-Japanese relationship was officially modernized with the conclusion of the Sino-Japanese Friendship and Trade Treaty in 1871, Japan's long-standing ties with China through Nagasaki had played a major role in its exposure to knowledge about the changing outside world. The news about the First Opium War brought by a Chinese trade ship to Nagasaki put the shogunate on high alert, while a wide array of Chinese translations of Western books and Chinese treatises on modern knowledge began to have a profound impact on Japanese literati. Numerous late Qing materials on modern knowledge were imported to Japan shortly after their original publication and circulated widely, often through domestic reprints.[20] On the eve of the Meiji Restoration, the shogunate dispatched newly acquired Western vessels to Shanghai in 1862 and 1864 for trade and took Japanese officials and merchants to the continent for the first time in about two centuries. Their reports on China's embattled situation warned the Japanese of the dangers of Western imperialism.[21]

Whereas classical Chinese was designated by the 1871 Treaty as the primary language to be used in diplomatic documents between China and Japan, it also enabled an increasing number of officials, literati, and merchants from both countries in contact to communicate via "brush talk" using Chinese writing. As travel picked up rapidly in both directions, those groups were aided by their shared cultural traditions to rediscover neighbors that they had long known only in books. In Japan, the Consulate of the Qing government, opened in 1878 in Tokyo, became a particularly lively venue for personal and textual exchanges. Huang Zunxian 黃遵憲 (1848–1905) was among the first generation of Chinese literati to witness the modernizing Japan and write seriously about its civilization. Drawing on his experience during his four-year tenure as an assistant to the inaugural Qing Minister to Japan He Ruzhang 何如璋 (1838–1891), Huang's writings were keenly read by Chinese intellectuals who were beginning to recognize the cultural merit of the island nation to the east, which they had traditionally disdained as civilizationally inferior. Evoking an anecdote about the Song dynasty's (960–1279) relationship to the Khitan people, Huang urged China to break away from its self-important disposition and raised awareness of its close neighbor just across the narrow seas.[22] While Huang and his peers who stayed in Japan, such as Wang Tao 王韜 (1828–1897), Yang Shoujing 楊守敬 (1839–1915), and Yao Wendong 姚文棟 (1853–1929), were intrigued by the nation's meteoric changes, they still enjoyed prestige as distinguished literati delegated by the time-honored center of civilization. They were eagerly sought out by Japanese Sinologists who craved firsthand Chinese criticism and correction of their compositions; asked to offer prefaces, postfaces, paratextual commentaries, and title calligraphies to books by the Japanese writers they befriended; and frequently invited to poetry gatherings, which resulted in the publication of many collections of exchanged poems.²³ They were also fascinated by Japan as a treasure trove of old Chinese books that had long since perished on the continent—an unlikely realization of the ancient lore of Xu Fu 徐福.²⁴

Even behind the scenes of the monumental arrival of the Black Ships in Japan was a seldom-mentioned episode that illustrates the lasting relevance of transregional literary traditions. When the Black Ships returned to Japan to obtain the shogunate's response to the U.S. demands for trade in 1854, Commodore Perry had Luo Sen 羅森 (1821–1899) on board to assist Samuel Williams, the English-Chinese interpreter who, together with an English-Dutch interpreter, facilitated the negotiations. While helping translate diplomatic documents and aiding in the historic negotiations on behalf of America, Luo Sen was welcomed by Japanese officials, literati, and Buddhist monks. They held discussions in writing, exchanged classical Chinese poems with Luo, and asked him to offer his calligraphy on hundreds of fans. As Luo reports in his travelogue *Riben riji* 日本日記 (Journal in Japan, 1854–1855), one Seki Kenji 関研次 presented him with a poem following the successful conclusion of the treaty:

橫濱相遇豈無因	How could our encounter in Yokohama be an accident?
和議皆安仰賴君	Peace talks have gone all well thanks to you.
遠方鴃舌今朝會	This morning, we met those from afar chirping in an exotic tongue;
幸觀同文對語人	But how fortunate we were to see a man with whom we shared writing and could exchange words!²⁵

The figurative fault line between "shared writing/culture" (*dōbun* 同文), on the one hand, and "exotic tongue" (*gekizetsu* 鴃舌; lit., shrike tongue), on the other, aligns with the classical distinction between civilization and its other (*huayi zhi bian* 華夷之辨).²⁶ The speaker expresses a sense of cultural community by virtue of sharing writing with the addressee—a community, however, evoked by the age-old Sinocentric worldview that is being shaken to the core by the praised "peace talks" which the addressee himself has facilitated as interpreter. But this salient irony does not seem to have raised either party's eyebrows. Luo Sen also received a letter from a shogunate official named Hirayama Kenjirō 平山謙二郎 (1815–1890), who expressed the hope that the newly opened trade would be driven not by profit (*li* 利) but by justice (*gi* 義) and that with the help of Luo, "the will of Confucius and Mencius shall be carried on for tens of thousands of years into the future so as to be expanded all over the world."[27] To this utopian vision, despite its conspicuous anachronism in view of the political reality unfolding right before their eyes, Luo replied with wholehearted endorsement.[28] They used idioms deriving from shared Confucian classics to exchange a coded message at the backstage of the signing of a modern treaty.[29]

Japanese travels to China likewise surged. Meiji Sinologists in particular wrote numerous travelogues about China, recording the experience of witnessing the land of letters in rapid transformation and conversing in writing with their Chinese counterparts on contemporary political affairs.[30] Apart from personal travels, textual exchanges gained steam. Japanese book traders imported more and more books from China, while Chinese booksellers opened stores in the Chinese settlement in Yokohama. Edo editions of Chinese texts were reprinted, and new reprints of Chinese classics and Ming-Qing fiction appeared; some of those Japanese editions were exported back to China. An Edo-era dictionary for reading vernacular Chinese fiction was augmented and reprinted.[31] Those publication activities catered to early Meiji scholars and students who continued to study Chinese classics and maintained an insatiable curiosity about Ming-Qing vernacular fiction. Japanese literati also tried to revitalize literary exchanges with China by translating vernacular Japanese literature into Chinese. Kikuchi Sankei 菊池三溪 (1819–1891), an eminent Sinologist, for example, echoed his contemporary Chinese counterparts in trying to awaken Chinese readers' long-dormant interest in Japanese culture.[32] It was in this context that some Japanese Sinologists reportedly tried to translate Shiba Shirō's *Chance Meetings* for a Chinese audience before Liang Qichao and his allies took on the work.[33] Modernization, to be sure, brought about unprecedented transformations in the Sino-Japanese cultural relationship, but amid the latter's revitalization, the cultural capital that had long accumulated around Chinese letters maintained its value across nations.

Korea entered a modern diplomatic and trade relationship with Japan with the signing of the 1876 Treaty of Amity, and with China with the 1899 Korea-China Commerce Treaty. Unlike Tokugawa Japan, which had restricted contacts with China to commerce through Nagasaki, Chosŏn Korea had maintained a tight diplomatic and trade relationship with China throughout its five-hundred-year history. Whereas the Chosŏn court sent a total of twelve "neighborhood" diplomatic missions called *t'ongsinsa* 通信使 to the Tokugawa shogunate, preceded by three to the Ashikaga shogunate (1336–1573) and two to Toyotomi Hideyoshi 豊臣秀吉 (1537–1598), it dispatched "tributary" delegates more than 1,200 times to the Ming and nearly 900 times to the Qing. Its commitment to tributary diplomacy ended only when the final delegation in 1894 had to return to Seoul midway through its mission due to the outbreak of the First Sino-Japanese War.[34] Having been built upon these thick ties with China, Korean engagement with Western knowledge maintained what Yi Chaesŏn has called a "twofold structure" involving mediation through both Chinese and Japanese materials especially until the colonization.[35]

The circulation of Western knowledge in Chinese translation into Korea beginning in the early seventeenth century paved the way for more copious and frequent arrivals in the post–Opium War era. The many Korean delegations to China brought home up-to-date late Qing publications in great numbers, including translations and writings by European and American missionaries as well as reform-minded Chinese literati. Many books on modern knowledge made their way to Korea shortly after their publication in China, some of which also reached Japan roughly contemporaneously. Widely circulated late Qing newspapers and magazines also played an important role in disseminating modern knowledge in the peninsula.[36] A pinnacle of the late Chosŏn Korean missions to China was the 1881 delegation of students and officials to inspect and learn about the burgeoning engineering and military technology at the Machine Factory and the Naval Academy in Tianjin, along with other modern institutions. Delegated by the court to lead the mission, Kim Yunsik 김윤식 (1835–1922) drew on the generic tradition of the *yŏnhaengnok* 燕行錄, the travelogue written on the tributary missions to Beijing, and reported on witnessing the transforming dynasty and conversing in writing with his Chinese counterparts on contemporary affairs. The account is a fascinating interweaving of exposure to modern civilization and the endurance of the traditional episteme, punctuated by exchanges of many poems and gifts, visits to historical sites, and reflections on time-honored moral values in turbulent times.[37]

Meanwhile, soon after the conclusion of the 1876 Treaty of Amity with Japan, the Chosŏn court dispatched the first of its diplomatic envoys to Meiji Japan, with the intention to normalize diplomacy that had been interrupted by the discontinuation of the *t'ongsinsa* missions in 1811. The ensuing delegations to Japan represent Korea's initial encounters with its rapidly modernizing neighbor.[38] They incubated reformist intellectuals such as Yu Kilchun 유길준 (1856–1914), who followed the *chosa sich'aldan* envoy in 1881 as a student and stayed on to enroll in Fukuzawa Yukichi's Keiō gijuku 慶應義塾 (now Keio University) as one of the first three Korean students to attend school in Japan. Yu later studied in the United States, toured Europe, and published *Sŏyu kyŏnmun* 西遊見聞 (Observations from a Journey to the West, 1895), in which he put forth his influential treatise on "levels of civilization." Drawing on the social Darwinian idea of the survival of the fittest under Fukuzawa's influence, it firmly inscribed Korea in a modern narrative of world history propelled by civilizational progress.[39]

While mediated by the modern discourse of civilization, Korea's early engagement with Japan was nevertheless often facilitated by the legacies of the countries' closely related literary traditions. Korean visitors frequently conversed with their Japanese hosts and Chinese literati-officials stationed in Japan in classical Chinese writing; they exchanged classical Chinese poems and organized poetry gatherings with Japanese Sinologists. The Japanese asked them to offer calligraphies, a tradition dating back to the *t'ongsinsa* era. Korean guests also desired up-to-date Japanese-language materials in Chinese translation and sought help from Japanese acquaintances willing to do such translation on their behalf.[40] It was against this backdrop that the Korean reformist Kim Okkyun 김옥균 (1851–1894), exiled in Japan after the failure of the Japanese-supported Gapsin coup d'état (1884), contributed a postface in classical Chinese to the first installment of Shiba Shirō's *Chance Meetings*, praising its literary elegance and benefit to society.[41] Important late Qing Chinese sources also reached Korea via Japan, including Zheng Guanying's 鄭觀應 (1842–1922) *Yi yan* 易言 (Discourse of Change, 1880), an encyclopedic treatise on modern institutions that circulated widely in Korea and would later appear in *hangul* translation. The book was handed to Kim Hongjip 김홍집 (1842–1896) by Huang Zunxian in 1880 in Tokyo, along with the latter's famous *Chaoxian celüe* 朝鮮策略 (Strategies for Korea, 1880), a policy recommendation influential in late Chosŏn diplomacy amid the intensifying American demands for trade.[42] Literary language in classical Chinese realized a mode of communication that was relatively independent from—and sometimes cut across—the widening gap in political power between Korea and Japan. Both sides evoked the idea of "shared writing/culture" to nurture friendship.[43] Broaching the common threats of Western imperialism kindled a sense of horizontal solidarity.[44] Technological spectacles and modern exotica in Meiji Japan laid bare the limits of the traditional episteme, but it was that very epistemological crisis that prompted the Korean envoys to produce travel narratives to configure a new subjectivity, while wavering between nostalgia for the lost past and vertiginous exposure to modernity. Their travelogues detailing busy tours of novel sites and institutions—from factories to ports, railways to military academies, hospitals to banks, newspaper bureaus to photo studios, ballrooms to museums—are in fact often counterbalanced by impromptu utterances of misgivings, suspicions, and criticisms. In acknowledging the exigencies of change in a new era, those writings constitute meaningful critiques of modernization.[45]

Intra–East Asian literary exchanges continued to be mediated by the traditional cultural capital well into the twentieth century. It was in its first decade that Liang Qichao's work in exile enjoyed a particularly broad readership in Korea. Beginning in 1897, numerous works by Liang were published, either in the original or in Korean translation, in various newspapers and magazines such as *Hwangsŏng sinmun* 皇城新聞 (Imperial Capital Gazette), *Taehan maeil sinbo* 大韓每日申報 (Korea Daily News), and *Sŏu* 西友 (Newsletter of the Society of the Western Provinces). More than a dozen books of Liang's writings were published; his works were translated either in the Sino-Korean mixed style or in *hangul*, and sometimes in both. The reprints and translations, however, represent just a fraction of the actual readership, for most Korean intellectuals were able to consume Liang's writings in the original. *The China Discussion* ran its own distribution branches in Seoul and Inchon, and *Xinmin congbao*

新民叢報 (New People's Journal), also edited by Liang, had one in Inchon. Liang's eloquent writing became an instant classic in Korea, as it was used, along with the orthodox Confucian classics, for instruction in classical Chinese writing.[46] His work engaged writers as diverse as Hyŏn Ch'ae 현채 (1856–1925), Pak Ŭnsik 박은식 (1859–1925), Chang Chiyŏn 장지연 (1864–1921), Chu Sigyŏng 주시경 (1876–1914), An Ch'angho 안창호 (1878–1938), and Sin Ch'aeho, among others, until it was suppressed under the Japanese colonial regime.

While Japan kept attracting literati from its neighbors as it emerged as a regional power, China, too, became home to numerous Korean exiles who escaped Japan's aggravating encroachment on their homeland. The Korean poet and historian Kim T'aekyŏng 김택영 (1850–1927) was among those who went into exile in China. Kim left the country in 1905, when Japan stripped Korea of diplomatic sovereignty, and lived in China for the rest of his life, working on compilations of Korean history and the history of Sino-Korean literature, while making connections with Chinese reformists such as Zhang Jian 張謇 (1853–1926) and Yan Fu 嚴復 (1854–1921), as well as Liang Qichao. In 1909, Kim received a copy of *Tianyan lun* 天演論 (On Evolution, 1898), Yan Fu's seminal translation of Thomas Huxley's *Evolution and Ethics* (1893), which is credited with introducing social Darwinism to China and then to Korea. On that occasion, he composed three poems, the first of which reads,

誰將漢宋作經師	Who would be a student of the Han or Song learning,
學術如今又轉移	Now that scholarship has once again transformed?
黃埔夜來江鬼哭	On the Huangpu, night falls and river ghosts cry,
一編天演譯成時	As a book called *Tianyan lun* has been translated.[47]

Unlike Yu Kilchun, Kim does not react conceptually to social Darwinism; rather, Yan Fu's archaist translation leads Kim to historicize it as yet another moment of transformation in the long history of Chinese thought, similar to what had taken place when Song Neo-Confucians challenged Han learning and caused a paradigm change.[48] In a highly personal voice, the poem implies apprehension that this transformation may lead to an ominous juncture foreshadowed by ghostly cries on the Huangpu River in Shanghai.[49]

A MULTILAYERED CONTACT SPACE

Kim T'aekyŏng's poetic engagement with Huxley's book via Yan Fu's translation, to be sure, does not remotely illustrate the conceptual sea change that this book caused in East Asia. Yet it encapsulates often-overlooked aspects of modern intra–East Asian cultural contacts. At stake were anachronistic entanglements of competing cultural dynamics: the opening to the West *and* the opening to each other; the dissemination of modern Western civilization *and* the shared cultural resources that enabled it; the investments in modern knowledge *and* the misgivings about the profound transformations it was causing; the embrace of new cultures *and* the reckoning with and making sense of the demise of time-honored values and norms. Cultural interfaces between the East Asian nations were not entirely coterminous with the modern political boundaries between imagined national communities, since they often evoked shared classical letters. Contact spaces not only produced identities but also associated them with each other, as intellectuals saw the fates of their own civilization in each other's modernity, carving out an important transnational locus for critical reflections on the epoch. Late nineteenth- to early twentieth-century transregional cultural contacts were therefore shaped as much by modernization as by the afterlives of shared cultures in the region. In the next two chapters, I argue that modern literature in East Asia emerged on this multilayered cultural stage.

CHAPTER ONE

Literature's Search for Itself

Liang Qichao and Meiji Political Fiction

Shortly after Liang Qichao settled into exile in Japan, he launched the journal *China Discussion*. This journal serialized the Chinese translation of Shiba Shirō's *Chance Meetings*, titled *Jiaren qiyu* 佳人奇遇 (Chance Meetings with Beautiful Women), beginning in its inaugural issue (published in December 1898) until it was terminated as of the thirty-fifth issue (published in February 1900) and replaced by the translation of another popular piece of Meiji political fiction: Yano Ryūkei's 矢野龍渓 (1851–1931) *Keikoku bidan* 經國美談 (The Beautiful Story of Statesmanship, 1883–1884), rendered as *Jingguo meitan* 經國美談. These two works are likely the first two Chinese translations of modern Japanese literature.[1]

This chapter zeros in on *Chance Meetings* and its interrupted Chinese translation published in *The China Discussion*.[2] These works have been noted as marking an important turning point in the respective nations' literary modernization, yet their modernity is markedly ambivalent.[3] On the one hand, *Chance Meetings* draws extensively on literary precedents, especially in the Chinese classics, and that provenance fundamentally informs its translation into Chinese. It is the proximity of their cultural roots that reportedly enabled Liang to take on the translation while still on board the ship between China and Japan. Yet on the other hand, the very affective power that these works draw from previous literatures is meant to serve the patently modern purpose of political reforms. In *Chance Meetings* and its Chinese translation, the received notion of what makes "literature," attributed to the latter's affective conveyance of moral values, is put to a serious test as they try to respond to the political exigencies of the time. The prolonged suspense of the narrative of *Chance Meetings* bespeaks the struggles of classical literature for contemporary relevance—the suspense whose aesthetic and political significance I shall explore through comparison with the idea of "aesthetic education." The narrative, however, is ultimately led to an anomic moment where the classical function of literature proves powerless in the face of modern political reality. Literature is thus driven to interrogate the very cultural context in which it gains its virtue *as* literature, thereby opening itself up to new modes of representation. This self-reflexive moment is also symptomized in the interruption of the Chinese translation in *The China Discussion*. The Meiji political novel and its Chinese translation, therefore, cause literature to deviate from its existing, culturally demarcated realm. This deviation is encapsulated in Liang Qichao's own attempt at political literature, *Xin Zhongguo weilai ji* 新中國未來記 (The Future of New China, 1902–1903), also an interrupted work.

USING OLD FORM FOR NEW CONTENT

Inspired by its popularization in nineteenth-century Britain, political fiction flourished in Japan in the 1880s amid the rise of the Freedom and People's Rights Movements.[4] During the late 1870s and 80s, disenfranchised samurai, affluent farmers, and the emerging urban bourgeoisie organized nationwide protests against the oligarchical Meiji government. Activists launched newspapers, assembled rallies and study groups, published rhetorical manuals for political speeches, formed political parties, and put together draft constitutions, demanding popular participation in the processes leading up to the promulgation of the Meiji Constitution in 1889 and the establishment of the Parliament in 1890. In response to the government suppression of these movements through censorship and the banning of political speeches, political novels thrived by taking advantage of fictional storytelling to create a much-needed discursive sphere in print media. Reflecting the idealist aspirations of the movements, this genre gained popularity with the publication of Toda

Gindō's 戸田欽堂 (1850–90) *Minken engi: Jyōkai haran* 民権演義: 情海波瀾 (The Romance of People's Rights: Swirling Sea of Feelings) in 1880 and reached its zenith when the movements were at their height around 1885. *Chance Meetings* was one of the most successful works of this genre.

Encouraged by the warm reception of the first installment of *Chance Meetings*, consisting of two volumes and published in 1885, Shiba Shirō put out eight more volumes of this novel by 1891. When its final six volumes appeared in 1897, political fiction had gone out of vogue in Japan, as politics became normalized under the new Constitution in the 1890s. Shiba himself was elected to the brand-new parliament in 1892. Works that had already fallen out of favor at home, however, regained relevance, this time in a transregional context, thanks to the translations in *The China Discussion*. Contemporaneously, politics became a popular subject in turn-of-the-century fiction in China and Korea.[5]

The Chinese and Korean intellectuals who took interest in Japanese political fiction perceived it first and foremost as a functional medium through which to modernize national politics. It was in this framework that Liang Qichao explained the rationale for translating *Chance Meetings* for a Chinese audience. He penned a seminal preface to the first installment of its serialization in *The China Discussion*, titled "Yi yin zhengzhi xiaoshuo xu 譯印政治小說序" (Preface to Political Fiction in Translation, 1898), and contended vigorously that the genre was "most responsible" for political modernization in the West and Japan and that translating one of its works would likewise fuel necessary reforms in China.[6]

Liang expected "fiction" (*xiaoshuo* 小說) to serve this political purpose specifically by working as the medium for what he termed the "renovation of people" (*xin min* 新民). This reconfiguration of subjectivity was to be prioritized over institutional modernization; as he argued through a rhetorical question in his "Xin min shuo 新民說" (Discourse on the New People, 1902–1906): "If there exist new people [*xin min* 新民], why would you worry about the absence of a new institution, a new government, or a new state?"[7] In the 1902 inaugural editorial of the journal he edited, *Xin xiaoshuo* 新小說 (New Fiction), he wrote "On the Relationship between Fiction and the Governance of Society" (Lun xiaoshuo yu qunzhi zhi guanxi 論小說與群治之關係) and famously contended, "In order to renovate the people of a nation, the fictional literature [*xiaosuho*

小說] of that nation must first be renovated"—that is, prior to the renovation of everything else: "morality," "religion," "politics," "customs," and "learning and arts." He continued, "Even in order to renovate the human mind and its character, fiction must be renovated. Why? That is because fiction has a mysterious power to control the way of humanity."[8] To make his case, he cites examples from previous literatures, especially Ming-Qing fiction and drama, from *Honglou meng* 紅樓夢 (Dream of the Red Chamber) and *Shuihu zhuan* 水滸傳 (Water Margin) to *Xixiang ji* 西廂記 (Romance of the Western Bower) and *Taohua shan* 桃花扇 (The Peach Blossom Fan). He then enumerates four powers by which fiction controls the human mind: "influence," "permeation," "stimulation," and "lifting." Fiction is the genre/style (*ti* 體) that, through these powers, can "affect" and "change" people's minds and that, by "heredity" and "infection" from birth, can eventually transform an entire "society" (*qun* 群). Traditional fiction (ab)uses these powers to convey immoral "ideas"; hence China's present corruption. But fiction's "poisonous" (*du* 毒) affective power, suggests Liang, can be repurposed by "new fiction" for the betterment of morals.[9] New fiction is thus expected to "attack poison by poison."[10]

New fiction, therefore, was an ambivalent genre, aesthetically grafted onto a literary tradition yet functionally self-conscious about its modern mission. Liang envisioned that it would exert on a contemporary readership the same kind of affective power that previous works in this tradition had—the power to make readers "surprised, astonished, sad, and moved, evoking an immeasurable number of nightmares and calling forth an infinite number of tears while they are reading."[11] Thus charged with alluring the reader, new fiction was to then use that affective ability to effect a proper transmission of moral values conducive to political modernization. For Liang, therefore, fiction's political function hinged on writing's power as a pharmakon—writing that at first seduces the reader into a logos while hiding behind it.[12] As a pharmakon, then, "this charm, this spellbinding virtue, this power of fascination can be—alternately or simultaneously—beneficial or maleficent."[13] This ambivalence is indeed corroborated by Liang himself, who, merely a decade after he discontinued the journal *New Fiction* in 1906, confessed, "In the last ten years morals and manners have declined tremendously, and what aspect of that degeneration has not been traceable to the influence of the so-called new fiction? If we drift astray in this fashion [*xun ci hengliu* 循此橫流], then in a few years, how would China not read its way into unstoppable sinking?"¹⁴ Indeed, as David Wang has contended, "new fiction decayed at the moment it arose; it was passé even before its newness was absorbed by the general public."¹⁵ New fiction may have failed to fulfill its prodigious purposes, but I would like to suggest that it is precisely in its incompleteness as an ethicopolitical medium "drift[ing] astray," in its suspension, or in its exile from a proper course of literary history that an origin of "literature" in its modern sense resides.

EXEMPLARY HEROES AND HEROINES

Chance Meetings is a political saga of exiled heroes and heroines from Japan, China, Spain, and Ireland who encounter each other in Philadelphia and forge transnational solidarity against the imperial powers wrecking their homelands. The Japanese hero, Tōkai Sanshi, is named after the author's own nom de plume and reflects his autobiography. Shiba Shirō was born into a retainer clan of the feudal domain Aizu in northeast Japan. At the Meiji Restoration, his clan chose to join many other Tokugawa vassals in maintaining loyalty to their feudal lords and the shogunate, refusing to recognize the legitimacy of the new rulers. The Meiji government waged a series of civil wars against Tokugawa loyalists, during which Aizu Domain became one of the loyalist strongholds and the battleground in the fierce War of Aizu in 1868. At the tender age of fifteen, Shiba served in the Aizu troops and experienced a terrible loss, witnessing his homeland devastated and many of his immediate relatives slaughtered or compelled to commit suicide. This experience left him with a deep-seated mistrust of the central government, which is articulated in the voice of the novel's Japanese hero, who identifies himself as a native of Aizu and calls himself "a loyal subject of a fallen country." As a disgraced clansman, Shiba struggled to continue his education, but financial support from the Iwasakis, the family of an emergent industrial tycoon, enabled him to go to the United States in 1879. There he spent almost six years studying business and finance, eventually obtaining one of the first five bachelor of finance degrees conferred by the Wharton School of the University of Pennsylvania. Shortly after returning to Japan, Shiba put together and published the first installment of *Chance Meetings*.¹⁶

The Chinese hero, Hankei, is a loyalist of the Ming dynasty in the original, while the Spanish heroine Yūran is the daughter of a general in the legitimist Carlist Party. The Irish heroine Kōren is a nationalist activist resisting British imperialism. With the story of these four fictional characters, embroidered biographies of historical anti-imperialist figures like Toussaint Louverture (c. 1743–1803), Aḥmad ʿUrābī Pasha (1839–1911), and Fanny Parnell (1848–1882) are interwoven. The narrative sets up a global stage for the protagonists' battles against the imperial powers embodied by Britain and France and evoked by the Meiji government's treatment of the Tokugawa loyalists and its espousal of wholesale Westernization. It imagines a world in which nationalist struggles cooperate to form a transnational alliance to eradicate imperialism and bring justice to the world. The success of this grand scheme is contingent on the fates of the four heroes and heroines, who wrestle with formidable adversaries and encounter testing misfortunes; they can only dream of realizing their ambitions at the brief moments of "chance meetings" scattered throughout the lengthy story. At its best, the novel gains its characteristic charm from its suspenseful narrative that projects utopian aspirations for a free and just world.

Written during an era when Japan was struggling to renegotiate unequal treaties with Western powers and translated as China was grappling with imperial encroachment, the novel could be read as a remote precursor of Fanonian postcolonialism, as Maeda Ai has suggested.[17] But unlike Fanon's writings, the novel portrays a global Manichean order based on a set of moral and aesthetic values deriving from literary precedents, especially canonical classical Chinese works. While the protagonists enact nationalisms particular to their countries, what gives legitimacy and international relevance to their battles are the age-old cultural values they collectively exemplify.

The indebtedness of *Chance Meetings* to Japanese literary tradition, which had long developed in tight relationship to Chinese letters, is profound. The prose style it adopts is derived from a traditional Japanese method of reading classical Chinese writing using Japanese pronunciation and grammar. Called *kanbun kundoku tai* 漢文訓読体, this style was used in a variety of publications in the early Meiji, from newspapers to translations of Western materials, from official documents to laws. Shiba was among the earliest writers to adopt it in fiction.[18] Thanks to its origin, this style made Meiji-era materials readily accessible to a Chinese readership as a handy medium to introduce modern knowledge. Liang, for instance, claimed that since "seventy to eighty percent of Japanese writing consists of Chinese characters," "those who learn Japanese writing can see initial results in a few days and totally master it in a few months." He even suspected that if his readers were unable to master the language in a few years, the reason must be that they had been abroad and had not mastered Chinese.[19] Kang Youwei, who was also exiled in Japan after the failure of the 1898 reforms, appreciated Japanese in like manner as a convenient intermediary providing quicker access to Western knowledge than directly tackling the original. He also believed that Japanese was relatively easy to read because "Japanese writing resemble[d] our writing" and contended, "The Japanese have already translated many of the essential books of European learning, so I can take advantage of their achievement, as though I were using the West as the cow, Japan as the farmer, and consume them in my armchair."[20] Japanese writing appeared to be a handy, and indeed transparent, intermediary—so transparent that Liang even asserted that "there is nothing in Eastern [i.e., Japanese] scholarship that does not come from the West."[21] This opinion stemmed from its close cultural relationship to Chinese writing and even crystalized in a popular reading manual that Liang helped compile around 1900. Titled *How to Read Japanese Writing in Chinese* (*Hewen handu fa* 和文漢讀法), it was edited on the eccentric premise that every Japanese sentence had a corresponding Chinese phrase from which it derived, and all that was necessary to read it was to recover that "original" Chinese phrase by following a fixed set of simple rules.[22]

Chance Meetings is also punctuated by about forty classical Chinese poems recited by the protagonists and the narrator. This feature, in addition to its prose style, allows the novel to weave numerous literary precedents into the text. The works alluded to include, to mention just a few, the pre-Qin classics *Analects*, *Mencius*, and *Zhuangzi* 莊子; the poetry classics *Shijing* 詩經 (The Book of Poems) and *Chuci* 楚辭 (The Songs of the Chu); many pieces from the sixth-century anthology *Wen xuan* 文選 (Selection of Refined Writings); and late imperial fiction, particularly in its "scholar and beauty" (*caizi jiaren* 才子佳人) romance subgenre. The published text also contains many prefaces, postfaces, and paratextual criticisms written in classical Chinese by prominent Japanese Sinologists and their peers.

The literary precedents catalyze affective communication among the multinational heroes and heroines and provide exemplars of the aesthetic-moral values they try to realize in modern times. Shared knowledge of these precedents underpins the characters' transnational solidarity as a cultural community, in which the novel tries to invite the implied readers to participate by having them appreciate their lyricism and affectively invest in their ethicopolitical idealism. Such a model readership is enacted in the beginning of the text, where two classical Chinese poems composed by Tōkai Sanshi in Philadelphia are coupled with reply poems penned by two of the contributors to the novel's paratextual commentary, both Meiji connoisseurs of Chinese verse and prose who studied in the United States when Shiba Shirō did. Just as shared literary precedents create aesthetic bonds among the protagonists within the story, so do they engage the reader, expected to be likewise versed in Chinese letters, in their imaginary affective solidarity, thereby mediating poetic communication across the novel's diegetic boundary.[23] *Chance Meetings* works *as* literature only for readers who possess the long-standing cultural capital of high letters in East Asia that accumulated around Chinese writings, and this prompted C. T. Hsia to declare that this novel is "unreadable by modern standards," bespeaking the difference in the cultural notions of "literature" between turn-of-the-century East Asia and what Hsia calls "modern."[24] Since that old cultural capital was regional, shared by the *China Discussion* translators and by the implied contemporary Chinese readership, *Chance Meetings* played its culturally expected function as literature just as well in Chinese translation.

Its fundamental rootedness in literary tradition notwithstanding, *Chance Meetings* is at the same time self-conscious about its intrinsic modernity. In the preface to the novel's first installment, Shiba suggests that his work falls outside the established literary genres he can think of and goes against all sorts of expectations that the reader might have. He admits that *Chance Meetings* may too often incline toward the style of popular fiction (*gesaku shōsetsu* 戯作小説) and may be too open to Western gender norms to satisfy orthodox Confucians; yet on the other hand, it may contain too little romance and too many serious discussions of political affairs to satisfy fiction writers (*haishika* 稗史家). One critic may deem it of low quality because of its insufficient attention to parallelism and refined phrasing, whereas another may criticize it for its rigid adherence to those very prose conventions. Shiba thus sarcastically anchors his argument in the disposition of literary genres in his time, within which he tries to position his work only to pronounce that it does not have a proper place in it. His work defies the standards of both high genres, represented by the Confucian classics and old-style prose from the Han, the Wei (220–266), and the Six Dynasties (222–589), and low genres like vernacular fiction in Japanese or Chinese. He hence expects that his readers will all have complaints, while redoubling his commitment to "those who tend to actual situations" and the pragmatism of employing "the contemporary writing of [his] country."[25] This preface may distantly resonate with the Bakhtinian characterization of the novel as a genre external to "the whole of literature" and defined by "forces [that] are at work before our very eyes"—a genre whose "birth and development . . . [take] place in the full light of the historical day."[26] Despite profuse allusions to classical precedents, therefore, *Chance Meetings* resolutely attends to the here and now, imbued with the recognition of its liminality as literature.

The narrative of *Chance Meetings* creates a fictional space in which age-old classics are evoked on the frontlines of life-and-death struggles; it makes allusions at times out of context, in eclectic, contrived, and even paradoxical manners, as if to scout out their relevance in the alien world of modernity. It is this battle for cultural relevance that the protagonists enact. They must prove the validity of the cultural past in modern times by defeating the corrupt imperial powers and surviving the contingencies of the open-ended world. The chance that they prevail, therefore, constitutes an allegory of the modern relevance of the literature that conveys their story. The fortuitous encounters scattered along the plotline where they can momentarily reaffirm their values to each other provide faint hopes, all while their realization continues to be deferred without a resolution. This protracted suspense engenders a labyrinthine narrative in which the protagonists and the cultural values that their story depends on to be told become trapped.

The novel's beginning and its Chinese rendition illustrate how the literary past is evoked to tell a story of modernity. In the opening scene,

Tōkai Sanshi visits Independence Hall in Philadelphia and ponders the history of the American Revolution.

ORIGINAL

東海散士一日費府ノ独立閣ニ登リ　仰テ自由ノ破鐘ヲ観　俯テ独立ノ遺文ヲ読ミ　当時米人ノ義旗ヲ挙テ英王ノ虐政ヲ除キ卒ニ能ク独立自主ノ民タルノ高風ヲ追懷シ俯仰感慨ニ堪ヘズ　愀然トシテ窓ニ倚テ眺臨ス会ゝ二姫アリ　階ヲ繞テ登リ来ル　<u>翠羅面ヲ覆ヒ暗影疎香白羽ノ春冠ヲ戴キ軽縠ノ短羅ヲ衣文華ノ長裾ヲ曳キ風雅高表実ニ人ヲ驚カス</u>

One day, Tōkai Sanshi climbed Independence Hall in Philadelphia, and looked up to observe the cracked Liberty Bell and down to read the Declaration of Independence. Profound emotion welled up as he recalled the nobility of the American people who had raised the banners of righteousness and removed the tyranny of the British king, successfully becoming an independent, self-governing nation. Deeply moved, he was looking out the window when two women suddenly climbed upstairs. They had their faces covered with emerald veils, trailing a subtle fragrance in the shades. Wearing hats with white feathers and short clothes made of silk crepe, they were dragging long, beautifully patterned skirts. Their elegance was really striking.[27]

CHINA DISCUSSION TRANSLATION

東海散士一日登費府獨立閣。仰觀自由之破鐘。俯讀獨立之遺文。愀然懷想。當時米人舉義旗。除英苛法。卒能獨立為自主之民。倚窓臨眺。追懷高風。俯仰感慨。俄見二妃繞階來登。<u>翠羅覆面。暗影疎香。戴白羽之春冠。衣輕縠之短羅。曳文華之長裾。風雅高表。駘蕩精目。</u>

One day, Tōkai Sanshi climbed Independence Hall in Philadelphia, and looked up to observe the cracked Liberty Bell and down to read the Declaration of Independence. Deeply moved, he recalled that at that time, American people had raised the banners of righteousness and removed the harsh British law, eventually gaining independence to become a self-governing nation. He looked out the window and remembered their nobility, filled with deep emotion. Suddenly, two women came climbing upstairs. They had their faces covered with emerald veils, trailing a subtle fragrance in the shades. Wearing hats with white feathers and short clothes made of silk crepe, they were dragging long, beautifully patterned skirts. Their elegance appeared carefree and subtle.[28]

Depicting the monuments of a historic event that marked the birth of a modern nation and imagining the righteousness of the heroes who realized it, the opening passage introduces some of the fundamental concepts of modern politics. *Jiyū* 自由 (freedom) and *dokuritsu* 獨立 (independence), as well as *dokuritsu jishu no tami* 獨立自主ノ民 (lit., an independent, self-governing nation), denoting the democratic nation, are neologisms that translate these Western-originated concepts. Aided by the fact that they are minted primarily in Chinese characters, the *China Discussion* translation is able to transpose those terms into Chinese simply by transcribing them. In a sense, this passage may be taken as a typical example of the Japanese intermediary helping transpose modern notions from the West into China. But as Tōkai Sanshi's eyes are drawn to the silhouettes of the two women, who soon turn out to be Yūran and Kōren, the Spanish and Irish expatriates, the perspective on modernity and its mediation become diverted. The original uses convoluted phrases to describe their elegant outfits, which the translation renders in literary prose that assumes the stylistic features of tetra- and hexasyllabic parallel prose (*pian ti wen* 駢體文).[29] The Chinese version appends an extra phrase (*daidang jingmu* 骀蕩精目) to form a balancing couplet with the preceding one, thereby maintaining orthodox prosody (see the underlined part). In translating an exotic landscape and cutting-edge notions for Chinese readers, it treats their ears to a familiar rhythm. In the very first scene, *Chance Meetings* and its translation drift away from the conceptual teleology of the rendition of modern ideas and instead reveal the aesthetic texture of their writing, beginning to tell a story of meandering, contingencies, and suspense.

As he overhears a conversation between Yūran and Kōren, Sanshi shifts his sensory focus from vision to hearing. The two women praise the heroism of the American people in fighting the War of Independence and admire their successful building of "a wealthy and strong country of civilization" (Jpn. *fukyō bunmei no hōkoku* 富強文明ノ邦国; Chn. *fuqiang wenming zhi bangguo* 富強文明之邦國).[30] But as they proceed to compare

Literature's Search for Itself 47

the American success with the embattled situations back home, their voices assume sorrowful tones, pushing the American scene into the background and instead conjuring up in Sanshi's mind a totally different landscape.

ORIGINAL

散士之ヲ聴テ以為ラク今這ノ嬋婉タル佳人自由ノ邦国ニ棲息シ文明ノ徳沢ニ沐浴シ而シテ慨歎悲哀此ノ如ク切ナル　恰モ晋廷ノ末路王導ガ諸人ト新亭ニ会合シ目ヲ挙ゲテ山河ノ異ナルヲ憤リ空ク南冠ヲ戴テ楚囚ノ涙ヲ灑グノ情アルガ如キハ何ゾヤ　怪訝自ラ禁ズル能ハズ

Overhearing [the conversation between the two women], Sanshi wondered why these elegant, beautiful women living in a country of freedom and enjoying the benefits of civilization had to express such pressing regrets and sorrows. They sounded reminiscent of the situation in the final days of the Jin court, when Wang Dao had gathered with his people at the New Pavilion and looked up to feel indignant at the sight of alien mountains and rivers, vainly shedding the tears of the Chu hostages wearing southern crowns. Sanshi could not but feel suspicious.[31]

CHINA DISCUSSION TRANSLATION

散士聽之。竊竊疑之。以為今此佳人棲息自由之邦國。沐浴文明之德澤。而慨歎悲哀如此。恰如晉廷末路諸名士新亭之會。作楚囚之對泣。歎山河之已非。甯非異事。

Overhearing [the conversation between the two women], Sanshi became secretly suspicious, and thought that it was indeed odd that these beautiful women now living in a country of freedom and enjoying the benefits of civilization nevertheless expressed such regrets and sorrows, just as in the final days of the Jin court, the worthy men had gathered at the New Pavilion and lamented over the already different mountains and rivers, shedding the face-to-face tears of the Chu hostages.[32]

While the two heroines talk about an archetypal event of modern civilization, the desolate tones of their voices remind Sanshi of a historical situation at the end of the Western Jin dynasty (265–316) in China, which the narrative represents through allusions to *Shishuo xinyu* 世說新語 (The New Accounts of the Tales of the World), the fifth-century Chinese compilation of tales. As the well-known episode goes, when the Western Jin fell due to the rebellions of Xiongnu and other ethnic groups and relocated its capital from the northern city of Luoyang to Jiankang in the unfamiliar south, the general Wang Dao 王導 (267–330) and his people gathered at the New Pavilion to feast. Someone remarked, "Though winds and sunshine are not unlike [those in Luoyang], the mountains and rivers look truly different," and "everybody looked at each other and shed tears." Wang Dao then told them not to "face each other like the hostages of the Chu" and to work together to restore the dynasty.[33] Wang Dao is known for his subsequent contribution to the foundation of the Eastern Jin dynasty (317–420) based in the south, which succeeded the Western Jin. These remarks by Wang Dao recorded in *The New Accounts* also allude to an ancient anecdote documented in the Zuo commentary to the *Spring and Autumn Annals* (*Chunqiu zuozhuan* 春秋左傳). The story has it that the hostages of the state of Chu (11th century?–223 BCE), when captured by its adversary Jin (11th century?–376 BCE), were "shackled while wearing the southern crown" to remember their homeland.[34] Comprehending the multilayered references to literary precedents, the Chinese translator renders the rather tortuous Japanese phrase into succinct prose based on hexasyllabic phrases (underlined). It also appends an additional four syllables, "*qieqie yizhi* 竊竊疑之" (secretly suspected), to adhere to the prosodic convention. The voices of the Spanish and Irish exiles resonate with Sanshi, who, also on foreign soil, identifies with his homeland of Aizu, which fell to the Meiji government forces. On the conceptual level, they uphold modern values such as freedom, independence, and self-governance, but precisely in doing so, they communicate to each other on the affective level the age-old virtue of loyalism. Their loyalist emotions are articulated in terms of the Wang Dao anecdote in *The New Accounts*, just as Wang Dao and his men, exiled to the south in fourth-century China, articulated their devotion to dynastic restoration by evoking the Chu hostages in the Zuo commentary. Thanks to sharing these classics, the Chinese translator is able to reproduce this affective communication, just as it translates modern concepts from the Japanese.

Thus steeped in poetic memory, Sanshi is lured into wandering farther; he leaves Philadelphia on a small boat on the Delaware River and heads toward Valley Forge. As he rows up a tributary, his poetic imagination, awakened by the heroines' voices, is quirkily projected onto late nineteenth-century America.

ORIGINAL

散士棹ヲ枉渚ニ弭メ笑テ曰ク　是レ真ニ今世ノ桃源ナリ　恨ムラクハ秦ヲ避クルノ人前朝ノ逸事ヲ話スル者ナキヲ　乃吟ジテ曰ク　扁舟来訪武陵春ト　未ダ聯ヲ成サズ　時ニ微風遥ニ琴声ヲ送ル　怪テ耳ヲ欹テ之ヲ聞ク　其声漸ク近シ　一小艇アリ上流ヨリ下リ来ル　一妃棹ヲ操リ一妃風琴ヲ弾ズ　綽約タル風姿之ヲ望メバ宛モ神仙ノ如シ

Resting his oar at a winding shore, Sanshi smiled and said, "This truly is a modern Peach Blossom Spring. I regret there is no one who fled the Qin and talked about unknown affairs of the previous dynasty." He was reciting, failing to make a couplet, "On a skiff, I have come to visit Wuling," when a gentle breeze carried the sound of a zither. Amazed, Sanshi listened to it carefully. As the sound gradually approached, a small boat sailed down from the upper stream, with one woman pulling on the oar, and the other playing the zither. They appeared as graceful as if they were immortals.[35]

CHINA DISCUSSION TRANSLATION

散士停舟而笑曰。是真今世之桃源也。恨無避秦人與之話前朝逸事耳。乃吟曰。扁舟來訪武陵春。覓句未成。忽聞微風。遙送琴聲。傾耳聽之。其聲漸近。瞥見一小艇。自上流來下。一妃操棹。一妃彈風琴。風姿綽約。望之若神仙。

Mooring his boat, Sanshi smiled and said, "This truly is a modern Peach Blossom Spring. I regret there is no one who fled the Qin and talked about unknown affairs of the previous dynasty." He then recited, "On a skiff, I have come to visit Wuling," failing to complete a phrase. Suddenly, he heard a gentle breeze carrying the sound of a zither. He listened to it carefully. As the sound gradually approached, a small boat sailed down from the upper stream, with one woman pulling on the oar, and the other playing the zither. They appeared as graceful as if they were immortals.[36]

As Sanshi goes up the Delaware River, a literary memory is once again kindled in his mind: Tao Yuanming's 陶淵明 (365?–471) "Taohuayuan ji 桃花源記" (Tale of the Peach Blossom Spring). The archi-topos of utopia in Chinese literature, the tale goes that during the Taiyuan era of the Eastern Jin dynasty, a fisherman from Wuling went upstream along a creek to reach a peach forest in full bloom. There he discovered a sequestered village where people who had fled the tumult during the Qin dynasty (221–207 BCE) had been living a peaceful life in exile for centuries. Sanshi's poetic memory, then, finds an echo in the real world, as his heptasyllabic verse, not yet forming a couplet, is serendipitously answered by the sound of a zither. The lyrical communication in Sanshi's mind is given a narratological embodiment in his fortuitous encounter with the two women he has just seen at Independence Hall. His literary memory is reenacted in the forests of Valley Forge where they learn about each other's identities as expatriates from crippled nations, exchange poems, and reaffirm their loyalist virtue together. This second encounter, in both the original and the translation, marks the beginning of the story of "chance meetings," which tests the protagonists' cultural values against the challenges of modernity.

The ensuing story sets the stage for the protagonists' political adventure, flavored by a romance between Sanshi and Yūran that draws from Ming-Qing scholar-and-beauty fiction, a genre that was avidly read and frequently adapted in Edo Japan.[37] Its beginning is set in the two heroines' clandestine residence in Valley Forge, where Sanshi is invited and meets the Chinese hero Hankei.[38] The four characters are instantly bonded as subjects loyal to nations in peril. They first identify themselves by telling their stories, which the narrative renders in such a way that they speak to each other politically, morally, and emotionally. Yūran says she was expelled from Spain with her father, a Carlist general who had opposed the liberalist policies of the allies of Isabella II (1830–1904, r. 1833–1868) and resisted the popular demand for republicanism in favor of constitutional monarchy. The political position of the Carlist Party is portrayed so that it agrees with Sanshi's legitimism and endorsement of constitutional monarchy for Japan. Kōren's suffering is also portrayed in a way that echoes Sanshi's experience and Japan's diplomatic circumstances. She expresses indignation at the "injustice" (不義 Jpn. *fu gi*; Chn. *bu yi*) of the British Empire, which killed her nationalist father in prison and trampled on the rights of the Irish, while also denouncing Britain's intervention in Japan, China, and India and its intrinsic lust for power and wealth. Kōren is surprised to learn that Sanshi was one of the Japanese men she had earlier read about in the newspaper pledging to aid Irish nationalists once they took up arms—another episode of fortuity. In the original, Hankei, disguised as a servant at the residence, reveals himself as a descendant of a general who fought with the Ming-dynasty loyalist Qu Shisi 瞿式耜 (1590–1650) to resist the Manchu invasion. Drawing on a popular perception in the late Edo, Hankei describes the Taiping Rebellion (1850–1864) as a Han loyalist uprising to restore the dynastic legitimacy broken by the Manchus. When the rebellion was crushed and his family members murdered by the Qing forces, Hankei was exiled to America, where he experienced racism. His loyalism and accusation of racist hypocrisy in America resonate with Sanshi. Responding to their stories, Sanshi announces, "[I] too am a loyal subject of a fallen country" (*bōkoku no ishin* 亡國ノ遺臣; *wangguo zhi yichen* 亡國之遺臣). Thus revealing his true identity, he states, "the hardships you have undergone and the sufferings you will endure are as though identical to mine," and he recalls the devastating War of Aizu, in which many of his clan members and compatriots died honorable deaths due to their unrelenting loyalty to the regime.[39] As a disgraced loyalist, he casts serious doubt on the legitimacy of the Meiji Restoration and lambasts the current government for its lukewarm diplomatic stance against the Western powers and unrestrained indulgence in high Western culture. Parts of his biting criticism were censored in the published text.

The fellow-feeling among the multinational heroes and heroines culminates in a poetry gathering. Inspired by the serendipitous occasion, Sanshi proposes to hold a banquet: "Someone in the past said, 'The good time and the beautiful scene, the appreciative minds and the joyful matters: these four things are rarely found complete.'"[40] This quaint comment is a reference to the fifth-century poet Xie Lingyun's 謝靈運 (385–433) acclaimed "Preface" to a series of poems he composed, called "Ni Wei taizi Yezhong ji 擬魏太子鄴中集" (Imitating the Poems of the Wei Crown Prince's Gathering at Ye). The *China Discussion* translation, recognizing this precedent, renders the phrase as a verbatim quote from the "Preface." Xie Lingyun's work consists of eight poems, each composed in imitation of the voice of a poet active during the Jian'an era (196–220), some two centuries before his time. The Jian'an poets are known for pioneering classical poetry in pentasyllabic lines, a form that Xie himself championed in the fifth century. By "imitating" the different styles of the Jian'an poets, Xie reimagined a gathering in Ye as an original scene of poetry composition, thereby historicizing and canonizing the tradition of classical poetry. Prefaced, so to speak, by the allusion to Xie's "Preface," the poetry gathering in *Chance Meetings* can be read as a further imitation of Xie's "Imitation." With this intertextual gesture, the narrative performatively positions itself in the canonical tradition of classical poetry, which has been transregionally passed on through Xie all the way to nineteenth-century Japan—the tradition in which the Chinese version, via the Japanese text, also registers itself.

The poetry exchange in the recesses of Valley Forge articulates the modern world in poetic language. The legacy of the American War of Independence inspires the protagonists' determination to again take up the lost cause. The poem attributed to Kōren, for instance, draws on the poetics of "mutual merging of the emotions and the landscape" (*qing jing xiang rong* 情景相融) to weave her moral sentiments with the background of the joyful banquet.

清夜会良友	In this pristine night I met with good friends;
花下酌芳罇	Under the flowers I poured flavorful wine.
春雁向北翔	Spring wild geese fly back to the north;
遙遙煙樹昏	Afar, the hazy trees appear dark.
落花隨風摧	Falling flowers break apart in the wind,
翩翩敷庭園	Dancing and carpeting the garden.
殘春看將尽	The remaining spring will be over in a blink;
難挽日月奔	No way to hold back the running time.
臂弱不堪戈	But my arms are too weak to hold a halberd;
幽憤空含冤	So my deep-seated anger vainly engenders hatred.
國仇未全雪	The enemies of my country have not been completely washed away;
甘心思喪元	I have indulged myself in the idea of giving away my head.

| 情悲絃声急 | As my emotion becomes sorrowful, the sounds of the strings speed up; |
| 和我慷慨言 | And they echo with my indignant words.[41] |

In the opening couplet, a retrospective gaze commemorates the fortuitous meeting and the cheerful banquet. Invited by the image of migrating birds, the speaker visualizes the vast late spring landscape, restoring a sense of reality to the utopian closure of the happy gathering. As if in slow motion, the speaker pictures flower petals breaking apart in the wind, carpeting the site of the banquet. The passing of time has always been inscribed on the heart of timeless joy; indeed, there is "no way to hold back the running time." The sense of time awakens the speaker to the onerous reality of being an Irish expatriate, symbolized by the image of arms too heavy to carry—a striking contrast with the floating petals. The precarious future suddenly looms large. Deprived of agency, the speaker cannot vent her resentment, with her "deep-seated anger vainly endanger[ing] hatred." But in the penultimate couplet, her inexpressible emotion finds its voice in a poetic precedent: Cao Zhi's 曹植 (192–232) canonical "Za shi 雜詩" (Miscellaneous Poems). The lines are an adaptation of a couplet in the sixth of the "Miscellaneous Poems," which reads, "The enemies of my country are truly persistent; / I have indulged myself in the idea of giving away my head" (*guo chou liang bu sai* 國讎亮不塞 / *gan xin si sang yuan* 甘心思喪元).[42] The voice of Cao Zhi, a representative Jian'an poet also featured in Xie Lingyun's "Imitation," articulates the speaker's nationalist feelings in terms of the classical virtue of self-sacrificial loyalty. The closing lines also quote the final couplet of Cao Zhi's poem, where the speaker's sorrow is echoed by music. Thus given a lyrical voice, her modern feelings are articulated in traditional poetics, and her nationalism is rendered into the paradigmatic topos of loyalist devotion.

THINGS FALL APART

This fictional poem, featured verbatim in the Chinese rendering, encapsulates a pivotal working of this novel's narrative, which translates the modern world back into the tropes of literary precedents. While relating the story of modern nationalists, it then represents their historical enterprises within a traditional metahistorical framework by positing "Heaven" as the agent of history. A speech by Yūran in the gathering epitomizes this narratology.

ORIGINAL

若シ天道果シテ善ニ幸セバ禍福循環シ卒ニ能ク志ヲ達スルノ時アラン不幸ニシテ時機到ラズンバ節ヲ守リテ道義ノ為メニ死スルモ亦好カラズヤ

If the Way of Heaven indeed benefits the good, then good times and bad times succeed each other, and in the end the time will come when I will be able to fulfill my will. Should such a time unfortunately not come, wouldn't it also be good even though I held onto my principles and died for the cause of righteousness?[43]

CHINA DISCUSSION TRANSLATION

若夫天道果善, 幸而禍福循環, 終有達志之時。不幸而時機未到, 則死守於道義之鄉, 不亦可乎。

If the Way of Heaven is indeed good, then fortunately good times and bad times succeed each other and the time will come when I will be able to fulfill my will in the end. Should such a time unfortunately not come, wouldn't it also be good if I defended to the death the kingdom of righteousness?[44]

The first conditional in this quote is in fact warranted by the precedents it alludes to, including the "Tang gao 湯誥" chapter of *Shangshu* 尚書 (The Book of Documents), which has it that "the Way of Heaven" (*tiandao* 天道) shall "benefit the good and punish the bad" (*fu shan huo yin* 福善禍淫).[45] The moralistic idea of the transcendental and fair working of the Way of Heaven, bolstered by Confucian orthodoxy, attunes the protagonists to the totality of the historical world as it is conceived of in the classical texts and propels their secular project of nation building that unfolds in it. They carry out their nationalist will by upholding the time-honored virtue of "righteousness" (道義 Jpn. *dōgi*; Chn. *daoyi*), which they trust Heaven will recognize. The literary precedents serve as essential exemplars through which they learn the meaning of virtue, and it is now their turn to exhibit it in a new world. If Cao Zhi is such an

Literature's Search for Itself 55

exemplar for Kōren, then she vies to become the next example, dead or alive, for the sake of other nationalists in Ireland and across the world.

Thanks to the shared literary precedents, this narrative structure also works in the Chinese version, presenting Chinese readers with modern examples to emulate. However, it did so only by removing the Chinese protagonist from the key scene of the "chance meeting" in Valley Forge and altering his identity. This translational decision, in fact, was the result of a notable wavering. The fourth issue of *The China Discussion* (January 22, 1899) initially carried a faithful translation of this scene where Hankei, disclosing his identity as a Ming loyalist, makes his first appearance. But in the fifth issue (February 1, 1899), this part was completely retranslated, removing the Chinese hero.[46] After the whole sequence of the banquet, he finally appears in the seventh issue (March 2, 1899) when the protagonists are taking leave of each other, promising a future reunion:

> Politely shaking hands [with the heroines], Sanshi was about to leave the gate when Yūran plucked a branch of white rose and stuck it in his collar, saying, "Sir, even though this flower withers, let us not abandon each other." Smiling, Sanshi turned to her and replied, "Of course I appreciate a person like a flower, but I don't know to whose home the word-understanding flower [i.e., Yūran] would want to fly away." Nodding and smiling, she sent him off for a long time. <u>Hankei was a man of ambition from China. Indignant at the world and loathing society, he had been secluded in the wild. He had been one of Sanshi's best friends, and they had visited each other frequently. He had long known the names of Yūran and Kōren, too. On the occasion of Sanshi's trip [to their residence], he had made an appointment earlier with him to meet at the moored boat. He had already been waiting for a long time at the shore.</u> As they greeted each other upon leaving, Sanshi boarded the boat. The two ladies said, "Please take care, sir." Taking his hat off, Sanshi replied, "We shall see each other again."[47]

The translator rather awkwardly appends to the romantic scene of separation a succinct introduction of the Chinese hero (the <u>underlined</u> part), transforming him from a Ming loyalist into an ambiguous "man of ambition from China." In the original, Sanshi and Hankei strike up a friendship "by chance," but in the translation, they are longtime friends; furthermore, Hankei already knows of Sanshi's visit to the residence, which in the original happens only by coincidence. Thus, in this Chinese version, not only does Hankei refrain from expressing himself lyrically or revealing his political identity, but he is also disengaged from the core narrative structure of "chance meetings."

Hankei's equivocal existence in the translated text indicates the latter's uncertainty about the identity of a modern Chinese hero in this story. The original implies that, together with a disgraced Aizu retainer, a Spanish legitimist, and an Irish nationalist, a Ming-dynasty loyalist should exemplify the virtue relevant to the modern world, an assumption with which the translation disagrees. With his identity left blank, the translated "Hankei" acts like an empty signifier. This revision points to the underlying question of what subject might be able to carry out a political enterprise to save China and, furthermore, whether the kind of virtue exemplified in classical letters is pertinent at all to modern political exigencies. These problems naturally interrogate the very authority of Heaven that allegedly legitimizes traditional virtue, thereby throwing into question the totality that the narrative transposes from the literary precedents and projects onto the late nineteenth-century globe.

These questions are already implied in the Japanese version, which struggles to constitute a totality of the represented world through a plethora of references to previous literatures. In addition to Wang Dao, Cao Zhi, and others we have identified, *Chance Meetings* alludes to numerous other cultural exemplars, such as Han Xin, Fan Zeng, Jing Ke, Nie Zheng, Ji Shao, Han Yu, Luo Binwang, and Li Ruoshui—the generals, thinkers, poets, and assassins whose stories were told and retold prominently in the Chinese classics. Another set of model characters mentioned are famous couples in Chinese letters. Sanshi expresses his feelings toward the heroines by evoking Wang Zhaojun and Emperor Yuan of Han, Yang Guifei and Emperor Xuanzong of Tang, and Lady Li and Emperor Wu of Han. Their romantic stories were canonized by literary works including Ma Zhiyuan's 馬致遠 (c. 1250–c. 1321) *Han gong qiu* 漢宮秋 (Autumn in the Han Palace), Bai Juyi's 白居易 (772–846) "Chang hen ge 長恨歌" (Song of Everlasting Sorrow), and Li Shangyin's 李商隱 (c. 813–858) "Li furen san shou 李夫人三首" (Three Poems on Lady Li). Then, as

Literature's Search for Itself 57

if to supplement the traditional reference points, the novel cites Western examples in an eclectic fashion. Besides Confucius, it mentions Jesus and Socrates as embodying righteousness; to describe female beauty, it brings up Helen of Troy and Mary, Queen of Scots in addition to the goddesses of Yunmeng and Luochuan; in illustrating the vastness of the universe, it touches on modern physics as well as Buddhist and Daoist concepts; in evoking the classical poetic topos about the transience of human institutions, it quotes from Herodotus and Thomas Babington Macaulay. The narrative abounds in instances of such eclecticism, which draws on the rhetoric of the East-West dichotomy to supplement "Eastern"—mostly classical Chinese—precedents with "Western" examples, in an effort to come up with an upgraded set of cultural exemplars for a newly conceived totality of the historical world.

The way *Chance Meetings* reconstructs the historical world may be symptomatic of *horror vacui*; its literary prose packed with allusions to archaic precedents, while supplemented by eclectic references, sometimes reads like a collection of fragments that fail to constitute a totality. This chasm finds its reflection in the struggles of the protagonists. After the merry gathering at Valley Forge, they plunge into protracted battles with no end in sight. Sanshi misses the promised reunion due to illness, and when he belatedly makes it back to the residence, he finds that his comrades have already departed for Europe to rescue Yūran's imprisoned father. Residing alone in Philadelphia, he worries about their whereabouts, betting the fate of his own political battle on their success. The news that reaches him, however, is mostly grim. Challenges are mounting and misfortunes piling up; only the sweet memories of the banquet can sustain his devotion to the political endeavor of righting the wrong of imperialism. Amid such adverse circumstances, he happens to meet Kōren at the grave of Fanny Parnell in Cambridge, Massachusetts. Having just returned to America, Kōren tells Sanshi the story of her adventure in Europe, which ended in a tragic shipwreck in the Mediterranean where Yūran and Hankei went missing. Separated from them, Kōren is especially delighted to see Sanshi again and invites him to her residence. They hold an all-night conversation and another round of poetry exchanges, hoping to revive the joy of the initial meeting. The cheerful reunion, however, cannot relieve Sanshi's deep-seated angst. The following morning, when he returns to his temporary abode, people notice his haggard face and soiled outfit and ask what he has been doing. Unable to invent an answer, he replies:

> Last night, tired of reading, I was seated alone, watching the bright moon. I was suddenly driven to come down the house and wander the garden. Inspired, I followed where my feet took me and reached the recesses of the wild. Reciting quietly and long, I wondered if there indeed was a Way of Heaven and pondered human life and death. The more I reflected, the more I lost myself. In a daze, I was enraptured as if in a dream. I can no longer remember where I went or what I did. That must have been what is called "fox possession" in Japan.[48]

Sanshi's voice betrays his perplexity as he tries to conceal his and his comrades' political scheme. Caught by surprise, he cannot translate between the authentic time he spent with friends and the alienating reality of life, and his bewilderment casts doubt on the relevance of their values to the broader world outside the imagined "peach blossom spring." By putting Sanshi's voice in dialogue with others that are alien to his culture, the narrative takes him out of the enclosed space in which it stages his idealist struggles, exposing the vulnerability, or even naïveté, of his ethicopolitical devotion. His acquaintances even wonder whether Sanshi "has at last had a nervous breakdown."[49] Questioning the protection of the Way of Heaven, he suffers from what, following Lukács, might be called "metaphysical homesickness," yet it is precisely in that open-ended modern world that the protagonists must now prove themselves.[50]

Chance Meetings and its translation were meant to convey classical ethical-aesthetic values as virtues necessary for realizing a better modern world, just as the various literary precedents they allude to imparted those values to the story's protagonists, and just as even older texts played the same function within those alluded-to precedents. Sanshi's suspected madness indicates a fateful exposure of the culture he inhabits and shares with his international allies to a broader world that calls its validity into question. This aporia of the hero, unresolvable in the framework of a story built on his culture, reflects a serious doubt cast on the medial function that *Chance Meetings* and its translation were intended to serve in the world where they circulated, causing them to deviate from the received notion of literature, which they derived from layers of precedents.

Indeed, following Sanshi's nervous breakdown, *Chance Meetings* departs from its ostensible literary function. With the fates of Yūran and Hankei still in limbo, Sanshi decides to return to Japan, determined to "devote himself to the nation and society far more than any ordinary person" and to "travel around Eastern countries to spread his ideas."[51] Just as he is about to undertake his project, however, he is offered a job in the Japanese government. Though at first he turns it down due to his "lack of interest in serving the government," he eventually accepts it at the cost of his idealism.[52] The novel's last six volumes then relate the official inspection trip to Europe and the Middle East in which Sanshi takes part. On the trip, he happens to meet Yūran and Hankei, who turn out to have survived the devastating shipwreck. Hankei has been working to overthrow the Qing dynasty in China, while Yūran has ended up in Egypt with her father, who has joined forces with ʿUrābī Pasha's nationalist army. Yūran and Sanshi are delighted about their chance meeting in Egypt, but Sanshi must soon leave her, saying, "I would be able to rescue you and go to Europe together, if only I were not bound by a governmental order. It is indeed a pity and regrettable." He leaves his sweetheart on the pretext of an official engagement, expecting aid to reach her from the remnant forces of the Carlist Party or Cuba.[53] The Japanese hero's heartless departure is symbolic of a structural shift in the novel's narratology. Its final six volumes replace the protagonists' labyrinthine struggles, marked by detours, suspense, and contingency, with a linear plot that punctually follows the scheduled itinerary of the official trip, defying the intrusion of romance or serendipity. Those readers who were enchanted by the suspense of the risky battles of virtue against power in the first ten volumes would have been disappointed by the loss of aesthetic taste and moral devotion in the final six. The latter part of the novel thus reads rather tediously and monotonously, and probably too much so for it to be serialized in a periodical. It was indeed shortly after this marked shift that *The China Discussion* cancelled the serialization of the translation.

The China Discussion's decision not to publish the latter part, which must have been ultimately made due to concerns about the literary qualities required of serialized fiction, is indicative of the radical change in the literary characteristics of the Japanese text. Fighting back from their degrading reduction to "loyal subjects of fallen countries" and driven by the desire to overturn imperial injustice, the heroes and heroines vied for political relevance by reenacting long-lived cultural values, and likewise, *Chance Meetings* wrestled to hold onto its status as literature by affirming and mediating those values anew to a contemporary readership. Yet in the final part of the Japanese version, Sanshi, while still upholding the old virtues, loses the utopian vision of a just world; now, as a government official, he serves the abstract, value-neutral goal of seeing Japan win an international competition with Western powers. The wretched subject's aspirational imagination shrinks, and amid the social Darwinian game of survival of the fittest, the raison d'état takes its place. Consequently, the tension between the classical literariness it conjures up, on the one hand, and the novelistic distance across which it tries to reaffirm that literariness in modern times, on the other, collapses. *Chance Meetings* abandons its attempts at fulfilling literature's assigned role of mediating ethical-aesthetic value and becomes something else. The anticlimax, therefore, throws into doubt the very status of *Chance Meetings* as literature in the accepted sense, forcing it to come full circle and return to the self-consciousness about marginality articulated in the preface. The text is left with the question: What is *Chance Meetings* if it is still called literature? While the Japanese text quickly left behind this self-reflexive moment and became a rather insipid narrative serving an extrinsic political agenda, the Chinese rendition, precisely by excising that latter portion, passed that suspense about literature's search for itself on to further experiments in new fiction.

AESTHETIC EDUCATION IN SUSPENSION

As it tried to prove its worth as literature, *Chance Meetings* sought to affirm and embody the surviving validity of the past culture that had nourished the long and powerful tradition of literature in a modernizing Japan. Relying on the transregional breadth of that culture, its Chinese translation carried this attempt on in a Chinese context. Yet as the story allegorizes, these anachronistic attempts eventually led literature away from its culturally accepted notion into a self-reflexive movement that calls its meaning into question. Just as the story's protagonists endure transcendental homesickness, literature leaves its cultural home for an open-ended world, indicating an origin of modern literature.

If observed with the benefit of hindsight, from the point of view of "modern literature" in the normalized sense of the term, then these works may represent little more than the last breaths of an obsolete culture. But the resonances of these works to contemporary concerns such as postcoloniality and philosophical reflections on modern political ideas in broader cultural contexts, urge us to reassess the implications of the ambivalent medium holding literariness in suspension that these works indicate. Such implications are significant, as they undercut at one stroke the constructed authority of modern culture *and* the fundamentalist anxiety to rejuvenate past culture uncritically. They bespeak, I would argue, the discursive significance of new fiction at its best. Inspired by the characterization of the effects of new fiction in terms of "affective education" (*chŏngyuk* 情育) by Sin Ch'aeho, to whom we will turn in chapter 2, I consider those implications through a comparison with the discourse of "aesthetic education" formulated by Friedrich Schiller. Literature and criticism in turn-of-the-century East Asia and aesthetic thought in eighteenth-century Europe have disparate conceptual constructs, but the political implications of the latter can help elucidate the former's stakes as cross-cultural discourse.

Schiller's notion of the state of "determinability" (*Bestimmbarkeit*), or the "aesthetic" state, can functionally describe the prolonged suspense that is characteristic of *Chance Meeting*'s narrative, where the aesthetic and moral values it expresses through allusion to previous literature are counterbalanced with an implied skepticism about their validity in modern times. In *On the Aesthetic Education of Man*, Schiller posits the psychic "middle disposition" in which "sense and reason are both active *at the same time*," and for this reason, "they cancel each other out as determining forces." "The middle disposition, in which the psyche is subject neither to physical nor to moral constraint, and yet is active in both these ways, pre-eminently deserves to be called a free disposition," he writes.[54] Through copious references to literary precedents, *Chance Meetings* evokes the reader's habitual responsiveness to literary topoi and moral investment in orthodox Confucian virtues like "loyalty" and "righteousness," yet as the lengthy narrative takes the reader through meandering twists and turns without direction and referential eclecticism without order, their sensational and moral attachment has to be held in suspension. This effect enacts Liang's contention that fiction is "able" (ke 可) not only to make the reader feel "pleasure and entertainment," but also to "surprise, startle, make us feel sad, and move us."[55] Fiction is a vehicle *capable* of conveying all sorts of emotion, as well as of exerting either good or bad moral influences. Fiction's potentiality thus consists in its ability to create a receptive state of mind that is in itself emotionally and morally undetermined—a sponge of determinability Liang wishes to create as the precondition for all the necessary renovations.

Schiller insists that it is exactly in this state of determinability that "something Infinite is achieved."[56] Considering this logic, Eagleton contends, "All of this, however, makes the aesthetic, that mighty force at the root of our moral humanity, sound like nothing so much as a simple *aporia*. Two strenuously antagonistic forces [sensation and morality] cancel each other out into a kind of stalemate or nullity, and this sheer suggestive nothingness is our pre-capacity for all value."[57] The enormous stakes of Schiller's aesthetic state resonate with the immensity of the possibility that Liang attributes to the affective power of fiction, which can "control the way of humanity," and from whose "renewal" emanate the reforms of all aspects of society, from "morality," "religion," "politics," "customs," and "learning and arts" to "the human mind and its character."[58] Yet if Schiller regards the state of determinability to be itself indicative of the realization of an "aesthetic State," then Liang, in contradistinction, adopts the anticipatory temporality of renovation (*yu xin* 欲新) and embraces that state in its sheer potentiality as the condition of possibility for China's coming reforms. For Schiller, the aesthetic state indicates the ideal State where humans, freed from indulgence in sensations and dictatorship by reason, realize themselves in their full diversity, all while the "parts" are "tuned up to the idea of the whole."[59] That aporetic leap from potentiality into actuality in Schiller hinges on, as De Man has pointed out, the proposition of an "absolute" category of "the human" that is not open to critique—an irony for a thought whose core stakes involve removing, by virtue of the aesthetic, a top-down definition of humanity.[60] Without the postulation of such an absolute category, Liang's discourse remains in pure suspension without sublimation, in an anticipatory mode that defers the realization of an ideal state and "new people" to the future—the work of a "transitional era."⁶¹ *Chance Meetings* likewise stays trapped in the "labyrinth of aesthetics,"⁶² whose detours and dead ends, contingent paths and unsuccessful routes constitute traces of its search-in-progress for an ideal state free of imperialism.

Without being sublimated into the "Infinite," the protracted suspension in *Chance Meetings* bespeaks its figuration of the ideal state as a mere example. Its political utopianism, to be sure, is articulated by modern ideas like "freedom," "independence," and "self-governance," but the convoluted path of the narrative prevents them from becoming its fixed telos as preconfigured concepts. The wandering and unforeseeable course of the narrative instead indicates literature attempting to tell the story of ideas that are heterogeneous to what it has conventionally been able to represent. That attempt implies literature's reflection on the realm of what it can represent; hence *Chance Meeting*'s self-consciousness about its marginality. At the same time, it points to a heuristic pursuit of the meaning of modern ideas without preempting them conceptually, from within a culture foreign to their provenance—a pursuit that resembles artistic striving for transcendental beauty without grasping it in advance as a concept, from within the realm of empirical expressions. In this sense, the way *Chance Meetings*, through the intensity of its literary marginality, indicates modern political ideas can be characterized in terms of "exemplary validity," tantamount to the way an artistic work, in its irreducible particularity, manifests a universal idea of beauty without conceiving it beforehand.⁶³

As in an aesthetic judgment, therefore, *Chance Meetings* constitutes one of the examples whose accumulation is to form a normative tradition from which those political ideas acquire their meaning. In so doing, the novel—if only through anachronism and cross-cultural misreading—endows the literary precedents it refers to with the same validity, thereby rendering, for instance, a classical Chinese poem as an example of national "independence." Because it shares this literary context, the Chinese translation too becomes such an exemplar. The protracted narrative of these works puts classical cultural values to the test, while leading modern political ideas to meet foreign examples and thus to transform themselves. It insists that those ideas are constituted, without having their meaning appropriated by any single culture, through a series of examples that can appear from within any cultural context. Drifting away from their cultural home, suspended between new and old cultures, these works point to the medium of modern literature, which can work as a conceptual laboratory driven by the utopian aspiration for an ideal state, where political ideas are freed from hegemonic definitions by embracing multiple culturally grounded examples, opening themselves to becoming *more* universal. These works thus transpose Western-originated political ideas not just conceptually but also *aesthetically*.

This narratology of suspension, however, disappears in the last ten volumes of the Japanese original, which *The China Discussion* mostly excises. It is succeeded by Liang's own political novel: *The Future of New China*.

After his engagement with the Meiji political novels, Liang, still in exile, pursued his literary endeavors in earnest, writing several fictional biographies of European and Chinese national heroes; advancing discourses of revolution in prose, verse, and drama; editing the literary journal *New Fiction*; and, above all, trying his pen on political fiction.[64] Liang serialized *The Future of New China* beginning in the first issue of *New Fiction*, published in 1902. According to an advertisement run a few months before the journal's launch, he intended it to be a colossal saga of China's modernization in the coming sixty years. It was, however, left incomplete, abandoned at a point when the story had barely begun.[65] Composed as it is in the style of classic cycle-chapter fiction, the novel is strikingly narrated from the vantage point of sixty years in the future.[66] The existing five chapters open with a future scene in which the imaginary Chinese state, which the author anticipates will be built ten years after his time, is hosting the World Expo to celebrate its fiftieth anniversary, showing off its industrial and cultural prosperity to delegates from all over the world. The illustrious sixty-year history of nation building is to be related by Kong Juemin, a descendant of Confucius, to an international audience. The nation building has been driven by heroes, namely Huang Keqiang and Li Qubing, who strove to advance modernization with the knowledge they had acquired through study in Europe. At a high point of the extant account, these heroes engage in heated debates about the course of China's modernization, with Huang advocating constitutional monarchy and Li revolutionary republicanism.

These enlightened heroes, however, are not culturally uprooted. In addition to being leading disciples of a prominent late Qing literatus,

Huang and Li are versed in classical literature. Upon returning home from study in Europe, the heroes witness Russia's occupation of the strategic Shanhai Pass region and express their indignation by alternately composing, phrase by phrase, a song lyric (*ci* 詞) to the stock tune of "He xinlang 賀新郎" (Congratulating the Bridegroom) and inscribing it on a wall. Later in the story, their poetic communication is extended to another character, who leaves next to their piece an additional *ci* piece that matches rhyme words with theirs, following the practice of *heyun* 和韻 (matching rhyme). There is yet another hero named Chen Meng, whom Huang and Li hear chanting lines from Byron's poems ("Don Juan" and "The Giaour") to a piano accompaniment. The narrative quotes those lines in the original English and then renders them into Chinese in a way that, as the author's interpolated comment explains, "translates the foreign meaning into the Chinese tune" (*yi Zhongguo diao yi waiguo yi* 以中國調譯外國意).[67] Just as Byron's lamentation over the ancient Greek civilization in decline touches the heartstrings of Huang and Li, Chen Meng's recitation, via the translation into the old tune, echoes their lyricism, mediating affective communication among the protagonists. The heroes are thus bonded together not only by ideas of Western origin and their passion for modernization, but also by a thick cultural habitus expressed in poetry.

The text of *The Future of New China* is woven with the warp of the epic of Chinese nation building and the weft of ethical-aesthetic values rooted in literary tradition. The heroes are at once enlightened modern intellectuals and lyrical poets; they have heated debates on the course of Chinese modernization, yet its success hinges on their solidarity through affective communication mediated by *ci* poetry. And the sixty years of the nation-building epic are as much about realizing universal political values as about giving them new meaning through their actual struggles grounded in a cultural-historical context. With the figures of Huang Keqiang and Li Qubing, Liang designed exemplary heroes for modern China, in a way taking up the question left unanswered in the *China Discussion* translation of *Chance Meetings*, which featured merely an ambiguous character as the Chinese hero.

The Future of New China resonates with *Chance Meetings* in that both texts put classical cultural values to the test of modern validity, while making modern political ideas more capacious by having them enacted by culturally rooted protagonists. *Chance Meetings* achieves this through its prolonged narrative, whereas Liang's work does so by being interrupted at the beginning. In the opening scene set in the future, the World Expo coincides with China's hosting of the signing of a peace treaty. The publication advertisement informs us that this was originally intended to be the occasion to celebrate the aversion of a war that China was about to wage as the "leader" of the "yellow race," including Japan and the Philippines, against the Western nations on account of the latter's racialized colonial oppression.[68] Yet this epic, which would have given China the sole privilege to reconfigure modern political ideas vis-à-vis the West, remained unwritten, leaving, despite Liang's plan, the beginning scene in its unapologetic utopianism that weds the projection of a new world order to the excavation of an ancient ideal—an emblematic example of the image of a peaceful and equitable world that is meant to free modern political ideas from being monopolized by the West, whose racism and imperialism were causing suffering in the rest of the world.[69]

Leaving aside circumstantial speculations about why Liang did not write the subsequent chapters, I argue that *The Future of New China* indicates an origin of modern literature precisely because it was abandoned in the beginning.[70] The absent chapters expose the limits of what literature as Liang practiced it could represent. Just as Sanshi in *Chance Meetings* lost his story after his literary culture proved bankrupt, so do the protagonists of *The Future of New China* fail to have their modern stories told in the still-relevant culture where *ci* poems would be exchanged as a vehicle of ethical-aesthetic value and ears would be treated well by the "Chinese tune." This conundrum puts the work out of place in the very culture where it exists as literature—the impossible status at which the author himself cannot but "laugh," as Liang writes in its preface: "Now that this work has seen the completion of its first two to three chapters, I have turned over its pages, and thought it reads like popular literature [*shuobu* 說部] but not really, like an unofficial history [*baishi* 稗史] but not really, or like a treatise [*lunzhu* 論著] but not really—I do not know what kind of style/genre [*ti* 體] it is. I cannot help laughing at myself."[71] *The Future of New China* does not properly belong to the disposition of genres in the current literary culture, haunted by the same self-consciousness about marginality that Shiba expressed about *Chance*

Meetings. Its liminal position in the existing order of literature is such that *The Future of New China* is unable to complete itself and, in its interrupted form, is left with the question about its status *as* literature—the ambivalence that makes it a quintessential example of modern literature, as a practice ingrained with self-reflection about what constitutes the realm of literature.

The Meiji political novels and the late Qing discourse and practice of new fiction constitute ambivalent moments. Shiba Shirō and Liang Qichao still relied heavily on classical literariness, yet they did not regard the received notion of literature in their present cultures as still relevant as is without renovations. In this intermediate state, they ventured to have the existing literature meet modern political exigencies, leading it to leave its established cultural confines and face the modern world with open horizons. Their works speak to the process by which existing literature responded to the contemporary sociopolitical demands, the process through which modern literature emerged in its core aesthetic sense in Japan and China. In the next chapter, we will further explore new fiction in Korea by considering Sin Ch'aeho's engagement with Liang's work.

CHAPTER TWO

Literature and Life in Exile
Sin Ch'aeho's Engagement with Liang Qichao's Work

In the "twofold structure" of Korea's exposure to modern discourse, Chinese texts, in addition to Japanese sources, had served as an essential interface since the mid–nineteenth century.[1] In the first decade of the twentieth century, as Japan's territorial ambition for the peninsula became ever more salient, Chinese materials gained renewed relevance. As Yŏp Kŏn'gon and U Imkŏl have demonstrated, Liang Qichao's writing was particularly admired against the backdrop of this national crisis.[2]

Korean reformists during that decade took Liang's work to be first and foremost a useful source of modern knowledge. Ch'oe Sŏkha 최석하 (1864–1912), for example, published an essay called "Chosŏn hon 朝鮮魂" (The Korean Soul) in *T'aegŭk hakpo* 太極學報 (T'aegŭk Scholarly Journal) in 1906, promoting nationalism in the face of the Japanese usurpation of sovereign rights.

> Liang Qichao, the Master of the Ice Drinker's Studio, is a famous man of ambition from the Qing. He earlier lamented that there was no national soul among the people of the Qing and wrote a book called *The Chinese Soul*, demanding loudly and indignantly that the Chinese soul be created. I can see he is a man of passion, concerned with the fate of his country. Judging from the current situation in Korea, we are now at a juncture where we need a national soul hundreds of times more than China. . . . Erect a Korean soul! Erect!

Once we erect a Korean soul in each compatriot, we will be able to recover the lost sovereign rights in politics, finances, and diplomacy.[3]

Alluded to here is Liang's 1899 essay "Zhongguo hun an zai hu 中國魂安在乎" (Where Is the Chinese Soul?), which adapted Meiji Japan's nationalistic discourse on the "Japanese soul" (*yamato damashii* 大和魂).[4] Ch'oe Sŏkha's essay goes on to discuss modernization in Japan, Russia, France, Britain, and America, contending that without a national soul, these countries would not have achieved their current prosperity in their respective areas of strength. To Ch'oe, Liang's impassioned discourse in the wake of the failure of the Hundred Days' Reform proved particularly pertinent to Korea's embattled situation.

For a Korean readership, however, Liang's writing was not just one of the available sources of modern ideas; it had a unique appeal and relevance thanks to Korea's long-standing cultural relationship with China. Hong P'ilju 홍필주 (1857–1917), for instance, relates an episode of his visit to Liang in Yokohama, who encouraged him to "translate many Western books to benefit [his] people." Hong claims that the West is "removed afar by the oceans and its customs are different, many of them incommensurate with those in East Asia"; yet, "since only Korea and China originally shared the same script and tracks [*mungwe pondong* 文軌本同], they also share their shortcomings, and the means to fix them cannot be different."[5] Hong's idiomatic expression alludes to the policy of the First Emperor of China to "unify the carriage tracks and written script" (*che tong gui, shu tong wenzi* 車同軌, 書同文字) for standardized communication and centralized power.[6] He evokes Korea's centuries-old relations to the Sinocentric sphere of influence and suggests that solutions to China's contemporary troubles would be particularly pertinent to the Korean situations and customs; hence the unique relevance of Liang's work. In the same vein, a short writeup introducing the idea of equality before the law, published in *Honam hakpo* 湖南學報 (Honam Scholarly Journal) in 1908, claims that in scholarship on modern politics, "some [theories] are applicable to the West but not to the East, and others are suitable for the past but not for the present," and "only what Mr. Liang Qichao writes" appears "exceptionally complete."[7] Whereas turn-of-the-century Korean intellectuals ascribed the nation's independence first and foremost to the dismantling of what they perceived as its age-old cultural and political dependence on China, the remainders of that rapidly withering tradition undergirded its engagement with the modern episteme through Liang's work. Like the cases of Sino-Japanese literary exchanges that we examined in chapter 1, the paradoxical structure of the regional cultural context, in which the mediation of modernity rested on the legacies of the cultural past it was to replace, underpinned the turn-of-the-century Korean engagement with Chinese materials.

Among the Korean intellectuals who most avidly interacted with Liang's writing was Sin Ch'aeho, whose literary works are the focus of this chapter.[8] Sin translated into Korean Liang's popular literary adaptation of the biographies of three founding heroes of modern Italy, *Yidali jianguo sanjie zhuan* 意大利建國三傑傳 (The Biographies of the Three Heroes of Italian Nation-Building, 1902, hereafter referred to as *Biographies*). Like *Chance Meetings* and its Chinese translation, Liang's work and Sin's translation employ a classical literary form—this time the *zhuan/chŏn* 傳 (lit., biography, story)—to relate a modern epic of nation-building, and through this anachronistic gesture they defy a teleological point of view and render history as a precarious process navigated by heroic subjects taking a blind, mythical leap forward. This translation informed Sin's works in the genre of hero biography, through which he grappled with the aporia of recovering a history written from the point of view of the Korean nation based on documents produced and preserved from what he perceived as a Sinocentric vantage point. In creating stories of national heroes, Sin took classical letters out of the traditional horizon of interpretation, exposing them to hermeneutic indeterminability. He thus presented existing literature in its irreducible semiotic ambiguity, as traces or signs anticipating the future revealing of a yet-to-be-told story of the nation. Exiled in China following Korea's colonization, Sin took his quest for national history further in a dream narrative titled "Kkum hanŭl 꿈하늘" (Dream Heaven, 1916), in which he reaffirmed the afterlives of existing letters, no matter how obsolete or even detrimental to modern culture they may be, as the sole ground on which to search for a Korean national history. Through his work, Sin wrested literature from the cultural context where it had been produced and read and revisited it in open-ended interpretative horizons, thereby indicating an origin of literary modernity that inherently straddles cultural-contextual boundaries.

MODERNIZATION AS A MYSTERY

Sin Ch'aeho was an intellectual of utmost importance for modern Korea. A fierce opponent of Japanese imperialism and an unrelenting nationalist, Sin is best remembered as a pioneer of national history in Korea. Ruthlessly criticizing traditional historiography for its alleged submission to the Sinocentric worldview, he explored new literature with which to convey history from a "subjective position" of the Korean nation. His work was marked by a profound social and cultural shift that Korea underwent in his time, which his biography reflects, providing the context for my analysis of his literary writings.

Sin was born in 1880 into a family of scholar-official background that was already in significant decline.[9] After the patriarch died in 1886, he began pursuing an orthodox education based on the Chinese classics under the auspices of the grandfather, who had retired from official service in the Chosŏn court and opened a village school. Among several mentors he studied with, Sin Kisŏn 신기선 (1851–1909), a prominent late Chosŏn scholar-official, let him also read late Qing books on modern knowledge and recommended him for admission to Sŏnggyungwan in 1898. Established in the late fourteenth century as the top Confucian academy and restructured with the Kabo Reforms (1894–1895) into a modern higher-education institution, Sŏnggyungwan gave Sin further exposure to the modern episteme. While joining the Independence Association and participating in the modernization movement in earnest, he devoted himself to education, publishing a number of essays promoting policy reforms and cautioning his compatriots against aggravating Japanese interventionism. In 1905, the year Japan usurped Korea's diplomatic sovereignty with the Eulsa Treaty, he was given the highest *paksa* chair by Sŏnggyungwan, yet against the backdrop of the dire political situation, he rushed to resign from the prestigious position and set the stage for his activism in the modern publishing world. Involved in the editorship of the *Imperial Capital Gazette* and the *Korea Daily News*, he sought outlets for his prolific writing in modern newspapers and journals. In 1907, he cofounded the New People's Association (*Sinmin hoe* 신민회), a clandestine organization aimed at recovering sovereign rights whose ambitious plan of action covered areas from publication to education, from financing industry to building a military school and constructing an overseas military base in preparation for an anticipated war of independence against Japan. Through those activities, he became a leading figure in the nationalist, anti-Japanese, and reformist campaign, known as the Patriotism and Enlightenment Movement (*aeguk kyemong undong* 애국계몽운동), which lasted through the first decade of the twentieth century until the nation was colonized in 1910.

During those years, Sin engaged in the discourse of new fiction (*sin sosŏl* 신소설). This genre flourished in modern print media in Korea in the first decade of the twentieth century in close contact with Meiji and late Qing fiction. Like its Japanese and Chinese counterparts, Korean new fiction displayed an eclectic style, inheriting features of premodern fiction while representing modernity in both form and content.[10] Liang Qichao's theory and practice of new fiction exerted a particularly significant influence, resulting in numerous discussions, translations, and adaptations. Sin was among those who most eagerly read Liang's literary work. He took seriously Liang's idea of making use of the affective power of fiction to reconfigure national subjectivity for the sake of modernization—the idea that, as we saw in chapter 1, Liang put forth in his 1902 essay "On the Relationship between Fiction and the Governance of Society." Alluding to this piece, as well as to Liang's 1898 "Preface to Political Fiction in Translation," Sin writes in a 1908 piece titled "Kŭn'gŭm kungmun sosŏl chŏja ŭi chuŭi 近今國文小說著者의 注意" (Admonition for the Authors of Recent Fiction in the National Script),

> Even though a worthy and upright man, talking from a rostrum with his naturally honest appearance, discusses some profound principles of mind and things or some histories of prosperity and decline in the past and the present, the audience surrounding him will be no more than a few learned men. Moreover, even though some knowledge can be developed in this way, it will be difficult for this man to make a bad folk good or to tame a wicked one by transplanting his own personality. But works of fiction, which are

based on street talk and colloquialisms, are not like that. All the women, children, and servants love them so much. Therefore, even with a little eccentricity of ideas or a bit of virility of words, their hundred readers and thousand listeners will all end up admiring them. How much more so when the author's spirit and soul are present on the pages? The reader then cannot help shedding tears upon reading something terrible and feeling their energies aroused upon reading something thrilling. By virtue of the lasting effects of edification and penetration [*ki hundo nŭng'yŏm ŭi kigu* 其熏陶凌染의 既久], their moral nature will naturally be affected and transformed [*kamhwa* 感化]. I therefore claim: the general propensity of society is to be rectified by fiction written in the national script.[11]

Following this argument, Sin further echoes Liang in denouncing the malicious influence that "old fiction" has on people's minds and customs, and suggests that it be renovated into and gradually replaced by "new fiction."[12] Just as Liang did, Sin proposes to employ fiction as a pharmakon to attack poison by poison, as a means to foster "affective education" (*chŏngyuk* 情育), which he advocates as one of the three branches of "new education"—along with "physical" and "academic education"—in order to cultivate the "patriotic heart."[13]

The Korean engagement with Liang's writing was indeed as much affective as conceptual. As a window onto modernity, Liang's work served especially as a medium capable of conveying the emotions of oppressed peoples vying for national independence. *Yuenan wangguo shi* 越南亡國史 (History of the Fall of Vietnam), which Liang helped the Vietnamese nationalist activist Phan Bội Châu (1867–1940) publish in 1905, drew particularly passionate responses from Korean readers.[14] A criticism in the *Imperial Capital Gazette* reads, "If you have a decent heart and understanding, who in this world would not beat the earth and cry out in sorrow, and look up to heaven and shout out pain after reading *History of the Fall of Vietnam*? . . . Imagining the people of Vietnam, I cannot but sob with tears washing down my face."[15] The critic even confesses that every time he picked up a pen to discuss this piece, he was "unable to write" with his "blood boiling up and tears gushing out."[16] Korean critics' poignant responses to Liang's work on Vietnam's colonization resonate with his writings on Korea's crisis as a harbinger of China's impending fall. Responding to the Japan-Korea Treaty of 1904, which became a precursor of the Eulsa Treaty, Liang wrote, "A country with three thousand years of history [i.e., Korea] suddenly passed away. Now, if you kept a close relationship with it, would you not write its story to honor its death? Alas! This [writing] will let you fathom and understand my grief."[17] Liang's discourses on Vietnam and Korea, to be sure, were not entirely innocent, for China's historical power over them was at stake. Yet in the transregional cultural context, they served as an important medium to communicate these nations' painful circumstances with emotional force.

It is in this affective communication that Sin's 1907 translation of Liang's *Biographies*, titled *Yit'aeri kŏn'guk samgŏl chŏn* 伊太利建國三傑傳 (The Biographies of the Three Heroes of Italian Nation-Building), became involved.[18] Reiterating Liang's discussions on the relationship between "new people" and "new fiction," the writer Chang Chiyŏn described how Sin's translation touched his heart: "Were it not for the heart [*sim* 心], studying politics, law, industry, artistic skills, or various sciences would be but a machine's or a slave's deed."[19] Another critic wrote,

> The three [Italian] heroes have been dead for only a few decades. Will their spirits descend on our country, bringing about an Italy of the East? I have the highest expectations of the newly published *Biographies of the Three Heroes*. How many readers might have the same feeling as me? The old saying goes: "If you do not shed tears after reading the 'Memorial on Sortie' [*Ch'ul sa p'yo* 出師表], you are definitely not a loyal subject [*sinja* 臣子]." So let me say this: If your blood does not boil up or your crying does not become loud after reading *The Biographies of the Three Heroes of Italy*, you are a man like wood or stone. Once our men of ambition keep a copy of these *Biographies* at their elbow, worshiping them every morning and dreaming about them every night, then there shall come a day when they will undertake an enterprise of patriotism.[20]

Biographies is a story of modern nation-building, featuring three Italian politicians and activists—Giuseppe Mazzini (1805–1872), Giuseppe Garibaldi (1807–1882), and Count Camillo di Cavour (1810–1861)—as heroes instrumental in enabling Italy to overcome the crisis of divided rule and intervention from the neighboring powers. Sin's translation moved this critic, who hopes that his readers will feel the same and be motivated to act toward national independence. Its affective power, however, is here analogized to that of a third-century Chinese text, Zhuge Liang's 諸葛亮 (181–234) "Chushi biao 出師表" (Memorial on Sortie), a canonical epitome of loyalty.[21] As an affective medium, Sin's translation evoked a nationalist emotion in the same way that this ancient text has long stirred the moral sentiment of loyalty.

The emotional anachronism stems from the narrative form that Liang employed to tell the story of Italian heroes, which informed the Korean translation thanks to its transregional circulation in premodern East Asia. *Biographies* reworks a few Japanese materials on modern Italian history, namely Hirata Hisashi's 平田久 (1872–1923) *Itarī kenkoku sanketsu* 伊太利建国三傑 (The Three Heroes of Italian Nation-Building, 1892), itself a translation of *The Makers of Modern Italy: Mazzini, Cavour, Garibaldi, Three Lectures Delivered at Oxford* (1889) by a British scholar-cum-politician named John Marriott (1859–1945).[22] In this reworking, *Biographies* adopts the classical genre of 傳 (Chn. *zhuan*; Kor. *chŏn*). The polysemic connotations of the *zhuan/chŏn* in East Asian letters include "biography," "story," and "commentary"; writings in this genre, in the broad sense of the term, can be considered supplements to history—supplements that remain on the margins of history, yet are indispensable for its transmission.[23] *Biographies* is grafted onto the contemporary global circulation of the nineteenth-century European discourse of the "hero" as a history-making individual, represented by Thomas Carlyle's *On Heroes, Hero-Worship, and the Heroic in History* (1841), whose Japanese translation came out in 1893 and inspired the publication of numerous hero biographies (*eiyūden* 英雄傳) in Meiji Japan.[24] This discourse captured Liang's attention, and he loosely adapted Japanese hero biographies to pen well-received biographies of Lajos Kossuth (1802–1894) and Madame Roland (1754–1793), as well as of the three Italian figures. All three of these hero biographies by Liang were contemporaneously translated into Korean.[25] Italian nation-building, meanwhile, had a worldwide impact on anti-imperial nationalism, including in India, in the late nineteenth to the early twentieth centuries.[26] East Asia found itself caught in this avid circulation of the figures of nation-building heroes through the world, and layered on top of the global flow of figures was a singular transregional structure in the Sino-Korean exchanges resulting from the usage of the classical form of *zhuan/chŏn*.

The adoption of the *zhuan* form in Liang's *Biographies* fundamentally transforms the narrative of modernization on which Hirata Hisashi's and John Marriott's accounts are based. Whereas Xiaobing Tang has argued that *Biographies* displays a "constant effort to generalize . . . about the implications and consequences of revolution and reform,"[27] that effort does not offer a model on which China's nation-building would materialize. Liang's work, indeed, narrates the Italian Risorgimento not as a generalizable historical process but as a unique mystery, the likes of which China—and, for Sin, Korea—must demand to resolve its grave crisis and achieve modern statehood despite terrible odds. It does not represent Italian history as a case of the totality of a historical process of modernization but as an exemplar for China to emulate through on-the-ground struggles in order to realize history's yet-to-be manifested course. Rather than generalizing the Italian experience, Liang furnishes it merely with exemplary validity in a universal history of modernization that is still to be written—a narratology that resonates with Meiji political fiction and its Chinese translation and adaptation, which we discussed in the previous chapter.

In contrast, the primary resource that Liang used in *Biographies*, Hirata's *Itarī kenkoku sanketsu*, represents the Risorgimento in a general scheme of modernization, which it transposes from Marriott's *The Makers of Modern Italy*. Marriott suggests that a well-defined "perspective" on a historical period be established by discerning its "dominant principle or institution"; he calls himself a "philosophic historian of the future" and argues that his century will be distinguished by two paramount ideas: "parliamentary democracy" and "nationality." Marriott's account is premised on a historical teleology, which he articulates thus: "In the attainment of national unity, some states were, I need not say, very much ahead of others. England, for example, compassed the realization of her national identity as early as the thirteenth century; France and Spain not until the sixteenth; while other states, like Germany and Italy, have reached the same goal only within the last few years."[28] Writing about Italy in a more advanced Britain, Marriott effectively finds himself in the "future" of his subject matter. Hirata adopts Marriott's perspective by calling himself "a historian of a hundred years from now," and he embeds Japan in this teleology by arguing that Napoleon is to Italy what Commodore Perry is to Japan and drawing a parallel between Italian and Japanese histories.[29] Hirata claims that Japanese modernization has just reached the "statesman" stage of progress, which in Italy was taken charge of by Cavour, preceded by Mazzini and Garibaldi, who had accomplished the "prophet" and "militant" stages, respectively.[30] In this general pattern, Japan is following closely in Italy's footsteps. The translation of Marriott's account gives Hirata an overall narrative framework in which to make sense of Japanese modernization on the model of Italian experience—a modernization that had by then, in 1892, reached the stage of normalization with the recent promulgation of the Constitution and the establishment of the Parliament.

Liang translates Hirata's account out of this teleological framework; Italian nation-building had something more to it than just belonging to a generalizable process. It was precisely to narrativize this excess that Liang had recourse to the *zhuan* form. Squarely defying linear progress, his storytelling weaves a complex temporal texture by using various narrative devices, such as omens to foreshadow a major turn of history, flashbacks, and flashforwards—devices that Sin meticulously translates into Korean.[31] "Heaven" (天 Chn. *tian*; Kor. *chŏn*) as a metahistorical agent is also prominently featured to make sense of the unintelligible working of history.[32] The perspective of the omniscient "future historian" is not available to Liang's and Sin's narrators, who are instead positioned as witnesses to unpredictable events unfolding before their eyes, to which they respond with various emotions. In 1859, for example, with the French military support that Cavour had secured from Napoleon III, the Kingdom of Sardinia waged a war against Austria to reclaim territories in Lombardy and Venetia (the Second War of Italian Independence). Following the sweeping victory of the Sardinian-French army in the month of June, history took an unexpected turn:

> It was at this [victorious] moment that Cavour's brave mind in an instant mounted to the highest of heavens. How can a hero become happier than when a project he has undertaken for several decades with tenacity, hardship, and imagination is finally being realized in front of his eyes?

> Why is the moonlight bothered by the floating clouds,
> Which often choose to appear when the moon is full?
>
> Good moments are easy to miss; fine dreams are hard to realize. Alas!... At the very moment when Cavour's brave mind reached the highest heaven, another storm erupted out of the blue. At the height of the battle, Napoleon was suddenly missing from the troops. Damn! Where the hell did he go?³³

Thus foreshadowed is the Armistice of Villafranca, which would be negotiated between Napoleon III and Emperor Franz Joseph I of Austria and signed in July behind closed doors, blasting Sardinia's hopes for a unified Italy. Liang writes this lengthy passage—including a rhetorical question, an ad-hoc heptasyllabic couplet, and an exclamation—in order to apply an almost exaggerated dramatization to this turn of events and express indignation over imperial injustice. His lavish rhetoric is illuminated in comparison with Marriott's flat "And then—" or Hirata's boilerplate "*shikashite koko ni itarite* 而して此に至りて" (lit., however, at this point), which introduces this momentous episode.³⁴

For Liang's narrator, modern Italian history reads as though it "brought together dramas of grandeur, vitality, misery, tragedy, danger, and ingenuity from all over the world, past and present, and staged them all in a single theater one after another." Thus he asks, "Alas! Why does it show such an extreme level of surprise, astonishment, and mystery?" On the flipside of this fascination is anxiety about China's future, for the latter's crisis is no less complex than Italy's and cannot be helped by previous models: "China's current situation, in comparison with late seventeenth-century England, eighteenth-century America or France, or late nineteenth-century Japan, is several times more difficult. Thus, it might only be the mutual matching of heavenly time and human endeavor that could enable Chinese heroes to accomplish the grand work—something that I cannot plan to do."³⁵ When a preexisting concept is useless for telling history, Liang employs the *zhuan* form to create a story that is to supplement and convey a yet-to-be written history of modernization. Modernization for Liang is not a ready-made goal but an open-ended, still unconceptualizable notion of which Italian experience offers a mere exemplar. And just as a work of art can inspire the production of another work through the virtue of exemplarity, Liang's political narrative is intended to engender the next heroes who will survive history without an end in sight, making blind leaps toward "modernization." This narrative, imbued with ample emotional expressions, is meant to cast the reader into that drama of survival, the call to which Sin responded by translating it, "with a brush of emotion" (*ujŏng ŭi ilp'il* 有情의一筆), into Korean.[36] "Having read *The Biographies of Three Italian Heroes*, I feel as though my body is straightened up and my brain is pierced through. It can make me sing, cry, dance, and leap! Oh, the three heroes! Who are they? Who on earth are they?" writes Sin.[37] Hence Sin's translation also claims in the Korean context exemplary validity for modernization. The "twisting and turning" and the "heartbreaking and painful, bitter and precarious shapes" of the Italian story, therefore, become an exemplar for both Chinese and Korean audiences.[38] Liang comments in conclusion,

> Why do we read history? It is in order to know the future by examining the past, and to admonish ourselves in light of others. When I read the modern histories of European countries and observe their enterprises and their peoples, there is nothing in them that does not make my spirit vigorous and ecstatic. But especially in the history of Italian nation-building, there is something worrisome that scratches my mind and something vibrant that stimulates my brain. That history makes me laugh, cry, get tipsy, and dance. I wonder why, but I am not sure. As I was writing *The Three Heroes*, I felt as if I were beginning to transform myself [*hua wu shen* 化吾身] and enter the stage where the three heroes had stood: I was a clerk in Cavour's camp, a soldier in Garibaldi's tent, and an activist in Mazzini's party. When they were angry, so was I; when they were happy, so was I; when they were worried, so was I; when they were sick, so was I. As I lay down my pen here and look to the west at my home country, however, I become depressed and feel bitter. Ah! Why does the Italy of a few decades ago resemble [*xianglei* 相類] my home country so much?[39]

Italian history takes the Chinese narrator back to his reality, exiled in Japan from his homeland to the west; it puts him on the same stage where the Italian heroes stood, thus "transforming" him into a subject of modern history. It is a history in suspense, as much in crisis as pregnant with radical change it may bring about victory at the most adverse junctures, as it did in Italy. Liang's writing prepares the reader to navigate this contingent history with the sole faculty of judgment informed by examples rather than guided by ready-made models or concepts. For Sin, too, the Italian crisis resembles the Korean situation, and so he, in concluding the translation, addresses the Korean audience: "Readers! You have just finished my *Three Italian Heroes*! If you do not worry about luck or care about fame, and rise under the heavens with just your burning sincerity, then this country will one day be saved by you. This is what I expect from my readers."[40]

Liang's attempt at making an old form tell a modern story represents modernization as an untrodden path without a conceivable direction. When the narrator states "I am not sure," he renders Italian nation-building relevant to China and, via Sin's translation, to Korea, not through a general concept but through unconceptualizable "resemblance." In this sense, the narrative's representation of modernization is as much aesthetic as utopian. Just as was the case with Meiji political fiction and its Chinese translation and adaptation, modernization is rendered as a myth that may or may not become history.

THE HERMENEUTIC FIGHT FOR MODERN HISTORY

In his translation of Liang's *Biographies* of the Italian heroes, Sin expressed the hope that "people, if inspired and encouraged by this book, will further produce biographies [*chŏn* 傳] of three, thirty, and three hundred heroes for the revival of Korea."[41] Following the translation, Sin himself put together three such hero biographies. They featured Ŭlji mundŏk 乙支文德 (fl. late 6th–early 7th centuries), the towering general of Koguryŏ (37 BCE?–668 CE) whose shrewd strategies helped expel repeated invasion attempts by the Sui (581–618); Yi Sunsin 李舜臣 (1545–1598), the naval commander known for his epic fights in the Imjin War (1592–1598) against Japan; and Ch'oe Yŏng 崔瑩 (1316–1388), the famed general of Koryŏ (918–1392) who led successful campaigns against the Yuan (1271–1369) to reclaim northern territories.[42] Among them, Ŭlji mundŏk figures most prominently in Sin's oeuvre.

Sin's *Ŭlji mundŏk* 乙支文德 (Ŭlji mundŏk, 1908) is a national allegory. Contrasted with Ŭlji mundŏk is Kim Ch'unch'u 金春秋 (603–661), the twenty-ninth King of Silla (57 BCE?–935 CE), who collaborated with the Tang (618–907) to assault Paekche (18 BCE?–660 CE) and Koguryŏ, laying the groundwork for the end of the Three Kingdoms and the unification of the Korean peninsula under Silla's rule. But Kim Ch'unch'u, suggests Sin, worked merely in the interest of his particular kingdom, not that of the Korean nation.[43] "Ŭlji surely is the great man who built our state, the progenitor who bore and nourished our nation, and the sacred god who bestowed the spirit of independence on us, his posterity," he writes.[44] What is remarkable about Ŭlji mundŏk is that he defended Koguryŏ against "the powerful and grand China," while Silla and Paekche competed with Japan and Mohe, which were but "small enemies."[45] An anachronistic analogy is drawn between the military theater in seventh-century East Asia and the modern world, equating "Koguryŏ two thousand years ago" with "England in the eighteenth century" because of their display of the spirit of independence against Emperor Yang of Sui (r. 604–617) and Napoleon, respectively.[46] "When the situation becomes increasingly troubling, suffering grows, and existential crisis looms just a hair away," writes Sin, "I believe, before long, Ŭlji mundŏk's lucid heroic soul shall leap out from the tomb after many years, once again mounting the saddle of his times and brandishing his mighty sword. His soul shall run on the six continents together with Peter the Great and [George] Washington and share eternal glory with [Horatio] Nelson and [Otto von] Bismarck to lay the groundwork for independence."[47]

As a historian himself, however, Sin describes a fundamental challenge in his narration of the nation: the paucity and biases of the extant historical records. He argues that Korean history is "contaminated" and great heroes are consigned to oblivion owing to the long-standing Confucian ideology that prioritizes civilian rule over military might and the deep-rooted Sinocentric diplomatic principle that "the small [i.e., Korea] should serve the great [i.e., China]" (*yi so sa dae* 以小事大). As a result, the deeds of impeccable individuals are passed on only in the "rustic talk of village kids" and grand achievements are transmitted only in the "street songs of woodcutter children."[48] As a spearhead of national history, Sin maintained in his groundbreaking *Toksa sillon* 讀史新論 (New Discourse on Reading History, 1908) that the task of the modern historian is to write a national history and criticized the existing histories for relegating "our nation" to "part of the Chinese," "the Xianbei," "the Mohe," "the Mongols," "the Jurchens," or "the Japanese." Modern historiography must instead "first present the people who are the masters of the state" and then "break the stubborn dream of the entire country by virtue of nationalism [*minjok chuŭi* 民族主義] and forge new brains for the youth by virtue of the idea of statehood [*kukka kwannyŏm* 國家觀念]."[49] Later in his seminal *Chosŏn sanggo sa* 朝鮮上古史 (History of Korean Antiquity, 1931, 1948), Sin established "history" as the record of "struggles between the 'I' and the 'non-I,'" defining the "I" as "those who stand in the subjective position" (*chukwanchŏk wich'i e sŭn cha* 主觀的位置에 슨 者).[50] "What is fortunate about Ŭlji mundŏk," Sin writes, "is that the few lines of history have still been passed on. What is unfortunate about him, however, is that only these few lines exist"—that is, the meager documents fraught with a long-standing Sinocentric ideology.[51] The challenge Sin tackles, therefore, is to reconstruct a history of the "I" (i.e., Korea) from the records written from a perspective heavily reliant on the culture of the "non-I" (i.e., China). His work thus consists of a hermeneutic struggle amid a cultural sea change—a change fundamentally concerned with the construct of literature in its broad sense, or the ideology that determines what is worth being recorded and transmitted in refined writing. This transition undermines the grounds for an objective or coherent point of view that would narrate "history" as a whole, and in the midst of it, Sin dwells on existing documents to read in them a story long deemed out of bounds for writing and suitable only for the "rustic talk of village kids" or the "street songs of woodcutter children": a story of the Korean nation. This hermeneutic intervention performs such an unorthodox reading, defying the established horizon of interpretation, that it exposes the inherent semantic ambiguity of the extant texts.

Extant history, indeed, tells us very little about Ŭlji mundŏk. Ŭlji mundŏk was an army general of Koguryŏ in the late sixth to the early seventh centuries, when the kingdom endured a series of attempted invasions by the Sui, which was intent on expanding its territories. Emperor Yang of Sui waged three campaigns against Koguryŏ, the first in 612, the second in 613, and the third in 614, only to fail to conquer it. Ŭlji mundŏk is credited with using astute strategies instrumental in fending off the persistent attacks. The most substantial, though still scant, record of this general is found in the "biography" section of *Samguk sagi* 三國史記 (History of the Three Kingdoms), the official history of the Three Kingdoms compiled in the twelfth century by the Koryŏ literatus Kim Busik 金富軾 (1075–1151). The account in this source draws on the "biography" of Yu Zhongwen 于仲文 (545–613) recorded in the seventh-century official history of the Sui dynasty, *Sui shu* 隋書 (History of the Sui).[52]

The account in the *History of the Three Kingdoms* can be outlined as follows.[53] In 612, Emperor Yang of Sui ordered a campaign against Koguryŏ. When the Sui army reached the Yalu River, Ŭlji mundŏk visited their camp by the order of the king to communicate fake submission, while in fact his true objective was to spy on the enemy. The Sui generals Yuwen Shu 宇文述 (546–616) and Yu Zhongwen had earlier received a secret order that they should capture the king or Ŭlji upon sight, but one of their subordinates let Ŭlji return to his camp, making the generals nervous. Yu Zhongwen insisted on pursuing Ŭlji despite the lack of food and crossed the Yalu River, whereas Ŭlji, knowing that the enemy appeared fatigued, tried to exhaust them by running away at every battle. After a whole day of consecutive wins, the Sui troops erected a camp near the Pyongyang fortress, Koguryŏ's stronghold. At that moment, Ŭlji had a poem delivered to Yu Zhongwen that read,

神策究天文	Your marvelous strategies master heaven's design;
妙算窮地理	Your clever calculations exhaust the earth's pattern.
戰勝功旣高	Your achievement in winning battles is already great;
知足願云止	So if you understand it is enough, please order a halt.

Upon receiving this poem, Yu Zhongwen sent a letter in reply, "instructing" (*yu* 諭) Ŭlji, who then once again communicated feigned capitulation, telling Yuwen Shu that he would go to the location of the Sui throne if he withdrew his troops. Observing that his soldiers were too fatigued to overpower the strong defense of the Pyongyang fortress, Yuwen Shu decided to retreat. Ŭlji then took advantage of the move and dispatched his men to chase the retreating army, attacking it from behind and destroying most of it. The account concludes with a comment attributing to Ŭlji's personal ability the fact that the small, remote state of Koguryŏ was able not only to defend itself but also to repeatedly repel the Sui's attacks on an unprecedented scale.

Sin's retelling of the biography of Ŭlji mundŏk, which draws on this exiguous "biography," has little to do with taking it as a usable past from an authoritative vantage point of the modern or inventing a tradition in a modern image of the Korean nation. Rather, his strategy resides precisely in resisting such a reduction of the text to a preconceived interpretative framework and in reencountering the extant record in its irreducible ambiguity in search of an untold story of the nation. It is with this approach that he criticizes Kim Busik, the historian of the *History of the Three Kingdoms*, for uncritically adopting the official Chinese history.

Sin's interpretative strategy is put into practice in the discussion on the "character" of Ŭlji mundŏk. Kim Busik's account includes a succinct observation about the general's character: "Ŭlji mundŏk. Genealogy unknown. His nature was composed and intrepid [*ch'imji* 沈鷙], and he had strategic talent [*chisu* 智數]. He also appreciated literature."[54] Sin questions whether "these four characters" (*saja* 四字)—*ch'im* 沈, *ji* 鷙, *kwon* 權 [*sic*], and *su* 數—are based on "an intelligent observation about the totality of Ŭlji mundŏk." He suggests that the existing portrayal tells only a half-truth and proposes an alternative set of adjectives: *chinsŏng* 真誠 (sincere), *kang'ŭi* 強毅 (relentless), *t'ŭngnip* 特立 (determined), and *mohŏm* 冒險 (adventurous). In doing so, he in fact makes the erroneous claim that "the four characters [by Kim Busik] originated from the appreciation offered [to Ŭlji mundŏk] by the historian of the *History of the Sui* and have been inherited [*sangjun* 相遵] in our history for generations."[55] The four characters in question are actually not used in the relevant passage of the Chinese history.[56] This Freudian slip, so to speak, is symptomatic of Sin's underlying accusation that the Korean history incorporated the Chinese history uncritically. Elsewhere in its biography of Ŭlji mundŏk, *History of the Three Kingdoms* indeed takes advantage of the common usage of Chinese script and simply transcribes passages from the *History of the Sui*. Sin's critical intervention does not constatively challenge the accuracy of Korean historiography per se due to the lack of counterevidence, but it performatively lays bare the ideological condition that enabled it to adopt Chinese depictions as a Korean history. It pulls the text out of a long-established culture of textual production and reception where the ideological premise of Chinese historiography was recognized as also valid for Korean historiography, and it performs a new mode of textual engagement that is conscious of the document's cultural constructs.

In Sin's account, Ŭlji mundŏk's fight against the Sui army can itself be read as a hermeneutic battle. Military prowess aside, what is at stake in the war is symbolic power. The tipping point comes when Ŭlji sends the classical pentasyllabic poem to the Sui general Yu Zhongwen. *History of the Three Kingdoms* suggests that the poem, filled with glowing praises of the opponent's strategy, was taken by the addressee as an expression of concession, for he "instructed" Ŭlji in reply. To this pivotal scene, Sin adds a comment: "[The poem in its first three lines] offered huge praises [to the enemy general], aggravating his arrogance. Only thereafter did it suggest [*kwon* 勸] that he should understand that it had been enough and halt."[57] Sin takes the poem to be a "suggestion" of a ceasefire under the guise of an admission of defeat. This interpretation hinges on the poem's ambivalent final line, which can also be read, "You should understand it is enough, and I hope you order a halt"—a warning against the adversary's hubris in fighting successive battles despite the troops' fatigue, which Ŭlji had already discovered. That the Sui general took it instead as Koguryŏ's declaration of surrender implies his greed and recklessness, as well as the strategic naïveté that clouded his judgment of the situation. In Sin's reinterpretation, it is Ŭlji, not Yu Zhongwen, who holds the moral high ground and can "instruct" his opponent. Ŭlji's and, by extension, Koguryŏ's moral superiority gives legitimacy to its power, while exposing the corruption of the power-hungry Sui, whose rule is characterized as "self-glorifying," "arrogant and disrespectful," "ferocious," and "insulting" and is disparaged throughout the account.[58] The Sui's subsequent defeat is therefore a necessary consequence of the moral illegitimacy of its power, whereas in contrast it is Koguryŏ, as represented by Ŭlji mundŏk, that would have been a legitimate ruler of all under heaven. Hence, Sin contends that had Ŭlji not died too early, Koguryŏ would have "made China into Korea," "expanding its territories and building a great Eastern empire," and that Ŭlji epitomizes nothing short of "imperialism."[59]

Sin's account reads Ŭlji's poem with its intrinsic ambiguity and thus presents it as a kind of litmus paper to test the morality of the recipient. It exposes the conceit of Yu Zhongwen, who failed to decipher Ŭlji's admonition, and reveals the fraudulence of both the Chinese and Korean histories, which likewise missed the hero's true voice—the voice long encrypted in the final five characters of this poem but silenced by the orthodox mode of reading. Sin's account is intended to reconstruct "an authentic picture of the true hero" that, given the Sui's eventual defeat, should have been discerned long ago.[60] Yet it is little concerned with the veracity of the interpretation, for it is impossible to reduce the ambivalence of Ŭlji's poem to either meaning; instead, it engages with the extant document in its irreducible semantic ambiguity in order to suspend the culturally established mode of textual interpretation. In so doing, it performatively undercuts the accepted signification of the text and presents it as a set of signs that are subject to decoding. If the traditional Sinocentric culture exerted the power and authority to domesticate such ambiguity and control the hermeneutic horizon of literature so that a Chinese record could be read as a Korean history, then Sin frees it from such culture to reveal its intrinsic openness to other modes of reading.

Those who expect to grasp the identity of the Korean nation in the reconstructed figure of the national hero in *Ŭlji mundŏk* will be disappointed. Quite uninterested in identity, Sin's account represents the hero in his untamed mercuriality, "metamorphosing like the dragon and transforming like the tiger." "Not only is he a great man, but he is also a heaven-sent marvel."[61] "Out of the blue, he appears as a messenger, a general, a poet, a minister, an explorer, and a diplomat; as a sincere subject, he suddenly pretends to be treacherous, and as an illustrious general, he abruptly disguises himself as defeated; he comes and goes, hides and appears, moves to and fro, and rises and lies down, all of a sudden. . . . In the single body of Ŭlji mundŏk, millions of Ŭlji mundŏk are incarnated."[62] The protean figure of Ŭlji mundŏk, whose identity is impossible to pin down, is symbolic of the textual ambiguity that Sin recovers from the existing literature. It bespeaks Sin's concern not so much with defining a story of the nation as with opening literature up to a broader context where it will unveil a yet-to-be-told national story.

Sin concludes his work with a commentary, quoting a friend who reports on his travels through Koguryŏ's former territories in Manchuria.

> The author earlier heard from a friend who had traveled west to China and come back. He told me, "When traveling to places like Fengtian [i.e., today's Shenyang], Jilin, and Lüshunkou in Manchuria,

many people often barely find traces [*yuch'ok* 遺躅] of our ancestors in discovered stone coffins or remaining royal artifacts. But a village called Koryŏ is where the people of Koguryŏ used to open the barren land and settle; a fort called Koryŏ is where they used to build walls and defenses. Centuries have already passed. Things have changed, and stars have moved; hills have each grown high and deep. Through the old land that my ancestors conquered with long spears and great swords and defended with tough forts and effective armor I, a distant descendent, now travel as a guest on horseback carrying a silk bag. Then my thoughts are often touched by the feeling of the passing of time." The Scholar of No Boundaries [i.e., Sin Ch'aeho] says, "Alas! Those are traces [*chinjŏk* 陳跡] of the rule of Ŭlji mundŏk and his men! Their unworthy posterity has ceded to the hands of foreigners the entire legacy of what was obtained and defended with blood and sweat, exhausted properties, and selfless sacrifices."[63]

Sin's hermeneutic battle against Sinocentric historiography in the end presents extant documents as such "traces" left on the land; it emancipates existing literature from its culture of origin that has determined the mode of reading and ushers it into the open horizons of the modern world. Through his search for national history, Sin ultimately posits the modern world, a boundary-defying space that intrinsically encompasses multiple cultural contexts, as a novel space for literary production and reception where literature is freed from the confines of the particular cultural context that has valorized it as "literature," and is led to incessant self-reflection on the conditions of its existence.

AFTERLIVES OF LETTERS

In 1910, while his third and last hero biography was still being serialized, Sin Ch'aeho followed the directions of the New People's Association and went into exile. He was initially based in Vladivostok, where he heard the news of the colonization of his homeland, and moved to China in 1913, where he spent most of the rest of his life. He was well connected with Korean exiles in that country, with whom he collaborated on nationalist activities while using Chinese archives to continue his research on

Korean history. He taught at Paktal Academy, established in the French concession in Shanghai to prepare the expatriate Korean youth for advanced education in China and the West in the hope of nourishing the next generation of independence activists. In 1914, Sin relocated for a year to Tongch'ang School, built by the religious society Daejonggyo in Huanren in the Sino-Korean border area of Manchuria, where he was in charge of teaching national history. While in Manchuria, he visited the remains of Koguryŏ tombs to search for archaeological materials to supplement the incomplete history and worked on the project that became his magnum opus *Chosŏn sa* 朝鮮史 (History of Korea). Having moved to Beijing in 1915, the exiled Sin wrote the fantastic story "Dream Heaven" in the following year. In this incomplete mid-length text loaded with symbolic images and fragments, Sin features an autobiographical persona named Hannom (한놈, lit., "a man"), who is identified as the author of *Ŭlji mundŏk*. Through this self-reference in the form of a dream narrative, Sin revisits the formidable challenge of writing a national history based on Sinocentric documents.

In "Dream Heaven," Hannom is afflicted with melancholy after publishing the biography of Ŭlji mundŏk: "When he goes out, he has nowhere to go; when he comes back, he has nowhere to sleep. When he cries, he has no one to trust; when he lies down, he has no one to love. He just comes and goes as a man [*hannom*]."[64] He ponders his lost ancestors, dreaming through the night and often losing himself in reveries during the day. And in this story, "written by the dream itself," he at last encounters the object of his desire: Ŭlji mundŏk.[65]

> Carefully examining his face, Hannom thought he looked like an elder he had met some time before. After hesitating for a while, he said, "Ah! Now I remember. This expression of the eyes, these muscles of the forehead, this light beard, as well as these clothes—they are all identical to the statue carved on the stone monument outside the south gate of the city of Anju in P'yŏng'an Province! He is Ŭlji mundŏk, whom I have yearned to see even in a dream!"[66]

The sight of Ŭlji mundŏk strikes Hannom as "uncanny" (*isang t'a* 異常타), as this elder from "two thousand years ago" appears to him as though he were a friend or family.

Upon the encounter, Hannom's lingering questions about Korean history that cannot be answered by the extant records gush out. As Hannom tries to choose a proper honorific to address his hero, Ŭlji mundŏk reveals his astonishing knowledge of ancient history:

> In Silla, they loved young soldiers and named them "*toryŏng* 도령"; the "*sŏnrang* 仙郎" that appears in the *History of the Three Kingdoms* is a translation of its meaning. In Paekche, they loved mature soldiers and named them "*sudu* 수두"; the "*sodo* 蘇塗" that appears in that history is a translation of its sound. In Koguryŏ, they loved soldiers who were also gentlemen and named them "*sŏnbae* 선배"; the "*sŏnin* 先人" that appears in that history is a translation of its sound and meaning. Since I am from Koguryŏ, you may call me "*sŏnbae*."[67]

Ŭlji knows exactly which native Korean notions, written in *hangul*, are "translated" by the Chinese-character terms that appear in the *History of the Three Kingdoms*. If Sin in *Ŭlji mundŏk* attempted to reread Sinocentric documents to reconstruct a lost figure of the Korean nation, then Ŭlji mundŏk in this dream appears to possess the precise key to perform such an interpretation. That key would decode the existing documents to reveal a lost history written from the nation's perspective, of which those documents are but a "translation"; it would turn the blurred lens of the remaining records into a perfect mirror to reflect the nation's self-defined identity. Hannom is thus naturally compelled to pose his questions about Korean history. He is obsessed with such trivia as the length of the ears of Dongmyŏng sŏngjo, the founder of Koguryŏ (r. 37–19 BCE), and the size of the eyes of Chinhŭng daeche, the twenty-fourth King of Silla (r. 540–576). He wonders about unknown details of famous historical events, such as how many palace ladies threw themselves off the cliff of the Nak'waam, which brave man assassinated Emperor Yang of Sui, how tall the Imryu Pavilion built by King Tongsŏng of Paekche (r. 479–501) was, and so on.[68]

Scholars have pointed out an affinity between Sin's "Dream Heaven" and the *mongyurok* 몽유록 (lit., dream record), a subgenre of classical Korean literature featuring dream sequences as the primary narrative device.[69] Sometimes interpreted as political allegory, *mongyurok* often uses the dream as a critical topos through which to picture a possible world to expose the injustices of the actual world.⁷⁰ Ŭlji's ultimate knowledge would have made "Dream Heaven" a modern example in this genre through its use of a dream to represent the realization of Sin's desire for a possible world in which Koreans would have always written and transmitted their national history. Yet the adaptation of this genre in "Dream Heaven" constitutes a criticism of just such an imagination of the dream as the fulfillment of an unrealized desire.

Despite the miraculous encounter, Hannom hesitates to pose his burning questions to Ŭlji mundŏk, as the latter tells him that the afterlife is a mere "projection" of the mortal life. The struggles in the mortal life are carried into the life after death; the winner goes to heaven and the loser to hell. Ŭlji suggests that the afterlife is governed by the same social Darwinian law as mortal life and that a belief in justice served after death is a source of national weakness. Ŭlji enjoys his afterlife only because of his actual victory in the Koguryŏ-Sui War, while Emperor Yang of Sui, in contrast, has to suffer as a loser. This lesson comes as a shock to Hannom, for it raises a suspicion that his hope of recovering lost history may be tantamount to a flimsy belief in afterlife redemption.⁷¹ Disappointed as he is, Hannom cannot stop wondering how many heroes and facts have disappeared without a trace, leaving posterity ignorant, and he finally comes up with ten questions about Korean history. Yet instead of answering them, Ŭlji shows him a golden casket marked "The 4240 Years of Korea." Within the box are hundreds of mirrors, and on the back of each mirror are the indication of a dynasty and the name of a place. Ŭlji picks up one marked "Koyrŏ, Songgyŏng" and has Hannom look into it. In the mirror, Hannom sees a landscape of Kaesŏng, the capital of Koryŏ, also known as Songgyŏng, in which he spots famous monuments like the Sŏnchuk Bridge and Mount Chinbong and structural remains like the foundation of the Koryŏ Palace. He cannot, however, see any of the buildings or people that should have existed back in the Koryŏ period. He also tries other mirrors:

> As Hannom tried looking at several mirrors, he took out the one for Koguryŏ's capital Pyongyang, only to hear the banging sound of washing clothes along the shore of the Taedong River. In the one for Paekche's capital Puyŏ, he saw Western-style houses in pointed shapes; in the one for Palhae's capital Yŏnggot'ap, he saw only

Chinese people passing by. Hannom could not overcome his feelings, and came forward to ask, "Because our people are so incapable of preservation, I would like to ask you questions about the history of Silla's capital and its territories."[72]

Hannom observes views of the places indicated on the mirrors, but, contrary to Ŭlji's expectations, all he can see are present rather than past scenes. The magical mirrors would have given Hannom an omniscient view of national history, breaking the clouded perspectives of the extant records, yet without the records' mediation, he can see nothing but the current reality of the nation—a nation that is already under the influence of Western culture and has already lost its northern territories to the Chinese. At the heart of the dream, he encounters reality.

Hannom nonetheless insists on asking questions about Silla. In the end, Ŭlji replies with tears in his eyes, "I cannot do that. What different books of history do you think the world of gods has? The books we read in the world of gods are all brought from the world of humans. So why would you look for books lost in the world of humans in the world of gods? You had better go back and ask people for them."[73] Through Hannom's repeated disappointments at his interactions with Ŭlji mundŏk, Sin delineates the domain of his writing vis-à-vis the existing documents. Rather than offering possibilities for imaginative exploration of Korean history, the dream narrative in this story works as a hyperbolic illustration of the sheer impossibility of subsuming history under a present perspective independent of the extant records. By insisting that the existing "books" are all that there is *even* in the dream, the narrative embodies the domain of modern writing, which is built only on the ruins of old literature, no matter how incompatible it may be with modern values.

This amounts to an absolute affirmation of new culture's irreducible difference from old culture as the sole condition of possibility for modern writing. The affirmed difference is categorical, in that it pertains to their disparate ideological constructs arising from the shift in the notion of what constitutes literature. What is meaningful in the new culture is writings for the Korean nation, whereas the earlier writings were created and circulated based on a different conception of value, which Sin attributes to Sinocentric ideology. The writings that are needed in today's literature were simply not produced in the past, while those that were produced are inadequate and even useless in light of the present concept of valuable writing. In the realms of old and new cultures, any text belonging to one cannot claim value in the other without serious efforts at interpretation. For the new, the old is already dead; for the old, the new exists only in its afterlives. Sin's dream narrative indicates a refusal to ascribe or reduce one to the other and an affirmation of the qualitative difference between them as the inescapable condition for the production of new literature.

Literature has already left the confines of classical culture, but Sin's dwelling on the difference indicates that it has not found a cultural home in a new domain separate from the past, nor has it been elevated to a transhistorical "literature" capable of capitalizing on the cultural past as a national "tradition," much less to a metahistorical, universal concept of Literature. As a result, literature in Sin's conception becomes a liminal practice, in the sense that it is neither confined in a past or present culture nor defined in cross-cultural or universal terms. Hannom's sober encounter with familiar books in a dream indicates Sin's entanglement with classical literature, which prevents him from embarking on a "new" creative pursuit without the haunting resonances of the old. His dwelling in this unsettling space nevertheless constitutes the sole condition of possibility for modern literature, which goes so far as to question what such "newness" means at all in relation to the past.

"Where should I go?" Hannom asks himself, as Ŭlji mundŏk leaves him to his ultimate disappointment.[74] The anticlimax of "Dream Heaven" continues as Hannom departs on a melancholic journey through hell and heaven. In hell, he learns about various sins, among which national betrayal is listed as the gravest; in heaven, he witnesses a pantheon of national heroes but realizes that those deities do nothing but make brooms and sweep the dirty sky. Learning that the sky has been completely covered by dust due to neglect of the nation, Hannom takes on the Sisyphean task of cleaning the sky, to no avail. At the end of his journey, he visits *toryŏnggun* 도령군, which he identifies with the ancient origin of Hwarang, the elite youth association in Silla whose records exist only in fragments. Eager to visit the legendary band of noble youths, which he calls the "bone" of Korean history, he arrives at a stone gate with letters in gold reading "The *Toryŏnggun* Banquet Place." The gatekeeper asks Hannom to offer his tears to enter, demanding that he display deep emotion (*chŏng* 情); he tells him that his guest rank shall be determined by the number of tears he has shed in "righteous indignation" for the nation. In the end, Hannom stands alone before the gate, watching his friends gather and suspecting that he will be the last to be admitted because he is by nature "heartless" (*mujŏng* 無情).[75] If the affective community of *toryŏnggun* is the epitome of Korean nationalism, then the "heartless" figure of Hannom left alone in front of the gate, sharing righteous tears with national heroes and yet unable to join their gathering, is an allegory for a writer still in pursuit of a medium for just such communication, a new literature that would be able to convey a shared history of the Korean nation.

POSTREVOLUTIONARY CULTURE

Sin Ch'aeho devoted his career as a modern intellectual to writing a history of the Korean nation, and in so doing he grappled with the ideological difference between the literature he pursued and the documents he had to draw on to do so. Liang Qichao's dramatization of Italian nation-building leveraged the supplementary function that the genre of *zhuan* had traditionally played vis-à-vis history *per se* and created a story of modernization outside the generalized course of history. Sin's transposition of this narrative into a *chŏn* informed his biography of Ŭlji mundŏk, written as a hermeneutic attempt at excavating a Korean story out of the Sinocentric histories. Through this work, he carved out a novel space for literary endeavor where writings open themselves to interpretational possibilities that have hitherto been culturally impossible. To be sure, Sin's was a literary enterprise of a transitional age that, on the one hand, freed literature from the premodern cultural context, yet, on the other, had not found itself in a new cultural home that, as we will see in part II, his contemporaries conceived of as separate from the cultural past. Yet in this state of cultural homelessness—a condition aggravated by Korea's colonization—his writings indicate all the more patently an origin of modern literature in Korea, remaining self-reflexively critical of the cultural context that determines what is worth counting as literature.

As if to reenact his literature's liminal existence, Sin's expatriation continued until his final days. He took part in the inauguration of the Korean Provisional Government in Shanghai following the vicious crackdown of the anti-Japanese March First Movement (1919) by the colonial authorities. Yet as he distanced himself from the mainstream political line of the provisional government, he launched the newspaper *Sin Taehan* 新大韓 (New Korea), where he published dissenting opinions, and he eventually left the circle and returned to Beijing in early 1920. He committed himself to preparing for a war of resistance against Japan, trying to unify the many Korean militias in northeast China under a single chain of command. In 1921, he published a Chinese-language journal titled *Ch'ŏn'go* 天鼓 (Heavenly Drum) in an effort to collaborate with his Chinese peers to form an anti-imperial united front.

During that time, Sin adopted anarchism as the ideological backbone for an alternative path toward Korean liberation. His initial exposure to this ideology dates back to the 1900s, when he studied works by Kōtoku Shūsui 幸徳秋水 (1871–1911), the eminent Japanese socialist and anarchist known for introducing the works of Peter Kropotkin to Japan. Sin's anarchism idiosyncratically drew on both Kropotkinian anarcho-communism and the utopianism of the "Great Community" (*datong* 大同) deriving from *Liji* 禮記 (The Book of Rites), the idea that Liang Qichao also adapted in his *Future of New China*.[76] In 1922, at the request of the Righteous Corps (*ŭiyŏldan* 의열단), an anti-Japanese association based in Manchuria, Sin drafted a pamphlet called "Chosŏn hyŏngmyŏng sŏn'ŏn 조선혁명선언" (The Manifesto of Korean Revolution), in which he lambasted "diplomacy" and "preparation" and instead supported "violence" as "the only weapon of our revolution"—"to smash the rule of Japan the robber, so that we shall reform all the irrational institutions and build an ideal Korea, where humans, as humans, shall not be oppressed and society, as society, shall not be undermined."[77] His anarchist activity crystalized in 1927 in the cofounding of the Anarchist Association of Asia, whose inaugural meeting in Beijing drew activists from Korea, China, Japan, Taiwan, Vietnam, and India. In 1928, Sin traveled to Taiwan to cash counterfeit foreign currency in an attempt to raise funds for this organization. He was withdrawing money at a post office in Keelung when the Japanese police arrested him, and he was sentenced to ten years in prison and sent to Lüshunkou. While imprisoned, he agreed to publish the historical research he had conducted in exile, culminating in *History of Korea*, which was serialized in *Chosŏn ilbo* 朝鮮日報 in 1931. He died in prison of a cerebral hemorrhage in 1936.

Shortly before his arrest, Sin wrote what would be his last literary work, titled "Yong kwa yong ŭi daegyŏkchŏn" 龍과 龍의 大激戰 (The Grand Battles Between Two Dragons). It is the allegorical story of the antagonism between twin dragon brothers named Miri 미리 (lit., "dragon") and Dŭraegon 드래곤. Miri, the dragon of the East, grows up in countries like Korea, India, and China and is revered by servants of the ruling class. Miri is appointed a minister of the God and produces from his mouth agents of power like emperors, generals, millionaires, landlords, and policemen. Dŭraegon, in contrast, is the dragon of the West, and it grows up in places like Greece and Rome and mingles with dissidents and revolutionaries. Dŭraegon sympathizes with nihilism and engages in revolutionary actions. Though they are polar opposites, "Miri and Dŭraegon, when written in Chinese characters, are both '*yong* 龍' [dragon], and they are translations [of this word]."[78] The epic fights between the two dragons allegorize an anarchist revolution that overthrows the ruling class and returns the land and resources to the hands of the "people" (*minjung* 民衆), which speaks to Sin's lifelong desire to establish the nation as the agent of history through a smashing of the old culture. If Ŭlji mundŏk and other hero figures in Sin's literature are meant to exemplify the nation that makes history, then Dŭraegon, as the symbol of revolution, epitomizes history-making in its most radical form, by means of the total destruction of the ruling institutions.

"The Grand Battles Between Two Dragons" is unique in Sin's oeuvre in that it envisions a postrevolutionary world. Inspired by Dŭraegon's heroism, the people annihilate the ruling class, which derives its power from the authority of Heaven, and build a secular "land State" (*chiguk* 地國) on Earth, whose communication with Heaven they completely shut down. In a survey of the world after the revolution, the angel looks for the missing God. He flies to the West and visits London, Paris, Rome, Berlin, and New York to see that the ruling class has totally vanished and customs and manners have all been transformed. Then he visits one destination in the East, Beijing, and observes an unlikely scene:

[The angel] arrived in Beijing in China and passed over the Altar of Heaven among pine trees about ten miles out of the Zhengyang Gate. There he saw spectators gathering to watch the great emperor of the great state of the Qing, wearing the Mianliu crown and the Gunlong robe, celebrating the Festival of Heaven.

"Aha! China is still a sacred country! It has reinstalled the emperor and revived the ritual of the Festival of Heaven," said the angel.

He then looked around for the God, but someone conspicuously opened his hand and said, "Stop dreaming, man! This is the theater for people's holidays. What God are you talking about?" And the angel had the cheek slapped again. Ah! Playing the role of God's loyal subject, the angel cannot forget about swollen cheeks.[79]

The Festival of Heaven (天祭, Kor. *ch'onje*, Chn. *tianji*), staged traditionally at the Altar of Heaven in Beijing, is the ritual of worshiping Heaven performed by the Chinese emperor in the name of the Son of Heaven. The garments mentioned—the mianliu crown (冕旒冠, Kor. *myŏllyugwan*, Chn. *mianliuguan*) and the gunlong robe (袞龍袍, Kor. *kollyongp'o*, Chn. *gunlongpao*)—are attributes of the Chinese imperial court and officialdom, which were also adopted in Korea. Judging based on what he sees, the angel feels relieved and belittles the people of the East who, unable in the end to smash classical culture to become modern, independent, or secular subjects, have apparently reinstated the imperial system under the auspices of Heaven. But to his surprise, the angel discovers that what he is witnessing is the "theater for people's holidays" (*minjung kyŏngjŏl ŭi yŏn'gŭk* 民眾慶節의演劇), a kind of popular parody of the imperial ritual.

The postrevolutionary people of "the East" do not abolish the ritual at the very heart of the Sinocentric world order, which Sin so vehemently despised for undermining Korean national subjectivity. His most radical vision of modernity—the world after an anarchist revolution—portrays not a completely new construction, but a parody of the very cultural past that was to be overcome.

In part I, we have explored how Shiba Shirō, Liang Qichao, and Sin Ch'aeho adopted and adapted elements of classical literature to respond to the contemporary sociopolitical exigencies produced by the injustices of imperialism and the need for nation-building to counter them. In those attempts at proving the relevance of past culture to the here and now, their works exhibited textual moments that defied literature's existing function. Those writers dwelled in the afterlives of the cultural past, rather than hastily burying it in oblivion, and affirmed them as the sole terrain for fresh creative struggles driven by idealist desires for a just world. Their struggles, situated between old and new cultures, generated new possibilities of literary expression that defied the traditional, culturally sanctioned realm of literature.

The ultimate imagery of the new world that Sin painted in the perplexing ending of "The Grand Battles" on the one hand encapsulates his literary endeavor as the pursuit of a coming modern culture without relying on a ready-made model, and on the other sheds light on the parody of old culture as a device for producing radical newness. In part II, I will take my inquiry further and analyze works that, unlike those in the transitional phases that we have discussed so far, are considered to have marked the proper beginnings of modern Chinese, Japanese, and Korean literatures defined as distinct from previous literatures. They expanded the expressive capacities of literature through parodic engagement with, rather than departure from, the cultural past.

PART II
Reforming Language and Redefining "Literature"

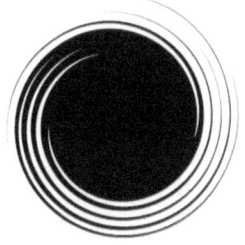

Almost contemporaneously with the efforts to pursue the relevance of past cultures to the new era, East Asian intellectuals undertook parallel yet often competing attempts at transforming literary culture itself through language reform, thus redefining "literature" for that new culture. Language reform—that is, the conception, formation, and institutionalization of "national language"—is a pivotal aspect of the cultural politics of nation-building in many parts of the world.[1] Yet the cases in China, Japan, and Korea are not simply separate examples of this global phenomenon, for the reformers in these nations had a shared understanding of the culture to be replaced. They conceived of modern literary culture by positing it especially against the traditional high letters built around the authority of classical Chinese writing, whose purported elitism, pedantry, and universalism were targeted as antithetical to the desired culture of a modern nation. The resonating battle cries in East Asian nations to cleanse the new writings of the stubborn influences of classical Chinese letters bespeak the echoing demands to "reorganize cultural hegemony" by smashing the cultural capital of the ailing ruling class and nurturing a new national culture for the emerging citizenry.[2]

In part II, I examine fictional works by Lu Xun, Mori Ōgai, and Yi Kwangsu that are positioned at the forefront of this cultural sea change and regarded as pinnacles of the nascent modern cultures in their respective nations. These writers produced their works in the cultural contexts that arose from the incipient processes of language reform involving style and script, as well as from the ensuing discourses on the redefinition of literature.

LANGUAGE REFORMS IN EAST ASIA

The interrelated courses of language reform in East Asia unfolded along a common discursive thread that depicted the needed change as a decisive departure from the omnipotent cultural capital of classical Chinese letters. Given the unmatched power that those letters had long held in the high cultures of East Asian nations, the groundbreaking works did not follow such a smooth path as the reformist discourses might have envisioned. The elevation of the status of the newly minted national languages involved contested and winding processes of legitimization.

The Korean case encapsulates the shared thrust of language reform in East Asia. As Hwang Hodŏk has illustrated by referring to the embarrassment that the reformist Yun Ch'iho 윤치호 (1865–1945) expressed in 1883 at a Korean diplomat's sheer ignorance of "the writing of his country" (*pon'guk munja* 本國文字), or "Korean writing" (*Chosŏn mun* 朝鮮文), into which diplomatic documents in English were to be translated, the discourse of language modernization in that country from the onset grappled with the deep-seated neglect of the cultural value of national writing vis-à-vis the enduring authority of Chinese letters.[3] The early attempts at modernizing writing in the 1880s were a collaborative endeavor involving intellectuals who embraced late Qing–style self-strengthening, such as Kim Yunsik, and those who advocated for more far-reaching reforms inspired by the Meiji Restoration, such as Yu Kilchun, Kim Okkyun, and Sŏ Chaep'il 서재필 (1864–1951).[4] Their efforts were concurrent with the growth of modern print media. The Pangmun guk 博文局, the newly established state bureau in charge of publication, launched Korea's first modern newspaper, *Hansŏng sunbo* 漢城旬報 (Seoul Trimonthly Gazette), in 1883. Yu Kilchun wrote an unpublished inaugural editorial for it in a novel style that used a mixture of Chinese and Korean scripts.⁵ Though the paper ended up adopting traditional Chinese writing, this "mixed style" (*kuk'anmun honyong ch'e* 국한문혼용체) came to be used in a majority of publications in turn-of-the-century Korea.⁶ Yu later defended his unorthodox choice of style, arguing that its "usage of plain word meanings [was] intended to help those with only a limited grasp of writing understand [his piece] with ease" and that he had modeled it on the long-established "technique of reading the seven [Chinese] classics in the [Korean] vernacular" (*ch'ilsŏ ŏnhae ŭi pŏp* 七書諺解의法).⁷ Besides making it accessible to a wider audience, this style's traditional provenance also gave it a modern utility. The mixed style is credited with facilitating the introduction into the Korean language of a plethora of neologisms coined in contemporary Japan to translate Western terms, since most of those new words used Chinese-character compounds, many of which had precedents in the Chinese classics.⁸ The mixed style is itself a heterogenous category designating a variety of Korean prose styles, from those heavily based on classical Chinese composition with just a few added Korean particles and phrase endings to those that further purged what is considered classical influence. This style played a crucial role in turn-of-the-century Korean language modernization, a project that engaged with both Chinese and Japanese, as well as Western, materials. Even as late as 1910, Yi Kwangsu, while expressing the hope to use only the vernacular style one day, had to concede that the mixed style was more pragmatic during the nation's "transitional age," citing the "extreme difficulty" of composing in the vernacular and the latter's unsuitability for translating new knowledge.⁹

When the need for a national language came to the fore, therefore, "Korean writing was too powerless as a medium to throw away Chinese characters entirely."¹⁰ Its status as a national medium had to be constructed through political, social, economic, and discursive processes. *Hangul*, or Korean script, initially received official recognition via a royal edict issued in 1894 in the wake of the Kabo Reforms, which stipulated that all laws and edicts be originally written in "national script" (*kungmun* 國文) and carry an accompanying translation in "Chinese script," or that they use a mixture of national and Chinese scripts.¹¹ The newspaper *Tongnip sinmun* 독립신문 (The Independent) broke the ground in 1896 for modern publication in *hangul*, articulating in its first editorial the intention to follow the lead of "various [modern] nations in which men and women all learn their national writing first before learning foreign writing" and to change the perverse situation in Korea in which "foreign writing"—that is, Chinese writing—enjoyed unnecessary primacy.[12] The linguist Chu Sigyŏng and his allies founded the Society for Unifying National Orthography (*kungmun tongsik hoe* 國文同式會) in the Independent Press in 1896 with the aim of standardizing Korean writing; the Ministry of Education opened the Institute for National Language Research (*kungmun yŏnguso* 國文硏究所) in 1907 to centralize the contested processes of standardization.[13] Orthography reform continued well into the colonial period and beyond. The Kabo Reforms also initiated the institutionalization of primary school education, which began to give priority to reading and writing in Korean script over those in the mixed style.[14] The key rhetoric that underpinned these endeavors was that of civilization. Chu Sigyŏng, for instance, contended in 1897 that the Korean script, thanks to the ease of learning it, brought convenience to "men and women, old and young, the high and low, the poor and rich, and the noble and vulgar" and hence would greatly benefit "our nation's politics of civilization [*munmyŏng chŏngch'i* 문명 정치] today."[15] An 1898 article in the *Imperial Capital Gazette* claimed,

> There are roughly two kinds of writing used in the world's nations today. One is ideographs, such as the Chinese characters used in the Qing; the other is phonetic script, such as our Eastern nation's [i.e., Korea's] alphabet and the Roman alphabet recently used in Western nations.... Why is it that the parts of the world that use ideographs are ignorant and those that use a phonetic script enlightened [*kaemyŏng* 開明]? That is surely because the ease or difficulty of a script [*muncha* 文字] determines whether a people's knowledge will be superior or inferior, and whether a people's knowledge is superior or inferior determines the strength or weakness of a nation.[16]

The writer resorts to the dichotomy of phonetic and ideographic scripts and deploys the discourse of civilization to legitimize Korean script, while relegating Chinese script to an embodiment of ignorance and weakness. This gaze renders Chinese script symbolic of that which Korea ought no longer to be—the "other" of modern civilization—following the idea of cultural modernization in turn-of-the-century Korea.

Calls to reform written language likewise mounted in China in the late nineteenth century. Intellectuals such as Huang Zunxian, Qiu Tingliang 裘廷梁 (1857–1943), Liang Qichao, Lin Xie 林獬 (1874–1926), and Liu Shipei 劉師培 (1884–1919) argued for vernacularization and popular literacy, drawing on an emergent notion of nationalism.[17] Huang Zunxian gave a prototypical formulation to the reformist spirit in a couplet: "My hand writes what I say; how could it be shackled by the ancient?"[18] Referring to the rise of the vernacular in early modern Europe and praising the pedagogical and cultural benefits of the Japanese phonetic *kana* script, Huang contended in 1887, "It is only natural that if speech and writing diverge, fewer people become literate, and if they converge, more become literate."[19] Qiu Tingliang also took the examples of the West and Japan and made an iconoclastic claim in 1896 that the vernacular (*baihua* 白話) "makes all under heaven knowledgeable," while the classical language (*wenyan* 文言) makes it "ignorant."[20] Qiu also suggested that true beauty in composition be bolstered by solid content and insisted that most classical writings displayed a mere "external" beauty that would disperse once they were translated into the vernacular. He thus attributed to the vernacular the force to break up classical writing's cultural aura of literariness and prestige, advocating for the shift of literary culture away from classical letters.[21] He put the nascent idea of vernacularization into practice by contributing to the establishment of the Vernacular Society (*baihua xuehui* 白話學會) in 1898, inaugurating the vernacular newspaper *Wuxi baihuabao* 無錫白話報 (Wuxi Vernacular Paper) in the same year, and editing an anthology of vernacular writing.

Late Qing periodicals increasingly adopted vernacular styles. The first such attempt is believed to be the short-lived *Minbao* 民報 (People's Paper), inaugurated as the vernacular supplement of the *Shenbao* 申報 (Shanghai News) in 1876. Vernacular journalism gained steam in the years leading to the Hundred Days' Reform as a novel medium to popularize modern knowledge for a broad public including the lower strata of society; it helped propagate reformist ideas and circulate news of the contemporary affairs of the world. A forerunner of the vernacular newspapers of the time, *Yanyi baihuabao* 演義白話報 (Vernacular Renditions, est. 1897), contended in its inaugural editorial that its usage of the vernacular was meant to translate not only foreign materials but also all kinds of useful books and news originally written in the inaccessible classical style.²² Following this initial surge, vernacular publishing was actively leveraged by anti-Qing revolutionaries during the first decade of the twentieth century, when some official publications also began employing the vernacular.²³ One important challenge for vernacular publication was posed by China's numerous and vastly diverse dialects. Some journals published in the south used local dialects, whereas most adopted Northern Mandarin (*guanhua* 官話), the common spoken language of Qing officialdom. In 1904 the Qing court gave Northern Mandarin formal endorsement with the Regulation of Schools, which stipulated the inclusion of its study in the school curriculum.²⁴ It became standard as vernacular publication was increasingly wedded to the promotion of "national language" (*guoyu* 國語) and "common speech" (*putongyu* 普通語 or *putonghua* 普通話) amid the rise of nationalist thought on the eve of the Republican Revolution (1911).²⁵

Vernacularization accompanied efforts at script reform in the late Qing era, when intellectuals began regarding Chinese script as a hindrance to the nation's modernization. Blaming the sheer number and difficulty of the characters for cultural elitism and the low literacy rate, they championed script reform and promoted simpler, easier-to-learn phonographic systems. Following some initial experiments with alphabetization by Western missionaries, the renovation of Chinese script gained traction amid the heightened calls for modernization after the failed Hundred Days' Reform. Dozens of novel systems of phonetic script were created in various regions to represent their dialects as well as Northern Mandarin. A Mandarin syllabary was adopted in some journals and reading materials and taught in schools, although its spread was limited.²⁶ The desire for a new script was shared by many turn-of-the-century intellectuals, including the young Liu Shipei, who identified in 1903 five shortcomings of Chinese characters that made Chinese writing "difficult to communicate" (*nantong* 難通). Besides the large number of strokes in a character, Liu focused his criticism on polysemy, taking issue with the existence of numerous homographs and homonyms in written Chinese and the morphological and semantic instability of the characters.²⁷ Yet, owing to the vast variety of dialects, the wholesale adoption of phonographic script in China turned out to result in the balkanization rather than the facilitation of written communication on a national scale. It would have defeated the purpose of fixing the flaws of

Chinese characters, which, precisely thanks to their nonphonetic nature, had long functioned as a universal, if elite, means of communication across a diverse linguistic landscape. After the Republican Revolution, script reform kept its relevance mainly as phonetic annotation indicating the standard pronunciation of the "national language"; the more widely adopted scripts like *zhuyin zimu* 注音字母 and *hanyu pinyin* 漢語拼音 continued to be employed as such methods.

The discourse of language reform also emerged in Japan in the late nineteenth century, as the deep historical indebtedness of the high styles of Japanese verse and prose to Chinese letters came to be perceived as a central obstacle to instituting a national culture. Mori Arinori 森有礼 (1847–1889), a diplomat and the first minister of education of Meiji Japan, for example, wrote in a letter to the American linguist William Dwight Whitney in 1872: "Written language now in use in Japan has little or no relation to the spoken language, but is mainly hieroglyphie [*sic*]—a deranged Chinese, blended in Japanese, all the letters of which are themselves of Chinese origin."[28] Mori also claimed, "The style of written language [in Japan] is like the Chinese. In all our institutions of learning the Chinese classics have been used.... Without the aid of the Chinese, our language has never been taught or used for any purpose of communication. This shows its poverty."[29] With this deep-seated problem, Mori expressed little hope for the survival of Japanese writing now that English had come to dominate the country; as he contended, "our meagre language, which can never be of any use outside of our islands, is doomed to yield to the domination of the English tongue, especially when the power of steam and electricity shall have pervaded the land."[30] Mori's stark diagnosis betrays the perception that national writing is feeble or even nonexistent in Japan and identifies "Chinese" as the primary culprit of that conundrum, aligning the search for a "national language," either conceptually or practically, with an obsessive cleansing of Chinese-oriented elements from writing.[31]

Japanese language reform initially focused on script, where Chinese characters became the main target of attacks. One of the earliest examples of this discourse appears in a memorial presented by Maejima Hisoka 前島密 (1835–1919) to the Tokugawa shogunate two years before the Meiji Restoration, which recommended that for the purpose of popular education, easy-to-learn "phonetic script be employed" as much as possible and that "the use of Chinese characters be abolished in everyday public and private writing."[32] While making the plea on practical grounds, Maejima also offered a value judgment on the merits of different literary cultures. Quoting the Episcopal missionary Channing Moore Williams, who worked in China and Japan, he criticized orthodox pedagogy in East Asia based on the recitation of Confucian classics and insisted that China's decline and its people's "barbaric and uncivilized" state were the result of ignorance caused by "the intoxication of pictographic script."[33] He resorted to the typical trope of language reform in East Asia, reading a civilizational hierarchy in the distinction between phonetic and nonphonetic scripts. Following Maejima, many ideologues proposed various solutions to Japanese writing's problematic reliance on Chinese letters throughout the Meiji era, with some calling for exclusive usage of *hiragana*, while others advocated for a complete switch to the Latin alphabet and still others supported the devising of a novel "national script."[34] Yet aided partly by the rediscovered utility of Chinese characters as a medium for regional communication amid the growth of Japan's territorial lust in the 1890s, the much-despised script survived. The prevalent usage of Chinese-character compounds in Japanese neologisms to translate Western-derived notions and the popularization of those new words through the modern media made it even more impractical to eliminate them from modern writing. Intervention in the end came in the form of restricting the number of Chinese characters to be learned in primary school, as was put forward in the revised State Ordinance on Primary School Education in 1900. This coincided with the implementation of the new subject *kokugo* 国語 (lit., national language) in primary school in the same year and the state-sponsored compilation of the first *kokugo* primer in 1904.

Following the discourse on script reform, Japanese intellectuals took up the question of style and set their goal as vernacularization, or *genbun itchi* 言文一致 (unification of speech and writing), which again took the influence of Chinese writing to be the foremost hindrance. In 1866, Fukuzawa Yukichi declared that in his project of enlightening the Japanese about the customs and institutions of Western nations, he chose to prioritize the "lucidity" (*tatsui* 達意) of writing rather than wasting time on perfecting stylistic elegance on the model of Confucian classics, and wrote that he "took special care to use colloquialisms [*zokugo* 俗語]" for that purpose.³⁵ Elsewhere, Fukuzawa explained that his writing was meant to disrupt old norms of literariness in Chinese-style writing and to frustrate literary distinction:

> Depending on the diction, I indeed don't mind using Chinese vocabulary. I insert Chinese words in colloquial phrases, making colloquial words touch Chinese words and mixing up the refined and the vulgar [*gazoku* 雅俗] like crazy, as if I am violating the holy land of the world of Chinese letters [*kanbun shakai* 漢文社会] and disturbing their rules of composition. I shall simply use a writing that can be understood quickly and easily, thereby letting a wide public comprehend new ideas of civilization.³⁶

Fukuzawa conceived of the newness of his writing in terms of shifting cultural hegemonies, envisioning a transfer of cultural capital to "a wide public" from "the world of Chinese letters," which had long monopolized it. Opening up a public sphere was tantamount to defying the distinctions of Chinese letters and reconfiguring "the distribution of the sensible" through new writings.³⁷ Later in the debates, as the issue of dialects came up, Nishimura Tei 西邨貞 (1854–1904) argued for adopting the Tokyo dialect as standard because "Tokyo is the center of assimilation."³⁸ The pursuit of a national vernacular indicated the desire for a national culture organized around a heart of "assimilation" capable of capitalizing on its geographical and historical differences across the nation.

REDEFINING "LITERATURE"

It was for the new national cultures thus desired, conceptualized, sought after, and institutionalized that Lu Xun, Mori Ōgai, and Yi Kwangsu produced literature. Writings that had long been regarded as literary, epitomized by Chinese letters, had to be dethroned from their normalized status as literature, and novel kinds of writing had to be created to claim distinction in their place. The sweeping shift in cultural hegemony prompted sociocultural processes of "legitimization," "manufacturing," or "formation" of modern literature—the processes built around the concept of redefining literature itself.³⁹ The greater the seismic shift of cultural hegemony in late nineteenth- to early twentieth-century East

Asia, the more the writers became obsessed with the question: What is literature?

Yi Kwangsu's contentions in his 1916 essay "What Is Literature?", which I touched on in the introduction, encapsulate the East Asian discourse of modern literature. "What is called '*munhak*' [文學] today signifies what the Westerners mean by it—that is, the term '*munhak*' is a translation of the Western term 'Literatur' or 'literature.' Therefore, the term '*munhak*' does not mean what people have long understood by it, but designates the '*munhak*' signified by the Western term."[40] The etymology of the term 文學 dates back to ancient China. One of the earliest usages of the term appears in a passage in the *Analects* where Confucius identifies four disciplines in which his close disciples excelled. One of those disciplines is *wenxue*, in which Confucius says "Ziyou and Zixia stand out." According to one of the oldest extant commentaries, *wenxue* in this quotation signifies "erudition in the classical writings of the old kings," and from this usage derives an original meaning of the compound: "broad learning in refined writing," roughly corresponding to the term "letters."[41] 文學 originally had a different semantic field from "literature" in its modern sense, and as that modern notion was transposed from the West into Chinese, Japanese, and Korean in the nineteenth century, the age-old term 文學 was recycled specifically to be used as the translation of that novel concept, which Yi designates in the Latin alphabet here as "'Literatur' or 'literature.'"[42] Yi affirms this recent reconfiguration of 文學 and remarks that his works aspire to make a Korean manifestation of the "literature" thus redefined.

Echoing Yi Kwangsu, Lu Xun likewise reconceptualized literature as a translated notion, inscribing a fine line between premodern and modern writings. While designating the former as 文, he makes it clear that the latter, 文學, is a concept not "cut out from" the *Analects*; as he writes in "Menwai wentan 門外文談" (Amateur Talk on Literature, 1934),

> Our ancestors called the essence of those old writings written in such difficult characters "*wen*," and those who have modernized a little now call them "*wenxue*." This term was not cut out from [the phrase in the *Analects*:] "In terms of '*wenxue*,' Ziyou and Zixia excel in it," but was imported from Japan as a translation of the English term "Literature." Those who can write a little "*wen*" can now write

even in the vernacular, and they are called *"wenxuejia"* or *"zuojia"* [writers].⁴³

What is alluded to here is "loanword" translation, the phenomenon in which Western notions are first translated into Japanese using Chinese-character compounds often borrowed from Chinese classics and then circulate back into China in that form.⁴⁴ Lu Xun's passage points to a paradigm change around the notion of "literature," in which the cultural distinction traditionally carried by the term *wen* was passed on to *wenxue*, all while the latter lost its classical connotation and took on a new meaning as the translation of the Western notion of "literature." Lu Xun, just like Yi Kwangsu, regarded this new literature as a national endeavor that was to give voice to the Chinese people and classical writing/script as the barrier to that goal. In his famed speech "Wusheng de Zhongguo 無聲的中國" (Voiceless China, 1927), he claimed, "China has its own writing/script [*wenzi* 文字], but it has nothing to do with us all anymore. It is only used for complex classical writing and signifies an outdated meaning. All the voices [it expresses] belong to the past, amounting to nothing. So people do not understand one another just like sand in a large dish."⁴⁵ In the 1930s, when he committed himself to leftist politics and took part in the debates over literature for the masses, Lu Xun went so far as to call Chinese characters a "tuberculosis infecting Chinese working people" and suggested that China "eradicate non-vernacular writing and squared characters [i.e., Chinese characters]" altogether in order to survive.⁴⁶

Like Yi Kwangsu and Lu Xun, intellectuals in Meiji Japan also argued for a radical redefinition of literature. Scholars such as Nakae Chōmin 中江兆民 (1847–1901), Tsubouchi Shōyō 坪内逍遥 (1859–1935), and Ernest Fenollosa (1853–1908), who was invited from the United States to teach at Tokyo Imperial University, introduced the modern discipline of aesthetics—rendered at first as *"shinbi gaku* 審美學"—from the West to redefine literature and art.⁴⁷ Wrestling with the perception that "what is called 'literature' in Sinology and what is called 'literature' in English are different in kind and cannot be subsumed under the same definition at all,"⁴⁸ Natsume Sōseki ventured to "fundamentally create, for myself, the concept of what literature is."⁴⁹ Mori Ōgai, who spent about four years in Germany studying hygiene and military medicine, spearheaded the introduction of aesthetics to Japan with his influential translation of Eduard von Hartmann's *Die Philosophie des Schönen* (The Philosophy of the Beautiful, 1887).[50] Brand-new concepts of modern European aesthetics enabled Ōgai to articulate the essence and function of literature and art in fresh terms, leading to a number of polemics with contemporary critics. He debated with the Britain-trained scholar Toyama Masakazu 外山正一 (1848–1900) on the nature of painting by borrowing von Hartmann's notion of "the ideality of aesthetic images."[51] He criticized Tsubouchi Shōyō for the blind promotion of fictional realism "without ideas" (*botsu risō* 沒理想), inspiring disputes over the nature of literature in general.[52] Through these debates, the terms of discourse on literature and art shifted to translated concepts deriving from Western aesthetics.

In their endeavors to redefine literature, Yi, Lu Xun, and Ōgai referred to the translations of Western discourses to conceive of a complete departure from previous literatures, symbolized by the authority of classical Chinese writing, thereby tethering their writings to the broader efforts at cultural modernization. Yet in their creative works, these authors engaged with the cultural past that their works were meant to render obsolete. This textual phenomenon is anachronistic in the context of the grand scheme of modernization in which they tried to legitimize their works, but as such, it is symptomatic of their deep obsession with newness that cut even across their own discourses, leaving them on the wasteland between past and present. In that comparative space, they initiated a movement of reconfiguring the literary realm, which involved a critique of the ideological constructs of the emerging modern cultures in their respective nations. It is in those writerly attempts that I locate the origins of modern literature. In chapter 3 I will revisit these authors' representative texts, credited as some of the "first" works of modern literature in their respective nations, and in chapter 4 I will examine their historical fiction as a generic allegory of their literary endeavors.

CHAPTER THREE

Parody and Repetition

Rereading the Works of Lu Xun, Mori Ōgai, and Yi Kwangsu

Some of the canonical works by Lu Xun, Mori Ōgai, and Yi Kwangsu are credited with marking the beginnings of, respectively, modern Chinese, Japanese, and Korean literatures. These works tend to be understood in terms of the ruptures they create with previous literatures to make a transition from premodern into modern. But instead of such a linear transition, they produce a new realm of literary representation through critical engagement with the cultural past.

The newness of these representative works by Lu Xun, Ōgai, and Yi in comparison with previous literatures could be explained in various ways. Even from the texts we analyzed in part I, they display obvious differences. Most of them, for example, use versions of what are now considered the standard modern vernaculars, whereas their precedents tend to retain more features of old literary composition deriving from classical Chinese writing. Implicit or explicit adaptations of Western literature are more salient in the works considered in this chapter. Such separations, to be sure, characterize some aspects of these works' modernity, but they cannot fully account for their *structural* constructs as modern literature—literature left on an open-ended semantic terrain where its definitions are in the making. My reading delves into those constructs by examining the critical relationships they establish with past cultures.

To conceptualize those relationships, I employ the notion of "parody" broadly defined. Thanks to its versatility, Linda Hutcheon's discussion is especially helpful: "Parody ... is a form of imitation, but imitation characterized by ironic inversion, not always at the expense of the parodied text.... Parody is, in another formulation, repetition with critical distance, which marks difference rather than similarity."[1] The notion of parody is useful first for illuminating the significance of the references that a work makes to previous texts, and second for considering a relationship between disparate cultural contexts that this critical gesture creates—a relationship that cannot be reduced either to simple rupture or continuity but needs to be discerned through dialectic interplays of past and present, or what Hutcheon has called a "bitextual synthesis."[2] Parody, in this sense, enables me to grasp the significance of the historical relationships that the works in question reconstruct to previous texts. This approach, then, leads me to shed light on the textual moments in which such relationships collapse into mere repetition. If parody functions by "self-referentiality" or "auto-reflexivity," then some of the works I analyze call into question the very identity of the "self" or "auto" in this gesture by virtue of the sheer forces of repetition that disturb differences that can be capitalized on by cultural history. To quote Deleuze: "In every respect, repetition is a transgression. It puts law into question, it denounces its normal or general character in favor of a more profound and more artistic reality."[3] My inquiry into parody will therefore be expanded by attention to instances at which a text presents itself in its utter "power" or as an "artistic reality" that, destabilizing the normalized "self" or "auto" of literature, demands new modes of reading.

My usage of "parody" is not intended to assess East Asian works against a global order of twentieth-century art in general or postmodernism in particular that pivots on self-referentiality. Instead, it aligns this study with the criticisms of major works of modern literature—including, to name just a few, *Don Quixote*, Shakespearean drama, and *Ulysses*—that analyze their critical references to past literature as integral to the emergence of new literary and even epistemic horizons.[4] In the introduction I pointed out the Orientalist construct of the discourse of cultural modernization that designates East Asia's transregional cultural past as obsolete and prehistoric. Beyond this framework, I undertake here to bring an earnest consideration of past literatures and other aspects of past culture into the reading of modern works.

The authors examined in part II all studied abroad in youth: Lu Xun in Japan from 1902 to 1909, Mori Ōgai in Germany from 1884 to 1888, and Yi Kwangsu in Japan from 1905 to 1910 and again from 1915 to 1919.[5] Lu Xun went to Japan on a Qing government scholarship to study medicine, only to quit medical school in 1906 and begin a literary career, whereas Ōgai stayed in Germany on an official mission to survey modern hygiene and military medicine. Yi attended middle school in Japan, and then returned there to enroll in college as a philosophy major. These experiences, with all the variations among them, exposed these writers to modern knowledge in general and, above all, world literature in particular. They read voraciously, often through translations, literatures from the broader world, which were, to be sure, centered on Western European works but nonetheless also included works from Eastern and Northern Europe, Russia, the United States, and, in the cases of Lu Xun and Yi Kwangsu, Japan. Their omnivorous reading, while inspiring Lu Xun and Ōgai in particular to produce copious translations themselves, urged all three of them to create novel literature in the open horizons of the modern world, where the cultural protections to circumscribe "literature" became subject to constant questioning.

LU XUN: RESIDUES OF MODERNIZATION

In his 1934 essay "Amateur Talk on Literature," Lu Xun described a transition from *wen* 文, the traditional notion of "letters" writ large, into *wenxue* 文學, the loanword translation, via Japanese, of the "English term 'Literature.'" This conceptualization indicates the typical notion of modern literature as a product, on one hand, of the severance from earlier literature and, on the other, of the embrace of equivalence or translatability with Western literatures. Yet in this essay, Lu Xun in fact describes this situation from an ironic distance, in the voice of an "amateur," or literally from "outside the gate" (*menwai* 門外). He envisions an even newer form of literature written in "the language of the masses" (*dazhongyu* 大眾語) that will defy even the "*wenxue*," which in his eyes has already been gatekept by elites by the time he writes this essay. Underpinning his discussion is the polemical contention that the established "*wenxue*" has carried over the kind of cultural distinction traditionally embodied by *"wen,"* and that *"wenxue,"* thanks to that inherited status, serves the privileged class and fails to become veritable modern literature, which he now sees in the literature of the masses. This contention echoes Qu Qiubai's 瞿秋白 (1899–1935) contemporary criticism of the May Fourth vernacular for becoming a de facto "new classical writing" (*xin wenyan* 新文言).[6] For Lu Xun in this essay, literature in the modern sense, despite its conceptual historical provenance, is something yet to be created.

Advancing a proposal to abolish and latinize Chinese characters, then, Lu Xun evokes folksongs, folktales, folk poetry, and folk theater as inspiration for this true modern literature. Among the examples he takes is a scene inserted in "Mulian xi 目連戲" (The Play of Mulian), a popular folk play put on during the Ghost Festival on the subject of the Buddhist legend of Mulian's (Maudgalyāyana) rescue of his mother from the realm of hell. The scene is a parody of the episode in *Water Margin* about Wu Song's fight with a man-eating tiger.

> One segment in it ["The Play of Mulian"] is "Wu Song beats the Tiger," where two actors, A and B, one strong and one weak, act playfully. First, A plays Wu Song and B the tiger. Beaten hard by A, B blames him. Then A says, "You are a tiger. So if I didn't beat you, wouldn't I be bitten to death by you?" So B can only ask to switch roles, but then he is again bitten hard by A and accuses him. Then A says, "You are Wu Song. So if I didn't bite you, wouldn't I be beaten to death by you?"[7]

Lu Xun praises this absurd act by comparing it to "the fables of Aesop from Greece or of [Fyodor] Sologub from Russia." Originally in *Water Margin*, the drunken and weaponless Wu Song singlehandedly defeats the tiger and shows his unassailable strength, whereas in this parody, narrative closure is broken and diegesis (i.e., Wu Song's fight with the tiger) is taken over by extradiegesis (i.e., actor A's apparent strength compared to actor B), wresting the original episode out of the normal literary context and exposing it to pure contextual indeterminacy.

This brief reference does not just indicate the author's interest in the "carnivalesque" imagination or even his leftist endorsement of popular art, but it also gestures toward the way his work relates itself to the cultural past.⁸ Rather than define and secure, in the name of "modern literature," a context in which texts are to be read, his references overturn unilateral contextual demarcations and open texts up to other possible readings. What is often seen as the "first" work of modern Chinese literature, Lu Xun's "Kuangren riji 狂人日記" (Diary of a Madman), originally published in the magazine *Xin qingnian* 新青年 (New Youth) in 1918, is concerned with such references in both form and content.

The bulk of this work consists of thirteen diary entries penned by the "madman," which are introduced by a pseudo-pathological preface that frames them as material for "medical research" showing symptoms of "a kind of persecution complex." This hypercanonical text has been singled out as one of the first literary works in China to adopt the modern vernacular—an unmistakable sign of its modernity.⁹ Yet while the vernacular style is employed in the diary proper, the preface that introduces it is penned in the orthodox classical style. The anachronism has invited many scholarly arguments over conflicts between the representing and the represented. Whereas, as Yi-tsu Mei Feuerwerker has pointed out, the prefatorial function of furnishing authority to the text is itself a reiteration of the convention in premodern vernacular fiction, the sheer heterogeneity of the frame with regard to its content has inspired reflections on representability per se.¹⁰ Echoing Marston Anderson's elucidation of the "disturb[ance]" of realism in Lu Xun's fiction, Theodore Huters has read "Diary of a Madman" as a "meta-discourse on the impossibilities of representation."¹¹ My reading instead illuminates the work's self-conscious foregrounding of semantic indeterminability and contends that the "Diary" symptomizes literature's departure from a cultural context that restrains or conceals such indeterminability and its move toward open interpretative horizons. Its ironic narrative structure engenders the very *possibility* of representation for modern literature.

The preface tells us that what follows are small, "barely coherent" portions selected from the original diary in two volumes, which presumably no one should bother to read since it is filled with so many "confused and disorderly words and absurdity of expressions"—the kind of writing that cannot be handled without "loud laughter" by ordinary readers, like the diarist's brother, who gives it to the preface's author. The preface also reveals that the presented excerpt is called "Diary of a Madman" after the title picked by the diarist himself following his "complete recovery," thanks to which he is now ready to take an official post.[12] This preface thus forms a narrative framework that professedly exposes its own biases resulting from the editorial interventions of abbreviation, titling, and quasi-medical judgment that renders the text presentable and legible—the biases of the norms against which the diarist is judged "mad."

In the diary proper, the voice of the "madman" resounds as the voice of a lucid, enlightened loner who cannot help discerning a deeply corrupt culture beneath the ostensible normalcy of Chinese society. As has been noted, this perspective is informed by Lu Xun's exposure to Western thought, namely the theory of evolution, Nietzsche's *Zarathustra*, and the works of Gogol and Andreyev.[13] The diarist's radical view is best epitomized in the epochal scene in which he examines history books during a sleepless night.

> Only by thorough research can one understand something. I seemed to remember, if rather vaguely, that people have been eating each other since ancient times. So I flicked through a history book, and found that it did not have dates but those Confucian virtues: benevolence, righteousness, and morality meandering across every single page. I could not fall asleep anyway, so I read with great care through the night, only to find out what emerged between the lines: the whole book was filled with two words, "Eat people!"[14]

This nocturnal epiphany inscribes a metaphysical rupture in Chinese history, denouncing the entire recorded past for concealing cannibalism under the guise of Confucian virtue. The "madman" eventually realizes that he himself is a product of four thousand years of cannibalism and wonders if there are any "children who have not yet eaten human flesh." This leads him to utter in the end the desperate plea: "Save the children..."[15]

Meanwhile, the diarist is ostracized by the paternalistic society because of his heretical views: he is isolated, locked up in his study by his elder brother, and subjected to an examination by a doctor of Chinese medicine. His modern, humane, or possibly even "sentimental" voice that attempts to open people's eyes to a new era and "change" them "from the bottom of [their] hearts" is never listened to in this world.[16] Yet what about this story itself? Is the text "Diary of a Madman," given the expressed biases involved in its presentation, suitable or "modern" enough to transmit a truth about this man in trouble? The preface implies that there might be complicity between, on the one hand, the power of social normalcy embodied in the classical style and, on the other, the power of modernization informing the pathologizing gaze. The captivity and silencing of the madman recorded in the diary ironically constitute a metonymy of the narrative closure that represents him as a "madman." This makes the narrative of "Diary of a Madman" a structural "irony," as Leo Ou-fan Lee has put it—irony in the proper sense of the term, which lays bare the "violently paradoxical" structure where "at all points the narrative can be interrupted."[17]

The relationship of "Diary of a Madman" to the cultural past is thus "dialectical," as Eileen Cheng has put it, displacing the radical rupture that the madman inscribes in Chinese history.[18] This work parodies the cultural past by evoking it to frame a content entirely alien to it; the cultural past is conjured up in a new context, where the relevance of its authority, its force to create and sustain narratological closure, is put to the test. As the diary conveys a singular, norm-defying, and "mad" voice, it increases the tension of that parody, thereby betraying the "violent paradox" of the irony, the impossibility of establishing a proper context to interpret this work between sanity and insanity, the modern and the premodern. The failure to account for this structure is tantamount to overlooking the existence of the diary's ur-text in two volumes, which is purportedly too absurd to be reproduced yet is perhaps the most authentic representation of the diarist's voice. Therefore, to hear the diarist's real voice, one needs to read this text with close attention to the less than transparent medium created by its parodic relationship to the cultural past.

This text, in other words, reveals itself as an orphan signifier drifting between possible semantic contexts. And such a confusion of signification indeed characterizes the terrible epistemological experience that the madman undergoes in the story. In his eyes, things, expressions, and idioms lose their ordinary meanings and expose themselves as horrifying "signs" (*anhao* 暗號).[19] He expresses suspicions about the people around him: "They seem to keep some secrets which I cannot guess at all, and once they turn on you [*fanlian* 翻臉], they will call you a bad person. I still remember when my eldest brother taught me composition, he would mark me up if I reversed [*fan* 翻] a few of the words by a virtuous person; if I excused villains, he would say, 'Exquisite! [*fantian miaoshou* 翻天妙手] It shows your originality.'"[20] The puns on the character *fan* 翻 (lit., flip, reverse, convert, translate) imply the arbitrariness of the existing order of meaning and value, as it is illustrated by the disingenuous instruction in composition by the elder brother as an embodiment of declining cultural authority. It is this chasm in signification that enables the madman to "flick through" (*fankai* 翻開) a history book and uncover the bankruptcy of such a strong currency in Chinese culture as "benevolence, righteousness, and morality" (*renyi daode* 仁義道德), laying bare its cannibalistic substance. If there were an allegorical meaning to "Diary of a Madman," it would be the exposure of the arbitrariness inherent in signification, or the corruption of the ideological power that sustains its normal stability. Not only is the madman unable to rely on cultural norms to read the history books, but he sees them as mere flippant "signs," even overshadowing a critical textual exegesis "central to the Confucian literary tradition."[21] Likewise, the reader, faced with the irreducible ambivalence of representation, cannot depend on either modern or premodern context to decipher his language literally. The madman's ultimate demand to save the children may call for a rupture, a fresh culture, or a new civilization to overcome this ruin of signification, but the "Diary" nevertheless dwells on that very ruin and affirms it as the sole *possibility* of representation between the old and new cultures—a possibility that appears an "impossibility" only if viewed from the vantage point of a presumed standard cultural context. For this reason, in its performance of—to use Lu Xun's own terms—an equivocal "intermediary" (*zhongjianwu* 中間物) that is unable to "shed" the "ancient ghosts" of the cultural past, the "Diary" generates and finds itself on a terrain that inherently deviates from a cultural context that tries to regulate the function of literature.[22]

Lu Xun's exploration of a new mode of representation, therefore, finds itself in a cultural in-between, the space he opened through parodic engagement with past cultures. And this endeavor is pursued, perhaps in the most developed form, in the only midlength fiction among the oeuvre of this master of short stories: "A Q zhengzhuan 阿 Q 正傳" (The Real Story of Ah Q). Originally serialized in the supplement of the newspaper *Chenbao* 晨報 (Morning Post) from 1921 to 1922, "The Real Story" is the satirical tragicomedy of an outcast of the village of Weizhuang set against the backdrop of the Republican Revolution.

Likely the most iconic character in modern Chinese literature, the protagonist named Ah Q lacks self-knowledge entirely. Dwelling in a local temple and hopping between dayworks, Ah Q is a favorite target of mockery from the villagers and reprimands from the village's gentry family, the Zhaos. He nevertheless remains optimistic and at times even cheerful thanks to his "method of spiritual victory," which amounts to a vicious circle: he mentally claims superiority over others by evoking the very social order—ultimately, the authority of the civil service examinations and the emperor—that relegates him to its lowest stratum. The absurdity of this reasoning is caricatured in, for example, Ah Q's speculation after a humiliation: "Could it be that, as he heard in the town, the emperor abolished the civil service examinations, and the successful candidates are of no use anymore; so the Zhaos have lost their authority and, by association, they began thinking little of him?" He is characterized by empty moralism, as he prides himself on heeding the teachings "passed down from the sacred sages" and espousing "Confucian orthodoxy" (*lijiao* 礼教). The hilarity of this character culminates when he turns defeat into victory by slapping himself and thinking that it was he who hit someone.[23]

This opportunistic, obsequious, and self-important outcast constitutes a potent caricature of Chinese society, including its upper echelons. When the Republican Revolution breaks out, Ah Q and those who hold power, likewise caged in the old system, both initially fear it, since it might smash their ways of life. Yet the powerful are able to weather the turmoil and maintain their status thanks to their vested resources, while Ah Q, despite his attempts at riding the tide and climbing up the ladder in revenge, remains lowly and stays an Ah Q. His tragicomedy thus satirizes the failure of the Republican Revolution to overturn the social order and allegorizes the China that needs to change. In this sense, as scholars since Fredric Jameson's controversial discussion of "third-world literature" have contended, "The Real Story" may be a quintessential "national allegory" or an expression of "Chinese national character," and it may even be safe to say, quite simply, that "Ah Q is China."[24]

This reading, however, must be counterbalanced by a consideration of the literary form in which Lu Xun creates such an allegory. "The Real

Story" is written as a parody of the traditional narrative form of *zhuan* 傳 and of the politics of literary "transmission" (*chuan* 傳).[25] Much like "Diary of a Madman," the preface plays an essential role in the narratology of "The Real Story." The importance of its beginning cannot be emphasized enough:

> It has already been more than one or two years that I have been meaning to write a real story for Ah Q. But while wanting to write, I have been in some trepidation, too. This is enough to show that I am not one of those people who "establish [their imperishable legacy by] words." For always an imperishable pen has had to write about an imperishable man, so that man becomes known to posterity through writing and writing known to posterity through man—until finally it is not so clear who is making whom known. But in the end, I end up writing a story of Ah Q, as if my thought is haunted by a ghost.
>
> But as I take up my pen to work on this rapidly perishable writing, I feel struck by extreme difficulties.[26]

In this self-reflection of the narrator, Lu Xun positions this work against existing literature. What he alludes to is the well-known argument in the Zuo commentary on the *Spring and Autumn Annals* about what kind of man will "not perish after death" (*si er bu xiu* 死而不朽). Those who "establish words" (*liyan* 立言) constitute the bottom of the three categories of imperishable men, the top being those who "establish virtue" and the middle those who "establish deeds."[27] The narrator says that literature has always been written by such a worthy writer about a likewise worthy man, and he satirizes this economy of existing literature as a tautological exercise in which "man becomes known to posterity through writing and writing known to posterity through man." Yet what the narrator now wants to make known to posterity (*chuan* 傳) is Ah Q, a mere outcast of a rural village, a subject that would normally be deemed undeserving of literary treatment. Ah Q should be outside the bounds of what can be spoken of in the language game of literature, but he is now demanding that the narrator give him a story, like a "ghost" haunting the realm that expelled it.[28] "The Real Story" is a hauntological practice, in the sense that it is a paradoxical undertaking of representing that which representation has excluded.

Ah Q, therefore, is someone who demands that the very realm of literature be expanded, and Lu Xun responds by creating a new form called "rapidly perishable writing" through parodying classical literature, especially the *zhuan* narrative. This genre has traditionally been understood in conjunction with adjacent genres like the *ji* 紀, the *jing* 經, and the *shi* 史. In relation to the *ji*, the main chronicles of emperors and extraordinary rulers, the *zhuan* designates the biographies of various individuals of import; to the *jing*, the classics, it means their commentary or exegesis; and to the *shi*, history, it signifies unusual or sometimes esoteric episodes that nevertheless deserve recording. The *zhuan*, therefore, remains external or superfluous to its superior terms, yet is necessary to convey their essence; it is a "supplement" in the classic Derridean sense of the term.[29] The narrator tries to use this form to write a story for Ah Q and, mimicking the Confucian doctrine of "rectifying names," to give it a proper title. Yet he immediately realizes that the intended work does not fall into any of the established subcategories of the *zhuan*, prompting him to come up with a makeshift title by cutting out "*zhengzhuan*," or "real story," from the boilerplate interpolation in traditional storytelling: "Enough of this digression, now return to the real story."[30] Unlike a mere "'new' variety" of the traditional *zhuan*, therefore, "The Real Story" is a *zhuan* only in name, excluded from its usual generic configuration and used outside its proper context.[31]

In this parodic performance of writing a "*zhuan*," the narrator tries to adopt some of its conventions by beginning the story with the protagonist's name, courtesy name, and native place—pieces of information that are often featured in an orthodox *zhuan* to determine the protagonist's identity through filiation. In the case of Ah Q, however, they are unavailable, as he does not have a place in the traditional social fabric of identification and is thus excluded from the standard order of the *zhuan*. Even the name "Ah Q" is the result of a compromise that attaches the commonplace prefix "Ah" to the first letter of a Latin transcription of his given name, whose proper character is unknown. The narrator nevertheless remains true to its generic function and scrupulously tries not to "go against history"[32] but to maintain a truth claim about it—a gesture that only intensifies the ambiguity about just what "history" this story might help convey. "The Real Story," thus, is a quasi-*zhuan*: the superior term it should serve to transmit is absent, while it floats in a paradoxical state of *pure supplement,* as it were, unaware of what to complement. And to underline this structure, the narrator ends the preface by mockingly alluding to the modern scientific historiography championed by Hu Shi 胡適 (1891–1962) during the May Fourth era. "As for the other problems [with regard to the identity of Ah Q], it is not for such unlearned people as myself to solve them, and I can only hope that the disciples of Mr. Hu Shi, who has such 'a passion for history and research,' may be able in future to throw new light on them. I am afraid, however, that by that time my 'Real Story of Ah Q' will have long since disappeared."[33] "Ah Q" is a ghostly figure of what remains external to both the premodern and modern (here, scientific) orders of representability; it embodies a residue of the transition from premodern to modern. Lu Xun's search of newness resulted in a parody of the *zhuan,* a transitory form unattributable either to the premodern or the modern, which he dubbed "rapidly perishable writing."

Critical references to past culture also inform the narrative. From the onset, the narrator makes it clear that he is telling this story after Ah Q's death. Thus, what we read in its nine chapters is a retrospective reconstruction, which involves, as critics have noted, a "distance" between the narrator and the subject, or the former's "superior position" against the latter.[34] Part of what creates the unsettling relationship between the narrator and the subject is the focalization of the point of view through the gaze of the villagers. Indeed, the reconstructed development of the ups and downs of Ah Q's life closely mimics his fluctuating reputations within Weizhuang. The story takes its first positive turn as Ah Q gets hit by the patriarch of the Zhaos, which, "because the beater was famous," brings him fame. This beating becomes a source of pride for him for several years, but the story enters a chapter of "tragedy" when the whole village begins to shun him after he is admonished for making awkward sexual advances to the maidservant of the Zhaos. Ostracized from village society, he has to leave for the town, yet after several months, his return to Weizhuang "makes news." "Everyone wanted to hear the revival story [*zhongxing shi* 中興史] of Ah Q, back with the ready cash and the new jacket—the story that gradually leaked out in the tavern, the teahouse, and under the temple eaves. As a result, Ah Q gained new respect."[35] As more gossip about Ah Q and the goods he has brought back from the town circulate in Weizhuang, the story opens a chapter titled "Revival and Decline." The revival, then, is followed by a decline, which begins when new rumors start to spread that Ah Q was involved in a robbery in town, and the villagers begin to keep their distance from him as "their respect suddenly changed."[36] Ah Q's fall culminates in his execution by firing squad after an accusation of looting and a cursory, politically motivated trial amid the turmoil of the Revolution. Despite this sad conclusion, the story's final chapter is entitled "A Happy Ending" to reflect the villagers' cynical perception of Ah Q's demise, with which the story comes to an ironic close: "Public opinion in Wenzhuang was unanimous, in that all naturally agreed that Ah Q was bad. The proof was that he had been shot. For if he was not bad, why would he have been shot? . . ."[37] A thug has been executed; hence, a "happy ending."

Thus adopting the perspective of the fictive villagers, the narrative mimics the circulation of rumors in Weizhuang in conveying Ah Q's story. And through the parody of the *zhuan*, combined with the loose adaptation of the form of traditional cycle-chapter fiction, this work invites the implied reader to appreciate it as they would normally do familiar literature.[38] The parody of existing literature renders this narrator quite reliable for the reader, enabling them to depend, without much critical distance, on the narrative point of view to read the story, even if it is focalized through the villagers' perspective. The reader, therefore, is led to consume Ah Q's hilarious tragicomedy just as the villagers spectate him. Through these calculated mediations, "The Real Story" aligns the mode of literary reading with that of rustic gossiping, if only to expose the former's ideological closure by revealing the latter's intrinsic violence, thereby calling into question the legitimacy of what is usually appreciated as "literature."

As is implied in his obsession with "spiritual victories," Ah Q internalizes the collective gaze of the villagers, to the point that he acts for the sole sake of "satisfying the spectators" even in his existential crisis.[39] He faithfully plays the role that people expect him to, even if the "happy ending" they want to see means his own death. When he is asked to sign a document that sentences him to death at his trial for looting, he "focuses all his energy" on drawing "a perfect circle" so as not to "look ridiculous to people" despite his illiteracy. He is ashamed of the distorted circle that is all he can draw and even consoles himself that "his grandsons should be able to draw a very round circle." His satirized actions come to a climax on his way to the execution ground, where he is paraded through the streets for public display and entertains the crowd by singing a few opera lines and showing off his good spirits.[40] The villagers whose collective gaze creates "Ah Q" put an end to it by staging the spectacle of his demise. Focalized through this exact gaze, the narrative betrays its apparent complicity in the violence inherent in what is visible and audible in Weizhuang's culture, and this in turn invites the reader to reflect on the ideological confines of what can be written and read in "literature," if they are to read this text as they ordinarily do, without a sense of ironic distance.

The parody of past cultures in "The Real Story," therefore, creates the same kind of narrative closure as it does in "Diary of a Madman"—a closure in which a subject has to be represented from a vantage point that may not recognize his internal voice. Yet Lu Xun goes a step further in "The Real Story" to crack an opening in this closure at the moment of Ah Q's death by representing the *absence* of his voice. At that moment, the narrative shifts its point of view to depict, at long last, the consciousness of the person it has been calling "Ah Q."

> Then, Ah Q looked back at the cheering crowd.
> At that moment, his thoughts revolved again in his head like a whirlwind. It was four years ago. At the foot of a mountain, he had encountered a hungry wolf that continued to follow him at a set distance, wanting to eat his flesh. He had felt almost dead with fear, and only the axe he happened to have with him had given him the courage to go back to Weizhuang. He had never forgotten the wolf's eyes, fierce yet cowardly, gleaming like two will-o'-the-wisps, as if boring through his flesh from a distance. But this time, he saw eyes that he had never seen, even more horrifying than the wolf's. Dull yet penetrating, they were already gulping down his words [*jujuele ta de hua* 咀嚼了他的話] and still eager to devour something other than his flesh, following him along at a set distance.
> These eyes seemed to have merged into one, already gnawing into his soul [*linghun* 靈魂] over there.

"Help..."

But Ah Q said nothing. His eyes had been hazy, and his ears buzzing, as if his whole body was scattered into so much dust.[41]

At the moment of his death, Ah Q finally realizes the ferocity of the crowd's gaze. Yet focalized through it, the narrative itself, along with the villagers, has been "gulping down his words" and "gnawing into his soul" by telling his "real story"—a troubling indication, to quote Anderson's words, of "the originary violence at the heart of Chinese society [being] perpetuated and disseminated."[42] As Ah Q finally grapples to break this discursive closure with his last plea ("Help..."), therefore, the narrative cannot represent it except by missing his voice ("But Ah Q said nothing"). "The Real Story" conveys the lone cry of Ah Q's soul only as a voiceless inscription through a chasm in the narrative closure, and this silence urges the reader to interrogate their complicity in creating "Ah Q," as literary readers no less violent than the Weizhuang crowd. The parody of an old literary form encourages the reader to maintain their accustomed mode of literary reading, only to estrange them from it and leave them in deafening silence. The silent inscription of "help..." reaches the reader as pure reverberations of an absent voice to which they must tune their ears to hear Ah Q—a self-reflexive practice tantamount to an examination of the condition of possibility for literary representation. For Lu Xun, therefore, the solution to the perpetuation of violence in representation, or the path to expanding literature and to its veritable "newness," consists not so much in the embrace of "an independent critical stance" or "sympathetic projection" as in the fictional *parody* of that culturally ingrained violence in such a way that it inspires the reader's self-transformation.[43] Parody in "The Real Story" thus ultimately leads to Ah Q's unuttered word that exerts its critical potency to fight against the exclusory forces of "literature" through *repetition* rather than meaningful differences—that is, the sheer force that the word in its voiceless inscription produces each time it meets the reader.

Parody complicates the idea that the way out of the satirized corruption of old culture is modernization. It epitomizes a modern literature that was, while embracing the progressive tides of history, born of attempts at reconstructing a relationship with the cultural past to produce transgressive newness. Lu Xun's literary endeavor sees one of its culminations in the 1924 short story "Zhu fu 祝福" (New Year's Sacrifice), which leverages its critical might—this time especially exploiting the form of storytelling—to envision modernity amid the dialectics of myth and enlightenment. If "Diary of a Madman" and "The Real Story" parody the discursive closures of past culture in their narratives, then "New Year's Sacrifice" attributes such a closure also to enlightenment by featuring a dramatized narrator as a modernized intellectual.

Published originally in the Shanghai-based journal *Dongfang zazhi* 東方雜誌 (The Eastern Miscellany), the story revolves around the narrator's encounter with a woman called "Xianglin's Wife." The narrator returns to his hometown Luzhen and stays with his uncle's family for the New Year celebration, but despite the jubilant holiday atmosphere enveloping the whole town, he feels alone and isolated. As if to add to his uneasiness, he meets Xianglin's Wife, a former maidservant in his uncle's household who, visibly frail and dejected, turns out to have been reduced to beggary. She abruptly asks him a philosophical question: "Is there a soul after a person dies?" The narrator is dumbfounded and finds himself miserably incapable of giving a proper reply, to the disappointment of Xianglin's Wife, who expected a reliable response from this "literate man." He convinces himself that he should not increase the suffering of a dying person and replies falteringly that there is a soul after death, but his angst only worsens as he cannot respond to her additional questions about the existence of hell and the fate of family in the afterlife. Eventually, he can only talk his way out by stammering, "That is . . . actually, I can't say for sure . . . Actually, I can't say for sure either whether there are souls or not."[44] The awkward conversation makes him realize that he is "an utter fool" and gives him premonitions about her fate. On the following day, his worst fear comes true when he overhears his uncle implying she has died. While the superstitious uncle avoids at all costs mentioning her death to keep inauspicious topics from tarnishing the holidays, the narrator retreats to his room, where he begins to reminisce about her life and tell her story.

Echoing "Diary of a Madman" and "The Real Story," this narrator betrays his own bias as he begins the story in an apathetic, detached voice:

> Seated alone in the amber light of the vegetable-oil lamp, I pondered on Xianglin's Wife, this helpless and forlorn woman who had been

abandoned in the dust like an old plaything of which people had wearied. When her body was still seen in the dust, those who enjoyed life, I am afraid, must have wondered why she still had to exist. But now, she had at least been swept away by Impermanence [*wuchang* 無常]. Whether souls existed or not I did not know; but in this world of ours the end of a futile existence, the removal of someone whom others are tired of seeing, was just as well both for them and for the individual concerned.[45]

With this rumination, the narrator gradually feels relaxed, and the fragments of what he knows about the life of Xianglin's Wife begin to come together. This oddly disengaged mode of narration has drawn critical attention. Anderson, for example, has read in the story Lu Xun's critique of realist representation, which could reproduce "at a formal level the relation of oppressor to oppressed," here realized between the narrator and Xianglin's Wife.[46] Huters has pointed out an urge for "the reader to examine the nature of his [i.e., the narrator's] complicity in the continuation of a rapacious society."[47] To be sure, the narrator's indifference seems to betray his lack of a critical view on the cruelty of the society that has mercilessly sacrificed Xianglin's Wife; yet it is also the case that he is the only hope, in this society that avoids even mentioning her, of giving her a story, however unsuitable he may be for the work.

Her story is one of despicable gender and class oppression in old Chinese society. As a widow, she is regarded as accursed but gains recognition through hard work in the uncle's household, only to be sold off in remarriage by her mother-in-law, who needs to finance her son's marriage. Her second husband rapes her, and she loses her baby son to a wolf attack. The stigma of remarriage brings her more humiliation and even a threat to her afterlife, where she is told that she will be sawed in half by the King of Hell to satisfy her two former husbands. She is, therefore, forsaken in both life and death—in life, because of her society's sexism and stigmatization of widowhood and remarriage; and in death, because of her lack of a proper place in a family lineage, a central social unit where ancestral worship is performed. Added to this all is the utter inability of modern knowledge to redeem her soul, bespoken by the impotent narrator, who, while at first futilely pretending to assure her of redemption after death, only ends up stammering and dodging the topic. The modernized narrator's avoidance of her question about death ironically resembles his uncle's superstitious evasion of the same topic on New Year's Eve—a powerful illustration of the "dialectic of enlightenment" formulated by Horkheimer and Adorno, the paradox that enlightenment's desire for demystification shares with myth the "taboo" or fear of the unknown "outside."[48] The narrator's ineptitude is due less to his personal "reluctance to think deeply and with compassion" or to particular issues in Chinese modernity than to the structure of the modern episteme in general.[49] For the narrator, then, the sole way to save her is not enlightenment or a "mythical fear radicalized,"[50] but storytelling.

Indeed, the narrator's story of Xianglin's Wife is itself about storytelling. It consists in large part of various characters' comments about Xianglin's Wife, and more importantly, it thematizes those people's responses to her own storytelling. Traumatized by the loss of her baby son, Xianglin's Wife tells everyone in Luzhen the devastating story of how a wolf killed him. Her story is initially "very effective": it moves men and women alike and effaces their contemptuous attitudes toward her. Some old women who have not heard it seek her out specifically to hear it. "Over and over she repeated it, often drawing a few audiences around her." Before long, however, people become used to it and stop showing sympathy; they even feel a "headache," as the whole village has "learned it by heart." No sooner does she begin the story than someone stops her and make her jump to the conclusion. They even preempt what she wants to say. Having been "masticated and savored for so many days," her story "had already become dregs, something worthy only of boredom and spitting out."[51] Though her story initially had the ability to arouse the audience's sympathy, it loses its strength as she tells it repeatedly; her story is reduced to mere "dregs" that people no longer care about. And almost corresponding to the attrition of her story's appeal, Xianglin's Wife herself declines and becomes once again a "plaything," an object of scorn and discrimination. However, in reproducing her iterative storytelling, the narrator, in a rather extraordinary gesture, repeats her entire story twice verbatim—all the way from her regret about not knowing the wolf's habit of coming down to the villages for food in spring, to her praise of her son for being so good that he had always done as he was told; from her panicked surprise at his disappearance from the doorstep where he was supposed to be shelling beans and the frantic search that ensued, to the gruesome depiction of the discovery of his body lying in the wolf's den with all his innards eaten away.[52] The narrator's word-by-word repetition of the story has the twofold effect of replicating the uncanny experience of hearing the exact same story compulsively repeated by Xianglin's Wife and of freeing her story from the present mode of narrativization to deliver it to the reader in its material intensity. It demands that the reader be critical of the constitutive forces of the narrative they read, and thereby hear her story *as if* it were told in her lost voice.

If the narrator's detached voice mobilizes the self-reflexive narratology that Lu Xun also deployed in the two previous stories we have analyzed, here specifically to lay bare the mythological closure of enlightenment, then his actual storytelling positively performs a new mode of representation called for by Xianglin's Wife's wandering soul. At the end of the story, we unexpectedly find out that the narrator has been in a dream or a dreamlike state during his recollection and storytelling. Having concluded the story by stating, "I was woken up by the noisy explosion of crackers close at hand," he feels "indolent and relaxed" and blissfully embraced by the atmosphere of "infinite happiness" that the holiday festivities bring to the whole of Luzhen.[53] The narrator's state of mind echoes some of Benjamin's conjectures on storytelling, that "sleep is the apogee of physical relaxation" conducive to the listener's "assimilation" to the storyteller's experience and that "boredom is the dream bird that hatches the egg of experience."[54] In this Benjaminian sense, Lu Xun's narrator, in his reminiscence and storytelling, may have been in a mode of "exchang[ing] experience," bypassing differences in class and levels of modernization, with Xianglin's Wife herself. And through this dramatized narrator, Lu Xun invites the reader to also participate in that exchange, forming a "community of listeners." "For storytelling is always the art of repeating stories."[55] By having the narrator repeat Xianglin's Wife's story, Lu Xun carves out a reenchanted realm of literature in which Xianglin's Wife's voice can be saved both from suppression by old social norms and mythology and from representation in an enlightened, disenchanted culture.

The newness of this realm is anachronistic, not just in the sense that it defies the notion of progress from mythology into enlightenment, but also in that it parodies the cultural past. In the beginning of the story, as the narrator commenced his storytelling, he stated that

Xianglin's Wife had been "swept away by Impermanence," or by *"wuchang* 無常." "Wuchang," in Buddhist doctrine, means the evanescence of all things in the world, but in the folklore of Lu Xun's hometown Shaoxing, it is the name of a deity that takes human souls to the underworld. In his essay "Wuchang 無常" (Impermanence, 1926), Lu Xun lovingly recollects the impersonation of that deity in "The Play of Mulian" put on during the village festival; he sees in "Wuchang" an arbiter of *"gongli* 公理," or the "universal principle" that is to be applied to human souls after death for fair and impartial judgment—something the disenfranchised "lowlifes," who "live, suffer, become victims of rumors and countercharges," cannot hope for in the social life of this world. So, writes Lu Xun, "When you think of life's happiness, you of course want to stick to life; but when you do life's pain, Wuchang may not necessarily be such an unwelcome guest."[56] The notion of *"gongli,"* to consult Wang Hui's discussion, implies a universality that emerged after the demise of traditional *"tianli* 天理," or the universal order within the particular ethicopolitical world that was premodern China.[57] Having Wuchang embody the universality that is quintessentially embodied by science in modernity is certainly an anachronism, yet it nonetheless indicates Lu Xun's self-reflexive program of creating a new realm of representation capable of conveying voices that the old culture suppresses and the new one also fails to save—a program through which he was able to envision justice, which in "New Year's Sacrifice" is demanded by the abject life and afterlife of Xianglin's Wife. That new realm is not created on the foundation of an existing concept like enlightenment but is only produced through a parody of the cultural past and the self-critical interrogation of representability. This leads to moments of repetition, where the texts read each time in a singular manner, inviting the reader to put down the armor of the received notions, old or new, of literature and encounter them as a vulnerable, dislocated subject, just as the narrator in "New Year's Sacrifice" embarrassingly stammered in the face of Xianglin's Wife, who was posing the aporia of the human soul.

MORI ŌGAI: CRITICAL ARCHAISM

Just as Lu Xun did in China, Mori Ōgai grappled with the cultural past at the origin of modern literature in Japan. His short story "Maihime 舞姫" (The Dancing Girl) ignited a famous polemic at the time of its publication in the journal *Kokumin no tomo* 国民之友 (The Nation's Friend) in 1890.[58] This polemic sheds light on the anachronistic construct of this work, now canonized as a foundational work of modern Japanese literature. One of the most prominent of Ōgai's opponents was the literary critic Ishibashi Ningetsu 石橋忍月 (1865–1926), who censured "The Dancing Girl" especially for the characterization of the heroine, the German dancer Erisu (i.e., Elise): "When I saw the title 'Dancing Girl' advertised in a newspaper last year, I thought [the heroine] would be a popular female performer... But in the actual work, the so-called dancing girl turns out to be but an illiterate and foolish woman who lacks discernment and integrity. That is my first disappointment."[59] The "dancing girl" as a fictional heroine made this critic anticipate a certain character type: a woman with erudition and wisdom, discernment and integrity. Ningetsu's horizon of expectation evoked the typical figure of the "beautiful woman" (佳人 Jpn. *kajin*; Chn. *jiaren*) in the classical fictional subgenre of romance between a scholar and a beauty, which was popularized through East Asia. In this critic's view, Ōgai's short story disappointingly lacked such a heroine.

This criticism would simply be misguided if it merely projected an old literary prototype onto an already modernized work. Scholars have indeed delineated how "The Dancing Girl" breaks away from previous literatures in a variety of ways, such as through the depiction of "the psychic interior of [the] character," "the influence of Ōgai's reading in Germany," "the story of spiritual transformation from a feudal man into a modern man," and even the establishment of a "geometric perspective" in narration.[60] Not only was Ōgai's exposure to European literature expansive, ranging from ancient Greek and Roman, English, French, and Russian to Danish, Norwegian, and Swedish literatures, but he was also a prolific and well-read translator, perhaps best known for his complete translation of Goethe's *Faust*.[61] However, Ōgai's defense against Ningetsu's criticism does not target the latter's anachronism, but instead doubles down on it, suggesting the inadequacy of considering the newness of "The Dancing Girl" solely in terms of departure from the literary past. In his refutation of Ningetsu, Ōgai argued,

> No other character would better embody an "illiterate and foolish woman who lacks in discernment" than Nana. But Zola, the great

French man of letters, titled his work with her name, and no one takes issue with it, although some might dislike its excessive inclination toward naturalism . . . But I for one only believe that Elise resembles Wenjun of the Zhuos or Hongfu from the Yang family. I don't think you would necessarily demand that the dancing girl should only be a popular female performer, and your disappointment might just come from the fact that you didn't see what you thought you should.[62]

While justifying the title by evoking the authority of Émile Zola, the "great French man of letters," Ōgai defends the characterization of Elise based not on its departure from but on its resemblance to prominent female characters in the classical Chinese canon: Zhuo Wenjun 卓文君 and Hongfu 紅拂. Their legends are featured in Chinese fiction compendia that had circulated widely in Japan since the Edo period, such as Feng Menglong's 馮夢龍 (1574–1646) *Qingshi* 情史 (Stories of Love), which sets their stories back-to-back among the four stories categorized under "romantic chivalry" (*qingxia* 情俠), or the stories of "chivalrous women [*xia nüzi* 俠女子] able to choose their spouses by themselves."[63] Ōgai's defense of his heroine by virtue of her genuine similarity to the prototypical female characters in old romances bespeaks the indebtedness of "The Dancing Girl" to classical Chinese letters, which the young Ōgai devoured, as abundantly evidenced by his writings and the collection in his personal archives.[64] The story's out-of-place archaism struck the critic Satō Haruo, who surmised, "Can it be that a sense of archaic oldness that I feel from 'The Dancing Girl' or 'Utakata no ki' [A Sad Tale, 1890] is the sense of oldness that I feel when I read legends [*ki* 記] or stories [*den* 傳] [in the traditional gerne of] strange-tale fiction [*denki shōsetsu* 傳奇小說]?"[65] The modernity of "The Dancing Girl" should thus be examined not simply by identifying the ways in which it differs from previous literatures but by considering how it engages with them. This approach brings to the fore the underdiscussed grounds for comparison between Ōgai's and Lu Xun's fictional works in terms of their common use of parody.

"The Dancing Girl" is Ōgai's quasi-autobiographical story about a romantic affair set in Berlin between Elise and a young Japanese bureaucrat named Ōta Toyotarō.[66] The narrative is constructed in a nested form in which Toyotarō recollects and writes down the story during the five years of his life in Germany in his private notebook in the middle of his sea journey back to Japan, alone in his cabin as his ship calls at the port of Saigon. Having graduated from law school at the top of his class, Toyotarō became an elite, up-and-coming bureaucrat in Japan, and his diligence earned him the long dreamed-of opportunity to travel to Europe on a prestigious governmental grant. Thrilled at this perfect chance to make his name and repay his family, he spends the first three years in Berlin conducting a survey for the ministry and auditing classes at university. While immersed in the liberal academic atmosphere, however, he begins to harbor doubts about his stellar career and realizes that he has been shackled by the expectations of his parents and superiors, reducing himself to a mere cog in the state bureaucracy. He reads Schiller and Schopenhauer and grows interested in the spirit of law, history, and literature rather than the minutiae of statutes; he feels as if his "real self, which has been lying dormant deep down, is gradually appearing on the surface."[67] Yet this realization alienates him from the community of Japanese students in Germany, who frown upon his independent thinking and slander him. Toyotarō's solitary figure echoes numerous protagonists in modern East Asian fiction who are modernized, yet by that very virtue isolated from their contemporary compatriots who are mechanically obsessed with modernization and extracting personal profits from it. Toyotarō is at a loss, enduring solitude and helplessness, when he encounters Elise on the street, and they fall in love.

But his courtship of Elise brings deeper troubles. As rumors spread within the Japanese community about their affair, Toyotarō's appointment is rescinded and his grant suspended, committing him to disgrace. It is indeed via this thematic of the conflict between love and society that "The Dancing Girl" grafts itself onto a tradition of romantic tales in Chinese letters. The story of Zhuo Wenjun, a prototype of the scholar and beauty romance set during the Western Han dynasty, relates Wenjun's elopement with Sima Xiangru 司馬相如 (c. 179–117 BCE) against her father's will. Xiangru was previously active in the literary circle around Prince Xiao of Liang (?–144 BCE), but after the prince dies, he loses his means of living due to a decline in his family fortune. Aided by a county magistrate, Xiangru is invited to a banquet hosted by Wenjun's wealthy father Zhuo Wangsun, where he plays the "Song of Phoenix" on the zither. Wenjun is so deeply moved by the song that she decides to elope with him that very night, infuriating her father, who reportedly yells, "Such a useless daughter! I wouldn't kill her, but I shall not give her a single dime, either!" Wenjun arrives at Xiangru's hometown only to find that his house is nothing but four walls. The couple takes on manual labor and sells wine to make ends meet.[68]

The legend of Hongfu (lit., "red whisk"), for its part, is set at the juncture of the dynastic transition from the Sui to the Tang. Hongfu is one of the courtesans of a powerful minister of Emperor Yang of Sui named Yang Su 楊素 (d. 606). One day, an official called Li Jing 李靖 (571–649) visits Yang Su in a commoner's outfit to provide strategic recommendations. But Su's disrespectful attitude at the reception prompts Jing to give an admonishment: "The world is in turmoil and heroes are vying to rise. You are an eminent servant of the court. Why don't you think about casting a wide net to gather brave men? You should not see a guest while reclining on a couch." Su has to apologize to Jing. Having intently observed the scene, Hongfu visits Jing's lodgings in disguise that night and tells him, "I have long served Minister of Works Yang and seen many people in the world. No one matches you. So I've come to become close to you." Though Jing is afraid of retaliation from the powerful minister, Hongfu reassures him that he is already like a dead man and his pursuit will not be far-reaching. Jing is struck by Hongfu's appearance and language, which seem to belong to a heavenly person, and takes her with him.[69]

If Zhuo Wenjun's affair with Sima Xiangru upsets the authority of a patriarch, then Hongfu's elopement with Li Jing undermines that of a prominent imperial minister. Both couples' affective attractions are incompatible with social norms, and in this sense, their stories provide a narrative prototype for "The Dancing Girl." Yet in the classical tales, the unorthodox love affairs eventually defeat those norms, and these miraculous reversals constitute the narratological heart of their literary merit. Wenjun's stubborn father in the end yields to his daughter and recognizes her marriage, providing the couple with abundant financial help. This lays the foundation for Xiangru's literary and political success, which even causes the father to regret that he did not marry his daughter to Xiangru earlier. The narrator of the *Stories of Love* comments, "Had Xiangru not met Wenjun, the strings of his zither would have perished.

Had Wenjun not met Xiangru, who would have written about her lotus-like cheeks for posterity?"[70] They turn out to be such a perfect match that they deserve a story that will be passed down. The Hongfu lore, for its part, derives its value from its take on political legitimacy at the juncture of dynastic transition. An epic sequel to the couple's elopement, Du Guangting's 杜光庭 (850–933) "Qiuranke zhuan 虯髯客傳 (Story of the Guest with Curly Whiskers), has it that Li Jing and Hongfu allied with a stranger with dragon-shaped whiskers and discovered Li Shimin 李世民 (599–649), who helped his father defeat the Sui and establish the Tang and became the new dynasty's second emperor. The legend builds on the theme of Hongfu's capacity of "consideration" (*zhenzhuo* 斟酌), to quote the commentary in *Stories of Love*, through which she was able to "understand Duke of Wei [i.e., Li Jing] at first sight and determine that Duke of Yue [i.e., Yang Su] was good at nothing."[71] Hongfu's attraction to Li Jing and abandonment of Yang Su, though upsetting her social obligations, allegorize the extraordinary discernment of a sign that heaven's mandate was shifting. The clashes of Zhuo Wenjun's and Hongfu's romances with social norms both constitute historical allegories for those norms' ultimate unfoundedness. History proves to be on the side of the chivalrous women, and it is precisely by virtue of the marvels of the prognostic abilities of their sensibilities that their otherwise private, if defiant, love affairs deserve to be recorded as "stories" and passed down. Their intrigues become literature as omens of history.

The courtship of Toyotarō and Elise, in contrast, ends in an utter tragedy. Thanks to the help of a friend named Aizawa Kenkichi, the disgraced Toyotarō is offered a position as a foreign correspondent for a Japanese newspaper and begins to live a modest but happy new life with Elise. But no sooner does Toyotarō learn she is pregnant with his child than Aizawa visits Berlin as a member of a ministerial delegation from Japan and gives Toyotarō a chance to "restore his name." Toyotarō translates German for the minister and accompanies him to Russia as an able interpreter of French. He earns the minister's trust, and Aizawa urges him to seize the chance to return to Japan. He is torn between Elise and Aizawa, between an uprooted yet free and happy life and allegiance to his family and nation, and he chooses the latter. The fateful decision causes him so much agony that he collapses when he tries to tell Elise about it and falls into a coma that lasts for weeks, during which time Elise finds out about his betrayal and loses her mind. Critics have condemned the protagonist for causing this devastating ending with his irresponsibility, heartlessness, and even "lack of ethics."[72]

A comparison with the traditional romances, however, throws light on the narratological stakes of this modern tragedy beyond mere moralism. Like its classical Chinese precedents, "The Dancing Girl" in fact hints at certain new norms foreshadowed by the new life that Toyotarō and Elise choose to live. Through his journalistic work, Toyotarō becomes an "expert in a different sphere—popular education [*minkan gaku* 民間学]," inspired by the writers of Young Germany.[73] "Rather than raking up onto paper the dead leaves of laws and statutes as I had done before, I would compose miscellaneous writings on, among other topics, the lively political scenes and the criticism of the latest trends in literature and the arts, carefully making connections between distant phenomena to the best of my ability and organizing my ideas more in the style of Heine than Börne."[74] Toyotarō's writings, indeed, might have resembled Heine's journalistic work, in which, according to Peter Uwe Hohendahl, "the apparent fragmentation, the leap from one topic to another, disguises . . . consistency" and "a totality" is achieved "through careful composition [where] heterogeneous elements are juxtaposed."[75] And if such a "negative" work of modern criticism ultimately "plays a role in an analysis of an era," then Toyotarō's "miscellaneous writings" could have sought to reconstruct a totality of the history of which his life was part, exiled yet lived together with his lover.[76] Yet as he leaves Elise, Toyotarō abandons that task. "If I did not take this chance [that Aizawa presents], I might lose not only my homeland but also the way to retrieve my good name. I was horror-struck to the core by the thought that I would drown in the sea of human beings, in this vast European capital. Alas! How spineless I am, that I agreed to go!"[77] He descends into a state of anomie and must cling to the "homeland" and his "good name"; he ceases not only to be a moral person but also to be a modern critic by abandoning Elise.

The conspicuously sad ending indicates that "The Dancing Girl" was composed in the absence of a conception of the course of history that would eventually legitimize the illegitimate romance, a metahistorical framework that underlies the classic scholar-and-beauty narratives. Ōgai's parody suggests that such a history, rather than being posited as a premise of literature, has yet to be written, as suggested by the protagonist's aborted work of "popular education." If dynastic history provided classic scholars and beauties with the stages for their courtship, then Ōgai's couple lacks one and is left in the open-ended horizons of the modern world ("I would drown in the sea of human beings, in this vast European capital"). And if an idea of history underpinned the literariness of the old romances, or their worth as "stories," then their parody leaves the literariness of "The Dancing Girl" in suspension. Its precarious status as literature is embodied in the form of its narrative, which presents the story as left in a private notebook. Toyotarō wakes up from the coma while Elise is still suffering from an incurable paranoia. He and Aizawa leave Elise's mother and the unborn child capital enough to eke out a bare living and board the ship for their homeland. With regret weighing heavy on his heart and giving him agonizing pain, Toyotarō "weave[s] a writing" (*fumi ni tsuzurite* 文に綴りて) with self-consciousness about the difficulty of doing so. He says that this regret is so deeply engraved on his heart that it cannot be "expressed in poetry or sung in songs"; he has not even written about it in his travel journal. He has to take up a pen with cynical self-deprecation: "To whom could I possibly show a record of fleeting impressions that might well be right one day and wrong the next?" The transient nature of his writing is emphasized in comparison to the travelogue he penned on his journey toward Europe five years ago, which amounted to "thousands of words a day" and enjoyed a good reception when it was published in a Japanese newspaper.[78] Toyotarō's story calls for a new form, neither poetry nor a song nor even an essay, without a warranted value in the existing order of literature. "The Dancing Girl" therefore frames the story proper as a text in suspension, left in a private notebook lying in a ship's cabin somewhere between Europe and Japan. Unlike his previous writings, or, for that matter, the numerous transpositions into contemporary Japan of European literature embodying the cultural capital of the West, Toyotarō's story, of dubious literary value, might not make it from the West to the East. "The Dancing Girl" presents itself as a text of ambivalent literariness, inscribed with self-consciousness about the possibility of its not being received as "literature." This narrative form indicates its self-reflexive questioning about what constitutes valuable literature, setting it as tangential to the established realms of both an old literature underpinned by a classical notion of history and a new literature carried by the world-historical tides of modernization. It is an uncanny resemblance to classical literature, rather than a progressive departure therefrom, that expands literature and produces a new mode of representation, here capable of freeing literature from history, of recording "fleeting impressions" without a clear historical significance "that might well be right one day and wrong the next" in search of their inherent meaning.

Ōgai's parody of classical fiction sees its most thorough manifestation in the novella "Gan 雁" (Wild Geese). Published in serial form in the literary magazine *Subaru* スバル (The Pleiades) from 1911 to 1913, this work has been noted for its complex dramatization of narration—the structure that I analyze here as a self-reflexive narrativization of the context into which classical literature is transported with a difference.[79] "Wild Geese" abounds in allusions to old texts. The unnamed first-person narrator and the protagonist Okada, both medical students in Tokyo, strike up a friendship through their shared literary tastes. They belong to a Japanese literary culture around 1880 that still felt the surviving appeal of age-old aesthetics. They share a used copy of a Chinese edition of *Jin ping mei* 金瓶梅 (The Plum in the Golden Vase), and they casually quote from Chinese classics like the Zuo commentary to the *Spring and Autumn Annals* and *Water Margin* in their conversations. They also enjoy early Meiji verse and prose, which were tangibly indebted to Chinese classics and not yet called "new" fiction, drama, or lyrical poetry—works by such Sino-Japanese poets as Mori Kainan 森槐南 (1863–1911) and Ue Mukō 上夢香 (1851–1937), who published in popular literary magazines like *Kagetsu shinshi* 花月新誌 (New Magazine of Flowers and the Moon) and *Keirin isshi* 桂林一枝 (A Branch in the Laurel Grove).[80] Fond of *Yuchu xinzhi* 虞初新志 (The New Records of Fiction), the seventeenth-century Chinese anthology of short stories, Okada identifies with the mysterious fighter with the iron awl featured in "Datiezhui zhuan 大鐵錐傳" (Story of the Great Iron Awl) and derives his image of an ideal woman from "Xiaoqing zhuan 小青傳" (Story of Xiaoqing), both collected in that anthology. Above all, his encounter with the woman named Otama, the chief event around which the novella revolves, is staged in explicit reference to *The Plum in the Golden Vase*. Okada reads that novel "for the whole morning" before going on a walk; he suspects he must have looked "awfully silly after reading that sort of book," which "usually after every ten or twenty pages of innocent description, always throws in an indecent scene as if trying quite punctually to fulfill a promise" of offering sexually explicit material.[81] Okada relates his chance encounter with Otama that afternoon to the narrator, who surmises that "Okada, who had been reading *The Plum in the Golden Vase*, might have met a [Pan] Jinlian."[82]

"Wild Geese" adapts the narrative of *The Plum in the Golden Vase* where the plot is driven by chance incidents, among which is the fateful meeting of Ximen Qing and Pan Jinlian, a classic scene of premodern Chinese romance. As the story goes:

> But this particular day was one of those occasions on which:
> Something was destined to happen.
> Just as she [Pan Jinlian] was about to take down the blind a certain person happened to walk by.
> Without coincidences there would be no stories;
> It is those who are predestined to do so who meet.
> The woman was in the very act of reaching up to take down the blind with a forked stick when a gust of wind dislodged it from her grip so that it fell,
> Neither correctly nor precisely,
> but right onto the hat of the passerby. As she hastened to put on an ingratiating smile she looked at him and saw that he was twenty-four or twenty-five years old and cut quite a dashing figure.[83]

The stock phrase "But this particular day was one of those occasions on which: / Something was destined to happen" (*yiri yeshi hedang youshi* 一日也是合當有事) is frequently interpolated in the narrative to introduce consequential events. It relates the encounter as coincidental on the surface yet "destined" in substance; fortuity is but the visible sign of a latent structure of necessity. In this sense, it espouses the proverbial saying derived from *Water Margin*: "Without coincidences there would be no stories" (*mei qiao bucheng hua* 沒巧不成話).[84] In "Wild Geese," the narrator's retelling of Okada's account of his encounter with Otama as a reenactment of the old topos of amorous rendezvous alludes to this traditional narratology—a gesture to represent contemporary events as

Parody and Repetition 139

enactments of patterns of necessity. And the obvious dramatization of their chance meeting, which involves Okada's chopping in half of the snake attacking Otama's two pet crimson linnets, an episode that the narrator calls "mythical," builds up the expectation that there should be a "story" to be told behind all this.[85]

Yet "Wild Geese" does not tell such a "story" in the traditional sense; it instead dramatizes the narrator's attempt to tell *a* story by stitching together two plot threads, one about the man and the other about the woman. The first-person narrator frequently inserts his voice to reveal that the related story is a retrospective reconstruction, an idea he repeats in the conclusion:

> Now that I have written this story, I have counted on my fingers and discovered that thirty-five years have passed since it happened. I witnessed half the story during my close association with Okada. And I heard the other half from Otama, with whom I accidentally became acquainted after Okada had left. In the same way that one receives an image through a stereoscope, with two pictures set together under a lens, I created this story by comparing and combining what I witnessed earlier and what I heard later.[86]

"Wild Geese" uses up more than half of its pages on the story of Otama, leading to the episode of how she obtained her crimson linnets, which become "the mediator" of her meeting with Okada.[87] It features a narrator who weaves together distinct stories to try to reconstruct a totality of the world in which their encounter occurs and the necessity behind that chance event may be revealed. It is an attempt to manifest through narrativization a latent dimension of necessity behind contingent worldly occurrences in much the same manner as a "stereoscope" restores the third dimension from two flat images. This dramatization constitutes a parody of the narratology of *The Plum in the Golden Vase*, which represents the world's underlying working through fictional composition.

The relation of Otama's story is lengthy and scrupulous, so much so that it constitutes a realistic account of the life of an ordinary woman who lives under the burden of gender inequality and class oppression. Otama is the concubine of a usurer named Suezō. Suezō was already a middle-aged man when he worked as a servant in the dormitory near the medical school that the narrator and Okada attended, and he earned the capital for usury through petty money lending to students. Canny and wily, but vain and fond of indulging in pricey outfits, Suezō decides to spend his surplus money on a concubine. He targets Otama, who has lived a humble life with her poor yet devoted single father, but recently had to cry herself to sleep over a marriage scam inflicted by a policeman too powerful for them to accuse. Suezō puts up a façade of being a respectable businessman and lures the father and the daughter with hard-to-resist financial incentives. With little leverage and driven by the filial obligation to repay her single father, Otama is compelled to agree to the deal and endure the disgrace of concubinage, which brings stability to her life while reducing her to the plaything of a banal petit bourgeois. Her unexpected discovery of Suezō's usury, a shameful fact he had hidden from both father and daughter, depresses her and glues her to the window on the street. As she melancholically and yearningly looks out at the passersby, she spots the handsome Okada. Meanwhile, Suezō is caught in a difficult relationship with his jealous wife, who suspects his infidelity, and a quarrel one day drives him to take a long walk, during which it occurs to him to buy two crimson linnets for his young, pretty concubine. The storytelling is meticulous in its psychological depictions, its realistic portrayals of the quarters, streets, and shops in the developing city of Tokyo, and its reflections of social discourses on student life, marriage, money, power, gender, and modernization.

Yet the narrative ultimately falls short of discerning necessity behind the encounter of Okada and Otama. Just as the meeting happens by sheer chance, so does it fail due to pure contingency. Taking advantage of Suezō's overnight business in the suburbs, Otama sends home her maidservant and braces herself for a second meeting with the man. But the latter, who normally passes by her house alone on his routine evening walks, happens to come out that day with the narrator, who disliked the miso-boiled mackerel served at their dormitory and took him out for supper. So "a mackerel boiled in miso had the same effect as that nail" in the Grimms' "The Nail," the tiny cause of a big consequence.[88] The narrator's presence prevents the romance from developing, and to deal it a final blow, they run into a classmate of theirs who insists on hunting a goose in a pond in the middle of the city. As a result, Okada's cloak assumes an unsightly conical shape with the hunted goose concealed under it, which keeps Otama from approaching him. The comical anticlimax leaves contingencies in place, in their sheer indifference to any divinable significance or necessity behind them.

The narrator's stereoscopic attempt at reconstructing a general structure of the world, therefore, results in a projection of the world in open horizons where multiple lives stumble across each other without dramatic consequences. The world is devoid of a metahistorical structure, represented merely by a modernizing cityscape in which shops, ways of life, and customs change over time and anonymous dwellers pass by each other. This world is topologically open-ended, for the very existence of the observer-narrator affects it—the self-reflexivity symbolized by the miscarriage of the romance due to such a random, minute fact as the narrator's dislike of the miso-boiled mackerel. The parody of old narratology fails by the very act of parodying, or by the dramatized existence of the narrator, who in old fiction is rendered reliable and transparent thanks to his self-ascribed omniscience about the totality of the world's working, the capacity to weave a "story" out of coincidences. Parody, therefore, collapses under its own weight. Romance becomes an inconsequential, undramatic, and purely contingent encounter that would have been forgotten without the narrator's unexplained, ambivalent intention to write a "story whose protagonist *ought* to be [shinakutewa naranu しなくてはならぬ] Okada" thirty-five years after it took place.[89] The parody of old literature fails to yield a new version of the classic romance, but that very failure opens literature to relating uneventful moments of everyday life that are to be savored in their own right.

In "Wild Geese" as well as "Dancing Girl," the parody of classical literature does not so much add value to existing literature as expands the expressive capacities of "literature" itself. This generative function of parody is indicated in the novella's ending. Okada, upon the request of a professor at Leipzig University researching Oriental epidemiology, readily translates several passages from the classics of ancient Chinese medicine into German and earns a rare opportunity to become the professor's assistant and continue his medical education in Germany, definitively forgoing his chance of meeting Otama again. But his otherwise able translation stumbles over the term "三焦 [Jpn. *sanshō*; Chn. *sanjiao*]" (the triple burner), the name of the sixth of the "six organs" in traditional Chinese medicine, which has no equivalent in Western anatomy.[90] He can only transcribe it as "chiao," a "phonetic transcription" of the Chinese term, undefined in Western medical knowledge.[91] If a difference in contexts sets the stage for the encounter between Okada and Otama as a parody of old romance, then Okada's smooth translation, by establishing equivalence between the old and new epistemes, bridges the contextual difference on which that parody depends—an allegory of the collapse of the parodied romance. Yet the difficulty of finding an equivalence, or the term "chiao" that has to be transcribed from the old into the new context, indicates not so much a difference that can be addressed by translation as an undefined, unconceptualized relationship between the premodern and the modern. The transcriptive repetition of "chiao" is indicative of the remainder of the transition from the premodern to the modern, for whose reckoning a new order of representation must emerge.[92] Ōgai employed parody to create newness in literature that expanded its domain, and in this sense, his works resonate with Lu Xun's in their pursuit of modern literature.

YI KWANGSU: THE TEMPORALITY OF MOURNING

We saw in the introduction to part II that Yi Kwangsu deployed the rhetoric of severance from past culture to explain "modern Korean literature." The same framework has often been used in the criticism of Yi's seminal novel *Mujŏng* 무정 (The Heartless, 1917) and his early stories.[93] Scholars have considered how Yi's early works are distinct from previous literatures in Korea and identified such traits as "the manufacturing of a modern, interiorized self," "the discovery of interiority" and "interior landscape," and "dramatic conflict [that is] internalized within the self."[94] Their assessments revolve around the idea that his work "reads like a totally new kind of fiction" that breaks radically from past literatures, if not "with no debt whatsoever to any previous Korean works."[95] This idea, moreover, mirrors an important plot line in *The Heartless* about the growth of the protagonist Yi Hyŏngsik into a "modern subject" through an agonizing separation from the old world, a plot that might warrant the characterization of this novel as a "Bildungsroman."⁹⁶

My critical intervention consists in drawing attention to the form in which this novel tells—or better, *attempts* to tell—a story of maturation or enlightenment, and reconceptualizing the modernity of this spearhead of modern Korean fiction in terms of the process of literature's self-transformation. This perspective enables me to reassess *The Heartless* in comparison with the works of Lu Xun and Mori Ōgai in their common use of parody as a device to expand the domain of literature.

The inherent complexity of this novel is first and foremost encapsulated in the serpentine path of the protagonist's growth and his incoherent, sometimes irritatingly indecisive character. As early as the 1930s, for example, the writer Kim Tongʻin (1900–1951) criticized this protagonist's "strange and contradictory" actions and censured the novel for failing to feature a coherent hero.⁹⁷ Yi Hyŏngsik's meandering development introduces a complex temporality into the narrative, as it is indicated in the final paragraph of this full-length novel:

> The world that has been dark should not be dark or heartless [*mujŏng* 무정] forever. With our own power, we shall make it bright, filled with feeling [*yujŏng* 유정], pleasurable, wealthy, and strong.
>
> With this happy smile and shout of cheers, let us end *The Heartless*—the mourning for [*chosang hanŭn* 조상하는] the world that has passed.⁹⁸

The narrative of progress out of the past world is at the same time one of "mourning" for the loss thereof. The temporality of progress into the modern is also one of residual attachment to the past, or, to use Freud's terminology, of the psychic "prolong[ation]" of "the existence of the lost object."⁹⁹ The story of progress is marked by an irresolvable duality, as its completion is iteratively deferred by the returns of what progress leaves behind. *The Heartless* is as much about progress as it is about the reassembly of that which progress has to destroy, an impossible task that ultimately leads to an experience of the sublime in the story's deus ex machina.

Yi Kwangsu was still a student at Waseda University in Japan when he serialized *The Heartless* in 1917 in *Maeil sinbo* 매일신보 (Daily News), the only Korean-language newspaper in colonial Korea sanctioned by the governor-general at the time. Like the author, the protagonist Yi Hyŏngsik is a colonial elite. Having been educated in the imperial metropole Tokyo, Hyŏngsik teaches English in the colonial capital and considers himself to be "the pioneer with the most advanced thought in Korea." He has read Rousseau's *Confessions* and *Émile*, Shakespeare's *Hamlet*, Goethe's *Faust*, and Kropotkin's *Conquest of Bread*; he knows of Tagore and Ellen Key. He peruses articles on politics and literature in the latest magazines, and the fiction he publishes in a Japanese journal even wins a prize. "He has confidence in having his own views on life, the universe, religion, and art, and his own opinions on education." He takes it as his mission to use his knowledge to educate the Koreans even as he feels hopeless about the lack of likeminded compatriots, giving him the attitude of a progressivist elite with "both pride and arrogance toward Korean society." This typical psychology, however, is satirized in the novel for the lack of affective appeal in his speech and writing:

> The words he uttered fervently as if telling some grand truths in fact did not particularly move the audiences. His only distinction was that he used a lot of English, dropped the names of famous Westerners and quoted them frequently, and rambled on things that were hard to understand. His speeches and writings sounded like literal translations [*chigyŏk* 직역] of Western texts. He would claim that deep and intricate thoughts could only be expressed in such speech or writing.[100]

The pedantic style of "literal translation" that Hyŏngsik's language assumes indicates, on the one hand, the common dilemma of a colonial elite whose modernized knowledge alienates him from the rest of the nation. Yet on the other, it manifests a crucial characteristic of the modernization he embodies, which is not only about introducing new terms and ideas but also about doing so in a novel style of speech and writing. Contrasted to Hyŏngsik is his friend Sin Usŏn, who is "educated in classical Chinese writing" and looks like "a man of taste right out of

Chinese novels," with "the manner of a bold and chivalrous young man of Suzhou or Hangzhou in the Tang dynasty." Usŏn's classical habitus and his old cultural capital deriving from erudition in the Chinese canon are still effective in Korean society, bringing him literary fame for his patriotic writing at the end of the story.[101] Yet Hyŏngsik, who is "educated in English or German writing,"[102] struggles because his language is new not only in content but also in form and hence fails to exert an emotional influence. His quandary embodies the difficulties of a cultural modernization that is not just about ideas and institutions but also about taste and manners.

This problem is thematized prominently in Yi Kwangsu's early short stories, in which the absence of affective communication leads to existential agony. Yi's debut piece, written in Japanese and entitled "Ai ka 愛か" (Perhaps Love? 1909), is the short story of a strained affective relationship. The protagonist, Bunkichi (Kor. Mungil), endured an abject childhood in Korea and obtained a chance to study in Tokyo, a unique opportunity he considers "the gate toward the ideal" and the way "out of darkness and into brightness." Yet he suffers from deep "desolation and loneliness," lamenting that "no one among the one-billion-and-six-hundred-million human beings would understand his heart." He has an intense crush on a male Japanese classmate called Misao and seeks his "love," but his visit to Misao does not go well. He is so dismayed that he attempts suicide on the railway track, exclaiming, "The stars are heartless!"[103] No less forlorn are the protagonists of two of the stories Yi wrote while *The Heartless* was being serialized, "Panghwang 방황" (Wandering) and "Yun Kwangho 윤광호" (Yun Kwangho), both published in the magazine *Ch'ŏngch'un* 청춘 (Youth) in 1918. "Wandering" features a Korean student who contemplates suicide during his studies in Japan. A friend of his admonishes him that his body also belongs to the nation that he must educate and lead, but he confesses that he "cannot 'marry Korea' as great patriots would do" and becomes a Buddhist monk as a last resort.[104] "Yun Kwangho," too, is the story of a Korean elite, the first to be granted a doctoral degree by a Japanese university. Despite the promise of becoming "a first-class gentleman in Korea," he feels that "there [is] a defect in his mind—a vast, deep hollow that seem[s] difficult to fill." It is an emptiness that fame and success, or even the love of "humanity," "compatriots," or "best friends," can never fill: "He cannot satisfy himself with a lukewarm, abstract love. He demands an ardent, concrete love." But because his homosexual love is not reciprocated, he chooses to take his life.[105] The theme of unrequited love not only encapsulates the subjectivity of colonial elites who are estranged from both the colonizer and the colonized, but also symbolizes affective alienation caused by cultural modernization. The characters may be "gentlemen" of modern society, yet they entirely lack an affective commitment to that new identity or habitus. Their aporia is indicative not only of the melancholia of the modern, but also of the inertia of the structure of feeling, which is hard to modernize.

Yi wrote the short story "Hŏnsinja 헌신자" (Devotee, 1910), in which he portrayed an ideal image of the modern educator, roughly contemporaneously to "Perhaps Love?" The hero is neither a *yangban* or colonial elite; he is from a humble family but makes a fortune through entrepreneurship and devotes all of it to building a private school. "He gains faith and adoration not on the grounds of knowledge, speech, or writings but of his sincere and ardent heart as well as his spirit of blindly marching forward once he makes up his mind."[106] The kind of intrinsic motivation Yi extols in this character is designated with "*chŏng* 정" in his criticism of the time. "*Chŏng*"—which can be roughly translated as "affect," "sentiments," "emotion," "feeling," or "heart"—"is the motive power of duties and the base of actions. It naturally endows humans with filial piety, respect for elder brothers, loyalty, faith, and love. Were it not for the guidance of reason, one probably could not be a worthy man; yet when it comes to true and profound endeavors, they originate [*yong hal* 湧할] from *chŏng*."[107] Certain just actions need to be taken outside the bounds of rights and duties and of ossified morality, and when Yi penned these words, just six months before the colonization, saving Korea was one of them. He praises *chŏng* as the driving force beyond reason and as the origin of human morality at the juncture of a national crisis, thereby calling for an education in the development of *chŏng*, or "*chŏngyuk* 정육" (affective education), echoing Sin Ch'aeho.[108] This articulation of the intrinsic motivation of modernization, however, also reads as archaic. For instance, "filial piety" (*hyo* 孝), "respect for elder brothers" (*che* 悌), "loyalty" (*ch'ung* 忠), and "faith" (*sin* 信) are among the cardinal virtues in Confucian doctrine, and his arguments on *chŏng* do not just resonate with Sin, but are even reminiscent of Mencian moral philosophy.[109] The not-so-subtle classicism of Yi's idea of *chŏng* seems to caution us against construing it simply as "a modern invention" or "the basis of interiority and thus of modern literature," as distinctive of the "modern" defined in terms of difference from the past.[110] As much as *chŏng* is the product of a dialectic of old and new, *The Heartless*—the novel on the "absence of *chŏng*" (*mujŏng*)—displays its characteristic as "a hybrid."[111] This may even justify the positioning of this work in a final phase of premodern literature or the emphasis on its indebtedness to "new fiction" in the previous era.[112]

The story of overcoming heartlessness and filling the world with "feeling" (*chŏng*) anew is, to be sure, a plot of modernization, yet as such, it is quite literally a narrative of impossibility. *The Heartless* embodies this problem in Hyŏngsik's affective relationships with two women: Kim Sŏnhyŏng and Pak Yŏngch'ae. Sŏnhyŏng is the daughter of a wealthy family who is learning English from Hyŏngsik in preparation for study in the United States. Yŏngch'ae is the daughter of a late Chŏson literatus in Pyongyang who took a young and orphaned Hyŏngsik under his wing and provided him with an education. Yŏngch'ae was considered Hyŏngsik's de facto fiancée before they had to separate when her father was imprisoned and his private academy was shut down due to an incident caused by a pupil of his. The story begins when Yŏngch'ae unexpectedly appears before Hyŏngsik in Seoul for the first time after seven years on the first day he is offering an English lesson to Sŏnhyŏng. There is little ambiguity about what this love triangle symbolizes. For Hyŏngsik, Sŏnhyŏng represents a fresh relationship that helps him realize his ambition of becoming a modern elite, as her powerful father promises full support of his college education in America once he becomes engaged to her. Yŏngch'ae, for her part, embodies a return of the old world that Hyŏngsik traumatically left behind seven years ago and has no reason to return to now that he is a Japanese-educated, up-and-coming modern intellectual. Hyŏngsik, in fact, leaves Yŏngch'ae for Sŏnhyŏng, and this constitutes a story of modernization and growth. But his "heart" (*chŏng*) does not so readily follow this rational course.

Yi Kwangsu wrote that he had originally planned to write a story about Yŏngch'ae based on his childhood before embarking on *The Heartless*, and that the present work prominently featured the relationship between Hyŏngsik and Yŏngch'ae that was lost forever and the tragedy that befell Yŏngch'ae.[113] The novel was reportedly received as a "tale of

Yŏngch'ae" by much of its contemporary readership.[114] This provenance is reflected in the scene where Hyŏngsik himself enacts an emotional engagement with the story of Yŏngch'ae. Having already met the attractive Sŏnhyŏng, Hyŏngsik at first does not particularly welcome Yŏngch'ae's return, and their emotional bonding is hindered by his obsessive suspicion that she "may not have studied anything" during those years and that she "may not be cultured enough to understand [his] mind and love."[115] But this barrier, a difference in the levels of modern cultivation, is broken down by the sheer beauty of Yŏngch'ae's classical storytelling. The story she tells of the past seven years is one of a virtuous, heroic woman in the traditional sense: she bravely survived many hardships and dangers after her father's imprisonment, and in order to fulfill the duties of a "filial daughter" (*hyonyŏ* 효녀) and help her captive and ailing father, she chose to become a *kisaen*, a performer and sometimes a prostitute in the traditional pleasure quarters. Being a *kisaen* was one of the rare ways for an unmarried woman to earn economic independence in the old society, though at the cost of social disdain. The dramatic content of Yŏngch'ae's story notwithstanding, it is above all the style of her storytelling that moves Hyŏngsik, along with the old lady at his lodgings, who listens to her with him.

> [While telling the story,] Yŏngch'ae did not appear the same even for a single moment, and the looks of her face and eyes were constantly changing as if thin mists were passing in front of her. Her metamorphosing appearances were beautiful and gentle beyond words.
>
> Her voice also became high and low, thick and thin, according to her emotions [*chŏng* 정] as if it were making subtle music. In fact, it was not so much Yŏngch'ae's pitiful story as her beautiful skill in telling [*mal somssi* 말솜씨] that story that moved Hyŏngsik and the old lady to sorrow and tears.[116]

Despite the ostensible gaps in their levels of education, Hyŏngsik and the old lady are no different in appreciating the "literary colors" of Yŏngch'ae's language.[117] The literariness of her storytelling stems from her cultivation. As a child, she studied readers in classical Chinese under her father's guidance, and as a lettered woman, she was able to appreciate classical literature when she worked as a *kisaeng*. Her role model was the top *kisaeng* in Pyongyang, named Wŏlhwa, who was versed in classical Chinese poetry and ink brush painting and enjoyed *sijo* and traditional Korean fiction. Wŏlhwa was fond of high-Tang poets like Li Bai 李白 (701–762), Gao Shi 高適 (c. 704–765), and Wang Changling 王昌齡 (698–c. 756); she despised greedy and licentious customers and regretted that she "was not born in Jiangnan 江南 during the high Tang era" but rather "in a country like Korea." She longed for archetypical heroes like Yang Ch'anggok in *Ongnumong* 옥루몽 (Dream in the Jade Chamber) and Yitoryŏng in *Ch'unhyang chŏn* 춘향전 (Story of Ch'unhyang); she would lament that "there was no Sima Xiangru who would seduce her with the 'Song of Phoenix,' although she would be a perfect Zhuo Wenjun."[118] Among the "ignorant and vulgar Korean men," she at last found a "true poet" in a school principal and fell in love with him, as she overheard his students sing a beautiful patriotic song he had composed and attended his fervent speech on nationalism. But she knew her love would not be reciprocated, and in despair, she drowned herself in the Taedong River.[119] Wŏlhwa's suicide symbolizes the bankruptcy of a particular ideal: the marriage of old virtue and nationalism, classical poetry and modern patriotic music—a utopian vision of modernity without any historical rupture or alienation. After seven years of separation, Hyŏngsik already knows the new age, on whose standards he regards Yŏngch'ae's cultivation, which is rooted in premodern Korean literary culture in close contact with Chinese letters, to be nothing but the source of doubt about her ignorance. Her story moves him to tears, nonetheless. The affective influence of Yŏngch'ae's storytelling bespeaks Hyŏngsik's old structure of feeling: he is indeed a man of "much emotion."[120] Conceptually, he believes he lives in a modern culture, but affectively, he is still very much attached to the old one. This ambivalence not only makes the idea of utopian modernity look naïve, but also complicates the project of modernization itself by bringing a tragedy to Yŏngch'ae.

After the awkward encounter with Yŏngch'ae, Hyŏngsik tries to ransom her out of the *kisaeng* business, only to realize the powerlessness of a young colonial intellectual. The only capital he has is modern knowledge, and he ponders how to cash it in. He would have to publish a book with a Western publisher to earn enough royalties to cover Yŏngch'ae's expensive ransom, but in order to do so, he would have to study English composition, produce a manuscript, send a draft to an American or British publisher, have it reviewed, and, if they accepted it for publication, finally have a check mailed all the way across the Pacific to Seoul. He is forced to conclude, "It's going to be too late."[121] The reality of cultural production—linguistic difference, physical distance from the centers of modern print culture, and the slowness of international shipping—exposes the powerlessness of "modern culture" in Korea despite Hyŏngsik's conceptual belonging to it. If his identity as a modern intellectual hinges on the perception of Korea as a backward yet potentially civilizable nation, then these material problems, all of which take a long time to deal with, introduce a sense of time into that idea of potentiality. The real lack of agency debunks the assumption of the nation's civilizability and the legitimization of his progressivist position. His helplessness is felt all the more poignantly because Yŏngch'ae's art and beauty are highly valued in the still powerful traditional—and, by modern standards, corrupt—culture, thus inflating her ransom. Overwhelmed by this problem, Hyŏngsik fails to take action, and this delay causes Yŏngch'ae to be raped by abusive patrons—the novel's tragic crux that symbolizes the aporia of modernization.

Following that devastating event, Yŏngch'ae is driven by the age-old female virtues instilled in her to take her own life. Her death note, addressed to Hyŏngsik, is replete with regrets and self-blame: she accuses herself of failing to save her father and defend her chastity, calling herself "a sinner" who has breached her duty to her father and fiancé.[122] Her only recourse is to follow Wolhwa's suit and drown herself in the Taedong River. Realizing her desperation, Hyŏngsik pursues her to Pyongyang to try to save her. In so doing, he is motivated by two contradictory forces. On the one hand, he thinks her belief that human life is to be entirely devoted to upholding moral laws is patently erroneous; as he reflects, "Human life in general does not reside in loyalty or filial piety, but loyalty and filial piety derive from human life. . . . Human life is greater than any single morality or law. Life is absolute; morality and law are relative."[123] One may discern in this line of contemplations on "human life" echoes of *Lebensphilosophie*, such as the thought of Bergson, by whom Yi Kwangsu is known to have been influenced in composing *The Heartless*. One could also point out gestures toward the idea of natural rights or human rights, a pinnacle of Enlightenment philosophy.[124] Based on his acquisition of the modern episteme, Hyŏngsik believes it is not right for Yŏngch'ae to sacrifice herself for moral laws. But on the other hand, as soon as he comes to this conclusion, he expresses a paradoxical approval of the very idea he has rejected; as he says to himself, "it is also the pride of life for a pure and impassionate person to stake their life on their cardinal duties." Thus "in theory [*iron* 이론], Hyŏngsik thought Yŏngch'ae's action was wrong, but according to his feelings [*chŏng* 정], he could not but shed tears for her."[125]

If Hyŏngsik owes his "theory" to the material condition of modern print culture and global transportation that carries knowledge, in this case, from the West to Korea via Japan, then his "feelings" are evoked by textual materiality rooted in the old culture. Yŏngch'ae's suicide note, written in "smooth vernacular script [*ŏnmun* 언문; i.e., *hangul*] in the palace lady style," moves Hyŏngsik to tears, which fall on the paper and make "the writing appear even more distinct." In an enclosed small envelope he discovers "something heavy," a bundle of papers wrapped in a red silk cloth. He severs the thread, opens the cloth, and finds "a wad of old, thick Korean papers" on which "the Korean letters *kiŭk*, *niŭn*, and *riŭl*, and the syllables *ka*, *na*, and *ta*" are written. Years ago, Yŏngch'ae's father asked her to "learn national script [*kungmun* 국문]" once she had mastered introductory readers in classical Chinese, and those characters are the model handwriting that Hyŏngsik offered to her. He stares at the papers and the writing and feels as if "each one of the characters tells a story of the past."[126] Melodramatic as it may read, this scene is indicative of a counterpoint to the modern culture that Hyŏngsik has aligned himself with. The materiality of writing—handwriting in different styles, the weight of papers, the cloth that wraps them, and so on—cuts across modern, rapid textual printing and circulation; it constitutes nostalgic moments that suspend the temporality of modern cultural flows, conjuring up cultural memories that are to be left behind by the new era, including the old-fashioned pedagogy in which the mastering of classical Chinese readers preceded the learning of *hangul* and even the ancient Confucian virtues that, by modern standards, are inhumane, paternalistic, and above all misogynistic—the "past" that Yi wanted to overcome with a "new civilization." The ambivalence of Hyŏngsik's attitude toward Yŏngch'ae's tragic decision, to be sure, may indicate the flaws of this self-proclaimed progressive, yet at the same time it epitomizes a story of modernization that contradicts itself in affective moments that bring back the cultural past.

Hyŏngsik arrives in Pyongyang only to lose track of Yŏngch'ae's whereabouts, and in one of the most counterintuitive moments of the novel, he prematurely gives up the search for her and decides to return to Seoul. He even feels little emotion on his first visit to the grave of Yŏngch'ae's father, his childhood mentor and benefactor, saying to himself, "I must take pleasure in seeing living people instead of feeling sad about dead ones."[127] On the night train bound for Seoul, he feels as if he has "awakened from a dream." "The mountains were one color, without valleys, trees, or stones, like an ink painting, a well-composed picture drawn on paper with a giant brush that mixes together the colors of moonlight, night, and clouds." "Hyŏngsik's spirit," too, "mixed and gathered together sorrow, suffering, desire, happiness, love, hatred, and all the spiritual workings, and melted and amassed them to the point that all distinctions were lost."[128] Hyŏngsik's experience on the train is a reiteration of the epistemological theme of *The Heatless*, which relates a few epiphanic moments where the protagonist realizes, in a manner not unlike phenomenological reduction, that the ordinary meanings of the world are bracketed out and the world lends itself to the divination of a "new meaning." The novel represents his self-reflective consciousness as an awakening to "the inner human," the free subjective agency that reconstructs the "inner meaning" of things.[129] This theme can be considered as indicating the desire to restore meaning and hence mark a fresh beginning to overcome the historical crisis of signification—the problem I discussed in reading Lu Xun's "Diary of a Madman." However, *The Heatless* also foregrounds what this experience cannot repeat, the lost cultural past that never presents itself as a monolithic, coherent meaning in the present but returns iteratively each time in a singular manner in the materiality of writing. Yŏngch'ae is an embodiment of this inexhaustible, haunting past. Her drowned body has to be left behind in order for Hyŏngsik to recognize and commit to a "new meaning" of the world, as he hears "a gallant military march" in the train's steady rattling that symbolizes modernization.[130] But if so, it is also the returns of this very past that threaten his new world. Indeed, as the night grows late on the train, memories of the past come flooding back, among which "Yŏngch'ae's figure appears for the longest time and most often." And as he visualizes her letter and belongings stored in his briefcase, he is assailed by haunting suspicions:

> Ah! Am I wrong? Am I too heartless [*mujŏng* 무정]? Should I have tried to locate Yŏngch'ae's whereabouts for a little longer?
>   Even if Yŏngch'ae had died, should I have tried to search for her body? Or at least should I have stood on the banks of the Taedong River and shed some warm tears? Yŏngch'ae died because she thought of me, but I do not even shed tears for her. Ah! I am so heartless! I am not a human![131]

Modernization seeks to free "human life" from the old culture, but it harms that value ("I am not a human!") through that very act of progress, in the "heartless" severance of affective ties with the past. Yŏngch'ae sacrifices herself because of the shackles of the old culture, but Hyŏngsik ignores it because of his commitment to the new culture. Yŏngch'ae's unsearched-for corpse pathetically represents the haunting residues of modernization, unable to be atoned for in either the old or the new culture. And its absent voice calls for nothing but a critique of the conception of modernity as a rupture from the past.

The Heartless explores a Korean modernity in a polyphonic space where the protagonist's cutting-edge progressivism sounds terribly backward vis-à-vis Yŏngch'ae's devout moralism, while her impassioned storytelling resonates with his ingrained "feelings" even though his acquired "theory" makes him pass unempathetic judgment on it. The doubling of Yŏngch'ae's voice in the scene of her storytelling by the interpolation of Hyŏngsik's listening ears invites the novel's readers to adjust their modes of literary reading. Just as he struggles between old and new cultures in response to her story, so are the readers called on to self-reflexively calibrate their modes of reading this novel between old and new cultures. *The Heartless* is thus a text that cannot be confined to the domains of modern or premodern literatures but exists to be read *between* them.

In recounting what actually happened to the missing Yŏngch'ae, the novel addresses the readers and lays bare this ambivalent mode of narration, urging them to appreciate the "differences" between Yŏngch'ae's episode and the typical plots of old stories, or, to take up our terminology, to read her story as a *parody* of familiar literature:

Now let us talk about Yŏngch'ae for a while. Did she plow through the blue water of the Taedong River and become a guest of the Dragon Palace [i.e., drown]?

Some of you, readers, might have felt sorry for Yŏngch'ae's death and shed tears. Others might have smiled to expect the cheap tricks of fiction writers, which would have Yŏngch'ae saved by a certain noble man just as she tries to drown herself, and have her live as a nun at a certain small temple until she and Hyŏngsik reencounter each other and happily exchange marriage vows, thus leading a life blessed with longevity, wealth, nobleness, and lots of sons. For in any old story books [*iyagi ch'aek* 이야기 책], those who do not have a son until old age do end up having one, sons do become noble, and those who drown do eventually survive.

Some of you might have thought that Yŏngch'ae's decision to drown herself was appropriate and praised her leaving for Pyongyang; others might have reckoned that she did not need to drown herself and regretted her deeds. No matter how the reader's diverse ideas and what I am now going to write about Yŏngch'ae's fate agree with or differ from each other, what if you compare your ideas and mine, and consider their differences? That should be a very interesting thing to do.[132]

The related story is one of affective communication across new and old. It reveals Yŏngch'ae's survival thanks to her fortuitous encounter with a female student named Kim Pyŏng'uk on the train she took to Pyongyang. Pyŏng'uk is studying music in Tokyo, and as a modernized woman, she calls the "teachings of old sages" instilled in Yŏngch'ae a "dream" and an "illusion." She "furiously attacks the old morality" and convinces Yŏngch'ae that she has been shackled by "the terrible few words" of obsolete female virtue that stipulate the "way of triple obedience," first to her parents, second to her husband, and finally to her son. She says that such a duty "kills the self" and calls it a "crime against humanity."[133] Pyŏng'uk thus destroys the old morality based on new values, but their encounter does not stop at a typical communication of enlightenment. Having dissuaded Yŏngch'ae from suicide, Pyŏng'uk takes her to her hometown in Hwangju, where they spend enough time together to "deeply sympathize with each other" (*kip'i chŏng i tŭrŏtta* 깊이 정이 들었다). From

Pyŏng'uk, Yŏngch'ae learns "new knowledge and Western-style feelings [*chŏng* 정]," whereas Pyŏng'uk learns from Yŏngch'ae "old knowledge and Eastern-style feelings." Pyŏng'uk has always "disliked everything old," but Yŏngch'ae inspires her to study the introductory Confucian reader *Sohak* 소학 (Minor Learning) and the classic stories of exemplary women *Yŏllyŏchŏn* 열녀전 (Biographies of Exemplary Women), as well as other examples of "Chinese verse and prose." She recites phrases from the anthology of old-style writings *Komun chinbo* 고문진보 (True Treasures of Old-Style Writing). Yŏngch'ae, for her part, is convinced that she has been reduced to a mere "model of certain moral principles" and unable to live as "an independent human." Thanks to Pyŏng'uk, she learns to appreciate Western music and comprehends for the first time the meaning of the word "art," which makes her realize that the music, dance, poetry, and painting practiced by *kisaeng* are "kinds of art" and see herself as "an artist."[134] Not only is Yŏngch'ae enlightened by modern values, but these women also influence each other affectively by exchanging literature and music. Just as Yŏngch'ae is awakened, so is Pyŏng'uk. This mutual representation has a therapeutic effect on Yŏngch'ae. "As she plucks the *kŏmungo* [the Korean zither] and tries her hand at the violin, all the sounds take on novel colors, and tears of joy and sorrow slowly gathered in her eyes."[135]

If Yŏngch'ae is victimized by modernity as a rupture from the past, she is saved by a modernity in transformation through engagement with the past. The modern notion of "art" becomes more capacious than the original Western sense of the term through its interaction with Korean arts—a transculturation that would dislocate Yi's own redefinition of literature as "a translation of the Western term."[136] This transcultural idea of modernity does not designate a civilizing of the world on a certain model but rather opens itself to a new world ("all the sounds take on novel colors"). The narrator's rather contrived suggestion to read these women's affective bonding by considering its difference from literary precedents ("old story books") might amplify its resonances with the classical topos of poetic communication, the topos exemplified, for instance, by the scholar-and-beauty lore of Sima Xiangru and Zhuo Wenjun. Yet, more important, the narrator's invitation prompts the reader to appreciate this entirely new kind of story, a hitherto unthinkable possibility of fictional narrative, not as a remote idea but as an actual experience of literary reading. The reader can rely on their usual literary taste—no matter how hackneyed and even irrelevant it is—only to find themselves needing to update it, just as the two women did through their affective cross-cultural encounter. It is this open-ended process of literary transformation—a clear antithesis to a preconceived idea of new literature—that the narratology of *The Heartless* tries to achieve through its parodic operation within differences between the old and the new.

And for that very reason, *The Heartless* must be left as an incomplete process, as it is enacted by Hyŏngsik agonizing over his path. Still believing that Yŏngch'ae is dead, he is torn between regret for forsaking her and expectation of the opportunities for which her death cleared the way. He admits that he "even felt relieved when Yŏngch'ae died," but out of remorse, he borrows five *won* from Usŏn and tries to return to Pyongyang to look for Yŏngch'ae's body once again.[137] Yet, just as he is about to put on his shoes to leave, he receives an official offer of engagement to Sŏnhyŏng and the chance to study in the United States with her. He forgoes the search for Yŏngch'ae and seizes the opportunity too good to miss. However, their modern-style engagement ceremony is performed as a formality, and the life-changing decisions are made "like jokes." The narrator comments on the "precariousness" of it all.[138] Meanwhile, Pyŏng'uk persuades Yŏngch'ae to study music in Tokyo, and, in the novel's final drama, they happen to depart on the same train as Hyŏngsik and Sŏnhyŏng. Astounded by Yŏngch'ae's survival, Hyŏngsik feels as though "the ghost of Yŏngch'ae, who drowned in the Taedong River, now appears to torment him."[139] Repentance for his heartless abandonment of the search wells up again and again.

> He did not confirm her safety after following her to Pyongyang, rushed back to get engaged on the very next day, and forgot about her after that—he thought he was a terrible sinner. He was, after all, heartless. He should have used the five *won* he had borrowed from Usŏn to go to Pyongyang. He should have looked for her body and arranged as generous a funeral as he could. He should have had the common sense [*injŏng* 인정; lit., human sensibilities] to wait at least a year before getting engaged. He should have shed scalding

tears and mourned for Yŏngch'ae, who had upheld lofty virtues for seven or eight years and, in the end, sacrificed her body and life, all for him.[140]

In agony, he returns to the original question: "Who do I love after all? Sŏnhyŏng or Yŏngch'ae?" and ends up declaring, "I won't go to America!"[141] The narrative form prolonged by Hyŏngsik's unresolvable oscillation between feeling and reason, old and new, and Yŏngch'ae and Sŏnhyŏng is an embodiment of the modern literature that Yi produced by means of the parody of classical culture, as a process of affective self-transformation.

It is only a deus ex machina that can put an end to this narrative-as-process, and it arrives in the form of a devastating flood. The protagonists' train is hit by torrential rain and grinds to a halt, and they witness nature's sublime power.

> This is indeed a great flood. Except for the mountains on both sides, everywhere is covered with muddy dark-red water. The sound of undulating water making a whirlpool in the middle of the river seems to be heard, and as the water erodes the curves of the hills lined up on both sides, the mountains seem about to collapse at any time. . . .
>
> Though the rain has stopped, the dark clouds, barely holding in the rain, float about in lumps in the sky. No sooner do the clouds charge toward the east than they flock toward the west as though they have changed their minds. Sometimes, as if the clouds cannot endure it any longer, large raindrops spill down. On the high, on bare mountains, falls and brooks are suddenly hanging upside-down, as though white strings were randomly placed here and there on a black background. The sound of those streams running down and scraping off the flesh of the bare mountains and scooping out their bones is combined with the sound of water running down horrifyingly, as if playing a sublime [*ung'dae* 웅대] music in concert.[142]

As the protagonists are overwhelmed by nature's brute forces, which pierce the land and ruin the lives of the peasants, "a kind of apprehension and fear that transcends the individual wells up in them," and they "forget about the ideas of an individual."[143] Then, as if "in a movement of negative transcendence" of the sublime, they realize "a common idea—the idea that every human being possesses."[144] Hyŏngsik, an indecisive, wavering man, "a [Korean] youth of the transitional period," is now baptized by nature's sublime power and gains a virile sense of mission: "Science! Science!" "Give them [the Koreans] power! Give them civilization!" "Teach them! Lead them! ... By education and by practice." His declaration reconciles and unifies the four youths, who feel as if "they have become one whole body and one mind without distinctions between you and me."[145] The catastrophe creates a state of exception that exposes bare life and unites the four together as one body around an urgent call for security.[146] With the help of the sublime, they leave behind the past and jump ahead to become quintessential modern subjects. This paves the way for the novel's conclusion with a "happy smile and shout of cheers," which looks at the future and reports on the successful completion of their studies abroad and their impending return to a Korea that is making rapid progress in modernization.[147]

The Heartless relies on the trope of the sublime to represent modernization, the discourse espoused by Yi and so many other East Asian intellectuals that conceives of modernity as progress away from the past. Yet in the same stroke, it also portrays a scene that foreshadows a culture of that envisioned modernity by evoking the cultural past *once again*. Trapped by the heavy rain, the protagonists organize a music concert to raise money for the affected peasants, an attempt to prove the real value of their cultural capital. Pyŏng'uk commences this ad hoc performance by playing "a sorrowful air from *Aida*" on the violin. Trying to describe the emotional effect of her tune on the victims, the narrator addresses the reader: "Rather than me describing at length what it was like to savor that sad melody, it would be most convenient for you to think of the 'Song of Pipa' composed in Sima of Jiangzhou."[148] What is alluded to is the canonical *yuefu* poem that the mid-Tang poet Bai Juyi is believed to have composed when he was demoted to a post in Sima in Jiangzhou Province. A consideration of "convenience" for the reader, of communicability to the readership to whose ambivalent frames of reference between old and new the novel has appealed, has to conjure up once again the literary past. While this climactic concert is symbolic of the affective community of an envisioned modern nation, the conveyance of that very affectivity—the resonances of the moving tune—complicates the idea of modernity as rupture. Following the air, Yŏngch'ae sings hymns she learned from Pyŏng'uk to her violin accompaniment, which the narrator says sounded "entrancing... even to those who did not understand the high-brow tune of the violin" thanks to the abundant freedom of Yŏngch'ae's voice, "trained for more than ten years [as *kisaeng*]." The concert concludes in a great success with the chorus of a Korean song that is "Hyŏngsik's translation of the lyrics that Yŏngch'ae had just composed in classical Chinese."[149]

The sublime has violently cut the protagonists' residual attachment to the past and hurled them into the modern, but in this final scene of the concert, the severed past makes yet another return. In the depiction of the concert, the literary past is alluded to just in form, without content or meaning derived from contextual differences. These formal references delineate a new affective medium that emerges from the repetition of literary tradition. This encapsulates the narratological form of *The Heartless* that iteratively evokes the cultural past that is to be forgotten, leading the story of growth, progress, and modernization to a fundamentally incomplete, open-ended process, as a gesture of envisioning the reader's self-transformation. The equivocal form of this novel bespeaks a new literature that emerged as a writerly response to the modern whose "heartless" ideological confines cannot but conjure up the moments of "mourning for the world that has passed."

The texts canonized as the spearheads of modern Chinese, Japanese, Korean literatures expanded the representational capacities of literature through parodic engagement with the cultural past. That expansion is not teleologically directed or conceptually defined, but critically self-reflexive, indicating the emergence of the mode of representation centrally attributed to modern literature—the mode that, in constant search of newness, drives literature to determine its own realm in potential defiance of its delineations in the dominant culture, either classical or modern.

Critical engagement with past cultures enabled Lu Xun to carve out a novel literary space for representing voices traditionally considered undeserving of literary treatment. For Mori Ōgai, it served to bring about forms of ambivalent literary value that offered a story to modern individuals living in open-ended historical and moral horizons. It disrupted the coming-of-age story in Yi Kwangsu's *Heartless* and ultimately produced new literature as an experience of self-transformation. These authors' works are modern not because of their severance from old culture, but because of the intensity with which they generated novel possibilities of expression from what had been culturally accepted as possible in literature.

In the next chapter, I will shift my focus to these writers' historical fiction. Our discussion so far will be especially useful in illuminating its significance as a generic embodiment of the origins of modern literature as a writerly effort to reconstruct the present's relationship to the past.

CHAPTER FOUR

History as Rewriting

The Historical Fiction of Lu Xun, Mori Ōgai, and Yi Kwangsu

Historical fiction (歷史小說; Chn. *lishi xiaoshuo*, Jpn. *rekishi shōsetsu*, Kor. *yŏksa sosŏl*) accounts for as much as half the corpus of fictional writing by Mori Ōgai and Yi Kwangsu, and Lu Xun produced works in this genre intermittently yet persistently through his career as a writer. Their historical fictions constitute some of the early examples of this major literary genre in modern East Asia, which was not only attempted by many of the eminent authors, but also carried great social and political import across high and low cultures, often inspiring transmedial adaptations. The sheer breadth and popularity of historical fiction are enough to call for a fresh look at its incipient examples.

We saw in the previous chapter that Lu Xun, Ōgai, and Yi produced modern literature through parodic engagement with past cultures. This argument lays the groundwork for my analysis of their historical fictions, which are writerly reckonings with the cultural past that appeared so patently and painfully incommensurable with the present owing to the radical cultural shifts of modernization. Historical fiction is a genre in which the depth of the past ungraspable in the present becomes wedded to the height of formal innovations in its search for the present's meaning in history. In this sense, it can be construed as a generic allegory of the task of modern literature in East Asia.

THE MODERNITY OF HISTORICAL FICTION

Lu Xun, Ōgai, and Yi commonly put forth an idea of marginality or imperfection with regard to their own works of historical fiction. This idea helps characterize these works in terms of their deviation from the Lukácsian concept of the historical novel, which has provided an important reference point for analyzing East Asian works in this genre.[1]

In his paradigmatic study, Lukács theorizes the historical novel as a quintessential art form in the post–French Revolution world; he argues that it relates stories of the "progress" of "the nation as a whole" by "bringing the past to life as the prehistory of the present, [by] giving poetic life to those historical, social and human forces which, in the course of a long evolution, have made our present-day life what it is and as we experience it."[2] At the heart of the genre is "necessary anachronism," which Lukács posits against "a chronicle-like, naturalistic reproduction of the language, mode of thought and feeling of the past." Drawing on Goethe's dictum that "all poetry in fact moves in the element of anachronism," Lukács elaborates on this idea through a reference to Hegel's aesthetics,[3] especially his formulation of the *"necessary* anachronism" of historical literature as a problem of aesthetics at large:

> He [the artist] is alone an artist because he knows what is true and brings it in its true form before our contemplation and feeling. Therefore, to express this, he has to take into account in each case the culture of his time, its speech, etc.... Such a transgression of so-called naturalness is, for art, a *necessary* anachronism. The inner substance of what is represented remains the same, but the development of culture makes necessary a metamorphosis in its expression and form.[4]

For the substance of the past to be represented in the art of the present, Hegel argues that the form of representation should constitute a dialectical unity with the content. His idea reflects his understanding of the "Beautiful," which he conceptualizes as "the Idea as the immediate unity of the Concept with its reality—the Idea, however, only in so far as its unity is present immediately in sensuous and real appearance."[5] For

History as Rewriting 163

Lukács, Scott's historical novel is precisely such an "Idea"—a contemporary form, "present in sensuous and real appearance," that creates a perfect "unity" with and thus manifests a past content that would otherwise remain latent or nonreal. For Lukács, Scott's work is so perfect that "'necessary anachronism' can emerge *organically* [my italics] from historical material." And by virtue of this, the novelist lets "his characters . . . express feelings and thoughts about real, historical relationships in a much clearer way than the actual men and women of the time could have done," thereby depicting the past as "the *necessary prehistory* of the present."⁶

Resonating with Lukács's discussion in the European context, historical fiction in East Asia emerged as an imaginative sandbox where writers tried to build a narrative to reckon with the meaning of the present in history. Yi Kwangsu, Mori Ōgai, and Lu Xun, to be sure, may well have conceptually sought what Lukács called the "Idea," a beautiful synthesis of the present form and the past content. Their actual works, however, give the impression that such an Idea loses the aura of authenticity and remains abstract; these writers seem to have conspicuously and even self-consciously abandoned the effort to generate an organic synthesis of form and content, even going so far as to undermine a coherent narrative point of view or leave narratological excesses unattended. They appear to have renounced the subjectivity of the heroic artist that Lukács saw in Scott, a grand synthesizer of past and present, capable of showing truth through fiction, by means of the latter's perfectly "necessary anachronism." Are the nascent works of East Asian historical fiction failures? Are those works not worthy of being considered serious historical literature, as some critics have contended?⁷

So ambivalent, indeed, was the status of these writers' historical fiction that they felt the necessity of almost apologetically justifying its *raison d'être* on the margins of "fiction" or "literature." Lu Xun wrote in the preface to the collection of his historical short stories *Gushi xinbian* 故事新編 (Old Stories Retold, 1936):

> Now, at last, I have finished compiling this book. It still contains many sketchy parts and does not deserve to be called a piece of "fiction" [*xiaoshuo* 小說] as it is defined in some *Introduction to Literature*. At times I ground myself in historical facts; at others, my

imagination roams free. And because I cannot convince myself that the ancients are as worthy of respect as my contemporaries, I have found myself periodically slipping into the quicksand of facetiousness [*youhua* 油滑]. . . . But as long as I have not made the ancients seem even more dead than they already are, there are perhaps margins on which this book can exist for the time being.[8]

The author's tongue-in-cheek acknowledgment of the "facetiousness" of his historical stories affirms his renunciation of a stable artistic judgment with which to strike a balance between factuality and fictionality, content and form. There is no expectation that "necessary anachronism" will emerge "organically" from historical material. His performative assertion of incompetence puts his work barely on the margins of the established domain of "fiction."

Mori Ōgai, for his part, wrote,

My friends would argue about whether any of my recent works treating historical figures belong to fiction [*shōsetsu* 小説] or not. That judgment, however, would be rather difficult in an era when fewer and fewer scholars uphold so-called normative aesthetics, asserting that fiction ought to be this or that. . . . While fiction usually shows the traces of picking and choosing facts at will and giving them an organization, [my historical works] do not have such traces. . . . In my recent fiction, I completely abandoned such a method. Why? My motivation was simple. First, it came to my mind that I should respect the "nature" [*shizen* 自然] that appeared in the historical documents I studied. I got tired of making changes to it on a whim. Second, I also thought I should be able to portray the past as it had been, if living authors could portray their present lives as they were.[9]

Karatani Kōjin has characterized this line of thoughts as an encapsulation of Ōgai's self-conscious "method" for writing historical fiction, by which the author "refused any vantage point from which to put [past] events in perspective."[10] Ōgai plays down compositional judgment as artificial and insists on "respect[ing] the 'nature' of the historical documents." He has to give up a coherent perspective from which to retell past events as a prehistory of the present in favor of retaining the contingency and even absurdity inherent in the "natural" unfolding of events. The idiosyncrasy of the method of his historical fiction is such that its literary merits can hardly be assessed by a "normative" judgment as to what does and what does not count as "fiction."

Finally, Yi Kwangsu, while underlining the factuality of the subject matter, affirmed emotional excess, the overabundance of the author's "righteous spirit" that vivified the story to the point that it read as if it were his "autobiography" or "self-portrait." As he argued in a postface to his popular *Tanjong aesa* 단종애사 (The Tragic Story of Tanjong, 1928–1929):

> This work is not a judgment of good and evil, nor a document of the author's lamentation. Such judgment or lamentation is the reader's business. The author, instead, writes down historical facts just as they took place.—But, even though I try to take this kind of cold, disinterested attitude, I cannot freeze my righteous spirit [*ŭigi* 의기] that would flare up like fire or take my own affairs as others'. [Writing this work has been] like penning an autobiography or painting a self-portrait. The tip of my brush cannot but heat up to the point of catching fire.[11]

Yi endorses as integral to the narrative his unquenchable passion, his ardent moral sentiments at the cost of aesthetic equilibrium ("disinterested attitude"); he indulges in the present passion rather than trying to bring the present to a Lukácsian synthesis with the past through novelistic composition. Yi elsewhere insisted that his historical fiction "served Korea and the Korean nation" as he defended it from contemporary attacks that called it a "vulgar/commercial fiction" (*t'ongsok sosŏl* 通俗小說).[12] Despite this characterization, he nonetheless affirms emotional excess at the cost of a properly distanced vantage point that would be capable of putting history in perspective, much less constructing a "homogeneous time" which the nation would navigate to make its history.[13]

The assessments by Lu Xun, Mori Ōgai, and Yi Kwangsu on their historical works align in implying their methodological withdrawals from achieving a beautiful synthesis of past and present. And indeed, the insuperable resistance of the past to the present perspective animates these authors' formal experiments in historical fiction, driving them to exploit the open realm of modern literature as a creative medium needed to revivify history.

HISTORY IN EXCESS: YI KWANGSU'S
TRAGIC STORY OF TANJONG

Yi Kwangsu serialized *The Tragic Story of Tanjong*, one of the most popular and representative of his many works of historical fiction, in the newspaper *Tong'a ilbo* 東亞日報 (East Asia Daily) from November 1928 to December 1929. Under the Government-General's so-called "cultural rule" in the aftermath of the March First movement, the 1920 launch of *East Asia Daily* along with *Korea Daily* provided fresh Korean-language venues for serial novels.[14] The compilation and publication of historical materials, undertaken both by Japanese-led historical research societies and by Korean nationalist organizations, gave modern writers unprecedented access to historical sources, leading to the popularization of "true records" (*silgi* 실기) stories featuring various Chosŏn-dynasty figures in the 1920s.[15] Particularly crucial to the subject matter of *The Tragic Story of Tanjong* was the publication of the critical editions of *Yŏllyŏsil kisul* 연려실기술 (Writings from the Burning Pigweed Studio), a compendium of unofficial history (*yasa* 야사) through the Chosŏn dynasty. Yi Kwangsu drew on this material, together with the official history *Chosŏn wangjo sillok* 조선왕조실록 (The True Records of the Chosŏn Dynasty) and other resources, to retell the story of King Tanjong (1441–1457, r. 1452–1455). In his career, Yi wrote full-length novels and short stories about a variety of major historical figures, which are credited with inaugurating the genre of historical fiction in colonial Korea.[16]

The sixth king of the Chosŏn dynasty, King Tanjong inherited the throne from his father King Munjong at the age of ten. The young king's reign quickly fell prey to power struggles in the court among ministers and Grand Princes. One of the king's uncles, Grand Prince Suyang (1417–1468), rose to power as he masterminded the purge of opposing ministers and the execution of Grand Prince Anp'yŏng (1418–1453) in the coup d'état of 1453. He forced Tanjong to abdicate the throne and established his reign as King Sejo (r. 1455–1468) in 1455. In the following year, ministers who remained loyal to Tanjong attempted his reinstatement, but the scheme was leaked, and the perpetrators and their family members were executed. As a result, Tanjong lost all of his royal titles and was reduced to a commoner; he was condemned to exile and finally executed in 1457 when he was only sixteen years old. Later, the leaders of the failed restoration plot were honored as the "six martyred ministers" (*sayuksin* 사육신), while the survivors of the purge who maintained their loyalty to Tanjong and refused to hold official posts for the rest of their lives were hailed as the "six alive ministers" (*saengyuksin* 생육신). The fate of the hapless Tanjong and the emotional drama of loyalty and betrayal encircling it were a favorite subject of historical stories during the colonial period. Those works, which sometimes intertextualized each other, adopted different styles and narrative points of view; some deviated liberally from the sources and featured imaginary characters.[17]

In a 1937 interview, Yi Kwangsu indicated that if Greek tragedy was the tragedy of fate, Shakespearean tragedy that of character, and Ibsenian tragedy that of society, then his tragedy was that of "reward and retribution" (*inkwa* 인과). Difference from European examples enabled Yi to articulate a metanarrative underlying his tragic works: "Goodhearted people will, not at all accidentally but *necessarily*, obtain happiness, while people who are not like them will *necessarily* obtain misery."[18] This simplistic moralism built on the traditional notion that Heaven rewards humans for good deeds seems to justify the criticism of his historical novels for their "immature historical consciousness."[19] Yet the actual story does not unfold that way, as the suffering of Tanjong, portrayed as a tenderhearted and blameless young man, patently displays. Yi's moralism indicates not how history works but how it *ought* to work: in his novel, history, rife with gross injustices and irrecoverable losses, is narrativized in its insurmountable distance from the moral idea about it. Historical phenomena are depicted in such a way that they do not simply interact with each other to form a chain of causality in reality, but also signify a deep-seated moral dynamic animating that reality. *The Tragic Story of Tanjong* is a melodrama that indulges in hyperrealistic descriptions, typification of characters, and overabundant explanation in order to render history as a surface below which unfolds a never-ending Manichean battle of morality between reward and retribution, salvation and condemnation, good and evil. Yi's metanarrative represents a "moral occulting" of "the melodramatic mode," as it is conceptualized by Peter Brooks as "the domain of operative spiritual values which is both indicated within and masked by the surface of reality."[20] Rather than Lukácsian realism, Yi's historical novel narrativizes history through a melodramatic imagination.

The example that best illustrates the narratology of *The Tragic Story of Tanjong* is the scene where the six martyred ministers are tortured and executed by Grand Prince Suyang's men when their plot to reinstate Tanjong is exposed. The narrative, for instance, provides horribly graphic details of the torture of Sŏng Sammun (1418–1456), one of the six martyred ministers: "As a red-hot iron after another touched Sammun's arms and legs, his flesh sizzled and scorched, and fat and blood dripped down.... [Suyang ordered to] pierce through his thigh and calf as well as arms and palms with blazing metal chopsticks. Burning flesh and fat made a smell like grilled meat that reached all the way to the palace yards, while yellow smoke rose into the chambers."[21] Pak P'aengnyŏn (1417–1456) is beaten and "throws up blood."[22] Yu Ŭngbu (?–1456), for his part, is skinned alive upon Suyang's order: "Soldiers rush in with glinting knives that looked like kitchen knives; they tear up Ŭngbu's clothes and peel off his skin, starting from the neck down to the back, the chest, and the arms, all while keeping him standing. Blood trickles down drop by drop following the knives' paths; his skinned flesh jerks and wiggles. It makes sticky sounds of skin dropping off. But Ŭngbu does not even complain of the pain and stands upright without moving his body."[23] The grotesque depictions of the visual, acoustic, and even olfactory details of torture are stylized and patterned, far exceeding the ordinary forms of realism. They present the phenomena in their visceral immediacy to sensation in a way that collapses historical perspective.

Inherent in these excessive descriptions is the need for interpretation, one that will discern a deeper and truer story behind the represented surface of reality. The interpolated gestures of interpretation contribute to the dramatization of the scene, whose depiction is scattered with multiple pieces of classical Chinese verse written by or sent to the martyred ministers. These poems are quoted from sources like Nam Hyoon's 남효온 (1454–92) *Yuksin chŏn* 육신전 (The Biography of the Six Ministers) and are accompanied by the narrator's brief translations into Korean to capture their main thrusts, so that the reader cannot fail to understand the moral innards of these characters existing below the visible reality. The narrator casts an interpretative gaze on his historical sources, just as he does on his depiction of reality. The story he thus attempts to decipher is indicated when Pak P'aengnyŏn tells Suyang the meaning of Sŏng Sammun's blood: "Sir, look at this blood. It is the blood of a loyal subject [*ch'ungsin* 충신]."[24] Underneath the surface of the gruesome and sadistic torment and killing is an ur-story of the battle between loyalty and self-interest. With Suyang in power and loyal ministers perishing, the battle in this scene clearly unfolds in favor of evil, yet Sŏng Sammun's blood and the entire extravagant drama of corporeal surfaces and fragments are meant to signify, through their lavish images, the faint yet surviving remainder of moral integrity in that darkest of times. Without the context of this underlying dynamic, the meaning of visible reality remains obscure. Thus, the decapitated heads of the executed ministers indicate not so much a tragic climax as the persisting forces of virtue in a cyclical working of the world. "The summer moonlight shines on the bloody heads, whose eyes will not shut but glimmer to make [Suyang's] soldiers realize the horripilation tingling down their bodies."[25] While reality fails to render justice, the battle of good and evil continues.

Characterization in *The Tragic Story of Tanjong* draws heavily on physical traits. The story abounds in depictions of physiognomy, facial expression, physicality, and physiological reactions such as sweating, trembling, and crying. Expanding on the records in the Chosŏn-era *Myŏng sin nok* 명신록 (The Who's Who of Illustrious Subjects), for instance, the narrator puts a particular emphasis on the physiognomy of Han Myŏnghoe (1415–1487), one of the main schemers behind the usurpation of Tanjong's throne: "His face had a wide bottom and a pointed top. His nose was big. His large eyes had a squint. His head was shaped as if someone had pulled it from above."[26] These deformations are presented as "omens" of certain underlying forces that define his character, which will prove fatal to the legitimacy of the dynasty. The narrator states, "They say the face is the catalogue of the mind," where the "mind" is a reflection of the opposing forces of moral dichotomy.[27] As the explicative, evaluative narratology reveals the clashing moral forces behind reality, the emphasis on the characters' physical features turns reality into metaphors of those forces. Gazed at by Kim Chongsŏ's (1383–1453) eyes "gleaming like a morning star" with solemnity, Hong

Yunsŏng (1425–1475) loses his strength and spontaneously bows down before him "like a rabbit stared at by the tiger."[28] In a rage, the tails of Suyang's eyes are "stretched upright" and his temples "throb."[29] Confronted by Sŏng Sammun, Kim Chil's (1422–1478) face gradually turns "pale," his lips become "dry and convulsed," and "numerous drops of cold sweat" drench his clothes. Every time Sŏng's and Kim's combative words resonate, those who hear them feel "cold and hot air alternately running down their spine."[30] Reality does not constitute a closure of signification but provides signs that point to something more real working in the characters' minds.

In this battle of morality, no one is entirely good or bad. The usurpers of the throne, though lured by "profit" (*i* 이), do have "righteousness" (*ŭiri* 의리) and "human feelings" (*injŏng* 인정), too.[31] Suyang, to be sure, might be "a force representing immorality [*pulŭi* 불의]" compared to Grand Prince Anp'yŏng, who is "a force representing morality [*ŭi* 의]."[32] Yet Suyang also has a conscience, as he "felt a little sorry for Tanjong" when he carried out the dethroning. "Otherwise, he might have hurt the king with the knife that he had used to slash the eunuchs. But that is something Grand Prince Suyang himself is not sure about."[33] Unsure of himself, Suyang is at the mercy of the forces of moral polarity, and eventually, "his unquenchable greed suppressed all his virtue and wisdom." "Riding the swift horse of ambition, he saw with his exceptional wisdom and foresight where that road would take him and felt regret after regret, but he just could not hold himself back and ended up dashing to the cliff, from which he would eventually tumble down."[34] Torn between the forces of good and evil, Suyang, in spite of his "exceptional wisdom and foresight," is helpless to resist the propensity of the times when evil is gaining ground. He is also "a tragic hero" because he finds himself at a particularly merciless juncture of this cardinal battle, just as Tanjong is "a tragic hero" who, despite his innocence, becomes a victim of that ruthless war.[35]

All the characters in *The Tragic Story of Tanjong* are subject to primordial moral forces; they are designed to play good or bad roles. The overtly explanatory depictions in the narrative are meant to ensure that the reader understands the moral combats being played out in the text. When he successfully insinuates himself into Suyang's good graces, Kwon Ram (1416–1465) sees "his wealth glimmering in front of his eyes"—a depiction to make sure the reader does not miss his avaricious character.[36] The narrative, for another example, carefully exposes Suyang's internal psychology as he mulls over the scheme to murder his good younger brother Grand Prince Anp'yŏng:

> To be sure, [Suyang] did not like Anp'yŏng and hoped someone else would kill him, but as his elder brother, he did not want to earn his place in history as a fratricide by killing him with his own hands. . . .
> "No, don't. No matter how sinful Anp'ŏng may be, killing him is outrageous."
> He wished he could forcefully say this just once. To say this was what Suyang at heart wanted, but his greed came in the way.
> *How could I realize my ambition by letting Anp'yŏng live?*
> With this thought in mind, Suyang shuts his eyes. By "realize his ambition," he meant satisfying his desire to seize the power of the state in his own hands.[37]

The explanatory narrator frequently interjects in conversations depicted in direct speech to explicate the interlocutors' inward thoughts, informed by either the virtuous force of righteousness or the evil force of greed.

This leads us to ask what ontological status the primordial moral battles in this story have. What determines good and bad in the first place? Rather than postulating a transcendental source of value, the narrative indicates a metahistorical moral order that manifests in exemplary figures in history and various phenomena in nature. While "heaven" (*ch'ŏn* 천) is invoked frequently in the story, its virtue is far from certain, as its name is abused by Suyang's entourage to justify the evil scheme and its evocation by Tanjong is merely a sign of his powerlessness. Reliable are instead the actual manifestations of good and evil in history, which are evoked particularly in reference to ancient China. The legendary sage kings Yao, Shun, and Yu; King Cheng of Zhou and his uncle and loyal regent Duke of Zhou; Guan Zhong, who aided Duke Huan of Qi to ascend to hegemony; Guan Zhong's confidant Bao Shuya; Zhang Liang, Zhang Yang, and Zhuge Liang, all known for strategic prowess; Emperor Jianwen of Ming, whose throne was seized by his uncle, who became the Yongle Emperor—all these and other exemplary historical figures are mentioned to illustrate the moral forces that are now working to animate the opposing forces surrounding the embattled reign in fifteenth-century Korea. If those historical characters are puppets of the moral forces, then nature is their stage, subject to the same dynamics. King Munjong, Tanjong's father whose premature passing led to the tragedy, began his reign in a spring when "bitter cold returned and the Han River froze again."[38] As Suyang's fateful scheme commences with Kwon Ram's aid, the narrator interjects, "Is it just a mishearing that the bowstring hung on the wall seems to make a sound?"[39] Depicting the day before Tanjong's forceful abdication, the narrative indulges in showing yellowing and withering grass leaves, chirping sparrows losing their breath, herons and ibises failing to find food, and a wheeling kite with its wing joints blackened and worn out from years of wind and frost. "Pieces of white cloud are reflected on the lotus pond by the Pavilion of Fortuitous Encounter, and their shadows are flickering with the waves. When even these waves seem to be bubbling and boiling, how heavy would the king's mind, full of sorrow larger than any other in a thousand years, be?"[40] The narrative does not depict external objects and sights as illustrative of the interior of the king's mind; rather, it draws a similized comparison between the two. Nature suffers from drought, withers, suffocates, and starves in the same process that enfeebles and depresses the king's mind; leaves, birds, clouds, and waves reflect the underlying metahistorical forces just as much as the king's fate is subject to them.

Just as nature has four seasons, therefore, the battle of virtue and evil unfolds in history with certain patterns. And like "autumn" in nature, moments of "great judgment" return in "a nation's history." Just as "the plants and trees reveal their true nature [evergreen or deciduous] when the frost falls in the autumn," so do "people shed the masks they have been wearing and show their true colors all at once" at such crucial historical junctures. These are moments that happen "once every few decades or centuries," when the primordial moral battles rise to the surface of historical reality. The period that the novel relates is "one such day of great judgment for the Korean nation as well as for those who lived in the era of Great King Tanjong. On that day, many Korean people showed their various true colors."[41] Then, in this inherent pattern of history, the narrative includes the present: "How clearly and similarly the advantages and disadvantages of our ancestors five hundred years ago appear to us today! Why are even the events that reveal our characters exactly the same after five hundred years? Herein might the amusement of reading history reside."[42] *The Tragic Story of Tanjong* retells the events of five hundred years ago so as to indicate a fundamental dynamic that has driven history from antiquity to the present, from the times of Yao and Shun through Chosŏn Korea all the way into the colonial era. It records examples of how individuals acted at a precarious historical juncture in order to illustrate the virtue that the Korean people should embody amid the current national crisis.

The upholding of Confucian virtues like "loyalty and righteousness" (*ch'ungŭi* 충의), to be sure, may seem "strange"[43] for a writer who had fiercely attacked "Chinese thought" for the sake of civilization in the 1910s, and this alone may well justify the criticism of its failure to represent the past as the present's "prehistory" in a proper perspective. But *The Tragic Story of Tanjong* nevertheless embodies a notion of history capable of reconstructing the present's relationship to the past—the problem that Yi Kwangsu grappled with in writing *The Heartless*, as we discussed in the previous chapter. In *The Tragic Story of Tanjong*, he approaches this fundamental task of modern literature through historical fiction, as a means to devise a story that can help reckon with a past made so incompatible with the present and thus hard to historicize in a coherent perspective by the ruthless exigencies of cultural modernization. More important, this work indicates that such a story, with all the Lukácsian function of historical fiction it serves, does not have to be written as one that endorses modern cultural norms such as progress. The novel, instead, unapologetically adopts a more classical style, introducing a cyclical notion of history, a moralizing perspective, Confucian virtues, examples from Chinese antiquity, and so forth—all that the discourse of modernization would have made passé. Anachronism in Yi's work, then, is not necessary for creating a realistic synthesis of past and present, but useful for producing melodramatic excess that invites the reader to see the historical world as a whole in moralizing terms. Yi wrote of *The Tragic Story of Tanjong*, "As long as people do not forget to cry when they see misery or to express anger when they see injustice, the story of this event [that happened to Tanjong and his men] will continue to draw people's interest."[44] The novel's narrator asserts, "Sorrows and regrets that are once deeply driven in the mind of the people will never disappear—forever."⁴⁵ The classicist style of this work conforms to cultural habitus and effectively evokes the present readers' moral sentiments about unrequited loyalty and righteousness five hundred years ago, rendering them as agents of the latent moral forces always working underneath the visible reality. The melodramatic mode, therefore, serves to display not only the past events but also the present reality as surfaces to be interpreted in order to know the *real* moral drama unfolding behind the scenes.

The absence of the trope of progress in Yi's historical novel may be symptomatic of the colonial condition of the nation in the post–March First Movement era, when the independence of the nation as the agent of history was made ideologically unrealistic. But it also points to the problem that inheres in East Asian modernity writ large: historical rupture caused by modernization. Yi's narrative rejects the representation of the past in the present's cultural terms, as something able to explain how "our present-day life" has been made "what it is and as we experience it"; rather, through dwelling and reflecting on history as an irrecoverable loss to be accounted for, it creates a melodramatic representation of the past whose interpreted meaning will enable the understanding of the present. That understanding should throw into relief the current Korean nation as an ethical entity capable of fighting moral battles and bringing about a "heartful" modernity in harmony with the past. That narrative relies on textual operations, the practices of rereading and rewriting through which age-old virtues like loyalty and righteousness are reconfigured in modern form.⁴⁶ The past, rather than being a prehistory of the present, becomes a text whose interpretation shapes the very meaning and value of the modern.

HISTORY AS EDITING: MORI ŌGAI'S HISTORICAL FICTION

The problem at the core of Yi Kwangsu's historical fiction also animates Mori Ōgai's prolific works in this genre. With a few exceptions, Ōgai treated the early modern period, ranging from the dawn of the Edo era to the Edo–Meiji transition; he mainly reworked accounts recorded in early modern sources in the "veritable records" (*jitsuroku* 実録) or "miscellaneous essays" (*zuihitsu* 随筆) genres, the kind of episodes that Edo-era playwrights or fiction writers had not chosen to feature in their works.⁴⁷ The subject matter bespeaks the author's interest in creating a new kind of literary work to historicize Japan's path to modernization.

Ōgai's initial attempt at the genre, "Okitsu Yagoemon no isho 興津弥五右衛門の遺書" (The Last Testament of Okitsu Yagoemon, 1912), was inspired by the suicide of the revered army general Nogi Maresuke 乃木希典 (1849–1912) on the day of Emperor Meiji's (1852–1912, r. 1867–1912) funeral. Nogi's death sparked an immense sensation throughout the nation, as it suddenly reminded the public of the obsolete practice of "honor suicide" (*junshi* 殉死), the ritual suicide committed by feudal vassals at the time of their lord's death in an ultimate display of loyalty. The practice had been prohibited by the Tokugawa Shogunate since the seventeenth century when its uncanny return of this bygone ritual at the end of the nation's first modern era elicited "deeply divided" responses among the public, some deeming it absurd in a modernizing nation, while others lauded it for reasserting time-honored virtue in a Westernizing country.⁴⁸ Nogi's anachronistic honor suicide confused temporality and exposed a gulf between the cultural norms of the past and the present.

If Yi used the melodramatic mode to reimagine the present's relationship to the past, then Ōgai wrote historical stories to leave that relationship as a sheer mystery to be valued in its own right. He retells past events loaded with odd, all-too-human, or simply absurd moments whose meaning is hard to comprehend from the present perspective—moments that linger as *je ne sais quoi* stuck in time. His historical fiction gives up on explaining the past in the present's terms, and vice versa, ultimately "refusing any vantage point from which to put events in perspective."⁴⁹ In Ōgai's own words, it refrains from "picking and choosing facts at will and giving them an organization" and instead "respect[s] the 'nature' that appear[s] in the historical documents."⁵⁰ Its idiosyncratic narratology eventually assumes the role of an "editor" that leaves the work of historicization to the reader.

Ōgai develops the theme of honor suicide in "Abe ichizoku 阿部一族" (The Abe Family, 1913). The short story relates a series of honor suicides that took place upon the death of the feudal lord of the Kumamoto domain, Hosokawa Tadatoshi (1586–1641), and the ensuing political strife that led to the massacre of the retainer Abe family in 1643. While quite faithfully following the extant sources, the story depicts the extreme show of loyalism as subject to caprices and contingencies without elucidating its significance for the modern reader.[51]

Tadatoshi's vassals pleaded with the lord on his deathbed for permission to commit honor suicide, and as many as eighteen of them were granted approval and followed him into death. The story focuses on Chōjūrō and depicts how this young retainer, for profoundly ambivalent reasons, becomes "obsessed" with the idea that he should repay the lord's favor with an honor suicide. The narrator ponders, "If we were to probe more deeply into his [Chōjūrō's] motives, however, it would seem that besides his compulsion to commit honor suicide at his own request, he felt with almost identical intensity that it was others who expected him to do so. He was thus left with no other recourse but to commit honor suicide, feeling as though he were leaning on others to move toward death."[52] The decision, as fatal as it is, is neither active nor passive; much about it hinges on ambivalent influences from the environment. No given ideas, whether they are meant to praise or despise Chōjūrō's decision, can help the reader fathom his state of mind.

Also ambivalent is the cause of the Abe family's tragedy. Abe Yaichiemon is one of Tadatoshi's retainers who wished to follow their lord into death, but for some reason, he was not granted permission. This unfair treatment leads malicious gossips to caricature Yaichiemon as a coward, and he takes his own life in a rage. Yet in the absence of the late lord's consent, Yaichiemon's death is wasted: it does not bring the Abe family the same benefits that the heirs of those who committed proper honor suicide enjoy. In defiance, Yaichiemon's eldest son Gombei stages a protest on the first anniversary of Tadatoshi's passing and is executed as punishment. The Abe family then entrench themselves in their house in protest, but all of their men are massacred by the lord's forces. What led to this devastation? Why did Tadatoshi not grant Yaichiemon permission in the first place? In an ironic yet matter-of-fact tone, the story reveals Tadatoshi's pure caprice: he simply did not like Yaichiemon. "Every man has natural likes and dislikes. If he tries to understand them, he often cannot tell exactly why he feels as he does. This was the case in Tadatoshi's dislike of Yaichiemon."[53] The exposure of the absurdly simple whim at the root of the tragedy foregrounds the fundamental contingency that drives the course of history. Far from providing a historical perspective, "The Abe Family" leaves it in a fog of ambiguity and unaccountable fickleness.

As a response to General Nogi's suicide, "The Abe Family" reads as out of place, for it does not clarify the significance of the contemporary event, nor does the latter offer a useful context for interpreting the story. As Ogata Tsutomu has argued, the sheer anachronism of Nogi's "honor suicide" may have reminded Ōgai of "his own urgent task of laying a path toward a harmonious resolution of the contradiction between the absolute authority of the imperial house symbolized by Emperor Meiji and the modern, rational and individual self. For the Emperor's absolute authority was, if you will, an extension of the feudal load's absolute authority in a different form."[54] While it may have been this political "task" that Ōgai's honor suicide stories tried to tackle, they do not offer a resolution to that "contradiction" at all. In spite, or even because, of this work, the past and the present, while apparently incompatible, remain anachronistically entangled with each other through an arcane course of history. The present is unable to distance itself from the uncanny returns of the past, much less attribute the latter to its prehistory. The present remains anachronistic in itself.

The unfathomability of the course of history also underlies "Sahase Jingorō 佐橋甚五郎" (Sahase Jingorō, 1913). Closely following the extant sources, the story relates the episode of Tokugawa Ieyasu (1543–1616), the founder of the Tokugawa regime who is now a retired shogun, receiving the first official mission from Korea to his government in 1607. Ieyasu unexpectedly recognizes that one of the Korean delegates is his former subject Sahase Jingorō. Sahase was originally a page waiting on Ieyasu's son Nobuyasu, but he killed another page and took his dagger in an altercation, which forced him to leave for Takeda Katsuyori's (1546–1582) domain. But when Sahase's cousin set out to convince Ieyasu that Sahase was not at fault in the quarrel, Ieyasu offered to save his life on the condition that he assassinate Amari Shirosaburō, a retainer of Takeda Katsuyori, with whom Ieyasu was vying for the unification of the nation at that time. Sahase skillfully terminated Ieyasu's stubborn enemy, which convinced Ieyasu to let him serve as his subject. However, when Ieyasu learned that Amari had earlier treated Sahase as his favorite subject, almost with the affection of a father for a son, and that Sahase had nonetheless swiftly terminated Amari, he harbored suspicion toward Sahase and kept him away from an important mission. Knowing Ieyasu's distrust, Sahase absconded from him and disappeared. All of this had happened before Ieyasu achieved the unification and became the shogun, but after about two decades, Sahase reappears in front of him disguised as an envoy from Korea. Whether it is actually Sahase himself or just someone Ieyasu misrecognizes, "no one knows for sure," the narrator adds, leaving a mystery at the heart of the story.[55]

Having betrayed his master Amari to serve Ieyasu, Sahase Jingorō embodies the groundlessness of the displayed virtue of loyalty at the basis of the feudal relationship. By failing to properly repay Sahase's service while profiting from it, Ieyasu himself becomes subject to that same groundlessness. Sahase is the figure of a defect inherent in the moral legitimacy of Ieyasu's power, a figure that reappears in the shogun's eyes as a Korean envoy as he tries to solidify the new government's legitimacy through regional diplomacy. Leaving the factuality of Sahase's reappearance undecided, Ōgai's narrative suspends the historiographical demand for evidence. Whether it depicted Sahase's return as an episode of a subject's amazing cunning or of an aging shogun's misrecognition, evidence-based history would relate Sahase's story as an incident of negligible importance compared to Ieyasu's epic ascent to power. Yet Ōgai's work, exactly by suspending the judgment of factuality, portrays Sahase as an eerie image that casts doubt on the new shogunate's moral legitimacy. It is precisely through such ambivalent factuality, or refusal to sort the past into facts and myths, that Ōgai's historical fiction obtains its characteristic power to convey an uncanny "truth" about history—a truth embedded at the origin of the shogunate's authority.[56]

The short story "Kano yōni かのように" (As If), which Ōgai wrote just a few months before he embarked on historical fiction, helps articulate his conception of history in entangled relationship to mythology. Set in the Meiji period, the story's protagonist is a young intellectual from an aristocratic family called Gojō Hidemaro, who researched ancient Indian history in college and, after graduating with distinction, studied for three more years in Berlin. Hidemaro realizes that his lifework is to write a "national history" (*kokushi* 国史), but for an unknown reason he suffers from a terrible writer's block and cannot embark on the work. "As If" depicts the existential agony of Hidemaro, "afflicted with boredom" as he "feels pressured by the dormant enterprise inside," which he has been delaying for over a year after returning from Europe.[57] He knows exactly what his book should look like. To begin with, he would need to make a clear distinction between history and mythology. So he would first examine the formation of the myths and study the faiths based on them and the institutions preaching those faiths, all modeled on Protestant historiography. Once this was done, he would then tackle history at his leisure. He can almost visualize the complete product. Yet he has "the perception that the circumstances around him will not likely let him dare to do it, to grasp in his hands that [product] which he can see."[58] "As If" uses its fictional space to depict those "circumstances," or the ideological situation that prevents the protagonist from making the past intelligible in modern terms.

Hidemaro's haunting "perception" stems from what he believes to be his father's view of history. He suspects that his father, Viscount Gojō, may be one of those "bigoted people" who believe that "materialist thinking" will sneak in and wreck the nation once it is clearly stated that mythology is not part of history. He thinks his father "misunderstands" him, for his position is far from the kind of simple secularism that he suspects his father sees in him. Indeed, he believes that "he can still preserve something important for life that is embraced by myths" even though "his conscience demands that it be unambiguously stated that myths are not history," and he tries to reconcile secular history particularly with "the doctrine and institution of ancestral worship."[59] However, he does not try to clear up his father's misunderstanding. The reader instead knows that Hidemaro in turn misunderstands his father, whose ideas are far more sophisticated than the son suspects. Viscount Gojō was earlier prompted by a letter Hidemaro sent from Berlin to undergo a lengthy and rambling "self-reflection" on his attitude toward history and ancestral worship. Having come of age during the era of the Meiji Restoration, Viscount Gojō himself understands that "mythology and history are not to be conflated." He believes ancestral worship is a mere "formality without content," as he does not necessarily believe in the existence of ancestral souls. But he does not agree with those secularists who do not see any merit in faith or religion, although he believes it should be out of the purview of "human ability" to censor them as "dangerous thinkers."[60] The viscount thus adheres to secular norms, while acknowledging the value of ritual and religion, whose authority, however, cannot be embodied by the state, much less by himself. His internal ruminations reveal that the father is in fact not the kind of traditionalist or a "bigot" that his son suspects he is, and that he would share much of his skepticism with his son should they have open conversations. But they exchange few words, just as "two armies encamped face-to-face, dispatching scouts who fire long-range shots at each sight of the enemy and retreat, do not clash with each other or come to a peaceful reconciliation."[61] Between them is that single letter in which the addresser "articulates his thoughts to himself" and onto which the addressee projects his self-examination.[62]

Hidemaro does not have a blank slate on which to write history in modern terms, yet Viscount Gojō's critical spirit revealed in the story suggests that the traditional authority prohibiting him from doing so is but a product of his own thinking. Just as the (mistaken) image of the father exerts real power over the son, so does the cultural past, in its actual demise, haunt the modern as a surviving image. And just as the father and the son never reconcile through candid talks, so do the past and the present never share a common cultural ground for sorting out their differences through discourse. Those cultural differences lay bare the limitations of secular historiography in making sense of the past and leave its exteriority in mythology. The powerlessness of the present to subsume the past under its discursive realm is unsettling, and Hidemaro in fact tries to find a solution to it in the "philosophy of as if" developed in Hans Vaihinger's *Die Philosophie des Als Ob* (1911). Hidemaro is very fond of Vaihinger's idea of "as if," since it gives a handy justification to his contradictory approach of upholding both traditional values and secular knowledge. "I shall advance with a light ahead on the path of humanity in sight. I shall advance with a light ahead in sight, while I look back and worship my ancestors as if there exist their souls and tread on a path of virtue [*tokugi* 徳義] as if there exist duties. . . . Could you think of a safer, less dangerous thought?"[63] The protection of "as if" should spare Hidemaro a confrontation with his father while allowing him to follow his "conscience" as a modern intellectual. This solution is roundly criticized by his friend Ayakōji, a European-trained painter who visits him for a chat. Ayakōji responds that people are not moved by the power of "as if" but by "something tangible" when they worship ancestors or fulfill duties, reminding Hidemaro that traditional values, even with the protection of "as if," are but images and, just as such, exert real effects.⁶⁴ Ayakōji thus brings the conversation full circle, and his urge to "charge forward" does not alleviate Hidemaro's conundrum and takes him back to the original state, "hemmed in on all sides" precisely by such images that cannot be exorcised.⁶⁵

"As If," I argue, is much more than a fictional commentary on "the suppression of intellectual freedom" in late Meiji Japan. It indicates the irreducible discursive condition in which Ōgai himself grappled with the cultural past.⁶⁶ In Hidemaro's agony, modern culture is unable to furnish itself with a self-sufficient secular realm and has to be threatened by the afterimages of the past that defy inclusion in it, and this structural weaving of the past into the present, myth into history, constitutes the one and only condition for writing history in modern times. The disorienting afterlives of the cultural past are neither properly modern nor premodern, but reside in between, arising from the historical documents that mediate them, just as the letter stuck between the father and the son who never share straightforward words engenders the aura of the authority of tradition. One of the primary foci in scholarship on Ōgai's historical fiction has been the degree of its faithfulness to the sources, or in the author's own terms, the question of "history as is" versus "departure from history."⁶⁷ But his method deconstructs this distinction and dwells on the uncanny function of "documents"—or their "nature," as he called it— that convey the past as lingering images without a cultural context that would make it possible to decipher their proper meaning. The author's intervention hinges not so much on the synthesis of fiction and history in the Lukácsian sense as on the reproduction of this haunting function of documents, or their "editing" to replicate their bizarre mediation.

Ōgai acts as just such an "editor" in "Tsuge Shirōzaemon 津下四郎左衛門" (Tsuge Shirōzaemon, 1915), in which he revisits the late Edo polemics over foreign policies from the unique vantage point of the son of the assassin of the prominent scholar-official Yokoi Shōnan 横井小楠 (1809–1869). The son tells a story from the first-person point of view, and in its postface, Ōgai speaks "as the editor" of his account.⁶⁸ The assassin Tsuge Shirōzaemon was born into the family of a village headman in Okayama, and in the midst of political turmoil and civil wars in late Edo, he became a zealous backer of the anti-Tokugawa, pro-imperial forces that gathered support through their exclusionist policy toward Western powers in opposition to the Tokugawa loyalists who championed the opening of the country. But as soon as it took power at the Meiji Restoration, the pro-imperial camp switched its platform and vigorously implemented open-country policies to introduce Western institutions and cultures for the sake of modernization. This apostasy seemed a flagrant betrayal to many pro-imperialists, including Tsuge Shirōzaemon. Shirōzaemon targeted Yokoi Shōnan, who from early on had argued for foreign trade and diplomacy and had a significant influence on contemporary literati and activists with his archaist doctrine of revivifying primordial thought during the eras of Yao and Shun and the Three Dynasties.[69] Upon the Meiji Restoration, he was appointed as a counselor to the new government, yet rumor had it that he was using his position to push radical measures like republicanism and the propagation of Christianity in Japan, although his actual position was pro-court in policy and Confucian in faith. He became an epitome of what was perceived to be the Meiji government's opportunistic obsequiousness toward the West. Galvanized by this public sentiment, Shirōzaemon took matters into his own hands and decapitated Yokoi in 1869, just one year after the Restoration, only to be arrested before long and executed.

Four and a half decades later, Shirōzaemon's son, Tsuge Masataka, speaking as the first-person narrator, commences his father's biography by acknowledging that Yokoi was a wise man, in stark contrast to his father, who "died without making any contribution to the world and perished like trees and plants." Masataka the narrator tries to "get to the bottom of" the disparate fates of the Yokoi and Tsuge clans, with the former enjoying "glory and happiness" and the latter enduring "shame and misfortune."[70] He was only a young boy when his father was executed for killing Yokoi, bringing disgrace and poverty to the family; yet having grown up believing that his father was a decent man, he collects testimonies and documents to reconstruct his father's life so that he can "vindicate" him.

Masataka attempts to fathom why at all his father made the "stupid" decision to murder Yokoi. First, he was young, much younger than Yokoi; second, he was of low birth and thus unable to mingle with wiser people and cultivate the knowledge necessary to understand the "secrets of the age." He grew up believing that "justice" lay in the pro-imperial, anti-foreigner camp, whereas the pro-shogunate, pro-opening camp stood for "irresolution." This ideology stemmed from the age-old notion in Chinese history books that talking peace with barbarians is tantamount to treason. Behind the hatred toward the pro-opening advocates was thus loathing for historical figures like Qin Hui 秦檜 (1091–1155), the Song dynasty minister notorious for profiting from making peace with the enemy state of the Jin (1115–1234). In this frame of reference, the father simply wanted to become a "man of justice."[71] Moreover, Yokoi was not careful enough in publishing his thought to avoid misunderstanding, which invited pro-imperial activists to misread his writings as arguments for wholesale Westernization and betrayal of imperial authority. This perception was so widespread that when the murder took place, "the word on the streets was mostly sympathetic to the band [of assassins] and tended rather to accuse the wrongdoing of Yokoi, who had been killed."[72]

"In retrospect, no one now thinks of Yokoi as bad," the narrator admits. Yet he deepens his contemplation: "Then, did my father kill a good man? No. . . . The criteria of good and bad change across time and place. My father, living in a certain age, killed a man who, in that age, was bad. Then why did my father have to be executed and his wife and son be reduced to social outcasts?"[73] Now, four and a half decades after the incident, when the new government has solidified its power and proven the validity of its open-country policy, no one questions the legitimacy of the law that executed Shirōzaemon. In retrospect, he is a terrorist, and there is no way to exonerate him. Yet back then, when the new government's power was still weak and the law contested, Shirōzaemon's action gained actual support and legitimacy. On what grounds, then, should we assess Shirōzaemon's life? "Such a rambling chain of thoughts, resembling a tautology or a vicious circle, entangled with my spirit like a spider web."[74] The narrator is not a revisionist who wants to rewrite history, nor is he a sycophant who would willingly submit to today's ideology and bury his father's legacy in oblivion, as someone on the wrong side of history whose sacrifice was needed for progress. Reviving the past perspective is little more than a form of defeatist nostalgia, whereas the present perspective is hopelessly incapable of doing justice to the real significance of this man's life. Faced with this dead end, the narrator's final recourse is to put his story in writing: "I have already given up. My compromises have piled up one on top of another, and my hope has now gradually shrunken to the point that I only want to have someone write down this story and leave it for future generations."⁷⁵

As the "editor" of this story, Ōgai does not resolve the narrator's *aporia* on his behalf but records it in writing "almost exactly" as he heard it.⁷⁶ This editorial gesture embodies the narratology of Ōgai's historical fiction. In relating history, it does not let the present be synthesized with the past into a uniform narrative. History ultimately resides in the documents handed to the present from the past, and Ōgai edits or rewrites them in such a way that his writing conveys history in its original resistance to the present meaning, folding in its mystery, without a cultural framework for explicating its significance to the modern reader. Because political legitimacy and moral criteria reversed themselves completely at the cultural threshold, no coherent point of view is able to bring the past and the present into a fine synthesis. Ōgai's historical fiction is an "editorial" attempt at nevertheless rebuilding, through textual mediation, a historical relationship across the ineffaceable cultural incommensurability.

In "Tsuge Shirōzaemon," the son's dilemma is not solved within the story, but Ōgai's afterword suggests that the son's acts of collecting materials and testimonies, organizing them into a biography, and telling it to the "editor" may have had a certain therapeutic effect on him. Ōgai describes Tsuge Masataka when they first met thirty years ago as "a pale young man with an oval face, with his eyebrows knitted in a perpetual frown," and he conjectures that "the misfortune of [his] family might have been inscribed, like the mark of Cain, on [his] countenance." Yet having spent years trying to reconstruct his father's life and having told it to Ōgai so that it may be written down, Tsuge now looks like "a robust and cheerful man without even a trace of the shadows of the past melancholy."⁷⁷ As his story ends in resignation, Masataka has not worked out a solution to his conundrum: he has not overcome it by conforming to progress, nor has he forged exoneration by refusing it. Beyond affirmation or denial of modernization, he finds a remedy in the temporality of textual transmission, which, while deferring resolution, opens history up to future readers' judgment.

Four years after the original publication, Ōgai added an appendix to a reprint of "Tsuge Shirōzaemon." In the appendix, he says that the original text served as an "intermediary" (*nakadachi* 媒) through which he acquainted himself with many people, including a friend of Shirōzaemon's, and gained access to additional anecdotes, correspondence, and documents that enabled him to revise parts of the original.[78] These additional resources, to be sure, still do not help resolve the aporia, yet the new communications mediated by Ōgai's text are symbolic of the function of his historical fiction. Rather than bring the past and the present into a reconciled story that would make a good national history, his work conveys the incompatible past in a text whose reading and rewriting constitute a continued collective endeavor to understand the meaning of the present in history. That readerly and writerly practice, albeit in the ultimate absence of a resolution, is expected to turn the historical aporia that is Japan's modernization into a chance to form a new community of remembrance.

LU XUN'S METAHISTORICAL FICTION

Although the historical fictions of Yi Kwangsu and Mori Ōgai can be construed as belonging to modern culture, their forms symptomize the inadequacy of modern cultural norms, values, and styles to historicize the past. Whereas Yi adopted elements of classical narratology to melodramatize history, Ōgai dwelled on irreducible cultural differences and reproduced the function of documents to convey history as a mystery that defied modern resolutions. Their historical fictions reflect the task of reconstructing the relationship between a past and a present that share little cultural ground, a problematic that also underlies Lu Xun's works in this genre. Lu Xun's historical stories are explorations of possible historical transmission in the cultural desert between past and present, and as such, they amount to a structural critique of Chinese civilization, whose existence depends on a particular regime of documentation, or of the power of culture, premodern *and* modern, that regulates what history is to be passed on. As Gao Yuandong has argued, Lu Xun's historical stories are part and parcel of his lifelong project of critiquing Chinese society and civilization.[79]

Reworking Chinese myths and historical legends, Lu Xun's historical short stories collected in *Old Stories Retold* frequently include contemporary references, inviting since its publication allegorical readings that try to decipher the author's satirical messages about present individuals or sociopolitical affairs.⁸⁰ While some of the pieces interpolate, implicitly or explicitly, such messages, they cannot be simply reduced to commentaries on the present, much less to a prehistory thereof. The frequent deviations of their referents from the past to the present, along with other disturbances of signification, create a self-consciously disruptive medium that gets in the way of conveying history. This performance constitutes a metacommentary on the construct of "history" that relies on a certain exclusionary order of documentary transmission, or to borrow from the Benjaminian formulation, the "barbarism" of the "document of civilization."⁸¹

Lu Xun's initial piece of historical fiction, the 1922 short story "Bu tian 補天" (Mending Heaven), originally titled "Bu zhou shan 不周山" (The Broken Mountain), illustrates the stakes of his critique. "Mending Heaven" rewrites the myths of the goddess Nüwa, the major cosmogonic deity to which the creation of humanity is attributed in Chinese mythology.⁸² The late second-century CE record of institutions, customs, and myths *Fengsu tongyi* 風俗通義 (Comprehensive Meaning of Customs and Mores) documents Nüwa's creation of humanity in two stages: first by kneading yellow earth, and second, because that hard work exhausted her energy, simply by dragging a rope in the mud and splashing it up.⁸³ *Huainanzi* 淮南子 (The Masters of Huainan), the second-century BCE compendium of philosophical essays, relates the legend of Nüwa quenching catastrophes on earth by mending the crumbling vault of heaven with smelted stones in five colors.⁸⁴ These myths are represented in Lu Xun's sarcastic, excessively colorful, and eerily realistic portrayal in "Mending Heaven."

In traditional representation, Nüwa is visualized in a figure with a human head and a serpent's body, often entangled with her brother and husband Fuxi, who is credited with originating human culture, namely primordial script. Yet in Lu Xun's rendition, Nüwa is a voluptuous, larger-than-life female figure with "perfectly rounded arms" and a "curvaceous form." The opening scene of creation is colored vividly and even ostentatiously, with "a mass of green serpentine clouds [weaving] their way through a powder-pink sky," "blood-red clouds on the horizon," "a frigid white moon in the color of pig iron," and the "ground carpeted in pastel green" with "a mass of pink and bluish-white flowers." The distant "heavens" respond to Nüwa's yawns by "paling to a mystical flesh pink," and her form melts into the "roseate ocean" as she walks through "the pink universe."[85] This exaggerated colorfulness confuses the sense of temporal distance, bringing the primordial past to the fore.

The sexual connotation of Nüwa's figure is emphasized when Lu Xun has a freshly created human being "stand between her legs, looking up at her."[86] On this particular detail, the author made an apologetic comment in the 1935 "Preface" to *Old Stories Retold*, asserting that he could not help but add it because of his revulsion at moralistic criticism.[87] He acknowledges, with a tongue-in-cheek tone, that this phrase was "the beginning of my slippery descent from earnestness into facetiousness—the archenemy of literary creation" and asserts that "after thirteen years, I have not progressed beyond 'The Broken Mountain.'" More than just an apology, Lu Xun's statement, despite its evocation of licentious material, suggests the self-conscious deviations of the works in *Old Stories Retold* from the established practice of "literary creation," foregrounding the "margins on which this book can exist for the time being."[88] If Lu Xun earlier dubbed the pieces collected in *Nahan* 呐喊 (Call to Arms, 1923) "fiction" whose "distance from works of art is great," then he characterizes *Old Stories Retold* as not even deserving of being called "'fiction' as it is defined in some *Introduction to Literature*."[89] *Old Stories Retold* thus recaptures the author's sustained formal experiments meant to expand the established domains of literature, the gesture *par excellence* of modern literature. And his pursuit of historical representation hinges precisely on the questioning of the constructs of the existing literary realms underpinning historical transmission.

Part of the challenge of interpreting *Old Stories Retold* is the capricious inclusion of references to contemporary affairs. The ad hoc allusions do not make an immediate contribution to the storytelling but destabilize the semantic horizon by mercurially shifting the referents away from the past. The anachronism of *Old Stories Retold* is conspicuously *unnecessary*. The narrative characterized by an unpredictable and self-dislocating signification makes the reading of its "relatively simple plots and descriptions" "feel like grabbing clouds," as Takeuchi Yoshimi complained.[90] In "Mending Heaven," the sexualized portrayal of Nüwa, along with the flamboyant colors in the scene of the creation of humanity, constitute superfluous signifiers pointing to the obvious inadequacy of the form for the content. They bespeak an opaque and even arbitrary mediality that, instead of serving as a mediator between past and present, produces an "estrangement" from history, as Chen Pingyuan has claimed.[91]

This idiosyncratic narratology in "Mending Heaven," indeed, is a critical repetition of Chinese fictional tradition, particularly the narratological framing of the Qing-dynasty masterpiece *Dream of the Red Chamber*. As Jing Wang has shown, the imagery of the stone in general and that of the stones used in Nüwa's mending of heaven in particular constitute a crucial narratological device in late imperial Chinese vernacular fiction.[92] In *Water Margin*, the removal of a stone tablet inscribed with illegible ancient-style characters releases the spirits of the 108 outlaws featured in the novel, whereas in *Xi you ji* 西遊記 (Journey to the West), Monkey King is born from an immortal stone. In *Dream of the Red Chamber*, the one leftover piece from the 36,501 stones that Nüwa used to repair the collapsing vault of heaven metamorphoses into the novel's hero Jia Baoyu, and the whole story is itself presented as transcribed from the inscription on that superfluous stone that was "rejected as unworthy."[93]

In *Dream of the Red Chamber*, the stone has to persuade a Daoist to "record" and "transmit" its story. The Daoist believes that the story does not have value and "no one would like to read it," for, without any "discoverable dynastic period" or any examples of "good governance" or "morality," it undercuts the received conventions of literature.[94] To this objection, the stone develops an elaborate rebuttal, censuring existing kinds of fiction for their adherence to "stale old convention," stilled and bombastic language, immorality, and obscenity, among other things. Affirming that its story has "freshness and a different kind of taste," the stone insists that its stories are "recorded exactly as they happened" (*zhui zong nie ji* 追踪躡跡; lit., following the traces and tracking the vestiges) and that it "has not dared to add the tiniest bit of contrived interpretation to vainly cater to people's appreciation for fear of losing the true story [*zhenzhuan* 真傳]."[95] In deploying this rhetoric, *Dream of the Red Chamber* asserts its value despite its departure from literary norms and conventions.

Old Stories Retold parodies this rhetoric by sarcastically referring to two different criteria—one based on moralistic and the other on aesthetic considerations—that have given "Mending Heaven" entirely

History as Rewriting 189

opposite evaluations as a literary work deemed worth publishing.⁹⁶ By doing so, *Old Stories Retold* manifests a crucial difference from the rhetoric in *Dream of the Red Chamber*, a difference that stipulates the modernity Lu Xun's work. The device of the stone in *Dream of the Red Chamber* aligns the textual production and circulation of this work with Nüwa's mending—or literally, "supplementing" (*bu* 補)—of heaven with the stones. Just as the stones in the mythology of Nüwa supplement heaven in crisis to reconstruct the totality of the world, so too in the narratology of *Dream of the Red Chamber* does the surplus stone left over from that endeavor supplement the out-of-date and indeed "self-contradictory" (*zixiang maodun* 自相矛盾) domain of literature to restore its wholeness—the self-assigned task, so to speak, of "mending" literature.⁹⁷ But *Old Stories Retold* foregrounds the idiosyncrasy of "Mending Heaven" that defies a preconceived notion of literature and gives grounds for its publication only on the "margins," where the book's existence is ostensibly uncertain and temporary. It does not posit a totality of literature that it intends to supplement as its cultural home and instead inspires a reconsideration of the significance of "literature" itself. Through this parody, *Old Stories Retold* inscribes itself in a literary space whose totality is out of sight, where it seeks an alternative historical transmission.

"Mending Heaven" situates its depiction of the mythological past against human culture at large. Nüwa shows motherly affection for and exchanges smiles with infantile human beings who utter "Nga! nga!," "Akon, Agon!," and "Uvu, Ahaha!," but as they grow and their culture advances, she loses touch with them.⁹⁸ The humans are portrayed as dwarfish creatures fond of trifling wars and obsessed with trivial rituals and rules; they even appropriate the lore of the goddess in the Daoist doctrine and frown upon her nudity on moralistic grounds, all while they depend on her mending labor to survive the crippled world. She can no longer understand their arcane language, which Lu Xun comically forges in archaist prose mimicking the style of the Confucian classic *Book of Documents*. After the goddess dies, the humans pitifully vie for the title of her only true descendants, making human culture desperately inadequate to pass down the goddess's larger-than-life enterprise. This is caricatured in the depiction of a Daoist priest who witnessed Nüwa instructing giant turtles to carry mountains on their backs out to sea:

The aged Daoist priest stranded on the seashore enlightened generations of disciples. Only on his deathbed, however, did he reveal that the magic mountains had been carried out to sea on the backs of giant turtles. And his disciples told their disciples, and so on it went, until an ambitious alchemist begged to inform the First Emperor of China, Qin shihuang, who sent him off in search.

The alchemist found nothing; the emperor died. Emperor Wu of the Han dispatched his own search party—but still nothing was found.[99]

Drawing on *Shiji* 史記 (Records of the Grand Historian), Lu Xun reworks the lore of the failed searches for the magic mountains commissioned by the founding emperors of the Qin and the Han dynasties. Its sardonic description of Nüwa's original deed passed on through the doctrinal lineage of Daoism all the way to imperial discourse culminates in an ironically nonchalant speculation about what might have happened to the sought-after mountains: "It was probably just happy coincidence that the turtles nodded when they did—probably they understood none of Nüwa's instruction. After swimming in aimless formation for a while, the shoal doubtless dispersed to sleep, leaving the magic mountains to sink. Thus, no one has discovered a trace of them since—only the occasional island of savages."[100]

With this renunciation of sure historical knowledge, "Mending Heaven" releases Nüwa from appropriation by documented human history. What is imagined is an ur-past that belongs to the historical world yet resists being recorded or transmitted in it. "Mending Heaven," therefore, undertakes to represent an exterior of recorded history constituted by the realm of extant documents and their circulation, an endeavor that calls for writing that escapes legitimization in that same cultural realm. Lu Xun's facetious style is a writerly performance that indicates just such alternative possibilities of historical transmission. His idiosyncratic historical fiction thus bespeaks a search for a new realm of literature and a pursuit of a novel path of historical transmission as two sides of the same coin.

Critique of the exclusionary cultural forces of historical transmission is a leitmotif that runs through the whole of *Old Stories Retold*.[101]

In it, the 1935 work "Chu guan 出關" (Leaving the Pass) displays perhaps the most developed exploration of this question.¹⁰² Drawing on sources including *Records of the Grand Historian* and the *Zhuangzi*, "Leaving the Pass" reworks the legend of the genesis of *Daodejing* 道德經 (The Classic of the Way and Virtue), the founding text of the Daoist canon. It interweaves the anecdote on the master-disciple relationship between Laozi and Confucius with the lore of Laozi's initial composition of *Daodejing* at the Hangu Pass on his way into seclusion. The documented interactions between Laozi and Confucius center on the significance of classical texts and the function of language in relationship to the Way. The "Tianyun 天運" (Movement of Heaven) chapter of the *Zhuangzi* relates an episode in which Confucius pays two visits to Laozi to seek his teaching. At their first meeting, the teacher Laozi criticizes Confucius for his complaints about the rulers who would not hire him despite his thorough mastery of the Six Classics, asserting that his disciple is indeed "lucky" not to have met a capable ruler. Laozi continues, "The Six Classics are but the traces [*chenji* 陳跡] of Old Kings. How could they be that which left those traces? What you are saying now is [also] like traces. Now, if traces are left by shoes, how could they be the shoes themselves?" With these remarks, the teacher suggests that one should not be concerned with mere texts but obtain the Way directly. For "if you obtain the Way, everything is possible by itself. If you don't, nothing is." Having received this wisdom, Confucius comes back for a second meeting, in which he convinces the teacher that he has actually "obtained the Way."¹⁰³ *Records of the Grand Historian* also documents an anecdote in its biography of Laozi that concerns his teaching's otherness to language: "Laozi studied the Way and virtue. His teaching took it as its task to occlude itself and not to be named."¹⁰⁴ There is, therefore, an irony in the legend of Laozi's writing of *Daodejing*: it is a text that conveys an obscure teaching that its author claims is fundamentally alien to language *per se*.

The genesis of *Daodejing* documented in *Records of the Grand Historian* recounts that Laozi, having witnessed the decline of the Zhou (11th century–256 BCE), leaves the state and on his way out meets a guard named Yin Xi, a disciple of Laozi's, at the Hangu Pass. Requested by Yin Xi to write a book before leaving for exile, Laozi agrees and composes five thousand words in two volumes, in which he discusses the meaning of the Way and virtue. Upon its completion, Laozi leaves the pass.¹⁰⁵ In the Daoist tradition, Yin Xi is known as Wenshi xiansheng 文始先生, or literally the master at the beginning of writing, and his receipt of Laozi's manuscript is considered the origin of the textual transmission of Daoist teaching.[106] In "Leaving the Pass," Lu Xun incorporates Zhang Taiyan's 章太炎 (1869–1936) fanciful theory about the reason for Laozi's westward exile and production of the manuscript, a theory whose veracity Lu Xun himself doubted.[107] Zhang conjectures that Confucius, knowing that his teaching derived from Laozi, did not want to revere Laozi as the original master, for Confucianism and Daoism were different. A few cryptic words that Confucius told Laozi gave the latter the fear that his disciple might come after him as "Feng Meng killed [his legendary archery teacher] Yi," so he left for the west, where Confucius's students were scarce, and in safety he began authoring the *Daodejing*.[108] In the Laozi legend reimagined by Lu Xun via Zhang Taiyan, Laozi counters Confucius's scheme to usurp and own the transmission of his teaching by going into exile and, more importantly, by *writing down* his teaching at the pass, despite his own disparagement of text as mere "traces."

Yet in "Leaving the Pass," the imagined scene of textual genesis foregrounds the profoundly precarious state of Laozi's original text. In the story, Yin Xi is a customs officer watching for smugglers at the pass, and he demands a manuscript from his teacher before letting him pass through the gate. Bothered and reluctant, Laozi nevertheless writes down his teaching on two sets of wood strips, which Yin Xi and other officials collect and store with other confiscated items like salt, sesame, cloth, beans, and bread. But they are not sure whether Laozi's text was even worth acquiring, for they may not be able to resell it for a profit, as they do the other products. The accountant inspects the two volumes Laozi left and predicts some interest on the market thanks to his "nice, clear handwriting," but the secretary belittles the cryptic opening: "Same boring old rubbish. Gives me a headache just reading it."[109] What Laozi leaves at the pass, then, is far from a canonical or even a literary or philosophical text. It is just one of those "goods" (*huose* 貨色), or even worse, a set of uncertain, risky letters whose value nobody understands. Thus permitted to pass the gate, Laozi mounts his black ox and disappears into the desert. No one knows his destination. Instead of repeating the Daoist tradition and identifying Laozi's writing as the legendary origin of textual transmission, "Leaving the Pass" satirically represents the original text as a mere stack of strips of wood stored with other, probably more valuable goods. The text remains at the gate, with the itinerary of its potential circulation in limbo. "Leaving the Pass," therefore, wrests Laozi's original text from the traditions that appropriate its transmission, recovering its original state as a material text open to precarious yet boundless routes of circulation and reading, just like Laozi's solitary journey into the desert.

But as such a document, Laozi's text has the potential to realize unexpected communications. In "Leaving the Pass," the border officials ask Laozi to put his teaching in writing because no one was able to comprehend his oral lecture. The audience members became bored and fell asleep, not only because his language was exceedingly abstruse, but also because "[his] lack of teeth, his poor enunciation, and his Shaanxi accent with its Hunan lilt—which mixed his l's with his n's, and prefaced everything with an 'errr'—ensured no one understood a thing he said." The clerk among the audience speaks in a Suzhou dialect, while the accountant uses speech that mixes northern and southern idioms. They cannot understand the master because "his national language [*guoyu* 國語] was not entirely pure," and neither can he understand them. It is in this desperate malfunctioning of communication on the borderland that the officials ask Laozi to "supplement [*bufa* 補發] the lecture" by writing it down—hence the birth of *Daodejing*.[110] In "Leaving the Pass," the original text thus becomes a figure of (mis)communication among disparate peripheral dialects on the border where they interface with each other—an antithesis to territorializing communication by means of a "national language." Laozi's writing mediates between those who are normally unable to communicate, symbolic, therefore, of possibilities of alternative historical transmission that undercut culturally sanctioned documentation. It epitomizes the history that Lu Xun tried to recover through historical fiction—history on the desert where the condition of possibility for transmission is always already questioned and documents are led to unpredictable destinations in defiance of cultural forces trying to regulate them.

With its attempts at reconstructing the present's relationship to the past, historical fiction by Yi Kwangsu, Mori Ōgai, and Lu Xun bespeaks through its formal experiments their critical reflections on whether their own writings, if institutionalized in modern culture as "literature," "fiction," and so on, are able to grasp the cultural past at all. Their works are imbued with a self-reflexive engagement with literary norms in treating this subject matter—an engagement that underlies their diverse forms: the melodramatic mode in Yi, the intervention as an editor in Ōgai, and the facetious mediality in Lu Xun. The otherness of the past they try to capture and the idiosyncrasy of their formal explorations meet in their historical fiction, echoing the modern practice of art where, as Rancière has formulated it, "writing history and writing stories come under the same regime of truth."[111] Their historical fiction, in this sense, flourished precisely in the perceived absence of a discursive ground on which to make sense of the rupture caused by cultural modernization.

"Modern literature," as long as it wants to be defined against the precedents, is itself fundamentally a "historical notion."[112] It would always have to be accompanied by a historical consciousness to make sure that it remains distinct from past literatures. As Hu Shi, in retrospectively distinguishing the May Fourth literary revolution he had spearheaded from late Qing vernacular literature, contended: "The history of vernacular fiction for the past fifty years displayed the same fundamental shortcomings as vernacular literature had had for one thousand years—that is, adoption of the vernacular was still unconscious [*wuyi de* 無意的] and arbitrary; it was not done consciously [*youyi de* 有意的] at all. The 'literary revolution' since 1917 has been a conscious statement. Unconscious evolution is slow and uneconomical."[113] Yet does not the past spill out of consciousness in the present? Are there not superfluous pasts that haunt the modern like "shadows of ghosts" (*guiying* 鬼影) and threaten its self-consciousness, self-definitions, and manifestos?[114] The past's irreducible resistance to the modern urges writers to take the sanctioned "modern literature" beyond its definitions and normalizations. The past that is older or deeper than a "history" representable in the present, therefore, meets the modern at its avant-garde moment, in its incessant pursuit of newness. The *arche* of history and that of modern literature become one and the same. Historical fiction, in this sense, is the generic allegory of modern literature in East Asia.

If, according to Lukács, Scott's historical novel tells a "necessary prehistory" of the post-1789, pre-1848 era of bourgeois revolution, then the idiosyncratic forms of historical fiction by Yi Kwangsu, Mori Ōgai, and

Lu Xun might indicate the struggles to locate such a prehistory for late nineteenth- to early twentieth-century East Asia. Yet the significance of these writers' historical fiction seems to go beyond this periodization as it evokes an ur-history that inspires the modern to break away from its self-identifications, to reexamine the meaning of the present in history— the ongoing task of reconceiving of modernity in broader, historically grounded contexts.

Allegorized in the forms of historical fiction in East Asia is modern literature as it originated in writerly attempts at reconstituting the present's relationship to the past that had become disarranged due to profound cultural transformations. Just as historical fiction lays bare the writers' strenuous endeavors to put the present in a historical perspective, modern literature finds itself, rather than safely housed in a defined culture, right on the contested boundaries between disparate cultures, trying to make sense of their relationship through inventing new modes of representation. In part III, I will explore how this working of modern literature to dislocate cultural confines provided semicolonial and colonial writers in wartime East Asia with agency to resist sanctioned cultures in the Japanese Empire, giving modern literature its transnational afterlives.

PART III
Japan's Imperial Mimicry and Its Critique

The East Asian discourse of cultural modernization closely reflects the region's *grand récit* of modernization, the story of a transfer of power from the old regional Sinocentric order to the new global Eurocentric order that China, Japan, and Korea vied to enter as nascent nation-states. One important turning point in this story was Japan's takeover of China's long-held position as the region's center of influence and its eventual rise as an imperial power. With the colonization of Taiwan in 1895, Japan took its territorial lust overseas, leading to the colonization of Korea in 1910, the establishment of the puppet state of Manchukuo in 1932, and the waging of an all-out war against China in 1937. It made a further foray into the south by starting the Asia-Pacific War in 1941. The new political realities caused by Japan's imperialist expansion forced the region's literary production to enter a new phase.

Japanese imperialism shared many basic features with Western imperialisms.[1] While it displayed as many of the vices of modern imperialism as its Western counterparts, the Japanese empire demands approaches that can analyze the specificities derived from its historical conditions. In her study of the transculturations of Japanese literature in its (semi)colonies, Karen Thornber has pointed out, "Part of what makes the cultural flows of the Japanese empire unusually fascinating and separates them from those of most European empires is Japan's long engagement with and oftentimes adulation of Chinese and Korean creative products."[2] The lengthy and tight cultural contacts between Japan and its (semi)colonies, indeed, constitute an aspect of Japanese imperialism that is fundamental to its formation yet often eludes the approaches based on colonial and postcolonial experiences in the contexts of Western imperialisms.

Japan recycled the regional universality of cultural resources centered on classical Chinese letters to forge a rhetoric to legitimize its imperial rule. It employed this discursive strategy to present itself as a virtuous ruler to be distinguished from Western empires, all while acting as an agent of the modern civilizing mission. The transregional comparative approach that this book adopts is useful for shedding light on this often-underappreciated aspect of Japanese imperialism that I call *imperial* mimicry, defined here as the discursive operation of legitimizing an imperial rule in East Asia by eclectically exploiting the resources of classical Chinese as well as modern Western civilizations.[3] If Japan's ascendency to power was a "success" in the East Asian story of modernization, then its eventual imperialization betrayed the return of the cultural past repressed in that story as obsolete. If so, then modern literature in East Asia, which, as we have seen, emerged through attempts at displacing just such a stark cultural divide, must have worked as a structural, historically grounded critique of Japanese imperialism. In the last two chapters, I explore how semicolonial Chinese and colonial Korean, Taiwanese, and Manchukuo works produced at the height of Japanese imperialism in the late 1930s to the early 1940s leveraged this critical capacity of modern literature to engender modes of representation in defiance of the sanctioned cultures of the imperium.

THE RECYCLING OF OLD UNIVERSALITY

In the early stages of Japan's territorial expansion, imperial agents ranging from colonial administrators to educators and scholars exploited the transregional cultural capital of Chinese letters. The first instances of this phenomenon can be observed in early colonial Taiwan, where Japanese officials rediscovered their cultural distinction as Meiji-era elites as useful for facilitating intra-imperial communication.

One fascinating case is the cultural activities that the fourth governor-general of Taiwan, Kodama Gentarō 児玉源太郎 (1852–1906, in office from 1898 to 1906), hosted to solidify his power. For example, he requested the presence of the elderly on the island at the rite of *xiang yinjiu* 鄉飲酒, or the time-honored local wine-drinking ritual stipulated in the Confucian classic *Yili* 儀禮 (Book of Ceremonies and Rites), in Taipei in 1898 and in Zhenghua and Tainan in the following year. In 1900, he organized *Yang wen hui* 揚文會 (Society for Elevating Letters), where he invited local literati who had passed the Qing-era civil service examinations to submit compositions on ethicopolitical themes, reenacting the classical practice of the political council.[4] He also held poetry gatherings at his retreat in Taipei suburbs, where poems were exchanged following the traditional protocol of matching meters and rhymes; the exchanged poems were published in imperial-sanctioned newspapers including *Taiwan nichinichi shinpō* 台灣日日新報 (Taiwan Daily) and circulated throughout the colony.[5] Qing-era Mandarin was employed in the early colonial period as the intermediary when Japanese officials who had no knowledge of local languages communicated with the indigenous population.[6] Kodama composed the following poem on the occasion of the new year in 1899:

雞報清晨萬象新	As the cock's crow announces dawn, everything becomes new;
邊城煙靄入陽春	In this border town, mists and hazes enter the balmy spring.
梅花野菊何嬌笑	Why are the plum blossoms and wild chrysanthemums showing such tender smiles?
草木皆知雨露仁	The plants must all know the benevolence of the rain and dew.[7]

Metaphorizing the advent of the new regime with the image of the first rooster crow of the day, the poem is unapologetically political; it fantasizes about people welcoming the new government through the figures of tame and smiling flowers gratefully quenching their thirst with

Part III: Japan's Imperial Mimicry

the "benevolence" of the long-awaited moisture, a metaphor for the virtue of Japanese rule. In this poet's voice, the location of the "border town" is meant to evoke the centrifugal dissemination of virtuous rule from the metropole into the southern island, but for the local audience, it could well have evoked the island's geographical distance from the imperial seat of the time-honored Chinese dynasty. Kodama's evocation of traditional Chinese culture signifies not just the strategic use of local culture by the foreign ruler but also Japan's imperial mimicry. The ritual of poetry exchanges, the classical form of heptasyllabic quatrain, the representation of imperial topology, the Confucian notion of "benevolence," and the commonplace floral metaphorization of cultural-political influence on people—all are instances of the Japanese governor's voice trying to mimic traditional imperial authority to further his modern imperialist agenda.

Similar poetry gatherings were held in Korea as well. In 1909, the inaugural resident-general of Korea, Itō Hirobumi 伊藤博文 (1841–1909), took the renowned Sinologist Mori Kainan to the peninsula and hosted a poetry gathering with Korean literati in Seoul. The exchanged poems in classical Chinese are compiled in *Suiun gashū* 翠雲雅集 (Elegant Collection from the Emerald Clouds, 1909), which opens with Itō's heptasyllabic quatrain followed by dozens of pieces composed by the Korean participants using the same meter and rhyme words as the host's. Along with Yu Kilchun, Kim T'aekyŏng was among the contributors.[8] Like the Taiwanese case, this practice mimics traditional poetry gatherings in the Chinese court, hosted by the monarch and attended by his subjects, an archaist attempt at staging the new power in an old style, facilitated by shared literary cultures in East Asia.

Education policy in early colonial Taiwan also reflects the Japanese Empire's use of shared cultural traditions. The Public School Regulation of 1898, which instituted modern elementary schools in place of the traditional Confucian academies, introduced a subject called "reading" separate from "national language" (i.e., Japanese).[9] Whereas the latter taught Japanese with the aid of side-by-side translation into Taiwanese transcribed in the *kana* script, the former instructed students in classical Chinese as well as related Japanese writings, adopting as the readers Confucian classics like *Xiaojing* 孝經 (The Classic of Filial Piety), *Daxue* 大學 (Great Learning), *Zhongyong* 中庸 (Doctrine of the Mean), and the *Analects*.[10] The uncannily archaic list of readers shows the perception of classical Chinese as an important discipline in elementary pedagogy, bespeaking the colonial policy that strategically took advantage of the age-old cultural capital. The many classical Chinese poetry societies organized by the settler Japanese throughout Taiwan, too, are a testimony to the surviving relevance of classical learning.[11] Isawa Shūji 伊沢修二 (1851–1917), the inaugural head of educational affairs in the colonial government, insisted on the value of Chinese characters as "an efficient instrument for communicating the thoughts of the five or six million souls in East Asia."[12] He also lauded the benefits of brush talk in Chinese script for communicating with locals who only spoke Taiwanese, a language his interpreters, versed only in Mandarin, were unable to handle.[13]

Emboldened by his experience in Taiwan, Isawa cofounded the Society for Unifying the Chinese Characters (*Kanji tōitsu kai* 漢字統一会) in 1907 with branches in China and Korea, and coedited *Dōbun shinjiten* 同文新字典 (New Dictionary in Shared Script, 1909). Grafted onto ancient Chinese lexicography, this dictionary picks about six thousand Sinographs deemed "the practical characters most needed for contemporary communication of thoughts on education, economy, politics, business, etc., among Japan, China, and Korea." The dictionary can be seen as embodying the Japanese political initiative to reconfigure the cultural capital for East Asia in the post–Russo-Japanese War era by determining the number of basic characters, standardizing their forms, and facilitating phonetic comparisons.[14] Here the notion of *dōbun* 同文 (shared script) even has an odd resonance with the legendary founding enterprise of China's First Emperor in "unifying the carriage tracks and written script [*shu tongwen* 書同文]" to facilitate transportation and communication within the new imperium on the Central Plain.[15] Isawa had in fact been a staunch advocate of the abolishment of Chinese characters amid the Japanese language reform movements, yet as a colonial administrator, he rediscovered their utility for intra-imperial contacts. His reversal of opinion is an epitome of the cultural irony of Japanese imperialism where the nation's much-maligned indebtedness to Chinese civilization was conjured up as an (ab)usable past now that it had expanded into the region. The society's project gained some sympathizers both in China and Korea, yet like all the other attempts at script reform, it implied a realignment of cultural hegemony for the benefit of the incumbent power, which, in this case, converged on Japan's imperialist ambitions.[16] Zhang Taiyan, for instance, lambasted the Society's mission, claiming that "Japan and China share script/culture in name, but their origins are actually entirely different." Zhang censured above all the imposition of arbitrary limits and standardizations on script and pronunciation, which he feared would cripple the philological reconstruction of China's intrinsic tradition.[17]

Chen Peifeng has contended that Chinese writing in colonial Taiwan was adopted both by the colonizer and the colonized and became "creolized," combining elements of classical Chinese proper, Sino-Japanese writing, and Taiwanese diction, as well as, after the 1920s, the May Fourth–style Chinese vernacular. In the 1930s, colonial writers undertook to create a novel prose style based on spoken Taiwanese, which, despite their nativist claims, still incorporated elements of those other styles. In the realm of writing in colonial Taiwan, the Manichean divide between the colonizer and the colonized was not only drawn between Japanese, on the other hand, and Taiwanese or Chinese, on the other, but it was also negotiated within a multilateral field of "creole Chinese writing."[18]

The education policies of early colonial Korea were devised on the heels of the marked shift in public education in Taiwan with the 1904 revision of the School Regulations, which allocated greater resources to "national language" (i.e., Japanese) and sharply limited the instruction of Chinese writing, removing the Confucian classics from the official curriculum.[19] The first Ordinance of Education in Korea, issued in 1911, set Japanese-language pedagogy as a principal objective of public primary education, while still allotting a small number of hours to reading courses covering "Korean and Chinese writings." Its second iteration in 1922 made "Chinese writing" an elective while keeping "Korean" as a required subject, and the third one in 1938 relegated "Korean" to an elective and effectively eliminated it in favor of more hours in Japanese, leading to its complete removal with the fourth and final ordinance put out in 1943.[20] These salient tendencies toward cultural assimilation and intra-imperial monolingualism point to their culmination in the wholesale "Japanization" that began in the late 1930s—a series of draconian biopolitical measures called *kōminka* 皇民化, which were aimed at turning colonial populations in Taiwan, Korea, and the occupied territories in China and Southeast Asia into loyal subjects of the Japanese emperor for the sake of wartime mobilization. It was implemented in Taiwan and Korea through means like severe restrictions on Chinese- and Korean-language publication, respectively; compulsory usage of Japanese in both public and private; forced adoption of Japanese-style surnames; coerced worship at Shinto shrines; and cross-monitored enforcement of Japanese-style customs.[21] The "Japanization" era laid bare a violent peak of the cultural policies under Japanese rule.

A central instrument that the modern Japanese state deployed for cultural assimilation through education was the Imperial Rescript of Education (*kyōiku chokugo* 教育勅語). The brief text of a mere three hundred or so characters composed in an archaist *kanbun kundoku* style, the rescript was originally promulgated in the form of an imperial bestowal and distributed to public schools throughout Japan in 1890, and it was applied further to colonial public schools in Taiwan in 1897 and in Korea in 1912.[22] The provenance of this text and its application to the colonies are instructive about how Japan's imperial mimicry underpinned its contrived attempts at cultural assimilation.

In the voice of the emperor himself, this text defines the cardinal virtues that all imperial subjects should uphold and proclaims the unbroken lineage of the Japanese imperial house to be the sole source of those virtues. An original copy of this text was safeguarded at each public school and used, together with photographic portraits of the emperor and the empress, as the central prop for national holiday rituals. A mandatory curriculum of moral education called *shūshin* 修身 (self-cultivation) à la Confucian doctrine was implemented for the purpose of explicating its meaning.[23]

As it was applied to the colonies, the rescript faced an obvious conundrum, for its assertion of Japan's particular royal lineage to be the only source of the universal virtues to be practiced by people beyond its imagined community was not quite persuasive.[24] To resolve this patent discrepancy between particularity and universality, the imperial ideologues conjured up the regional cultural traditions which they saw Japan had been part of. Isawa Shūji, in discussing public education in Taiwan, insisted that portions of the rescript were "almost the same" as the teachings of "Confucianism practiced in Taiwan," and that "the blessings of the [Japanese] imperial house" should not be limited to the narrow confines of "the Yamato nation" but applied to people all over the world by "impartially conferring benevolence upon them" (*isshi dōjin* 一視同仁). He also declared that Taiwan "completely shared the same script/culture" with Japan and recommended that the rescript's interpretation be produced in Chinese writing.[25] In Korea, imperial officials argued for grounding moral education at public school on Confucianism, trying to resolve differences between the contents of Confucian teaching and the rescript. Eight years into the colonial era, public-school textbooks deployed the rhetoric to designate the Japanese emperor as the provider of "benevolent governance" (*jinsei* 仁政), the pivotal Confucian notion of good rule deriving from the *Mencius*. The need for legitimization only increased in the aftermath of the anti-imperial March First Movement, prompting the philosopher Inoue Tetsujirō 井上哲次郎 (1856–1944) to propose an exegesis of the rescript that attributed Japanese rule to the "kingly way" (*ōdō* 王道; Chn. *wangdao*), the ancient Confucian ideal of rule by virtue as opposed to rule by force, or the "hegemon way" (*hadō* 霸道; Chn. *badao*).[26] In these efforts to bolster universal moral authority at the cost of national particularity, Inoue's theory was not put into practice; yet it throws into relief the fundamental rhetorical weakness of the rescript, which, despite its insistence on the supremacy of the Japanese imperial house, needed to be supplemented by Confucian ideas to assert universal relevance.

The reading of Confucianism into the rescript, attempted in both Taiwan and Korea, is not as far-fetched as it might appear, however. In content, the virtues that it stipulates pivot on two of the cardinal Confucian virtues, "loyalty" (*chū* 忠) and "filial piety" (*kō* 孝), and draw on the three foundational human relationships—ruler/subject, father/son, and husband/wife—that underlie Confucian moral orthodoxy.[27] In spirit, its promulgation was informed by the classical idea of the emperor's direct administration by virtue. At the height of nation-building in the 1880s, the Meiji government's conservative faction clashed with the proponents of secular statehood and insisted that the latter be counterbalanced by setting forth the state's identity in moral and cultural terms. Central to this movement was the state ideologue Motoda Nagazane 元田永孚 (1818–1891), who expected the emperor to fulfill "rule by virtue" (*tokuchi* 德治) and helped draft the rescript as the key vehicle for the people's "cultivation" (*kyōka* 教化) by means of the imperial good grace.²⁸ Against the backdrop of the fledgling efforts to institutionalize a modern state, "that the Imperial Rescript of Education was promulgated right before the convening of the inaugural session of the Imperial Diet amounted to an open proclamation that the state of Japan, as an embodiment of morality, was the sole arbiter of value," as Maruyama Masao famously put it.²⁹ This idea resulted in the ostensible representation of Japanese imperialism as a centrifugal overseas expansion of ethicocultural rule from the imperial throne.³⁰ The rescript embodies the incipient Japanese state's ideological oscillations between rule of law and rule by virtue, secularism and moralism, process and value—a duality carried over to colonial politics. And its provenance, deeply indebted to Confucianism in content and in spirit, encouraged the Japanese ideologues to believe in its effectiveness as a tool for cultural assimilation in the regional colonies. The evocation of Confucianism, however, was a double-edged sword, since it posited a higher source of legitimacy than any particular political entity. Korean literati indeed took this avenue of critique and cast doubt on the empire's legitimacy, claiming that its actual rule undercut "benevolent governance" as it had been understood in orthodox Confucian exegesis.³¹

Manchukuo, the Japanese puppet state that existed in northeastern China from 1932 to 1945, embodied Japan's imperial mimicry perhaps most saliently. The ideological debates over its legitimacy echoed with contemporary discourses on cultural identity, civilization, and modernity in East Asia; as Prasenjit Duara has put it, "Manchukuo reveals the lineaments of a *regional* understanding of how older formations are culturally constructed as sovereign nations in East Asia."³² The recycling of regional cultural resources informed the advertisement of Manchukuo as a "utopian land of the kingly way" (*ōdō rakudo* 王道楽土) where the Japanese, the Koreans, the Mongols, the Manchu Chinese, and the Han Chinese would thrive together, and as a state built by a heaven-mandated "revolution" capable of resolving political chaos in northeast China. Tachibana Shiraki 橘樸 (1881–1945), a journalist and Sinologist who became a vocal proponent of the Manchukuo project, evoked Sun Yat-sen's (1866–1925) talk on "Great Asianism" from 1924, which distinguished the "kingly way" of "Eastern culture" based on "benevolence and morality" (*renyi daode* 仁義道德) from the "hegemon way" of "Western culture." Whereas Sun had entrusted interwar Asian nationalism with the hope of constructing a new anti-imperialist civilization and revived the old resources of Confucian universalism to articulate it, Tachibana exploited this idea to legitimize Japanese imperialism.[33] Echoing Sun and Kang Youwei's late Qing political philosophy, Tachibana also revived the ancient Chinese utopian notion of the "great community" (*datong* 大同) to articulate the moral cause of Manchukuo. The reverberations of old notions helped veil the puppet state in an aura of authenticity to placate its opponents, recruit collaborators, and manufacture public consent.[34]

The "kingly way" ideology was also applied to education. The Manchukuo government gave orders in 1932 to abolish KMT-distributed materials and adopt the *Four Books* and the *Classic of Filial Piety* as readers. Zhu Xi's 朱熹 (1130–1200) commentary accompanied them in official textbooks, reviving Neo-Confucian orthodoxy in modern schools. Manchukuo's archaism culminated in the reinstalment of the disgraced last emperor of China Puyi as chief executive of the state in 1932 and his eventual crowning as emperor of Manchukuo in 1934. Manchukuo even revivified the ancient tribute ritual for Confucius, the *shidian li* 釋奠禮, and had Puyi perform it at the Hall of Letters in the state capital Shinkyō (today's Changchun) according to the formal protocol of three kneelings and nine prostrations, mimicking the dynastic Chinese regime in the wedding of political power to moral authority.[35]

In Manchukuo, amid the worsening antagonism between Japan and China in the late 1930s, the utopian rhetoric of the "kingly way" lost ground to Japanization. The Confucian classics were banned from schools in 1937, and Puyi officially proclaimed Shintoism as the state's religious foundation in 1940. The shift away from Confucian universalism to Japanese particularism was part of the sweeping Japanization pursued throughout the imperium during the Second Sino-Japanese War. This wartime political radicalization only revived the fundamental ideological challenge of Japanese imperialism: How to affirm the universality of Japanese civilization as an alternative to Western civilization, now without reference to Chinese civilization? Numerous Japanese intellectuals tackled this problem during the wartime era, some under the banners of "overcoming the modern" and Japan's "world-historical mission."[36] Symptomatic of the complexity of this problem, and of the desire to resolve it discursively, was the reliance on the quasi-sublimity of "nothingness." The Kyoto school philosopher Nishitani Keiji 西谷啓治 (1900–1990), for instance, attributed free human subjectivity to what he called "the subjective position of nothingness," which was devoid of all worldly possessions and even personae. As such, human subjectivity at its core became perfectly slated for assimilation into a monolithic whole, and Nishitani named that all-embracing totality "Japan," the only nation able to take, by virtue of the radical self-negation at its heart, the position of nothingness from which to "overcome" the entire modern world. The pure formality of nothingness collapsed any real tensions between the universal and the particular without the mediation of revived Confucianism, while escalating the position of "Japan" to an absolute self-identity to which all alterity was to be violently reduced.[37]

As much as the Japanese Empire showed the evils of modern imperialism in general, its curious discursive construct bespoke the conundrum of affirming the universal relevance of a particular culture whose historical provenance was not in the West. Modernization urged Japan to reconfigure its culture to proclaim its national particularity by erasing its traditional indebtedness to Chinese civilization, but as it hastily sought recognition beyond its borders, it ironically evoked the repressed past as a convenient resource. Japanese imperialism was therefore as much a version of modern imperialism as it was a symptom of East Asian modernization's troubled relationship to the cultural past. It could well even be analyzed as a phenomenon of the return of the repressed. The exploration of an alternative relationship to past culture is thus as imperative as the general framework of postcolonial criticism for the sake of the structural critique of Japanese imperialism. And if modern literature, as we saw in parts I and II, emerged through reconstructing just such a relationship across cultural divide, then it should function as a critical discourse against Japanese imperialism. Zhou Zuoren's wartime cultural criticism, which I explore in chapter 5, and the late colonial Korean, Taiwanese, and Manchukuo works that I examine with a focus on their intertextualizations of Lu Xun's works in chapter 6, put this function into practice, and as such, they enable us to consider the historical significance of the origins of modern literature in East Asia beyond cultural imperialism or nationalism.

CHAPTER FIVE

Archaeology of Resistance

Zhou Zuoren's Cultural Criticism in Wartime East Asia

The question of Chinese thought is an important issue. Important as it is, however, this is not a serious issue at all. I usually do not take anything rashly or optimistically, but the question of Chinese thought is the one and only area that I feel totally optimistic about. I do believe there is much hope in its future. There are indeed confusions recently in the world of Chinese thought, but these are only superficial and temporary phenomena. Seen from a far-reaching and in-depth perspective, in fact, the thought of the Chinese people is intrinsically very healthy. With this essential foundation, there will necessarily be growth if you keep up careful cultivation. Based on this healthy thought, we can create a healthy nation.[1]

Zhou Zuoren, a towering essayist, an unparalleled scholar and translator of Japanese and Greek literature, and a powerful social critic and satirist in modern China, wrote this passage at the beginning of his essay "Zhongguo de sixiang wenti 中國的思想問題" (The Problem of Chinese Thought) in 1942. The political climate at that time made this essay sound out of place. It irritated Japanese cultural agents active in the occupied regions of China, inviting, for instance, opprobrium from the writer Kataoka Teppei 片岡鉄兵 (1894–1944) in his speech at the Congress of the Writers of the Greater East Asia (*daitōa bungakusha taikai* 大東亜文学者大会). The infamous Congress had held its inaugural meeting in Tokyo in 1942 on the initiative of the Japanese Association for Literature in the Nation's Service (*Nihon bungaku hōkoku kai* 日本文学報国会) to discuss "collaboration among writers in the co-prosperity sphere for the achievement of the purpose of the Greater East Asian War [i.e., the Asia-Pacific War]" and "the establishment of Greater East Asian literature."[2] Kataoka took part in the Congress's second meeting in the following year and spoke on the topic of "the demand for the establishment of Chinese literature," alluding to Zhou as "an old reactionary authority in the liberated zone" and censuring his "extremely passive" attitude that poured cold water on the "youthful ideal" of "building a Greater East Asia."[3]

Zhou's ostensibly nonchalant expression of "optimism" and his affirmation of the intrinsic "health" of "Chinese thought" cut across the agenda of the organizers of the congress, who had failed to invite Zhou to take part in their effort to "establish" and "build" or to mark a new beginning of literature that would serve Japan's novel "world-historical mission" of constructing a new order in East Asia.[4] In his autobiography *Zhitang huixianglu* 知堂回想録 (The Memoir of Zhitang [Zhou Zuoren], 1970), Zhou recalls this essay and explains its implicit motif; as he writes, "I actually tried to hamper the scheme of the fake New Citizen's Society, which was making a fuss back then about founding a central thought and working with the new Greater East Asian order."[5] The New Citizen's Society (*xin min hui* 新民會) was organizing propaganda activities on behalf of the collaborationist government in besieged Beijing, which Kataoka called a "liberated zone."[6] Zhou even refers to "The Problem of Chinese Thought" and Kataoka's attack on it in an apologetic letter he sent to Zhou Enlai shortly before the inauguration of the People's Republic in 1949 to make the case that he "may have, to be sure, betrayed the sagely Way or harmed the Confucian doctrine, but never intended to hurt the nation" during the anti-Japanese war period.[7] Dong Bingyue has noted the distance between Zhou Zuoren's wartime discourse on "Chinese thought," on the one hand, and the collaborationist ideology of the Wang Jingwei government and Japan's imperialist worldview, on the other, and identified in Zhou's discourse a "cultural resistance against Japan."[8]

Despite the Japanese castigation and his own retrospective apology, however, Zhou Zuoren's wartime political record is far from clean, and has been regarded as one of the high-profile cases of "national treason" (*hanjian* 漢奸) in China.⁹ When Beijing fell to the Japanese army shortly after the Marco Polo Bridge Incident in July 1937, most intellectuals in the capital fled to the anti-Japanese strongholds in the south. Beijing University, where Zhou had taught since 1917, and Tsinghua University moved to Changsha and then to Kunming to form the National Southwestern Associated University. Despite mounting pleas and invitations from his colleagues and students in the south, Zhou decided to remain in the fallen capital with his extended family. For several months, he was able to keep a low profile, making ends meet by translating Greek literature. In a letter he sent to Tao Kangde 陶亢德 (1908–1983) in September, Zhou insisted that anyone remaining in Beijing be seen as a Su Wu, alluding to the lore of the Han dynasty general who staunchly refused to surrender to the Xiongnu barbarians for nineteen years in exile, and not as a Li Ling, who defected to them.¹⁰ However, in April 1938, media in resistance districts reported on Zhou's appearance with Japanese and puppet government officials in the Forum for Building the Culture of Renewed China (*kōsei Chūgoku bunka kensetsu zadankai* 更生中國文化建設座談會) hosted in Beijing by *Ōsaka mainichi shinbun* 大阪每日新聞 (Osaka Daily), igniting a huge scandal that came to be known as the "Zhou Zuoren affair."¹¹ Among a range of responses expressed by intellectuals, the most iconic came in the form of an open letter signed by eighteen major writers, who described Zhou's behavior as "a disappointing event that indeed amounted to a betrayal of the nation and kneeling before the foe."¹² To be sure, signs of Zhou's lukewarm attitude toward the Japanese occupiers and the collaborationist regime abound. He declined, for instance, several invitations from universities, including the brand-new Kenkoku University in Manchukuo's capital Shinkyō, and later, to the disappointment of the organizers, refused to take part in the Congress for the Writers of the Greater East Asia.¹³ But his relationship with the authorities deepened after he became target of a failed assassination attempt on New Year's Day in 1939, which he suspected was perpetrated by Japanese agents.¹⁴ He took several key posts, starting with the position of Dean of the Faculty of Letters at Beijing University (1939) and culminating in his installment as a standing member of the State Council and the Deputy Minister of Education in Wang Jingwei's puppet government (1941). He gave speeches and participated in cultural activities in support of Japanese rule. Upon Japan's defeat and retreat in 1945, Zhou was arrested and tried by the nationalist authorities. He was convicted of treason and sentenced to fourteen years in prison, only to be released in 1949 on the eve of the Communist victory in the Chinese Civil War.

Zhou's questionable behavior and even blatant collaboration with the occupation authorities have perplexed those who have sought to assess him. On this issue, I agree with Susan Daruvala that there is little merit in explaining, in a "teleological narrative," his wartime conduct via his literature, or vice versa.[15] A more interesting ambivalence resides in the observation that the kind of detached optimism Zhou articulates in "The Problem of Chinese Thought" should have sounded just as incompatible with China's contemporary rallying cries for "national defense literature" as it did with the Japanese imperial ideology.[16] The profound ambiguity of Zhou's work, unable to align either with nationalism or imperialism, calls for its reassessment in a transnational comparative context. This is not to discount the significance of national literature vis-à-vis imperialism and even regionalism—a significance explained, for example, in Frantz Fanon's exemplary and still relevant "On National Culture."[17] Nor is this to gloss over the idiosyncrasy of Zhou's discourse, which cannot but beg the question of how it made any sense of the actual atrocities and persecution of the war. Instead, my comparative perspective seeks to explore the significance of Zhou's work as an example of modern literature in East Asia, especially in terms of its reconfiguration of modernity's relationship to cultural pasts that show resistance to inclusion in nationalized traditions. My reassessment teases out in Zhou's cultural criticism a structural critique of the archaist universalism inherent in the Japanese imperial mimicry—its politically motivated recycling of the universality of premodern East Asian letters—and a reconceptualization of the relationship between Chinese and Japanese cultures beyond cultural nationalism or regionalism.

Zhou's wartime writings are preceded by a series of essays he penned on Japanese culture as the Sino-Japanese relationship quickly deteriorated in the mid-1930s. In what follows, I read this group of writings in the 1930s and 1940s in relation to Zhou's more iconic criticism and essays from earlier periods, writings in which his wartime oeuvre is firmly rooted. I therefore situate his idiosyncratic practice of modern literature in a broad context and discuss its implications for the critique of Japanese imperialism and the understanding of the Sino-Japanese cultural relationship.

MODERN LITERATURE IN HISTORY

What did Zhou Zuoren mean by the intrinsic "health" of Chinese thought? What enabled him to opine optimistically about its fate in the middle of a national crisis? Zhou's basic argument in "The Problem of Chinese Thought" is that "China's principal thought . . . is Confucian thought."[18] This is a striking statement coming from the pen of one of the most prominent intellectuals of the May Fourth generation, which was known for its staunch anti-traditionalism.[19] Yet Zhou distinguishes "Confucianism"—or "archi-Confucianism" (*yuanshi rujia* 原始儒家), as he calls it elsewhere—from its dogmatized and institutionalized form in later periods and traces it back to a fundamental continuum that "has not changed at all for thousands of years," since "before the name 'Confucian' [*ru* 儒] had even existed."[20] He identifies the exemplary manifestation of Confucianism in the *Mencius* and characterizes it as a kind of universal "humanism" (*rendao zhuyi* 人道主義) encapsulated in the concept of "*ren* 仁*,*" which in brief means to "treat others as humans."[21] He emphasizes that Confucianism in this sense recognizes "life's basic instincts" such as "food and sex," traditionally designated as "the great human desires" in the *Book of Rites*, and that the sagely way consists of making sure that people realize their desires in harmony without hampering others. Zhou insists that this ethics "does not have anything unnatural about it," and continues,

> This is why I call it a healthy thought. It derives from human nature and differs from something artificially injected from outside. Thus, scholars who read books and investigate principles certainly understand it more, but those ordinary, illiterate people who have not read a single phrase from books by the sages also understand it. The human relationship with other humans and things naturally has orders and rules [*lifa* 禮法], and nothing about it goes against the sagely way. This is the reason why I say I am optimistic.[22]

Several questions immediately arise. How, for example, are we to ensure that morality is rooted in human nature? Are "orders and rules" not artificial, at least to some extent? If so, how do they gain legitimacy? What if different forms of human desire cause conflicts? As a moral philosophy, Zhou Zuoren's archi-Confucianism seems underdeveloped, if not entirely naïve, preceded as it was by a lengthy history of Chinese philosophy that had developed sophisticated debates over these and other fundamental questions.[23] But this discourse, I argue, can be reevaluated in the modern context as an attempt at reconceiving of Chinese culture in history in relationship to a universal value rather than national particularity.

There is a marked ellipsis at the heart of Zhou's argument, namely the ambiguity of the definition of "humanism," of which "Chinese thought" is to be an expression. Rather than give it a clear definition, Zhou refers to a few examples of cultures in the broader historical world that manifest it in different forms. He claims that "the Jewish and Indian inclinations toward religion" are expressions of the instinctual human need for collective life "culminating in demands for eternal life and emancipation," that "the establishment of imperialism in Rome" is indicative of the same need recast as "demands for power," and that "in China," that need is affirmed in "a simple secularism."[24] Zhou represents Chinese culture as an expression of a certain universal value rooted in innate human nature, where the latter, however, is not conceptualized per se but manifested in particular cultures as examples. He regards individual cultures as particularities through which the universal manifests itself in actual forms. He uses the same logic when he contends, "Some say we need to preserve the national essence [*guocui* 国粹] and promote Chinese thought. But this kind of argument is a bit different from mine, for national thought proper to China—that is, Confucian thought—is in the first place healthy. Unless China vanishes, this kind of thought will not vanish. Hence, no need of preservation or promotion."[25] The compound "national essence" (Jpn. *kokusui*) was originally coined in Japanese as a translation of the English term "nationality" and throughout the Meiji period gained currency with a strong connotation of anti-Westernization and jingoistic nationalism.[26] When he contends that there is no need for promoting China's national thought, Zhou reconceives of it as a signifier beyond conceptual delineations prone to reifying it as an "essence." He deploys the metaphor of pine trees: if each Chinese individual is a pine tree, then Confucius would be a particularly tall and luxuriant one. The idea of "pine tree," coded in its "seeds" and "roots," is not defined as such or reduced to any one of the actual trees, but a "representative" one like Confucius is helpful in making it understood. Similarly, "Chinese thought" is exemplified in Confucian thought but cannot be grasped in itself independently of its actualizations in living individuals. Chinese thought surpasses and survives particular definitions and achieves healthy "growth"—"unless," that is, "China vanishes."[27]

Zhou had made a similar argument in his 1922 essay "Guocui yu ouhua 国粹與歐化" (National Essence and Europeanization). There he holds that he does not see the point in opposing Europeanization to national essence. He understands "national essence" as "national character [*guominxing* 國民性] as a whole"—or "Chinese thought," in his words from the 1940s—and embraces Europeanization as "a kind of new atmosphere" where it grows, rather than "an injection of new blood into veins."[28] Zhou conceives of "national essence" as national *becoming*, as it were, espousing its "changes" in new environments and envisioning "the creation of an eternal yet always-new national character." He thus imagines China's national identity not in predefined terms but as something in the making, and in this line of reflection, his paradigm is literature. He claims that "national essence" consists of "the inheritance of taste," where "taste" (*quwei* 趣味) is a key concept in his aesthetic thought deriving from late Ming literary theory.[29] He then identifies that which makes its "inheritance" (*yichuan* 遺傳) possible and thus gives it a certain identity in transformation: Chinese characters. He sketches his idea of literary modernity by endorsing "Europeanization" "to the fullest possible extent that the monosyllabic nature of Chinese characters can accept." While championing "free development," he holds that "the possibilities of couplets on both the semantic and acoustic levels cannot be ignored in the national language, and I do believe that the development of parallel regulation is a fatal necessity" even in modern free verse and prose in order to "smelt musical and colorful language."[30] Couplets are a major feature of classical Chinese verse and prose, and he assumes that the feature derives from the nature of Chinese characters and speculates that as long as Chinese literature uses that script, the old prosodic scheme will continue to be developed and featured in new writing, however profoundly it may be "Europeanized."

Zhou arrives at "Chinese characters" as he reflects on Chinese literature and looks for its intrinsic foundational principles separate from external authority—principles that can survive such radical sociopolitical transformations as modernization. He undertakes to identify the unique conditions of Chinese literature by wresting the latter from extrinsic grounds such as politics and moral norms, following in large part the modern idea of aesthetic autonomy. His conjectures thus gesture toward the path of Chinese literature's self-critique, its search for the bare-bones conditions that give it a generic identity. In his criticism, "Chinese characters" do not demarcate a defined realm of Chinese literature but rather constitute an open-ended plane on which Chinese literature incessantly redefines its realm through reflections on its conditions of possibility in response to changing sociopolitical realities. It is safe to say, thus, that "Chinese character" is to Chinese literature in Zhou's criticism what, for instance, "flatness" is to painting in modernist aesthetics.[31] This idea then serves as a paradigm for reconceiving of China's national identity—or "national essence" and "thought"—independent of extrinsic interventions to delineate, "guide," "establish," "preserve," or "promote" it, either for nationalist or imperialist purposes.

The positing of "Chinese characters" as the material condition for Chinese literature implies a view of the literary past that distinguishes Zhou from the mainstream May Fourth discourse of literary revolution. Encapsulating Zhou's idiosyncratic position is his assessment of the much-maligned "eight-legged essay" (*ba gu wen* 八股文), the highly technical and stylized composition genre used in the imperial civil service examinations during the Ming and Qing dynasties. Chen Duxiu 陳獨秀 (1879–1942), for example, in his iconic "Wenxue geming lun 文學革命論" (On Literary Revolution, 1917), singled out this genre as an epitome of the "ornate, sycophantic, pompous, and hollow classical literature" of the past that is shackled with outdated "regulations" and "parallelisms."[32] Many aspects of this genre clash with Hu Shi's well-known eight rules for modern writing advanced in his seminal "Wenxue gailiang chuyi 文學改良芻議" (Some Modest Proposals for the Reform of Literature, 1917).[33]

Vis-à-vis these standard characterizations of the genre as a typical case of obsolete and corrupt literature to be overcome by modernization, Zhou maintained in 1926, "I have always said that literature written in the national language [*guoyu wenxue* 國語文學] is nothing but a new name for literature written in Chinese script [*han wen xue* 漢文學], which contains whatever literature is composed in Chinese script [*han wen* 漢文], even the eight-legged essay and [civil service] examination verse. For these are works that represent special kinds of writing styles, even if they may naturally not have any literary value [by modern standards]."[34] Zhou redefines China's national literature as just a new name for "literature written in Chinese script," or Sinographic literature, and in the same stroke, conjures up the eight-legged essay as an integral part of it, against his May Fourth peers' arguments for dispensing with it. Zhou's defiant evocation of the infamous genre has its roots in his distinct conception of literary history. He suggests that this genre, and the literary culture that it crystalizes, must be carefully remembered and understood because of, rather than instead of, its radical heterogeneity to modern literature. As he writes in 1930,

> The literary revolution in the first years of the Republic, according to my interpretation, may well be considered as a reaction to the "eight-legged essay" culture.... If you ever try to understand the significance of that movement [of literary revolution] without first elucidating what this thing called the eight-legged essay is, then you will be no different from someone ignorant of the history of the Qing dynasty trying to understand the significance of the Republican Revolution. That is entirely impossible.[35]

Hence, "if you do not master the pinnacle of old tradition, then you cannot understand the origin [*qiyuan* 起源] of the new reaction."[36] For Zhou, the eight-legged essay, to the precise extent that the old culture that has already become obsolete culminates in it, is the *origin* of modern Chinese literature. The origin of modern literature resides but in the ruined cultural past.

Zhou's historicization of modern literature squarely undercuts the notion that modern literature pivots on a rupture from the past. He develops the idea of literary tradition in the lecture-based book *Zhongguo xinwenxue de yuanliu* 中國新文學的源流 (Sources of Modern Chinese Literature, 1932), in which he disagrees with Hu Shi's teleological historiography in *Baihua wenxueshi* 白話文學史 (History of Vernacular Literature, 1928). "He [Hu Shi] posits vernacular literature as the only goal of Chinese literature and believes that the previous literatures have also been developing in that direction. With too many obstacles, only now has it entered the right track, but from now on, it will certainly continue to follow it."[37] This is an accurate summary of Hu Shi's idea of literary history, corroborated by the description of Chinese literature as an evolution of vernacular literature from its "seeds" in the Tang dynasty into its full-fledged form in modern times along "a single consecutive line without interruption all the way to the present" (*yixian xiangcheng zhijin bujue* 一線相承，至今不絕).[38] This is but the projection onto the past of a modern idea of literature ("vernacular literature") defined in the first place by a rupture from the past; any previous literatures heterogeneous to that idea are deemed superfluous or "obstacles." Plainly rejecting this narrative, Zhou argues, "literature in China never took a straight path in the past. Instead, like a winding river, it flowed from point A to point B, then again from point B to point A. Every time it encountered resistance, it changed its course."[39]

According to Zhou, Chinese literature has always developed through an oscillation between two opposite tendencies: expressionism or *"shi yan zhi"* 詩言志 (lit., poetry expresses intention) and didacticism or *"wen yi zai dao"* 文以載道 (lit., literature carries the Way). It has advanced in a zigzag path as these two tendencies occurred alternately with one appearing in "reaction" to the previous one. This meandering movement arguably encompasses all genres and forms from pre-Qin classics to modern literature in the Republican period, reflecting the changing literary cultures through history. Expressionism dominates literature when politics descends into turmoil; when the state's power weakens and society's moral norms disappear, literature is cut loose from restraining forces, and everyone can say whatever they want. Didacticism, in contrast, comes to the fore when politics stabilizes and functions so well that it can provide the authority to bolster cultural standards that literature has to abide by. Thus, "the rise and fall in literature generally unfold in the opposite direction of the good and bad in political situations," contends Zhou.[40] Below the surface of this sweeping, and quite notably oversimplifying, categorization into dualistic tendencies, Zhou puts forward a clear and forceful picture of Chinese literary history "based upon contingencies and necessities of a particular historical moment ... constantly reshaping and reorienting itself to adapt to the changing terrain of social life," as Xudong Zhang has put it.[41] Chinese literature in a given era creates a new mode of representation in reaction to its manifestations in the previous period as it engages with new social and political realities. As much as those realities occur unpredictably—and often in ways that appear unjust and absurd to many living individuals, as is the case with dynastic transitions—Chinese literature holds its undulating course. Zhou's description implies a prescription for "modern Chinese literature," which, rather than demarcating itself by temporal severance or by a preconceived notion, should explore new forms that are needed in novel sociopolitical conditions through "reaction" to previous literatures. The Republic's political crisis is but a futile ground for nourishing a new "expressionist" literature in response to previous literatures that have lost all their relevance.

Zhou's reconfiguration of Chinese literature might resonate with Wei-ming Tu's well-known notion of a "cultural China" metaphorized by "a majestic flowing stream." But whereas Tu's mapping, in its championing of the crucial role of the peripheries, still relies on a geopolitical topology to identify its "first" "symbolic universe" with "the societies populated predominantly by cultural and ethnic Chinese" in "mainland China, Taiwan, Hong Kong, and Singapore," Zhou's "winding river" lacks a center in the first place.[42] The diagram in *Sources of Modern Chinese Literature* presents a dotted line passing through the middle of Chinese literature's zigzagging path, with only the remark that "this straight direction ... can only be imagined and does not exist in reality at all."[43] Dislocating the obsession with pinning down a cultural identity, Zhou's cultural criticism posits script as the sole material condition for Chinese culture's identity-in-transformation. Zhou explains how modern literature is unable to sever itself from its Qing-dynasty polar opposite in the eight-legged essay.

> The eight-legged essay, to be sure, is already dead, but it is precisely like that ghost in children's literature; it is chopped into pieces by the hero and becomes completely inactive, but its pieces are still

alive and show ghostly shapes and powers that prove it is not dead. We need to begin by paying attention to Chinese characters. Chinese characters are unlike any other scripts in the world, including those used in Japan or Korea. They have what is known as "the six classifications"; hence pictographs and compound ideographs. They have what is known as "the four tones"; hence level and oblique tones. From these features necessarily emerge quite a few kinds of tricks [*baxi* 把戲] in composition [such as parallelism and regulated prosody]. . . . The eight-legged essay includes all sorts of subtle playfulness [*youxi* 遊戲] that derive from the unique characteristics of Chinese characters themselves.[44]

Chinese literature's self-critique, which leads to a focus on "Chinese characters" as its inalienable condition, allows, on the one hand, for telling its autonomous history while accommodating radical alterations and, on the other, for affirming its fundamental openness to the contingencies of down-to-earth realities as moments for its vital self-transformations. To the extent that Zhou embraces the ghostly haunting of past literature—or even of "Chinese culture" in its entirety, as it is "crystalized" in the eight-legged essay[45]—as an indispensable condition of possibility for literary modernity, he calls for Chinese literature's existential engagement with open-ended reality here and now. At its most advanced moment facing the present world, literary modernity is fundamentally anachronistic. What Zhou deconstructs is dogmatic traditionalism, on the one hand, and the fantasy of a tabula rasa for a new beginning of Chinese literature, on the other.

The paradox resides in the fact that modern literature, no matter how adamantly it endorses novel cultural values, would become yet another version of "Confucianism or Classicism" if that endorsement reflected a pre-conceived "universal demand" or "a ready-made concept" to be realized in writing.[46] Modernity should not become yet another authority to replace classicism. In the 1923 essay "Difang yu wenyi 地方與文藝" (Locality and Literature), Zhou's diagnosis of a shortcoming of China's emergent literature is that it is "too abstract." Accordingly, he calls for "shedding these self-imposed shackles and freely expressing individuality nourished on the ground [*tu* 土]" and continues,

The norms of Confucians and Classicists can produce a kind of universal thought and writing, but since there are no further changes within that universality, they do not have artistic value. This sole fact is enough to give us a lesson. In the fields of thought and literature today, we also have a kind of universal restraint, a certain new conception of life and style, but if we customarily follow them, then they will end up being a modern version of Confucianism or Classicism, initiating a stagnation of thought and literature. What we hope is that we will shed all the restraints and just follow our feelings and sing. No matter how seriously people may write or optimistically they think, and no matter how they talk about patriotism or repaying moral debts, I shall maintain my elegance and lambency. Maybe some satire or exposé? Sure, that's my call, too. Whether I write is for seclusion or resistance, as long as it truly captures my heart that is an amalgamation of the environment I inherited and does not willfully forge something out of prejudicial adherence to opinions or sectarianism, then it by all means has the right and value to be published. That kind of work naturally has the characteristics that it ought to have—that is, it represents the nation, the local, and the individual. All of these are its life.[47]

The "ground," which Zhou adapts from Nietzsche's *"Erde"* in *Zarathustra*, is an anachronistic space where writers can set their individual voices free as they consent to embrace "the inheritance of taste," thereby pushing literature toward a new horizon. It is in this movement that Zhou sees the creation of "artistic value" and pronounces that "literature is universal," where "the universal is simply the greatest extension" that "can encompass vastly many changes, and is never something unaccommodating like a single indivisible number."[48]

Back to the wartime era: Zhou did not alter his position on literature or national essence from the earlier periods but reiterated many of his chief contentions. He repeated his observations on Chinese script as he expressed a preference for the term "Sinographic literature" (*han wen xue* 漢文學) over "Chinese literature" (*Zhongguo wenxue* 中國文學) and attributed its identity not to a "people" but to the script used. For not only the Han but also "the Manchu, the Mongol, and the Muslim peoples as well as quite a few southern and northern ethnic groups" all used Chinese script and produced "a grand current" of literature in China.[49] He also wrote he was concerned only with literature written in Chinese script and not with that penned in a transliteration system like the *zhuyin* or the Roman alphabet. It was script that carried the tradition of Sinographic literature, and if a different script system was adopted, that literature could gradually "leave its tradition."[50] Zhou moreover emphasized the importance of the "political success" of the new literature movement for circulating publications in Chinese script to a broad audience and enabling young people separated by great geographical distances to communicate their feelings and thoughts, regardless of the pedantic strife between traditionalists and modernists over the merits of vernacularization.[51]

Zhou's wartime focus on Chinese script recaptures his earlier conception of Chinese literature as a "universal" tradition embracing radical differences and transformations, while keeping it from being subsumed under extrinsic concepts. Yet with the nation's survival imminently at stake, his position became politically ambivalent. On the one hand, Zhou seems to have genuinely believed that Chinese literature would survive the Japanese invasion and emerge from the crisis in a new form, just as it had reinvented itself throughout history, outlasting every dynasty and outliving numerous foreign invasions and regime changes. Kiyama Hideo has even compared Zhou under Japanese rule to "a Han person serving the Manchu Qing dynasty."[52] For Zhou, Japanese imperialism might have been but yet another round of the sociopolitical turmoil Chinese literature had to survive through its creativity, which he discerned in its long tradition, and ultimately in the medium of Chinese script itself. He regarded it as the ultimate task of a writer to prevent that intrinsic resiliency from being suppressed by an extrinsic authority, be it nationalism or imperialism, and to confront new historical circumstances and express their feelings and thoughts by working the medium into a new form. This idea was premised on the autonomy of literature, which derived from modern aesthetics but also stemmed from the classical distinction between the civil (*wen* 文) and the military (*wu* 武). Chinese thought would sustain itself "unless China vanishes," he wrote; so "what is important about Chinese thought is nothing but avoiding disorder [*luan* 亂]," which, however, is the work of "politics" and not culture or "cultivation" (*jiaohua* 教化)—something "writing and language" cannot do.[53] Disorder was rampant and the nation's existence at stake, but Zhou held politics accountable for the resolution of the crisis. The best a writer could do, then, was to carry on with creating works that would redefine literature in the new era, and the minimum security a writer needed was a personal space behind closed doors, even if, in Zhou's case, it required a reluctant collaboration with the occupiers. The Japanese may have won Zhou's collaboration, but he secured a space for Chinese literary creativity. Collaboration was wrong, and it entailed political risks, personal costs, and moral transgressions. Yet it nevertheless might have been a necessary evil that allowed him to defend the "national essence" defined by the identity-in-transformation of its culture.

On the other hand, Chinese script was also used elsewhere in East Asia, including in Japan, and the Japanese Empire even abused the age-old cultural capital of Chinese letters and ethicopolitical notions of Confucianism in order to assert its universality as distinct from Western-originated civilization. In discussing Chinese script as a powerful medium for communication, Zhou also halfheartedly noted that it would play "not a small role" "in the East Asian cultural sphere" (*dongya wenhua quan* 東亞文化圈), which he marked as "an important problem" to reflect on later.[54] But the "universality" of the Chinese culture that Japanese imperialism recycled is categorically distinct from and indeed deconstructed by the universality Zhou recovered for Chinese literature. The latter is an open-ended movement in which literature transforms itself through reflection on its own conditions of possibility in contingent sociopolitical realities, and in light of it, the former reveals itself as a mere reifying dogmatism that does not allow for such changes but rather is fixated on revivifying the obsolete authority of an old universality. From Zhou's perspective, Japanese imperialism appears as a symptom of modernization and its obsessive severance from the past, leading to a reactionary, fundamentalist revival of the cultural past; the "universalist" exigencies of modernization and regression to fundamentalism share the same allergy to tradition-in-movement that can defy a fixed set of modern cultural norms. Grounding Chinese modernity upon its indissoluble relationship to just such a heterogeneous past, Zhou was able to devise an alternative criticism of Japanese imperialism—one distinguished from nationalist politics and yet uniquely capable of targeting its eclectic, archaist discourse.

THE MORALITY OF EVERYDAY LIFE

On the eve of the outbreak of the Second Sino-Japanese War, Zhou Zuoren penned a group of essays on Japanese culture. This corpus of texts, in light of his idiosyncratic view of cultural tradition, indicates his distinctive thought on regional cultural relationships in East Asia. His ties with Japan were long and deep, dating back to 1906, when he followed his elder brother Lu Xun (Zhou Shuren) and went to Japan on a Qing government scholarship. During the five years he spent in Tokyo, he was active as a young critic and a translator; his translation work culminated in *Yuwai xiaoshuo ji* 域外小說集 (Collection of Short Stories from Beyond Borders, 1909), an anthology with a special focus on Russian, Eastern European, and Northern European short stories that he compiled in collaboration with Lu Xun. Zhou also studied the Greek language at Rikkyo University, laying the foundation for his lifelong interest in ancient Greece. He returned to China in 1911 with a Japanese wife.

Tokyo was a burgeoning modern city for Zhou, serving as a window onto Western civilization as it did for many other students from China and elsewhere in East Asia.[55] Yet unlike many of his peers, Zhou did not view Japan as a mere intermediary. He criticized the widely held notion that "Japanese culture imitated China in premodern times and the West in modern times and it is not worth paying attention to," arguing instead that "Japan has its own civilization" and that "China, due to its particular position, especially has the necessity and possibility of understanding Japan."[56] He further maintained in 1927,

> Whether in studying past culture or creating modern art, China cannot ignore Japan, for [these countries] have formed a kind of inextricable cultural relationship thanks to their communication for over a millennium. If one tries to study Chinese history, culture, literature, or art without knowing this particular situation regarding that country, then topics related to our country in the end will not be very clearly understood and will leave areas that are hard to elucidate. Although Greek studies constitute foundational knowledge for the scholars of Rome, they can also obtain huge information and help from Rome. This precisely resembles the Sino-Japanese relationship in cultural studies.[57]

Japanese literature constitutes the second-largest portion of Zhou's prolific translation work, coming only after Greek literature. The works he translated from Japanese include the eight-century record of myths and historical accounts *Kojiki* 古事記 (Records of the Ancient Matters), medieval *kyōgen* comic plays, and a wide array of modern short stories and criticisms. In 1925, Zhou became the inaugural chair of the Department of Eastern Literature at Beijing University dedicated at that time to research on Japanese literature. In his lasting commitment to the translation and study of Japanese literature, Zhou stood aloof and defiant amid China's turbulent relationship to Japan, filled with calls for boycotting and resistance, especially after the Twenty-One Demands (1915) laid bare Japan's imperialist intentions. He lambasted agents of Japanese imperialism in the military, politics, business, journalism, and education and firmly sided with the popular anger about Japan's arrogance, hubris, and lust for profit and power. Nevertheless, "hoping that scholarship and the study of art should transcend politics," he staunchly continued to advocate for understanding Japanese culture well into the late 1930s.[58]

Reacting to the rapid deterioration of Sino-Japanese relationship into an all-out war, Zhou regretted that "Japan and China, which originally resembled Rome and Greece in terms of their cultural relationship, [had] now become Germany and France in the East."[59] The comparison of the Sino-Japanese and Greco-Roman cultural relationships stems from an observation that China and Greece played comparable roles in the formation of the Japanese and Roman cultures, respectively.[60] This understanding implies Zhou's attempt at teasing out a Sino-Japanese cultural relationship that was not entirely modeled on the relationships between national cultures in the modern sense, especially when Germany and France were on the verge of descending into another war.

Zhou's gaze on Japanese culture was not simply transnational but also archaeological. "In Japan, we [the Chinese] feel as if we are half in a foreign territory and half in the ancient past, and that ancient past actually lives a healthy life in that foreign territory," he wrote.[61] He discovered traces of old customs already lost in China in the everyday life of the ordinary Japanese people; he called that uncanny sense of longing for the lost past "the obscure sensation of nostalgia" (*sigu de youqing* 思古的幽情) after Ban Gu's 班固 (32–92) "Xidu fu 西都賦" (Poetic Exposition on the Western Capital). In the 1935 essay "Riben de yi shi zhu 日本的衣食住"

(Clothing, Food, and Housing in Japan), Zhou weaves Proustian reminiscences of rustic life in his hometown of Shaoxing in southern China with a quasi-ethnography of Japanese customs, drawing on Huang Zunxian's *Riben zashi shi* 日本雜事詩 (Poems on Miscellaneous Aspects of Japan, 1879), among other sources. In this essay, Zhou reveals his fondness for the simplicity and functionality of traditional Japanese houses and perceives Japanese conduct in interior spaces as resonating with the "old rituals" (*guli* 古禮) recorded in classical Chinese materials. He provides a semi-archaeological sketch of the Japanese trousers called *hakama*: "People in ancient Japan wore trousers as in China and the West, and as Japan introduced the culture of the Tang dynasty and reformed its clothes, cylinder-shaped trousers became lamp-shaped; then the bottom of the trousers became even wider and their crotch lower, making today's *hakama*, which is almost shaped like a skirt."[62] He enjoys finding Chinese counterparts to Japanese dishes and ingredients and compares the customs of consuming raw fish in Japan and China: "*Sashimi* is exactly what they call *yusheng* in Canton, while *sushi* is nothing other than what used to be called *yuzha* in the past, whose recipe appears in *Qimin yaoshu* 齊民要術 [The Key Technologies of People's Livelihood]."[63] It is through the impressions of shapes, tastes, movements, and other minute moments in everyday life that he reconstructs an "entirely subjective" cultural archaeology.[64]

In the 1920s, Zhou characterized China's cultural modernity as a "restoration" (*fugu* 復古) or "renaissance" (*fuxing* 復興) of its ancient civilization, which, as he observed, shared a common philosophy about the ideal life with ancient Greek civilization.[65] Inspired by Havelock Ellis's psychology of sex, Zhou sees "the harmony of asceticism and hedonism" at the heart of the ideal way of life and calls it "the art of life." He argues, "China today sorely needs a kind of new freedom and moderation. To build a new Chinese civilization is to revive [*fuxing*] its old civilization from a thousand years ago, and it is also to become one with Greek civilization, which is the foundation of Western civilization." "These words may perhaps sound too big and too lofty," he adds, "but in my opinion, there is no other way to save China."[66] He thus sets the task of China's new culture as revivifying its antiquity that has not yet been "poisoned"[67] by Confucian dogmatism, which he traces back to the rise of Neo-Confucianism in the Song dynasty. Agreeing with Gu Hongming's 辜

鴻銘 (1857–1928) translation of the *Analects*, Zhou proposes the "art of life" as the rendition of the Confucian notion of *li* 禮 (more commonly translated as "ritual"). He holds that the archaic *li* was lost due to its subsequent institutionalization into *liyi* 禮儀 (decorum) and *lijao* 禮教 (Confucian teaching); he implies that the new civilization built on a balance between order and desire, reason and nature should not be "such a strange thing" to the Chinese people, whose philosophical tradition has long understood *li* as conforming to human nature.[68]

None of this means that Zhou was a revivalist. As we saw earlier, he grounded culture on "basic human desire" or human nature as the metaphysical origin of its creativity, considered separately from its historical origin. The imagined antiquity, either in China or in Greece, was a figure of the amalgamation of these two kinds of origins in one. Of further interest here is that Zhou perceived the contemporary way of life in Japan as a tangible and real route back to this idealized antiquity. As Zhou maintains, "Japan, to be sure, received much influence from Song-dynasty scholarship, but life in that country inherits the lineage of the Heian period [794–1185] and retains many flavors of the elegance of the Tang dynasty. This is why Japan more easily understands the art of life. Japan indeed preserves flavors of that art in many of its customs, which is hard to emulate for us the Chinese."[69] Alluding to ancient Japan's avid adoption of Chinese cultures, Zhou discerns in that nation's contemporary everyday life remnants of Chinese antiquity that are unsullied by the later-era dogmatization of Confucianism and the ossified or corrupt institutions and customs like eunuchs, foot-binding, the eight-legged essay, and opium, which, as he claims, Japan did not introduce into its culture.[70]

Zhou's unflagging cross-cultural and archaeological attention to Japanese culture points to a transregional perspective of his cultural criticism that bespeaks a distinctive approach to cultural comparison in general and an unconventional envisioning of "new Chinese civilization" in particular. The 1936 piece titled "Huai Dongjing 懷東京" (Remembering Tokyo) helps elucidate his perspective. This essay is an affectionate and nostalgic recollection of life in Tokyo some three decades ago when he studied in that city. Building upon "Clothing, Food, and Housing in Japan," it combines excerpts from Japanese authors' writings on the city with his own "personal miscellanea and occasional feelings."[71] Among the quoted works is Nagai Kafū's 永井荷風 (1879–1959) essay "Ukiyoe no kanshō 浮世絵の鑑賞" (Appreciation of *Ukiyoe*, 1913) from his *Edo geijutsu ron* 江戸芸術論 (On Edo Art, 1920). Zhou cites Kafū's understanding of the Japanese woodblock painting *ukiyoe* in comparison to seventeenth-century Dutch painting as it is depicted in the Belgian symbolist poet Émile Verhaeren's (1855–1916) poem "Art Flamand" in *Les flamandes* (1883).[72]

In "Appreciation of *Ukiyoe*," Kafū extols "the abundance of worldly desires," particularly the carnal imagery of female figures, depicted in Verhaeren's poetic homage to Dutch painting. "Art Flamand" renders queens, goddesses, and other mythological characters as voluptuous and sensuous female bodies, "sweat[ing] health" that is "red of blood, white of fat" ("suaient la santé, / Rouge de sang, blanche de graisse"). Kafū dismisses the notion of obscenity and commends Verhaeren's materialistic representation of the bodies, arguing that the poet "freed himself from the conventional moral and religious barriers centered on purity and asceticism and regarded the fulness of life [*seikatsu* 生活] and the elevation of will as the true significance of human life [*jinsei* 人生]."[73] In Verhaeren's poeticization of Dutch painting, Kafū praises portrayals of life that are liberated from moral and religious confines and appreciates material depictions of textures and colors as the utmost expression of the meaning of secular life. For this, Kafū calls Verhaeren a poet from "a free nation," which has "recently made a great leap toward seizing the civilization of the nineteenth century after breaking the shackles of Spanish rule."[74]

Kafū's reading of Verhaeren's poem echoes with the pages of Hegel's *Aesthetics* that also treat Dutch painting. In Hegel's account, Dutch painting is positioned in the most modern phase of the secularization and humanization of art in the post-Reformation era, when art sought to "get a sure footing in the prose of life, to make it absolutely valid in itself independently of religious associations, and to let it develop in unrestricted freedom."[75] Freed from religious subject matter, Dutch art is able to portray the prosaic details of everyday life, attending to "the most transitory and fugitive material," giving it "permanence for our contemplation in the fullness of its life." Art becomes "mastery in the portrayal of all the secrets of this ever profounder pure appearance of external realities"; "the chief thing now—independently of the topic itself—is the subjective re-creation of the external world in the visible element of colors and lighting."[76]

Kafū characterizes *ukiyoe* by contrasting it with Dutch painting, pointing to its colors that show "pale, dull hues" like "a flicker of lamplight," as opposed to oil painting's "dazzling colors" like "the glare of the scorching sun." In these polar-opposite tones, Kafū recognizes two different kinds of national "spirits" allegorized: on the one hand, there are Dutch tones with strong meanings and statements indicating the spirit of a free nation, and on the other, there are Japanese "sleepy colors" that are but a reflection of "the people's shrunken minds in an authoritarian age."[77] However, in a quintessentially dialectical move, Kafū turns this dichotomy upside down and discloses his twisted affection for Japanese *ukiyoe* in the passage that Zhou cites in "Remembering Tokyo."

> But I look back at who I am and find that I was not a Belgian like Verhaeren but a Japanese. I am an Asian [*tōyōjin* 東洋人], whose fates and circumstances are naturally different. I live under laws that render all carnal sensations with regard to the opposite sex, not to mention the sincerest feeling of love, into the greatest evil of society. I was told that I should not rival the landlord or a crying child. I belong to a nation that knows that "arguments make your lips chilled." I do not care about the juicy lamb meat, the flavorful wine, or the fleshy beautiful women that excite Verhaeren. Ah! Instead, I love *ukiyoe*. The picture of a prostitute, sold by her parents, enduring a decade of suffering makes me shed tears. The image of a geisha idly watching running water through a bamboo lattice makes me pleased. The night scene of the waterfront lit by the lonesome lamps of a nocturnal noodle stall makes me tipsy. The cuckoo crying under the moon in a rainy night, the autumn leaves falling in a drizzle, the sound of a bell fading in the winds carrying flower petals, the snow on the hilly path in the dusk—these things are transient, unreliable, and hopeless, making me lament in vain that the world is but a dream. I am attached to them all; I yearn for them all.[78]

Kafū distinguishes himself from Verhaeren using the conventional dichotomy between the East (authoritarianism) and the West (freedom), but that distinction liberates him from the authority—or a constructed aesthetic standard—of Dutch painting, allowing him to cast an appreciative gaze on *ukiyoe*.

Indeed, Kafū's affectionate sensitivity to *ukiyoe*'s "transient, unreliable, and hopeless" scenes and images in turn resonates with Hegel's loving attention to "the most transitory and fugitive material" in Dutch genre painting. Like Kafū, Hegel especially values everyday scenes of "the down-to-earth life of the lower class" portrayed in Flemish and German painting—such as "scenes in the tavern," "weddings and other merrymaking peasants," "domestic affairs," and "portraits and objects in nature such as landscapes, animals, flowers, etc."[79] Dutch painting thus raises the question of what constitutes a work of art. Before this movement, art's subject matter was never "inherently arbitrary or transient" and its mode of portrayal was "fully in correspondence" with the content, but Dutch painting foregrounds "the artist's subjective conception and execution"—that is, "the aspect of the individual talent which can remain faithful both to the manifestations of spirit and also to the inherently substantial life of nature, even in the extreme limits of the contingency which that life reaches, and can make significant even what is in itself without significance."[80] This analysis, in its discernment of the aesthetic will to form in Dutch painting's grasping of significance in the insignificance of the everyday, is repeated in Kafū's appreciation of *ukiyoe*. Hegel sees in Dutch painting, through its emancipation from past religious authority, the emergence of art's intrinsic aesthetic value and artistic attention to the contingent and transient realities of everyday life. Kafū discovers in Edo *ukiyoe*, through its differentiation from the authority of Western art, the aesthetic value particular to this genre and its singular capacity to portray the on-the-ground life of Edo commoners, afflicted as it is by oppression and misery. By the standards of art in the Renaissance and before, Dutch genre painting "undoubtedly fall[s] far short,"[81] and likewise by the criteria of Dutch painting (as presented by Verhaeren), *ukiyoe* is so "pale," so "dull," and displays so "shrunken" a mind that it would not qualify as art. If Hegel rediscovers Dutch painting in a secular age when religious authority is dead, Kafū reaffirms the intrinsic value of *ukiyoe* on an "Asian" land where European-originated values like "freedom" and "justice"[82] die because of ingrained "authoritarianism." Kafū claims that "rational eyes" will unveil "the spirit of military rule unaltered at all from a hundred years ago" below the surface of the rampant "mimicry of Western civilization" in modern Japan, and that, in contrast to the survival of authoritarianism beneath Westernization, "the sorrowful colors of Edo woodblock painting seep into the bottom of my heart and always convey intimate whispers without a slightest temporal distance."[83] Thus for Kafū, the *ukiyoe* creators' pictorial execution, capable of giving aesthetic expression ("intimate whispers") to everyday life under social oppression—of "mak[ing] significant even what is in itself without significance"—provides an exemplar for envisioning a "new national music" and "new national art" that have yet to be created for modern Japan.[84] It is therefore in *ukiyoe*, "produced by townspeople as minute as insects in rented houses in sunless alleys," that Kafū distinguishes "the victory of true and free art," an expression of "the will of the commoners defying persecution by the government"—a victory that the academic Kanō school, which was patronized by the shogunate, was unable to attain.[85] Kafū's dialectical admiration of aesthetic freedom in *ukiyoe*, therefore, repeats Hegel's illumination, in the dusk of the history of Western art, of a manifestation of *"Humanus"* as art's "new holy of holies; i.e., the depths and heights of the human heart as such, mankind in its joys and sorrows, its strivings, deeds, and fates."[86]

Having cited Kafū, Zhou Zuoren remarks that foreign readers do not have to feel the same "lament and resentment" that the Japanese writer articulates toward his own country. Yet he adds, "That is true, but indeed, not quite true. For there are many similar aspects in the background lives, and artistic expressions coming out of them often make one feel as if 'you and I are like them.'"[87] Referring to a phrase ("you and I are like them") attributed to the Ming dynasty philosopher Wang Yangming 王陽明 (1472–1529), who reportedly uttered it to tell his subordinates to take time to bury dead bodies on the roadside, Zhou suggests that *ukiyoe* as Kafū appreciates it should provoke empathy and has existential implications that would not be "foreign" to the Chinese audience. Zhou continues,

> China and Japan are now in the positions of enemies, but setting aside their current relationship and considering their eternal natures, they are both Asian peoples whose fates and circumstances are naturally vastly different from the West. Some fascism addicts in Japan may be thinking their nation's happiness has become at

least equal to, if not greater than, that of the West and feeling a bit of regret at not having been able to annex Asia yet. But artists are meanwhile feeling the sorrow of "arguments make your lips chilled." And that is precisely the sorrow of the Asians [*dongyangren zhi beiai* 東洋人之悲哀]. I personally cannot but feel bewildered by hearing it.... I can secretly feel the sorrow concealed [in Edo music and art]. They do not represent the sorrow of the Chinese people, but it cannot be said that they do not include part of it in them. For what they indicate ... is in the end the sorrow of the Asians.[88]

Drawing on the notion of "Asia" in Kafū, Zhou carefully probes ways to make sense of China's relationship to Japan that can account for his deeply felt sympathy with Edo art. Being "Asians" means that China is not entirely "foreign" to Japan, but it does not make a firm self-identity with which they could "represent" each other; instead, it consists in a certain resemblance, here articulated in terms of living a life ("fates and circumstances") in submission, short of the freedoms of a modern individual. This life should not evoke a desire to emulate the West in a way that preserves authoritarianism and entails self-denial, as some "fascism addicts" in Japan do by "annex[ing] Asia," but should rather become uniquely ripe grounds for self-affirmation through creating novel modes of representation as a critique of powerful cultural norms, modes capable of "secret[ly]" imparting the "concealed" feelings of their lived lives. Zhou, through Kafū's perspective, appreciates that the "art of the ordinary people [*pingmin yishu* 平民藝術] in Japan seems to be good at embracing deep sorrow in a beautiful form."[89]

"Ordinary people" is a key concept in Zhou's criticism from early on, designating the agent of modern literature and art. In 1919, he defined "literature of the ordinary people" as "literature that studies ordinary people's lives, or human life" and proclaimed that its objective was not to "try to forcefully push down a thought or taste of humanity to make it fit the ordinary people" but to "elevate ordinary people's lives to their suitable [*shidang* 適當] places."[90] Put in the context of this early discussion, Zhou's reading of Kafū's art criticism implies his prescription for a "new Chinese civilization," for whose creation the culture of ordinary Japanese people in general and *ukiyoe* in particular serve as examples. Zhou elsewhere admired "the beauty of human feelings" expressed in "the way the Japanese drink tea and look after trees and flowers" and agreed with Watsuji Tetsurō 和辻哲郎 (1889–1960) in praising its ancient history *Kojiki* as an "artwork" displaying an "affective view of human life."[91] Zhou's appreciation of Japanese culture indicates a critique of the kind of modern culture that claims its distinction by espousing external universal values or an abstract "thought or taste of humanity," and endorses a new culture that originates as it should in ordinary life and "elevates" it by expressing its significance as human life in a form of special beauty. For to live an ordinary life is to be a human enduring particular fates and circumstances.

Whereas Zhou liked to put into his essays the rustic life and customs of his hometown and its environs in southern China and the lifestyle of Beijing, quite uniquely among his contemporary peers he expressed a particular fondness for life in Tokyo.[92] That Japan served as an exemplary location for his envisioning of a new Chinese culture has a twofold implication. First, Zhou's discourse precludes the locations of culture from being appropriated by a defined national space. It conceives of those locations as rooted in the lives of ordinary people who seek affirmation of their ways of life in actual sociopolitical realities in new forms of culture yet to be created. Those ways of life are the sedimentation of past customs and tastes, and in the case of China and Japan, they are formed through long-term cultural exchanges across borders rather than simply molded in an imagined national community, and thus present curious resemblances, subtle sympathy, and even nostalgia. Zhou's cultural criticism conceives of "Asia" as an archaeological topology where such cultural terrains exist in a palimpsestic relationship with each other without being completely territorialized by a national historical consciousness. Against the modern identification that bred political enmity and human suffering, Zhou rescues such border-defying cultural localities as indispensable grounds for new culture via its methodological detour through Japan.

Zhou's cultural criticism thus affirms cultural locations in historically grounded, multilayered relationships that are irreducible to self-conscious nation-to-nation relations in their modern sense. This leads to the second implication of his transregional perspective: the envisaging of an organization of the modern world as an alternative to the Eurocentric status quo. In one of his most idealistic moments, Zhou wrote about Japan in 1919,

Before the [Meiji] Restoration, Japan learned many things from China and nourished a "Confucian" country, causing all sorts of harm to family and society; after the Restoration, it learned things from Germany and nourished a "statist" country, bringing about many different kinds of damage domestically and internationally. Now that these two teachers—China and Germany—themselves have collapsed . . ., what will Japan do? Will it still collect scrap materials in their ruins to support the old building? Will it instead seek a third teacher and learn to rebuild? For the sake of the interests of the people of their neighboring country and those of their own, I hope—and indeed believe—that Japan's new people [*xinren* 新人] will follow a peaceful and just path. The third teacher will be able to lead humanity to build a "third land" or heaven on earth, where human life [*renjian de shenghuo* 人間的生活] will be realized. Japan and China doubtless share the character and opportunity to enjoy this happiness.[93]

"Whether this hope may end up as a fanciful 'ideal,' it is too early to know," Zhou remarks, "but today I have a very strong belief in it."[94] Put back in the context of the rise of anti-Japanese nationalism in the aftermath of the First World War, Zhou's comment here might sound as hollow as it does utopian, and in historical hindsight, his idealism betrays a certain political naïveté, given Japan's ensuing imperialization in the name of making East Asia into a "co-prosperity" sphere. Yet this ambivalence enables us to assess the critical stakes of Zhou's discourse by considering what it is about his idealism that was not realized in actual history.

For Zhou Zuoren, it is because Japan also finds itself in the minor position of "Asia" that its culture serves as an exemplar for what he prescribes for Chinese modernity. Yet Japan's eventual fall into imperialism indicates that it suppressed, in the course of its cultural self-affirmation, the possibility for other Asian peoples to pursue it in their ordinary lives in their particular sociopolitical circumstances. As Japan worked itself into a successful nation-state, it turned its pasts into a self-conscious narrative of history that, as Stefan Tanaka has argued, invented "Japan's Orient" as "an object, an idealized space and time from which Japan developed" into a modern subject.[95] This new episteme projected assumed "cultural difference[s]" onto Asia and included them in a synthetic story of Japan's development in world history: Asia, to adapt Okakura Tenshin's 岡倉天心 (1863–1913) famous formulation, was reduced to a mere "museum of Asiatic civilization" that was itself Japan.[96] This discourse repeated Hegel's philosophy of history, which, while recognizing secular society in Europe as an agent of world history, deprived Asia of freedom and hence of historical agency.[97] In contradistinction, Zhou's discourse explores historically sedimented relationships between ordinary people's lives in China and Japan that are irreducible to simple "cultural difference" or to a relationship between self-conscious national cultures, committing to the universal ethical value of "human life" that calls for every people's unconditional right to enjoyment of intrinsic happiness in their ordinary lives and to cultural self-affirmation. It then reimagines the world not as a "world history" in the Hegelian sense but as an open-ended universality ("a third land") to which no subject has an exclusive claim at any historical moment—a universality that cannot be conceptually appropriated but is only aesthetically suggested by exemplars or cultural expressions of subtle beauty that defy the established aesthetic norms. Neither Japan, China, nor any other nation has a privileged view of the world thus reimagined; only an anonymous "third teacher" might.

Zhou's archaeological interest in the inextricable cultural relationship between the East Asian neighbors and his personal admiration of the beauty of Japanese culture distinguish his discourse from cultural nationalism. It proclaims Japanese culture to be a mere example of the coming "peaceful and just" world in which China will also take part, and it thereby casts Japan out of its self-appointed role of carrying out a "world-historical mission." Zhou's wartime essays on Japanese culture are distinctly personal, ad hoc, and even impressionistic, but as modest as they appear on the surface, they constitute a powerful structural critique of the imperialism into which Japan was quickly descending.

The two aspects of Zhou Zuoren's work are, if not exactly two sides of the same coin, complementary: the reconceptualization of modern literature in China in its fundamental ties to previous literatures, on the one hand, and the appreciation of Japanese culture as an exemplar of cultural creativity in Asia, on the other. He envisions modern literature in

China in the inalienable material condition of Chinese characters, which locates literary creativity at the intersection of the present sociopolitical exigencies and the surviving cultural habitus. His staunch defense of creativity unrestrained by imposed values or norms, namely politicized national consciousness, informs his archaeological recovery of multilayered cultural pasts and motivates his humanist commitment to a universalism of "human life." In the border-defying reality of the sedimentation of ways of life, he acknowledges every ordinary people's right to happiness and cultural self-affirmation—an unconditional universalism that constitutes a critique of the particular universalism of modern civilization in its status quo. His appreciation of the aesthetic expressions of ordinary lives, whose example he sees in Japan, crystalizes in his conceptualization of Asia as a space pregnant with creative potentialities, where the affirmation of one people's secular freedom does not fall into imperialism against another. His critical discourse on modern literature in China in its inextricable reaction to previous writings, originating on the ruins of the cultural past, provides a model for his cultural criticism, which he stubbornly upheld despite its dubious political implications on the eve of and into the wartime era as the practice of an archaeology of resistance to Japanese imperialism in a transnational *longue dureé* of culture in East Asia.

But against the backdrop of the rise of the Japanese Empire, what attitude did Zhou have toward his own work, which seems to be shot through with an unapologetic spirit of criticism divorced from concern for political action? In a sequel to "Clothing, Food, and Housing in Japan," Zhou wrote in 1936 "Riben guankui zhi san 日本管窺之三" (My Humble View on Japan III), where he redoubled his attention to the expression of "the beauty of human feelings" (*renqing zhi mei* 人情之美) in Japanese culture, this time even in the life of *samurai* (*wushi* 武士). He concludes this essay on a pessimistic note, however:

> Understanding a country's culture is of course difficult, but it also makes you melancholic [*jimo* 寂寞]. If you always pay attention only to cultures of the past, you cannot help but become overeager. However, they often not only disagree but quite simply conflict with reality, and this likely makes you feel contradicted and disappointed. . . . Those who study culture would like to see culture everywhere, but

that is impossible. Japanese culture is not an exception. Thus, those who cannot endure melancholy should not begin to study it, for if you are overenthusiastic, you will want to match the culture in mind to the reality in front of you—a recipe for abandoning your study due to contradiction and disappointment.... This sort of conclusion may sound dark and discouraging, but it is absolutely sincere and truthful, as it derives from my own experience.[98]

Zhou regards *jimo*, which I translate here as "melancholy" to suggest its distant echo with Benjamin's study of Baroque tragedy, as a necessary attitude for the cultural critic (see chapter 6). Melancholy is a symptom of the work of recollecting cultural pasts that have been ruined in modernity; as Zhou articulates, it means the endurance of irreducible conflicts between past and present as the sole ground for the work of a critic. As I have been arguing in this book, such endurance—or attempts to reconstruct, out of contradictions and disappointment, the present's historical relationship with the past—underpins the creation of modern literature. Zhou's cultural criticism in this sense embodies an origin of this genre in East Asia and its potency as a structural critique of Japanese imperialism.

Zhou's advice to the cultural critic to "endure melancholy" will inform my inquiry in this book's final chapter on transregional literary exchanges in Korea, Taiwan, and Manchukuo in the late colonial period.

CHAPTER SIX

Transnational Allegory

Intertextualizing Lu Xun in Late Colonial Korean, Taiwanese, and Manchukuo Literatures

Upon the outbreak of the Second Sino-Japanese War in 1937, Japan enhanced its policies for cultural integration across the imperium to bolster its escalating war efforts in mainland China, Southeast Asia, and the Pacific. Literary productions in colonial Korea and Taiwan, as has been demonstrated in previous scholarship, had formed multilingual fields involving various forms of the Korean and Sinitic languages, in addition to Japanese as the imperial language.[1] Those productions were put under ever-tightening restrictions, and colonial authors were more and more compelled to adopt the Japanese language and write for Japanese-language outlets.[2] As a result, literature in colonial Korea and Taiwan became increasingly integrated into the literary culture of the metropole. Beyond linguistic assimilation, a growing number of translations, anthologies, and criticisms enabled "colonial literature" to circulate among metropolitan audiences.[3] Literary prizes awarded to colonial authors also played an important role in including colonial literatures in the broader field of "Japanese-language literature."[4]

Manchuria, the area that is now northeastern China, became a battleground for competing warlords upon the collapse of the Qing dynasty in 1911 and was nominally subsumed under the sovereignty of the Republic of China in 1928. It offered a multilingual terrain for literary production for Chinese-, Japanese-, and Korean-speaking settler writers in the 1920s, and linguistic diversity remained a hallmark of literature in this borderland even after the Japanese military occupation commenced with the Manchurian Incident in 1931 and the puppet state Manchukuo was established in the following year.[5] Unlike in Korea and Taiwan, the imperial authorities did not impose linguistic assimilation on Manchukuo, and instead allowed the residents to use their native tongues while expecting them to learn Japanese.[6] The Dalian-based faction of Japanese ideologues even argued for the autonomous development of literature in Manchuria independent of imperial policies.[7] They posited the "distinctiveness" of literature in Manchukuo as separate from literature in mainland Japan; a radical opinion suggested that even literature written by Japanese settlers should "transmute into a Manchukuo national literature [*manshū minzoku bungaku* 満洲民族文学]."[8]

In the late 1930s, however, these positions supporting the autonomy and distinctiveness of Manchukuo literature gradually lost ground to more centralized control and imperial guidance, advocated by ideologues based in Shinkyō (Chn. Xinjing), the then capital of Manchukuo and today's Changchun.[9] The statewide artists' association Bunwakai 文話會 began working closely with the authorities and eventually became the state-sanctioned Bungeika kyōkai 文藝家協會 in 1941. This society was founded following the infamous "Outline for the Guidance of Art and Literature" (*geibun shidō yōkō* 藝文指導要綱) put forward by Kōhōsho 弘報處, the newly incorporated state bureau in charge of the centralized administration of propaganda and censorship. The "Outline" explicitly stipulated that art and literature in Manchukuo must manifest the spirit of the Japanese Empire and asserted that Japanese art and literature were "the best" and should "guide" the arts and literatures of the world. Meanwhile, multiple translations and anthologies were published to introduce literature written by multiethnic writers in Manchukuo to metropolitan readers.[10] In the late colonial period, multilingual Manchukuo literature was thus put under tight ideological control and increasingly circulated into mainland Japan, contributing, together with colonial Korean and Taiwanese literatures, to the creation of the integrated literary sphere of a broader imperium. This happened against the backdrop of the promulgation of the "New East Asian Order" by the first Konoe Cabinet in 1938, which called for cooperation among Japan and its colonies (Korea and Taiwan), Manchukuo, and the collaborationist government in China to aid in the protracted war in mainland China. This

Transnational Allegory 239

policy laid a stepping-stone for the notorious proclamation of the "Greater East Asian Co-Prosperity Sphere" by the second Konoe Cabinet in 1940, which envisioned an expanded imperial bloc in preparation for a total war against the Western powers.[11]

The growing circulation and representation of colonial literatures in the metropole integrated Korea, Taiwan, and Manchukuo into an enlarged literary field centered on the imperial capital Tokyo. Colonial literatures were appreciated for meaningful *differences* they brought to the empire's literature, increasing the value of the cultural capital of Japanese-language literature. The aggravating political interventions in the late colonial period, therefore, engendered a caricatured "regional empire of letters" in which literary representation, circulation, and reception all risked adding further value to the empire-sanctioned cultural capital. As colonial literatures were reduced to mere expressions of "local color" (*chihō shoku* 地方色) or to works from the "outer territories" (*gaichi* 外地) as opposed to the "inner territories" (*naichi* 内地; i.e., mainland Japan), those literatures were led to become complicit with the "strategies of differential inclusion" that underpinned the Japanese Empire's racial ideology.[12]

Yet the emergent "East Asian literary field" involved complex textual motions that are not entirely accounted for by the interplays between the center and the peripheries.[13] One symbolic example is the anthology *Shanling: Chaoxian Taiwan duanpian ji* 山靈: 朝鮮台灣短篇集 (The Mountain Soul: A Collection of Korean and Taiwanese Short Stories, 1936) edited by Hu Feng 胡風 (1902–1985), which collects in Chinese translation Japanese-language short stories by colonial Korean and Taiwanese authors that were originally published and well received in the metropole. In editing this anthology, Hu Feng was echoing the discourse of the "literatures of weak nations," which had its roots in Lu Xun's early criticism and translation work and stirred up avid interest among a left-wing readership in Shanghai in the 1930s.[14] Hu gleaned otherwise inaccessible works by Korean and Taiwanese authors from Japanese publications and presented them to Chinese audiences, hoping that they would "read 'foreign' stories as [their] own situations." Through Hu's translation and editing, works that had presented colonial literature to a metropolitan readership were re-presented as works that allegorized the common realities of oppressed peoples, as literature necessary for saving

China and "securing peace in Asia."[15] Another example of transcolonial exchanges appeared in Manchukuo in 1940. A Chinese-language literary journal based in Fengtian (today's Shenyang) called *Zuofeng* 作風 (Style) ran a special issue on translated literature that featured three Korean short stories in Chinese translation. Likely relay-translated via existing Japanese renditions, those works joined five more Korean works in translation in the anthology *Chaoxian duanpian xiaoshuo xuan* 朝鮮短篇小說選 (Collection of Korean Short Stories) edited by Wang He 王赫 (years unknown) and published in Xinjing in 1941. In putting together *Style*'s special issue, which was the journal's only published tome due to censorship, the editor, probably familiar with Hu Feng's compilation, indicated that it followed the model of the collections of literature from weak nations popularized in Shanghai in the 1930s.[16] Wang He, in the postface to his anthology, expressed the belief that his work would send "one of the greatest expressions of empathy and encouragement" to Korean writers who had endured three decades of hardship under Japanese rule.[17] Japanese oppression raised awareness of the need for transcolonial literary exchanges and gave new allegorical significance to colonial Korean literature for Manchukuo's Chinese readership.

These examples of interperipheral textual exchanges are at once enabled by and in conflict with the construct of the imperial literary field centered on the metropole. Through transcolonial translation and anthologizing, texts stop presenting themselves to metropolitan audiences and begin assuming new meanings for colonized people. On a conceptual level, these examples cogently bespeak texts' inalienable ability to transgress contextual boundaries and its intrinsic openness to allegorical meanings. Through dissemination into a distant context, texts alter their cultural belonging and political allegiances.

Inspired by these cases, I explore in this chapter the allegorical functions of late colonial Korean, Taiwanese, and Manchukuo literatures by focusing on their intertextualizations of Lu Xun's works. I use the notion of "intertextuality" to draw on the concept's original implication of resistance to monologism and to illustrate how Lu Xun's writings as intertexts open the late colonial works to semantic resonances that undercut the imperial desire for unified signification.[18] My focus on these intertextualizations is also meant to invite reflection on the significance of the origins of modern literature in East Asia beyond established concepts of history. Through their late colonial disseminations, Lu Xun's writings reveal themselves as a *transnational* allegory. Here I want to evoke Walter Benjamin's notion of the "origin" as particularly pertinent to this final stage of our inquiry:

> Origin [*Ursprung*], although an entirely historical category, has, nevertheless, nothing to do with genesis [*Entstehung*]. The term origin is not intended to describe the process by which the existent came into being, but rather to describe that which emerges from the process of becoming and disappearance. Origin is an eddy in the stream of becoming, and in its current it swallows the material involved in the process of genesis. That which is original is never revealed in the naked and manifest existence of the factual; its rhythm is apparent only to a dual insight. On the one hand it needs to be recognized as a process of restoration and reestablishment, but, on the other hand, and precisely because of this, as something imperfect and incomplete. There takes place in every original phenomenon a determination of the form in which an idea will constantly confront the historical world, until it is revealed fulfilled, in the totality of its history. Origin is not, therefore, discovered by the examination of actual findings, but it is related to their history and their subsequent development.[19]

Benjamin's idea is especially relevant to the way "modern literature" as a genre originated in East Asia. This literature was not an "existent" object that appeared on a readymade stage of history; instead, it was a process that tried to make sense of the very history from which it emerged. No extraliterary concept can fully define modern literature in East Asia and thus capture its origin "in the naked and manifest existence of the factual." Its origin has rather had to be elucidated within the process of its critical engagement with past cultures: it reused, parodied, and repeated the cultural past so as to find historical grounds for reconsidering "literature" itself, as if it "emerge[d] from the process of becoming and disappearing" or formed a "current" that "swallow[ed] the material involved." We have not only witnessed moments of "restoration and reestablishment" but also attended to "something imperfect and incomplete" in the works whose newness could not entirely be explicated by their adherence to extrinsic models or standards. By exploring this process, we have illuminated the "determination of the form[s]" that the idea of "modern literature" took in confronting "the historical world" involving the transnational sedimentations of East Asian cultures.

Having thus examined modern literature as it originated in the afterlives of classical cultures, I will in this chapter delve into its "subsequent development" (*Nachgeschichte*) by considering the transcolonial afterlives of Lu Xun's works. In doing so, I seek to further refine our picture of the process by which modern literature took form in East Asia without postulating its totality in a grand narrative of modernization. If the classic Jamesonian interpretation of Lu Xun's works as a Chinese case of "national allegory" is premised on a Hegelian-Marxist idea of world history,[20] then my concept of *transnational* allegory makes it possible to revisit them against the backdrop of the utter futility of Japan's self-assigned "world historical" mission to create an alternative modernity, or amid the broken totality of the historical world. Allegory for Benjamin can be illustrated by the figure of the "ruin" where the dead elements of antiquity were used, "item by item," to "reconstruct" a "new whole" by the melancholic Baroque allegorists.[21] Echoing this image, Lu Xun's texts were disseminated and brought into a new constellation by colonial writers as allegories that, beyond an established conception of history, illuminate a transnational formation of modern literature in East Asia.

Hu Feng, in the preface to his anthology *Mountain Soul*, described his translation work as taking place in a collapsing world:

> I still remember I grabbed moments late at night to work on almost all of these translations. Tranquility surrounded me; urban noises left me afar. Only occasionally did I hear the sad and weak voices of street snack vendors. I gradually found myself among the characters in the story, crushed under that grand devilish palm that they were enduring; I was suffering and struggling with them. And I sometimes even felt as if the whole world [*zhengge shijie* 整個世界] was falling apart around me.[22]

Facing the looming arrival of a "new order" propagated by the imperialists, the translator, alone on a deserted night in Shanghai, finds himself in a world that is falling apart. The foreign story he renders appears to his melancholic gaze to be an allegory of his own embattled situation in a declining world, visualized as "crushed under [a] grand devilish palm." His transcolonial anthology, then, may be construed as an assemblage of stories to reconstruct a new historical whole. Wang He, for his part, emphasizes that "we and Korea, whether historically or geographically, have an everlasting and tight relationship" and positions his anthology as part of a wider Sino-Korean relationship beyond particularities of modern times, where each nation regrettably knows little about the lives and minds of the other.[23] Inspired by those attempts, my transcolonial inquiry will be guided by Lu Xun's works as intertexts and will examine Korean, Taiwanese, and Manchukuo writings as allegories that together point to a disposition where those texts manifest the historical significance of modern literature in the region.

Lu Xun was introduced to colonial Korea and Taiwan, often via Japanese materials, shortly after the May Fourth movement (1919).[24] Lu Xun played an instrumental role in publishing in Shanghai works by writers who were exiled from northeastern China in the aftermath of the 1931 Japanese military occupation, and his writings, despite censorship, continued to be received by a Chinese readership in the region after the puppet state was founded.[25] Lu Xun's oeuvre thus constituted a crucial thread in the literary interplays in and around the Japanese Empire.[26] My focus in this chapter is on the intertextualization of Lu Xun's works in late colonial writings by Kim Saryang, Long Yingzong, and Gu Ding, who were active in colonial Korea, Taiwan, and Manchukuo, respectively. These writers, to different degrees and in different manners, adapted to the ideological construct of the literary fields in the Japanese Empire and attained prominent recognition in them. Yet the intertextuality in their writings, especially their references to Lu Xun's works, provides a window onto the dialogic workings of their language, and hence their resistance to imperial cultural intervention.

LU XUN AND TRANSCOLONIAL INTERTEXTUALITY

I begin my inquiry with a rare documentation of transcolonial literary exchanges in the form of personal correspondence. The letter was penned in Japanese by Kim Saryang and sent to Long Yingzong in 1941.[27] Born in 1914 in Pyongyang, Kim Saryang went to Japan to attend high school in Kyushu in 1933 and entered Tokyo Imperial University in 1935, where he majored in German literature and graduated with a thesis on Heinrich Heine while participating in the activities of the Tokyo-based Korean drama company Korean Artistic Theater (*Chōsen geijutsu za* 朝鮮藝術座). Kim began writing stories as a student and gained overnight fame when his debut piece "Hikari no nakani 光の中に" (Into the Light), written in Japanese and published in the journal *Bungei shuto* 文藝首都 (Literary Capital), was nominated for the prestigious Akutagawa Literary Prize in 1939. While he also wrote in Korean, Kim had gained recognition by the time he sent this letter as one of the most prolific and established colonial Korean writers in the Japanese-language literary field.

The letter's addressee Long Yingzong, born in 1911 into a Hakka family in Hsinchu, received most of his education in Japanese-built public schools. His literary talent was discovered early on by his school teachers and flourished when he began writing stories in Japanese while working for a bank after graduating from a commercial college in Taipei. In 1937, Long sent his maiden short story, titled "Papaiya no aru machi パパイヤのある街" (A Village with Papaya Trees), to the magazine *Kaizō* 改造 (Reform) based in Tokyo and won second place in its fiction competition. He is said to have submitted his debut manuscript to *Reform* because of the honorable mention that the Korean writer Chang Hyŏkchu 장혁주 (1905–1997) had obtained in its 1932 fiction competition for his Japanese-language story "Gakidō 餓鬼道" (Hell of Starving). The success of "A Village with Papaya Trees" launched a fertile career for Long as a Japanophone author in late colonial Taiwan; he published numerous stories, poems, and criticisms in Japanese-language venues in the colony and the metropole.[28]

In 1941, both Kim and Long were enjoying prominent recognition as colonial writers in the broader Japanese-language literary field. But in his letter to Long, Kim calls their creative language "a foreign language" that they both have to use "even though [they] were born in very remote places" and reflects on their works from a critical distance. Kim approvingly refers to Long's criticism of his debut story "Into the Light" and discounts the acclaim it received in the metropole by acknowledging that "it is a work intended for the mainland Japanese audience." He feels "terrified" as he is aware of the chasm between public reception and personal perception, casting a light on his own work that undercuts monologic appropriation by the imperial readership. Kim's gaze thus dislocates the text's forced semantic stability and opens it up to dialogic reading, and this gesture also informs his comments on Long's piece "Evening Moon," or "Yoizuki 宵月," which came out in *Literary Capital* in 1940. "When I read your 'Evening Moon,' I felt something very intimate to me. I shuddered at the thought that the place you live and the place I live are in fact no different in terms of their realities. That piece, of course, is not intended to expose reality and is written in a perfect matter-of-fact style, but I feel as if I saw your shivering hand in it. This might just be my arbitrary judgment, or sentimentalism.... Please forgive me, forgive me." Kim carefully discerns the author's "shivering hand" behind the story's "matter-of-fact style" that is ostensibly not intended to "expose reality." He unleashes the story's allegorical significance in indicating the common "realities" that he intimately shares with the addressee, reading it as much about Korea as about Taiwan. He then insists that "tradition is very important" and suggests, "You indeed practice literature for the Taiwanese people as you should; I practice literature for the Korean people as I should." It is through dialogic reading that he, having to write and be read in the colonizer's language, envisions literature for the colonized.

It is in this context that Kim mentions Lu Xun. "I like Lu Xun very much. Lu Xun was admirable. You should establish yourself as Taiwan's Lu Xun [*Taiwan no Ro Jin* 台灣の魯迅]. I might be sounding impolite here, but what I only mean is that I hope you create works that bear significance to the whole of literature as Lu Xun did. I also want to write good works as much as I can, and I am trying to do so step-by-step, without haste." Kim indeed took an intense interest in Lu Xun's works and adapted them in several of his fictional works written between 1940 and 1942. He did so most prominently in the short story "Yuch'ijang esŏ mannan sanai 留置場에서 만난 사나이" (A Man Whom I Met in a Detention Cell), which I discuss in detail later in this chapter. He wrote and published this story in Korean in 1941, and translated it himself into Japanese in the following year and published it in Tokyo with a revised title: "Kyū hakushaku Q 伯爵" (Count Q, 1942)—an evident allusion to Lu Xun's "The Real Story of Ah Q." Not only did Kim's own fascination with Lu Xun underlie the suggestion for Long to become "Taiwan's Lu Xun," but Long himself had already displayed an avid interest in the Chinese writer. Long evoked

"The Real Story of Ah Q" as well as "Guxiang 故鄉" (My Hometown, 1921) in his debut piece "A Village with Papaya Trees" and put together in 1940 a criticism of Lu Xun's "Diary of a Madman" in comparison to Gogol's 1835 short story of the same title.[29] Kim's private letter lays bare an interpretative horizon that reveals Lu Xun's works as intertexts that wrest late colonial texts away from appropriation by the imperial gaze and leads them to be read in each other's light to uncover their alternative significances.

Almost contemporaneously in Manchukuo, Gu Ding was also encouraged to "become Manchuria's Lu Xun [*Manshū no Ro Jin* 満洲の魯迅]." Gu Ding, born Xu Changji 徐長吉 in Changchun in 1914, was sent by his wealthy father to Japanese-managed primary and middle schools built by the South Manchuria Railway Company, where he learned Japanese in earnest. The Manchurian Incident in 1931 forced him to continue his college education in Beijing; he joined the League of Leftist Writers, in whose founding Lu Xun was centrally involved, and emerged as an up-and-coming left-wing figure and translator of Japanese materials. But his early activities were cut short to a mere few months due to the KMT-led crackdown on the League's northern branch in 1933. He was accused of betraying the League and enabling the suppression and returned in disappointment to his hometown Changchun, which had become the capital of the puppet state. There he leveraged his Japanese proficiency, obtained a post in the Manchukuo government, and resumed his literary pursuits under the new pseudonym Gu Ding as a staunch advocate of Chinese-language "new literature" in the archaist, colonialist, and anticommunist regime of the puppet state. As a fertile writer, critic, translator, and editor, Gu Ding became one of the most celebrated, albeit controversial, Chinese-language literary figures in Manchuria.[30]

By the early 1940s, Gu Ding's prominence was widely recognized among Manchukuo's cultural establishment and officials, and his literary works had been translated and introduced into mainland Japan. The statement that he should "become Manchuria's Lu Xun" was made by the former leftist and imperialist convert Hayashi Fusao 林房雄 (1903–1975) in his conversation with Gu Ding published in 1942 in the journal *Geibun* 藝文 (Art and Literature), which was launched under the auspices of the "Outline for the Guidance of Art and Literature."[31] The ideological context of the statement is patently reflected in the published tête-à-tête, which rather reads as Hayashi's monologue on his personal opinions on politics and culture, exhibiting, according to Mei Ding'e, "the usual pattern of interaction between Japanese and Chinese writers [in Manchukuo]."[32] Hayashi urges Gu Ding in a heavily patronizing tone to "shut down" the Yiwen Publishers, which he had founded just the year before, and write fiction "with nothing in possession." Hayashi's condescending urging to "become Manchuria's Lu Xun," then, is met with Gu Ding's perfunctory response that he "is now more occupied with administrative work than artistic work."[33] The power dynamic in their conversation invites us to interpret Gu Ding's reticence.

As we will see in a moment, Gu Ding played a pivotal role in introducing Lu Xun's work to the literary scene in Manchukuo. Given his long-term admiration of the Chinese writer, his muted response to the encouragement to write like Lu Xun appears all the more eloquent. His taciturnity vis-à-vis Hayashi Fusao's wordiness not only throws into relief their stark power imbalance in the sanctioned literary culture, but also unveils "Lu Xun" as an index for escape from that discursive order. Gu Ding's suppressed response thus aligns precisely with Kim Saryang's urging for Long Yingzong to become "Taiwan's Lu Xun" in a transcolonial private correspondence concealed from imperial readership. These labored evocations of "Lu Xun" point to the ambivalent statuses of the late colonial writers' works in the sanctioned realm of literature in the empire. Their texts, on the one hand, existed and circulated in this realm despite imperial censorship, yet on the other, they could, once read from a critical distance, convey prohibited voices through dialogic resonances. Treating Lu Xun's works as intertexts, then, allows us to perform precisely the kind of allegorical reading that Kim did privately on Long's work, to attune our ears to the polyphonic openness of the writings and attend to their textual gestures through which they express what is inexpressible in the sanctioned literature. The intertextualizations of Lu Xun uncover those late colonial works' probing of the boundaries of what could be spoken of in the accepted practice of literature, the critical endeavor that reiterated Lu Xun's work to bring about an origin of modern literature through critical engagement with the established literary culture.

GU DING AND ELLIPSIS

Gu Ding spearheaded the introduction of Lu Xun's works into Manchukuo shortly after his death in 1936.[34] Just a few months after he made the terse response to Hayashi Fusao's suggestion, Gu Ding, as if to pronounce a belated reply, published a historical short story called "Zhulin 竹林" (The Bamboo Grove, 1942). It is a reworking of the legend of the Seven Sages of the Bamboo Grove recorded namely in the fifth-century *New Accounts of the Tales of the World* and *Jin shu* 晉書 (History of the Jin), and it thematically intertextualizes Lu Xun's celebrated talk from 1927 titled "Wei-Jin fengdu ji wenzhang yu yao ji jiu zhi guanxi 魏晉風度及文章與藥及酒之關係" (The Wei-Jin Period's Spirit and Writing and Their Relationship to Drug and Wine). This piece sheds light on the stakes of Gu Ding's reference to Lu Xun in his conception of new literature in Manchukuo and suggests the significance of ellipsis in his literary practice.

The Seven Sages were reclusive literati active in the third century and are known for their eccentric, norm-bending discourse and behavior as well as their espousal of the arcane Lao-Zhuang thought. Foregrounding the two most prominent of those men, Ji Kang 嵇康 (223–262) and Ruan Ji 阮籍 (210–263), Gu Ding's adaptation depicts their elusive words and deeds against the implicit backdrop of political turbulence caused by the Sima clan's assaults against the Wei court and eventual usurpation of the throne by force to establish the Jin dynasty. Ji Kang indulges himself in steel forging and zither playing to evade the labor of composition, declares a breakup with a friend who recommended him for a ministry position, and luxuriates in a psychoactive drug whose lethal side effects need to be counteracted by taking cold food and lengthy walks. Ruan Ji defies the mourning ritual in public, receives those he despises by looking at them only with the whites of his eyes, and drinks away months to avoid marrying his daughter into the Sima clan.[35] These episodes, based on well-known classical accounts on these figures, are contextualized in "Bamboo Grove" in the perilous political situation amid the dynastic transition, where literati fall victim to malicious slander and arbitrary persecutions and executions. The cryptic prophecy that a Daoist Sun Deng gives Ji Kang in the story encapsulates the situation:

Do you know fire? It is alive and bright, but it preserves brightness by not using it. Man is alive and has talent, but he preserves talent by not using it. If, then, brightness is used with firewood, then its illumination can be preserved. And if talent is used with knowledge, then man can live out his life. But you have ample talent and scant knowledge such that it will be hard for you to avoid disaster. You had better not seek much.[36]

The prediction comes true in the end and Ji Kang is executed by Sima Zhao 司馬昭 (211–265) for his defense of an ally accused of the violation of "filial piety." The risky political climate (the lack of "firewood") and the sequestered and idiosyncratic sages who try to "preserve brightness by not using it" in Gu Ding's story have been read since its publication as a political allegory for Chinese intellectuals in Manchukuo in Japan's ever-tightening grip in the 1940s.[37]

Critics have underlined Lu Xun's long-term admiration of essays by writers from the Wei and Jin eras and pointed out characteristics of his works, such as their "nonconformism" and their "lucid and aloof, straightforward and unconstrained" style, that show resemblance to the works of the third-century literati.[38] The author's "Wei-Jin Period's Spirit and Writing," moreover, analyzes the idiosyncrasy of the Wei-Jin writers and points out the paradox that their outward "resistance to old Confucian orthodoxy" in fact belies their "extremely obstinate belief" in it.[39] The contradiction symptomizes a discursive confusion of the era: "In the Wei-Jin era, those who followed Confucian orthodoxy and looked respectable actually corrupted it, whereas those who destroyed it on the surface in fact recognized it, or believed in it deeply."[40] Because notions such as "filial piety" were exploited by politicians for their personal profit, ignoring them was an ironic gesture of upholding them. When an illegitimate power exposed the ideological forces that corrupted their discursive culture, the Wei-Jin writers retreated to an alternative space—the "bamboo grove"—and treated the expressions appearing in the official culture with deep irony. It is such an ironic spirit that Lu Xun discerns in that era's writings; as he contends about Ruan Ji, "[His] verse and prose are excellent. His writings are imbued with passion, but many meanings are hidden and do not show."[41] If the Seven Sages' ostensible defiance of morality reflected the nihilistic spirit of the age ("everything is empty"[42]), then the elliptic rhetoric of their writing was meant to repair the fraudulent signification in the sanctioned literary culture. The Wei-Jin literature as Lu Xun observed it leveraged ellipsis to challenge undue political intervention in culture.

Lu Xun takes the abuse of Sun Yat-sen's "Three Principles of the People" by the northern warlords as a contemporary example of such meddling.[43] One could readily extrapolate to pinpoint the exploitation of Confucian ideals, namely the "kingly way," by the Japanese occupier and the numerous other rhetorical devices they used to purchase legitimacy as instances of cultural corruption in Manchukuo. Gu Ding's "Bamboo Grove" is hence as much an allegory of Manchukuo's cultural situation as an ironic manifesto of the kind of literature that he envisioned and practiced in it. Gu Ding's terse response to the suggestion by an imperial cultural agent to "become Manchuria's Lu Xun," therefore, can be understood as a potent expression of his deeply felt endorsement of Lu Xun's critical "spirit and writing." And in this precise sense, his introduction of Lu Xun to Manchukuo had to dislocate the authorized order of "literature" and thus entail asking whether "Manchuria has literature at all"—the question he raised in the postface to his "Lu Xun zhushu jieti 魯迅著書解題" (Introduction to Lu Xun's Books, 1937).[44] Lu Xun inspired Gu Ding to consider what was taken as "literature" in his culture with a spirit of scathing irony and to radically question its significance as it became a target of political interventions.

As much as Gu Ding took the task of introducing Lu Xun into Manchukuo seriously, he regarded Lu Xun not just as a writer but also as a "warrior" whose writings—especially his *zawen* or "miscellaneous essays"—were "the daggers with which [he] struggled with society" to carve out a new domain for literature. And society in Manchukuo was nothing but "a great desolation" or "a grand wasteland," for the necessary books were banned or in short supply, freedom of speech was nonexistent, and intellectuals idly led hedonistic lives, often without even reading the newspapers. Few, to begin with, understood what kind of writer Lu Xun was.[45] So Gu Ding wrote satirically,

> If you really want to become "a writer like Lu Xun," then first, you must be confused. Second, regardless of how "a writer like Lu Xun" might come about, you should break through the great desolation

and gallop across the grand wasteland. And third, regardless of how the emergence of "a writer like Lu Xun" might save those unsavable mute and deaf [intellectuals], you might as well rush headlong in a direction that you don't know.[46]

This last phrase, which encapsulates Gu Ding's thought on literature, resonates with the canonical ending of Lu Xun's short story "My Hometown": "I thought: hope cannot be said to exist, nor can it be said not to exist. It is just like roads across the earth. For actually the earth had no roads to begin with, but when many people tread one way, a road is made."[47] Citing from this same passage, Gu Ding noted elsewhere, "A road in literature is also made this way, by treading."[48] "Lu Xun," therefore, does not designate a model to emulate, an idea or thought to heed, or even texts to allude to, but indicates the spirit of existential "struggle[s]" to pursue possibilities of representation that oppose what is representable in a given culture.

At the heart of Gu Ding's pursuit of representation were people's "lived lives" (*huo de rensheng* 活的人生),[49] so much so that he rejected any "thought," "color," or "morality" that would try to give direction to "literature in Manchuria," which was only "in its nascent stage." He even put between brackets powerful critical notions like "masses," "reality," and "the dominant class," as well as literary movements like "indigenous literature."[50] It is in this sense that he claimed that "literature, like other cultural disciplines, cannot totally abandon the tradition of the previous generation or begin on a tabula rasa," for such a desire for a fresh start would divorce work from people's lives in favor of a readymade direction or notion.[51] The writer's "self" should not be "buried" in tradition but should "emerge from within it" through encounters with the present realities of people's lives.[52]

Because it did not make it possible to represent people's "lived lives," the culture of the puppet state was as much of a "desolation" and "wasteland" for Gu Ding as China's culture in the 1920s had been for Lu Xun. Hence Gu Ding remarks: "But there are only two words that describe our literature and writers: no voice [*wusheng* 無聲]."[53] This alludes to Lu Xun's eminent 1927 talk "Voiceless China," in which he deplored the alienating silence that plagued China due to the burden of classical writing and advocated for writing in a living vernacular.[54] Gu Ding's deploring of a similar voicelessness in Manchuria, on the one hand, grafts his search for literature onto the spirit of Chinese literary revolution, yet on the other, it projects an imagined community in Chinese-speaking Manchuria as at least partly distinct from the greater China that May Fourth ideologues imagined. The ambivalent identity of "our literature and writers" is also reflected in Gu Ding's discourse on language. Whereas he refuses to create in Japanese, he calls for "opening up the front gate" of the Chinese language to welcome the "vocabulary, grammar, and style" of other languages that would "enrich, refine, and embellish" it. He calls attention to the language "closely embedded in the actual lives [of people]" in Manchuria where Japanese and Russian words are being incorporated, and to facilitate such incorporation, he even backs the usage of the phonetic *zhuyin* alphabet in Chinese writing.[55] Gu Ding thus argues for representing social and cultural realities particular to Manchuria, where speech hybridization is an everyday affair. In so doing, he follows Lu Xun's advocacy of vernacularism, even if it means undercutting the authority of the kind of standardized *baihua* writing that May Fourth intellectuals had in mind to institute for China.

To Gu Ding, the call to become a "Lu Xun" must have sounded hollow in Manchukuo's cultural circumstances, but he took struggling in that desolate lack of resonance where "literature" lost its significance to be the first step toward answering that call. Through literature, he sought representation against what was representable within the culture of Manchukuo—a practice that fundamentally echoed Lu Xun's pursuit of modern literature between the dominant old and new cultures. It was a practice of creating a new mode of representation for the voiceless "lived lives" in Manchukuo, rushing "headlong toward a direction that you don't know" with "the sole purpose of finding hope" that does not belong to the present.[56]

Gu Ding's satirical novella "Yuanye 原野" (Wasteland, 1938) is illustrative of the literature he envisioned. It first appeared in the journal *Mingming* 明明 (Brightness) in 1938 and was included in the author's collection of stories *Fenfei* 奮飛 (Strenuous Flight, 1938). *Strenuous Flight* won the literary prize awarded by the Japanese-owned Chinese-language newspaper *Shengjing shibao* 盛京時報 (Shengjing Times) for "works published by a Manchukuo national [*Manzhouguo ren* 滿洲國人] within Manchukuo."[57] Thus praised in Manchukuo's literary establishment,

"Wasteland" is regarded as Gu Ding's "representative work."[58] The novella caricatures three generations of a landlord family in Manchuria. Qian Jingbang returns to his hometown with a bachelor's degree in law from a college in Tokyo. His grandfather, the patriarch Qian Caishen, migrated to the northeast decades ago and acquired enough wealth to own land, but he now keeps a rapacious concubine who is younger than his grandson and squanders his fortune on her as she elopes with a lover. Jingbang's father, called Qian the Chief after his previous position, was sent to the United States to receive education as a young man and still mixes crude English expressions into his conversation, but now he chain-smokes opium while barely scraping out a living by having a subordinate run a sketchy pawn business. Having been educated in the metropole, Jingbang tries to separate himself from his contemptible father and grandfather, but his struggles prove futile and become the subject of satire in the story. Jingbang's inflated self-confidence lets him deride "everything at home" as "feudalistic," from sycophantic servants to metal chopsticks, old-style toilets, and even his "illiterate" wife.[59] Yet his college degree was accompanied by the "first-prize certificate" from the "Japan Mahjong Association," and back at home, he barely lands a position as a petty clerk in a government office, only to find himself wearied by the tedious bureaucracy and falling in love with the manager's daughter Yuzhen, who devours hackneyed *yanqing* romances. The roots of the problem run deep, as the story exposes how primitive accumulation originally occurred for migrant farmers in the northeast thanks to a simple combination of economic necessity and chance. There is "nothing amazing" about the current landlords.[60] Regarding the "wasteland" that is Manchukuo, the narrative portrays Jingbang as caught in the same trap of banality that ensnared the previous generations, a trap that continues to prevent them from making any meaningful contribution to history.

"Let me put it straight: humanity did not feel any urgent need for this group of people. But they all do live or have lived—Is this still a stage in human history?"[61] As the narrator thus pronounces the underlying question of the novella, his biting satire is bolstered by an idea of history as an arbiter of value in life. Yet the related episodes present such decadence, platitudes, and nihilism that the narrator wonders if at all they can claim a place ("stage") in that posited totality. The story of the "wasteland" seems to be simply divorced from history. Thus, "the many miserable people on this wasteland of ours cling to their happiness after death, even though they cannot live a satisfactory life before death."[62] The ironic inversion of life and death informs the sarcastic portrayal of Yuzhen's vain suicide attempt with a reference to Lu Xun. To protest her father's prohibition of the love affair with Jingbang, Yuzhen overdoses on opium, and this ostentatious performance, which ends up a failure, "reminds" the narrator "of a quote from Lu Xun."[63] What this interpolation refers to are the hilarious comments on suicide that Lu Xun reportedly made the day before his own death, in which he told a joke about a woman who worries about the whereabouts of her ring after a failed attempt at taking her life by swallowing it.[64] Discussing this humorous "chitter-chatter" along with a few essays on death that the late Lu Xun penned and mentioned in that conversation, Qian Liqun has pointed out an underlying theme of "the 'resistance' of 'life' against 'death'" in them.[65] But the humor that colors Lu Xun's late writings on death seem to instead gesture toward death's eerie entanglement with life.

For instance, one of Lu Xun's last essays, "Nüdiao 女吊" (Hung Woman, 1936), which is mentioned in the conversation alluded to in "Wasteland," depicts the folk theater performed in the author's hometown, featuring the spirit of a woman who hanged herself to escape suffering in life.[66] During the festival, wandering specters are summoned from the potter's field to join the villagers to watch the play of the spirits of people who died regretful deaths, and that theatrical space is meanwhile carefully maintained to make sure that "real" ghosts do not appear to haunt the actual performers or audiences and that grudge-bearing ghosts do not find their "replacement" in a living person. The essay reports on an interesting case of the play "hanged man," in which an acrobat is suspended on stage from ropes at forty-nine points on the body, but the whole scene needs to be carefully watched in a mirror by a backstage observer dressed as the Daoist deity Wanglingguan because "if two men appear in the mirror, then one is a real ghost." Should that happen, the observer will have to drive "the fake ghost" off the stage, and will have him wash off the makeup and watch the play among the crowd before he slowly returns home, so that he does not actually get hanged on stage and the real ghost does not remember his face and haunt him.[67] What is documented here is a fear of the confusion of signification, in which the signifier (the actor, life) does not represent the signified (the ghost, death) but rather becomes it. The fascinating protocol involving a backstage observer suggests an effort to repair a breached theatrical framework, a fine line between the representing and the represented, life and death, humans and ghosts. If theatrical representation was meant to appease stray ghosts and keep them from causing harm in real life, then it implied an inevitable ambiguity in which representation can conjure up apparitions through images, creating a world where "'humans' and 'ghosts' infiltrate into each other."[68]

In "Wasteland," Lu Xun's jest about death is evoked by a ludicrous combination of Yuzhen's overdramatized suicide attempt and the seriousness of the barely averted consequence. This episode satirizes a decaying society where life and death have become almost interchangeable: people lead indolent lives, "but," remarks the narrator, they "eventually need to die." "However, people often turn death into life" rather than trying to derive meaning for life from the finitude thereof.[69] Such an inversion of life and death makes it impossible for the narrator to tell a story that furnishes significance to the lived lives in Manchukuo. The intertext of Lu Xun's discourse on death thus exposes the crumbling narrative framework of "Wasteland," which fails to depict life in a totality like "history" that would give meaning to it—a symptom of the dissolving form of life in the puppet state. The enchanted confusion of life and death in "Hung Woman" is reduced into a vapid colonized existence where death feigns life. Just as the American-educated "chief" becomes as corrupt as his feudalistic father, so does the Japanese-educated Jingbang turn as lifeless as his opium-addicted father. The apathetic three generations symbolize the nihilism of a society in which oppositions such as feudalism/modernization, East/West, and nation/empire are as pointless as a decadent life that is tantamount to death. The novella as a result becomes a series of hollow signifiers stuck in an iron house of utter banality that as a whole amounts to a general ellipsis revolving around the unanswered rhetorical question: "Is this still a stage in human history?"

"Wasteland," therefore, constitutes a paradoxical story that contains resistance to meaningful storytelling. Gu Ding's intertextualization of Lu Xun prompts an ironic reading of this ellipsis as a biting critique of what can be written about, or what is accepted as "literature," within the forged culture of Manchukuo. The novella's ellipsis is thus symptomatic of its ambivalent existence in a culture in which it gained critical acclaim yet against which it envisioned an alternative, yet still nonexistent, mode of literary representation. Its intrinsic critique is articulated in its ending, where the "wasteland" itself becomes the subject: "Oh, Wasteland, you should dance! / Oh, Wasteland, you should roar!"[70] Gu Ding's elliptic writing implies a utopian envisioning of an entirely new culture, echoing the ethicopolitical significance of Lu Xun's literary endeavor.

LONG YINGZONG AND CRITICAL REALISM

Just as Gu Ding did in Manchukuo, Long Yingzong attained prominent recognition in the Japanese-sanctioned literary field in late colonial Taiwan. He joined Gu Ding in taking part in the inaugural meeting of the Congress of the Writers of Greater East Asia, which was organized in 1942 on the initiative of the imperial government for the purpose of establishing a "Greater East Asian Literature."[71] Long represented colonial Taiwan and Gu Ding Manchukuo in this political pageant of staging a literature in the service of the Japanese Empire. Yet through his late colonial literary activities, Long also shared with Gu Ding the fundamental ambivalence of colonial writers. On the one hand, Long on several occasions argued for producing a distinct literature for Taiwan; as he claimed in 1941, "outer-territory [i.e., colonial] literature should not aim at the literary world of mainland Japan but should be one that is particular to the land. . . . It must be a literature for the sake of those who live on that land and bury their bones in it; it must love that land and enhance its culture." Yet on the other, he added in the same stroke, "Outer-territory literature, just like inner-territory [i.e., mainland Japanese] literature, is thus the healthiest literature for ordinary people, and it is such a beautiful literature that possesses unique features while being able to form a wing of the broader culture of the state, adding diversity [tayōsei 多様性] to it while being integrated into it."[72] He also affirmed his literary identity by contending that someone like him who did not inherit Japan's tradition could "form a new Japanese language" capable of "adding freshness with a different color of hair" to that language.[73] Within the accredited metropole-centered culture, literature particular to a colony was prone to being reduced to a mere factor ("wing") that would add "diversity" or "freshness" to Japanese literature as a whole. Even the affirmation of ordinary life and the expression of the "love" of the land, as long as they were rendered in "literature" in that existing culture, could be tantamount to declaring complicity in and even reinforcing the cultural status quo that deprived the colonized of their voices. Amid this ambivalence, Long wrote works that self-critically dislocated the representative function that they were supposed to play in the culture where they were produced and read. Treating Lu Xun's works as intertexts helps uncover in Long's writings this self-reflexive movement.

The critical stakes of Long Yingzong's late colonial works already appear in his award-winning debut story "A Village with Papaya Trees" (hereafter designated as "Papaya Trees"). It is the story of a youthful and ambitious middle-school graduate named Chen Yousan, who moves to a small rural village to take a job as an assistant accountant in the town hall. Despite his advanced education and diligence, he is assigned to petty work and paid poorly, and he quickly finds that his living conditions are no better than those of the indigenous villagers. Nonetheless, he believes that effort will lift him out of the stagnant life and decides to devote himself to studying for the civil service examination and eventually the bar examination. He regards himself as part of "the new intellectual class" and "looks down on" the native people, who appear to him "like subservient weeds growing on the gloomy plane of life without any advancement or progress." Always wearing Japanese-style clothes and speaking in Japanese, and afire with the desire for ideals and advancements, he draws "a sense of self-consolation" from finding himself "different from his kind."[74] As obsession with colonial mimicry drives him to put ever more effort into his studies, however, he is met with overwhelming skepticism from his Taiwanese peers, who suggest that his struggles will never pay off in the present social conditions. "You are forgetting the position you occupy," a friend warns Chen Yousan, who expresses the hope of leading a "creative" life.[75] Chen gradually becomes preoccupied with the idea that "unhappiness in society is always caused by excessive knowledge."[76] He is becoming increasingly desperate and tempted by wine and women when he meets the sick eldest son of a colleague named Lin Xingnan, who tells him:

> True knowledge may drag us into deep suffering as it interprets [social] phenomena, but I believe we should not curse these phenomena, for they are but manifestations of the law of history.

> Happiness will not be achieved without suffering and effort. But I believe we should discern based on correct knowledge how history unfolds and live a proper life without being trapped by vain despair or decadence so that we can survive in this dark society.[77]

Lin Xingnan's ailing son thus tries to awaken Chen to "true knowledge" of the "law of history" that would allow him to observe the present phenomena from an objective perspective and find a proper direction for his efforts and struggles. So affirming the value of knowledge, Lin's son mentions "the deep impression" that was made on him when he read Lu Xun's "My Hometown" in Satō Haruo's 佐藤春夫 (1892–1964) Japanese translation. He also hopes to read "The Real Story of Ah Q," which he says he has not yet been able to afford. He expresses admiration for Engels and wishes to read Gorky and Lewis H. Morgan. His words, however, are dismissed by Chen, to whom they "sound only like empty words." Chen is instead distracted by the sight of Lin Xingnan's daughter.[78] He is devastated as she rejects his marriage proposal, and at the end of the story, when he learns that Lin's eldest son is dead and Lin goes mad, he becomes more isolated and hopeless than ever before.

In the contemporary criticism published in response to its sensational winning of a prestigious Kaizō award in 1937, "Papaya Trees" is often characterized as a realistic portrayal of Taiwanese society and intellectuals. A Japanese critic active in Taiwan points out, "I rather believe this work should be highly appreciated as a great piece of literature.... What is impressive is that it exposes a patent reality, the simplicity of the thought [of many Taiwanese youths], in a realistic style."[79] An anonymous critic even urges the Japanese government to draw lessons for its education policies from the "unfortunate social situations" depicted in this work.[80] Others mention the representation of Taiwan's "local color" in the story.[81] An interview with Long Yingzong that introduces him as a "rising star of the central [i.e., metropole] literary world" quotes him: "I wrote 'A Village with Papaya Trees' to feature realistically the depiction of an intellectual on this island who graduated middle school and the socioeconomic relations in the background."[82]

While this work was thus frequently acclaimed for its colonial realism in the Japanophone literary field, however, the narrative itself, despite its ostensible realist mode, implies a critical self-consciousness about that

Transnational Allegory 259

very characterization. In several instances, the narrative lays bare the sheer artificiality of the reality that the protagonist and his Taiwanese peers have to endure, a reality constructed by colonial ideology to make them consent to the modern lifestyle and strive for personal advancement. Reality constitutes a closure that blinds them to structural issues and puts them on a path to progress, without which there is nothing but stagnation, poverty, and meaninglessness. Long uses a sarcastic voice to describe the industrious hero's willing confinement to this fabricated space. To start a new life with a new job, Chen Yousan covers the walls of his cheap rented lodging with white wallpaper that makes "the room suddenly look brighter." He writes on a wall "with thick characters slanted right-side up" a slogan in a couplet: "What Wouldn't Be Achievable / If You Devoted Your Spirit?" He pairs it with "a portrait of Napoleon, who appeared as if he were thinking something, with his hands crossed behind his back." His preoccupation with effort and success, moreover, derives from "the books on self-cultivation, the hero biographies, and the stories of success and ambition that he had read in middle school besides school textbooks." The narrative caricatures this hero: "Chen Yousan in Japanese-style clothes lying on a Taiwanese-style platform made of bamboo in the three-*yen*-a-month dirt-floored room that was no better than a shed created an awfully comical scene."[83] The narrator's satirical gaze exposes the fact that it is objects and clothes, books and slogans that stage reality for the protagonist, undercutting the constative "realism" for which this work became known among imperial critics. The narrative thus implies a critique of the ideological premises for appreciating this work as realist, the same premises that make the protagonist believe in the manufactured "reality" of his life.

Long's critical self-consciousness about literary representation was explored in his 1939 novella "Chō fujin no giga 趙夫人の戯画" (A Caricature of Madame Zhao). Serialized in the newspaper *Taiwan xinmin bao* 台灣新民報 (The New Taiwan People's Paper), which was published exclusively in Japanese after 1937 due to the assimilation policies, it is the melodramatic satire of a loveless husband and wife, Zhao Junma and Madame Zhao. It features a self-reflexive narrative structure in which Madame Zhao reads the novella "A Caricature of Madame Zhao," which she suspects "Long Yingzong" wrote based on her actual life. The snobbish Zhao Junma boasts about his comfortable and eventful life, declaring, "my life is itself a novel and I am its protagonist" and despising the novelist for having to rely on fancy.[84] Madame Zhao accuses the novella of spreading "lies" "divorced from the facts" in her life and calls it "a pure fabrication" of "such indecency and vulgarity."[85] The story proper, then, is little more than a vapid domestic drama, in which the philandering husband acquires a pretty maid with the intention of making her his concubine and the jealous wife begins an ostentatious flirtation with a handsome butler. Yet the nested narrative form produces a caricature of Madame Zhao's desperate lack of self-knowledge about the banality of her life and, more importantly, suggests that literature—the novel, in particular—is part and parcel of the construct of the characters' desires, mindset, self-image, and, quite simply, reality. By featuring himself as the author of the trite melodrama, Long Yingzong betrays a self-critical understanding that his work was circulated and consumed in the same privileged circles as he hyperbolically satirizes in this story. Long thus views himself as confined to and complicit in the vicious cycle of perpetuating an idea of what reality should look like and implies that a culture that shares that idea is the sole terrain where he is able to publish his works and gain a readership. The satire of this metafiction is therefore concerned less with its realism or fictionality than with the sheer vanity of the culture that gives it an identity as circulated literature.

Lin Xingnan's son in "Papaya Trees," with an allusion to Marxist criticism, points to the "true knowledge" that would enable Chen Yousan to regard reality as mere "phenomena" or as manifestations of a general law of history. Such knowledge, should it exist, would smash the ideological confines of colonial culture and show a way out of it toward true realism. While Lu Xun's works are also evoked as conducive to such a path, their intertextual significance, I contend, lies in the protagonist's utter neglect of it. In that he imagines a better future by setting up around him the same theater of reality that traps him in the present colonial Manichean order, Chen Yousan reenacts Ah Q's "spiritual victory." Then, in that Long Yingzong's narrative positions a vantage point within that same theater and recounts Chen's tragicomedy in an apparent realist mode, it adapts the narratology of "The Real Story of Ah Q," which draws its point of view from the spectating gazes of Weizhuang villagers.[86] The protagonist's hopeless imprisonment in colonial reality, culminating in his neglect of Lu Xun, indicates the intrinsic inability of the very literary

Transnational Allegory 261

medium of this story to represent a way out of that ideological confinement. In "Papaya Trees," Lu Xun's works thus do not symbolize an idolizable hope for a new reality but reveal the present culture where "hope" strikes but a hollow note, just as it did for the narrator of Lu Xun's "My Hometown" in the end of the story. As they did for Gu Ding, Lu Xun's texts for Long indicate a new literature that is to emerge in a culture yet to be created, like a "road" that cannot be *said* to exist or not but can only be made "when many people tread one way."[87]

In "Papaya Trees," Lin Xingnan's son leaves a note for Chen Yousan when he dies. Having earlier disregarded his words, Chen "jam[s]" the note "in his pocket" and does not bother to read it. But at the end of the story, he takes it out, "smooth[s] out the crumpled paper and read[s]" it. Lin's son has expressed a utopian hope: "Though I feel bottomless sorrow now, a beautiful society will arrive someday. I wish to have a long sleep under the cold ground while pondering images of a land filled with happiness."[88] By articulating hope in the already disappeared voice of a deceased character, barely preserved on a piece of crushed paper, Long makes another allusion to "The Real Story of Ah Q." Just like Ah Q's unuttered plea for "help," the voice of Lin's son remains silent and ignored in the colonial culture that "Papaya Trees" depicts as "reality" and in which it exists as literature. Long's work, like "The Real Story," thus implies a self-critical questioning of what can be written, transmitted, and read in that which is accepted as literature. It can only convey the dead character's voice by opening itself to allegorical readings. That openness squarely undermines the imperial consumption of "Papaya Trees" as mere colonial realism and envisions a new culture where literature will gain new expressive possibilities.

In his transcolonial letter, Kim Saryang performed just such an allegorical reading of Long's story "Evening Moon," behind whose "matter-of-fact style" he discerned the author's "shivering hand." The adaptation of Lu Xun's short stories is also evident in the narrative of "Evening Moon," especially in its featuring of a first-person narrator who is patently inadequate to tell the story he does. Centered on the death of a demoralized colonial elite named Peng Yingkun, this story might be read as a sequel to "Papaya Trees." It begins with the unnamed narrator's encounter with Peng's abject death in a poverty-stricken house visited by petty debt collectors until the very end of his life. On Peng's deathbed, the narrator regrets in a contemptuous tone that Peng did not try hard enough to live a decent life and that the "village's intellectual class" has to die such an unsightly death.[89] Peng's death leaves his widow and four children in dire poverty, and the narrator helps them sort out Peng's posthumous affairs out of pity. Yet as he reflects on his generous conduct, the narrator is assailed by a profound sense of guilt and shame and begins to tell Peng's story.

> "Stay strong. Don't grieve too much." So I would tell his wife from time to time, and worked in an active and ostensibly friendly manner, sending telegrams to family members, calling for acquaintances, and ordering a death certificate.
>
> Recalling my clownish, moralistic behavior, I was suddenly overwhelmed by a strong sense of self-disgust.
>
> "What a hypocrite!" I murmured.
>
> I had been content until a moment ago, imbued with the good feeling of satisfaction and pride after putting morality into practice, but I felt as though I had been suddenly tripped up and fallen into mud.
>
> Yes, I had been looking for an outlet for my sentimentality or a cheap impulse of morality, and I finally took advantage of Peng Yingkun's death and satisfied my moral vanity.
>
> I did not grieve Peng Yingkun's death from the bottom of my heart. I just encountered his death by chance and satisfied the vanity lurking in me.
>
> Mrs. Peng should be thankful for me. But meanwhile, I was devouring the pleasure of a good deed as I would food.
>
> I saw myself as obscene and blushed with shame, and an unpleasant, turbid emotion circulated like dirty blood.
>
> However, I think here I must tell a story of the relationship between Peng Yingkun and me.[90]

The ensuing storytelling is thus overshadowed by the narrator's regret and shame and characterized by his confessed inability, despite that room for self-reflection, to fathom Peng's troubled mind.

The narrator went to the same middle school as Peng, who was three years his senior and appeared a hero to him. He presents himself as a mediocre student and depicts the young Peng as a smart, mature, active, and aspiring young man. Peng penned a biography of Byron and wrote a free verse poem to praise youth; he gave an impassioned speech called "Youth and Effort" in a speech contest, which made an argument that "effort" could "overcome any difficulty and achieve goals" and that "young people . . . should work toward society's development and progress as well as their individual advancement and success."[91] The once-ardent Peng, however, appeared visibly frail and sad when the narrator reunited with him after five years, when he became a teacher in the public school in a village where Peng had been teaching. "The Peng Yingkun in middle school who looked like a fine horse and the shabby Peng Yingkun now who looks like a scarecrow seem to be different people."[92] Peng earned a negative reputation in the village for squandering money on prostitution and drinking and at school for indolent work. He never read and even used his middle-school language arts textbook as toilet paper for his children. While the narrator says he cannot entirely understand Peng's youthful idealism, he shows disdain for the late Peng's decadent lifestyle. Now that he is dead, the narrator expresses "regret" because he "should have had closer contact" with Peng and claims that it is already "too late" to understand "why Peng changed so much."[93]

While the narrator is thus no longer able to comprehend Peng's "desperate view of life," his sense of guilt and shame also distances him from Peng's widow. He convinces himself that her economic hardships are the "affairs of another person and have nothing to do with me" and that he "shall just mind [his] own business." Yet as "the problems that arose from Peng Yingkun's death stick with [his] head," the narrator nevertheless decides to help her put the family's finances in order by claiming Peng's life insurance and severance benefits and negotiating discounts with one of the creditors, who happens to be his former colleague at the school.[94] The negotiation fails, however, and the narrator in the end has to give the bad news to Peng's widow, whose economic prospects now look even more dire.

The dramatized narrator of "Evening Moon" thus wavers between worry and a sense of guilt, on the one hand, and contempt and indifference, on the other, in a way that evokes the narrator in Lu Xun's "New Year's Sacrifice." Just as the storytelling in Lu Xun's piece is informed by the enlightened narrator's inability to sympathize with the suffering of Xianglin's Wife, so does the narrator in "Evening Moon"—a Taiwanese elite represented as adaptable enough to be able to lead a "proper life" under colonial conditions—tells Peng's story while confessing his moral vanity and inability to fully feel or understand Peng's mental ordeal. The awkward relationship between the narrator and the subject is foregrounded by the former's response to the latter's confused interaction with their school's principal. Peng lambasted the principal for only caring about avoiding trouble and failing to show any passion or devotion to education, but he immediately retracted the censure and began to criticize himself for lethargy. In the end, he found himself having to thank the principal for supporting him instead of firing him for laziness, and "hugging the principal's legs as if he were kissing them." The narrator depicts his response to this tense scene elliptically with a mere indication of a "warm something welling up in my eyes," which made him "feel embarrassed" since he did not want "other people" to see his tears. He also downplays his tears back then as "effeminate" and attributes them simply to his young age and drinking.[95] Elsewhere, he expresses a realization that "Peng's melancholic gaze could have had something in common with me," but he hurries to add the reservation that "their relationship is still vague until now."[96] The narration of "Evening Moon" thus internalizes the collective gaze of colonial society, paying only scarce attention to Peng's troubled mind and the narrator's own covert sympathy with him, for they are underestimated or disavowed in that society.

The "shivering hand" that Kim Saryang said he had noticed in "Evening Moon" should have pointed to Long's struggle with possible representation in colonial literature. The "matter-of-fact style" that Kim perceives bespeaks the ostensible readability of Long's text as a kind of normal representation, a narratological equivalent of the narrator's wish to normalize Peng's death by showing due pity and helping liquidate his debts and assets in order to pull his family's lives back into the ordinary economy. His failure at liquidation is then symbolic of the impossibility to remain in a mode of normativity when it comes to reading Long's work. Just as the storytelling is underpinned by the narrator's self-reflective confessions of the inadequacy of his point of view, so does the reading need to linger over and endure moments of suspension in signification.

And just as the narrator tries to repay the deceased Peng by storytelling, so must the reader attend to what eludes the given representation through allegorical reading.

The story concludes with the narrator returning to Peng's widow to tell her that the negotiations with the usurer did not materialize:

> The windows of the house of Peng's widow were sunk in thick darkness, while the windows of other houses were lit by yellow lights.
> I casually looked back.
> Without my realizing it, the round evening moon had risen above the village.
> I thought that my pity for this neighbor was as cold and wretched as the evening moon.
> I couldn't move my feet when I realized that I had to speak ominous words to the grieving widow.
> The leaves of the pomelo tree cast shadows on the mud wall. The pale moonlight and the shadows of the leaves were tirelessly moving in the occasional breezes.[97]

The cold and wretched image of the evening moon that shines from behind the speechless narrator as he hesitates to bring his words to the widow allegorizes the voices that the "literature" Long practices in late colonial Taiwan was unable to convey.

KIM SARYANG AND THE POLITICS OF SELF-TRANSLATION

The image of pale moonlight at the end of "Evening Moon" constitutes a narratological counterpoint to the figure of "light" toward which the protagonist of Kim Saryang's acclaimed "Into the Light" is depicted as moving. Mirroring the story, the nomination of "Into the Light" for a 1939 Akutagawa Prize shot Kim into the literary limelight; he was welcomed to the imperial literary field as a new member from the colony.[98] His representation and self-representation in this field, however, suffered from an ambivalence similar to that of Gu Ding and Long Yingzong.

In an essay catered to a Japanese audience, Kim on the one hand unequivocally affirmed the self-identity of modern Korean literature as "something on the soil of the tradition of national literature cultivated over a long period of time that blossomed in the winds of modernity." The essential part of that identity is language, as he staunchly insisted: "It is an undeniable truth that Korean literature must be written in the Korean language."[99] On the other hand, however, he asserted that "the existence of Korean literature undoubtedly adorns a wing of Japanese literature," just as "British literature increases its glory because it embraces Irish literature under its wings." He even declared that "only through literature can the true spiritual integration of Japan and Korea [*naisen ittai* 内鮮一体] be realized," referring unapologetically to the wartime imperial slogan for uniting the metropole and the colony into "one body."[100] The identity of Korean literature, which the bilingual writer Kim believed was first and foremost attributable to the use of the Korean language, is here reduced to a difference or adornment that increases the value of imperial literature's cultural capital. To ensure the working of the logic of differentiation, Kim proposed that an "authoritative institute of translation" sponsored by the governor-general be established and put in charge of systematically translating premodern and modern Korean literature into Japanese. This institute would help foster and gatekeep exchanges between Japanese and Korean literatures and, ultimately, make Japanese audiences understand "the true reason for which Korean literature ought to be written in Korean."[101] Kim took advantage of Japan's increased interest in Korea in general and in Korean literature and culture in particular, prompted by the wartime need for cultural integration. Yet in this discursive situation, his strategy, even its affirmation of national identity, risked bolstering the empire's sanctioned multiculturalism.

Kim's ambivalent position as a budding colonial writer, grappling with the contradictory forces of inclusion and exclusion and of identity and difference, is embodied in the story "Into the Light." A student of the imperial university, the first-person narrator teaches English in evening classes to factory workers as a resident of the S co-op. The narrator is called "Mr. Minami" by children at the co-op, but this appellation immediately makes him explain to the reader in an apologetic tone why he accepts it. "Come to think of it," he addresses the reader, "before I knew it I was passing as Mr. Minami at the co-op. As you may know, my surname should be read 'Nam,' but for a variety of reasons, I was addressed in Japanese style as 'Minami.'"[102] Thus involving the readers, who are first and foremost a Japanese audience expected at least to know the Korean and Japanese pronunciations of the surname "南," the narrator from the onset finds himself in the politically charged, existentially taxing theater of identification in the culture that this text both depicts and exists in. The conflation of the diegetic and extradiegetic games of recognition thematizes the reader's horizon of expectation, which arises from the known identity of the author. The chief interlocutor of the narrator, a boy named Yamada Haruo, first gives him the impression that "something is odd:" "The figure of Haruo—his hunched back, his face, the shape of his mouth, even the way he held his chopsticks—reminded me of something I couldn't quite put my finger on."[103] The narrator's—and by extension, the reader's—hypersensitive, if inarticulate, intuition then develops into an assumption that, judging from Haruo's mockery of Koreans, the boy must be "from a poor family of settlers recently returned from Korea" and that he has come back with "a warped sense of superiority" like "the majority of children who travel to the colonies."[104] This then gives way to a suspicion that Haruo might in fact be a Korean child. But when the narrator witnesses an incident of domestic violence inflicted upon Haruo's mother, he in the end realizes that Haruo is the child of a Korean mother and a Japanese father. Then in a final twist, Haruo's abusive father, a gambler named Hanbei whom the narrator earlier met in a police detention cell and thought he was "mainland Japanese," turns out to have a Korean mother himself. The narrative thus reenacts the intrusive politics of identification in colonial representation, which, in turn, agonizes the narrator. He tries to convince himself that passing as "Mr. Minami" among children does not amount to "hypocrisy" or "cowardice" but rather reflects his simple hope to "get along well with the children" without provoking unnecessary "morbid curiosity." Yet to the young nationalist Yi, who demands clarity about the narrator's identity and attributes his Koreanness to physiognomic traits like "[his] eyes, [his] cheekbones, the shape of [his] eyes," he ought to declare: "I am of course Korean."[105] The colonial ambivalence tears the narrator apart:

> Of course, I told myself that Yi's naïveté was understandable; I had gone through a similar stage in my life once, too. But the next instant, I remembered that my current name was Minami, a fact that reverberated through my entire five senses like the peal of an

electric bell. Instinctively, I scrambled to think of my usual array of excuses. But it did not work anymore.

"You hypocrite. You're at it again, I see," said a voice from beside me. "Now that you can't hold out much longer, you're starting to lose your nerve, aren't you?"

I was stunned, but I shot back scornfully, "Why am I always vowing never to be a coward, never to be a coward. Doesn't that just prove I'm knee-deep in the swamp of cowardice already? . . . "

But I didn't have the courage to finish my sentence.[106]

The incomplete sentence that signifies the profundity of the narrator's mental torment also serves on the extradiegetic level as a demarcation of the extent of the stories he is able to tell. The textual interruption suggests that further fathoming of the "swamp" of his internal conflicts is beyond the bounds of the stories worth relating in the present medium. The story falls silent in front of a gaze obsessed with its ambivalent identity, the inquisitive eyes of the Japanese-language readers of colonial literature.

In the rest of the story, then, the narrator tries to resolve this conflict through his intimate relationship with Haruo. Haruo is afflicted with a "tragic estrangement of . . . two irreconcilable elements," "torn between an unconditional devotion to something paternal and a blind aversion to anything maternal."[107] The narrator, for his part, is trapped in the depths of the "solitary mudslinging" of "being Korean in this country."[108] The narrator helps Haruo reconcile with his Korean mother and takes him out for a walk in the bustling downtown of Tokyo. They shop in a department store and eat at a restaurant; they take the air in a crowded park and stroll down a wide boulevard. They encounter a happy-looking Yi in a new hat who has just received his driver's license and begun to work as a driver. Haruo reveals to the narrator that his dream is to become a dancer. He likes dancing with the lights off, and the narrator, who is himself fond of dancing in darkness and used to want to become a dancer and experiment with choreography, cannot help but imagine: "This young boy, who'd been hurt and warped by his unusual family background, was standing on a stage with his legs spread wide and his arms stretched out as he danced around into the light, caught up in a blur of red, green, and other colors." "I felt a wave of joy and admiration wash over me. He, too, was beaming with pleasure as he gazed up at me."[109] Remaining incognito in the urban crowds and embracing race-blind consumerism, they provide each other with temporary relief, and that moment allows the narrator to project the image of an ideal social space where self-representation and spectatorship are in harmony, symbolized by Haruo's dance "into the light." Kim's optimism envisions a successful performance of colonial identity on the public stage, through which the "hurt and warped" self of the colonized will be sublimated into an aesthetic representation, the dancing movements of extended limbs in colorful lights. Haruo's corporal movements are an idealized metonymy of the textual circulation of colonial literature among imperial audiences.

Yet in "Into the Light," the performances of colonial identity, or the "performative identities"[110] of the characters, are gendered. Indeed, Haruo's Korean mother Teijun/Chŏngsun is excluded from that exact performativity. She was handed over to Hanbei from a "Korean restaurant" in a red-light district in Tokyo to become his wife and, having suffered a major injury inflicted by her husband, she sees the "serious scar" on her face as a reason to stay with her violent husband. She believes that he would not be able to "sell [her] away" as no one would be willing to "purchase" her, and she chooses that precarious assurance over fleeing back to her hometown in Korea.[111] In contrast to Haruo's and the narrator's protean performing bodies, the ineffaceable scar left on Haruo's mother, while prohibiting the commercialization of her body, bespeaks her desperate lack of agency. Unlike Haruo's mind that has been "hurt and warped" by imperial violence, his mother's "scar," left *also* by gendered violence, remains hopelessly the same, unable to be differentiated or sublimated into a performative identity, as she is kept away from the space of representation that the narrator carves out. "Yeah, one of these days we'll move into an apartment or something near the co-op. For once, it'll just be the two of us," says the narrator to himself, considering taking Haruo under his wing so that the boy can receive dance lessons.[112] The narrator thus betrays exclusion inherent in colonial representability, which keeps Haruo's mother away from the "light" and confines her to the obscurity of Hanbei's dangerous household.

The narrator of "Into the Light," therefore, ironically inflicts the same kind of exclusionary forces on Haruo's mother that the imperial gaze does on him. The text leaves traces of such forces. For one, the narrator has to "leave the room" before he can overhear Haruo's mother telling Yi's mother of her decision to stay with her husband, implying the inadequacy of the narrator's presence to convey the full range of Haruo's mother's voice. More importantly, if Kim Saryang's Japanophone text is composed in such a way that it normalizes colonial bilingualism by representing Korean speech by the narrator and Yi, as well as Japanese speech, in standard Japanese prose, then it foregrounds the exclusion of Haruo's mother from that normalcy by marking her Korean utterance with nonstandard Japanese pronunciation with a Korean accent. Kim specifically represents the Korean interjection "aigo" in *katakana* and portrays her saying "*tesu*" instead of "*desu*," which would be the standard pronunciation. Along with those and other accented phrases, the text uses numerous points of suspension to reproduce her weak and wounded voice.[113] Kim made minor revisions to her speech and used furigana to further highlight her Korean accent when he reprinted this work in his first collection of Japanese-language short stories *Hikari no nakani* 光の中に (Into the Light, 1940). For "worried," she is portrayed as saying "*sunpai*" instead of the standard "*shinpai*." She calls her husband "*sujin*" rather than "*shujin*," which would be the standard pronunciation. She does not say "*onegai*" but "*onekai*" to make a plea.[114] These textual features indicate self-critical moments in Kim's Japanophone writing, pointing to what the "literature" he produces cannot convey in its normal mode of representation embodied in his skillful literary Japanese capable of embracing bilingualism. Beneath the performativity of bilingualism and the ambivalence of identities between Korean and Japanese, the colonized and the colonizers, "Into the Light" is haunted by the sheer forces of exclusion exerted by that performance of hybridity itself.

Kim's transcolonial letter to Long Yingzong, in which he agreed with the latter's criticism of "Into the Light" and admitted that it was a mere "work intended for the mainland Japanese audience," suggests his private awareness of this contradiction. Kim, indeed, was led to further tackle the exclusionary forces inherent in the literature he practiced, and he did so through intertextualizing Lu Xun's works, namely in his short story "A Man Whom I Met in a Detention Cell" (hereafter referred to as "A Man in a Detention Cell").

This story was originally published in the leading Seoul-based Korean-language literary journal *Munjang* 문장 (Composition) in 1941, just a few months before it was shut down due to intervention by the colonial government. Kim retitled it "Count Q" when he published it in his second collection of Japanese-language stories *Kokyō* 故郷 (My Hometown, 1942) in his own translation, foregrounding the work's indebtedness to Lu Xun's "The Real Story of Ah Q." The detained man in the story is the son of a Korean provincial governor and is nicknamed "Count Wang" by his fellow detainees and the officials due to his privileged status. The story is related by a Japanese-educated Korean newspaper reporter talking to his three Korean friends—all, including the reporter himself, alumni of the same college in Tokyo—on an express train from Pusan bound for the capital of Manchukuo, Shinkyō (Kor. Sin'gyŏng). The work's first-person narrator, the "I," is featured as one of these three men on board listening to the reporter's story.

The reporter depicts his first encounter with Count Wang a while ago in a police detention center in Tokyo, where, it is suggested, they were arrested on anti-regime charges. The reporter from the onset stresses the "strange pronunciation" of the Japanese that Count Wang speaks to a guard, which he recognizes as an unmistakable sign of his Korean identity. In a treatment similar to the depiction of the voice of Haruo's mother in "Into the Light," Kim reproduces Count Wang's speech through transcription into Korean.

「탄나 탄나상」
이렇게 그는 밖으로 向해 부르기가 일쑤였다.
　留置場에 들어간 바롯날 나는 이 奇異한 發音에 퍽이나 놀래었다. 그것은 바로 마즌편쪽 房으로 부터였으나 아모래도 그 목소리의 임자가 朝鮮사나이임에 틀림없기 때문이다.
「포쿠데스요. 포쿠 便所, 便所에 가구싶어요」
「王伯爵인가」
「하이 하잇」
그것이 아주 질겁할만치 황송한 목소리이다.

"Saar, saar."

It was his habit to speak to the outside in this manner.

On the day I entered the detention cell, I was very surprised at this strange pronunciation. It was because the owner of this voice, which came from a cell on the opposite side, must have been a Korean man.

"It'z mee. Mee, bathroom. I want to go to the bathroom."
"Is that Count Wang?"
"Ye, yess."
It is a surprisingly ceremonious voice.¹¹⁵

Careful attention is paid to emphasizing Count Wang's accent. He says "*t'annasang*" for "sir," indicating a deviation from the standard "*danna-san*." A similar accent with voiced consonants appears in the first-person pronoun "*p'oku*," which he uses instead of the standard "*boku*." His words sound markedly clumsy, as they are denoted by the stammered "*hai hait*" ("Ye, yess").

"A pitiful anarchist," as the reporter calls him, Count Wang has been arrested and detained dozens of times for his bizarre involvement in unlawful activities against the imperial authorities. Instead of taking part in direct action, he writes a letter to an arrested activist exaggerating the circumstances, only to annoy the police when they discover that the letter is forged. He is found by the police lying in the middle of the items of evidence he has recovered from a friend's room when he learns that the friend's illegal activities are being investigated. He feigns participation in resistance schemes to confuse the authorities, knowing that he will be released thanks to his powerful collaborationist father.

The reporter spends a year in jail, and shortly after he is released, he encounters Count Wang again, this time on a northbound train from Pusan to Manchuria packed with Korean peasants migrating to the northern land. Fresh out of prison, the reporter is trying to move on from the past, as he tells himself to "think no more" and forget the past that "needs to be buried." The prospect of a new life excites him, making him feel "the blood and power of new life springing out in the body." The sight of migrating farmers encourages him: "Having lost all of their fields and houses to the waters due to the hateful damages of winds and floods, those farmers were just beginning to discover new light and migrating to the wild plains far away. I looked at them and pledged that I must be reborn with ever more courage, and I must regain a new life." The excitement sends a rush of blood to his head.¹¹⁶ Since the takeover of Manchuria, the Japanese government had advertised the new puppet state as the frontier of opportunity and multiethnic coexistence and actively promoted the settlement of Korean farmers. Forced migration was common throughout the colonial period. The Japanese-implemented land reform in the peninsula increased the number of Korean tenant farmers, who were often compelled by natural disasters to abandon the lands and migrate to Manchuria and Siberia.[117] The reporter's gaze ideologically aligns with the imperial propaganda, as he discerns a "new light" in Manchuria and draws a parallel between their northbound exile and his renunciation of the political commitment in his dark past.

On the train, Count Wang addresses the newspaper reporter in the same accented Japanese as before and perceives himself and the migrants in an entirely different light. Count Wang is tormented by himself:

> "No, well . . ." he [Count Wang] moaned again in distress. "Alas! I am being avenged and choked up by myself right at this moment. There is no hope, no pleasure, no sadness, and even no purpose. . . . Alas! I can't help feeling happy only when I ride this immigration train. I can cry and wail with them."
>
> "But they are relocating with hope. They are not relocating to feel sad."
>
> "I don't care. I just feel extreme pleasure that I am moving in the same car in the same direction as them. They cry and wail together, but how about me? What should I do when these people cross the national borders and I cannot do anything but come back alone? When I think of that moment . . ."[118]

Count Wang ignores whether the migrating peasants harbor hope as propagandized by the state and feels "extreme pleasure" just because he can temporarily join them in crying and wailing and move "in the same direction in the same car" as them, until the train crosses the Korea–Manchuria border and he has to return. When the train leaves the station, "wailing and screaming arose all at once as if to move the heavens" among the migrants, and Count Wang "chuckled and giggled like a crazy man and then all of a sudden began to weep aloud." The train departs and the passengers calm down before long, but Count Wang's weeping only gets louder, and "as if suffering a seizure," he switches language and "exclaims in Korean": "I want to wail, too. I want to wail out loud. I like to cry, just cry. So I always board this immigration train."[119] The imperial narrative of auspicious frontier migration allowed the reporter to live in imagination the same official story of progress as the peasants, yet overwhelming that sanctioned ideology are the resounding lamentations and howls of the suffering, uprooted colonized. Count Wang's echoing cries and wails forge affective ties with the migrants.

The reporter empathizes with Count Wang. As he conjectures, "I understood that that frenzied man was seized by the hopeless despair that we also often fall into. Yes, he was always buried under absolute solitude." Count Wang thus mediates the voices of the agonized peasants, via the reporter, to the latter's three listeners ("we"), all colonial elites. Yet the reporter immediately adds, "I hoped that he would calm down soon."[120] As Count Wang's weeping does not stop, he further ponders, "In coolheaded eyes, of course, he was such a miserable fellow. It is such a man that is gradually going to perish." He finally silences him: "Stop it. It is so unsightly." Count Wang protests but, as if deprived of "the last pleasure," he falls down on the floor and becomes silent, which lets the reporter "feel relieved and fall asleep."[121] When he is about to get off the train, he tries to wake Count Wang, who remains unresponsive, yet he is so occupied with leaving the train on time that he no longer cares about Count Wang. Upon leaving the train, he gives a sigh of relief. It remains unknown whether Count Wang is alive or dead.

Relating this story, the reporter admits deep regret for feeling relieved when Count Wang finally fell silent on the train. He also remains repentant for leaving the train without making sure that he was alive and has been troubled by contrition ever since. "Yes, I think I committed another major sin at the onset of my rebirth or the restart of my life," confesses the reporter, revealing the emotional toll that his unsettling encounter with Count Wang has taken on the fresh beginning of life out of prison.[122] Telling the story does not release him from this pain. Still unaware of Count Wang's whereabouts, he mentions a few instances when he believed he might have seen his shadows after the encounter on the train, once in the middle of a flooded river and again during an air-raid drill. Then, to the depressed reporter, the "I" narrator, who has been listening to his whole story, makes reassuring comments: "Yes, that [person at the air-raid drill] must have been Count Wang. I believe he is pleased that the war has begun, because our country, despite some actual hardships, is now advancing further and further in national unity. He may have now realized the purpose and meaning of life. He could comfortably serve as something like the squad leader of a civil air-defense unit." To this optimistic opinion, the listeners all give "nods," yet the reporter in reply appends an eerie remark at the very end of the story, evoking one last time the haunting image of Count Wang: "But then after that, again on another day..."[123]

The nested structure of the narrative uncovers the ideological construct of the literary medium in which this story is conveyed. Just as the newspaper reporter is annoyed by and tries to suppress Count Wang's wails, weeping, and cries, so does the space of storytelling, consisting of four Tokyo-educated colonial elites, drive away his lingering afterimage. Bolstering the narration of this work is an underlying force at work to encompass all of the voices in one story, the sublime state power that provides all life—even that of a "pitiful anarchist"—with a "purpose and meaning," the power metaphorized by the transcolonial railway. Count Wang's cacophonic and inarticulate voice reverberates with the wailing and screaming of the crowd of Korean peasants in such a way that they defy inclusion in the imperial orchestra of war, progress, and new life. Kim's work conveys them only by featuring a repentant narrator who has missed and suppressed them, perhaps for good, in addition to unsympathetic audiences who also want to reduce them to ideological normalcy.

In that it employs this inadequate narration, "A Man in a Detention Cell" intertextualizes Lu Xun's stories, namely "The Real Story of Ah Q." Count Wang's eccentric simulation of resistance amounts to a caricature of Ah Q's "spiritual victory," while Kim's protagonist is all too aware of the futility of such an act, leading to the tormenting realization that he is "being avenged and choked up" by himself. Whereas Ah Q had to play his role until the very end of his life before he could finally cry "Help," Count Wang's groans and moans abound. But just as Ah Q was unable to verbalize his cry and his inner voice failed to resonate with the narrator, so does Count Wang's voice fail to move the storyteller and his listeners. The returning silent afterimages of Count Wang evoke Ah Q's muted plea for rescue, as both images demand that the reader self-reflectively question their abilities to hear their voices through the literary medium. Just as Lu Xun parodied existing literature to tell a story about the kind of subject that has always been excluded from it, so too Kim parodies in the nested narrative the institutionalized "literature" in the imperium to give voice to that which is suppressed in it. The self-reflexive mode of literary representation that Lu Xun practiced, therefore, inspires Kim to convey the voices of the colonized not as a literary theme or an identity but as an allegory whose significance is missed in the current regime of literature.

Kim Saryang gave the Japanese version of this story the new title "Count Q" and featured the eponymous protagonist in lieu of Count Wang. As he undertook this otherwise quite faithful self-translation in order to publish the work in the metropole, Kim assumed the role of intra-imperial translator. This act of self-translation, then, could have resulted in the addition of yet another restrictive layer of authorized representation, further banishing Count Wang/Count Q into the abyss of voicelessness. Yet just as the parody of imperial literary production in the Korean original engendered an allegorical mode, essential for self-critically imparting voiceless voices, so does the self-translation enhance Kim's pursuit of novel literature within a prohibitive literary culture.

Like the Korean original, the Japanese text characterizes the protagonist through scrupulous representations of his voice.

「たん那、たん那さん」と、彼はよく外に向つて呼ぶ。
はいつたばかりの日、僕はこのひょうきんな舌廻りに随分と驚いた。それは、筋向ひあたりの房からであるが、何分その聲主が朝鮮の男であるに違ひないからだ。
「ぼくですよ、ぼく、便所、便所へ行きたいですよ」
「Q伯爵か」と看守は眠さうな聲で唸る。
「は、はい」
それが又いかにも畏つた軍隊式の聲なのだ。
"Saar, saar."
He frequently calls to the outside in this manner.
On the day I entered the detention cell, I was very surprised at this funny turn of the tongue. It was because the owner of this voice, which came from a cell on the opposite side, must have been a Korean man.
"It'z mee. Mee, bathroom. I want to go to the bathroom."
"Is that Count Q?" groans the guard in a sleepy voice.
"Ye, yess."
It was a ceremonious military-style voice.[124]

Kim portrays Count Q's accented Japanese in the same manner as he did in the Korean original of this passage, which we have seen above, by reproducing his distinctive pronunciation of voiced consonants—"*poku*" and "*tannasan*," instead of the ordinary "*boku*" and "*dannasan*"—as well as by foregrounding his stammers. In this translational gesture, Count Q's voice stands out for it is uncannily preserved *as is*, whereas other portions in the Korean original, including the Japanese guard's speech, are rendered into standard Japanese.

The scene of the newspaper reporter's initial encounter with Count Wang/Count Q deserves particular attention in this regard:

「東京의同志!」
이렇게 그는 아무 꺼리낌 없이 닷자로 부르지졌다. 술기운 때문에 <u>以前</u>보다도 더욱 혀가 돌아가지않는 국어를 쓴다.
「응. 이게 웬일인가 大體 자네는 그後 無事했는가. 얼굴 빛이 아주 나뿌구먼」
「어서 여기라도 좀 앉게나.」
하고 나는 그에게 자리를 내 주려고 일어났다.
 . . .
「아니 나는 여기가 더 좋을세 여기가. 응 그런데 여보게 東京의同志 나는 자 자네가 送局될때 근심하였다네. 아주 크게 걱정을 했었다네. 저것이 처음이 되어 금시에 헤타바루 하지나 않을까하구 응」
「고마웁세 그러나 자네 지금 좀 쉬이는게 좋을것같은데」
하며 나는 그를 타일르듯이 조용히 달래였다. 그런즉 그는 두말 안짝으로 유순히 물꽉을 모아 세우고 머리를 숙였다. 그리고는 괴로운듯이 呻吟소리를 내기始作한다.

"Comrade of Tokyo!"

He abruptly called me in a loud voice without any consideration for others. Because he was drunk, he spoke in the national language even more clumsily than the last time.

"Um, hey, what's going on here? Have you been all right since then? You look so pale."

"Come on, sit down here," I said.

And I made room for him. . . .

"No don't worry. I'm fine here. Um, but hey Comrade of Tokyo, I was so worried when you, you were sent to jail. I was hugely concerned. You were sent there for the first time, so I thought you would soon be worn out, um."

"Thanks. But you'd better have some rest now."

I said to him quietly as if I were admonishing him. But then he stopped talking, and meekly held his knees and hid his head. Then he started to groan painfully.[125]

Count Wang's Japanese is designated as "national language," yet its clumsiness is salient, as represented by the frequent interjections of "*ŭng*" ("um") and the stammering "you, you," as well as the *hangul* transcription of the Japanese term "*het'abaru*" ("worn out"). Annoyed by Count Wang's "loud" and inept Japanese, the reporter, trying to silence him, speaks in accurate Japanese, which is rendered in smooth Korean, and asks him to "have some rest" in a "quiet" and "admonishing" tone. Suppressed by the standard Japanese, Count Wang's awkward Japanese becomes a painful groan.

Kim renders this passage as follows:

「東京の同志!」と、彼はあたりかまはず大きな声で唸った。酒気のため以前より余計舌の廻らない内地語を使ってゐる。私はいささかはらはらした。「え、これはどうしたことだよ。きみーー君はその後元気かい? 顔色が悪いぞ!」

「まあ、ここにでも落着きよ」と云って、僕は彼に席を譲らうとして立ち上がった。

. . .

「いや、ぽくはここでええ。ここでええんだ。ぽくはよ東京の話がしてえんだ。よう、東京の同志、ぽくは君、きみーーが送られる時は心配したぞう。大いに心配したぞう。野郎ははじめてだから、きっとへたばるだらうってな」

「ありがとう、だが君は寝んだ方がよさそうだ」

と、僕は彼をいたはるやうに物静かに云った。と、彼は素直に膝小僧を抱いて頭をうな垂れた。そして苦しさうに呻き出した。

"Comrade of Tokyo!" he yelled in a loud voice without any consideration for others. Because he was drunk, he spoke in the mainland language that was even clumsier than the last time. I got a little nervous. "Hey, what's going on here? You—have you been all

Transnational Allegory 279

right since then? You look so pale!" "Come on, sit down here," I said, and stood up to make room for him. . . .

"No don't worry. I'm fine here. I'm all right here. I want to talk about Tokyo. Hey Comrade of Tokyo, I was so worried when you, you were sent [to jail]. I was hugely concerned. You were sent there for the first time, so I thought you would soon be worn out."

"Thanks. But you'd better have some rest now."

I said to him quietly as if I were consoling him. But then he meekly held his knees and hid his head. Then he started to groan painfully.[126]

Still speaking in Japanese, or "the mainland language," Count Q sounds slightly clumsier in the translation, as Kim uses the same technique as he does in the above-quoted detention center scene to illustrate his accented voiced consonants: "*tōshita*" and "*poku*" for "*dōshita*" and "*boku*." Elsewhere, his stammer—"*kimi, kimi*" ("you, you")—is reproduced, and the term "*hetabaru*" ("worn out"), which in the original is transcribed in *hangul*, is employed verbatim. Against the backdrop of the standard-sounding Japanese that the reporter speaks in his speeches and narration, Count Q's language sounds as odd as Count Wang's in the original.

While Kim, just like the bilingual newspaper reporter in the story, therefore translates himself adroitly between two standard languages, he preserves a distinction between fluency and clumsiness, normality and abnormality, through that process. Count Wang/Count Q's queer language evades proper translation and confuses the distance between languages, eventually turning into a "groan" that defies linguistic articulation. At stake in Kim's self-translation, thus, is not only the relationship between Korean and Japanese, but also the separation between those who are able to perform bilingualism between them, on the one hand, and those who speak them only incompetently, blur their distinctions, and find themselves stuck in between, on the other hand.

Count Wang/Count Q's language undermines the function of intra-imperial translation to furnish Korean literature with proper representation in the imperial literary field. It fundamentally eludes and dislocates the proper linguistic difference that the translation is meant to bridge; it sounds equally "strange" in both languages, thereby engendering an eerie *repetition* between the original and the translation. His voice, if you will, is too translatable to generate a difference that could be capitalized upon. Silenced both in the Korean and Japanese texts, then, his voice becomes a prelinguistic, wordless weeping and wailing, which reverberate with the resounding cry of the suffering Korean peasants. His exclamation: "I want to wail, too. I want to wail out loud. I like to cry, just cry. So I always board this immigration train," which the storyteller, in both the original and the translation, designates as uttered "in Korean," no longer indicates a national language that could be properly conveyed in the sanctioned literary medium or translated into the imperial language.[127] Instead, it becomes an allegory of the voice of a nation whose expression requires a new literature that would come into existence when the imperial culture playing with bilingualism and identities is to be smashed altogether.

Kim's self-translation thus bespeaks a self-critical resistance to the imperial cultural integration that he endorsed both in theory and practice as a bilingual colonial writer. Like the story's first-person narrator "I," who attempts to reduce Count Wang/Count Q's haunting figures to characters in the imperial propaganda, Kim translated his work to give it a proper place in the broader imperial literary field. Yet just as the reporter's ambiguous final remark ("But then after that, again on another day . . .") hauntingly arrests the working of the state ideology, so do the voices of Count Wang and Count Q, uncannily repeating each other, dislocate the politics of intra-imperial representation. Kim's self-translation is reminiscent of a sharply critical view of the relationship between Korean and Japanese that he published in 1936 before his major debut. The young Kim, while stating the ambition to write "the reality of Korea faithfully," expressed bewilderment at his usage of Japanese: "Just as I am writing these words, I still start to worry about the language. I even try to think of rather killing off Japanese from my writing. What if I transpose my mother tongue into a stiff literal translation [*seikōna chokuyaku* 生硬な直譯] using *kana* characters? I have written seventy pages but now I am stuck. Give me time until the next issue so I can write something."[128] While exhibiting the desire to eliminate Japanese from his writing, Kim suggests reinventing it through a "stiff literal translation" of his "mother tongue" into a Japanese writing that only employs the *kana* alphabet, i.e.,

Transnational Allegory 281

without the Chinese characters, which both the Japanese and Korean writing systems used at that time. Kim's program of envisioning a new kind of literary medium through tensions between the two languages, without the help of the shared characters, lays bare a modernist idea of literary translation that squarely undercuts his later support of imperial literary politics based on differences.[129]

"A Man in a Detention Cell" and its Japanese translation embody the author's self-reflexive attempts at representing the voice of the colonized in the imperial institution of literature in which he was eminently involved. In this sense, they constitute a creative response to his self-criticism of "Into the Light" in his letter to Long Yingzong. Intertextualizing Lu Xun's endeavor to engender a new realm of literature through parodic intervention in the existing literature, Kim uses the sign "Q" as the symbol of a quintessential movement of modern literature, one that continues to redraw the realm of literature from within, driven by interrogations of what "literature" can and cannot convey as it exists in the present cultural situations.

Viewed from the vantage point of the early history of modern literature in East Asia, with the intertextualization of Lu Xun's works as a key point of reference, late colonial literatures in Manchukuo, Taiwan, and Korea display aspects that cut across the center/periphery dynamics of textual movements in the Japanese Empire. The works by Gu Ding, Long Yingzong, and Kim Saryang create textual moments at which they suspend the significances assigned to them in the sanctioned literary culture where they were produced, circulated, and received and begin to exist as allegories. The transregional adaptations of Lu Xun's works in the late colonial period inform our comparative reading that offers a semantic horizon where those allegories align in a constellation to throw light on modern literature in the region as a persistent self-reflexive movement of redefining literature amid the sociopolitical realities that test its received function and meaning.

We examined in chapter 3 how Lu Xun, like his Japanese and Korean counterparts, created an origin of this movement in East Asia through critical engagement with the cultural past. The newness of his works was not defined by preconceived values or norms of the modern culture that was being created; rather, it was produced by the forces of their critique and expansion of the accepted realm of what literature was able to represent. His works' defiance of ideological determinations, while complicating their cultural allegiance, informed the late colonial writers' efforts to convey colonial voices through the very literary medium that suppressed them. Through their intertextualizations of Lu Xun's texts, these writers' works bespeak the transcolonial afterlives of modern literature in East Asia, conjuring up its intrinsically transnational origins and illuminating its historical significance as an interminable endeavor of border-bending critique.

Conclusion

This book has explored the origins of modern literature in East Asia through a transregional comparative approach. In the late nineteenth to early twentieth centuries, literature in the region freed itself from its culturally determined functions and became an open concept, or an aesthetic endeavor in the modern sense that self-reflexively defines its own realm in response to sociopolitical situations. We have examined this process and demonstrated that it took place through writerly attempts at reconstructing the present's historical relationship to the past across the radical cultural changes caused by modernization. Modern literature originated in East Asia from cultural in-betweenness, wresting itself from confinement in a modern culture delineated by severance from the past.

Based on this study, I suggest that the following three tasks are mutually complementary: (1) elucidating a regional structure of modern literature that arises from the legacies of classical culture; (2) grasping modern literature in its conceptual openness; and (3) conceiving of world literature with open horizons. Our comparative approach has shed light on the region's cultural pasts that were deemed obsolete and unusable as a nationalized tradition and recovered their afterlives as integral to the formations of modern literature in East Asia. This approach has enabled modern literature to maintain its conceptual openness as an aesthetic endeavor beyond the ideological confines of cultural modernization. Modern literature thus reveals itself as fundamentally marked by, in addition to national and other transnational formations, a *regional* structure attributable to the remaining effects of the classical literary world. So grasped as a modern, aesthetic concept, literature reclaims its original potential to defy its culturally defined realms and opens itself to diverse examples taken from beyond cultural boundaries. Inherent in literary modernity is resistance to literature's appropriation by a fixed set of privileged examples, be they from the West or the East. Its conceptual openness is therefore precisely coterminous with the open horizons of the world from which its examples are gleaned. To the extent that the examination in this book is based on close reading rooted in East Asian archives, it in turn allows us to capture world literature in its fundamental openness.

I owe the conception of this project to the rise of new approaches to East Asian literatures beginning in the late 1980s. Against the backdrop of the waning Cold War and the growth of postcolonial and postmodern studies, scholars began in earnest to reconsider modern East Asian literatures beyond the grand narratives of national literature, which had been shaped and institutionalized in the postwar period often under the structural influence of the Cold War politics.[1] They called for attention to underrepresented literary formations that had tended to be excluded from the hegemonies of postwar national cultures. In the context of the democracy movement in Korea, diverse manifestations of the nation's modern literature began to be revisited to elicit insights into the imaginations of a coming post–Cold War, postcolonial era. The lifting of the four-decade-old martial law in Taiwan initiated reckonings with the island's history and reassessments of its multifaceted literatures. The era of reforms in China inspired the globalization of Chinese literary studies and the expansion of the field into ideological, linguistic, historical, ethnic, and other diversities. The rise of the region's economies prompted Japanese literary studies to grapple with the nation's wartime responsibility anew and reassess its modern literature from postcolonial and postmodern perspectives.

But in the early twenty-first century, despite the tremendous diversifications of the field, East Asia seems to witness the classic contradictions of modernity concentrated once again in the region. Nearly eighty years after the collapse of the Japanese Empire, intractable clashes between nationalisms remain a major concern; even the specters of a new Cold War appear to be looming on the horizons of a region drenched in discontent with the current form of globalization. At this juncture, I have returned to one of the most fundamental thrusts of post-1980s scholarship: the reclamation of literature's intrinsic resistance to conceptual definition and its fundamental capacity to attend to minor voices excluded from dominant orders of representation. I have thus delved into the origins of literature in this modern sense, which has led me to revisit interplays between literatures in the region, yet this time in a way that is more firmly grounded on the historical contexts of East Asian letters than the previous studies. This approach has enabled me to offer a new response to the perennial question: What is modern literature in East Asia? I have tried to respond to it by examining its origins, which are inherently transnational and anachronistic; it came into being through the attempts at reconstructing meaning in the middle of the wasteland between cultures deemed incompatible, rather than reinforcing particular cultural norms. It was born endowed with the ability to provide space and time for the difficult task of cultural co-being and co-transformations.

This study's return to the origins of modern literature in East Asia is intended, on the one hand, to inspire further diversification of the field. One obvious lacuna in this study is a consideration of modern literature in Vietnam, which faced similar cultural-historical situations at its origin, yet with the added intervention of French imperialism. Further studies are needed on the minor formations of modern literature in the subnational regions and communities as well as on the borderlands of East Asian nations. On the other hand, this study seeks to generate dialogue with the growing explorations of the thoughts and imaginations of classical East Asian civilizations as resources to cast critical light on the conceptual premises that are taken for granted in the modern way of organizing the world. More and more scholars are drawing on East Asian sources to gain philosophical insights into universal questions such as justice, governance, the good life, and happiness—projects prompted by the challenges of modernity that have been vividly laid bare by the global issues of the twenty-first century.[2] How should we reestablish interfaces through which to engage with cultural pasts that are rendered obsolete? How can we hear the resonances of the past without reducing them to normalcies of our modern culture or to a mere cultural fundamentalism? How can we present the resources of East Asian civilizations as philosophical moments capable of inspiring our common pursuit of moral community? We face, in different sociopolitical circumstances, questions similar to those that late nineteenth- to early twentieth-century East Asian intellectuals wrestled with as they created modern literature. Revisiting the origins of modern literature offers us a critical frame of reference for comparative examinations of philosophical resources in cultural pasts that may not be immediately commensurable with modern values or norms.

In concluding this study, I would like to delineate the critical stakes of our present's engagement with the cultural past by once again returning to Lu Xun. I opened this book with Lu Xun's prose poem "After Death" as an epigraph for my revisionary approach, drawing on the ironic light it casts on modernity's incessant movement toward newness. The ambivalent rise of the dead speaker at the end of this dream poem allegorized the origins of modern literature, the emergence of a new horizon of representation in the midst of the ineluctable cycles of the new and the old.

Having thus begun this study with "After Death," I close it with Lu Xun's "Resurrection," or "Qi si 起死" (1935). The sole piece written in the style of a short play in *Old Stories Retold*, "Resurrection" rewrites a well-known parable on life and death in the *Zhuangzi*. In the original tale, Zhuangzi is on his way to the state of Chu when he discovers an ancient, parched skull and addresses it with his conjectures on the reason for its owner's death. As he finishes speaking, Zhuangzi uses the skull for a pillow and lies down to sleep. He then has a dream in which the skull's owner appears to bestow a moral on him. The skull notices in Zhuangzi's speculations "the entanglements of a living man" and lectures him on death, insisting that death, "with no rulers above, no subjects below, and no chores of the four seasons," amounts to the ultimate "happiness" that even the south-facing king is unable to match. Zhuangzi tries to confirm the skull's meaning by asking whether he would want to come back alive if he could have the Arbiter of Fate give him a body and return him to his family, neighbors, and friends. The skull appears genuinely worried, wondering why he would ever renounce the happiness of the south-facing king for the travails of the human.[3]

By incorporating a few references to the seminal "Qiwulun 齊物論" (Discourse on Making All Things Equal) chapter of the *Zhuangzi*, Lu Xun reworks this anecdote into a satire of Zhuangzi the master. In "Resurrection," the skull is actually resurrected by the Arbiter of Fate summoned by Zhuangzi. Yet rather than appearing as a meaningful interlocutor for the master, the revived man is—quite understandably—stark naked, since his clothes have decomposed, and he is preoccupied with his embarrassing public nudity and the business of delivering dates and white sugar to his relatives, which his untimely death had prevented him from completing. Zhuangzi, for his part, belittles the man's worldly concerns and ridicules his ignorance of the purported "principles" (*daoli* 道理) behind the miraculous resuscitation, mocking him as "a barbarian without the understanding of philosophical principles [*zheli* 哲理]."[4] Zhuangzi acts as a self-important agent of knowledge and inquires about the man's provenance in the style of "evidential investigation" (*chakao* 查考), concluding that he is from the era of the last king of the Shang dynasty, more than five hundred years before Zhuangzi's time, and that he was killed by a robber on his way to see his relatives. The uneasy pairing of the "philosophical principles" and "evidential investigation" is meant to caricature a metaphysical interpretation of the thought in the *Zhuangzi* that posits a transcendental gaze capable of "making all things equal" and encompassing life and death as somehow commensurable with one another. Lu Xun's piece exposes the idealism of such a notion by revealing the material reality of the revived man and staging the sheer absurdity of communication, one imposing a philosophical lesson and the other looking for his lost things, which results in a skirmish that ultimately needs to be quelled by the police, who are called by Zhuangzi himself and mobilized by his authority as a "master."

"Resurrection," in the conclusion of this book, prompts us to reflect once more on the present's relationship to the cultural past. It reveals, hyperbolically through the critique of the Zhuangzi-esque transcendental gaze of "making all things equal," the absence of any real grounds on which to recover the lost past as immediately commensurate with the present. It instead lays bare the incompatibility of the characters' worlds, as indicated by the preposterousness of the communication, a sign of the gulf between two entirely disparate language games. This absurd play insists that the resurrection of the dead, or the endeavor to reconstruct a relationship to the past, must entail real friction—not necessarily without violence—that calls our epistemological premises into question, a process essentially distinct from the satirized attitude that postulates, from the authoritative point of view of the present, the whole historical world as inherently intelligible, either positivistically or metaphysically. As Lu Xun's ridicule shows, this subtly exclusionary attitude dismisses unsettling resonances of the past that resist intelligence in present culture—resonances that the play's ending expresses in the voice of the revived man demanding that the policeman help him and arrest his robber, indicating a form of life that irretrievably lost its relevance centuries ago: "Otherwise, I can't visit my relatives or live as a decent man. Two pounds of dates and a pound and a half of white sugar... You let him go; I shall with all my might have you...."[5] Modern literature, in its emergent moments in East Asia, constituted attempts at conveying just such reverberations of the lost past, as an art of leaving our present culture with questions about what can be spoken of in it.

Today, our engagement with the cultural past can benefit from the examples of late nineteenth- and early twentieth-century East Asian writers. They tell us to remain critical of the premise of commensurability, whether in the form of scientific positivism or metaphysical idealism. They also suggest that we should not exoticize or essentialize the past, a mistake that tends to render past cultures as mere "others" of modernity. We must instead attend to the past in ways that endure the cacophonies and philosophical questions it raises in our ordinary use of language, questions whose resolution should alter our forms of life and result in our self-transformation. Our engagement, therefore, requires forms that indicate exteriorities of our cultural norms—forms that we have been attributing to "modern literature" in this study.

This particular kind of positive relationship to the past—neither appropriation nor othering—is conceptually underexplored. I propose, inspired by "Resurrection," to make my last anachronistic move in this study by revisiting the *Zhuangzi* itself. Lu Xun's criticism of the metaphysical interpretation of its thought indeed distantly echoes the classic commentary to this text by Guo Xiang 郭象 (252–312). Commenting on the skull parable, Guo Xiang interprets the notion of "making all things equal": "Old theories contended that Zhuangzi enjoyed death and hated life, but they are fraudulent! If they were right, then how could one make [all things] equal? To 'make equal' means to be satisfied with life when alive, and to be satisfied with death when dead. Since life and death are equal in terms of their states, you don't worry about death when you're alive. This is Zhuangzi's meaning."[6] Guo Xiang does not argue that life and death are objectively "equal," but that they are "equal" in that each one constitutes a self-sufficient world where one can be "satisfied" (*an* 安) with being in it. He then explores the relationship between life and death in terms of their being "equal" in this sense through the doctrine of the "transformation of things" (*wuhua* 物化). He analogizes the distinction between life and death to that between wakefulness and dreaming in his commentary on the famous "butterfly dream" parable of the *Zhuangzi*, which Lu Xun also alludes to in "Resurrection."[7] The parable goes as follows:

> Once Zhuang Zhou [i.e. Zhuangzi] dreamt he was a butterfly, a butterfly flitting and fluttering around, happy with himself and doing as he pleased. He didn't know he was Zhuang Zhou. Suddenly he woke up and there he was, solid and unmistakable Zhuang Zhou. But he didn't know if he was Zhuang Zhou who had dreamt he was a butterfly, or a butterfly dreaming he was Zhuang Zhou. Between Zhuang Zhou and a butterfly there must be distinction. This is called the transformation of things.[8]

"Between Zhuang Zhou and a butterfly there must be distinction." So the transformation of things is not concerned with a transformation within an existing world but with the affirmation of a radically transformed world that Zhuang Zhou had never imagined before he happened upon this dream about the happiness of the life of a butterfly—a world in which Zhuang Zhou would have been a butterfly. Like the dream that reveals the groundlessness of Zhuang Zhou's self-identical world, modern literature in East Asia derives from the distinction between past and present the intensity to destabilize our world's identity and open it to a possible transformation, into a world that recognizes the happiness of others.

Notes

INTRODUCTION

1. Lu Xun, "Si hou," in *Lu Xun quanji* (Beijing: Renmin wenxue chubanshe, 2005), 2:214–18. Translations from Chinese, Japanese, and Korean in this book are mine unless otherwise noted. I have benefited from existing English translations that I have listed in the bibliography.
2. Lu Xun, "Si hou," 217–18.
3. Leo Ou-fan Lee, *Voices from the Iron House: A Study of Lu Xun* (Bloomington: Indiana University Press, 1987), 69–88. In the 1925 essay "Zhanshi he cangying" (The Warrior and the Flies), Lu Xun contrasts the "warrior" with the gossipy "flies"—a figure of the "crowd"—that use their "perfect" "imperishable voice" to find fault with the warrior's legacy (*Lu Xun quanji*, 3:40–41). He also attributes the figure of the warrior in this essay to "Sun Yat-sen [1866–1925] and the martyrs who died for the country and yet were mocked and trampled on by the slavish people around the first year of the Republic." See "Zhe shi shenme yige yisi," in *Lu Xun quanji*, 7:275.
4. See Lu Xun's seminal "Preface" to *Nahan* (Call to Arms), in *Lu Xun quanji*, 1:441.
5. Lu Xun, "Moluo shili shuo," in *Lu Xun qianji*, 1:65. Lu Xun quotes from Friedrich Nietzsche, *Also Sprach Zarathustra*, Pt. 3, Ch. 12, §25. English translation in *Thus Spoke Zarathustra: A Book for All and None*, ed. Adrian Del Caro and Robert B. Pippin, trans. Adrian Del Caro (Cambridge: Cambridge University Press, 2006), 170. For "On the Power of Mara Poetry" and its usage of the

notion of "origin," see Pu Wang, "Poetics, Politics, and 'Ursprung/Yuan': On Lu Xun's Conception of 'Mara Poetry,'" *Modern Chinese Literature and Culture* 23, no. 2 (Fall 2011): 34–60.
6. Lu Xun, "Moluo shili shuo," in *Lu Xun qianji*, 1:65.
7. Friedrich Nietzsche, "On the Uses and Disadvantages of History for Life," in *Untimely Meditations*, ed. Daniel Breazeale, trans. R. J. Hollingdale (Cambridge: Cambridge University Press, 1997), 64.
8. Jacques Derrida, *Of Grammatology*, trans. Gayatri Chakravorty Spivak, corrected ed. (Baltimore, MD: Johns Hopkins University Press, 1997), 17.
9. Jacques Derrida, *Spurs: Nietzsche's Styles / Éperons: Les styles de Nietzsche*, trans. Barbara Harlow (Chicago: University of Chicago Press, 2017), 130–33.
10. For the notion of the worldliness of text, see Edward Said, "The World, the Text, and the Critic," in *The World, the Text, and the Critic* (Cambridge, MA: Harvard University Press, 1983), 31–53.
11. See Michael Nylan, "The 'Chin Wen/Ku Wen' Controversy in Han Times," *T'oung Pao* 80, nos. 1–3 (1994): 83–145; Benjamin A. Elman, *Classicism, Politics, and Kinship: The Ch'ang-chou School of New Text Confucianism in Late Imperial China* (Berkeley: University of California Press, 1990).
12. The Gongyang school, via its revival by Kang Youwei, has been avidly revisited once again by contemporary Chinese intellectuals as an important philosophical resource. See conclusion, note 2.
13. See Eric J. Hobsbawm and Terence O. Ranger, eds., *The Invention of Tradition* (Cambridge: Cambridge University Press, 1992). For Lu Xun's practice of classical poetry, see Jon Eugene von Kowallis, *The Lyrical Lu Xun: A Study of His Classical-Style Verse* (Honolulu: University of Hawai'i Press, 1996).
14. See the introduction to part II.
15. For example, some of the field-defining histories include C. T. Hsia, *A History of Modern Chinese Fiction*, 3rd ed. (Bloomington: Indiana University Press, 1999); Donald Keene, *Dawn to the West: Japanese Literature of the Modern Era* (New York: Columbia University Press, 1998); Kwon Yŏngmin, *Han'guk hyŏndae munhaksa* (Seoul: Minŭmsa, 2002).
16. Karatani Kōjin, *Origins of Modern Japanese Literature* (Tokyo: Iwanami shoten, 2008).
17. The writers I will examine in part II of this book have particularly often been discussed in a similar framework. See chapter 3.
18. For a comparative study of the modern genre of "literary history" in East Asia, see Cho Tong'il, *Tong asia munhaksa pigyoron* (Seoul: Sŏul taehakkyo ch'ulp'anbu, 1993). See also Emmanuel Lozerand, *Littérature et génie national: Naissance d'une histoire littéraire dans le Japon du XIXe siècle* (Paris: Belles lettres, 2005).

19. See Trevor Ross, "Copyright and the Invention of Tradition," *Eighteenth-Century Studies* 26, no. 1 (1992): 1–27.
20. Recent examples in the English language include Kang-i Sun Chang and Stephen Owen, eds., *The Cambridge History of Chinese Literature* (Cambridge: Cambridge University Press, 2010); Haruo Shirane et al., eds., *The Cambridge History of Japanese Literature* (Cambridge: Cambridge University Press, 2015); and Peter H. Lee, ed., *A History of Korean Literature* (Cambridge: Cambridge University Press, 2003).
21. Paul De Man, "Literary History and Literary Modernity," *Daedalus* 99, no. 2 (Spring 1970): 391.
22. In much of Karatani's discussion, the emergence of "modern Japanese literature" can be conceptually attributed to the introduction of "perspective," which he draws from Panofsky's *Perspective as Symbolic Form*, into narratives. Karatani, however, privileges "geometrical perspective" developed in the Renaissance and does not fully take into account Panofsky's historicization of "perspective" as "symbolic form." As Panofsky explains by referring to Ernst Cassirer, "perspective" is "symbolic form" through which "spiritual meaning is attached to a concrete, material sign and intrinsically given to this sign," and so "it is essential to ask of artistic periods and regions not only whether they have perspective, but also which perspective." Erwin Panofsky, *Perspective as Symbolic Form* (Cambridge, MA: MIT Press, 1991), 41. Panofsky's argument would call for interrogating what "perspective" premodern Japanese literature had had and what new "perspective" emerged in a new transcultural space in modern Japan, unlike Karatani's approach, which perceives "the absence of 'depth' in premodern literature" and considers the emergence in modern times of that which had been absent. Karatani, *Nihon kindai bungaku*, 204.
23. See Satoru Hashimoto, "World Literature and East Asian Literatures," in *The Routledge Companion to World Literature*, 2nd ed., ed. Theo D'haen, David Damrosch, and Djelal Kadir (New York: Routledge, 2022), 425–33.
24. See Terry Eagleton, *Literary Theory: An Introduction* (Minneapolis: University of Minnesota Press, 2008), 16; Raymond Williams, *Marxism and Literature* (Oxford: Oxford University Press, 1977), 45–54; Michel Foucault, *The Order of Things: An Archaeology of the Human Sciences* (New York: Routledge Classics, 2002), 321–27; Trevor Ross, "The Emergence of 'Literature:' Making and Reading the English Canon in the Eighteenth Century," *ELH* 63, no. 2 (1996): 397–422.
25. For the modern etymology of the term 文學 in East Asia, see Suzuki Sadami, *Nihon no "bungaku" gainen* (Tokyo: Sakuhin sha, 1998) and Ch'oe Wŏnsik, *Han'guk kaenyŏmsa ch'ongsŏ: Munhak* (Seoul: Sohwa, 2012).

26. Immanuel Kant, *Critique of the Power of Judgment*, ed. Paul Guyer, trans. Eric Matthews (Cambridge: Cambridge University Press, 2000), 66–68. See Hannah Arendt, *Lectures on Kant's Political Philosophy*, ed. Ronald Beiner (Chicago: University of Chicago Press, 1982), 76–77, 79–85.
27. Eagleton, *Literary Theory*, 8.
28. Northrop Frye, *Anatomy of Criticism: Four Essays* (Princeton, NJ: Princeton University Press, 1957), 345.
29. René Wellek, *Theory of Literature* (New York: Harcourt, Brace and Company, 1949), 17.
30. Foucault, *The Order of Things*, 327.
31. Natsume Sōseki, "Watashi no kojinshugi," in *Teihon Sōseki zenshū* (Tokyo: Iwanami shoten, 2016–20), 16:611.
32. Natsume Sōseki, *Bungaku ron*, in *Teihon Sōseki zenshū*, 14:9. On *Theory of Literature*, see Natsume Sōseki, *Theory of Literature and Other Critical Writings*, ed. Michael K. Bourdaghs et al. (New York: Columbia University Press, 2009), 1–35.
33. Natsume, "Watashi no," 16:614.
34. Jacques Derrida, "This Strange Institution Called Literature," in *Acts of Literature*, ed. Derek Attridge (New York: Routledge, 1992), 36.
35. This insight underpins sociological studies of modern literature and art. See in particular Pierre Bourdieu, *Distinction: A Social Critique of the Judgement of Taste*, trans. Richard Nice (New York: Routledge & Kegan Paul, 1986). For examples of sociological approaches to modern East Asian literatures, see Lydia Liu, *Translingual Practice: Literature, National Culture, and Translated Modernity—China, 1900–1937* (Stanford, CA: Stanford University Press, 1995), 214–38; Michel Hockx, *Questions of Style: Literary Societies and Literary Journals in Modern China, 1911–1937* (Leiden: Brill, 2003); Hoyt Long, *On Uneven Ground: Miyazawa Kenji and the Making of Place in Modern Japan* (Stanford, CA: Stanford University Press, 2011); Young Min Kim, *The History of Modern Korean Fiction (1890–1945): The Topography of Literary Systems and Form*, trans. Rachel Min Park (Lanham, MD: Lexington Books, 2020).
36. Frye, *Anatomy of Criticism*, 345.
37. Stanley Cavell, "Aesthetic Problems of Modern Philosophy," in *Must We Mean What We Say?* (Cambridge: Cambridge University Press, 2002), 86. Italics in original.
38. Theodor Adorno, *Ästhetische Theorie*, vol. 7 of *Gesammelte Schriften* (Frankfurt: Suhrkamp, 1970), 11–12; *Aesthetic Theory*, trans. Robert Hullot-Kentor (Minneapolis: University of Minnesota Press, 1997), 2–3. Translation slightly modified.
39. T. S. Eliot, "Tradition and the Individual Talent," *Perspecta* 19 (1982), 37.
40. See Pierre Bourdieu, *The Logic of Practice*, trans. Richard Nice (Stanford, CA: Stanford University Press, 1990), 52–65.

41. Chinese script and writing are estimated to have reached Korea in the second century BCE and Japan at least by the fifth century CE and probably by the end of the fourth. See Lee, *A History of Korean Literature*, 87; Peter F. Kornicki, *The Book in Japan: A Cultural History from the Beginnings to the Nineteenth Century* (Leiden: Brill, 1998), 278–79. For the notion of "reference culture," see Wiebke Denecke, *Classical World Literatures: Sino-Japanese and Greco-Roman Comparisons* (Oxford: Oxford University Press, 2014), 1–19.
42. Yi Kwangsu, "Munhak iran hao?", in *Yi Kwangsu chŏnjip* (Seoul: Samjungdang, 1962–64), 1:507. "Literatur" and "literature" are written as is in the original.
43. Yi, "Munhak," 512.
44. Yi, "Munhak," 512.
45. Yi, "Munhak," 518.
46. Fukuzawa Yukichi, "Datsu a ron," in *Fukuzawa Yukichi chosakushū* (Tokyo: Keiō gijuku shuppankai, 2002–03), 8:262–63.
47. Fukuzawa Yukichi, *Fukuō jiden*, in *Fukuzawa Yukichi chosakushū*, 12:6. See Ichikawa Mototarō, *Nihon jukyō shi* (Tokyo: Kyūko shoin, 1989–95).
48. See Wang Hui, *The Politics of Imagining Asia*, ed. Theodore Huters (Cambridge, MA: Harvard University Press, 2011), 10–62.
49. Fukuzawa, "Datsu a ron," 264–65.
50. G. W. F. Hegel, *Lectures on the Philosophy of World History: Manuscripts of the Introduction and the Lectures of 1822–3*, ed. and trans. Robert F. Brown and Peter C. Hodgson (Oxford: Oxford University Press, 2011), 135–37.
51. For the modernization of historiography in East Asia, see, for example, Prasenjit Duara, *Rescuing History from the Nation: Questioning Narratives of Modern China* (Chicago: University of Chicago Press, 1995); Margaret Mehl, *History and the State in Nineteenth-Century Japan* (London: Macmillan, 1998); and Henry Em, *The Great Enterprise: Sovereignty and Historiography in Modern Korea* (Durham, NC: Duke University Press, 2013).
52. Erich Auerbach, *Mimesis: The Representation of Reality in Western Literature* (Princeton, NJ: Princeton University Press, 2003); Ernst Robert Curtius, *European Literature and the Latin Middle Ages* (Princeton, NJ: Princeton University Press, 2013); Karen Thornber, *Empire of Texts in Motion: Chinese, Korean, and Taiwanese Transculturations of Japanese Literature* (Cambridge, MA: Harvard University Asia Center, 2009); Sheldon Pollock, *The Language of the Gods in the World of Men: Sanskrit, Culture, and Power in Premodern India* (Berkeley: University of California Press, 2006); Ronit Ricci, *Islam Translated: Literature, Conversion, and the Arabic Cosmopolis in South and Southeast Asia* (Chicago: University of Chicago Press, 2011).
53. Charles Wagley, *Area Research and Training: A Conference Report on the Study of World Areas* (New York: National Conference on the Study of World Areas,

1948), 1, quoted in Gayatri Chakravorty Spivak, *Death of a Discipline* (New York: Columbia University Press, 2003), 7. This problematic is shared with, for instance, Dipesh Chakrabarty, *Provincializing Europe: Postcolonial Thought and Historical Difference* (Princeton, NJ: Princeton University Press, 2008), 3–23.

54. Satoru Hashimoto and Karen Thornber, "Trans-Regional Asia and Futures of World Literature," *Journal of World Literature* 4 (2019): 459–65.
55. Jing Tsu, "New Area Studies and Languages on the Move," *PMLA* 126, no. 3 (May 2011): 699.
56. I am borrowing the notion of "universalizing" from François Jullien, *On the Universal, the Uniform, the Common and Dialogue Between Cultures*, trans. Michael Richardson and Krzysztof Fijalkowski (Cambridge: Polity Press, 2014), 100–120.

PART I: A MULTILAYERED CONTACT SPACE IN TURN-OF-THE-CENTURY EAST ASIA

1. Shiba Shirō, *Kajin no kigū*, in *Seiji shōsetsu shū 2*, ed. Ōnuma Toshio and Nakamaru Nobuaki, vol. 17 of *Shin Nihon koten bungaku taikei: Meiji hen* (Tokyo: Iwanami shoten, 2006). On this book's reception in Meiji Japan, see Atsuko Sakaki, "*Kajin no Kigū*: The Meiji Political Novel and the Boundaries of Literature," *Monumenta Nipponica* 55, no. 1 (Spring 2000): 83–108; and *Obsessions with the Sino-Japanese Polarity in Japanese Literature* (Honolulu: University of Hawai'i Press, 2006), 143–76. See also Ai Maeda, "Meiji rekishi bungaku no genzō: Seiji shōsetsu no baai," *Tenbō* 213 (1976): 108–33.
2. This anecdote is mentioned in Ding Wenjiang and Zhao Fengtian, eds., *Liang Qichao nianpu changbian* (Shanghai: Shanghai renmin chubanshe, 1983), 1:158.
3. See the papers collected in Joshua A. Fogel, ed., *The Role of Japan in Liang Qichao's Introduction of Modern Western Civilization to China* (Berkeley: Center for Chinese Studies, Institute of East Asian Studies, University of California, 2004); and Hazama Naoki, ed., *Kyōdō kenkyū Ryō Keichō: Seiyō kindai shisō juyō to meiji Nihon* (Tokyo: Misuzu shobō, 1999). See also Xia Xiaohong, *Jueshi yu chuanshi: Liang Qichao de wenxue daolu* (Beijing: Zhonghua shuju, 2006), 169–259. For the Korean engagement with Liang's works, see chapter 2.
4. It is estimated that Japan attracted in total several hundred thousand students from across Asia until 1945. See Karen Thornber, *Empire of Texts in Motion: Chinese, Korean, and Taiwanese Transculturations of Japanese Literature* (Cambridge, MA: Harvard University Asia Center, 2009), 34–42.

5. Fogel, ed., *Role of Japan*, 3–12.
6. See Immanuel C. Y. Hsü, *China's Entrance Into the Family of Nations* (Cambridge, MA: Harvard University Press, 1960), 21–145.
7. See Jonathan D. Spence, *The Search for Modern China*, 3rd edition (New York: W. W. Norton, 2013), 191-96. *Wanguo gongfa* is the translation by the American missionary William Martin of Henry Wheaton's *Elements of International Law* (1836). For the Korean and Japanese reception of this book, see So Hyonsopu (Sŏ Hyŏnsŏp), *Kindai Chōsen no gaikō to kokusaihō juyō* (Tokyo: Akashi shoten, 2001), 69–97.
8. For the activities of the Tongwen guan, see Lawrence Wang-chi Wong, "Entrance Into the Family of Nations: Translation and the First Diplomatic Missions to the West, 1860s–1870s," in *Translation and Modernization in East Asia in the Late Nineteenth and Early Twentieth Centuries*, ed. Lawrence Wang-chi Wong (Hong Kong: The Chinese University of Hong Kong Press, 2018), 165–217.
9. See W. G. Beasley, *The Meiji Restoration* (Stanford, CA: Stanford University Press, 1972), 74–116.
10. See Numata Jirō, *Bakumatsu yōgaku shi* (Tokyo: Tōkō shoin, 1951).
11. On late Edo to early Meiji envoys and students sent abroad, including a list of them, see Ishizuki Minori, *Kindai Nihon no kaigai ryūgaku shi* (Kyoto: Mineruba shobō, 1972).
12. See Bruce Cumings, *Korea's Place in the Sun: A Modern History*, updated ed. (New York: Norton, 2005), 86–138.
13. For the early history of modern education in Korea, see Klaus Dittrich, "The Beginnings of Modern Education in Korea, 1883–1910," *Paedagogica Historica* 50, no. 3 (2014): 265–84; Son Yinsu, *Han'guk kaehwa kyoyuk yŏngu* (Seoul: Ilchisa, 1980).
14. Shi Meng, *Wan Qing xiaoshuo* (Shanghai: Shanghai guji chubanshe, 1989), 11, quoted in David Wang, *Fin-de-Siècle Splendor: Repressed Modernities of Late Qing Fiction, 1849–1911* (Stanford, CA: Stanford University Press, 1997), 3.
15. Tarumoto Teruo, "Shinmatsu-minsho shōsetsu no futakobu rakuda," in *Shinmatsu shōsetsu ronshū* (Kyoto: Hōritsu bunka sha, 1992), 308. Tarumoto's augmented catalogue lists more than 8,000 translations among the total of more than 33,000 works of fiction published in the late Qing through the early Republican periods. See Tarumoto Teruo, *Shinmatsu minsho shōsetsu mokuroku*, 6th ed. (Ōtsu: Shinmatsu shōsetsu kenkyūkai, 2014).
16. Guo Tingli, *Zhongguo jindai fanyi wenxue gailun* (Wuhan: Hubei jiaoyu chubanshe, 1998), 15.
17. Tarumoto's study based on his list compiled in 1988 includes 103 translations of Japanese-language works, among which as many as 78 are Chinese renderings of Japanese translations of Western texts. See Tarumoto Teruo, "Shinmatsu

minsho no hon'yaku shōsetsu," *Ōsaka keidai ronshū* 47, no. 1 (May 1996): 45–49.
18. Michiaki Kawato et al., eds., *Meijiki hon'yaku bungaku sōgō nenpyō* (Tokyo: Ōzora sha, 2001). This list includes poetry and drama as well as fiction.
19. Kim Pyŏngch'ŏl, *Segyemunhak pŏnyŏk sŏji mongnok ch'ongnam: 1895-1987* (Seoul: Kukhak charyowŏn, 2002), 3-12. See also Kim Pyŏngch'ŏl, *Han'guk kŭndae pŏnyŏk munhak sa yŏngu* (Seoul: Ŭryu munhwasa, 1975) and Pak Chin'yŏng, *Pŏnyŏkka ŭi t'ansaeng kwa tongasia segyemunhak* (Seoul: Somyŏng chu'ulp'an, 2019). For the significance of *T'aesŏ munye sinbo*, see Kim Haengsuk, "*T'aesŏ munye sinbo* e nat'anan kŭndaesŏng ŭi tu kaji ch'ŭngwi," *Kugŏ munhak* 36 (January 2001): 5–33.
20. Masuda Wataru, *Seigaku tōzen to Chūgoku jijyō* (Tokyo: Iwanami shoten, 1979); Ōba Osamu, *Kanseki yu'nyū no bunkashi: Shōtoku Taishi kara Yoshimune e* (Tokyo: Kenbun shuppan, 1997), 326–37.
21. Joshua A. Fogel, *The Literature of Travel in the Japanese Rediscovery of China, 1862–1945* (Stanford, CA: Stanford University Press, 1996), 43–65.
22. See Huang Zunxian, "Riben guozhi xu," in *Huang Zunxian quanji* (Beijing: Zhonghua shuju, 2005), 2:819.
23. See Wang Xiaoqiu, *Jindai Zhong-Ri wenhua jiaoliu shi* (Beijing: Zhonghua shuju, 1992), 214–86; Chin Shō (Chen Jie), *Meiji zenki nitchū gakujutsu kōryū no kenkyū: Shinkoku chūnichi kōshikan no bunka katsudō* (Tokyo: Kyūko shoin, 2003), 63–146; Chō Iyū (Zhang Weixiong), *Bunjin gaikōkan no meiji Nihon: Chūgoku shodai chūnichi kōshidan no ibunka taiken* (Tokyo: Kashiwa shobō, 1999).
24. Xu Fu is a legendary alchemist who is said to have been sent by the First Emperor of Qin to the eastern seas on a journey to seek the elixir of life, only to settle permanently overseas with his three thousand crew members. Later, a celebrated poem attributed to Ouyang Xiu 歐陽脩 (1007–1072), "Riben dao ge 日本刀歌" (Song of the Japanese Sword), surmised that since Xu Fu left before the book burning by the First Emperor, books lost in China should exist in Japan. On the discovery of lost Chinese books in Japan and the late nineteenth-century Sino-Japanese book trade, see Wang, *Jindai Zhong-Ri*, 287–312; Chin, *Meiji zenki*, 205–571.
25. Luo Sen, *Riben riji*, in Luo Sen et al., *Zaoqi Riben youji wu zhong* (Hunan: Hunan renmin chubanshe, 1983), 39.
26. One can invoke a line in the chapter Duke Wen of Teng of the *Mencius*: "今也南蠻鴃舌之人，非先王之道。" "Now here is this shrike-tongued barbarian of the south, whose doctrines are not those of the ancient kings." Translation by James Legge, *The Works of Mencius* (New York: Dover Publications, 1970), 255.

27. Luo, *Riben riji*, 32–34.
28. Luo Sen's reply to Hirayama Kenjirō is included in Matthew Calbraith Perry, *Perī kantai Nihon ensei ki*, trans. Office Miyazaki (Tokyo: Eikō kyōiku bunka kenkyūjo, 1997), 2:399–400.
29. For more on Luo Sen's visit to Japan, see Wang Xiaoqiu, *Jindai Zhong-Ri guanxi shi yanjiu* (Beijing: Zhongguo shehui kexue chubanshe, 1997), 263–74.
30. See Fogel, *Literature of Travel*, 43–125.
31. Maeda Ai, *Maeda Ai chosakushū* (Tokyo: Chikuma shobō, 1989–90), 2:297–300.
32. Kikuchi Sankei, *Yakujun kigo*, reprint ed. (Tokyo: Shōshidō, 1911), 16–17. Kikuchi Sankei compiled *Yakujun kigo* 訳準綺語 (Refined Writings in Translation), an anthology of Japanese vernacular fiction in Chinese translation. A similar attempt is Kayanoki Hironori's 榧木寬則 (1852–1927) *Enka bunsō* 艶華文叢 (Collection of Colorful Writings, 1881), an anthology of *jōruri* stories translated into vernacular Chinese.
33. See Yanagida Izumi, *Seiji shōsetsu kenkyū* (Tokyo: Shunjyū sha, 1967), 1:380–81.
34. Fuma Susumu, *Chōsen enkōshi to Chōsen tsūshinshi* (Nagoya: Nagoya daigaku shuppankai, 2015), 4–6.
35. Yi Chaesŏn, *Han'guk kaehwagi sosŏl yŏngu* (Seoul: Ilchogak, 1972), 145.
36. Yi Kwanglin, *Han'guk kaehwasa yŏngu* (Seoul: Ilchogak, 1977), 40–46; Hŏ Chaeyŏng, "Kŭndae kyemonggi chisik yut'ong ŭi t'ŭkching kwa yŏksul munhŏn e taehayŏ," *Ŏmun nonjip* 63 (September 2015): 7–36.
37. Kim Yunsik, *Ŭm ch'ong sa*, in *Chongjŏng yŏnp'yo; Ŭm ch'ŏng sa* (Seoul: Kuksa p'yŏnch'an wiwŏnhoe, 1958). See Liu Shunli, *Wangchao jian de duihua: Chao-xian lingxuanshi Tianjin laiwang riji daodu* (Yinchuan: Ningxia renmin chubanshe, 2006). Liu comments on poetry exchanges, "Exchanging poems and songs was an essential means of communication between Kim Yunsik and Chinese officials.... Both in China or Korea, the position and status of an official as well as his reputation among colleagues derive entirely from [his ability in] writing" (202).
38. See Martina Deuchler, *Confucian Gentlemen and Barbarian Envoys: The Opening of Korea, 1875–1885* (Seattle: University of Washington Press, 1977).
39. Yu Kilchun, *Sŏyu kyŏnmun*, in *Yu Kilchun chŏnsŏ* (Seoul: Ilchogak, 1971), 1:396–97, 1:404. *Sŏyu kyŏnmun* is known for broadly incorporating translated excerpts of Fukuzawa's *Seiyō jijō* 西洋事情 (Things and Situations in the West, 1866–1870). Fukuzawa puts forth the three-tier theory of civilization in his seminal *Bunmeiron no gairyaku* 文明論之概略 (Essence of the Discourse of Civilization, 1875). See *Bunmeiron no gairyaku* (Tokyo: Iwanami shoten, 1995), 25–27. For the relationship between Yu's conception of civilization and that of Fukuzawa, see Yi Kwanglin, "Yu Kilchun ŭi kaehwa sasang: *Sŏyu kyŏnmun* ŭl

chungsimŭro," *Yŏksa hakpo* 75–76 (December 1977): 199–250; Li Ginson (Yi Ŭnsong), "Yu Kitsushun no *Seiyū kenbun* ni okeru shakai shinkaron teki keikō: Nihon no shakai shinkaron tono kanren wo chūshin toshite," *Kyōikugaku ronshū* 2 (March 2006): 23–41.

40. Akizuki Nozomi, "Suematsu Jirō hitsudanroku in mirareru 'kindai': 1881 nen no 'shinshi yūran dan' tono kōryū wo chūshin ni," in *Kindai kōryū shi to sōgo ninshiki I*, ed. Miyajima Hiroshi and Kim Yongdŏk (Tokyo: Keiō gijuku daigaku shuppankai, 2001), 3–33.

41. Shiba, *Kajin*, 101.

42. On *Yi yan*'s influential reception in Korea, see Yi Kwanglin, *Han'guk kaehwasa*, 19–30.

43. See Pak Yŏngmi, "Sam Koenam ŭi kyŏng'uro pon aeguk kyemonggi chisigin ŭi taeil insik," *Hanmunhak nonjip* 33 (2011): 181–202.

44. Akizuki, "Suematsu Jirō." The Japanese Sinologist Suematsu Jirō 末松二郎 (years unknown), who helped translate Japanese materials into Chinese for Korean delegates, conversed with the reformist Hong Yŏngsik 홍영식 (1855–1884), a member of the 1881 mission, in writing and praised Korea's spirit of independence. See Suematsu's brush talk with Hong on July 23, 1881, quoted at 22.

45. See Fuan Hodoku (Hwang Hodŏk), "Sansui to fūkei no aida: Kankoku kaikō kaikaki no kenbunroku ni okeru kanbunkateki jikohyōshō," in *Zenkindai ni okeru higashi ajia sangoku no bunka kōryū to hyōshō: Chōsen tsūshinshi to enkōshi wo chūshin ni*, ed. Ryū Kenki (Liu Jianhui) (Kyoto: Kokusai Nihon bunka kenkyū sentā, 2006), 125. For more on the Korean travelogues of Meiji Japan, see Sō Bin (Song Min), *Meiji shoki ni okeru Chōsen shūshinshi no Nihon kenbun* (Kyoto: Kokusai Nihon bunka kenkyū sentā, 2000).

46. U Imkŏl, *Han'guk kaehwagi munhak kwa Yang Kyech'o* (Seoul: Pagijŏng, 2002), 27–28, 35.

47. Kim T'aekyŏng, *Kim T'aekyŏng chŏnjip* (Seoul: Asea munhwasa, 1978), 1:270.

48. On the significance of Yan Fu's *Tianyan lun*, see Wang Hui, *Xiandai Zhongguo sixiang de xingqi* (Beijing: Sanlian shudian, 2004), 833–923; Theodor Huters, *Bringing the World Home: Appropriating the West in Late Qing and Early Republican China* (Honolulu: University of Hawai'i Press, 2005), 43–73; Huang Kewu, "He wei tianyan? Yan Fu 'tianyan zhi xue' de neihan yu yiyi," *Zhongyang yanjiuyuan jindaishi yanjiusuo jikan* 85 (2014): 129–87. Despite the salient contrast with Kim T'aekyŏng, Yu Kilchun also reacted to modern civilization in a highly personal and reflective voice in his classical Chinese poems, of which he was known as a prolific writer. See Kyo Seiichi (Hŏ Sŏng'il), "Kanshi bunshū ni arawareta Yu Kitsushun no kaika ishiki," *Bukkyō daigaku sōgō kenkyū kiyō*, special issue (2000): 59–79.

49. In reply to Kim, Yan Fu composed five poems and presented them to him just as Kim was about to sail back to Korea for a short sojourn for archival research. In the second poem, Yan alluded to two other of his translations, *Yuanfu* 原富 (Pursuing the Origin of Wealth, 1902; translation of Adam Smith's *The Wealth of Nations*, 1776) and *Mingxue qianshuo* 名學淺說 (Introduction to Logic, 1908; translation of William Jevons's *The Primer of Logic*, 1879), which he would offer to Kim. See Yan Fu, *Yan Fu ji* (Beijing: Zhonghua shuju, 1986), 1:375. For more on Kim T'aekyŏng's poetry exchange with Yan Fu, see Yang Sŏl, "Kim T'aekyŏng ŭi Chungguk mangmyŏnggi kyoyusi yŏngu: Chang Kŏn kwa ŭi kyoyurŭl chungsimŭro" (MA thesis, Seoul National University, 2017), 74–92. For more on Kim's poetry in exile, see Ho Kwangsu, "Ch'anggang Kim T'aekyŏng ŭi mangmyŏng hansi e nat'anan sanghwangsŏng," *Chungguk inmun kwahak* 32 (June 2006): 213–48.

1. LITERATURE'S SEARCH FOR ITSELF

1. See Tan Ruqian et al., eds., *Zhongguo yi Riben shu zonghe mulu* (Hong Kong: Zhongwen daxue shubanshe, 1980); Kuroko Kazuo and Kō Tōgen (Kang Dongyuan), eds., *Nihon kingendai bungaku no Chūgokugo yaku sōran* (Tokyo: Bensei shuppan, 2006). The interrupted translation of *Chance Meetings* was later augmented with the omitted final chapters, where some significant changes were made owing to political concerns, and was reprinted several times in book format. My analysis is based on the version in *The China Discussion*. For an analysis of the alterations in the Chinese reprint versions, see Ōmura Masuo, "Ryō Keichō no Chōsenkan to '*Kajin no kigū*,'" in *Chōsen kindai bungaku to Nihon* (Tokyo: Ryokuin shobō, 2003), 244–51. There have been debates about who, besides Liang Qichao, contributed to the translation. See Kyo Jōan, "*Shin gi hō* tōsai no *Kajin kigū* ni tsuite: Tokuni sono yakusha," *Kanbun gakkai kaihō* 30 (1971): 39–53; Ōmura Masuo, "Ryō Keichō oyobi '*Kajin no kigū*,'" *Jinbun ronshū* 11 (1973): 103–33.
2. For *The Beautiful Story of Statesmanship* and its Chinese and Korean translations, see Satoru Hashimoto, "Regional Literary Tradition in Modern World Literature: The Allegorization of Democracy in Yano Ryūkei's *Beautiful Story of Statesmanship* and Its Chinese and Korean Translations," *Comparative Literature Studies* 59, no.4 (2022): 768–86. I have put forward, in an early form, some of the ideas underlying my discussion in this chapter in "February 10, 1900: Liang Qichao's Suspended Translation and the Future of Chinese New Fiction," in *A New Literary History of Modern China*, ed. David Der-Wei Wang (Cambridge, MA: Harvard University Press, 2017), 161–66.

3. See, for instance, Maeda Ai, "Meiji rekishi bungaku no genzō: Seiji shōsetsu no baai," *Tenbō* 213 (1976): 108–33; Atsuko Sakaki, "*Kajin no Kigū*: The Meiji Political Novel and the Boundaries of Literature," *Monumenta Nipponica* 55, no. 1 (Spring 2000): 83–108; C. T. Hsia, "Yan Fu and Liang Ch'i-ch'ao as Advocates of New Fiction," in *Chinese Approaches to Literature from Confucius to Liang Ch'i-ch'ao*, ed. Adele Austin Rickett (Princeton, NJ: Princeton University Press, 1978), 221–57.
4. For an overview of Meiji political fiction, see Yanagida Izumi, *Seiji shōsetsu kenkyū* (Tokyo: Shunjyū sha, 1967), 1:32–47; Yamada Shunji, "Seiji shōsetsu no ichi," in *Seiji shōsetsu shu 1*, ed. Yamada Shunji and Rinbara Sumio, vol. 16 of *Shin Nihon koten bungaku taikei: Meiji hen* (Tokyo: Iwanami shoten, 2003), 539–56.
5. On the introduction of political fiction into China, see Hiroko Willcock, "Meiji Japan and the Late Qing Political Novel," *Journal of Oriental Studies* 33, no.1 (1995): 1–28; Catherine Vance Yeh, *The Chinese Political Novel: Migration of a World Genre* (Leiden: Brill, 2015), 53–161; and on its introduction into Korea, see Kim Yunsik and Kim Hyŏn, *Han'guk munhak sa* (Seoul: Minŭmsa, 1996), 96–105; Kim Sunjŏn, *Han-Il kŭndae sosŏl ŭi pigyo munhakchŏk yŏngu* (Seoul: T'aehaksa, 1998), 106–54. On the circulation of political fiction from Japan to Korea, see Shin Konje (Sin Kŭnjae), *Nikkan kindai shōsetsu no hikaku kenkyū: Tetchō, Kōyō, Roka to hon'an shōsetsu* (Tokyo: Meiji shoin, 2006), 41–108. *Chance Meetings* was also translated via Chinese into Vietnamese by Phan Châu Trinh (1872–1926). See Vĩnh Sính, "'Elegant Females' Re-Encountered: From Tokai Sanshi's *Kajin no kigū* to Phan Châu Trinh's *Giai Nhân Kỳ Ngô Diễn Ca*," in *Essays Into Vietnamese Pasts*, ed. K. W. Taylor and John K. Whitmore (Ithaca, NY: Southeast Asia Program, Cornell University, 1995), 195–206. Works by Liang Qichao, along with those by Kang Youwei, were widely circulated among anti-French activists in Vietnam in the beginning of the twentieth century. See David G. Marr, *Vietnamese Anticolonialism, 1885–1925* (Berkeley: University of California Press, 1971), 98–155.
6. Liang Qichao, "Yi yin zhengzhi xiaoshuo xu," *Qing yi bao* 1, reprint (Taibei: Chengwen chubanshe, c. 1967), 1:54. For Korean cases, see chapter 2.
7. Liang Qichao, *Xin min shuo*, in *Yinbingshi heji: Zhuanji* (Beijing: Zhonghua shuju, 1989), 4:2.
8. Liang Qichao, "Lun xiaoshuo yu qunzhi zhi guanxi," in *Yinbingshi heji: Wenji*, 10:6.
9. Liang, "Lun xiaoshuo," 10:6–10.
10. Wang Dewei, "Cong moluo dao nuobeier," in *Cong moluo dao nuobeier: Wenxue, jingdian, xiandai yishi*, ed. Gao Jiaqian and Zheng Yuyu (Taipei: Maitian chuban,

2015), 58. The Korean discourse of new fiction also hinged on such a double-edged effect of this ambivalent genre. See chapter 2.

11. Liang, "Lun xiaoshuo," 10:6.
12. Wang Dewei points out the "similarity" of Liang's conception of fiction to Jacques Derrida's "pharmakon." See "Xiaoshuo zuowei 'geming': Chongdu Liang Qichao *Xin Zhongguo weilai ji*," *Suzhou jiaoyu xueyuan xuebao* 31, no. 4 (August 2014): 5. See also Jacques Derrida, "Plato's Pharmacy," in *Disseminations*, trans. Barbara Johnson (Chicago: University of Chicago Press, 1981), 72.
13. Derrida, "Plato's Pharmacy," 70.
14. Liang Qichao, "Gao xiaoshuojia," in A Ying, ed., *Wan Qing wenxue congchao: Xiaoshuo xiju yanjiu juan* (Beijing: Zhonghua shuju, 1960), 21. Quoted in Hsia, "Yan Fu," 257.
15. David Wang, *Fin-de-Siècle Splendor: Repressed Modernities of Late Qing Fiction, 1849–1911* (Stanford, CA: Stanford University Press, 1997), 25.
16. See an account by the author's brother, Shiba Gorō, *Aru Meijijin no kiroku: Aizujin Shiba Gorō no isho* (Tokyo: Chūō kōron sha, 1971). See also Ōnuma Toshio, "Tōkai Sanshi Shiba Shirō ryakuden: Hito to shisō," in *Seiji Shōsetsu shū 2*, ed. Ōnuma Toshio and Nakamaru Nobuaki, vol. 17 of *Shin Nihon koten bungaku taikei: Meiji hen* (Tokyo: Iwanami shoten, 2006), 667–82.
17. Maeda Ai contends that *Chance Meetings* "shows the possibility of an alternative world history written from a non-European point of view" and illustrates its significance by quoting Frantz Fanon: "That same Europe where they were never done talking of Man, and where they never stopped proclaiming that they were only anxious for the welfare of Man: today we know with what sufferings humanity has paid for every one of their triumphs of the mind." The quotation is from *The Wretched of the Earth* (New York: Grove Press, 2004), 312. Maeda, "Meiji rekishi bungaku," 459.
18. For an overview of the *kanbun kundoku* style in Meiji Japan, see Saitō Mareshi, "Kindai kundokutai to higashi ajia," in *Kindai higashi ajia ni okeru buntai no hensen: Keishiki to naijitsu no sōkoku wo koete*, ed. Chin Kokui (Chen Guowei) and Uchida Keiichi (Tokyo: Hakutei sha, 2010), 109–120. See also Shimizu Ken'ichirō, "Ryō Keichō to 'teikoku kanbun,'" *Ajia yūgaku* 13 (2000): 22–37.
19. Liang Qichao, "Lun xue Riben wen zhi yi," in *Yinbingshi heji: Wenji*, 4:81.
20. Kang Youwei, "Riben shumu zhi, zixu," in *Kang Youwei quanji* (Beijing: Zhongguo renmin daxue chubanshe, 2020), 3:264.
21. Liang Qichao, "Dongji yuedan, xulun," in *Yinbingshi heji: Wenji*, 4:82. The underlying concept of *Hewen handufa* was criticized by Zhou Zuoren some three and a half decades later, who blamed this manual for having caused much misunderstanding and demanded the plain recognition that "Japanese, at the end

of the day, [was] a foreign language." Zhou Zuoren, "Hewen handu fa," in *Zhou Zuoren sanwen quanji* (Guilin shi: Guangxi shifan daxue chubanshe, 2009), 6:640–41. See chapter 5.

22. This method received its inspiration from the practice called *fukubun* in Japanese Sinology. See Kodajima Yōsuke, "Ryō Keichō *Wabun Kandoku Hō* (Rohon) kanchū: Fukubun wo toita Nihongo sokushūsho," *Meisei daigaku kenkyū kiyō* 16 (2008): 29–64. See also Xia Xiaohong, "Hewen handu fa," *Shinmatsu shōsetu kara* 53 (April 1999): 9–16.

23. Corroborating the popularity of *Chance Meetings* and the readers' poetic engagement with it, Tokutomi Roka's 徳富蘆花 (1868–1927) retrospective novel *Kuroi me to chairo no me* 黒い目と茶色の目 (Black Eyes and Brown Eyes, 1914) portrays three hundred youths studying in a dorm as "absorbed and enthralled" by the recitation of a poem from this novel. Tokutomi Kenjirō, *Kuroi me to chairo no me, Shinshun,* in *Roka zenshū* (Tokyo: Roka zenshū kankōkai, 1928), 10:239.

24. Hsia, "Yan Fu," 235.

25. Shiba Shirō, *Kajin no kigū,* in *Seiji shōsetsu shū* 2, 5–7.

26. Mikhail Bakhtin, "Epic and Novel: Toward a Methodology for the Study of the Novel," in *The Dialogic Imagination: Four Essays* (Austin: University of Texas Press, 1981), 3–4.

27. Shiba, *Kajin,* 8. Here and elsewhere, all underlining is mine.

28. *Qing yi bao* 1, 1:55.

29. See Saitō Mareshi's analysis of this translation, which points out this characteristic. "Shōsetsu no bōken: Seiji shōsetsu to sono kayaku wo megutte," *Jinbun gakuhō* 69 (1991): 4–5.

30. Shiba, *Kajin,* 16; *Qing yi bao* 1, 1:57.

31. Shiba, *Kajin,* 17.

32. *Qing yi bao* 1, 1:57.

33. "Yuyan di er," in *Shishuo xinyu jianshu,* comp. Liu Yiqing, annot. Liu Xiaobiao (Scripta Sinica: Hanji dianzi wenxian ziliaoku [digital database]).

34. "Chenggong jiu nian" in *Chunqiu zuozhuan.* See Du Yu et al., eds., *Chunqiu zuozhuan zhengyi* (Shanghai: Shanghai guji chubanshe, 1990), 449.

35. Shiba, *Kajin,* 19–20.

36. *Qing yi bao* 1, 1:57–58.

37. For the Japanese reception of Ming-Qing scholar-and-beauty fiction, see En Shōmai (Yan Xiaomei), "Nihon ni okeru saishi kajin shōsetsu no juyō ni tsuite: Torai saishi kajin shōsetsu mokuroku," in *Yomihon kenkyū shinshū,* ed. Yomihon kenkyū no kai, vol. 4 (Tokyo: Kanrin shobō, 2003), 124–44.

38. Shiba, *Kajin,* 53; *Qing yi bao* 4, 1:250.

39. Shiba, *Kajin,* 65–66; *Qing yi bao* 5, 1:316.

40. Shiba, *Kajin*, 84; *Qing yi bao* 6, 1:383.
41. Shiba, *Kajin*, 85; *Qing yi bao* 6, 1:384.
42. Cao Zhi, "Zashi liu shou," *Cao Zijian shi zhu* (Beijing: Renmin wenxue chubanshe, 1957), 28.
43. Shiba, *Kajin*, 62.
44. *Qing yi bao* 5, 1:314.
45. "Tang gao di san," in *Shangshu* (Scripta Sinica: Hanji dianzi wenxian ziliaoku [digital database]).
46. Kang Youwei may have been involved in this retranslation. See Kyo Jōan, "Shin gi hō dai yon satsu yakusai no *Kajin kigū* ni tsuite," *Nihon Chūgoku gakkaihō* 24 (1972): 193–208.
47. *Qing yi bao* 7, 1:444–45.
48. Shiba, *Kajin*, 279; *Qing yi bao* 18, 3:1173. The last phrase is omitted in the translation.
49. Shiba, *Kajin*, 279; *Qing yi bao* 18, 3:1173.
50. Georg Lukács, *The Theory of the Novel: A Historico-Philosophical Essay on the Forms of Great Epic Literature*, trans. Anna Bostock (Cambridge, MA: MIT Press, 1971), 61.
51. Shiba, *Kajin*, 437–38; *Qing yi bao* 28, 4:1849.
52. Shiba, *Kajin*, 506; *Qing yi bao* 32, 4:2117.
53. Shiba, *Kajin*, 566.
54. Friedrich Schiller, *On the Aesthetic Education of Man: In a Series of Letters*, ed. and trans. Elizabeth M. Wilkinson and L. A. Willoughby (Oxford: Clarendon Press, 1982), 141.
55. Liang, "Lun xiaoshuo," in *Yinbingshi heji: Wenji*, 10:6.
56. Schiller, *Aesthetic Education*, 147.
57. Terry Eagleton, *Ideology of the Aesthetic* (Oxford: Blackwell, 1990), 107.
58. Liang, "Lun xiaoshuo," in *Yinbingshi heji: Wenji*, 10:6.
59. Schiller, *Aesthetic Education*, 21.
60. Paul de Man, *Aesthetic Ideology* (Minneapolis: University of Minnesota Press, 1997), 150.
61. See Liang Qichao, "Guodu shidai lun," in *Yinbingshi heji: Wenji*, 6:27–31.
62. Schiller, *Aesthetic Education*, 123.
63. See Hannah Arendt's analysis of "exemplary validity" in *Lectures on Kant's Political Philosophy*, ed. Ronald Beiner (Chicago: University of Chicago Press, 1982). Arendt derives this concept from aesthetic judgment. "[The] exemplar is and remains a particular that in its very particularity reveals the generality that otherwise could not be defined" (77).
64. For an overview of Liang's literary endeavor in exile, see Xia, *Jueshi*.
65. Xia, *Jueshi*, 40–42.

66. Two possible sources of inspiration for this narrative format have been pointed out: Edward Bellamy's *Looking Backward: 2000–1887*, whose Chinese rendition by Timothy Richard was serialized in *Wanguo gongbao* 萬國公報 (A Review of the Times) from 1891 to 1892; and Suehiro Tetchō's 末広鉄腸 (1849–1896) political novel *Setchūbai* 雪中梅 (The Plum Tree in the Snow), published in 1886.
67. Liang Qichao, *Xin Zhongguo weilai ji*, in *Yinbingshi heji: Zhuanji*, 89:45.
68. Xia, *Jueshi*, 40–42.
69. The climax is intended to be a modern incarnation of the old Confucian ideal of *datong* 大同, or the Great Community, expressed in the Confucian classic *Liji* 禮記 (The Book of Rites). See Ban Wang, "Geopolitics, Moral Reform, and Poetic Internationalism: Liang Qichao's *The Future of New China*," *Frontiers of Literary Studies in China* 6, no. 1 (2012): 2–18.
70. It has been speculated that Liang stopped working on this novel because of his trip to the United States in 1903; yet, more important, by that year, Liang gave up on the idea of revolution as a possible means for Chinese modernization. See Xia, *Jueshi*, 69.
71. Liang, *Xin Zhongguo*, in *Yinbingshi heji: Zhuanji*, 89:2.

2. LITERATURE AND LIFE IN EXILE

1. See the introduction to part I. See also Yi Chaesŏn, *Han'guk kaehwagi sosŏl yŏngu* (Seoul: Ilchogak, 1972), 145.
2. Yŏp Kŏn'gon, *Yang Kyech'o wa kuhan mal munhak* (Seoul: Pŏpchŏn ch'ulp'ansa, 1980); U Imkŏl, *Han'guk kaehwagi munhak kwa Yang Kyech'o* (Seoul: Pagijŏng, 2002). The examples of the Korean responses to Liang's work discussed here appear in Yŏp, *Yang Kyech'o*, 123–26.
3. Ch'oe Sŏkha, "Chosŏn hon," in *T'aegŭk hakpo* 5 (December 24, 1906), reprint, vol. 13 of *Han'guk kaehwagi haksulji* (Seoul: Asea munhwasa, 1978), 301–304.
4. For Liang Qichao's concept of "the Chinese soul" and its Japanese sources, see Wu Chunming, "Liang Qichao 'Zhongguo hun' jianlun," *Huanan shifan daxue xuebao* (February 2007): 99–103.
5. Hong P'ilju, "Bing chip chŏllyak," *Taehan hyŏphoebo* 1, no. 2 (May 25, 1908), reprint, vol. 3 of *Han'guk kaehwagi haksulji* (Seoul: Asea munhwasa, 1976), 97.
6. See, for instance, "Qin shi huang benji," in Sima Qian, *Shiji* (Scripta Sinica: Hanji dianzi wenxian ziliaoku [digital database]).
7. Yi Ki, "Chŏngch'i haksŏl" in *Honam hakpo* 2 (July 25, 1908), reprint, vol. 17 of *Han'guk kaehwagi haksulji* (Seoul: Asea munhwasa, 1978), 97.
8. See the introduction to part I for Liang Qichao's influence in Korea.
9. For Sin Ch'aeho's biography in this chapter, I consulted Yi Horyong, *Sin Ch'aeho tasi ilki: Minjokchuŭija esŏ anak'isŭt'ŭ ro* (Kyŏnggi-do P'aju-si:

Tolbegae, 2013), and Kim Sam'ung, *Tanjae Sin Ch'aeho p'yŏngjŏn* (Seoul: Sidae ŭi ch'ang, 2011).

10. For an overview of the emergence of *sin sosŏl*, see Yi Chaesŏn, *Han'guk kaehwagi*, 2–37. Kim Chungha discusses the inheritance of the styles of premodern fiction in this genre. See *Kaehwagi sosŏl yŏngu* (Seoul: Kukhak charyowŏn, 2005), 345–73. For the relationship of *sin sosŏl* to contemporary works of Meiji and late Qing fiction, see Yi Chaesŏn, *Han'guk kaehwagi*, 108–73; Shin Konje (Sin Kŭnjae), *Nikkan kindai shōsetsu no hikaku kenkyū: Tetchō, Kōyō, Roka to hon'an shōsetsu* (Tokyo: Meiji shoin, 2006); Sŏng Hyŏnja, *Sin sosŏl e mich'in manch'ŏng sosŏl ŭi yŏngyang* (Seoul: Chŏng'ŭmsa, 1985).

11. Sin Ch'aeho, *Tanjae Sin Ch'aeho chŏnjip* (Ch'ungnam Ch'ŏnan-si: Tongnip kinyŏmgwan Han'guk tongnip undongsa yŏn'guso, 2007), 6:639. Liang's discourse was echoed by a number of contemporary intellectuals, including Pak Ŭnsik. See Pak Ŭnsik, "Sŏ," *Sŏsa kŏn'gukchi*, in *Paekam Pak Ŭnsik chŏnjip* (Seoul: Tongbang midiŏ, 2002), 5:185–87.

12. Sin, *Chŏnjip*, 6:639.

13. Sin Ch'aeho, "Chŏngyuk kwa aeguk," in *Chŏnjip*, 7:624–26.

14. Hyŏn Ch'ae's mixed-style translation *Wŏllam mangguk sa* 越南亡國史 (History of the Fall of Vietnam) came out in 1906. Hyŏn Ch'ae appended translations of several other writings by Liang on Korea and Vietnam, including "Riben zhi Chaoxian 日本之朝鮮" (Korea in Japan's Possession, 1903) and an excerpt of "Chaoxian wangguo shilüe 朝鮮亡國史略" (Brief History of the Fall of Korea, 1904), drawing an explicit analogy between the political perils faced by these nations. Hyŏn Ch'ae's translation was further rendered into *hangul* twice in 1907 by Chu Sigyŏng and Yi Sang'ik 이상익 (1881–?). U, *Han'guk kaehwagi munhak*, 37–50.

15. "Tok Wŏllam mangguk sa," in *Hwangsŏng sinmun* (August 28, 1906), reprint (Seoul: Kyŏng'in munhwasa, 1971–81), 13:406. Quoted in U, *Han'guk kaehwagi munhak*, 46.

16. "Tok Wŏllam mangguk sa (sok)," in *Hwangsŏng sinmun* (September 5, 1906), reprint, 13:430. Quoted in U, *Han'guk kaehwagi munhak*, 47.

17. Liang Qichao, "Chaoxian wangguo shilüe," in *Yinbingshi heji: Zhuanji*, 17:1.

18. Liang's *Biographies* was translated into Korean at least four times. Sin's was the first to translate Liang's text in its entirety and is recognized as "the most influential" among the four. U, *Han'guk kaehwagi munhak*, 51–65.

19. Chang Chiyŏn, "Yit'aeri kŏn'guk samgŏl chŏn sŏ," in Sin, *Chŏnjip*, 4:357. See chapter 1 for Liang's discourse on the new people and new fiction.

20. "Tok Yit'aeri samgŏl chŏn ugam," in *Hwangsŏng sinmun* (November 16, 1907), reprint, 16:50. Quoted in U, *Han'guk kaehwagi munhak*, 61–62.

21. This is an allusion to An Zishun's 安子順 (1158–1227) saying featured in the popular writing manual of old-style prose *Wenzhang guifan* 文章軌範 (Collection

of Exemplary Composition). "Memorial at Sortie" is a canonical piece attributed to Zhuge Liang, who submitted it Emperor Liu Shan 劉禪 (r. 223–263) of the Shu (221–263) when he went out to the battle front for a campaign against the Wei.

22. For the Japanese sources of this work, see Yōji Matsuo, "Ryō Keichō to shiden," in *Kyōdō kenkyū Ryō Keichō: Seiyō kindai shisō juyō to meiji Nihon*, ed. Hazama Naoki (Tokyo: Misuzu shobō, 1999), 257–95.

23. Traditionally glossed by the verb *chuan* 傳 (to transmit), *zhuan* etymologically means text that is written to transmit something to later generations. A *zhuan* of *Chunqiu* (The Spring and Autumn Annals), for example, is established in order to carry the otherwise obscure meaning of those annals. Liu Xie's 劉勰 (c. 465–c. 532) *Wenxin diaolong* 文心雕龍 (The Literary Mind and the Carving of Dragons) takes the *Zuo zhuan*, the Zuo commentary, of *Chunqiu* to be the origin of the "*zhuan* form/genre" (*zhuanti* 傳體), examining the rhetoric by which the subtle meaning of this classic is passed on. "*Zhuan* is to transport [*zhuan* 轉]. Receiving the meaning of the classic, it bestows it upon later generations. Indeed, it becomes the wings of the sacred text; it records that text in books, thereby crowning it." Liu Xie, *Wenxin diaolong yizheng*, ed. Zhan Ying (Shijiazhuang: Hebei jiaoyu chubanshe, 2016), 2:8–9. The *zhuan* is indispensable for conveying the meaning of the classic, all the while remaining external ("wings," "books," "crown") to it. Beginning with *Shiji* 史記 (Records of the Grand Historian), Chinese official histories include a *liezhuan* 列傳 section dealing with the biographies of diverse individuals whose records must be kept to transmit history, whereas they remain external to the history-making emperors and kings covered in the *benji* 本紀 section. The *zhuan* was also written for unofficial histories, such as the *biezhuan* 別傳 (alternative records) and the *jiazhuan* 家傳 (family records). Some unofficial pieces of *zhuan* related personal affairs and fantastic anecdotes, stories too private, episodic, or mysterious to warrant representation in history *per se*. Sometimes titled *waizhuan* 外傳 (outer records) or *neizhuan* 內傳 (inner records), many such works were later categorized into *xiaoshuo* 小說. Many *chuanqi* 傳奇 (lit., conveying the strange) short stories from the Tang dynasty were works of *zhuan*, and some fictional narratives in later imperial periods were also written in this genre, such as, most notably, in *Shuihu zhuan* 水滸傳 (Water Margin). Grafted onto the Chinese tradition, works of *chŏn* are considered to have been written in Korea beginning in the eighth century. *Samguk sagi* 三國史記 (History of the Three Kingdoms) adopted the style of official Chinese historiography, including the "biographies" (*yŏlchŏn* 列傳) section. See Kim Kyunt'ae, "Chŏn munhak," in *Han'guk kojŏn sosŏllon*, ed. Han'guk kojŏn sosŏl p'yŏnch'an wiwŏnhoe (Seoul: Saemunsa, 1990), 91–119; So Chaeyŏng, "'Chŏn' ŭi kŭndae munhakchŏk

sŏngkyŏk," in *Kŭndae munhak ŭi hyŏngsŏng kwajŏng*, ed. Han'guk kojŏn munhak yŏnguhoe (Seoul: Munhak kwa chisŏngsa, 1983), 133–52; Kondō Haruo, *Tōdai shōsetsu no kenkyū* (Tokyo: Kasama shoin, 1978).

24. For the nineteenth-century discourse on the hero in Europe, see Eric Bentley, *A Century of Hero-Worship: A Study of the Idea of Heroism in Carlyle and Nietzsche, with Notes on Wagner, Spengler, Stefan George, and D. H. Lawrence* (Boston: Beacon Press, 1957). The Japanese hero biographies featured figures from Oliver Cromwell, George Washington, Napoleon, and Otto von Bismarck to Lajos Kossuth, Enver Pasha, Alexander Gorchakov, Li Hongzhang 李鴻章 (1823–1901), and Saigō Takamori 西郷隆盛 (1828–1877).

25. U, *Han'guk kaehwagi munhak*, 30–35.

26. See Gita Srivastava, *Mazzini and His Impact on the Indian National Movement* (Allahabad: Chugh Publications, 1982); C. A. Bayly and Eugenio F. Biagini, eds., *Giuseppe Mazzini and the Globalisation of Democratic Nationalism 1830–1920* (Oxford: Oxford University Press, 2008).

27. See Xiaobing Tang, *Global Space and the Nationalist Discourse of Modernity: The Historical Thinking of Liang Qichao* (Stanford, CA: Stanford University Press, 1996), 88.

28. John Marriott, *The Makers of Modern Italy: Mazzini, Cavour, Garibaldi, Three Lectures Delivered at Oxford* (London: Macmillan, 1908), 1–3.

29. Hirata Hisashi, *Itarī kenkoku sanketsu* (Tokyo: Min'yūsha, 1892), 4, 8.

30. Hirata, *Itarī*, 150–51.

31. Liang, *Yinbingshi heji: Zhuanji*, 11:19, 11:21, 11:24; Sin, *Chŏnjip*, 4:394, 4:397, 4:403.

32. The births of the heroes are described as a realization of heaven's will. See Liang, *Yinbingshi heji: Zhuanji*, 11:4–5; Sin, *Chŏnjip*, 4:367. Other usages of the figure of "heaven" include Liang, *Yinbingshi heji: Zhuanji*, 11:15, 11:29; Sin, *Chŏnjip*, 4:386, 4:410.

33. Liang, *Yinbingshi heji: Zhuanji*, 11:37; Sin, *Chŏnjip*, 4:422–23.

34. Marriott, *Makers*, 47; Hirata, *Itarī*, 92–93.

35. Liang, *Yinbingshi heji: Zhuanji*, 11:57.

36. Sin, *Chŏnjip*, 4:365.

37. Sin, *Chŏnjip*, 4:453–54.

38. Liang, *Yinbingshi heji: Zhuanji*, 11:57.

39. Liang, *Yinbingshi heji: Zhuanji*, 11:56–57.

40. Sin, *Chŏnjip*, 4:455.

41. Sin, *Chŏnjip*, 4:365.

42. *Taedong Sach'ŏn chae cheil dae wiin Ŭlji mundŏk* 大東四千載第一大偉人乙支文德 (Ŭlji mundŏk: The Greatest Hero in Korea in Four Thousand Years) was published in 1908. This work, written in the mixed style, was rendered in

hangul in the same year. My discussion uses the original mixed-style version. *Sugun cheil wiin Yi Sunsin* 水軍第一偉人李舜臣 (Yi Sunsin: The Greatest Man of the Navy) was first serialized in the *Korea Daily News* from May to August 1908. Finally, *Tongguk kŏgŏl Ch'oe Tot'ong* 東國巨傑崔都統 (Ch'oe Tot'ong: The Towering Hero of the Eastern Country) was also serialized in the same newspaper from December 1909 to May 1910, just three months before Korea was annexed by Japan.

43. Sin, *Chŏnjip*, 4:91–93.
44. Sin, *Chŏnjip*, 4:94.
45. Sin, *Chŏnjip*, 4:31–32.
46. Sin, *Chŏnjip*, 4:40–41.
47. Sin, *Chŏnjip*, 4:95. The Chosŏn navy general Yi Sunsin is also compared to Horatio Nelson. Sin, *Chŏnjip*, 4:198–99.
48. Sin, *Chŏnjip*, 4:24–25.
49. Sin, *Chŏnjip*, 3:309–10. On Sin's discourse on national history, see Yi Manyŏl, *Tanjae Sin Ch'aeho ŭi yŏksahak yŏngu* (Seoul: Munhak kwa chisŏngsa, 1990), 23–33; Michael Robinson, "National Identity and the Thought of Sin Ch'aeho: *Sadaejuŭi* and *Chuch'e* in History and Politics," *Journal of Korean Studies* 5 (1984): 121–42; Andre Schmid, "Rediscovering Manchuria: Sin Ch'aeho and the Politics of Territorial History in Korea," *Journal of Asian Studies* 56, no. 1 (February 1997): 26–46.
50. Sin, *Chŏnjip*, 1:601. *Chosŏn sanggo sa* first appeared as "Chosŏn sa 朝鮮史" (History of Korea) in *Chosŏn ilbo* 朝鮮日報 (Korea Daily) in 1931. It was then published in book format in 1948 as *Chosŏn sanggo sa*.
51. Sin, *Chŏnjip*, 4:26.
52. On the sources and interpretation of *Ŭlji mundŏk*, I consulted Pak Kibong, *Ŭlji mundŏk chŏn: Tongnip chŏngsin kwa minjok chajon ŭi p'yosang* (Seoul: Pibong ch'ulp'ansa, 2006).
53. *Samguk sagi*, comp. Kim Busik, trans. Chŏng Kubok et al. (Sŏng'nam: Han'guk chŏngsin munhwa yŏnguwŏn, 1996), 1:421–22. An account on the Koguryŏ-Sui War based on *History of the Three Kingdoms* also appears in the eighteenth-century *Tongsa kangmok* 東史綱目 (The Compendium of the Eastern history), which Sin may have consulted.
54. *Samguk sagi*, 1:421.
55. Sin, *Chŏnjip*, 4:88–89.
56. *Sui shu*, comp. Wei Zheng et al. (Beijing: Zhonghua shuju, 1973), 1455.
57. Sin, *Chŏnjip*, 4:70.
58. Sin, *Chŏnjip*, 4:34–35, 40, 48.
59. Sin, *Chŏnjip*, 4:53, 4:80, 4:83.
60. Sin, *Chŏnjip*, 4:95, 4:19.

61. Sin, *Chŏnjip*, 4:67.
62. Sin, *Chŏnjip*, 4:70–71.
63. Sin, *Chŏnjip*, 4:96–97.
64. Sin, *Chŏnjip*, 7:520.
65. Sin, *Chŏnjip*, 7:513.
66. Sin, *Chŏnjip*, 7:517–18.
67. Sin, *Chŏnjip*, 7:518.
68. Sin, *Chŏnjip*, 7:520.
69. See, for instance, Sŏ Hyŏngbŏng, "'Kkum hanŭl' ŭi sosach'ŭngwibunsŏk kwa mongyuyangsik sŏnt'aek ŭi ŭimi," *Han'guk hyŏndae munhak yŏngu* 16 (December 2004): 111–34; Min Ch'an, "Tanjae sosŏl ŭi kyŏngno wa chŏnt'ong ŭi chajang," *Inmun kwahak nonmunjip* 34 (2002): 147–62.
70. For an overview of this subgenre, see Chang Hyohyŏn, "Mongyurok ŭi yŏksajŏk sŏngkyŏk," in *Han'guk kojŏn sosŏllon*, ed. Han'guk kojŏn sosŏl p'yŏnch'an wiwŏnhoe (Seoul: Saemunsa, 1990), 145–55; Sŏ Taesŏk, "Mongyurok ŭi changnŭjŏk sŏngkyŏk kwa munhaksajŏk ŭiŭi," *Han'gukhak nonjip* 3 (March 1980): 511–42. For the relevance of this genre to modern Korean literature, see Chŏng Haksŏng, "Mongyudam ŭi uŭijŏk chŏnt'ong kwa kaehwagi mongyurok," *Kwan'ak ŏmun yŏngu* 3 (1978): 431–43.
71. Sin, *Chŏnjip*, 7:519.
72. Sin, *Chŏnjip*, 7:530.
73. Sin, *Chŏnjip*, 7:530.
74. Sin, *Chŏnjip*, 7:537.
75. Sin, *Chŏnjip*, 7:559–60.
76. Yi Horyong, *Sin Ch'aeho tasi ilki*, 153–88.
77. Sin, *Chŏnjip*, 8:901.
78. Sin, *Chŏnjip*, 7:341.
79. Sin, *Chŏnjip*, 7:348.

PART II: REFORMING LANGUAGE AND REDEFINING "LITERATURE"

1. See, for example, Renée Balibar and Dominique Laporte, *Le français national: Politique et pratiques de la langue nationale sous la revolution française* (Paris: Hachette, 1974); Niloofar Haeri, *Sacred Language, Ordinary People: Dilemmas of Culture and Politics in Egypt* (New York: Palgrave Macmillan, 2003).
2. Antonio Gramsci's remark is relevant to the discourses of language and literary reforms in turn-of-the-century East Asia: "every time that the language question appears, in one way or another, it signifies that . . . other problems are

beginning to impose themselves: the formation and enlargement of the ruling class, the need to stabilize the most intimate and secure links between that ruling group and the popular national masses, that is, to reorganize cultural hegemony." Antonio Gramsci, *Quaderni del carcere* (Torino: Giulio Einaudi, 1975), 3:2346, quoted in Jonathan Steinberg, "The Historian and the *Questione della Lingua*," in *The Social History of Language*, ed. Peter Burke and Roy Porter (Cambridge: Cambridge University Press, 1987), 206.

3. Yun Ch'iho, *Yun Ch'iho ilki* (Seoul: Kuksa p'yŏnch'an wiwŏnhoe; pŏn'gak panp'och'ŏ T'amgudang, 1973–89), 1:8. See Hwang Hodŏk, *Kŭndae neisyŏn kwa kŭ p'yosangdŭl* (Seoul: Somyŏng ch'ulp'an, 2005), 255–61.

4. See Hwang, *Kŭndae neisyŏn*, 399–493.

5. Yu Kilchun, "Sinmun ch'anggan sa," in *Yu Kilchun chŏnsŏ* (Seoul: Ilchogak, 1971), 4:5–11. This is considered one of the first modern writings to adopt the "mixed style." See Ross King, "Nationalism and Language Reform," in *Nationalism and the Construction of Korean Identity*, ed. Hyung Il Pai and Timothy R. Tangherlini (Berkeley: Institute of East Asian Studies, University of California, 1998), 36–37.

6. See Andre Schmid, *Korea Between Empires, 1895–1919* (New York: Columbia University Press, 2002), 64–72.

7. Yu Kilchun, *Sŏyu kyŏnmun*, in *Yu Kilchun chŏnsŏ*, 1:7–8.

8. Yu Kilchun's *Sŏyu kyŏnmun*, in which he adopted the "mixed style," is recognized for introducing nearly three hundred Meiji Japanese neologisms. See Yi Hansŏp, "*Sŏyu kyŏnmun* e padadŭlyŏjin Ilbon ŭi hanjaŏ e taehayŏ," *Ilbonhak* 6 (1987): 85–107. See also Hwang, *Kŭndae neisyŏn*, 373–96; Lydia Liu, *Translingual Practice: Literature, National Culture, and Translated Modernity—China, 1900–1937* (Stanford, CA: Stanford University Press, 1995), 302–42.

9. Yi Kwangsu, "Kŭmil a-Han yongmun e taehayŏ," in *Hwangsŏng sinmun* (July 24, 26, and 27, 1910). Reprint in Ha Tong'ho et al., eds., *Kungmunnon chipsŏng* (Seoul: T'ap ch'ulp'ansa, 1985), 189–92.

10. See Hwang, *Kŭndae neisyŏn*, 260.

11. See King, "Nationalism and Language Reform," 37.

12. "Nonsŏl," in *Tongnip sinmun* (April 7, 1896), reprint in Ha, *Kungmunnon*, 2.

13. Yi Kimun, *Kaehwagi ŭi kungmun yŏngu* (Seoul: Ilchogak, 1970), 35–64.

14. Yun Yŏt'ak et al., eds., *Kugŏ kyoyuk 100 nyŏn sa* (Seoul: Sŏul taehakkyo ch'ulp'anbu, 2006), 1:164–76.

15. Chu Sangho (Sigyŏng), "Kungmunnon," *Tongnip sinmun* (April 24, 1897), reprint in Ha, *Kungmunnon*, 12.

16. "Kungmun hanmun non," *Hwangsŏng sinmun* (September 28, 1898), reprint in Ha, *Kungmunnon*, 31–32. Discussed in Schmid, *Korea Between Empires*, 67.

17. See Xia Xiaohong, "Wusi baihua wenxue de lishi yuanyuan," *Zhongguo xiandai wenxue yanjiu congkan* 3 (1985): 22–41; "Wan Qing baihuawen yundong de guanfang ziyuan," *Beijing shehui kexue* 2 (2010): 4–17.
18. Huang Zunxian, "Zagan 2," *Renjinglu shicao*, vol. 1, in *Huang Zunxian quanji* (Beijing: Zhonghua shuju, 2005), 1:75.
19. Huang Zunxian, *Riben guozhi*, in *Huang Zunxian quanji* (Beijing: Zhonghua shuju, 2005), 2:1420.
20. Qiu Tingliang, "Lun baihua wei weixin zhi ben," in *Zhongguo jindai wenlun mingpian xiangzhu*, ed. Huo Songlin (Guiyang: Guizhou renmin chubanshe, 1986), 174.
21. Qiu, "Lun baihua," 167–68.
22. Elisabeth Kaske, *The Politics of Language in Chinese Education, 1895–1919* (Leiden: Brill, 2008), 104–5.
23. Kaske, *Politics of Language*, 161–201.
24. Ping Chen, "Establishment and Promotion of Modern Written Vernacular," in *The Oxford Handbook of Chinese Linguistics*, ed. William S-Y. Wang and Chaofen Sun (Oxford: Oxford University Press, 2015), 533.
25. Kaske, *Politics of Language*, 202–14; Ping Chen, "China," in *Language and National Identity in Asia*, ed. Andrew Simpson (Oxford: Oxford University Press, 2007), 141–67. By some estimates, about 10 percent of the late Qing periodicals employed the vernacular. See Kaske, *Politics of Language*, 190.
26. Elisabeth Kaske identifies twenty-four kinds of phonetic script invented between the 1890s and the 1900s. See *Politics of Language*, 132–59. For various late Qing discourses on script reform, see Wenzi gaige chubanshe, ed., *Qingmo wenzi gaige wenji* (Beijing: Wenzi gaige chubanshe, 1958).
27. Liu Shipei, "Zhongguo wenzi liubi lun," in *Liu Shipei wenxuan*, ed. Li Miaogen (Shanghai: Shanghai yuandong chubanshe, 2011), 2–3.
28. Mori Arinori, "Hoitoni ate shokan" (Letter to Whitney, dated May 21, 1872), in *Mori Arinori zenshū* (Tokyo: Senbundō shoten, 1972), 1:309. Original in English. For an overview of the Meiji-era language reforms, see Atsuko Ueda, *Language, Nation, Race: Linguistic Reform in Meiji Japan, 1868–1912* (Berkeley: University of California Press, 2021), 19–59.
29. Mori Arinori, "Introduction" to *Education in Japan* (1873), in *Mori Arinori zenshū*, 3:265–66. Original in English.
30. Mori, "Introduction," 3:266. Original in English.
31. See I Yonsuku (Lee Yeounsuk), *"Kokugo" toiu shisō: Kindai Nihon no gengo ninshiki* (Tokyo: Iwanami shoten, 1996), 12.
32. Maejima Hisoka, "Kanji onhaishi no gi," in *Kokugo kokuji kyōiku shiryō sōran*, ed. Nishino Minoru and Hisamatsu Sen'ichi (Tokyo: Kokugo kyōiku kenkyūkai, 1969), 17.

33. Maejima, "Kanji," 18.
34. I, "Kokugo," 26–46 and 148–151; Nanette Twine, *Language and the Modern State: The Reform of Written Japanese* (New York: Routledge, 1991), 224–56. For more on the complex cultural significance of Chinese script in Japan, see Yasuda Toshiaki, *Kanji haishi no shisōshi* (Tokyo: Heibonsha, 2016); Koyasu Nobukuni, *Kanji ron: Fukahi no tasha* (Tokyo: Iwanami shoten, 2003).
35. Fukuzawa Yukichi, *Seiyō jijō*, in *Fukuzawa Yukichi chosakushū* (Tokyo: Keiō gijuku shuppankai, 2002–03), 1:11–12.
36. Fukuzawa Yukichi, "Fukuzawa zenshū shogen," in *Fukuzawa Yukichi chosakushū*, 12:413.
37. See Jacques Rancière, *The Politics of Aesthetics: The Distribution of the Sensible*, trans. Gabriel Rockhill (London: Continuum, 2004).
38. Quoted in Yamamoto Masahide, *Kindai buntai hassei no shiteki kenkyū* (Tokyo: Iwanami shoten, 1965), 440. "Assimilation" is in English in the original.
39. Liu, *Translingual Practice*, 183–238; Edward Mack, *Manufacturing Modern Japanese Literature: Publishing, Prizes, and the Ascription of Literary Value* (Durham, NC: Duke University Press, 2010); and Kwon Boduerae, *Han'guk kŭndae sosŏl ŭi kiwŏn*, 2nd ed. (Seoul: Somyŏng ch'ulp'an, 2012). For more on the matter of the sociocultural processes of the establishment of modern literature as an institution, see Robert Culp, "Teaching *Baihua*: Textbook Publishing and the Production of Vernacular Language and a New Literary Canon in Early Twentieth-Century China," *Twentieth-Century China* 34, no. 1 (2008): 4–41; Atsuko Ueda, "The Production of Literature and the Effaced Realm of the Political," *Journal of Japanese Studies* 31, no. 1 (2005): 61–88.
40. Yi Kwangsu, "Munhak iran hao?", in *Yi Kwangsu chŏnjip* (Seoul: Samjungdang, 1962–64), 1:507. "Literatur" and "literature" are written as in the original.
41. Cheng Shude, *Lunyu jishi* (Beijing: Zhonghua shuju, 1990), 3:744. See also the entry *"wenxue"* in *Hanyu da cidian*, 2nd ed. (Shanghai: Hanyu dacidian chubanshe, 2001).
42. See Suzuki Sadami, *Nihon no "bungaku" gainen* (Tokyo: Sakuhin sha, 1998); Ch'oe Wŏnsik, *Han'guk kaenyŏmsa ch'ongsŏ: Munhak* (Seoul: Sohwa, 2012). See also Kōno Kimiko et al., eds., *"Bun" kara "bungaku" e: Higashi ajia no bungaku wo minaosu* (Tokyo: Bensei shuppan, 2019).
43. Lu Xun, "Menwai wentan," in *Lu Xun quanji* (Beijing: Renmin wenxue chubanshe, 2005), 6:95–6. "Literature" is written as in the original.
44. On the phenomenon of loanword translation, see Liu, *Translingual Practice*, 32–36. Unlike what Lu Xun suggests, the modern term *"wenxue"* is in fact a direct translation from English by an American missionary, but it was through a process of "roundtrip diffusion via Japan" that this term became the standard translation for "literature" in China (35).

45. Lu Xun, "Wusheng de Zhongguo," in *Lu Xun quanji*, 4:11–12.
46. Lu Xun, "Guanyu xinwenzi," in *Lu Xun quanji*, 6:165; Lu Xun, "Zhongguo yuwen de xinsheng," in *Lu Xun quanji*, 6:119.
47. For an overview of modern aesthetic discourses in Meiji Japan, see Kanbayashi Tsunemichi, *Kindai Nihon "bigaku" no tanjō* (Tokyo: Kōdansha, 2006).
48. Natsume Sōseki, *Bungaku ron*, in *Teihon Sōseki zenshū* (Tokyo: Iwanami shoten, 2016–20), 14:8.
49. Natsume Sōseki, "Watashi no kojinshugi," in *Teihon Sōseki zenshū*, 16:611.
50. Kanbayashi, *Kindai Nihon*, 5. Ōgai's translation was first serialized in an abbreviated form with the title "Shinbi ron 審美論" (On Aesthetics) in *Shigarami zōshi* しがらみ草紙 (Drafts of Obstructions) from 1892 to 1893. A complete version was published in book form as *Shinbi kōryō* 審美綱領 (Principles of Aesthetics) in 1899. See also Bruno Lewin, "Mori Ōgai and German Aesthetics," in *A History of Modern Japanese Aesthetics*, trans. and ed. Michael F. Marra (Honolulu: University of Hawai'i Press, 2001), 68–92.
51. Mori Ōgai, "Toyama Masakazu shi no garon wo bakusu," in *Ōgai zenshū* (Tokyo: Iwanami shoten, 1971–1975), 22:175–207. For an analysis of the polemics between Ōgai and Toyama, see Kanbayashi, *Kindai Nihon*, 92–98.
52. The year-long debate ignited by Ōgai's criticism is known as "the polemics of non-ideas" (botsu risō ronsō 没理想論争). See Mori Ōgai, "*Shigarami zōshi* no sanbō ronbun," in *Ōgai zenshū*, 23:1–87. For a discussion on the significance of these debates for the fledgling modern Japanese literature, see Karatani Kōjin, *Nihon kindai bungaku no kigen* (Tokyo: Iwanami shoten, 2008), 193–216.

3. PARODY AND REPETITION

1. Linda Hutcheon, *A Theory of Parody: The Teachings of Twentieth-Century Art Forms* (Urbana: University of Illinois Press, 2000), 6.
2. Hutcheon, *Theory of Parody*, 35.
3. Gilles Deleuze, *Difference and Repetition*, trans. Paul Patton (New York: Columbia University Press, 1994), 3.
4. Rachel Schmidt, *Forms of Modernity: Don Quixote and Modern Theories of the Novel* (Toronto: University of Toronto Press, 2011), 17–29, 69–73, 257–60; Michel Foucault, *The Order of Things: An Archaeology of the Human Sciences* (New York: Routledge Classics, 2002), 51–55; Charles Martindale and A. B. Taylor, eds., *Shakespeare and the Classics* (Cambridge: Cambridge University Press, 2004); Richard Ellmann, "Joyce and Homer," *Critical Inquiry* 3, no. 3 (Spring 1977): 567–82.
5. For biographies of these writers, see, for instance: Lin Fei and Liu Zaifu, *Lu Xun zhuan* (Beijing: Zhongguo shehui kexue chubanshe, 1981); Yamazaki

Kuninori, *Hyōden Mori Ōgai* (Tokyo: Taishūkan shoten, 2007); Kim Yunsik, *Yi Kwangsu wa kŭŭi sidae* (Seoul: Hangil sa, 1986).

6. Qu Qiubai, "Dazhong wenyi de wenti," in *Qu Qiubai wenji: Wenxue bian* (Beijing: Renmin wenxue chubanshe, 1989), 3:13.
7. Lu Xun, "Menwai wentan," in *Lu Xun quanji* (Beijing: Renmin wenxue chubanshe, 2005), 6:103.
8. On the carnivalesque aspects of the folk culture that Lu Xun praised, see Eileen Cheng, *Literary Remains: Death, Trauma, and Lu Xun's Refusal to Mourn* (Honolulu: University of Hawai'i Press, 2013), 194–98. On Lu Xun's commitment to popular art, especially in the form of woodcuts, see Xiaobing Tang, *Origins of the Chinese Avant-Garde: The Modern Woodcut Movement* (Berkeley: University of California Press, 2008), 82–89, 103–10.
9. Xiaobing Tang, "Lu Xun's 'Diary of a Madman' and a Chinese Modernism," *PMLA* 107, no. 5 (October 1992): 1229.
10. Yi-tsu Mei Feuerwerker, *Ideology, Power, Text: Self-Representation and the Peasant "Other" in Modern Chinese Literature* (Stanford, CA: Stanford University Press, 1998), 62.
11. Marston Anderson, *The Limits of Realism: Chinese Fiction in the Revolutionary Period* (Berkeley: University of California Press, 1990), 92; Theodor Huters, "Lives in Profile: On the Authorial Voice in Modern and Contemporary Chinese Literature," in *From May Fourth to June Fourth: Fiction and Film in Twentieth Century China*, ed. Ellen Widmer and David Der-wei Wang (Cambridge, MA: Harvard University Asia Center, 1993), 280.
12. Lu Xun, "Kuangren riji," in *Lu Xun quanji*, 1:444.
13. See Lu Xun, "*Zhongguo xin wenxue daxi* xiaoshuo erji xu," in *Lu Xun quanji*, 6:246–47; Andrew Johns, *Evolutionary Fairy Tales: Evolutionary Thinking and Modern Chinese Culture* (Cambridge, MA: Harvard University Press, 2011), 105–11; Patrick Hanan, "The Technique of Lu Hsün's Fiction," *Harvard Journal of Asiatic Studies* 34 (1974): 55–96.
14. Lu Xun, "Kuangren riji," 1:447.
15. Lu Xun, "Kuangren riji," 1:454–55.
16. C. T. Hsia sees in the madman's final plea an "insidious form of sentimentality." *A History of Modern Chinese Fiction*, 3rd ed. (Bloomington: Indiana University Press, 1999), 52–53. Lu Xun, "Kuangren riji," 1:453.
17. Leo Ou-fan Lee, *Voices from the Iron House: A Study of Lu Xun* (Bloomington: Indiana University Press, 1987), 53–57. The quotation on the concept of irony is from Paul de Man, "The Concept of Irony," in *Aesthetic Ideology* (Minneapolis: University of Minnesota Press, 1997), 179.
18. Cheng, *Literary Remains*, 44.
19. Lu Xun, "Kuangren riji," 1:446.

20. Lu Xun, "Kuangren riji," 1:446–47.
21. Cheng, *Literary Remains*, 41.
22. Lu Xun "Xie zai *Fen* houmian," in *Lu Xun quanji*, 1:301–2. Wang Hui focuses on the concept of the "intermediary" as a key to understanding Lu Xun's self-reflexive relationship to tradition. See Wang Hui, *Fankang juewang: Lu Xun ji qi wenxue shijie* (Beijing: Sanlian shudian, 2008), 181–255.
23. Lu Xun, "A Q zhengzhuan," in *Lu Xun quanji*, 1:519, 521, 525.
24. Fredric Jameson, "Third-World Literature in the Era of Multinational Capitalism," *Social Text* 15 (Fall 1986): 65–88. For the controversies around Jameson's essay, see Aijaz Ahmed, "Jameson's Rhetoric of Otherness and the 'National Allegory,'" *Social Text* 17 (Fall 1987): 3–25. Lydia Liu, *Translingual Practice: Literature, National Culture, and Translated Modernity—China, 1900–1937* (Stanford, CA: Stanford University Press, 1995), 64–76; Xudong Zhang, "Zhongguo xiandai zhuyi qiyuan de 'ming' 'yan' zhi bian: Chongdu *A Q zhengzhuan*," *Lu Xun yanjiu yuekan* 1 (2009): 5.
25. See Lee, *Voices*, 76–77.
26. Lu Xun, "A Q," 1:512.
27. "Xianggong ershisi nian" in *Chunqiu zuozhuan*. See Du Yu et al., eds., *Chunqiu zuozhuan zhengyi* (Shanghai: Shanghai guji chubanshe, 1990), 609.
28. On the understanding of "Ah Q" as a ghost figure, see Maruo Tsuneki, *Ro Jin: "Jin" "ki" no kattō* (Tokyo: Iwanami shoten, 1993), 103–210.
29. Jacques Derrida, *Of Grammatology*, trans. Gayatri Chakravorty Spivak, corrected edition (Baltimore, MD: Johns Hopkins University Press, 1997), 141–64. I discussed the generic characteristics of the *zhuan* in chapter 2.
30. Lu Xun, "A Q," 1:512.
31. The quotation is from Martin Weizong Huang, "The Inescapable Predicament: The Narrator and His Discourse in 'The True Story of Ah Q,'" *Modern China* 16, no. 4 (October 1990): 433.
32. Lu Xun, "A Q," 1:514.
33. Lu Xun, "A Q," 1:515.
34. Huang, "Inescapable Predicament," 434; Cheng, *Literary Remains*, 75; Feuerwerker, *Ideology*, 75.
35. Lu Xun, "A Q," 1:533.
36. Lu Xun, "A Q," 1:537.
37. Lu Xun, "A Q," 1:552.
38. See Zhang, "Zhongguo xiandai zhuyi," 4.
39. Lu Xun, "A Q," 1:523.
40. Lu Xun, "A Q," 1:549–51.
41. Lu Xun, "A Q," 1:550–51.
42. Anderson, *Limits of Realism*, 84.

43. The quoted matter is from Anderson, *Limits of Realism*, 84.
44. Lu Xun, "Zhu fu," in *Lu Xun quanji*, 2:7.
45. Lu Xun, "Zhu fu," 2:10.
46. Anderson, *Limits of Realism*, 88–91.
47. Theodore Huters, "Blossoms in the Snow: Lu Xun and the Dilemma of Modern Chinese Literature," *Modern China* 10, no. 1 (1984): 65–68.
48. Max Horkheimer and Theodor W. Adorno, *Dialectic of Enlightenment: Philosophical Fragments*, ed. Gunzelin Schmid Noerr, trans. Edmund Jephcott (Stanford, CA: Stanford University Press, 2002), 8–10. For Lu Xun's critique of enlightenment, see "Po e'sheng lun," in *Lu Xun quanji*, 8:25–40, and Wang Hui's interpretation of it: "The Voices of Good and Evil: What Is Enlightenment? Rereading Lu Xun's 'Toward a Refutation of Malevolent Voices,'" *boundary 2* 38, no. 2 (2011): 67–123.
49. Lee, *Voices*, 75. See Lydia Liu, "Life as Form: How Biomimesis Encountered Buddhism in Lu Xun," *Journal of Asian Studies* 68, no. 1 (February 2009): 44–51.
50. Horkheimer and Adorno, *Dialectic of Enlightenment*, 11.
51. Lu Xun, "Zhu fu," 2:17–18.
52. See the verbatim repetition in Lu Xun, "Zhu fu," 2:15–16, 17.
53. Lu Xun, "Zhu fu," 2:21.
54. Walter Benjamin, "The Storyteller," in *Illuminations*, ed. Hannah Arendt, trans. Harry Zohn (New York: Schocken Books, 1969), 91.
55. Benjamin, "The Storyteller," 83, 91.
56. Lu Xun, "Wuchang," in *Lu Xun quanji*, 2:278–79.
57. For this distinction, see Wang Hui, *Xiandai Zhongguo sixiang de xingqi* (Beijing: Sanlian shudian, 2004), 47–71.
58. For more on this polemic, see Usui Yoshimi, *Kindai bungaku ronsō* (Tokyo: Chikuma shobō, 1975), 1:27–50.
59. Ishibashi Ningetsu, "Maihime," in *Yamada Bimyō, Ishibashi Ningetsu, Takase Bunen shū*, vol. 23 of *Meiji bungaku zenshū* (Tokyo: Chikuma shobō, 1971), 273.
60. Mori Ōgai, *Youth and Other Stories*, trans. J. Thomas Rimer (Honolulu: University of Hawai'i Press, 1994), 7; Richard John Bowring, *Mori Ōgai and the Modernization of Japanese Culture* (Cambridge: Cambridge University Press, 1979), 47; Satō Haruo, *Kindai Nihon bungaku no tenbō* (Tokyo: Dainihon yūbenkai kōdansha, 1950), 27; Karatani Kōjin, *Nihon kindai bungaku no kigen* (Tokyo: Iwanami shoten, 2008), 61.
61. Satō, *Kindai Nihon bungaku*, 22–23; Nagashima Yōichi, *Mori Ōgai no hon'yaku bungaku: "Sokkyō shijin" kara "Perikan" made* (Tokyo: Shibundō, 1993).

62. Mori Ōgai, "Maihime ni tsukite Kidorihannojō ni atauru sho," in *Ōgai zenshū* (Tokyo: Iwanami shoten, 1971–1975), 22:159.
63. Feng Menglong, *Qingshi*, vols. 37–38 of *Feng Menglong quanji*, ed. Wei Tongxian (Shanghai: Shanghai guji chubanshe, 1993), 1:227. Sasagawa Yūichi conjectures that the stories on Zhuo Wenjun and Hongfu in *Qingshi* were a source of "Maihime." See *Meiji Taishō bungaku no bunseki* (Tokyo: Meiji shoin, 1970), 96–97.
64. On Ōgai's wide-ranging reading of classical Chinese literature, see Maeda Ai, "Ōgai no Chūgoku shōsetsu shumi," in *Maeda Ai chosakushū* (Tokyo: Chikuma shobō, 1989–90), 2:74–87; Yamane Hiroko, "Mori Ōgai seinenki no kanshibun juyō: Ōgai bunko chōsa wo meguri 1, 2," *Kindai bungaku chūshaku to hihyō* 1 (1994): 2–14; 2 (1995): 1–18; Rin Shukutan (Lin Shudan), *Mori Ōgai to Chūgoku koten bungaku*. PhD diss., Ochanomizu University, 2003.
65. Satō, *Kindai Nihon bungaku*, 31–32.
66. For the debates over the autobiographical nature of "Maihime," see Bowring, *Mori Ōgai*, 47–55.
67. Mori Ōgai, "Maihime," in *Ōgai zenshū*, 1:428. I quote, with some modifications, from Richard Bowring's translation: "The Dancing Girl," in *Youth and Other Stories*, 6–24.
68. "Sima Xiangru liezhuan," in Sima Qian, *Shiji* (Scripta Sinica: Hanji dianzi wenxian ziliaoku [digital database]). The *Qingshi* version is largely based on *Shiji*. "Zhuo Wenjun," in Feng Menglong, *Qingshi*, 1:278–85.
69. "Hongfu ji," in Feng Menglong, *Qingshi*, 1:285–87.
70. "Zhuo Wenjun," 1:282–83.
71. "Hongfu ji," 1:287.
72. Komori Yōichi, *Buntai toshite no monogatari* (Tokyo: Chikuma shobō, 1988), 157.
73. Ōgai's interest in Young Germany is pointed out in the annotations in *Ōgai kindai shōsetsu shū* (Tokyo: Iwanami shoten, 2012–13), 1:73, 75.
74. Ōgai, "Maihime," 1:436.
75. Peter Uwe Hohendahl, *The Institution of Criticism* (Ithaca, NY: Cornell University Press, 1982), 119. For Heine's journalistic work, see 117–25. See also Susan Bernstein, "Journalism and German Identity: Communiqués from Heine, Wagner, and Adorno," *New German Critique* 66 (Autumn 1995): 65–93.
76. Hohendahl, *Institution of Criticism*, 121.
77. Ōgai, "Maihime," 1:444.
78. Ōgai, "Maihime," 1:425–26.
79. See namely Stephen Snyder, "Ōgai and the Problem of Fiction: Gan and Its Antecedents," *Monumenta Nipponica* 49, no. 3 (Autumn 1994): 353–73; Atsuko

Sakaki, *Recontextualizing Texts: Narrative Performance in Modern Japanese Fiction* (Cambridge, MA: Harvard University Asia Center, 1999), 137–80.

80. Mori Ōgai, "Gan," in *Ōgai zenshū*, 8:494. For quotes from this work, I use with slight modifications the translation in *The Wild Geese*, trans. Kingo Ochiai and Stanford Goldstein (Rutland, VT: Tuttle Publishing, 1959).

81. Ōgai, "Gan," 8:566.

82. Ōgai, "Gan," 8:573. These explicit allusions to *Jin ping mei* have drawn scholarly attention. See, for instance, Chiba Shunji, "'Mado no onna' kō: 'Gan' wo megutte," *Mori Ōgai kenkyū* 2 (1988): 26–47; Rin Shukutan (Lin Shudan), "Mori Ōgai 'Gan' to *Kin pei bai*: Monogatari no kōsaku," *Ōgai* 69 (2001): 118–29.

83. Lanling xiaoxiaosheng, *Jin ping mei cihua chongjiaoben*, ed. Mei Jie (Hong Kong: Mengmeiguan, 1993), 1:22. Translation in David Tod Roy, trans., *The Plum in the Golden Vase; Or, Chin P'ing Mei* (Princeton, NJ: Princeton University Press, 1993), 1:48–50.

84. Shi Nai'an and Luo Guanzhong, *Shui hu zhuan: Li Zhuowu ping ben*, annot. Li Zhi (Shanghai: Shanghai guji chubanshe, 1988), 1:340.

85. Ōgai, "Gan," 8:573.

86. Ōgai, "Gan," 8:603.

87. Ōgai, "Gan," 8:564.

88. Ōgai, "Gan," 8:589.

89. Ōgai, "Gan," 8:499. My italics.

90. See Giovanni Maciocia, *The Foundations of Chinese Medicine: A Comprehensive Text*, 3rd ed. (Edinburgh: Elsevier, 2015), 219–32.

91. Ōgai, "Gan," 8:596.

92. The phonetic transcription "chiao" can be understood in terms of what Haun Saussy calls the "boundary-object" indicating the "internal limit of translation." See *Translation as Citation: Zhuangzi Inside Out* (Oxford: Oxford University Press, 2017), 22, 82–83.

93. Portions of discussion in this section appear, in an early version, in Satoru Hashimoto, "Kindaisei to jō no seijigaku: I Gwansu *Mujō* ni okeru chōsō no jikansei," *Tōyō bunka kenkyūjo kiyō* 170 (2016): 88–126.

94. John Whittier Treat, "Introduction to Yi Kwangsu's 'Maybe Love' (Ai ka, 1909)," *Azalea: Journal of Korean Literature and Culture* 4 (2011): 320; Michael D. Shin, "Interior Landscape and Modern Literature: Yi Kwangsu's 'The Heartless' and the Origins of Modern Literature," in *Colonial Modernity in Korea*, ed. Gi-Wook Shin and Michael Robinson (Cambridge, MA: Harvard University Asia Center, 1999), 248–87; Ann Lee, "Yi Kwangsu and Korean Literature: The Novel 'Mujŏng' (1917)," *Journal of Korean Studies* 8 (1992): 100.

95. Kichung Kim, "'Mujŏng': An Introduction to Yi Kwangsu's Fiction," *Korean Studies* 6 (1982): 129.

96. See Shin, "Interior Landscape," 278; Kim Yunsik, *Yi Kwangsu*, 2:537, 685–86; Hatano Setsuko, *I Gwansu, "Mujō" no kenkyū: Kankoku keimō bungaku no hikari to kage* (Tokyo: Hakuteisha, 2008), 260.
97. Kim Tong'in, "Ch'unwŏn yŏn'gu," in *Kim Tong'in chŏnjip* (Seoul: Chosŏn ilbosa, 1998), 16:51, 56–63.
98. Yi Kwangsu, *Mujŏng*, in *Yi Kwangsu chŏnjip* (Seoul: Samjungdang, 1962–1964), 1:318.
99. Sigmund Freud, "Mourning and Melancholia," in *The Standard Edition of the Complete Psychological Work of Sigmund Freud* (London: Hogarth Press, 1957), 14:245.
100. Yi, *Mujŏng*, 1:181–82.
101. Yi, *Mujŏng*, 1:99, 121, 317.
102. Yi, *Mujŏng*, 1:121.
103. Yi Kwangsu, "Ai ka," *Shirogane gakuhō* 19 (December 1909): 35–41, reprint in *"Gaichi" no Nihongo bungakusen 3: Chōsen*, ed. Kurokawa Sō (Tokyo: Shinjuku shobō, 1996), 21–26.
104. Yi Kwangsu, "Panghwang," in *Yi Kwangsu chŏnjip*, 14:61–68.
105. Yi Kwangsu, "Yun Kwangho," in *Yi Kwangsu chŏnjip*, 14:69–82.
106. Yi Kwangsu, "Hŏnsinja," in *Yi Kwangsu chŏnjip*, 1:537.
107. Yi Kwangsu, "Kŭmil a-Han ch'ŏngnyŏn kwa chŏng'yuk," in *Yi Kwangsu chŏnjip*, 1:475.
108. Sin Ch'aeho, "Chŏng'yuk kwa aeguk," in *Sin Ch'aeho chŏnjip* (Ch'ungnam Ch'ŏnan-si: Tongnip kinyŏmgwan Han'guk tongnip undongsa yŏn'guso, 2007), 7:626. See chapter 2.
109. For this aspect of Mencian moral philosophy, see François Jullien, *Fonder la morale: Dialogue de Mencius avec un philosophe des Lumières* (Paris: B. Grasset, 1995).
110. Sheila Miyoshi Jager, *Narratives of Nation Building in Korea: A Genealogy of Patriotism* (New York: M. E. Sharpe, 2003), 23. Jagar cites Christian Wolf as a source of Yi's discourse on *chŏng*. Korean students in Japan received Wolf's thought through translations by early Meiji philosophers such as Nishi Amane 西周 (1829–1897). See Hwang Jong-yon, "The Emergence of Aesthetic Ideology in Korea: An Essay on Yi Kwang-su," *Korea Journal* 39, no. 4 (Winter 1999): 19; Shin, "Interior Landscape," 278.
111. Ann Sung-hi Lee, "Introduction," in *Yi Kwangsu and Modern Korean Literature: Mujŏng* (Ithaca, NY: Cornell East Asia Series, 2005), 42.
112. Cho Tong'il, *Han'guk munhak t'ongsa*, 2nd ed. (Seoul: Chisik sanŏpsa, 1989), 4:436–41; Yi Chaesŏn, "Han'guk hyŏndae sosŏl ŭi ryaksa," in *Han'guk kŭndae sosŏl chakp'umron*, ed. Cho Tong'il and Yi Chaesŏn (Seoul: Munjang, 1987), 16–18.

113. Yi Kwangsu, "Tananhan pansaeng ŭi tojŏng," in *Yi Kwangsu chŏnjip*, 14:399.
114. Hatano, *I Gwansu*, 101.
115. Yi, *Mujŏng*, 1:34.
116. Yi, *Mujŏng*, 1:47.
117. Yi, *Mujŏng*, 1:34.
118. Yi, *Mujŏng*, 1:81–82.
119. Yi, *Mujŏng*, 1:83–84.
120. Yi, *Mujŏng*, 1:48.
121. Yi, *Mujŏng*, 1:67.
122. Yi, *Mujŏng*, 1:130–32.
123. Yi, *Mujŏng*, 1:139.
124. Hatano, *I Gwansu*, 184–257.
125. Yi, *Mujŏng*, 1:140.
126. Yi, *Mujŏng*, 1:133–34.
127. Yi, *Mujŏng*, 1:168.
128. Yi, *Mujŏng*, 1:169. Hatano Setsuko sees echoes of Bergsonian "pure perception" in the description of Hyŏngsik's experience. Hatano, *I Gwansu*, 250.
129. Yi, *Mujŏng*, 1:73–76.
130. Yi, *Mujŏng*, 1:169.
131. Yi, *Mujŏng*, 1:173.
132. Yi, *Mujŏng*, 1:221.
133. Yi, *Mujŏng*, 1:230–32.
134. Yi, *Mujŏng*, 1:234–42.
135. Yi, *Mujŏng*, 1:242.
136. See the introduction to part II.
137. Yi, *Mujŏng*, 1:194.
138. Yi, *Mujŏng*, 1:216.
139. Yi, *Mujŏng*, 1:285.
140. Yi, *Mujŏng*, 1:268.
141. Yi, *Mujŏng*, 1:288–89.
142. Yi, *Mujŏng*, 1:299–300.
143. Yi, *Mujŏng*, 1:301.
144. Yi, *Mujŏng*, 1:301. The quotation on the sublime is from Terry Eagleton, *The Ideology of the Aesthetic* (Oxford: Blackwell, 1990), 91. Many echoes can be identified between the problematic of the sublime in *The Heartless* and that in modern Chinese literature and aesthetics. See Ban Wang, *The Sublime Figure of History: Aesthetics and Politics in Twentieth-Century China* (Stanford, CA: Stanford University Press, 1997).
145. Yi, *Mujŏng*, 1:273, 311–12.

146. I am alluding to Giorgio Agamben's discussion on bare life and sovereignty in *Homo Sacer: Sovereign Power and Bare Life*, trans. Daniel Heller-Roazen (Stanford, CA: Stanford University Press, 1998).
147. Yi, *Mujŏng*, 1:318.
148. Yi, *Mujŏng*, 1:308.
149. Yi, *Mujŏng*, 1:308–9.

4. HISTORY AS REWRITING

1. Resonances of the Lukácsian notion of the historical novel frequently inform the studies of historical fiction in modern East Asia. See, for example, Li Chenghua, *Chuantong xiang xiandai de shanbian: Zhongguo xiandai lishi xiaoshuo yu Zhong–wai wenhua* (Nanning: Guangxi jiaoyu chubanshe, 1996), 100–106; Ōoka Shōhei, "Rekishi shōsetsu no hassei," in *Ōoka Shōhei zenshū* (Tokyo: Chikuma shoten, 1994–2003), 16:117–25; Kang Yŏngju, *Han'guk yŏksa sosŏl ŭi chaeinsik* (Seoul: Ch'angjak kwa pip'yŏng sa, 1991), 11–21; Yu Chaeyŏp, *Han'guk kŭndae yŏksa sosŏl yŏngu* (Seoul: Kukhak charyowon, 2002), 11–27.
2. Georg Lukács, *The Historical Novel*, trans. Hannah and Stanley Mitchell (Lincoln: University of Nebraska Press, 1983), 53.
3. Lukács, *Historical Novel*, 61.
4. G. W. F. Hegel, *Aesthetics: Lectures on Fine Art*, trans. T. M. Knox (Oxford: Oxford University Press, 1975), 1:278. Italics in original.
5. Hegel, *Aesthetics*, 1:116.
6. Lukács, *Historical Novel*, 61–63. Italics in original.
7. Historical fiction by Lu Xun, Mori Ōgai, and Yi Kwangsu has sometimes been a target of criticism in contrast to their canonized "modern" works. Leo Oufan Lee acknowledges only a "partial success" of Lu Xun's *Old Stories Retold* because of its occasional slippage into "vacuous parody." *Voices from the Iron House: A Study of Lu Xun* (Bloomington: Indiana University Press, 1987), 32–33. Takeuchi Yoshimi, if hesitantly, regarded *Old Stories Retold* as uniquely "superfluous" and "completely unsuccessful" in Lu Xun's entire oeuvre. *Ro Jin*, in *Takeuchi Yoshimi zenshū* (Tokyo: Chikuma shobō, 1980), 1:108–10. Mori Ōgai's historical stories have been criticized for their lack of "a self-conscious grasp of history," for "distorting" history for political purposes, and for their failure in "abstracting truth from the historical process." See, respectively, Iwakami Jun'ichi, *Rekishi bungaku ron* (Tokyo: Chūō kōron sha, 1942), 54–55; Ōoka, *Rekishi shōsetsu ron*, 228–30; and Irokawa Daikichi, *Rekishi no hōhō* (Tokyo: Yamato shobō, 1992), 38–39. Besides accusations of adherence to commercialism or popularity, Yi Kwangsu's *Tragic Story of Tanjong* has been

censured for its "immature historical consciousness" and for its reliance on the early genre of "biography" (*chŏn'gi munhak* 전기문학) during the Patriotism and Enlightenment period, which "inherited the traditional style of *chŏn* 전." See Paek Nakch'ŏng, "Yŏksa sosŏl kwa yŏksa ŭisik: Sin munhak esŏ ŭi ch'ulbal kwa munjejŏm," *Ch'angjak kwa pip'yŏng* 2, no. 1 (1967): 18; Kang, *Han'guk yŏksa sosŏl*, 52.

8. Lu Xun, "Xuyan," *Gushi xinbian*, in *Lu Xun quanji* (Beijing: Renmin wenxue chubanshe, 2005), 2:354.
9. Mori Ōgai, "Rekishi sono mama to rekishi banare," in *Ōgai rekishi bungaku shū* (Tokyo: Iwanami shoten, 1999), 3:361–62.
10. Karatani Kōjin, "Rekishi to shizen: Mori Ōgai ron," in *Karatani Kōjin bungaku ronshū* (Tokyo: Iwanami shoten, 2016), 166.
11. Yi Kwangsu's postface to the final installment of *The Tragic Story of Tanjong*, in *East Asia Daily*, August 20, 1929, quoted in *Yi Kwangsu chŏnjip* (Seoul: Samjungdang, 1962–1964), 5:554.
12. Yi Kwangsu argues against the writer Chu Yosŏp's 주요섭 (1902–1972) criticism of *The Tragic Story of Tanjong* for being "vulgar/commercial fiction." See "Yŏ ŭi chakka chŏk t'aedo," in *Yi Kwangsu chŏnjip*, 16:194–95.
13. See Benedict Anderson's classic discussion on nationalism and "homogeneous, empty time." *Imagined Communities: Reflections on the Origin and Spread of Nationalism*, rev. ed. (London: Verso, 2006), 22–31.
14. Han Wŏnyŏng, *Han'guk sinmun yŏnjae sosŏl ŭi sajŏk yŏngu* (Seoul: P'urŭn sasang, 2010), 1:260–309.
15. Kim Sŏngch'ŏl, "*Tanjong taewang silgi* wa '*Tanjong aesa*' ŭi hŏgujŏk yŏsŏng inmul ege t'uyŏng toen chakka ŭisik," *Uri munhak yŏngu* 43 (July 2014): 74–75.
16. Kim Yunsik, "Uri yŏksa sosŏl ŭi 4 kaji yuhyŏng," *Sosŏl munhak* 11, no. 6 (1985): 150–67; Kang, *Han'guk yŏksa sosŏl*, 47–63.
17. Kim Sŏngch'ŏl, "*Tanjong taewang*," 75–78.
18. Yi Kwangsu, "*Mujŏng* tŭng chŏnchakp'um ŭl ŏhada," in *Yi Kwangsu chŏnjip*, 16:303–4. Italics in original.
19. Paek, "Yŏksa sosŏl," 18.
20. Peter Brooks, *The Melodramatic Imagination: Balzac, Henry James, Melodrama, and the Mode of Excess* (New York: Columbia University Press, 1985), 5. The melodramatic characteristic of Yi's historical novels has been pointed out in relation to their mass appeal. See Kim Pyŏnggil, "Yi Kwangsu yŏksa sosŏl *Wŏnhyo daesa* nŭn ŏttŏk'e ilk'yŏnnŭn'ga?: Shinmun yŏnjae sosŏl rosŏŭi taejungsŏng ŭl chungshimŭro," *Ch'unwŏn yŏngu hakpo* 12 (June 2018): 37–63.
21. Yi Kwangsu, *Tanjong aesa*, in *Yi Kwangsu chŏnjip*, 5:302.

22. Yi, *Tanjong aesa*, 5:304.
23. Yi, *Tanjong aesa*, 5:305–6.
24. Yi, *Tanjong aesa*, 5:304.
25. Yi, *Tanjong aesa*, 5:312.
26. Yi, *Tanjong aesa*, 5:62.
27. Yi, *Tanjong aesa*, 5:232.
28. Yi, *Tanjong aesa*, 5:104.
29. Yi, *Tanjong aesa*, 5:163.
30. Yi, *Tanjong aesa*, 5:300.
31. Yi, *Tanjong aesa*, 5:242.
32. Yi, *Tanjong aesa*, 5:186.
33. Yi, *Tanjong aesa*, 5:134.
34. Yi, *Tanjong aesa*, 5:225.
35. Yi, *Tanjong aesa*, 5:225, 5:270.
36. Yi, *Tanjong aesa*, 5:60.
37. Yi, *Tanjong aesa*, 5:178.
38. Yi, *Tanjong aesa*, 5:15.
39. Yi, *Tanjong aesa*, 5:90.
40. Yi, *Tanjong aesa*, 5:270.
41. Yi, *Tanjong aesa*, 5:219.
42. Yi, *Tanjong aesa*, 5:220.
43. Kim Chong'uk, "Yi Kwangso, sinmin hoe, kŭrigo Ryang Ch'ich'ao," *Ch'unwŏn yŏngu hakpo* 12 (June 2018): 65.
44. Yi Kwangsu, "Chakka ŭi mal," in *Yi Kwangsu chŏnjip*, 16:273.
45. Yi, *Tanjong aesa*, 5:342.
46. This operation also underpins Yi's biography of An Ch'angho 안창호 (1878–1938), in which the Confucian virtue of "sincerity" (*song* 성) is adapted to furnish the core virtue of this quintessential independence activist. Yi writes, "When I become a sincere [*song* 성] person, that alone already means I'm helping the nation. So to be a patriot of utmost sincerity, you should first of all cultivate yourself to be a person of utmost sincerity." Yi Kwangsu, *Tosan An Ch'angho*, in *Yi Kwangsu chŏnjip*, 13:96.
47. Ogata Tsutomu, *Ōgai no rekishi shōsetsu: Shiryō to hōhō* (Tokyo: Iwanami shoten, 2002), 3–4.
48. Doris G. Bargen, *Suicidal Honor: General Nogi and the Writings of Mori Ogai and Natsume Soseki* (Honolulu: University of Hawai'i Press, 2006), 3.
49. Karatani, "Rekishi to shizen," 166.
50. Ōgai, "Rekishi sono mama," 3:361–62.
51. See Ogata, *Ōgai*, 63–125.

52. Mori Ōgai, "Abe ichizoku," in *Ōgai rekishi bungaku shū*, 2:34–35. For my quotes from Ōgai's historical fiction, I consulted translations in David Dilworth and J. Thomas Rimer, eds., *The Historical Fiction of Mori Ōgai* (Honolulu: University of Hawai'i Press, 1991).
53. Ōgai, "Abe ichizoku," 2:50.
54. Ogata, *Ōgai*, 139.
55. Mori Ōgai, "Sahase Jingorō," in *Ōgai rekishi bungaku shū*, 2:98.
56. Ōgai, "Sahase Jingorō," 2:98.
57. Mori Ōgai, "Kano yōni," in *Ōgai kindai shōsetsu shū* (Tokyo: Iwanami shoten, 2012–13), 6:30.
58. Ōgai, "Kano yōni," 6:34–35.
59. Ōgai, "Kano yōni," 6:32, 35.
60. Ōgai, "Kano yōni," 6:15–20.
61. Ōgai, "Kano yōni," 6:34.
62. Ōgai, "Kano yōni," 6:21.
63. Ōgai, "Kano yōni," 6:49.
64. Ōgai, "Kano yōni," 6:50–51.
65. Ōgai, "Kano yōni," 6:52.
66. Helen M. Hopper, "Mori Ōgai's Response to Suppression of Intellectual Freedom, 1909–12," *Monumenta Nipponica* 29, no. 4 (Winter 1974): 404–13.
67. Ōgai, "Rekishi sono mama," 3:361–65. See, for instance, Ogata, *Ōgai*; and Gamō Yoshirō, *Ōgai no rekishi shōsetsu: Sono shi to shinjitsu* (Tokyo: Shunjū sha, 1983).
68. Mori Ōgai, "Tsuge Shirōzaemon," in *Ōgai rekishi bungaku shū*, 3:158. "Editor" is written in French ("éditeur") in the original.
69. On Yokoi's thought, see, for example, Motoyama Yukihiko, *Yokoi Shōnan no gakumon to shisō* (Osaka: Osaka kōritsu daigaku kyōdō shuppankai, 2014); Mikami Kazuo, *Yokoi Shōnan: Sono shisō to kōdō* (Tokyo: Yoshikawa kōbunkan, 1999).
70. Ōgai, "Tsuge Shirōzaemon," 3:129–30.
71. Ōgai, "Tsuge Shirōzaemon," 3:132–35.
72. Ōgai, "Tsuge Shirōzaemon," 3:148.
73. Ōgai, "Tsuge Shirōzaemon," 3:153–54.
74. Ōgai, "Tsuge Shirōzaemon," 3:154.
75. Ōgai, "Tsuge Shirōzaemon," 3:158.
76. Ōgai, "Tsuge Shirōzaemon," 3:159–60.
77. Ōgai, "Tsuge Shirōzaemon," 3:159–60.
78. Ōgai, "Tsuge Shirōzaemon," 3:160.
79. Gao Yuandong, *Xiandai ruhe "nalai?": Lu Xun de sixiang yu wenxue lunji* (Shanghai: Fudan daxue chubanshe, 2009), 3–4.

80. See Lu Xun's criticism of such readings by contemporary critics in "'Chu guan' de 'guan,'" in *Lu Xun quanji*, 6:536–40. See Lin Fei, *Lun "Gushi xinbian" de sixiang yishu ji lishi yiyi* (Tianjin: Tianjin renmin chubanshe, 1984), 116–42.
81. Consider Walter Benjamin's famous dictum, "There is no document of civilization which is not at the same time a document of barbarism." "Theses on the Philosophy of History," in *Illuminations*, ed. Hannah Arendt, trans. Harry Zohn (New York: Schocken Books, 1969), 256.
82. Anne Birrell, *Chinese Mythology: An Introduction* (Baltimore, MD: Johns Hopkins University Press, 1993), 163–65.
83. See Li Fang et al., eds., *Taiping yulan* (Beijing: Zhonghua shuju, 1960), 1:365.
84. Zhang Shuangdi, *Huainanzi jiao shi* (Beijing: Beijing daxue chubanshe, 2013), 1:688.
85. Lu Xun, "Bu tian," *Gushi xinbian*, in *Lu Xun quanji*, 2:357–58. For this story, I use, with modifications, Julia Lovell's translation.
86. Lu Xun, "Bu tian," 2:364.
87. Lu Xun alludes to Hu Menghua's 胡夢華 criticism of Wang Jingzhi's 汪靜之 (1902–1996) poetry collection *Hui de feng* 蕙的風 (Orchid Breeze, 1922). Lu Xun expresses his revulsion against this criticism in "Fandui 'hanlei' de pipingjia," in *Lu Xun quanji*, 1:425–28.
88. Lu Xun, "Xuyan," *Gushi xinbian*, in *Lu Xun quanji*, 2:354.
89. Lu Xun, "Zixu," *Nahan*, in *Lu Xun quanji*, 1:442; Lu Xun, "Xuyan," 2:354.
90. Takeuchi Yoshimi, *Ro Jin nyūmon*, in *Takeuchi Yoshimi zenshū*, 2:167–68.
91. Chen Pingyuan, "Lu Xun de *Gushi xinbian* yu Bulaixite de 'Shishi xiju,'" in *Chen Pingyuan zixuanji* (Guilin: Guangxi shifan daxue chubanshe, 1997), 30–32.
92. Jing Wang, *The Story of Stone: Intertextuality, Ancient Chinese Stone Lore, and the Stone Symbolism in Dream of the Red Chamber, Water Margin, and The Journey to the West* (Durham, NC: Duke University Press, 1992), 1–33.
93. Cao Xueqin, *Zhiyanzhai chongping shi tou ji* (Hong Kong: Zhonghua shuju Xianggang fenju, 1977), 4. I use, with minor modifications, translation in *The Story of the Stone: A Chinese Novel in Five Volumes*, trans. David Hawkes (London: Penguin Books, 1979).
94. Cao, *Zhiyanzhai*, 6.
95. Cao, *Zhiyanzhai*, 6–7.
96. Lu Xun, "Xuyan," 2:353–54.
97. Cao, *Zhiyanzhai*, 7–8.
98. Lu Xun, "Bu tian," 2:358.
99. Lu Xun, "Bu tian," 2:366.

100. Lu Xun, "Bu tian," 2:366.
101. For more on this matter, see Satoru Hashimoto, "Science, History, Fiction: Mediality in Lu Xun's *Old Stories Retold*," *Frontiers of Literary Studies in China* 13, no. 3 (2019): 385–404.
102. The following discussion of "Chu guan" is adapted from Satoru Hashimoto, "World of Letters: Lu Xun, Benjamin, and *Daodejing*," *Journal of World Literature* 1, no. 1 (March 2016): 39–51.
103. The *"Tian yun"* chapter of *Zhuangzi*. See Guo Qingfan, ed., *Zhuangzi jishi* (Scripta Sinica: Hanji dianzi wenxian ziliaoku [digital database]).
104. "Laozi Han Fei liezhuan," in Sima Qian, *Shiji*, Scripta Sinica: Hanji dianzi wenxian ziliaoku (digital database). See also the opening phrases of *Daodejing*: "道可道，非常道；名可名，非常名," which can be translated: "The Way that can be spoken of is not the enduring and unchanging Way; the name that can be named is not the enduring and unchanging name." Zhu Qianzhi, ed., *Laozi jiaoshi* (Scripta Sinica: Hanji dianzi wenxian ziliaoku [digital database]).
105. "Laozi Han Fei liezhuan," in Sima Qian, *Shiji*.
106. Livia Kohn, "Yin Xi: The Master at the Beginning of the Scripture," *Journal of Chinese Religions* 25 (1997): 83–139.
107. Lu Xun, "'Chu guan' de 'guan,'" 6:539.
108. Zhang Taiyan, "Zhuzixue lüeshuo," in *Guocui xuebao*, year 2, vol. 4, 5–6.
109. Lu Xun, "Chu guan," *Gushi xinbian*, in *Lu Xun quanji*, 2:462.
110. Lu Xun, "Chu guan," 2:459–60.
111. Jacques Rancière, *The Politics of Aesthetics: The Distribution of the Sensible*, trans. Gabriel Rockhill (London: Continuum, 2004), 38.
112. Hu Shi, "Lishide wenxue guannian lun," in *Hu Shi quanji* (Anhui: Anhui jiaoyu chubanshe, 2003), 1:30–33.
113. Hu Shi, "Wushi nianlai de Zhongguo zhi wenxue," in *Hu Shi quanji*, 2:262.
114. Hu Shi, "Guogu zhengli yu 'dagui,'" in *Hu Shi quanji*, 3:145.

PART III: JAPAN'S IMPERIAL MIMICRY AND ITS CRITIQUE

1. See, for instance, W. G. Beasley, *Japanese Imperialism, 1894–1945* (Oxford: Clarendon Press, 1987), 1–13.
2. Karen Thornber, *Empire of Texts in Motion: Chinese, Korean, and Taiwanese Transculturations of Japanese Literature* (Cambridge, MA: Harvard University Asia Center, 2009), 7.
3. Here I am adapting Homi Bhabha's notion of "colonial mimicry." See "Of Mimicry and Man," in *The Location of Culture* (New York: Routledge, 2004), 85–92.

A few scholars have attempted this adaptation, yet solely to illustrate Japan's mimicry of Western imperialism. See Robert Thomas Tierney, *Tropics of Savagery: The Culture of Japanese Empire in Comparative Frame* (Berkeley: University of California Press, 2010), 16; Jini Kim Watson, "Imperial Mimicry, Modernisation Theory and the Contradictions of Postcolonial South Korea," *Postcolonial Studies* 10, no. 2 (2007): 174.

4. Saitō Mareshi, "Dōbun no poritikusu," *Bungaku* 10, no. 6 (2009): 42–43. See also Shukuri Shigeichi, *Kodama Gentarō* (Tokyo: Taikyōsha, 1938).
5. Saitō, "Dōbun," 44–45.
6. Ri Shōrin (Li Shanglin), "Taiwan shokuminchi jidai shoki ni okeru Nihon tōchi to shindai kanwa: 'Fukutsūyaku sei' ka no Taiwan kanwa shiyōsha wo chūshin ni," in *Nihon tōchiki Taiwan ni okeru yakusha oyobi "hon'yaku" katsudō: Shokuminchi tōchi to gengo bunka no sakusō kankei*, ed. Yō Shōshuku (Yang Chengshu) (Taipei: Taiwan daxue chuban zhongxin, 2015), 55–84.
7. Quoted in Saitō, "Dōbun," 43.
8. Suematsu Kenchō, ed., *Zenrin shōwa dai ni shū; Suiun gashū* (Tokyo: Suematsu Kenchō, 1909), 58, 60. In the same year, the Korean resistance activist An Chunggŭn 안중근 (1879–1910) assassinated Itō at Harbin Station, and Kim T'aekyŏng composed impassioned poems and wrote a biography in honor of An.
9. For the significance of the notion of "national language" (i.e., Japanese) in the Japanese Empire at large, see Yasuda Toshiaki, *Teikoku Nihon no gengo hensei* (Tokyo: Seori shobō, 1997).
10. Komagome Takeshi, *Shokuminchi teikoku Nihon no bunka tōgō* (Tokyo: Iwanami shoten, 1996), 51–57. Komagome notes that they used a modified version of *San zi jing* 三字經 (The Classic in Three Characters) to redact the passages on the Qing Empire and avoided the *Mencius* to censor the idea of "revolution," which would undercut the Japanese ideology of an unbroken imperial line.
11. Huang Mei'e, *Gudian Taiwan: Wenxueshi, shishe, zuojialun* (Taipei: Guoli bianyiguan, 2007), 183–227.
12. The quotation is from Isawa Shūji, "Iwayuru saikin no kokugo mondai ni tsukite," in *Isawa Shūji senshū* (Nagano: Shinano kyōiku kai, 1958), 727. See Komagome, *Shokuminchi*, 53–54. This was by no means Isawa's unique contention. In 1895, for example, Miyake Setsurei 三宅雪嶺 (1860–1945) wrote, "The benefit of Chinese characters resides in grasping East Asian thought and in facilitating the strategies of conquering and doing business in East Asia, which is why we must study Chinese writing and learn Chinese characters." "Kanji ridō setsu," in Nishio Minoru and Hisamatsu Sen'ichi, eds., *Kokugo kokuji kyōiku shiryō sōran* (Tokyo: Kokugo kyōiku kenkyūkai, 1969), 81.

13. See Chin Baihō (Chen Peifeng), *Nihon tōchi to shokuminchi kanbun: Taiwan ni okeru kanbun no kyōkai to sōzō* (Tokyo: Sangensha, 2012), 16–17.
14. Isawa Shūji, "Jo," in Isawa Shūji et al., eds., *Dōbun shinjiten* (Tokyo: Taitō dōbun kyoku, 1909), 1–12.
15. See Zhu Xi, ed., *Zhongyong zhangju* (Scripta Sinica: Hanji dianzi wenxian ziliaoku [digital database]).
16. Among the prominent sympathizers were Yu Kilchun in Korea, who aided in the compilation of the dictionary with regard to Korean pronunciation, and Zhang Zhidong 張之洞 (1837–1909) in China, who lent backing to the society. See Kim Soyŏng, "Hanja t'ong'il hoe hwaldong kwa 'tongmun' ŭisik," *Han'guksa yŏngu* 177 (2017): 1–35; Ryū Senka, "Kanji tōitsu kai ni kansuru ichi kōsatsu: Shinkoku to Kankoku no hannō wo chūshin to shite," *Gengo shakai* 13 (2019), 280–96.
17. Zhang Taiyan, "Lun hanzi tongyi hui zhi huanglou," *Minbao* 17 (1907): 5–10.
18. Chin, *Nihon tōchi*, 37–234.
19. Komagome, *Shokuminchi*, 63–71, 79–83.
20. Ch'oe Yong'gi, *Han'gugŏ chŏngch'aek ŭi ihae* (Seoul: Han'guk munhwasa, 2010), 36–55; Lee Sunyoung (Yi Sŏnyŏng), "Shokuminchi Chōsen ni okeru gengo seisaku to nashonarizumu: Chōsen sōtokufu no Chōsen kyōikurei to Chōsengo gakkai jiken wo chūshin ni," *Ritsumeikan kokusai kenkyū* 25, no. 2 (2012): 495–519. See also Hŏ Chaeyŏng, *Ilche kangjŏmgi ŏmun chŏngch'aek kwa ŏmun saenghwal* (Kyŏnggi-do Kwangmyŏng-si: Kyŏngjin, 2011).
21. Wu Micha et al., eds., *Diguo li de "difang wenhua": Huangminhua shiqi Taiwan wenhua zhuangkuang* (Taipei: Bozhongzhe chuban youxian gongsi, 2008), 1–48; Miyata Setsuko, *Chōsen minshū to "kōminka" seisaku* (Tokyo: Miraisha, 1985). Chen Peifeng points out that even in the *kōminka* era, Chinese writing barely survived in some publications in Taiwan, and its usefulness was again invoked as Taiwan bore the role of the strategic outpost for the empire's further expansion into southern China as well as Southeast Asia. The survival of Chinese writing came at the cost of "standardization," purging Taiwanese diction in particular, so that it better served the function of an imperial *lingua franca*. See Chin, *Nihon tōchi*, 235–307.
22. Hirata Yūji, *Kyōiku chokugo kokusai kankeishi no kenkyū: Kantei hon'yaku kyōiku chokugo wo chūshin to shite* (Tokyo: Kazama shobō, 1997), 35–77, 404–421.
23. See Soeda Yoshiya, *Kyōiku chokugo no shakaishi: Nashonarizumu no sōshutsu to zasetsu* (Tokyo: Yūshindō kōbunsha, 1997), 189–243. *Shūshin*, or *xiushen* in Chinese, is one of the steps in the process of arriving at "manifestation of bright virtue to all under heaven" beginning from "perfecting knowledge through investigation of things" described in the Confucian classic *Great Learning*.
24. Komagome, *Shokuminchi*, 52, 95.

25. Isawa Shūji, "Taiwan kōgakkō setchi ni kansuru iken," in *Isawa Shūji senshū*, 615–16.
26. Komagome, *Shokuminchi*, 95–100, 198–208.
27. For how *chū* and *kō* in particular came to the fore of the Japanese interpretation of Confucianism through Edo Sinology, see Zhang Kunjiang, *Dechuan Riben 'zhong' 'xiao' gainian de xingcheng yu fazhan: Yi bingxue yu yangmingxue wei zhongxin* (Taipei: Ximalaya yanjiu fazhan jijinhui, 2003).
28. Morikawa Terumichi, *Zōhoban kyōiku chokugo eno michi: Kyōiku no seijishi* (Tokyo: Sangensha, 2011), 171–207; Umetani Noboru, *Kyōiku chokugo seiritsushi: Tennōsei kokkakan no seiritsu ge* (Tokyo: Seishi shuppan kabushiki gaisha, 2000), 3–129.
29. Maruyama Masao, "Chō kokkashugi no ronri to shinri," in *Chō kokkashugi no ronri to shinri hoka hachi hen*, ed. Furuya Jun (Tokyo: Iwanami shoten, 2015), 21.
30. Maruyama, "Chō kokkashugi," 32–36. Maruyama analyzed this structure in terms of "the transfer of oppression."
31. See Komagome, *Shokuminchi*, 99–100.
32. Prasenjit Duara, *Sovereignty and Authenticity: Manchukuo and the East Asian Modern* (Lanham, MD: Rowman & Littlefield, 2003), 2. Italics in original.
33. Prasenjit Duara, "Transnationalism and the Predicament of Sovereignty: China, 1900-1945," *The American Historical Review* 102, no. 4 (1997), 1030–51.
34. Lincoln Li, *The China Factor in Modern Japanese Thought: The Case of Tachibana Shiraki, 1881–1945* (Albany: State University of New York Press, 1996), 69–70. See also Komagome, *Shokuminchi*, 240–68. On the idea of *datong* in modern Chinese thought, see "The Moral Vision in Kang Youwei's *Book of the Great Community*," in *Chinese Visions of World Order: Tianxia, Culture, and World Politics*, ed. Ban Wang (Durham, NC: Duke University Press, 2017), 87–105.
35. Yamamuro Shin'ichi, *Kimera: Manshūkoku no shōzō* (Tokyo: Chūōkōron shinsha, 2004), 137–56, 221–35; Komagome, *Shokuminchi*, 269–82.
36. On the Japanese discourse of "overcoming modernity," see Harry Harootunian, *Overcome by Modernity: History, Culture, and Community in Interwar Japan* (Princeton, NJ: Princeton University Press, 2000), 34–93; and Naoki Sakai and Isomae Jun'ichi, eds., *"Kindai no chōkoku" to Kyōto gakuha: Kindaisei, teikoku, fuhensei* (Kyoto: Ningen bunka kenkyū kiko kokusai Nihon bunka kenkyū sentā, 2010). For a discussion on Japanese imperialism and the discourse of "world history," see Christian Uhl, "What Was the 'Japanese Philosophy of History?': An Inquiry Into the Dynamics of the 'World-Historical Standpoint' of the Kyoto School," in *Political Philosophy in Japan: Nishida, the Kyoto School, and Co-Prosperity*, ed. Christopher Goto-Jones (New York: Routledge, 2005), 113–33.

37. See Nishitani Keiji, "'Kindai no chōkoku' shiron," in *Kindai no chōkoku*, ed. Kawakami Tetsutarō (Tokyo: Fuzanbō, 1979), 18–37. This is Nishitani's position paper for the famous roundtable on the theme of "overcoming the modern" (*kindai no chōkoku*) organized by the magazine *Bungakukai* (Literary World) in 1942.

5. ARCHAEOLOGY OF RESISTANCE

1. Zhou Zuoren, "Zhongguo de sixiang wenti," in *Zhou Zuoren sanwen quanji* (Guilin shi: Guangxi shifan daxue chubanshe, 2009), 8:708.
2. See Ozaki Hideki, *Kindai bungaku no shōkon* (Tokyo: Iwanami shoten, 1991), 1–57. For the Japanese Association for Literature in the Nation's Service, see Sakuramoto Tomio, *Nihon bungaku hōkoku kai: Daitōa sensō ka no bungakusha tachi* (Tokyo: Aoki shoten, 1995).
3. Nihon Bungaku Hōkokukai, *Bungaku hōkoku* (Tokyo: Fuji shuppan, 1990), 15. See also Liu Anwei, *Shū Sakujin den: Aru chinichiha bunjin no seishinshi* (Tokyo: Mineruva shobō, 2011), 300–301; Edward Gunn, *Unwelcome Muse: Chinese Literature in Shanghai and Peking, 1937–1945* (New York: Columbia University Press, 1980), 165–68.
4. The Kyoto school philosopher Kōyama Iwao 高山岩男 (1905–1993) used this notion to characterize Japan's war effort. See *Sekaishi no tetsugaku* (Tokyo: Iwanami shoten, 1942). See Christian Url, "What Was the 'Japanese Philosophy of History'?: An Inquiry into the Dynamics of the 'World-Historical Standpoint' of the Kyoto School," in *Political Philosophy in Japan: Nishida, the Kyoto School, and Co-Prosperity*, ed. Christopher Goto-Jones (New York: Routledge, 2005), 113–33.
5. Zhou Zuoren, *Zhitang huixianglu* (Shijiazhuang: Hebei jiaoyu chubanshe, 2002), 2:656.
6. See Wang Qiang, *Hanjian zuzhi xinmin hui* (Tianjin: Tianjin shehui kexueyuan chubanshe, 2006), 77–112.
7. This letter, first published in *Xin wenxue ziliao* 2 (June 1987), is reprinted as "Yijiusijiu nian de yi feng xin" in Zhou Zuoren, *Zhou Zuoren wenlei bian* (Changsha: Hunan wenyi chubanshe, 1998), 10:63–71. The quotation is at 67.
8. Dong Bingyue, *"Guomin zuojia" de lichang: Zhong-Ri xiandai wenxue guanxi yanjiu* (Beijing: Sanlian shudian, 2006), 197.
9. For Zhou's biography, see Qian Liqun, *Zhou Zuoren zhuan* (Beijing: Huawen chubanshe, 2013); Liu, *Shū Sakujin den*. See also Kiyama Hideo, *Shū Sakujin "tainichi kyōryoku" no tenmatsu* (Tokyo: Iwanami shoten, 2004).
10. Zhou Zuoren, *Zhou Zuoren ji wai wen*, ed. Chen Zishan and Zhang Tierong (Haikou: Hainan guoji xinwen chuban zhongxin, 1995), 504.

11. On the political interventions in literature and culture in Beijing under Japanese rule, including the activities of the Chinese-language edition of *Osaka Daily*, see Zhang Quan, *Lunxian shiqi Beijing wenxue banian* (Beijing: Zhongguo heping chubanshe, 1994), 25–55. See also Sugino Yōkichi's edited volume *Kōsō suru Chūgoku bungaku to Nihon bungaku: Rinkanka Pekin 1937–45* (Tokyo: Sangensha, 2000).
12. Mao Dun et al., "Gei Zhou Zuoren de yi feng gongkai xin," in *Guonan shengzhong*, vol. 3 of *Huiwang Zhou Zuoren*, ed. Sun Yu and Huang Qiaosheng (Kaifeng: Henan daxue chubanshe, 2004), 5.
13. Zhang Juxiang and Zhang Tierong, eds., *Zhou Zuoren nianpu* (Tianjin: Nankai daxue chubanshe, 1985), 543–64, 645.
14. Thanks to new testimonies and documents, we know the most probable perpetrators were agents of an underground anti-Japanese organization. Sun Yu and Huang Qiaosheng, eds., *Guonan shengzhong*, 82–97.
15. Susan Daruvala, *Zhou Zuoren and an Alternative Chinese Response to Modernity* (Cambridge, MA: Harvard University Asia Center, 2000), 2.
16. On "national defense literature," see Wanshan Sheng, *Lu Xun, geming, lishi: Wanshan Sheng xiandai Zhongguo wenxue lunji*, trans. Wang Junwen (Beijing: Beijing daxue chubanshe, 2005), 120–65.
17. Franz Fanon, "On National Culture," in *The Wretched of the Earth* (New York: Grove Press, 2004), 145–80.
18. Zhou, "Zhongguo de sixiang," 8:708.
19. For Zhou's discourse on Confucianism in the wartime political context, see Dong, *Guomin zuojia*, 171–206.
20. Zhou, *Zhitang huixianglu*, 2:656; Zhou, "Zhongguo de sixiang," 8:708.
21. Zhou, "Zhongguo de sixiang," 8:710.
22. Zhou, "Zhongguo de sixiang," 8:712.
23. For the first question, refer, for example, to the discussion of the "four beginnings" in the "Gongsun Chou" chapter of the *Mencius*. See François Jullien, *Fonder la morale: Dialogue de Mencius avec un philosophe des Lumières* (Paris: B. Grasset, 1995). The second and third questions are implied in the discussion in the "Xing e" chapter of the *Xunzi*. See Michael Puett and Christine Gross-Loh, *The Path: What Chinese Philosophers Can Teach Us About the Good Life* (New York: Simon & Schuster, 2016), 163–81.
24. Zhou, "Zhongguo de sixiang," 8:711.
25. Zhou Zuoren, "Zhongguo de guomin sixiang," in *Zhou Zuoren sanwen quanji*, 8:583.
26. See the entry "kokusui" in Nihongo gakkai ed. *Nihon kokugo daijiten* (Tokyo: Tōkyōdō shuppan, 2018).
27. Zhou, "Zhongguo de guomin," 8:583–84.

28. Zhou Zuoren, "Guocui yu ouhua," in *Zhou Zuoren sanwen quanji*, 2:515–17.
29. See Daruvala, *Zhou Zuoren*, 138–52.
30. Zhou, "Guocui yu ouhua," 2:517.
31. I am referring to Clement Greenberg's paradigmatic discussion in "Modernist Painting," in *Modern Art and Modernism: A Critical Anthology*, ed. Francis Franscina and Charles Harrison (London: P. Chapman, 1988), 5–10.
32. Chen Duxiu, "Wenxue geming lun," in *Chen Duxiu xuanji*, ed. Hu Ming (Tianjin: Tianjin renmin chubanshe, 1990), 48–51.
33. Hu Shi, "Wenxue gailiang chuyi," in *Hu Shi quanji* (Hefei: Anhui jiaoyu chubanshe, 2003), 1:4–15.
34. Zhou Zuoren, "Guoyu wenxue tan," in *Zhou Zuoren sanwen quanji*, 4:484.
35. Zhou Zuoren, "Lun baguwen," in *Zhou Zuoren sanwen quanji*, 5:658–59.
36. Zhou, "Lun baguwen," 5:657.
37. Zhou Zuoren, *Zhongguo xinwenxue de yuanliu*, in *Zhou Zuoren sanwen quanji*, 6:63.
38. Hu Shi, "Lishi de wenxue guannian lun," in *Hu Shi quanji*, 1:30–1.
39. Zhou, *Zhongguo xinwenxue*, 6:63.
40. Zhou, *Zhongguo xinwenxue*, 6:63–64.
41. Xudong Zhang, "A Radical Hermeneutics of Chinese Literary Tradition: On Zhou Zuoren's *Zhongguo xinwenxue de yuanliu*," in *Classics and Interpretations: The Hermeneutic Traditions in Chinese Culture*, ed. Ching-I Tu (New Brunswick, NJ: Transaction Publishers, 2000), 436.
42. Wei-Ming Tu, "Cultural China," in *Sinophone Studies: A Critical Reader*, ed. Shu-mei Shih, Chien-hsin Tsai, and Brian Bernards (New York: Columbia University Press, 2013), 147–48.
43. Zhou, *Zhongguo xinwenxue*, 6:63.
44. Zhou, "Lun baguwen," 5:658.
45. Zhou writes, "The eight-legged essay forever constitutes part of Chinese literature; or I would dare to just say that it is a crystallization of Chinese culture. This is an undeniable, obvious fact whether today's people accept it or not." "Lun baguwen," 5:658.
46. Zhou Zuoren, "Difang yu wenyi," in *Zhou Zuoren sanwen quanji*, 3:101–2.
47. Zhou, "Difang yu wenyi," 3:102–3.
48. Zhou, "Difang yu wenyi," 3:101.
49. Zhou Zuoren, "Han wen xue de chuantong," in *Zhou Zuoren sanwen quanji*, 8:407.
50. Zhou Zuoren, "Han wen xue de qiantu," in *Zhou Zuoren sanwen quanji*, 8:778.
51. Zhou, "Han wen xue de qiantu," 8:785.
52. Kiyama, *Shū Sakujin*, 195.
53. Zhou, "Zhongguo de sixiang," 8:713, 715.

54. Zhou, "Han wen xue de qiantu," 8:784.
55. Thornber, *Empire of Texts*, 34–58.
56. Zhou Zuoren, "Riben yu Zhongguo," in *Zhou Zuoren sanwen quanji*, 4:302.
57. Zhou Zuoren, "Pairi pingyi," in *Zhou Zuoren sanwen quanji*, 5:247.
58. Zhou, "Pairi pingyi," 5:249.
59. Zhou Zuoren, "Riben de yi shi zhu" (a.k.a. "Riben guankui zhi er"), in *Zhou Zuoren sanwen quanji*, 6:666.
60. See Wiebke Denecke, *Classical World Literatures: Sino-Japanese and Greco-Roman Comparisons* (Oxford: Oxford University Press, 2014), 4–10.
61. Zhou, "Riben de yi shi zhu," 6:658.
62. Zhou, "Riben de yi shi zhu," 6:661.
63. Zhou, "Riben de yi shi zhu," 6:663–64. *Qimin yaoshu* is a work from around the sixth century on agriculture and cuisine.
64. Zhou, "Riben de yi shi zhu," 6:666.
65. For Zhou Zuoren's understanding of ancient Greek culture, see Jingling Chen, "An Acropolis in China: The Appropriation of Ancient Greek Tradition in Modern Chinese Literature" (PhD diss., Harvard University, 2016), chapter 4.
66. Zhou Zuoren, "Shenghuo de yishu," in *Zhou Zuoren sanwen quanji*, 3:513–14. On Zhou Zuoren's engagement with Havelock Ellis's work, see Dai Weina, *Weiwancheng de beiju: Zhou Zuoren yu Ailishi* (Nanjing: Jiangsu fenghuang wenyi chubanshe, 2018).
67. Zhou Zuoren, "Zhina minzuxing," in *Zhou Zuoren sanwen quanji*, 4:583.
68. Zhou, "Shenghuo de yishu," 3:513–14.
69. Zhou, "Shenghuo de yishu," 3:514.
70. Zhou, "Riben de yi shi zhu," 6:666.
71. Zhou Zuoren, "Huai Dongjing," in *Zhou Zuoren sanwen quanji*, 7:325.
72. Zhou, "Huai Dongjing," 7:330–31. Quote from Kafū is "Ukiyoe no kanshō," in *Kafū zenshū* (Tokyo: Iwanami shoten, 1992), 10:152. Verhaeren's "Art Flamand" is in *Choix de poèmes* (Paris: Mercure de France, 1917), 13–17.
73. Kafū, "Ukiyoe no kanshō," 10:151.
74. Kafū, "Ukiyoe no kanshō," 10:152.
75. G. W. F. Hegel, *Aesthetics: Lectures on Fine Art*, trans. T. M. Knox (Oxford: Oxford University Press, 1975), 1:598.
76. Hegel, *Aesthetics*, 1:598–600.
77. Kafū, "Ukiyoe no kanshō," 10:147.
78. Kafū, "Ukiyoe no kanshō," 10:152. The saying "arguments make your lips chilled," which originated in a haiku by Matsuo Bashō 松尾芭蕉 (1644-1694), is a proverbial admonishment against excessive talking and arguing.
79. Hegel, *Aesthetics*, 2:886–87.

80. Hegel, *Aesthetics*, 1:596.
81. Hegel, *Aesthetics*, 1:596.
82. Kafū, "Ukiyoe no kanshō," 10:147.
83. Kafū, "Ukiyoe no kanshō," 10:148.
84. Kafū, "Ukiyoe no kanshō," 10:154–55.
85. Kafū, "Ukiyoe no kanshō," 10:146–47.
86. Hegel, *Aesthetics*, 1:607.
87. Zhou, "Huai Dongjing," 7:331. The expression "you and I are like them" is a reference to Wang Yangming's "Yilüwen 瘞旅文" (Essay on Burring on the Road).
88. Zhou, "Huai Dongjing," 7:331–32.
89. Zhou, "Huai Dongjing," 7:332.
90. Zhou Zuoren, "Pingmin de wenxue," in *Zhou Zuoren sanwen quanji*, 2:104.
91. Zhou Zuoren, "Riben de renqing mei," in *Zhou Zuoren sanwen quanji*, 4:32–33.
92. Among the many examples are "Guxiang de yecai" (Vegetables in My Hometown, 1924) and "Beijing de chashi" (Sweetmeats in Beijing, 1924).
93. Zhou Zuoren, "You Riben zagan," in *Zhou Zuoren sanwen quanji*, 2:194.
94. Zhou, "You Riben," 2:194.
95. Stefan Tanaka, *Japan's Orient: Rendering Pasts Into History* (Berkeley: University of California Press, 1993), 12–13.
96. Okakura Tenshin famously said, "Japan is a museum of Asiatic civilization." Kakuzō Okakura, *The Ideals of the East with Special Reference to the Art of Japan* (New York: Dutton, 1920), 7.
97. Consider the notion infamously put forth by Hegel that "the *Orientals* do not know that spirit, or the human being as such, is intrinsically free" and that "they are not themselves free." G. W. F. Hegel, *Lectures on the Philosophy of World History: Manuscripts of the Introduction and the Lectures of 1822–3*, ed. and trans. Robert F. Brown and Peter C. Hodgson (Oxford: Oxford University Press, 2011), 87.
98. Zhou Zuoren, "Riben guankui zhi san," in *Zhou Zuoren sanwen quanji*, 7:16.

6. TRANSNATIONAL ALLEGORY

1. For Korea, see Kim Sunjŏn et al., eds., *Han'gugin Ilbonŏ munhak sajŏn* (Seoul: Cheiaenssi, 2018); Nayoung Aimee Kwon, *Intimate Empire: Collaboration and Colonial Modernity in Korea and Japan* (Durham, NC: Duke University Press, 2015), 17–40; Ōmura Masuo and Hotei Toshihiro, eds., *Kindai Chōsen bungaku Nihongo sakuhinshū, 1901–1938* (Tokyo: Ryokuin shobō, 2004). For Taiwan, see Chen Fangming, *Taiwan xinwenxue shi* (Taipei: Lianjing, 2011),

1:43–88; Fujii Shōzō, *Taiwan bungaku kono hyakunen* (Tokyo: Tōhō shoten, 1998), 25–67; Satoru Hashimoto, "Japanese-Language Literature in the Colonial Period," in *Encyclopedia of Taiwan Studies*, ed. Michael Hsiao (Leiden: Brill, forthcoming); Chen Peifeng, "Shizi, shuxie, yuedu yu rentong: Chongxin shenshi 1930 niandai xiangtu wenxue lunzhan de yiyi," in *Taiwan wenxue yu kuawenhua liudong*, ed. Qiu Guifen and Liu Shuqin (Taipei: Xingzhengyuan wenhua jianshe weiyuanhui, 2007), 83–110; Hoan Chichun (Huang Qichun), "Shakai shugi shichō no eikyōka ni okeru kyōdo bungaku ronsō to Taiwan gobun undo," in *Yomigaeru Taiwan bungaku: Nihon tōchiki no sakka to sakuhin*, ed. Shimomura Sakujirō et al. (Tokyo: Tōhō shoten, 1995), 47–72. See also Kimberly Tae Kono, *Romance, Family, and Nation in Japanese Colonial Literature* (New York: Palgrave Macmillan, 2010). Some expatriate writers adopted English. See Son Chŏngsu, "Kŭndae ch'ogi Miguk ch'eryu chishigindŭl ŭi Yŏng'ŏ kŭlssŭgi e nat'anan sŏsulchŏk chŏngch'esŏng ŭi munje: Yu Kilchun ŭi p'yŏnji, Yun Ch'iho ŭi ilgi, Sŏ Chaep'il ŭi sosŏl," *Han'gukhak nonjip* 79 (2020): 93–137; Wook-Dong Kim, *Global Perspectives on Korean Literature* (Singapore: Springer Singapore, 2019), 195–214.

2. Kim Yunsik, *Ilche malgi Han'guk chakka ŭi Ilbonŏ kŭlssŭgi ron* (Seoul: Sŏul taehakkyo ch'ulp'anbu, 2003), 3–68; Cho Chin'gi, *Ilche malgi kukch'aek kwa ch'eje sunŭng ŭi munhak* (Seoul: Somyŏng ch'ulp'an, 2010), 13–18; Pang Minho, *Ilche malgi Han'guk munhak ŭi tamnon kwa t'eksŭt'ŭ* (Seoul: Yeok, 2011), 23–78; Chen, *Tanwan xinwenxue*, 1:157–78; Faye Yuan Kleeman, *Under the Imperial Sun: Japanese Colonial Literature of Taiwan and the South* (Honolulu: University of Hawai'i Press, 2003), 160–227; Kawahara Isao, "The State of Taiwanese Culture and Taiwanese New Literature in 1937: Issues of Banning Chinese Newspaper Sections and Abolishing Chinese Writings," in *Taiwan Under Japanese Colonial Rule, 1895–1945: History, Culture, Memory*, ed. Ping-hui Liao and David Der-wei Wang (New York: Columbia University Press, 2006), 122–40.

3. Japanese anthologies of Korean and Taiwanese literatures published in this period include: the 1939 special issue of the journal *Modan Nihon* (Modern Japan) on Korean literature; Sin Kŏn, ed., *Chōsen shōsetsu daihyō shū* (Representative Korean Fiction, 1940); Chang Hyŏkchu et al., eds., *Chōsen bungaku senshū* (Collection of Korean Literature, 1940) in three volumes; Kayama Mitsurō (a.k.a. Yi Kwangsu) et al., *Hantō sakka tanpenshū* (Collection of Short Stories by Writers in the Peninsula, 1944); Ishii Kōzō (a.k.a. Ch'oe Chaesŏ), ed., *Shin hantō bungaku senshū* (New Collection of Peninsula Literature, 1944) in two volumes; Nishikawa Mitsuru, ed., *Taiwan bungaku shū* (Collection of Taiwanese Literature, 1942). See Yun Taesŏk, "1940 nyŏndae Han'guk munhak esŏŭi pŏnyŏk," *Minjok munhaksa yŏngu* 33 (2007): 312–36; Izumi Tsukasa,

Nihon tōchiki Taiwan to teikoku no bundan: Bungaku kenshō ga tsukuru Nihongo bungaku (Tokyo: Hitsuji shobō, 2012), 15–108.

4. See Izumi, *Nihon tōchiki Taiwan*.
5. Miya Qiong Xie, *Territorializing Manchuria: The Transnational Frontier and Literatures of East Asia* (Cambridge, MA: Harvard University Asia Center, 2023), 35–68.
6. Shi Kan (Shi Gang), *Shokuminchi shihai to Nihongo: Taiwan, Manshūkoku, tairiku senryōchi ni okeru gengo seisaku* (Tokyo: Sangensha, 2003), 48–83.
7. Okada Hideki, *Bungaku ni miru "Manshūkoku" no isō* (Tokyo: Kenbun shuppan, 2000), 7–24.
8. Yoshino Haruo, aka. Ehara Teppei, "Futatabi Manshū bungaku wo," in *Manshū nichinichi shinbun*, March 31 and April 4, 1939, quoted in Okada, *Bungaku ni miru*, 10–11.
9. Okada, *Bungaku ni miru*, 25–64; Annika A. Culver, *Glorify the Empire: Japanese Avant-Garde Propaganda in Manchukuo* (Vancouver: UBC Press, 2013), 134–67.
10. *Manjin sakka shōsetsu shū* (Collection of Fiction by Chinese Writers), for example, anthologizes Chinese-language short stories from Manchukuo in Ōuchi Takao's 大内隆雄 (1907–1980) translation, published in Tokyo in two volumes in 1939 and 1940. *Nichi Man Ro zaiman sakka tanpen senshū* (Collection of Short Stories by Manchukuo Japanese, Manchu, and Russian Writers), ed. Yamada Seizaburō 山田清三郎 (1896–1987), was published in Tokyo in 1940. *Manshūkoku kaku minzoku sōsaku senshū* (Collection of Writings by Each Ethnic Group in Manchukuo) was published in Tokyo in two volumes in 1942 and 1944 under the editorship of Kawabata Yasunari 川端康成 (1899–1972) et al.
11. W. G. Beasley, *Japanese Imperialism, 1894–1945* (Oxford: Clarendon Press, 1987), 198–250.
12. Christopher P. Hanscom and Dennis Washburn, "Introduction," in *The Affect of Difference: Representations of Race in East Asian Empire*, ed. Christopher P. Hanscom and Dennis Washburn (Honolulu: University of Hawai'i Press, 2016), 2–4.
13. See Liu Shuqin's edited volumes: *Dongya wenxue chang: Taiwan, Chaoxian, Manzhou de zhimin zhuyi yu wenhua jiaoshe* (Taipei: Lianjing, 2018) and *Zhanzheng yu fenjie: "Zonglizhan" xia Taiwan, Hanguo de zhuti chongsu yu wenhua zhengzhi* (Taipei: Lianjing, 2011). See also Lin Peijie, *Taiwan wenxue zhong de "Manzhou" xiangxiang ji zaixian* (Taipei: Xiuwei zixun keji gufen youxian gongsi, 2015). Li Wenqing has used the term "greater East Asian literary sphere." See Li Wenqing, *Gongrong de xiangxiang: Diguo, zhimindi yu da dongya wenxue quan, 1937–1945* (Taipei: Daoxiang chubanshe, 2012). These studies are part of the growing body of scholarship that attends to multidirectional literary

and artistic exchanges in the Japanese Empire, often calling into question the scheme of center vs. periphery.

14. Song Binghui, *Ruoshi minzu wenxue zai Zhongguo* (Nanjing: Nanjing daxue chubanshe, 2007), 33–57.
15. Hu Feng, trans. and ed., *Shanling: Chaoxian Taiwan duanpian ji* (Shanghai: Wenhua shenghuo chubanshe, 1936), ii.
16. Miya Qiong Xie, "'Borderland Translation': Manchuria and the Multilingual Translations of the Korean Short Story 'The Red Hill,'" *Journal of World Literature* 4, no. 4 (2019): 570–71; Kim Changsŏn, "Manjuguk munhakchang e iiptoen Han'gk munhak: *Chosŏn tanp'yŏn sosŏl sŏn* ch'ulgan ŭl chungshimŭro," *Han-Chung inmunhak yŏngu* 62 (March 2019): 23–42; Kim Changsŏn, *Manju munhak yŏngu* (Seoul: Yŏngnak, 2009), 87–95.
17. Wang He, ed., *Chaoxian duanpian xiaoshuo xuan* (Xinjing: Xin shidai she, 1941), 118.
18. Julia Kristeva, "Word, Dialogue, and Novel," in *Desire in Language: A Semiotic Approach to Literature and Art*, ed. Leon S. Roudiez, trans. Thomas Gora et al. (New York: Columbia University Press, 1980), 64–91.
19. Walter Benjamin, *The Origin of German Tragic Drama*, trans. John Osborne (New York: Verso, 1998), 45–46.
20. Fredric Jameson, "Third-World Literature in the Era of Multinational Capitalism," *Social Text* 15 (Fall 1986): 65–88.
21. Benjamin, *Origin of German*, 178–79.
22. Hu, *Shanling*, ii.
23. Wang, *Chaoxian duanpian*, 117.
24. See, for example, Hong Sŏkp'o, *Ru Swin kwa kŭndae Han'guk: Tong asia kongjon ŭl wihan sangsang* (Seoul: Ihwa yŏja daehakkyo ch'ulp'an munhwa wŏn, 2018); Lu Xun bowuguan, ed., *Hanguo Lu Xun yanjiu lunwenji* (Zhengzhou: Henan wenyi chubanshe, 2005); Im Myŏngsin, "Kankoku kindai seishinshi ni okeru Ro Jin: 'A kyū seiden' no Kankoku teki juyō" (Ph.D. diss., University of Tokyo, 2001); Nakajima Toshirō, ed., *Taiwan shinbungaku to Ro Jin* (Tokyo: Tōhō shoten, 1997).
25. Jiao Heran, "Lu Xun yu dongbei lunxianqu Haerbin diqu zuoyi wenxue huodong zhi guanxi," *Lu Xun yanjiu yuekan* 1 (2019): 79–88; Xie Chaokun, "Lu Xun zai Weimanzhouguo de chuanbo, jieshou yu yingxiang," *Mingzuo xinshang* 26 (2016): 8–12; Li Wenqing, "Lu Xun zhi hou: 'Zhanzheng qi' (1937–1945) de manxi wentan yu wenyi," *Nanfang wentan* 6 (2014): 43–53.
26. The dissemination of Lu Xun's works reached well beyond the region. See Wang Jiaping, *Lu Xun yuwai bainian chuanbo shi, 1909–2008* (Beijing: Beijing daxue chubanshe, 2009); Wang Runhua and Pan Guoju, eds., *Lu Xun zai dongnan ya* (Singapore: Bafang wenhua chuangzuoshi, 2017).

27. This letter, dated February 8, was discovered by the Japanese researcher Shimomura Sakujirō in Long Yingzong's private archive and is cited in its entirety in Shimomura Sakujirō, *Bungaku de yomu Taiwan* (Tokyo: Tabata shoten, 1994), 210–12. Shimomura estimates that the letter was sent in 1941. The original letter is reproduced as a photocopy in Kwon, *Intimate Empire*, 62–64. For the significance of this letter, see also Hwang Hodŏk, "Cheguk Ilbon kwa pŏnyŏk (ŏmnŭn) chŏngch'i: Ru Swin, Rung Ingtchung, Kim Saryang, 'a kyu' chŏk sam kwa chukwŏn," *Taedong munhwa yŏngu* 63 (2008): 375–423.
28. For these writers' biographies, see An Ushiku, *Kin Shiryō: Sono teikō no shōgai* (Tokyo: Iwanami shoten, 1972) and Long Yingzong, *Long Yingzong quanji: Ribenyu ban*, ed. Chen Wanyi et al. (Tainan: Guoli Taiwan wenxueguan, 2008), 6:155–69.
29. Long Yingzong, "Futatsu no kyōjin nikki," in *Long Yingzong quanji: Ribenyu ban*, 4:65–69.
30. For Gu Ding's biography, see Mei Ding'e, *Ko Tei kenkyū: "Manshūkoku" ni ikita bunkajin* (Kyoto: Kokusai Nihon bunka kenkyū sentā, 2012), 11–71.
31. Gu Ding and Hayashi Fusao, "Hayashi Fusao, Ko Tei taidan," *Geibun* 1, no. 5 (April 1942): 146–56. On the journal *Geibun*, see Shan Yuanchao, "Zasshi *Geibun* no seiritsu to hensen ni tsuite: 'Bunka sōgō zasshi' kara 'jun geibun zasshi' e," *Kokyō: Nihongo bungaku kenkyū* 1 (2014): 73–88.
32. Mei, *Ko Tei*, 49.
33. Gu and Hayashi, "Hayashi Fusao," 155–56.
34. Li Bin, *1931–1945: Dongbei lunxianqu wenxue yu "wailai" wenxue guanxi yanjiu* (Changchun: Jilin renmin chubanshe, 2011), 178–85; Xie Chaokun, "Lu Xun"; Li Wenqing, "Lu Xun zhi hou."
35. Gu Ding, "Zhulin," in *Gu Ding zuopinxuan*, ed. Li Chunyan (Shenyang: Chunfeng wenyi chubanshe, 1995), 350–68. The sources of those episodes are found in "Qiyi di shiba," "Rendan di ershisan," and "Jian'ao di ershisi" in *Shishuo xinyu jianshu*, comp. Liu Yiqing, annot. Liu Xiaobiao (Scripta Sinica: Hanji dianzi wenxian ziliaoku [digital database]); "Ruan Ji zhuan" and "Ji Kang zhuan" in *Jin shu*, comp. Fang Xuanling et al., ed. Yang Jialuo et al. (Scripta Sinica: Hanji dianzi wenxian ziliaoku [digital database]); and "Yu Shan Juyuan juejiao shu" in *Wen xuan*, comp. Xiao Tong et al. annot. Li Shan (Scripta Sinica: Hanji dianzi wenxian ziliaoku [digital database]).
36. Gu, "Zhulin," 366. Source in "Qiyi di shiba."
37. Mei, *Ko Tei*, 195; Okada Hideki, *"Manshūkoku" no bungaku to sono shūhen* (Tokyo: Tōhō shoten, 2019), 46–47.
38. Chen Pingyuan, "Xiandai Zhongguo de 'Wei-Jin fengdu' yu 'Liuchao sanwen,'" *Zhongguo wenhua* 15–16 (1997): 273–305; Qian Liqun, "Shinian chenmo de Lu

Xun," *Zhejiang shehui kexue* 1 (2003): 138; Wang Yao, "Zhongguo xiandai wenxue yu gudian wenxue de lishi guanxi," *Beijing daxue xuebao* 5 (1986): 10.
39. Lu Xun, "Wei-Jin fengdu ji wenzhang yu yao ji jiu zhi guanxi," in *Lu Xun quanji* (Beijing: Renmin wenxue chubanshe, 2005), 3:532, 537.
40. Lu Xun, "Wei-Jin fengdu," 3:535.
41. Lu Xun, "Wei-Jin fengdu," 3:533.
42. Lu Xun, "Wei-Jin fengdu," 3:533.
43. Lu Xun, "Wei-Jin fengdu," 3:535–36.
44. Gu Ding, "Lu Xun zhushu jieti," in *Gu Ding zuopinxuan*, 562. This essay is a translation of the introductions to Lu Xun's works in the Kaizō sha edition of his complete works, *Dai Ro Jin zenshū*, edited by Inoue Kōbai et al. and published in 1936 and 1937.
45. Gu Ding, *Tan*, in *Gu Ding zuopinxuan*, 30–33.
46. Gu Ding, *Tan*, 33.
47. Lu Xun, "Guxiang," in *Lu Xun quanji*, 1:510.
48. Gu Ding, *Yizhi banjie ji*, in *Gu Ding zuopinxuan*, 26.
49. Gu Ding, *Tan*, 87.
50. Gu Ding, *Yizhi banjie ji*, 52–56; *Tan*, 87–88, 103.
51. Gu Ding, *Tan*, 88.
52. Gu Ding, *Tan*, 91.
53. Gu Ding, "Lu Xun zhushu jieti," 562.
54. Lu Xun, "Wusheng de Zhongguo," in *Lu Xun quanji*, 4:11–17.
55. Gu Ding, *Tan*, 129–31.
56. Gu Ding, "Lu Xun zhushu jieti," 562.
57. Dajiubao Mingnan (Ōkubo Akio) et al., *Wei Manzhouguo wenxue yanjiu zai Riben* (Harbin: Beifang wenyi chubanshe, 2017), 5.
58. Okada, *Bungaku ni miru*, 76.
59. Gu Ding, "Yuanye," in *Gu Ding zuopinxuan*, 264.
60. Gu Ding, "Yuanye," 278–79.
61. Gu Ding, "Yuanye," 317.
62. Gu Ding, "Yuanye," 316.
63. Gu Ding, "Yuanye," 307.
64. Lu Xun xiansheng jinian weiyuanhui, ed., *Lu Xun xiansheng jinian ji: Daowen dierji* (Shanghai: Shanghai shudian chubanshe, 1979), 55.
65. Qian Liqun, *Lu Xun zuopin shiwu jiang* (Beijing: Beijing daxue chubanshe, 2003), 15.
66. Lu Xun, "Nüdiao," in *Lu Xun quanji*, 6:637–44.
67. Lu Xun, "Nüdiao," 6:639–40.
68. Maruo Tsuneki, *Ro Jin: "Jin" "ki" no kattō* (Tokyo: Iwanami shoten, 1993), 42.
69. Gu Ding, "Yuanye," 317.

70. Gu Ding, "Yuanye," 317.
71. See Ozaki, *Kindai bungaku*, 52.
72. Long Yingzong, "Taiwan bungaku no tenbō," in *Long Yingzong quanji: Ribenyu ban*, 4:86.
73. Long Yingzong, "Sōsaku sentosuru tomoe," in *Long Yingzong quanji: Ribenyu ban*, 4:25.
74. Long Yingzong, "Papaiya no aru machi," in *Long Yingzong quanji: Ribenyu ban*, 1:15–16.
75. Long, "Papaiya," 1:33–34.
76. Long, "Papaiya," 1:39.
77. Long, "Papaiya," 1:52.
78. Long, "Papaiya," 1:52–53.
79. Nakayama Yū, "Genjitsu no mondai," originally published in *Ōsaka asahi shinbun* on April 25, 1937, reprinted in *Long Yingzong quanji: Ribenyu ban*, 6:139.
80. Anonymous, "'Papaiya no aru machi' de chūi wo hiku futatsu no ten," originally published in *Tōkyō nichinichi shinbun* on April 13, 1937, reprinted in *Long Yingzong quanji: Ribenyu ban*, 6:138.
81. See *Long Yingzong quanji: Ribenyu ban*, 6:133, 144.
82. See *Long Yingzong quanji: Ribenyu ban*, 6:132.
83. Long, "Papaiya," 1:14–16.
84. Long Yingzong, "Chōfujin no giga," in *Long Yingzong quanji: Ribenyu ban*, 1:71.
85. Long, "Chōfujin," 1:82.
86. See chapter 3.
87. Lu Xun, "Guxiang," in *Lu Xun quanji*, 1:510.
88. Long, "Papaiya," 1:56–57.
89. Long Yingzong, "Yoizuki," in *Long Yingzong quanji: Ribenyu ban*, 1:142.
90. Long, "Yoizuki," 1:143.
91. Long, "Yoizuki," 1:143–44.
92. Long, "Yoizuki," 1:147.
93. Long, "Yoizuki," 1:149.
94. Long, "Yoizuki," 1:152–55.
95. Long, "Yoizuki," 1:151–52.
96. Long, "Yoizuki," 1:147.
97. Long, "Yoizuki," 1:162.
98. On the Japanese reception and criticism of "Into the Light," see Kwon, *Intimate Empire*, 41–58.
99. Kim Saryang, "Chōsen bunka tsūshin," in *Kin Shiryō zenshū*, ed. Kin Shiryō zenshū henshū iinkai (Tokyo: Kawade shobō shinsha, 1973), 4:25–27.
100. Kim, "Chōsen bunka," 4:28–29. On the imperial slogan, see Miyata Setsuko, *Chōsen minshū to "kōminka" seisaku* (Tokyo: Miraisha, 1985), 148–92.

101. Kim, "Chōsen bunka," 4:29–30.
102. Kim Saryang, "Hikari no nakani," *Bungei shuto* (October 1939), reprint in *Kindai Chōsesn bungaku Nihongo sakuhinshū, sōsaku hen*, ed. Ōmura Masuo and Hotei Toshihiro (Tokyo: Ryokuin shobō, 2001), 1:55. For quotes from this story, I use, with slight modifications, the translation in Melissa L. Wender, ed., *Into the Light: An Anthology of Literature by Koreans in Japan* (Honolulu: University of Hawai'i Press, 2011), 15–38.
103. Kim, "Hikari no nakani," 1:54.
104. Kim, "Hikari no nakani," 1:58.
105. Kim, "Hikari no nakani," 1:56.
106. Kim, "Hikari no nakani," 1:67.
107. Kim, "Hikari no nakani," 1:65.
108. Kim, "Hikari no nakani," 1:67.
109. Kim, "Hikari no nakani," 1:79.
110. Nayoung Aimee Kwon has referred to Judith Butler to emphasize the performative constructs of identities in this story. See Kwon, *Intimate Empire*, 65n6.
111. Kim, "Hikari no nakani," 1:75.
112. Kim, "Hikari no nakani," 1:80.
113. Kim, "Hikari no nakani," 1:72–75.
114. Kim Saryang, "Hikari no nakani," in *Hikari no nakani* (Tokyo: Koyama shoten, 1940), 37-42.
115. Kim Saryang, "Yuch'ijang esŏ mannan sanai," in *Munjang* (February 1941), 290. My underlines.
116. Kim, "Yuch'ijang," 295–96.
117. See Matsumura Takao, "Nihon teikoku shugi ka ni okeru 'Manshū' eno Chōsenjin idō ni tsuite," *Keio Journal of Economics* 63, no. 6 (1970): 479–595; Jin Yongzhe, *"Manshūkoku" ki ni okeru Chōsenjin manshū imin seisaku* (Kyoto: Shōwadō, 2012).
118. Kim, "Yuch'ijang," 298.
119. Kim, "Yuch'ijang," 297.
120. Kim, "Yuch'ijang," 297.
121. Kim, "Yuch'ijang," 298–99.
122. Kim, "Yuch'ijang," 295.
123. Kim, "Yuch'ijang," 301.
124. Kim Saryang, "Kyū hakushaku," in *Kokyō* (Kyoto: Kōchō shorin, 1942), 109. My underlines.
125. Kim, "Yuch'ijang," 296–97. My underlines.
126. Kim, "Kyū hakushaku," 122. My underlines.
127. Kim, "Yuch'ijang," 297; "Kyū hakushaku," 124.
128. Kim Saryang, "Zatsuon," in *Kin Shiryō zenshū*, 4:53.

129. Kim's discussion on "stiff literal translation" reminds one of Lu Xun's idea of "stiff translation" (*yingyi* 硬譯). For more on this idea, see Satoru Hashimoto, "Intra-Asian Reading; or, How Lu Xun Enters Into a World Literature," in *The Making of Chinese-Sinophone Literatures as World Literature*, ed. Yingjin Zhang and Kuei-fen Chiu (Hong Kong: Hong Kong University Press, 2022), 83–102.

CONCLUSION

1. I owe this study to the numerous scholarly works from this period, including but not limited to those by Paek Nakch'ŏng, Ch'oe Wŏnsik, Kim Yunsik, Chen Fang-ming, Peng Hsiao-yen, Ke Qingming, Leo Ou-fan Lee, Shu-mei Shih, Jing Tsu, David Der-wei Wang, Xudong Zhang, Kawamura Minato, Katō Norihiro, and Naoki Sakai.

2. The Gongyang commentary on the *Spring and Autumn Annals*, whose uncanny return to Lu Xun's poem "After Death" I began this book with, has been avidly revisited, via Kang Youwei's late Qing restoration. See Wang Hui, *Xiandai Zhongguo sixiang de xingqi* (Beijing: Sanlian shudian, 2004), 737–829, and Gan Yang et al., "Kang Youwei yu zhiduhua ruxue," *Kaifang shidai* 5 (2014): 12–41. The "new discourse of all-under-heaven" (*xin tianxia zhuyi* 新天下主義) has ignited debates over the question of universality in East Asia. See Xu Jilin, "Xin tianxia zhuyi yu Zhongguo de neiwai zhixu," *Zhishifenzi luncong* 1 (2015): 3–35, and Zhao Tingyang, *Tianxia tixi: Shijie zhidu zhexue daolun* (Nanjing: Jiangsu jiaoyu chubanshe, 2005). See also Paek Yŏngsŏ's critique of this discourse in Peku Yonso (Paek Yŏngsŏ), *Kyōsei eno michi to kakushin genba: Jissen kadai toshite no higashi ajia*, ed. Nakajima Takahiro, trans. Chō Kyonhi (Cho Kyŏnghŭi) (Tokyo: Hōsei daigaku shuppankyoku, 2016), 1–22, and Kyo Kirin (Xu Jilin), *Fuhenteki kachi wo motomeru: Chūgoku gendai shisō no shin chōryū*, trans. and ed. Nakajima Takahiro and Ō Zen (Wang Qian) (Tokyo: Hōsei daigaku shuppankyoku, 2020), 295–329. Also notable is the recasting of "East Asia" as a critical concept. See, for example, Chŏng Mun'gil et al., eds., *Chubyŏn esŏ pon tong asia* (Seoul: Munhak kwa chisŏngsa, 2004). See also Ban Wang, ed., *Chinese Visions of World Order: Tianxia, Culture, and World Politics* (Durham, NC: Duke University Press, 2017), and Kuan-Hsing Chen, *Asia as Method: Toward Deimperialization* (Durham, NC: Duke University Press, 2010).

3. "Zhile di shiba," in *Zhuangzi jishi*, ed. Guo Qingfan (Scripta Sinica: Hanji dianzi wenxian ziliaoku [digital database]). I refer to Burton Watson's translation in *The Complete Works of Chuang Tzu* (New York: Columbia University Press, 1968). For this parable's afterlives in the history of Chinese literature

up to Lu Xun, see Wilt L. Idema, *The Resurrected Skeleton: From Zhuangzi to Lu Xun* (New York: Columbia University Press, 2014).
4. Lu Xun, "Qisi," in *Lu Xun quanji* (Beijing: Renmin wenxue chubanshe, 2005), 1:490–91.
5. Lu Xun, "Qisi," 1:490–91.
6. "Zhile di shiba," in *Zhuangzi jishi*. My interpretation of the doctrine of "making all things equal" in the *Zhuangzi* is inspired by Takahiro Nakajima, *Sōji: Tori to natte toki wo tsugeyo* (Tokyo: Iwanami shoten, 2009), 111–95.
7. Lu Xun, "Qisi," 1:487.
8. "Qiwulun di er," in *Zhuangzi jishi*.

Bibliography

A Ying, ed. *Wan Qing wenxue congchao: Xiaoshuo xiju yanjiu juan* (An Anthology of Late Qing Literature: The Volume on Studies of Fiction and Theater). Beijing: Zhonghua shuju, 1960.

Adorno, Theodor. *Aesthetic Theory*. Trans. Robert Hullot-Kentor. Minneapolis: University of Minnesota Press, 1997.

———. *Ästhetische Theorie*. Vol. 7 of *Gesammelte Schriften*. Frankfurt: Suhrkamp, 1970.

Agamben, Giorgio. *Homo Sacer: Sovereign Power and Bare Life*. Trans. Daniel Heller-Roazen. Stanford, CA: Stanford University Press, 1998.

Ahmed, Aijaz. "Jameson's Rhetoric of Otherness and the 'National Allegory.'" *Social Text* 17 (Fall 1987): 3–25.

Akizuki Nozomi. "Suematsu Jirō hitsudanroku in mirareru 'kindai': 1881 nen no 'shinshi yūran dan' tono kōryū wo chūshin ni" ("Modernity" in Suematsu Jirō's Brush Talks: With a Focus on His Exchanges with the 1881 "Delegation of Gentlemen"). In *Kindai kōryū shi to sōgo ninshiki I* (History of the Exchanges and Mutual Understanding in Modern Times), ed. Miyajima Hiroshi and Kim Yongdŏk, 3–33. Tokyo: Keiō gijuku daigaku shuppankai, 2001.

An Ushiku (An Usik). *Kin Shiryō: Sono teikō no shōgai* (Kim Saryang: A Life of Resistance). Tokyo: Iwanami shoten, 1972.

Anderson, Benedict. *Imagined Communities: Reflections on the Origin and Spread of Nationalism*. Rev. ed. London: Verso, 2006.

Anderson, Marston. *The Limits of Realism: Chinese Fiction in the Revolutionary Period*. Berkeley: University of California Press, 1990.

Arendt, Hannah. *Lectures on Kant's Political Philosophy*. Ed. Ronald Beiner. Chicago: University of Chicago Press, 1982.

Auerbach, Erich. *Mimesis: The Representation of Reality in Western Literature*. 50th anniversary ed. Princeton, NJ: Princeton University Press, 2003.

Bakhtin, Mikhail. "Epic and Novel: Toward a Methodology for the Study of the Novel." In *The Dialogic Imagination: Four Essays*, 3–40. Austin: University of Texas Press, 1981.

Balibar, Renée, and Dominique Laporte. *Le français national: Politique et pratiques de la langue nationale sous la revolution française*. Paris: Hachette, 1974.

Bargen, Doris G. *Suicidal Honor: General Nogi and the Writings of Mori Ogai and Natsume Soseki*. Honolulu: University of Hawai'i Press, 2006.

Bayly, C. A., and Eugenio F. Biagini, eds. *Giuseppe Mazzini and the Globalisation of Democratic Nationalism 1830–1920*. Oxford: Oxford University Press, 2008.

Beasley, W. G. *Japanese Imperialism, 1894–1945*. Oxford: Clarendon Press, 1987.

——. *The Meiji Restoration*. Stanford, CA: Stanford University Press, 1972.

Benjamin, Walter. *Illuminations*. Ed. Hannah Arendt. Trans. Harry Zohn. New York: Schocken Books, 1969.

——. *The Origin of German Tragic Drama*. Trans. John Osborne. New York: Verso, 1998.

Bentley, Eric. *A Century of Hero-Worship: A Study of the Idea of Heroism in Carlyle and Nietzsche, with Notes on Wagner, Spengler, Stefan George, and D. H. Lawrence*. Boston: Beacon Press, 1957.

Bernstein, Susan. "Journalism and German Identity: Communiqués from Heine, Wagner, and Adorno." *New German Critique* 66 (Autumn 1995): 65–93.

Bhabha, Homi K. "Of Mimicry and Man." In *The Location of Culture*, 85–92. New York: Routledge, 2004.

Birrell, Anne. *Chinese Mythology: An Introduction*. Baltimore, MD: Johns Hopkins University Press, 1993.

Bourdieu, Pierre. *Distinction: A Social Critique of the Judgement of Taste*. Trans. Richard Nice. New York: Routledge & Kegan Paul, 1986.

——. *The Logic of Practice*. Trans. Richard Nice. Stanford, CA: Stanford University Press, 1990.

Bowring, Richard John. *Mori Ōgai and the Modernization of Japanese Culture*. Cambridge: Cambridge University Press, 1979.

Brooks, Peter. *The Melodramatic Imagination: Balzac, Henry James, Melodrama, and the Mode of Excess*. New York: Columbia University Press, 1985.

Cao Xueqin. *The Story of the Stone: A Chinese Novel in Five Volumes*. Trans. David Hawkes. London: Penguin Books, 1979.

———. *Zhiyanzhai chongping shi tou ji* (The Story of the Stone: The Re-Annotated Text by the Rouge Inkstone Studio). Hong Kong: Zhonghua shuju Xianggang fenju, 1977.

Cao Zhi. *Cao Zijian shi zhu* (The Poems of Cao Zhi: The Annotated Edition). Beijing: Renmin wenxue chubanshe, 1957.

Cavell, Stanley. "Aesthetic Problems of Modern Philosophy." In *Must We Mean What We Say?*, 68–90. Cambridge: Cambridge University Press, 2002.

Chakrabarty, Dipesh. *Provincializing Europe: Postcolonial Thought and Historical Difference*. Princeton, NJ: Princeton University Press, 2008.

Chang Hyohyŏn. "Mongyurok ŭi yŏksajŏk sŏngkyŏk" (The Historical Characteristics of the Dream Stories). In *Han'guk kojŏn sosŏllon* (Studies of Classical Korean Fiction), ed. Han'guk kojŏn sosŏl p'yŏnch'an wiwŏnhoe, 145–55. Seoul: Saemunsa, 1990.

Chang, Kang-i Sun, and Stephen Owen, eds. *The Cambridge History of Chinese Literature*. Cambridge: Cambridge University Press, 2010.

Chen Duxiu. *Chen Duxiu xuanji* (The Selected Works of Chen Duxiu). Ed. Hu Ming. Tianjin: Tianjin renmin chubanshe, 1990.

Chen Fangming. *Taiwan xinwenxue shi* (A History of Taiwanese New Literature). Taipei: Lianjing, 2011.

Chen Jingling. "An Acropolis in China: The Appropriation of Ancient Greek Tradition in Modern Chinese Literature." PhD diss., Harvard University, 2016.

Chen Peifeng. "Shizi, shuxie, yuedu yu rentong: Chongxin shenshi 1930 niandai xiangtu wenxue lunzhan de yiyi" (Literacy, Writing, Reading, and Identity: Revisiting the Significance of the 1930s Debates on Nativist Literature). In *Taiwan wenxue yu kuawenhua liudong* (Taiwanese Literature and Cross-Cultural Movements), ed. Qiu Guifen and Liu Shuqin, 83–110. Taipei: Xingzhengyuan wenhua jianshe weiyuanhui, 2007.

Chen Pingyuan. "Lu Xun de *Gushi xinbian* yu Bulaixite de 'Shishi xiju'" (Lu Xun's *Old Stories Retold* and Brecht's "Epic Theater"). In *Chen Pingyuan zixuanji* (The Works of Chen Pingyuan Selected by Himself), 23–42. Guilin: Guangxi shifan daxue chubanshe, 1997.

———. "Xiandai Zhongguo de 'Wei-Jin fengdu' yu 'Liuchao sanwen'" (The "Wei-Jin Style" and "Six-Dynasty Essays" in Modern China). *Zhongguo wenhua* (Chinese Culture) 15–16 (1997): 273–305.

Chen, Kuan-hsing. *Asia as Method: Toward Deimperialization*. Durham, NC: Duke University Press, 2010.

Chen, Ping. "China." In *Language and National Identity in Asia*, ed. Andrew Simpson, 141–67. Oxford: Oxford University Press, 2007.

———. "Establishment and Promotion of Modern Written Vernacular." In *The Oxford Handbook of Chinese Linguistics*, ed. William S-Y. Wang and Chaofen Sun, 532–40. Oxford: Oxford University Press, 2015.

Cheng, Eileen. *Literary Remains: Death, Trauma, and Lu Xun's Refusal to Mourn.* Honolulu: University of Hawai'i Press, 2013.

Cheng Shude. *Lunyu jishi* (The Analects: The Text with Compiled Annotations). Beijing: Zhonghua shuju, 1990.

Chiba Shunji. "'Mado no onna' kō: 'Gan' wo megutte" (Reflections on the "Woman at the Window": On "Wild Geese"). *Mori Ōgai kenkyū* (Mori Ōgai Studies) 2 (1988): 26–47.

Chin Baihō (Chen Peifeng). *Nihon tōchi to shokuminchi kanbun: Taiwan ni okeru kanbun no kyōkai to sōzō* (Japanese Rule and the Colonial Sinograph: The Boundaries and Imaginations of Sinographic Writing in Taiwan). Tokyo: Sangensha, 2012.

Chin Shō (Chen Jie). *Meiji zenki nitchū gakujutsu kōryū no kenkyū: Shinkoku chūnichi kōshikan no bunka katsudō* (The Study of Sino-Japanese Scholarly Exchanges in the Early Meiji: The Cultural Activities of the Consulate of the Qing Government in Japan). Tokyo: Kyūko shoin, 2003.

Cho Chin'gi. *Ilche malgi kukch'aek kwa ch'eje sunŭng ŭi munhak* (State Policy and the Literature of Submission to the System in the Late Japanese-Imperial Period). Seoul: Somyŏng ch'ulp'an, 2010.

Chō Iyū (Zhang Weixiong). *Bunjin gaikōkan no meiji Nihon: Chūgoku shodai chūnichi kōshidan no ibunka taiken* (Literati Diplomats in Meiji Japan: The Cross-Cultural Experience of the First Chinese Official Envoy to Japan). Tokyo: Kashiwa shobō, 1999.

Cho Tong'il. *Han'guk munhak t'ongsa* (A Complete History of Korean Literature). 2nd ed. Seoul: Chisik sanŏpsa, 1989.

——. *Tong asia munhaksa pigyoron* (A Comparative Study of Literary Histories in East Asia). Seoul: Sŏul taehakkyo ch'ulp'anbu, 1993.

Ch'oe Wŏnsik. *Han'guk kaenyŏmsa ch'ongsŏ: Munhak* (Studies on Korean Conceptual History: Literature). Seoul: Sohwa, 2012.

Ch'oe Yong'gi. *Han'gugŏ chŏngch'aek ŭi ihae* (An Understanding of the Korean Language Policies). Seoul: Han'guk munhwasa, 2010.

Chŏng Haksŏng. "Mongyudam ŭi uŭijŏk chŏnt'ong kwa kaehwagi mongyurok" (The Allegorical Tradition of the Dream Tale and the Dream Stories in the Era of Modernization). *Kwan'ak ŏmun yŏngu* (The Kwan'ak Journal of Linguistic and Literary Studies) 3 (1978): 431–43.

Chŏng Mun'gil et al., eds. *Chubyŏn esŏ pon tong asia* (East Asia Seen from the Peripheries). Seoul: Munhak kwa chisŏngsa, 2004.

Culp, Robert. "Teaching *Baihua*: Textbook Publishing and the Production of Vernacular Language and a New Literary Canon in Early Twentieth-Century China." *Twentieth-Century China* 34, no. 1 (2008): 4–41.

Culver, Annika A. *Glorify the Empire: Japanese Avant-Garde Propaganda in Manchukuo*. Vancouver: UBC Press, 2013.
Cumings, Bruce. *Korea's Place in the Sun: A Modern History*. Updated ed. New York: Norton, 2005.
Curtius, Ernst Robert. *European Literature and the Latin Middle Ages*. Princeton, NJ: Princeton University Press, 2013.
Dai Weina. *Weiwancheng de beiju: Zhou Zuoren yu Ailishi* (The Incomplete Tragedy: Zhou Zuoren and Havelock Ellis). Nanjing: Jiangsu fenghuang wenyi chubanshe, 2018.
Dajiubao Mingnan (Ōkubo Akio) et al. *Wei Manzhouguo wenxue yanjiu zai Riben* (A Collection of Japanese Studies on the Literature of the Puppet State of Manchukuo). Harbin: Beifang wenyi chubanshe, 2017.
Daruvala, Susan. *Zhou Zuoren and an Alternative Chinese Response to Modernity*. Cambridge, MA: Harvard University Asia Center, 2000.
Deleuze, Gilles. *Difference and Repetition*. Trans. Paul Patton. New York: Columbia University Press, 1994.
De Man, Paul. *Aesthetic Ideology*. Minneapolis: University of Minnesota Press, 1997.
——. "Literary History and Literary Modernity." *Daedalus* 99, no. 2 (Spring 1970): 384–404.
Denecke, Wiebke. *Classical World Literatures: Sino-Japanese and Greco-Roman Comparisons*. Oxford: Oxford University Press, 2014.
Derrida, Jacques. *De la grammatologie*. Paris: Éditions de Minuit, 1967.
——. *Of Grammatology*. Trans. Gayatri Chakravorty Spivak. Corrected ed. Baltimore, MD: Johns Hopkins University Press, 1997.
——. "Plato's Pharmacy." In *Disseminations*, trans. Barbara Johnson, 67–172. Chicago: University of Chicago Press, 1981.
——. *Spurs: Nietzsche's Styles / Éperons: Les styles de Nietzsche*. Trans. Barbara Harlow. Chicago: University of Chicago Press, 2017.
——. "This Strange Institution Called Literature." In *Acts of Literature*, ed. Derek Attridge, 33–75. New York: Routledge, 1992.
Deuchler, Martina. *Confucian Gentlemen and Barbarian Envoys: The Opening of Korea, 1875–1885*. Seattle: University of Washington Press, 1977.
Dilworth, David, and J. Thomas Rimer, eds. *The Historical Fiction of Mori Ōgai*. Honolulu: University of Hawai'i Press, 1991.
Ding Wenjiang and Zhao Fengtian, eds. *Liang Qichao nianpu changbian* (The Long Chronology of Liang Qichao). Shanghai: Shanghai renmin chubanshe, 1983.
Dittrich, Klaus. "The Beginnings of Modern Education in Korea, 1883–1910." *Paedagogica Historica* 50, no. 3 (2014): 265–84.

Dong Bingyue. *"Guomin zuojia" de lichang: Zhong-Ri xiandai wenxue guanxi yanjiu* (The Position of the "National Writer": Studies of the Modern Sino-Japanese Literary Relationship). Beijing: Sanlian shudian, 2006.

Du Yu et al., eds. *Chunqiu zuozhuan zhengyi* (The Rectified Meanings of the Zuo Commentary to the *Spring and Autumn Annals*). Shanghai: Shanghai guji chubanshe, 1990.

Duara, Prasenjit. *Rescuing History from the Nation: Questioning Narratives of Modern China*. Chicago: University of Chicago Press, 1995.

———. *Sovereignty and Authenticity: Manchukuo and the East Asian Modern*. Lanham, MD: Rowman & Littlefield, 2003.

———. "Transnationalism and the Predicament of Sovereignty: China, 1900-1945." *The American Historical Review* 102, no. 4 (1997): 1030-51.

Eagleton, Terry. *Ideology of the Aesthetic*. Oxford: Blackwell, 1990.

———. *Literary Theory: An Introduction*. Minneapolis: University of Minnesota Press, 2008.

Eliot, T. S. "Tradition and the Individual Talent." *Perspecta* 19 (1982): 36–42.

Ellmann, Richard. "Joyce and Homer." *Critical Inquiry* 3, no. 3 (Spring 1977): 567–82.

Elman, Benjamin A. *Classicism, Politics, and Kinship: The Ch'ang-chou School of New Text Confucianism in Late Imperial China*. Berkeley: University of California Press, 1990.

Em, Henry. *The Great Enterprise: Sovereignty and Historiography in Modern Korea*. Durham, NC: Duke University Press, 2013.

En Shōmai (Yan Xiaomei). "Nihon ni okeru saishi kajin shōsetsu no juyō ni tsuite: Torai saishi kajin shōsetsu mokuroku" (The Reception of Scholar-and-Beauty Romance in Japan: A List of Imported Works of Scholar-and-Beauty Romance). In *Yomihon kenkyū shinshū* (The New Collection of Studies on *Yomihon*), ed. Yomihon kenkyū no kai, 4:124–44. Tokyo: Kanrin shobō, 2003.

Fanon, Frantz. *The Wretched of the Earth*. New York: Grove Press, 2004.

Feng Menglong. *Qingshi* (Stories of Love). Vols. 37–38 of *Feng Menglong quanji* (The Complete Works of Feng Menglong). Ed. Wei Tongxian. Shanghai: Shanghai guji chubanshe, 1993.

Feuerwerker, Yi-tsu Mei. *Ideology, Power, Text: Self-Representation and the Peasant "Other" in Modern Chinese Literature*. Stanford, CA: Stanford University Press, 1998.

Fogel, Joshua A. *The Literature of Travel in the Japanese Rediscovery of China, 1862–1945*. Stanford, CA: Stanford University Press, 1996.

———, ed. *The Role of Japan in Liang Qichao's Introduction of Modern Western Civilization to China*. Berkeley: Center for Chinese Studies, Institute of East Asian Studies, University of California, 2004.

Foucault, Michel. *The Order of Things: An Archaeology of the Human Sciences*. New York: Routledge Classics, 2002.

Freud, Sigmund. "Mourning and Melancholia." In *The Standard Edition of the Complete Psychological Work of Sigmund Freud*, 14:243–58. London: Hogarth Press, 1957.

Frye, Northrop. *Anatomy of Criticism: Four Essays*. Princeton, NJ: Princeton University Press, 1957.

Fujii Shōzō. *Taiwan bungaku kono hyakunen* (The Recent Hundred Years of Taiwanese Literature). Tokyo: Tōhō shoten, 1998.

Fukuzawa Yukichi. *Bunmeiron no gairyaku* (Essence of the Discourse of Civilization). Tokyo: Iwanami shoten, 1995.

———. *Fukuzawa Yukichi chosakushū* (Selected Works of Fukuzawa Yukichi). Tokyo: Keiō gijuku shuppankai, 2002–03.

Fuma Susumu. *Chōsen enkōshi to Chōsen tsūshinshi* (The Korean Missions to Imperial China and to Japan). Nagoya: Nagoya daigaku shuppankai, 2015.

Gamō Yoshirō. *Ōgai no rekishi shōsetsu: Sono shi to shinjitsu* (The Historical Fiction of Ōgai: Its Poetry and Truth). Tokyo: Shunjū sha, 1983.

Gan Yang et al. "Kang Youwei yu zhiduhua ruxue" (Kang Youwei and the Institutionalization of Confucianism). *Kaifang shidai* (The Era of Opening) 5 (2014): 12–41.

Gao Yuandong. *Xiandai ruhe "nalai?": Lu Xun de sixiang yu wenxue lunji* (How Do You "Import" Modernity?: A Collection of Essays on the Thought and Literature of Lu Xun). Shanghai: Fudan daxue chubanshe, 2009.

Gramsci, Antonio. *Quaderni del carcere*. Torino: Giulio Einaudi, 1975.

Greenberg, Clement. "Modernist Painting." In *Modern Art and Modernism: A Critical Anthology*, ed. Francis Franscina and Charles Harrison, 5–10. London: P. Chapman, 1988.

Gu Ding. *Gu Ding zuopinxuan* (The Selected Works of Gu Ding). Ed. Li Chunyan. Shenyang: Chunfeng wenyi chubanshe, 1995.

Gu Ding and Hayashi Fusao. "Hayashi Fusao, Ko Tei taidan." *Geibun* 1, no. 5 (April 1942): 146–56.

Gunn, Edward. *Unwelcome Muse: Chinese Literature in Shanghai and Peking, 1937–1945*. New York: Columbia University Press, 1980.

Guo Qingfan, ed. *Zhuangzi jishi* (The Zhuangzi: The Text with Compiled Annotations). Scripta Sinica: Hanji dianzi wenxian ziliaoku (digital database).

Guo Tingli. *Zhongguo jindai fanyi wenxue gailun* (A Survey of Translated Literature in Modern China). Wuhan: Hubei jiaoyu chubanshe, 1998.

Ha Tong'ho et al., eds., *Kungmunnon chipsŏng* (Selected Essays on National Language). Seoul: T'ap ch'ulp'ansa, 1985.

Haeri, Niloofar. *Sacred Language, Ordinary People: Dilemmas of Culture and Politics in Egypt*. New York: Palgrave Macmillan, 2003.

Han Wŏnyŏng. *Han'guk sinmun yŏnjae sosŏl ŭi sajŏk yŏngu* (A Study of the History of Korean Fiction Serialized in Newspapers). Seoul: P'urŭn sasang, 2010.

Hanan, Patrick. "The Technique of Lu Hsün's Fiction." *Harvard Journal of Asiatic Studies* 34 (1974): 55–96.

Hanscom, Christopher P., and Dennis Washburn. "Introduction." In *The Affect of Difference: Representations of Race in East Asian Empire*, ed. Christopher P. Hanscom and Dennis Washburn, 1–18. Honolulu: University of Hawai'i Press, 2016.

Hanyu dacidian (The Grand Chinese Dictionary). 2nd ed. Shanghai: Hanyu dacidian chubanshe, 2001.

Harootunian, Harry. *Overcome by Modernity: History, Culture, and Community in Interwar Japan*. Princeton, NJ: Princeton University Press, 2000.

Hashimoto Satoru. "February 10, 1900: Liang Qichao's Suspended Translation and the Future of Chinese New Fiction." In *A New Literary History of Modern China*, ed. David Der-Wei Wang, 161–66. Cambridge, MA: Harvard University Press, 2017.

——. "Intra-Asian Reading; or, How Lu Xun Enters Into a World Literature." In *The Making of Chinese-Sinophone Literatures as World Literature*, ed. Yingjin Zhang and Kuei-fen Chiu, 83–102. Hong Kong: Hong Kong University Press, 2022.

——. "Japanese-Language Literature in the Colonial Period." In *Encyclopedia of Taiwan Studies*, ed. Michael Hsiao. Leiden: Brill, forthcoming.

——. "Kindaisei to jō no seijigaku: I Gwansu *Mujō* ni okeru chōsō no jikansei" (Modernity and the Politics of Affect: Temporality of Mourning in Yi Kwangsu's *Heartless*). *Tōyō bunka kenkyūjo kiyō* (The Memoirs of Institute for Advanced Studies on Asia) 170 (2016): 88–126.

——. "Regional Literary Tradition in Modern World Literature: The Allegorization of Democracy in Yano Ryūkei's *Beautiful Story of Statesmanship* and Its Chinese and Korean Translations." *Comparative Literature Studies* 59, no. 4 (2022): 768–86.

——. "Science, History, Fiction: Mediality in Lu Xun's *Old Stories Retold*." *Frontiers of Literary Studies in China* 13, no. 3 (2019): 385–404.

——. "World Literature and East Asian Literatures." In *The Routledge Companion to World Literature*, ed. Theo D'haen, David Damrosch, and Djelal Kadir, 2nd ed., 425–33. New York: Routledge, 2022.

——. "World of Letters: Lu Xun, Benjamin, and *Daodejing*." *Journal of World Literature* 1, no. 1 (March 2016): 39–51.

Hashimoto, Satoru, and Karen Thornber. "Trans-Regional Asia and Futures of World Literature." *Journal of World Literature* 4 (2019): 459–65.

Hatano Setsuko. *I Gwansu: Kankoku kindai bungaku no so to "shinnichi" no rakuin* (Yi Kwangsu: The Father of Modern Korean Literature and His "Pro-Japanese" Stigma). Tokyo: Chūō kōron shinsha, 2005.

———. *I Gwansu, "Mujō" no kenkyū: Kankoku keimō bungaku no hikari to kage* (A Study of Yi Kwangsu's *Heartless*: The Bright and Dark Sides of Korean Enlightenment Literature). Tokyo: Hakuteisha, 2008.

Hazama Naoki, ed. *Kyōdō kenkyū Ryō Keichō: Seiyō kindai shisō juyō to meiji Nihon* (A Collaborative Study of Liang Qichao: The Introduction of Modern Western Thought and Meiji Japan). Tokyo: Misuzu shobō, 1999.

Hegel, G. W. F. *Aesthetics: Lectures on Fine Art*. Trans. T. M. Knox. Oxford: Oxford University Press, 1975.

———. *Lectures on the Philosophy of World History: Manuscripts of the Introduction and the Lectures of 1822–3*. Ed. and trans. Robert F. Brown and Peter C. Hodgson. Oxford: Oxford University Press, 2011.

Hirata Hisashi. *Itarī kenkoku sanketsu* (The Three Heroes of Italian Nation-Building). Tokyo: Min'yūsha, 1892.

Hirata Yūji. *Kyōiku chokugo kokusai kankeishi no kenkyū: Kantei hon'yaku kyōiku chokugo wo chūshin to shite* (The Imperial Rescript of Education and the International Relations: With a Focus on the Official Translations of the Imperial Rescript of Education). Tokyo: Kazama shobō, 1997.

Hŏ Chaeyŏng. *Ilche kangjŏmgi ŏmun chŏngch'aek kwa ŏmun saenghwal* (The Language Policy and Life in the Japanese Colonial Period). Kyŏnggi-do Kwangmyŏng-si: Kyŏngjin, 2011.

———. "Kŭndae kyemonggi chisik yut'ong ŭi t'ŭkching kwa yŏksul munhŏn e taehayŏ" (Characteristics of Knowledge Circulation and Translated Publications in the Modern Age of Enlightenment). *Ŏmun nonjip* (Journal of Language and Literature) 63 (September 2015): 7–36.

Ho Kwangsu. "Ch'anggang Kim T'aekyŏng ŭi mangmyŏng hansi e nat'anan sanghwangsŏng" (The Contextual Situations Expressed in the Chinese Poems of Ch'anggang Kim T'aekyŏng in Exile). *Chungguk inmun kwahak* (Journal of the Chinese Humanities) 32 (June 2006): 213–48.

Hoan Chichun (Huang Qichun). "Shakai shugi shichō no eikyōka ni okeru kyōdo bungaku ronsō to Taiwan gobun undo" (The Polemics of Nativist Literature and the Taiwanese Writing Movement Under the Influence of Socialist Thought). In *Yomigaeru Taiwan bungaku: Nihon tōchiki no sakka to sakuhin* (Taiwanese Literature Redux: Writers and Works Under Japanese Rule), ed. Shimomura Sakujirō et al., 47–72. Tokyo: Tōhō shoten, 1995.

Hobsbawm, Eric J., and Terence O. Ranger, eds. *The Invention of Tradition*. Cambridge: Cambridge University Press, 1992.

Hockx, Michel. *Questions of Style: Literary Societies and Literary Journals in Modern China, 1911–1937.* Leiden: Brill, 2003.

Hohendahl, Peter Uwe. *The Institution of Criticism.* Ithaca, NY: Cornell University Press, 1982.

Honam hakpo (Honam Scholarly Journal). Vol. 17 of *Han'guk kaehwagi haksulji* (The Scholarly Journals in the Era of Modernization in Korea). Seoul: Asea munhwasa, 1978.

Hong Sŏkp'o. *Ru Swin kwa kŭndae Han'guk: Tong asia kongjon ŭl wihan sangsang* (Lu Xun and Modern Korea: Imaginations for Coexistence in East Asia). Seoul: Ihwa yŏja daehakkyo ch'ulp'an munhwa wŏn, 2018.

Hopper, Helen M. "Mori Ōgai's Response to Suppression of Intellectual Freedom, 1909–12." *Monumenta Nipponica* 29, no. 4 (Winter 1974): 381–413.

Horkheimer, Max, and Theodor W. Adorno. *Dialectic of Enlightenment: Philosophical Fragments.* Ed. Gunzelin Schmid Noerr. Trans. Edmund Jephcott. Stanford, CA: Stanford University Press, 2002.

Hsia, C. T. *A History of Modern Chinese Fiction.* 3rd ed. Bloomington: Indiana University Press, 1999.

———. "Yan Fu and Liang Ch'i-ch'ao as Advocates of New Fiction." In *Chinese Approaches to Literature from Confucius to Liang Ch'i-ch'ao,* ed. Adele Austin Rickett, 221–57. Princeton, NJ: Princeton University Press, 1978.

Hsü, Immanuel C. Y. *China's Entrance Into the Family of Nations.* Cambridge, MA: Harvard University Press, 1960.

Hu Feng, trans. and ed. *Shanling: Chaoxian Taiwan duanpian ji* (The Mountain Soul: A Collection of Korean and Taiwanese Short Stories). Shanghai: Wenhua shenghuo chubanshe, 1936.

Hu Shi. *Hu Shi quanji* (The Complete Works of Hu Shi). Hefei: Anhui jiaoyu chubanshe, 2003.

Huang Kewu. "He wei tianyan?: Yan Fu 'tianyan zhi xue' de neihan yu yiyi" (What Is "Tianyan"?: The Connotations and Significances of Yan Fu's "Theory of Evolution"). *Zhongyang yanjiuyuan jindaishi yanjiusuo jikan* 85 (2014): 129–87.

Huang, Martin Weizong. "The Inescapable Predicament: The Narrator and His Discourse in 'The True Story of Ah Q.'" *Modern China* 16, no. 4 (October 1990): 430–49.

Huang Mei'e. *Gudian Taiwan: Wenxueshi, shishe, zuojialun* (The Classical Taiwan: Literary History, Poetry Society, and Author Studies). Taipei: Guoli bianyiguan, 2007.

Huang Zunxian. *Huang Zunxian quanji* (The Complete Works of Huang Zunxian). Beijing: Zhonghua shuju, 2005.

Huo Songlin, ed. *Zhongguo jindai wenlun mingpian xiangzhu* (The Representative Texts of Modern Chinese Literary Criticism with Detailed Annotations). Guiyang: Guizhou renmin chubanshe, 1986.

Hutcheon, Linda. *A Theory of Parody: The Teachings of Twentieth-Century Art Forms*. Urbana: University of Illinois Press, 2000.

Huters, Theodor. "Blossoms in the Snow: Lu Xun and the Dilemma of Modern Chinese Literature." *Modern China* 10, no. 1 (1984): 49–77.

———. *Bringing the World Home: Appropriating the West in Late Qing and Early Republican China*. Honolulu: University of Hawai'i Press, 2005.

———. "Lives in Profile: On the Authorial Voice in Modern and Contemporary Chinese Literature." In *From May Fourth to June Fourth: Fiction and Film in Twentieth Century China*, ed. Ellen Widmer and David Der-wei Wang, 269–94. Cambridge, MA: Harvard University Asia Center, 1993.

Hwang Hodŏk. "Cheguk Ilbon kwa pŏnyŏk (ŏmnŭn) chŏngch'i: Ru Swin, Rung Ingtchung, Kim Saryang, 'a kyu' chŏk sam kwa chukwŏn" (The Japanese Empire and the Politics of (Non-)Translation: Lu Xun, Long Yingzong, Kim Saryang, the Life of Ah Q, and Sovereignty). *Taedong munhwa yŏngu* (Journal of Korean Culture) 63 (2008): 375–423.

———. *Kŭndae neisyŏn kwa kŭ p'yosangdŭl* (The Modern Nation and Its Representations) Seoul: Somyŏng ch'ulp'an, 2005.

——— (Fuan Hodoku). "Sansui to fūkei no aida: Kankoku kaikō kaikaki no kenbunroku ni okeru kanbunkateki jikohyōshō" (Between *Shanshui* and Landscape: The Cross-Cultural Self-Representations in the Travelogues in the Era of Opening and Modernization in Korea). In *Zenkindai ni okeru higashi ajia sangoku no bunka kōryū to hyōshō: Chōsen tsūshinshi to enkōshi wo chūshin ni* (The Premodern Cultural Exchanges and Representations Among the Three East Asian Nations: With a Focus on the Korean Missions to Imperial China and Japan), ed. Ryū Kenki (Liu Jianhui), 109–37. Kyoto: Kokusai Nihon bunka kenkyū sentā, 2006.

Hwang, Jong-yon. "The Emergence of Aesthetic Ideology in Korea: An Essay on Yi Kwang-su." *Korea Journal* 39, no. 4 (Winter 1999): 5–35.

Hwangsŏng sinmun (The Imperial Capital Gazette). Seoul: Kyŏng'in munhwasa, 1971–81.

I Yonsuku (Lee Yeounsuk). *"Kokugo" toiu shisō: Kindai Nihon no gengo ninshiki* ("National Language" as a Thought: The Understanding of Language in Modern Japan). Tokyo: Iwanami shoten, 1996.

Ichikawa Mototarō. *Nihon jukyō shi* (The History of Confucianism in Japan). Tokyo: Kyūko shoin, 1989–95.

Idema, Wilt L. *The Resurrected Skeleton: From Zhuangzi to Lu Xun*. New York: Columbia University Press, 2014.

Im Myŏngsin. "Kankoku kindai seishinshi ni okeru Ro Jin: 'A kyū seiden' no Kankoku teki juyō" (Lu Xun in the Spiritual History of Modern Korea: Korean Receptions of "The Real Story of Ah Q"). PhD diss., University of Tokyo, 2001.

Irokawa Daikichi. *Rekishi no hōhō* (The Method of Historiography). Tokyo: Yamato shobō, 1992.

Isawa Shūji. *Isawa Shūji senshū* (The Selected Works of Isawa Shūji). Nagano: Shinano kyōiku kai, 1958.

Isawa Shūji et al., eds. *Dōbun shinjiten* (New Dictionary in Shared Script). Tokyo: Taitō dōbun kyoku, 1909.

Ishibashi Ningetsu. "Maihime" (The Dancing Girl). In *Yamada Bimyō, Ishibashi Ningetsu, Takase Bunen shū* (The Selected Works of Yamada Bimyō, Ishibashi Ningetsu, and Takase Bunen). Vol. 23 of *Meiji bungaku zenshū*, 272–73. Tokyo: Chikuma shobō, 1971.

Ishizuki Minori. *Kindai Nihon no kaigai ryūgaku shi* (The History of Study Abroad in Modern Japan). Kyoto: Mineruba shobō, 1972.

Iwakami Jun'ichi. *Rekishi bungaku ron* (A Study of Historical Literature). Tokyo: Chūō kōron sha, 1942.

Izumi Tsukasa. *Nihon tōchiki Taiwan to teikoku no bundan: Bungaku kenshō ga tsukuru Nihongo bungaku* (Taiwan Under Japanese Rule and the Imperial Literary Field: Japanese-Language Literature Formed by Literary Awards). Tokyo: Hitsuji shobō, 2012.

Jager, Sheila Miyoshi. *Narratives of Nation Building in Korea: A Genealogy of Patriotism*. New York: M. E. Sharpe, 2003.

Jameson, Fredric. "Third-World Literature in the Era of Multinational Capitalism." *Social Text* 15 (Fall 1986): 65–88.

Jiao Heran. "Lu Xun yu dongbei lunxianqu Haerbin diqu zuoyi wenxue huodong zhi guanxi" (The Relationship Between Lu Xun and the Leftist Literary Activities in Harbin in the Occupied Territories in the Northeast). *Lu Xun yanjiu yuekan* (Lu Xun Studies Monthly) 1 (2019): 79–88.

Jin shu (History of the Jin). Comp. Fang Xuanling et al. Ed. Yang Jialuo et al. Scripta Sinica: Hanji dianzi wenxian ziliaoku (digital database).

Jin Yongzhe. *"Manshūkoku" ki ni okeru Chōsenjin manshū imin seisaku* (The Manchukuo Immigration Policy for Korean Migrants in Manchuria). Kyoto: Shōwadō, 2012.

Jones, Andrew F. *Evolutionary Fairy Tales: Evolutionary Thinking and Modern Chinese Culture*. Cambridge, MA: Harvard University Press, 2011.

Jullien, François. *Fonder la morale: Dialogue de Mencius avec un philosophe des Lumières*. Paris: B. Grasset, 1995.

——. *On the Universal, the Uniform, the Common and Dialogue Between Cultures*. Trans. Michael Richardson and Krzysztof Fijalkowski. Cambridge: Polity Press, 2014.

Kanbayashi Tsunemichi. *Kindai Nihon "bigaku" no tanjō* (The Birth of "Aesthetics" in Modern Japan). Tokyo: Kōdansha, 2006.

Kang Yŏngju. *Han'guk yŏksa sosŏl ŭi chaeinsik* (Revisiting Korean Historical Fiction). Seoul: Ch'angjak kwa pip'yŏng sa, 1991.

Kang Youwei. *Kang Youwei quanji* (The Complete Works of Kang Youwei). Beijing: Zhongguo renmin daxue chubanshe, 2020.

Kant, Immanuel. *Critique of the Power of Judgment*. Ed. Paul Guyer. Trans. Eric Matthews. Cambridge: Cambridge University Press, 2000.

Karatani Kōjin. *Nihon kindai bungaku no kigen* (Origins of Modern Japanese Literature). Tokyo: Iwanami shoten, 2008.

———. "Rekishi to shizen: Mori Ōgai ron" (History and Nature: On Mori Ōgai). In *Karatani Kōjin bungaku ronshū* (The Selected Writings on Literature of Karatani Kōjin), 159–220. Tokyo: Iwanami shoten, 2016.

Kaske, Elisabeth. *The Politics of Language in Chinese Education, 1895–1919*. Leiden: Brill, 2008.

Kawahara, Isao. "The State of Taiwanese Culture and Taiwanese New Literature in 1937: Issues of Banning Chinese Newspaper Sections and Abolishing Chinese Writings." In *Taiwan Under Japanese Colonial Rule, 1895–1945: History, Culture, Memory*, ed. Ping-hui Liao and David Der-wei Wang, 122–40. New York: Columbia University Press, 2006.

Keene, Donald. *Dawn to the West: Japanese Literature of the Modern Era*. New York: Columbia University Press, 1998.

Kikuchi Sankei. *Yakujun kigo* (Refined Writings in Translation). Reprint ed. Tokyo: Shōshidō, 1911.

Kim Changsŏn. *Manju munhak yŏngu* (A Study of Literature in Manchuria). Seoul: Yŏngnak, 2009.

———. "Manjuguk munhakchang e iiptoen Han'gk munhak: *Chosŏn tanp'yŏn sosŏl sŏn* ch'ulgan ŭl chungshimŭro" (Korean Literature Introduced to the Literary Field of Manchukuo: With a Focus on the Publication of *A Selection of Korean Short Stories*). *Han-Chung inmunhak yŏngu* (Journal of the Korean and Chinese Humanities) 62 (March 2019): 23–42.

Kim Chong'uk. "Yi Kwangsu, sinmin hoe, kŭrigo Ryang Ch'ich'ao" (Yi Kwangsu, the Society of New Citizens, and Liang Qichao). *Ch'unwŏn yŏngu hakpo* (Journal of Ch'unwŏn Studies) 12 (June 2018): 65–87.

Kim Chungha. *Kaehwagi sosŏl yŏngu* (A Study of Fiction in the Era of Modernization). Seoul: Kukhak charyowŏn, 2005.

Kim Haengsuk. "*T'aesŏ munye sinbo* e nat'anan kŭndaesŏng ŭi tu kaji ch'ŭngwi" (The Two Dimensions of Modernity Seen in the *Journal of European Literature*). *Kugŏ munhak* (Journal of National-Language Literature) 36 (January 2001): 5–33.

Kim, Kichung. "'Mujŏng': An Introduction to Yi Kwangsu's Fiction." *Korean Studies* 6 (1982): 125–39.

Kim Kyunt'ae. "Chŏn munhak" (The *Chŏn* in Literature). In *Han'guk kojŏn sosŏllon* (A Study of Classical Korean Literature), ed. Han'guk kojŏn sosŏl p'yŏnch'an wiwŏnhoe, 91–119. Seoul: Saemunsa, 1990.

Kim Pyŏngch'ŏl. *Han'guk kŭndae pŏnyŏk munhak sa yŏngu* (A Study of the History of Translated Literature in Modern Korea). Seoul: Ŭryu munhwasa, 1975.

——. *Segyemunhak pŏnyŏk sŏji mongnok ch'ongnam: 1895–1987* (The Comprehensive List of the Translated Works of World Literature, 1895–1987). Seoul: Kukhak charyowŏn, 2002.

Kim Pyŏnggil. "Yi Kwangsu yŏksa sosŏl *Wŏnhyo daesa* nŭn ŏttŏk'e ilk'yŏnnŭn'ga?: Shinmun yŏnjae sosŏl rosŏŭi taejungsŏng ŭl chungshimŭro" (How Was Yi Kwangsu's *Master Wonhyo* Read?: With a Focus on Its Mass Appeal as a Newspaper Serial Fiction). *Ch'unwŏn yŏngu hakpo* (Journal of Ch'unwŏn Studies) 12 (June 2018), 37–63.

Kim Sam'ung. *Tanjae Sin Ch'aeho p'yŏngjŏn* (Tanjae Sin Ch'aeho: A Critical Life). Seoul: Sidae ŭi ch'ang, 2011.

Kim Saryang. "Hikari no nakani" (Into the Light). *Bungei shuto* (Literary Capital) (October 1939): 2–29, reprint in *Kindai Chōsen bungaku Nihongo sakuhinshū, sōsaku hen* (A Collection of Japanese-Language Works in Modern Korean Literature: Creative Writing), ed. Ōmura Masuo and Hotei Toshihiro, 53–80. Tokyo: Ryokuin shobō, 2001.

——. "Hikari no nakani" (Into the Light). In *Hikari no nakani* (Into the Light), 1–56. Tokyo: Koyama shoten, 1940.

——. *Kin Shiryō zenshū* (The Complete Works of Kim Saryang). Ed. Kin Shiryō zenshū henshū iinkai. Tokyo: Kawade shobō shinsha, 1973.

——. "Kyū hakushaku." In *Kokyō* (My Hometown), 105–32. Kyoto: Kōchō shorin, 1942.

——. "Yuch'ijang esŏ mannan sanai" (A Man Whom I Met in a Detention Cell). *Munjang* (Literature) (February 1941): 289–301.

Kim Sŏngch'ŏl. "*Tanjong taewang silgi* wa 'Tanjong aesa' ŭi hŏgujŏk yŏsŏng inmul ege t'uyŏng toen chakka ŭisik" (*The True Records of Great King Tanjong* and the Author's Ideology Reflected in the Fictional Female Characters in *The Tragic Story of Tanjong*). *Uri munhak yŏngu* (Journal of Korean Literature) 43 (July 2014): 73–97.

Kim Soyŏng. "Hanja t'ong'il hoe hwaldong kwa 'tongmun' ŭisik" (The Activities of the Society for Unifying the Chinese Characters and the Notion of "Shared Script"). *Han'guksa yŏngu* (Journal of Korean History) 177 (2017): 1–35.

Kim Sunjŏn. *Han-Il kŭndae sosŏl ŭi pigyo munhakchŏk yŏngu* (A Comparative Literary Study of Modern Fiction in Korea and Japan). Seoul: T'aehaksa, 1998.

Kim Sunjŏn et al., eds. *Han'gugin Ilbonŏ munhak sajŏn* (Dictionary of Japanese-Language Literature by Korean Authors). Seoul: Cheiaenssi, 2018.

Kim T'aekyŏng. *Kim T'aekyŏng chŏnjip* (The Complete Works of Kim T'aekyŏng). Seoul: Asea munhwasa, 1978.
Kim Tong'in. *Kim Tong'in chŏnjip* (The Complete Works of Kim Tong'in). Seoul: Chosŏn ilbosa, 1998.
Kim, Wook-Dong. *Global Perspectives on Korean Literature*. Singapore: Springer Singapore, 2019.
Kim, Young Min. *The History of Modern Korean Fiction (1890–1945): The Topography of Literary Systems and Form*. Trans. Rachel Min Park. Lanham, MD: Lexington Books, 2020.
Kim Yunsik. *Ilche malgi Han'guk chakka ŭi Ilbonŏ kŭlssŭgi ron* (A Study of Japanese-Language Works by Korean Authors in the Late Colonial Period). Seoul: Sŏul taehakkyo ch'ulp'anbu, 2003.
——. *Ŭm ch'ong sa* (History in Shadows and Lights). In *Chongjŏng yŏnp'yo; Ŭm ch'ŏng sa* (The Chronology of Official Service; History in Shadows and Lights). Seoul: Kuksa p'yŏch'an wiwŏhoe, 1958.
——. "Uri yŏksa sosŏl ŭi 4 kaji yuhyŏng" (Four Types of Korean Historical Fiction). *Sosŏl munhak* (Journal of Fictional Literature) 11, no. 6 (1985): 150–67.
——. *Yi Kwangsu wa kŭŭi sidae* (Yi Kwangsu and His Times). Seoul: Hangil sa, 1986.
Kim Yunsik and Kim Hyŏn. *Han'guk munhak sa* (A History of Korean Literature). Seoul: Minŭmsa, 1996.
King, Ross. "Nationalism and Language Reform." In *Nationalism and the Construction of Korean Identity*, ed. Hyung Il Pai and Timothy R. Tangherlini, 33–72. Berkeley: Institute of East Asian Studies, University of California, 1998.
Kiyama Hideo. *Shū Sakujin "tainichi kyōryoku" no tenmatsu* (A Detailed Account of Zhou Zuoren's Collaboration with the Japanese). Tokyo: Iwanami shoten, 2004.
Kleeman, Faye Yuan. *Under the Imperial Sun: Japanese Colonial Literature of Taiwan and the South*. Honolulu: University of Hawai'i Press, 2003.
Kodajima Yōsuke. "Ryō Keichō *Wabun Kandoku Hō* (Rohon) kanchū: Fukubun wo toita Nihongo sokushūsho" (Concise Annotations of Liang Qichao's *How to Read Japanese Writing in Chinese?* (Ro Edition): The Fast-Learning Manual of Japanese Based on the Idea of "Fukubun"). *Meisei daigaku kenkyū kiyō* (The Memoires of Meisei University) 16 (2008): 29–64.
Kohn, Livia. "Yin Xi: The Master at the Beginning of the Scripture." *Journal of Chinese Religions* 25 (1997): 83–139.
Komagome Takeshi. *Shokuminchi teikoku Nihon no bunka tōgō* (Cultural Integration in the Colonies of the Japanese Empire). Tokyo: Iwanami shoten, 1996.
Komori Yōichi. *Buntai toshite no monogatari* (The Monogatari as a Style). Tokyo: Chikuma shobō, 1988.
Kondō Haruo. *Tōdai shōsetsu no kenkyū* (A Study of Tang Fiction). Tokyo: Kasama shoin, 1978.

Kono, Kimberly Tae. *Romance, Family, and Nation in Japanese Colonial Literature.* New York: Palgrave Macmillan, 2010.

Kōno, Kimiko, et al., eds. *"Bun" kara "bungaku" e: Higashi ajia no bungaku wo minaosu* (From *"Bun"* to *"Bungaku"*: Revisiting Literature in East Asia). Tokyo: Bensei shuppan, 2019.

Kornicki, Peter F. *The Book in Japan: A Cultural History from the Beginnings to the Nineteenth Century.* Leiden: Brill, 1998.

Kōyama Iwao. *Sekaishi no tetsugaku* (Philosophy of World History). Tokyo: Iwanami shoten, 1942.

Koyasu Nobukuni. *Kanji ron: Fukahi no tasha* (Theory of Kanji: The Unavoidable Other). Tokyo: Iwanami shoten, 2003.

Kristeva, Julia. "Word, Dialogue, and Novel." In *Desire in Language: A Semiotic Approach to Literature and Art,* ed. Leon S. Roudiez, trans. Thomas Gora et al., 64–91. New York: Columbia University Press, 1980.

Kuroko Kazuo and Kō Tōgen (Kang Dongyuan), eds. *Nihon kingendai bungaku no Chūgokugo yaku sōran* (A Comprehensive List of the Works of Modern and Contemporary Japanese Literature Translated Into Chinese). Tokyo: Bensei shuppan, 2006.

Kwon Boduerae. *Han'guk kŭndae sosŏl ŭi kiwŏn* (The Origins of Modern Korean Fiction). 2nd ed. Seoul: Somyŏng ch'ulp'an, 2012.

Kwon, Nayoung Aimee. *Intimate Empire: Collaboration and Colonial Modernity in Korea and Japan.* Durham, NC: Duke University Press, 2015.

Kwon Yŏngmin. *Han'guk hyŏndae munhaksa* (A History of Modern Korean Literature). Seoul: Minŭmsa, 2002.

Kyo Jōan. "*Shin gi hō* tōsai no *Kajin kigū* ni tsuite: Tokuni sono yakusha" (*Chance Meetings with Beautiful Women* Published in *The China Discussion*: With a Focus on the Translators). *Kanbun gakkai kaihō* (Journal of Kanbun Studies) 30 (1971): 39–53.

———. "*Shin gi hō* dai yon satsu yakusai no *Kajin kigū* ni tsuite" (The Translation of *Chance Meetings with Beautiful Women* Published in the Fourth Issue of *The China Discussion*). *Nihon Chūgoku gakkaihō* (Journal of the Japanese Society of Chinese Studies) 24 (1972): 193–208.

Kyo Seiichi (Hŏ Sŏng'il). "Kanshi bunshū ni arawareta Yu Kitsushun no kaika ishiki" (The Idea of Modernization in Yu Kilchun's Collection of Chinese Verse and Prose). *Bukkyō daigaku sōgō kenkyū kiyō* (The Integrated Research Journal of Bukkyo University), special issue (2000): 59–79.

Lanling xiaoxiaosheng. *Jin ping mei cihua chongjiaoben* (The Plum in the Golden Vase: The Version by Revised Textual Critique). Ed. Mei Jie. Hong Kong: Mengmeiguan, 1993.

Lee, Ann. "Yi Kwangsu and Korean Literature: The Novel 'Mujŏng' (1917)." *Journal of Korean Studies* 8 (1992): 81–137.

Lee, Ann Sung-hi. *Yi Kwangsu and Modern Korean Literature: Mujŏng*. Ithaca, NY: Cornell East Asia Series, 2005.

Lee, Leo Ou-fan. *Voices from the Iron House: A Study of Lu Xun*. Bloomington: Indiana University Press, 1987.

Lee, Peter H., ed. *A History of Korean Literature*. Cambridge: Cambridge University Press, 2003.

Lee Sunyoung (Yi Sŏnyŏng). "Shokuminchi Chōsen ni okeru gengo seisaku to nashonarizumu: Chōsen sōtokufu no Chōsen kyōikurei to Chōsengo gakkai jiken wo chūshin ni" (Language Policy and Nationalism in Colonial Korea: The Ordinances of Education in Korea Issued by the Governor-General of Korea and the Incident of the Korean Language Society). *Ritsumeikan kokusai kenkyū* (Ritsumeikan International Studies) 25, no. 2 (2012): 495–519.

Legge, James. *The Works of Mencius*. New York: Dover, 1970.

Lewin, Bruno. "Mori Ōgai and German Aesthetics." In *A History of Modern Japanese Aesthetics*, trans. and ed. Michael F. Marra, 68–92. Honolulu: University of Hawai'i Press, 2001.

Li Bin. *1931–1945: Dongbei lunxianqu wenxue yu "wailai" wenxue guanxi yanjiu* (1931–1945: A Study of the Relationship Between Literature in the Occupied Areas in the Northeast and Literature from "Outside"). Changchun: Jilin renmin chubanshe, 2011.

Li Chenghua. *Chuantong xiang xiandai de shanbian: Zhongguo xiandai lishi xiaoshuo yu Zhong–wai wenhua* (The Evolution from Tradition Into Modernity: Modern Chinese Historical Fiction and Chinese and Foreign Cultures). Nanning: Guangxi jiaoyu chubanshe, 1996.

Li Fang et al., eds. *Taiping yulan* (The Imperial Reader of the Taiping Era). Beijing: Zhonghua shuju, 1960.

Li Ginson (Yi Ŭnsong). "Yu Kitsushun no *Seiyū kenbun* ni okeru shakai shinkaron teki keikō: Nihon no shakai shinkaron tono kanren wo chūshin toshite" (The Tendency Toward Social Darwinism in Yu Kilchun's *Observations from a Journey to the West*: With a Focus on Its Relationship to Social Darwinism in Japan). *Kyōikugaku ronshū* 2 (March 2006): 23–41.

Li, Lincoln. *The China Factor in Modern Japanese Thought: The Case of Tachibana Shiraki, 1881–1945*. Albany: State University of New York Press, 1996.

Li Wenqing. *Gongrong de xiangxiang: Diguo, zhimindi yu da dongya wenxue quan, 1937–1945* (Imaginations of Co-Prosperity: Empire, Colonies, and the Greater East Asian Literary Sphere, 1937–1945). Taipei: Daoxiang chubanshe, 2012.

———. "Lu Xun zhi hou: 'Zhanzheng qi' (1937–1945) de manxi wentan yu wenyi" (Post-Lu Xun: The Literary Field and Literature in Manchuria in the "Wartime Period," 1937–1945). *Nanfang wentan* (The Southern Literary World) 6 (2014): 43–53.

Liang Qichao. *Yinbingshi heji* (The Combined Collection of the Works of Ice Drinker's Studio, Liang Qichao). Beijing: Zhonghua shuju, 1989.

Lin Fei. *Lun "Gushi xinbian" de sixiang yishu ji lishi yiyi* (The Art of Thinking and the Historical Significance of *Old Stories Retold*). Tianjin: Tianjin renmin chubanshe, 1984.

Lin Fei and Liu Zaifu. *Lu Xun zhuan* (A Biography of Lu Xun). Beijing: Zhongguo shehui kexue chubanshe, 1981.

Lin Peijie. *Taiwan wenxue zhong de "Manzhou" xiangxiang ji zaixian* (The Imagination and Representation of Manchuria in Taiwanese Literature). Taipei: Xiuwei zixun keji gufen youxian gongsi, 2015.

Liu Anwei. *Shū Sakujin den: Aru chinichiha bunjin no seishinshi* (A Biography of Zhou Zuoren: The Spiritual Journey of a Japanophile Intellectual). Tokyo: Mineruva shobō, 2011.

Liu, Lydia. "Life as Form: How Biomimesis Encountered Buddhism in Lu Xun." *Journal of Asian Studies* 68, no. 1 (February 2009): 21–54.

———. *Translingual Practice: Literature, National Culture, and Translated Modernity—China, 1900–1937*. Stanford, CA: Stanford University Press, 1995.

Liu Shipei. "Zhongguo wenzi liubi lun" (On the Shortcomings of Chinese Writing). In *Liu Shipei wenxuan* (Selected Works of Liu Shipei), ed. Li Miaogen, 1–4. Shanghai: Shanghai yuandong chubanshe, 2011.

Liu Shunli. *Wangchao jian de duihua: Chaoxian lingxuanshi Tianjin laiwang riji daodu* (Dialogue Between Kingdoms: A Guided Reading of the Journal of the Korean Official Envoys Visiting Tianjin). Yinchuan: Ningxia renmin chubanshe, 2006.

Liu Shuqin, ed. *Dongya wenxue chang: Taiwan, Chaoxian, Manzhou de zhimin zhuyi yu wenhua jiaoshe* (The East Asian Literary Field: Colonialism and Cultural Exchanges Between Taiwan, Korea, and Manchukuo). Taipei: Lianjing, 2018.

———. *Zhanzheng yu fenjie: "Zonglizhan" xia Taiwan, Hanguo de zhuti chongsu yu wenhua zhengzhi* (War and Boundaries: The Reconfiguration of Subjectivity and the Cultural Politics in Taiwan and Korea during the "Total War"). Taipei: Lianjing, 2011.

Liu Xie. *Wenxin diaolong yizheng* (The Literary Mind and the Carving of Dragons: The Text with Evidentiary Critique of Interpretation). Ed. Zhan Ying. Shijiazhuang: Hebei jiaoyu chubanshe, 2016.

Long Yingzong. *Long Yingzong quanji: Ribenyu ban* (The Complete Works of Long Yingzong: The Japanese Version). Ed. Chen Wanyi et al. Tainan: Guoli Taiwan wenxueguan, 2008.

Long, Hoyt. *On Uneven Ground: Miyazawa Kenji and the Making of Place in Modern Japan*. Stanford, CA: Stanford University Press, 2011.

Lozerand, Emmanuel. *Littérature et génie national: Naissance d'une histoire littéraire dans le Japon du XIXe siècle*. Paris: Belles lettres, 2005.

Lu Xun. *The Complete Stories of Lu Xun*. Trans. Gladys Yang and Yang Hsien-yi. Bloomington: Indiana University Press, 1981.

———. *Lu Xun quanji* (The Complete Works of Lu Xun). Beijing: Renmin wenxue chubanshe, 2005.

———. *The Real Story of Ah-Q and Other Tales of China: The Complete Fiction of Lu Xun*. Trans. Julia Lovell. London: Penguin, 2009.

———. *Yeh Cao*. Trans. Xianyi Yang and Gladys Yang. Xianggang: Zhongwen daxue chubanshe, 2003.

Lu Xun bowuguan, ed. *Hanguo Lu Xun yanjiu lunwenji* (A Collection of Korean Studies on Lu Xun). Zhengzhou: Henan wenyi chubanshe, 2005.

Lu Xun xiansheng jinian weiyuanhui, ed. *Lu Xun xiansheng jinian ji: Daowen dierji* (Essays in Memory of Mr. Lu Xun: The Second Volume of Homages). Shanghai: Shanghai shudian chubanshe, 1979.

Lukács, Georg. *The Historical Novel*. Trans. Hannah and Stanley Mitchell. Lincoln: University of Nebraska Press, 1983.

———. *The Theory of the Novel: A Historico-Philosophical Essay on the Forms of Great Epic Literature*. Trans. Anna Bostock. Cambridge, MA: MIT Press, 1971.

Luo Sen. *Riben riji* (The Journal on Japan). In Luo Sen et al., *Zaoqi Riben youji wu zhong* (Five Early Journals of Journeys to Japan). Hunan: Hunan renmin chubanshe, 1983.

Maciocia, Giovanni. *The Foundations of Chinese Medicine: A Comprehensive Text*. 3rd ed. Edinburgh: Elsevier, 2015.

Mack, Edward. *Manufacturing Modern Japanese Literature: Publishing, Prizes, and the Ascription of Literary Value*. Durham, NC: Duke University Press, 2010.

Maeda Ai. *Maeda Ai chosakushū* (The Selected Works of Maeda Ai). Tokyo: Chikuma shobō, 1989–90.

———. "Meiji rekishi bungaku no genzō: Seiji shōsetsu no baai" (The Original Images of Meiji Historical Literature: The Case of the Political Novel). *Tenbō* (Perspective) 213 (1976): 108–33.

Mao Dun et al. "Gei Zhou Zuoren de yi feng gongkai xin" (An Open Letter to Zhou Zuoren) In *Guonan shengzhong* (Amid the Voices in National Crisis). Vol. 3 of *Huiwang Zhou Zuoren* (Zhou Zuoren Retrospective), ed. Sun Yu and Huang Qiaosheng, 5–6. Kaifeng: Henan daxue chubanshe, 2004.

Marr, David G. *Vietnamese Anticolonialism, 1885–1925*. Berkeley: University of California Press, 1971.

Marriott, John. *The Makers of Modern Italy*. London: Macmillan, 1908.

Martindale, Charles, and A. B. Taylor, eds. *Shakespeare and the Classics*. Cambridge: Cambridge University Press, 2004.

Maruo Tsuneki. *Ro Jin: "Jin" "ki" no kattō* (Lu Xun: The Struggles Between "Humans" and "Ghosts"). Tokyo: Iwanami shoten, 1993.

Maruyama Masao. "Chō kokkashugi no ronri to shinri" (The Logic and Psychology of Ultra-Nationalism). In *Chō kokkashugi no ronri to shinri hoka hachi hen* (The Logic and Psychology of Ultra-Nationalism and Eight Other Essays), ed. Furuya Jun, 11–40. Tokyo: Iwanami shoten, 2015.

Masuda Wataru. *Seigaku tōzen to Chūgoku jijyō* (The Travel of Western Learning to the East and the Situations in China). Tokyo: Iwanami shoten, 1979.

Matsumura Takao. "Nihon teikoku shugi ka ni okeru 'Manshū' eno Chōsenjin idō ni tsuite" (A Study of Korean Migration to Manchuria Under Japanese Imperial Rule). *Keio Journal of Economics* 63, no. 6 (1970): 479–595.

Matsuo Yōji. "Ryō Keichō to shiden" (Liang Qichao and Historical Stories). In *Kyōdō kenkyū Ryō Keichō: Seiyō kindai shisō juyō to meiji Nihon* (A Collaborative Study of Liang Qichao: The Introduction of Modern Western Thought and Meiji Japan), ed. Hazama Naoki, 257–95. Tokyo: Misuzu shobō, 1999.

Mehl, Margaret. *History and the State in Nineteenth-Century Japan*. London: Macmillan, 1998.

Mei Ding'e. *Ko Tei kenkyū: "Manshūkoku" ni ikita bunkajin* (A Study of Gu Ding: A Cultural Intellectual Who Lived in Manchukuo). Kyoto: Kokusai Nihon bunka kenkyū sentā, 2012.

Michiaki Kawato et al., eds. *Meijiki hon'yaku bungaku sōgō nenpyō* (A Comprehensive Chronology of Translated Literature in the Meiji Era). Tokyo: Ōzora sha, 2001.

Mikami Kazuo. *Yokoi Shōnan: Sono shisō to kōdō* (Yokoi Shōnan: His Thought and Action). Tokyo: Yoshikawa kōbunkan, 1999.

Min Ch'an. "Tanjae sosŏl ŭi kyŏngno wa chŏnt'ong ŭi chajang" (The Path of Tanjae Sin Ch'aeho's Fiction and the Magnetic Field of Tradition). *Inmun kwahak nonmunjip* (Journal of the Humanities) 34 (2002): 147–62.

Miyata Setsuko. *Chōsen minshū to "kōminka" seisaku* (The Korean People and the Japanization Policy). Tokyo: Miraisha, 1985.

Mori Arinori. *Mori Arinori zenshū* (The Complete Works of Mori Arinori). Tokyo: Senbundō shoten, 1972.

Mori Ōgai. *Ōgai kindai shōsetsu shū* (The Selected Modern Stories of Ōgai). Tokyo: Iwanami shoten, 2012–13.

———. *Ōgai rekishi bungaku shū* (The Selected Historical Literature of Ōgai). Tokyo: Iwanami shoten, 1999.

———. *Ōgai zenshū* (The Complete Works of Ōgai). Tokyo: Iwanami shoten, 1971–75.

———. *The Wild Geese*. Trans. Kingo Ochiai and Stanford Goldstein. Rutland, VT: Tuttle, 1959.

———. *Youth and Other Stories*. Trans. J. Thomas Rimer. Honolulu: University of Hawai'i Press, 1994.

Morikawa Terumichi. *Zōhoban kyōiku chokugo eno michi: Kyōiku no seijishi* (The Path Toward the Imperial Rescript of Education: The Political History of Education, Augmented Edition). Tokyo, Sangensha, 2011.

Motoyama Yukihiko. *Yokoi Shōnan no gakumon to shisō* (The Learning and Thought of Yokoi Shōnan). Osaka: Osaka kōritsu daigaku kyōdō shuppankai, 2014.

Nagai Kafū. *Kafū zenshū* (The Complete Works of Kafū). Tokyo: Iwanami shoten, 1992.

Nagashima Yōichi. *Mori Ōgai no hon'yaku bungaku: "Sokkyō shijin" kara "Perikan" made* (Translated Literature in Mori Ōgai: From *The Improvisatore* to *The Pelican*). Tokyo: Shibundō, 1993.

Nakajima Takahiro. *Sōji: Tori to natte toki wo tsugeyo* (The Zhuangzi: Announce the Time as a Bird!). Tokyo: Iwanami shoten, 2009.

Nakajima Toshirō, ed. *Taiwan shinbungaku to Ro Jin* (Taiwanese New Literature and Lu Xun). Tokyo: Tōhō shoten, 1997.

Natsume, Sōseki. *Teihon Sōseki zenshū* (The Complete Works of Sōseki: The Definitive Edition). Tokyo: Iwanami shoten, 2016–20.

———. *Theory of Literature and Other Critical Writings*. Ed. Michael K. Bourdaghs et al. New York: Columbia University Press, 2009.

Nietzsche, Friedrich Wilhelm. *Thus Spoke Zarathustra: A Book for All and None*. Ed. Adrian Del Caro and Robert B. Pippin. Trans. Adrian Del Caro. Cambridge: Cambridge University Press, 2006.

———. *Untimely Meditations*. Ed. Daniel Breazeale. Trans. R. J. Hollingdale. Cambridge: Cambridge University Press, 1997.

Nihon Bungaku Hōkokukai. *Bungaku hōkoku* (Literature in the Nation's Service). Tokyo: Fuji shuppan, 1990.

Nihongo gakkai, ed. *Nihon kokugo daijiten* (The Grand Dictionary of Japanese). Tokyo: Tōkyōdō shuppan, 2018.

Nishino Minoru and Hisamatsu Sen'ichi, eds. *Kokugo kokuji kyōiku shiryō sōran* (A Compendium of Sources on the Education of National Language and Script). Tokyo: Kokugo kyōiku kenkyūkai, 1969.

Nishitani Keiji. "'Kindai no chōkoku' shiron" (An Essay on Overcoming the Modern). In *Kindai no chōkoku* (Overcoming the Modern), ed. Kawakami Tetsutarō, 18–37. Tokyo: Fuzanbō, 1979.

Numata Jirō. *Bakumatsu yōgaku shi* (A History of Western Learning in the Late Edo Period). Tokyo: Tōkō shoin, 1951.

Nylan, Michael. "The 'Chin Wen/Ku Wen' Controversy in Han Times." *T'oung Pao* 80, nos. 1–3 (1994): 83–145.

Ōba Osamu. *Kanseki yu'nyū no bunkashi: Shōtoku Taishi kara Yoshimune e* (The Cultural History of Imported Chinese Books: From Shōtoku Taishi to Yoshimune). Tokyo: Kenbun shuppan, 1997.

Ogata Tsutomu. *Ōgai no rekishi shōsetsu: Shiryō to hōhō* (Historical Fiction of Ōgai: Sources and Methods). Tokyo: Iwanami shoten, 2002.

Okada Hideki. *Bungaku ni miru "Manshūkoku" no isō* (Aspects of Manchukuo Seen through Literature). Tokyo: Kenbun shuppan, 2000.

——. *"Manshūkoku" no bungaku to sono shūhen* (Manchukuo Literature and Its Environs). Tokyo: Tōhō shoten, 2019.

Okakura, Kakuzō. *The Ideals of the East with Special Reference to the Art of Japan*. New York: Dutton, 1920.

Ōmura Masuo. "Ryō Keichō no Chōsenkan to '*Kajin no kigū*'" (Liang Qichao's View on Korea and *Chance Meetings with Beautiful Women*). In *Chōsen kindai bungaku to Nihon* (Modern Korean Literature and Japan), 241–63. Tokyo: Ryokuin shobō, 2003.

——. "Ryō Keichō oyobi 'Kajin no kigū'" (Liang Qichao and *Chance Meetings with Beautiful Women*). *Jinbun ronshū* 11 (1973): 103–33.

Ōmura Masuo and Hotei Toshihiro, eds. *Kindai Chōsen bungaku Nihongo sakuhinshū, 1901–1938* (A Collection of Japanese-Language Works in Modern Korean Literature, 1901–1938). Tokyo: Ryokuin shobō, 2004.

Ōnuma Toshio. "Tōkai Sanshi Shiba Shirō ryakuden: Hito to shisō" (A Concise Biography of Tōkai Sanshi Shiba Shirō: Life and Thought). In *Seiji Shōsetsu shū 2* (A Collection of Historical Novels, Volume 2), ed. Ōnuma Toshio and Nakamaru Nobuaki, vol. 17 of *Shin Nihon koten bungaku taikei: Meiji hen* (The New Compendium of Classical Japanese Literature: The Works of the Meiji Era), 667–82. Tokyo: Iwanami shoten, 2006.

Ōoka Shōhei. *Ōoka Shōhei zenshū* (The Complete Works of Ōoka Shōhei). Tokyo: Chikuma shobō, 1994–2003.

Ozaki Hideki. *Kindai bungaku no shōkon* (The Trauma of Modern Literature). Tokyo: Iwanami shoten, 1991.

Paek Nakch'ŏng. "Yŏksa sosŏl kwa yŏksa ŭisik: Sin munhak esŏ ŭi ch'ulbal kwa munjejŏm" (Historical Fiction and Historical Consciousness: The Departure from New Fiction and Its Problems). *Ch'angjak kwa pip'yŏng* (The Quarterly Changbi) 2, no. 1 (1967): 5–40.

Pak Chin'yŏng. *Pŏnyŏkka ŭi t'ansaeng kwa tong asia segyemunhak* (The Birth of the Translator and World Literature in East Asia). Seoul: Somyŏng chu'ulp'an, 2019.

Pak Kibong. *Ŭlji mundŏk chŏn: Tongnip chŏngsin kwa minjok chajon ŭi p'yosang* (The Biography of Ŭlji mundŏk: The Representation of the Spirit of Independence and National Self-Sustenance). Seoul: Pibong ch'ulp'ansa, 2006.

Pak Ŭnsik. *Paekam Pak Ŭnsik chŏnjip* (The Complete Works of Paekam Pak Ŭnsik). Seoul: Tongbang midiŏ, 2002.

Pak Yŏngmi. "Sam Koenam ŭi kyŏng'uro pon aeguk kyemonggi chisigin ŭi taeil insik" (The Intellectuals' View of Japan in the Era of Patriotism and Enlightenment, Based on the Case of Mori Kainan). *Hanmunhak nonjip* (Journal of Sino-Korean Literature) 33 (2011): 181–202.

Pang Minho. *Ilche malgi Han'guk munhak ŭi tamnon kwa t'eksŭt'ŭ* (The Discourse and Texts of Korean Literature in the Late Colonial Period). Seoul: Yeok, 2011.

Panofsky, Erwin. *Perspective as Symbolic Form*. Cambridge, MA: MIT Press, 1991.

Peku Yonso (Paek Yŏngsŏ). *Kyōsei eno michi to kakushin genba: Jissen kadai toshite no higashi ajia* (The Path Toward Coexistence and the Core Sites: East Asia as a Practical Task). Ed. Nakajima Takahiro. Trans. Chō Kyonhi (Cho Kyŏnghŭi). Tokyo: Hōsei daigaku shuppankyoku, 2016.

Perry, Matthew Calbraith. *Perī kantai Nihon ensei ki* (The Documents of Commodore Perry's Mission to Japan). Trans. Office Miyazaki. Tokyo: Eikō kyōiku bunka kenkyūjo, 1997.

Pollock, Sheldon. *The Language of the Gods in the World of Men: Sanskrit, Culture, and Power in Premodern India*. Berkeley: University of California Press, 2006.

Puett, Michael, and Christine Gross-Loh. *The Path: What Chinese Philosophers Can Teach Us About the Good Life*. New York: Simon & Schuster, 2016.

Qian Liqun. *Lu Xun zuopin shiwu jiang* (Fifteen Lectures on Lu Xun's Works). Beijing: Beijing daxue chubanshe, 2003.

———. "Shinian chenmo de Lu Xun" (Lu Xun's Ten-Year Silence). *Zhejiang shehui kexue* (The Zhejiang Journal of Social Sciences) 1 (2003): 133–39.

———. *Zhou Zuoren zhuan* (A Biography of Zhou Zuoren). Beijing: Huawen chubanshe, 2013.

Qing yi bao (The China Discussion). Reprint. Taipei: Chengwen chubanshe, c. 1967.

Qu Qiubai. *Qu Qiubai wenji: Wenxue bian* (The Selected Writings of Qu Qiubai: Literature). Beijing: Renmin wenxue chubanshe, 1989.

Rancière, Jacques. *The Politics of Aesthetics: The Distribution of the Sensible*. Trans. Gabriel Rockhill. London: Continuum, 2004.

Ri Shōrin (Li Shanglin). "Taiwan shokuminchi jidai shoki ni okeru Nihon tōchi to shindai kanwa: 'Fukutsūyaku sei' ka no Taiwan kanwa shiyōsha wo chūshin ni" (Japanese Rule and the Qing Mandarin in Taiwan in the Early Colonial Period: With a Focus on the Taiwanese Speakers of Mandarin in the Practice of Dual Interpretation). In *Nihon tōchiki Taiwan ni okeru yakusha oyobi "hon'yaku" katsudō: Shokuminchi tōchi to gengo bunka no sakusō kankei* (Translators and Translation Activities in Taiwan Under Japanese Rule: The Inextricable Relationship Between Colonial Rule and Language Culture), ed. Yō Shōshuku (Yang Chengshu), 55–84. Taipei: Taiwan daxue chuban zhongxin, 2015.

Ricci, Ronit. *Islam Translated: Literature, Conversion, and the Arabic Cosmopolis in South and Southeast Asia*. Chicago: University of Chicago Press, 2011.

Rin Shukutan (Lin Shudan). "Mori Ōgai 'Gan' to *Kin pei bai*: Monogatari no kōsaku" (Mori Ōgai's "Wild Geese" and *The Plum in the Golden Vase*: Interwoven Stories). *Ōgai* 69 (2001): 118–29.

———. "Mori Ōgai to Chūgoku koten bungaku" (Mori Ōgai and Classical Chinese Literature). PhD diss., Ochanomizu University, 2003.

Robinson, Michael. "National Identity and the Thought of Sin Ch'aeho: *Sadaejuŭi* and *Chuch'e* in History and Politics." *Journal of Korean Studies* 5 (1984): 121–42.

Ross, Trevor. "Copyright and the Invention of Tradition." *Eighteenth-Century Studies* 26, no. 1 (1992): 1–27.

———. "The Emergence of 'Literature': Making and Reading the English Canon in the Eighteenth Century." *ELH* 63, no. 2 (1996): 397–422.

Roy, David Tod, trans. *The Plum in the Golden Vase; Or, Chin P'ing Mei*. Princeton, NJ: Princeton University Press, 1993.

Ryū Senka. "Kanji tōitsu kai ni kansuru ichi kōsatsu: Shinkoku to Kankoku no hannō wo chūshin to shite" (A Reflection on the Society for Unifying the Chinese Characters: With a Focus on the Responses from the Qing and Korea). *Gengo shakai* (Language and Society) 13 (2019): 280–96.

Said, Edward W. "The World, the Text, and the Critic." In *The World, the Text, and the Critic*, 31–53. Cambridge, MA: Harvard University Press, 1983.

Saitō Mareshi. "Dōbun no poritikusu" (The Politics of Shared Script). *Bungaku* (Literature) 10, no. 6 (2009): 38–48.

———. "Kindai kundokutai to higashi ajia" (The Modern "Kundoku" Style and East Asia). In *Kindai higashi ajia ni okeru buntai no hensen: Keishiki to naijitsu no sōkoku wo koete* (The Transformations of Writing Styles in Modern East Asia: Beyond the Contradictions Between Form and Content), ed. Chin Kokui (Chen Guowei) and Uchida Keiichi, 109–120. Tokyo: Hakutei sha, 2010.

———. "Shōsetsu no bōken: Seiji shōsetsu to sono kayaku wo megutte" (The Adventures of Fiction: The Political Novels and Their Chinese Translations). *Jinbun gakuhō* (Journal of the Humanities) 69 (1991): 1–29.

Sakai, Naoki, and Isomae Jun'ichi, eds. *"Kindai no chōkoku" to Kyōto gakuha: Kindaisei, teikoku, fuhensei* ("Overcoming the Modern" and the Kyoto School: Modernity, Empire, and Universality). Kyoto: Ningen bunka kenkyū kikō kokusai Nihon bunka kenkyū sentā, 2010.

Sakaki, Atsuko. "*Kajin no Kigū*: The Meiji Political Novel and the Boundaries of Literature." *Monumenta Nipponica* 55, no. 1 (Spring 2000): 83–108.

——. *Obsessions with the Sino-Japanese Polarity in Japanese Literature*. Honolulu: University of Hawai'i Press, 2006.

——. *Recontextualizing Texts: Narrative Performance in Modern Japanese Fiction*. Cambridge, MA: Harvard University Asia Center, 1999.

Sakuramoto Tomio. *Nihon bungaku hōkoku kai: Daitōa sensō ka no bungakusha tachi* (The Japanese Association for Literature in the Nation's Service: Writers During the Greater East Asian War). Tokyo: Aoki shoten, 1995.

Samguk sagi (History of the Three Kingdoms). Comp. Kim Busik. Trans. Chŏng Kubok et al. Sŏng'nam: Han'guk chŏngsin munhwa yŏnguwŏn, 1996.

Sasagawa Yūichi. *Meiji Taishō bungaku no bunseki* (An Analysis of Literature in the Meiji and Taishō Eras). Tokyo: Meiji shoin, 1970.

Satō Haruo. *Kindai Nihon bungaku no tenbō* (Perspectives on Modern Japanese Literature). Tokyo: Dainihon yūbenkai kōdansha, 1950.

Saussy, Haun. *Translation as Citation: Zhuangzi Inside Out*. Oxford: Oxford University Press, 2017.

Schiller, Friedrich. *On the Aesthetic Education of Man: In a Series of Letters*. Ed. and trans. Elizabeth M. Wilkinson and L. A. Willoughby. Oxford: Clarendon Press, 1982.

Schmid, Andre. *Korea Between Empires, 1895–1919*. New York: Columbia University Press, 2002.

——. "Rediscovering Manchuria: Sin Ch'aeho and the Politics of Territorial History in Korea." *Journal of Asian Studies* 56, no. 1 (February 1997): 26–46.

Schmidt, Rachel. *Forms of Modernity: Don Quixote and Modern Theories of the Novel*. Toronto: University of Toronto Press, 2011.

Shan Yuanchao. "Zasshi *Geibun* no seiritsu to hensen ni tsuite: 'Bunka sōgō zasshi' kara 'jun geibun zasshi' e" (The Establishment and Changes of the Journal *Geibun*: From a "General Cultural Journal" to a "Pure Literary Journal"). *Kokyō: Nihongo bungaku kenkyū* (Border-Crossings: Journal of Japanese-Language Literature) 1 (2014): 73–88.

Shangshu (The Book of Documents). Scripta Sinica: Hanji dianzi wenxian ziliaoku (digital database).

Shi Kan (Shi Gang). *Shokuminchi shihai to Nihongo: Taiwan, Manshūkoku, tairiku senryōchi ni okeru gengo seisaku* (Colonial Rule and Japanese: The Language Policies in Taiwan, Manchukuo, and the Occupied Territories in Mainland China). Tokyo: Sangensha, 2003.

Shi Meng. *Wan Qing xiaoshuo* (The Late Qing Novel). Shanghai: Shanghai guji chubanshe, 1989.

Shi Nai'an and Luo Guanzhong. *Shui hu zhuan: Li Zhuowu ping ben* (Water Margin: The Text with Commentary by Li Zhuowu). Annot. Li Zhi. Shanghai: Shanghai guji chubanshe, 1988.

Shiba Gorō. *Aru Meijijin no kiroku: Aizujin Shiba Gorō no isho* (The Memoir of a Meiji Man: The Last Will and Testament of Shiba Gorō, an Aizu National). Tokyo: Chūō kōron sha, 1971.

Shiba Shirō. *Kajin no kigū* (Chance Meetings with Beautiful Women). In *Seiji shōsetsu shū* 2 (A Collection of Historical Novels, Volume 2), ed. Ōnuma Toshio and Nakamaru Nobuaki, vol. 17 of *Shin Nihon koten bungaku taikei: Meiji hen* (The New Compendium of Classical Japanese Literature: The Works of the Meiji Era). Tokyo: Iwanami shoten, 2006.

Shimizu Ken'ichirō. "Ryō Keichō to 'teikoku kanbun'" (Liang Qichao and the Imperial Kanbun). *Ajia yūgaku* (Intriguing Asia) 13 (2000): 22–37.

Shimomura Sakujirō. *Bungaku de yomu Taiwan* (Taiwan Read through Literature). Tokyo: Tabata shoten, 1994.

Shin Konje (Sin Kŭnjae). *Nikkan kindai shōsetsu no hikaku kenkyū: Tetchō, Kōyō, Roka to hon'an shōsetsu* (A Comparative Study of Modern Japanese and Korean Fiction: Tetchō, Kōyō, and Adapted Fiction). Tokyo: Meiji shoin, 2006.

Shin, Michael D. "Interior Landscape and Modern Literature: Yi Kwangsu's 'The Heartless' and the Origins of Modern Literature." In *Colonial Modernity in Korea*, ed. Gi-Wook Shin and Michael Robinson, 248–87. Cambridge, MA: Harvard University Asia Center, 1999.

Shirane, Haruo, et al., eds. *The Cambridge History of Japanese Literature*. Cambridge: Cambridge University Press, 2015.

Shishuo xinyu jianshu (The New Accounts of the Tales of the World: The Text with Commentary and Annotation). Comp. Liu Yiqing. Annot. Liu Xiaobiao. Scripta Sinica: Hanji dianzi wenxian ziliaoku (digital database).

Shukuri Shigeichi. *Kodama Gentarō*. Tokyo: Taikyōsha, 1938.

Sima Qian. *Shiji* (Records of the Grand Historian). Scripta Sinica: Hanji dianzi wenxian ziliaoku (digital database).

Sin Ch'aeho. *Tanjae Sin Ch'aeho chŏnjip* (The Complete Works of Tanjae Sin Ch'aeho). Ch'ungnam Ch'ŏnan-si: Tongnip kinyŏmgwan Han'guk tongnip undongsa yŏn'guso, 2007.

Sính, Vĩnh. "Elegant Females Re-Encountered: From Tokai Sanshi's *Kajin no kigū* to Phan Châu Trinh's *Giai Nhân Kỳ Ngô Diễn Ca*." In *Essays Into Vietnamese Pasts*, ed. K. W. Taylor and John K. Whitmore, 195–206. Ithaca, NY: Southeast Asia Program, Cornell University, 1995.

Snyder, Stephen. "Ōgai and the Problem of Fiction: Gan and Its Antecedents." *Monumenta Nipponica* 49, no. 3 (Autumn 1994): 353–73.

Sŏ Bin (Song Min). *Meiji shoki ni okeru Chōsen shūshinshi no Nihon kenbun* (The Korean Envoy's Journeys to Japan in the Early Meiji Period). Kyoto: Kokusai Nihon bunka kenkyū sentā, 2000.

So Chaeyŏng. "'Chŏn' ŭi kŭndae munhakchŏk sŏngkyŏk" (The Characteristics of "*Chŏn*" as Modern Literature). In *Kŭndae munhak ŭi hyŏngsŏng kwajŏng* (The Process of the Formation of Modern Literature), ed. Han'guk kojŏn munhak yŏnguhoe, 133–52. Seoul: Munhak kwa chisŏngsa, 1983.

Sŏ Hyŏngbŏm. "'Kkum hanŭl' ŭi sŏsach'ŭngwibunsŏk kwa mongyuyangsik sŏnt'aek ŭi ŭimi" (A Narrative Analysis of "Dream Heaven" and the Significance of the Adoption of the Style of the Dream Stories). *Han'guk hyŏndae munhak yŏngu* (Journal of Modern Korean Literature) 16 (December 2004): 111–34.

So Hyonsopu (Sŏ Hyŏnsŏp). *Kindai Chōsen no gaikō to kokusaihō juyō* (Modern Korean Diplomacy and the Reception of International Law). Tokyo: Akashi shoten, 2001.

Sŏ Taesŏk. "Mongyurok ŭi changnŭjŏk sŏngkyŏk kwa munhaksajŏk ŭiŭi" (The Generic Characteristics and Literary Historical Significance of the Dream Stories). *Han'gukhak nonjip* (Journal of Korean Studies) 3 (March 1980): 511–42.

Soeda Yoshiya. *Kyōiku chokugo no shakaishi: Nashonarizumu no sōshutsu to zasetsu* (Social History of the Imperial Rescript of Education: The Creation and Failure of a Nationalism). Tokyo: Yūshindō kōbunsha, 1997.

Son Chŏngsu. "Kŭndae ch'ogi Miguk ch'eryu chishigindŭl ŭi Yŏng'ŏ kŭlssŭgi e nat'anan sŏsulchŏk chŏngch'esŏng ŭi munje: Yu Kilchun ŭi p'yŏnji, Yun Ch'iho ŭi ilgi, Sŏ Chaep'il ŭi sosŏl" (The Issues of the Narrative Identity in the English Writings of Early Modern Korean Intellectuals in the United States: With a Focus on Yu Kilchun's Letters, Yun Ch'iho's Diary, and Sŏ Chaep'il's Fiction). *Han'gukhak nonjip* 79 (2020): 93–137.

Son Yinsu. *Han'guk kaehwa kyoyuk yŏngu* (A Study of Education in Korea in the Era of Modernization). Seoul: Ilchisa, 1980.

Song Binghui. *Ruoshi minzu wenxue zai Zhongguo* (Literature of the Weak Nations in China). Nanjing: Nanjing daxue chubanshe, 2007.

Sŏng Hyŏnja. *Sin sosŏl e mich'in manch'ŏng sosŏl ŭi yŏngyang* (The Influence of Late Qing Fiction on New Fiction in Korea). Seoul: Chŏng'ŭmsa, 1985.

Spence, Jonathan D. *The Search for Modern China*. 3rd ed. New York: W. W. Norton, 2013.

Spivak, Gayatri Chakravorty. *Death of a Discipline*. New York: Columbia University Press, 2003.

Srivastava, Gita. *Mazzini and His Impact on the Indian National Movement*. Allahabad: Chugh Publications, 1982.

Steinberg, Jonathan. "The Historian and the *Questione della Lingua*." In *The Social History of Language*, ed. Peter Burke and Roy Porter, 198–209. Cambridge: Cambridge University Press, 1987.

Suematsu Kenchō, ed. *Zenrin shōwa dai ni shū; Suiun gashū* (The Second Collection of Poems for Neighborhood Friendship; The Elegant Collection of Emerald Clouds). Tokyo: Suematsu Kenchō, 1909.

Sugino Yōkichi, ed. *Kōsō suru Chūgoku bungaku to Nihon bungaku: Rinkanka Pekin 1937–45* (The Struggles Between Chinese and Japanese Literatures: Beijing Under Occupation, 1937–1945). Tokyo: Sangensha, 2000.

Sui shu (History of the Sui). Comp. Wei Zheng et al. Beijing: Zhonghua shuju, 1973.

Sun Yu and Huang Qiaosheng, eds. *Guonan shengzhong* (Amid the Voices in National Crisis). Vol. 3 of *Huiwang Zhou Zuoren* (Zhou Zuoren Retrospective). Kaifeng: Henan daxue chubanshe, 2004.

Suzuki Sadami. *Nihon no "bungaku" gainen* (The Concept of "Literature" in Japan). Tokyo: Sakuhin sha, 1998.

T'aegŭk hakpo (T'aeguk Scholarly Journal). Vol. 13 of *Han'guk kaehwagi haksulji* (Korean Scholarly Journals in the Era of Modernization). Seoul: Asea munhwasa, 1978.

Taehan hyŏphoebo (Journal of the Korean Association). Vol. 3 of *Han'guk kaehwagi haksulji* (Korean Scholarly Journals in the Era of Modernization). Seoul: Asea munhwasa, 1976.

Takeuchi Yoshimi. *Takeuchi Yoshimi zenshū* (The Complete Works of Takeuchi Yoshimi). Tokyo: Chikuma shobō, 1980.

Tan Ruqian et al., eds. *Zhongguo yi Riben shu zonghe mulu* (A Comprehensive List of Japanese Books Translated Into Chinese). Hong Kong: Zhongwen daxue shubanshe, 1980.

Tanaka, Stefan. *Japan's Orient: Rendering Pasts Into History*. Berkeley: University of California Press, 1993.

Tang, Xiaobing. *Global Space and the Nationalist Discourse of Modernity: The Historical Thinking of Liang Qichao*. Stanford, CA: Stanford University Press, 1996.

——. "Lu Xun's 'Diary of a Madman' and a Chinese Modernism." *PMLA* 107, no. 5 (October 1992): 1222–34.

——. *Origins of the Chinese Avant-Garde: The Modern Woodcut Movement*. Berkeley: University of California Press, 2008.

Tarumoto Teruo. "Shinmatsu minsho no hon'yaku shōsetsu" (Translated Literature in the Late Qing and the Early Republican Periods). *Ōsaka keidai ronshū* (Journal of the Osaka University of Economics) 47, no. 1 (May 1996): 25–74.

——. *Shinmatsu minsho shōsetsu mokuroku* (A List of Literary Works in the Late Qing and the Early Republican Periods). 6th ed. Ōtsu: Shinmatsu shōsetsu kenkyūkai, 2014.

———. "Shinmatsu-minsho shōsetsu no futakobu rakuda" (A Two-Bump Structure of the Number of Published Works of Literature in the Late Qing and the Early Republican Periods). In *Shinmatsu shōsetsu ronshū* (Studies of Late Qing Fiction). Kyoto: Hōritsu bunka sha, 1992.

Thornber, Karen. *Empire of Texts in Motion: Chinese, Korean, and Taiwanese Transculturations of Japanese Literature*. Cambridge, MA: Harvard University Asia Center, 2009.

Tierney, Robert Thomas. *Tropics of Savagery: The Culture of Japanese Empire in Comparative Frame*. Berkeley: University of California Press, 2010.

Tokutomi Kenjirō. *Kuroi me to chairo no me, Shinshun* (Black Eyes and Brown Eyes, The New Year). Vol. 10 of *Roka zenshū* (The Complete Works of Roka). Tokyo: Roka zenshū kankōkai, 1928.

Treat, John Whittier. "Introduction to Yi Kwangsu's 'Maybe Love' (Ai ka, 1909)." *Azalea: Journal of Korean Literature and Culture* 4 (2011): 315–20.

Tsu, Jing. "New Area Studies and Languages on the Move." *PMLA* 126, no. 3 (May 2011): 693–700.

Tu, Wei-Ming. "Cultural China." In *Sinophone Studies: A Critical Reader*, ed. Shumei Shih, Chien-hsin Tsai, and Brian Bernards, 145–57. New York: Columbia University Press, 2013.

Twine, Nanette. *Language and the Modern State: The Reform of Written Japanese*. New York: Routledge, 1991.

U Imkŏl. *Han'guk kaehwagi munhak kwa Yang Kyech'o* (Korean Literature in the Era of Modernization and Liang Qichao). Seoul: Pagijŏng, 2002.

Ueda, Atsuko. *Language, Nation, Race: Linguistic Reform in Meiji Japan, 1868–1912*. Berkeley: University of California Press, 2021.

———. "The Production of Literature and the Effaced Realm of the Political." *Journal of Japanese Studies* 31, no. 1 (2005): 61–88.

Uhl, Christian. "What Was the 'Japanese Philosophy of History'?: An Inquiry Into the Dynamics of the 'World-Historical Standpoint' of the Kyoto School." In *Political Philosophy in Japan: Nishida, the Kyoto School, and Co-Prosperity*, ed. Christopher Goto-Jones, 113–33. New York: Routledge, 2005.

Umetani Noboru. *Kyōiku chokugo seiritsushi: Tennōsei kokkakan no seiritsu ge* (The Birth of the Imperial Rescript of Education: Emergence of Imperial State Ideology 2). Tokyo: Seishi shuppan kabushiki gaisha, 2000.

Usui Yoshimi. *Kindai bungaku ronsō* (The Polemics of Modern Literature). Tokyo: Chikuma shobō, 1975.

Verhaeren, Émile. *Choix de poèmes*. Paris: Mercure de France, 1917.

Von Kowallis, Jon Eugene. *The Lyrical Lu Xun: A Study of His Classical-Style Verse*. Honolulu: University of Hawai'i Press, 1996.

Wagley, Charles. *Area Research and Training: A Conference Report on the Study of World Areas*. New York: National Conference on the Study of World Areas, 1948.

Wang, Ban, ed. *Chinese Visions of World Order: Tianxia, Culture, and World Politics*. Durham, NC: Duke University Press, 2017.

——. "Geopolitics, Moral Reform, and Poetic Internationalism: Liang Qichao's *The Future of New China*." *Frontiers of Literary Studies in China* 6, no. 1 (2012): 2–18.

——. "The Moral Vision in Kang Youwei's *Book of the Great Community*." In *Chinese Visions of World Order: Tianxia, Culture, and World Politics*, ed. Ban Wang, 87–105. Durham, NC: Duke University Press, 2017.

——. *The Sublime Figure of History: Aesthetics and Politics in Twentieth-Century China*. Stanford, CA: Stanford University Press, 1997.

Wang, David Der-wei (Wang Dewei). "Cong moluo dao nuobeier" (From Mara to the Nobel). In *Cong moluo dao nuobeier: Wenxue, jingdian, xiandai yishi* (From Mara to the Nobel: Literature, the Classics, and Modern Consciousness), ed. Gao Jiaqian and Zheng Yuyu, 30–62. Taipei: Maitian chuban, 2015.

——. *Fin-de-Siècle Splendor: Repressed Modernities of Late Qing Fiction, 1849–1911*. Stanford, CA: Stanford University Press, 1997.

—— (Wang Dewei). "Xiaoshuo zuowei 'geming': Chongdu Liang Qichao *Xin Zhongguo weilai ji*" (Fiction as "Revolution": Revisiting Liang Qichao's *Future of New China*). *Suzhou jiaoyu xueyuan xuebao* (Journal of the Suzhou Academy of Education) 31, no. 4 (August 2014): 1–10.

Wang He, ed. *Chaoxian duanpian xiaoshuo xuan* (Collection of Korean Short Stories). Xinjing: Xin shidai she, 1941.

Wang Hui. *Fankang juewang: Lu Xun ji qi wenxue shijie* (Resistance and Desolation: Lu Xun and the World of His Literature). Beijing: Sanlian shudian, 2008.

——. *The Politics of Imagining Asia*. Ed. Theodore Huters. Cambridge, MA: Harvard University Press, 2011.

——. "The Voices of Good and Evil: What Is Enlightenment? Rereading Lu Xun's 'Toward a Refutation of Malevolent Voices.'" *boundary 2* 38, no. 2 (2011): 67–123.

——. *Xiandai Zhongguo sixiang de xingqi* (The Rise of Modern Chinese Thought). Beijing: Sanlian shudian, 2004.

Wang Jiaping. *Lu Xun yuwai bainian chuanbo shi, 1909–2008* (A Hundred-Year History of the Circulation of Lu Xun's Works, 1909–2008). Beijing: Beijing daxue chubanshe, 2009.

Wang, Jing. *The Story of Stone: Intertextuality, Ancient Chinese Stone Lore, and the Stone Symbolism in Dream of the Red Chamber, Water Margin, and The Journey to the West*. Durham, NC: Duke University Press, 1992.

Wang, Pu. "Poetics, Politics, and 'Ursprung/Yuan': On Lu Xun's Conception of 'Mara Poetry.'" *Modern Chinese Literature and Culture* 23, no. 2 (Fall 2011): 34–60.

Wang Qiang. *Hanjian zuzhi xinmin hui* (The New Citizen's Society; or, an Anti-Chinese Organization). Tianjin: Tianjin shehui kexueyuan chubanshe, 2006.

Wang Runhua and Pan Guoju, eds. *Lu Xun zai dongnan ya* (Lu Xun in Southeast Asia). Singapore: Bafang wenhua chuangzuoshi, 2017.

Wang Xiaoqiu. *Jindai Zhong-Ri guanxi shi yanjiu* (A Study of the History of the Modern Sino-Japanese Relationship). Beijing: Zhongguo shehui kexue chubanshe, 1997.

——. *Jindai Zhong-Ri wenhua jiaoliu shi* (History of Modern Sino-Japanese Cultural Exchanges). Beijing: Zhonghua shuju, 1992.

Wang Yao. "Zhongguo xiandai wenxue yu gudian wenxue de lishi guanxi" (The Historical Relationship Between Chinese Modern Literature and Classical Literature). *Beijing daxue xuebao* (Journal of Beijing University) 5 (1986): 1–14.

Wanshan Sheng (Maruyama Noboru). *Lu Xun, geming, lishi: Wanshan Sheng xiandai Zhongguo wenxue lunji* (Lu Xun, Revolution, and History: Selected Essays of Maruyama Noboru on Modern Chinese Literature). Trans. Wang Junwen. Beijing: Beijing daxue chubanshe, 2005.

Watson, Burton, trans. *The Complete Works of Chuang Tzu*. New York: Columbia University Press, 1968.

Watson, Jini Kim. "Imperial Mimicry, Modernisation Theory and the Contradictions of Postcolonial South Korea." *Postcolonial Studies* 10, no. 2 (2007): 171–90.

Wellek, René. *Theory of Literature*. New York: Harcourt, Brace and Company, 1949.

Wen xuan (Selection of Refined Writings). Comp. Xiao Tong et al. Annot. Li Shan. Scripta Sinica: Hanji dianzi wenxian ziliaoku (digital database).

Wender, Melissa L., ed. *Into the Light: An Anthology of Literature by Koreans in Japan*. Honolulu: University of Hawai'i Press, 2011.

Wenzi gaige chubanshe, ed. *Qingmo wenzi gaige wenji* (A Collection of Essays on Late Qing Script Reforms). Beijing: Wenzi gaige chubanshe, 1958.

Willcock, Hiroko. "Meiji Japan and the Late Qing Political Novel." *Journal of Oriental Studies* 33, no. 1 (1995): 1–28.

Williams, Raymond. *Marxism and Literature*. Oxford: Oxford University Press, 1977.

Wong, Lawrence Wang-chi. "Entrance Into the Family of Nations: Translation and the First Diplomatic Missions to the West, 1860s–1870s." In *Translation and Modernization in East Asia in the Late Nineteenth and Early Twentieth Centuries*, ed. Lawrence Wang-chi Wong, 165–217. Hong Kong: Chinese University of Hong Kong Press, 2018.

Wu Chunming. "Liang Qichao 'Zhongguo hun' jianlun" (A Brief Study of Liang Qichao's "Chinese Soul"). *Huanan shifan daxue xuebao shehui kexue ban* (Journal of South China Normal University: Social Sciences Edition) 1 (2007): 99–103.

Wu Micha et al., eds. *Diguo li de "difang wenhua": Huangminhua shiqi Taiwan wenhua zhuangkuang* ("Local Cultures" in the Empire: The Situations of Taiwanese

Culture in the Era of Japanization). Taipei: Bozhongzhe chuban youxian gongsi, 2008.

Xia Xiaohong. *"Hewen handu fa"* (How to Read Japanese Writing in Chinese). *Shinmatsu shōsetu kara* (From Late Qing Fiction) 53 (April 1999): 9–16.

———. *Jueshi yu chuanshi: Liang Qichao de wenxue daolu* (The Realization and Transmission of the Epoch: Liang Qichao's Literary Path). Beijing: Zhonghua shuju, 2006.

———. "Wan Qing baihuawen yundong de guanfang ziyuan" (The Official Resources of the Late Qing Vernacularization Movement). *Beijing shehui kexue* (Journal of the Beijing Academy of Social Sciences) 2 (2010): 4–17.

———. "Wusi baihua wenxue de lishi yuanyuan" (The Historical Sources of May-Fourth Vernacular Literature). *Zhongguo xiandai wenxue yanjiu congkan* (Journal of the Studies of Modern Chinese Literature) 3 (1985): 22–41.

Xie Chaokun. "Lu Xun zai Weimanzhouguo de chuanbo, jieshou yu yingxiang" (The Dissemination, Reception, and Influence of Lu Xun's Works in the Puppet State of Manchukuo). *Mingzuo xinshang* (Journal of Appreciating Great Works) 26 (2016): 8–12.

Xie, Miya Qiong. "'Borderland Translation': Manchuria and the Multilingual Translations of the Korean Short Story 'The Red Hill.'" *Journal of World Literature* 4, no. 4 (2019): 552–80.

———. *Territorializing Manchuria: The Transnational Frontier and Literatures of East Asia*. Cambridge, MA: Harvard University Asia Center, 2023.

Xu Jilin (Kyo Kirin). *Fuhenteki kachi wo motomeru: Chūgoku gendai shisō no shin chōryū* (Toward Universal Values: New Tendencies in Contemporary Chinese Thought). Trans. and ed. Nakajima Takahiro and Ō Zen (Wang Qian). Tokyo: Hōsei daigaku shuppankyoku, 2020.

———. "Xin tianxia zhuyi yu Zhongguo de neiwai zhixu" (The New Discourse of All-Under-Heaven and China's Domestic and International Orders). *Zhishifenzi luncong* (Journal of Intellectuals) 1 (2015): 3–35.

Yamada Shunji. "Seiji shōsetsu no ichi" (The Position of the Political Novel). In *Seiji shōsetsu shu 1* (A Collection of Historical Novels, Volume 1), ed. Yamada Shunji and Rinbara Sumio. Vol. 16 of *Shin Nihon koten bungaku taikei: Meiji hen* (The New Compendium of Classical Japanese Literature: The Works of the Meiji Era), 539–56. Tokyo: Iwanami shoten, 2003.

Yamamoto Masahide. *Kindai buntai hassei no shiteki kenkyū* (A Historical Study of the Emergence of the Modern Prose Style). Tokyo: Iwanami shoten, 1965.

Yamamuro Shin'ichi. *Kimera: Manshūkoku no shōzō* (Chimera: A Portrait of Manchukuo). Tokyo: Chūōkōron shinsha, 2004.

Yamane Hiroko. "Mori Ōgai seinenki no kanshibun juyō: Ōgai bunko chōsa wo meguri 1, 2" (Mori Ōgai's Reception of Chinese Verse and Prose in His Youth: A

Survey of the Ōgai Archives). *Kindai bungaku chūshaku to hihyō* (Modern Literature: Commentary and Criticism) 1 (1994): 2–14, and 2 (1995): 1–18.

Yamazaki Kuninori. *Hyōden Mori Ōgai* (Mori Ōgai: A Critical Biography). Tokyo: Taishūkan shoten, 2007.

Yan Fu. *Yan Fu ji* (Selected Works of Yan Fu). Beijing: Zhonghua shuju, 1986.

Yanagida Izumi. *Seiji shōsetsu kenkyū* (A Study of the Political Novel). Tokyo: Shunjyū sha, 1967.

Yang Sŏl. "Kim T'aekyŏng ŭi Chungguk mangmyŏnggi kyoyusi yŏngu: Chang Kŏn kwa ŭi kyoyurŭl chungsimŭro" (A Study of Exchanged Poems by Kim T'aekyŏng in Exile in China: With a Focus on the Exchanges with Zhang Jian). MA thesis, Seoul National University, 2017.

Yasuda Toshiaki. *Kanji haishi no shisōshi* (An Intellectual History of the Abolition of Chinese Characters). Tokyo: Heibonsha, 2016.

———. *Teikoku Nihon no gengo hensei* (The Organization of Languages in Imperial Japan). Tokyo: Seori shobō, 1997.

Yeh, Catherine Vance. *The Chinese Political Novel: Migration of a World Genre*. Leiden: Brill, 2015.

Yi Chaesŏn. *Han'guk kaehwagi sosŏl yŏngu* (A Study of Korean Fiction in the Era of Modernization). Seoul: Ilchogak, 1972.

———. "Han'guk hyŏndae sosŏl ŭi ryaksa (An Abbreviated History of Modern Korean Fiction)." In *Han'guk kŭndae sosŏl chakp'umron* (Studies of the Works of Modern Korean Fiction), ed. Cho Ton'gil and Yi Chaesŏn, 10–45. Seoul: Munjang, 1987.

Yi Hansŏp. "Sŏyu kyŏnmun e padadŭlyŏjin Ilbon ŭi hanjaŏ e taehayŏ" (A Study of Japanese Words in Chinese Characters Introduced Into *Observations from a Journey to the West*). *Ilbonhak* (Journal of Japanese Studies) 6 (1987): 85–107.

Yi Horyong. *Sin Ch'aeho tasi ilki: Minjokchuŭija esŏ anak'isŭt'ŭ ro* (Revisiting Sin Ch'aeho: From Nationalist to Anarchist). Kyŏnggi-do P'aju-si: Tolbegae, 2013.

Yi Kimun. *Kaehwagi ŭi kungmun yŏngu* (A Study of Hangul Writing in the Era of Modernization). Seoul: Ilchogak, 1970.

Yi Kwanglin. *Han'guk kaehwasa yŏngu* (A Study of the History of Korean Modernization). Seoul: Ilchogak, 1977.

———. "Yu Kilchun ŭi kaehwa sasang: *Sŏyu kyŏnmun* ŭl chungsimŭro" (Yu Kilchun's Thought of Modernization: With a Focus on *Observations from a Journey to the West*). *Yŏksa hakpo* (Journal of Historical Studies) 75–76 (December 1977): 199–250.

Yi Kwangsu. "Ai ka" (Perhaps Love?). *Shirogane gakuhō* (Shirogane Alumni Journal) 19 (December, 1909): 35–41, reprint in *"Gaichi" no Nihongo bungakusen 3: Chōsen* (A Selection of Japanese-Language Literary Works from "Outer Territories" 3: Korea), ed. Kurokawa Sō, 21–26. Tokyo: Shinjuku shobō, 1996.

———. *Yi Kwangsu chŏnjip* (The Complete Works of Yi Kwangsu). Seoul: Samjungdang, 1962–64.

Yi Manyŏl. *Tanjae Sin Ch'aeho ŭi yŏksahak yŏngu* (A Study of Tanjae Sin Ch'aeho's Historical Research). Seoul: Munhak kwa chisŏngsa, 1990.

Yŏp Kŏn'gon. *Yang Kyech'o wa kuhan mal munhak* (Liang Qichao and Literature in the Late Chosŏn Period). Seoul: Pŏpchŏn ch'ulp'ansa, 1980.

Yu Chaeyŏp. *Han'guk kŭndae yŏksa sosŏl yŏngu* (A Study of Modern Korean Historical Fiction). Seoul: Kukhak charyowon, 2002.

Yu Kilchun. *Yu Kilchun chŏnsŏ* (The Complete Works of Yu Kilchun). Seoul: Ilchogak, 1971.

Yun Ch'iho. *Yun Ch'iho ilki* (The Diary of Yun Ch'iho). Seoul: Kuksa p'yŏnch'an wiwŏnhoe; pŏn'gak panp'och'ŏ T'amgudang, 1973–89.

Yun Taesŏk. "1940 nyŏndae Han'guk munhak esŏŭi pŏnyŏk" (Translation in Korean Literature in the 1940s). *Minjok munhaksa yŏngu* (Journal of National Literary History) 33 (2007): 312–36.

Yun Yŏt'ak et al., eds. *Kugŏ kyoyuk 100 nyŏn sa* (The Hundred-Year History of National Language Education). Seoul: Sŏul taehakkyo ch'ulp'anbu, 2006.

Zhang Juxiang and Zhang Tierong, eds. *Zhou Zuoren nianpu* (The Chronology of Zhou Zuoren). Tianjin: Nankai daxue chubanshe, 1985.

Zhang Kunjiang. *Dechuan Riben 'zhong' 'xiao' gainian de xingcheng yu fazhan: Yi bingxue yu Yangming xue wei zhongxin* (The Emergence and Development of the Concepts of "Loyalty" and "Filial Piety" in Edo Japan: With a Focus on Military Science and Yangming Learning). Taipei: Ximalaya yanjiu fazhan jijinhui, 2003.

Zhang Quan. *Lunxian shiqi Beijing wenxue banian* (Beijing Literature in the Eight-Year Occupation). Beijing: Zhongguo heping chubanshe, 1994.

Zhang Shuangdi. *Huainanzi jiaoshi* (The Masters of Huainan with Textual Critique and Interpretation). Beijing: Beijing daxue chubanshe, 2013.

Zhang Taiyan. "Lun hanzi tongyi hui zhi huanglou" (On the Absurdity of the Society for Unifying the Chinese Characters). *Minbao* (People's News) 17 (1907): 5–10.

———. "Zhuzixue lüeshuo" (Brief Words on Neo-Confucianism). *Guocui xuebao* (The Scholarly Journal of National Essence), year 2, vol. 4.

Zhang Xudong. "A Radical Hermeneutics of Chinese Literary Tradition: On Zhou Zuoren's *Zhongguo xinwenxue de yuanliu*." In *Classics and Interpretations: The Hermeneutic Traditions in Chinese Culture*, ed. Ching-I Tu, 427–55. New Brunswick, NJ: Transaction Publishers, 2000.

———. "Zhongguo xiandai zhuyi qiyuan de 'ming' 'yan' zhi bian: Chongdu *A Q zhengzhuan*" (The Distinction Between "Name" and "Language" at the Origin of Chinese Modernism: Rereading *The Real Story of Ah Q*). *Lu Xun yanjiu yuekan* (Lu Xun Studies Monthly) 1 (2009): 4–20.

Zhao Tingyang. *Tianxia tixi: Shijie zhidu zhexue daolun* (The System of All Under Heaven: Introduction to the World Philosophy of Institutions). Nanjing: Jiangsu jiaoyu chubanshe, 2005.

Zhou Zuoren. *Zhitang huixianglu* (The Memoir of Zhitang). Shijiazhuang: Hebei jiaoyu chubanshe, 2002.

———. *Zhou Zuoren ji wai wen* (The Uncollected Writings of Zhou Zuoren). Ed. Chen Zishan and Zhang Tierong. Haikou: Hainan guoji xinwen chuban zhongxin, 1995.

———. *Zhou Zuoren sanwen quanji* (The Complete Prose of Zhou Zuoren). Guilin shi: Guangxi shifan daxue chubanshe, 2009.

———. *Zhou Zuoren wenlei bian* (The Writings of Zhou Zuoren Collected by Topics). Changsha: Hunan wenyi chubanshe, 1998.

Zhu Qianzhi, ed. *Laozi jiaoshi* (Laozi: The Critical and Annotated Edition). Scripta Sinica: Hanji dianzi wenxian ziliaoku (digital database).

Zhu Xi, ed. *Mengzi jizhu* (The Mencius: The Text with Compiled Annotations). Scripta Sinica: Hanji dianzi wenxian ziliaoku (digital database).

———. *Zhongyong zhangju* (The Doctrine of the Mean with Phrase-by-Phrase Annotation). Scripta Sinica: Hanji dianzi wenxian ziliaoku (digital database).

Index

A Ying, 27
"Abe Family, The" ("Abe ichizoku"). See Mori Ōgai
"Admonition for the Authors of Recent Fiction in the National Script" ("Kŭn'gŭm kungmun sosŏl chŏja ŭi chuŭi"). See Sin Ch'aeho
Adorno, Theodor, 10, 128
aesthetic/aesthetics: and Asia, 229–31; classical, 40, 42, 44, 47, 66, 67, 138; and education, 38, 61–68; judgment, 8, 9, 10, 64, 81, 165–66; and modern literature, 2, 8–9, 10, 68, 216, 284–85; and Mori Ōgai, 109–10, 165; and new fiction, 40, 62–64; and political ideas, 65, 235; state, 63–64; sublimation, 270; and translation, 65; and virtue, 59, 60, 61, 66, 67; and Zhou Zuoren, 215, 216, 222. See also Hegel, G. W. F.: Aesthetics; sublime, the
Aesthetics. See Hegel, G. W. F.
affect/affective, 94, 134, 145–48, 150, 153–54, 155–58, 160, 233, 275;

alienation, 147; chŏng as, 147; cross-cultural encounter, 157; education (chŏngyuk), 62, 74, 147–48; function of literature, 17, 37–38, 40, 44, 49, 63, 66, 73–76, 149–50; self-transformation, 158
"After Death" ("Si hou"). See Lu Xun
afterlife, 91; of cultural pasts, 5, 8, 10, 11, 18, 20, 25, 35, 71, 93, 98, 118, 153, 181–82, 217, 236, 243, 284; and literature, 10, 196, 243, 283; suffering in, 126–27, 130
Agamben, Giorgio, 323n146
agency, 54, 151, 153, 196, 235, 270
Aizu (Japanese feudal domain), 41, 49, 52; War of (1868), 41, 52
all under heaven, 86, 103, 330n23; new discourse of, 344n2. See also heaven
allegory, 96–97, 118, 135, 229; and colonial literature, 240–41; of literature, 4, 19, 21, 45, 61, 94, 110, 143, 162, 195, 251, 277, 282, 287; national, 82, 119, 243, 281; political, 90, 135,

allegory (*continued*)
  240, 250; and reading, 241, 246, 248, 262, 266, 277; transnational, 20, 240, 241–44, 282; and Walter Benjamin, 242–43
Amari Shirosaburō, 178–79
"Amateur Talk on Literature" ("Menwai wentan"). *See* Lu Xun
America/United States (U.S.), 50, 58, 70, 79, 151; areas studies in, 15–16; demanding trade in East Asia, 25–27, 29, 33; East Asian envoys to, 25–26; literature of, 27, 113; missionaries from, 31, 297n7, 314n44; racism in, 52; Revolution in, 46–48, 53; scholars from, 105, 109; study in, 25, 32, 41, 44, 148, 157–58, 254, 256
An Ch'angho, 34, 325n46
An Chunggŭn, 329n8
An Zishun, 307n21
anachronism, 82, 289; emotional, 76; and engagement with classical culture, 2, 35, 64, 71, 76, 115, 129–30, 131; of modern literature, 2, 4, 5, 7, 8, 115, 131, 220, 221, 286; and modernization, 7, 71, 110, 176, 178; necessary, 163–64, 165, 174; of political fiction, 17, 30, 61, 64; unnecessary, 188
Analects, the, 43, 108, 200, 227
anarchism/anarchist, 95–97, 273, 276
Anarchist Association of Asia, 95
ancestral worship, 127, 180–81
Anderson, Marston, 115, 125, 127
Andreyev, Leonid, 116
Anp'yŏng, Grand Prince, 167, 171–72
anthologies, 224; classical, 43, 132, 138; of colonial literature, 238, 239, 241, 337n3, 338n10; transcolonial, 240–41, 243–44; of vernacular

Japanese fiction in Chinese, 299n32; of vernacular writings in China, 103
"Appreciation of *Ukiyoe*" ("Ukiyoe no kanshō"). *See* Nagai Kafū
archaeology, 89, 225–26, 227, 233, 235, 236
Arendt, Hannah, 305n63
Armistice of Villafranca, 79
Art and Literature (*Geibun*), 247
"Art Flamand." *See* Verhaeren, Émile
"As If" ("Kano yōni"). *See* Mori Ōgai
Ashikaga shogunate (Japan), 31
Asia: and modern literature, 229–33, 235–36; Orientalist notion of, 13–14, 234–35. *See also* East Asia
Asia-Pacific War (1941–1945), 197, 210
assimilation: cultural, 202, 203, 205, 207, 260; linguistic, 238, 239; and national language, 107. *See also* Japanization
Auerbach, Erich, 15
Autumn in the Han Palace (*Han gong qiu*). *See* Ma Zhiyuan
award, literary. *See* prize, literary

Bai Juyi, 159; "Song of Everlasting Sorrow" ("Chang hen ge"), 57
Bakhtin, Mikhail, 45
"Bamboo Grove" ("Zhulin"). *See* Gu Ding
Ban Gu: "Poetic Exposition on the Western Capital" ("Xidu fu"), 225
Bao Shuya, 172
Beautiful Story of Statesmanship, The (*Keikoku bidan*; trans. as *Jingguo meitan*). *See* Yano Ryūkei
Bellamy, Edward: *Looking Backward: 2000–1887*, 306n66
Benjamin, Walter, 129, 187, 237, 242–43, 327n81
Bergson, Henri, 151, 322n128
Bhabha, Homi, 328n3
Bildungsroman, 144

bilingualism, colonial, 146, 267, 271, 280–81; critique of, 271, 281
biographies, 183, 185, 324, 329; of heroes, 17, 65, 71, 76, 81, 260, 264, 309n24. *See also zhuan/den/chŏn*
Biographies of Exemplary Women (Yŏllyŏchŏn), 156
Biographies of the Three Heroes of Italian Nation-Building, The (*Yidali jianguo sanjie zhuan*; Liang Qichao), 71, 75–81, 94; and classical letters, 76–77; and hero biographies, 76, 81; Japanese sources of, 76; Korean translation of, 75, 76–81, 307n18
Biographies of the Three Heroes of Italian Nation-Building, The (*Yit'aeri kŏn'guk samgŏl chŏn*; trans. Sin Ch'aeho), 75, 76–81; and Chinese original, 75, 76–81, 307n18; and classical letters, 76–77; and hero biographies, 81
Biography of Six Ministers (*Yuksin chŏn*). See Nam Hyoon
Bismarck, Otto von, 82, 309n24
Black Eyes and Brown Eyes (*Kuroi me to chairo no me*). See Tokutomi Roka
Book of Ceremonies and Rites (*Yili*), 199
Book of Documents (*Shangshu*), 55, 190
Book of Poems (*Shijing*), 43
Book of Rites (*Liji*), 95, 213, 306n69
Börne, Ludwig, 136
Bourdieu, Pierre, 11, 294n35
Branch in the Laurel Grove, A (*Keirin isshi*), 138
Brightness (*Mingming*), 253
Britain, 26, 70, 76–77, 110, 151; imperialism of, 42, 46, 52; and Irish literature, 267; literature of, 267; and political fiction, 38. *See also particular authors and works*

"Broken Mountain" ("Bu zhou shan"). *See* "Mending Heaven"
Brooks, Peter, 169
Buddhism/Buddhist, 29, 58, 114, 130, 146
Bungeika kyōkai (writers' association; Manchukuo), 239
Bunwakai (writers' association; Manchukuo), 239
Butler, Judith, 343n110
Byron, George Gordon, Lord, 3, 66, 264

Call to Arms (*Nahan*). *See* Lu Xun
Cao Zhi, 55, 57; "Miscellaneous Poems" ("Za shi"), 54
"Caricature of Madame Zhao" ("Chō fujin no giga"). *See* Long Yingzong
Carlyle, Thomas: *On Heroes, Hero-Worship, and the Heroic in History*, 76
Cassirer, Ernst, 293n22
Cavell, Stanley, 10
Cavour, Count Camillo di, 75, 78, 79, 80
censorship: in Japan, 38, 52, 180; in Korea, 238, 271–72; in Manchukuo, 239, 241, 244, 248; in Taiwan, 238, 260
Chance Meetings with Beautiful Women (*Kajin no kigū*; Shiba Shirō; trans. as *Jiaren qiyu* by Liang Qichao et al.), 23–24, 37–68, 71, 303n17, 304n23; and aesthetic education, 61–65; ambivalent status of, 44–45; Chinese translation of, 23, 30, 39, 44, 45–61, 301n1; and classical letters, 42–61; and Freedom and People's Rights Movements, 38–39; and Kim Okkyun, 32; and Liang Qichao, 23–24, 63–64, 65–68; and new fiction, 39–41; Vietnamese translation of, 302n5
Chang Chiyŏn, 34, 75

Chang Hyŏkchu, 337n3; "Hell of Starving" ("Gakidō"), 245
Chen Duxiu: "On Literary Revolution" ("Wenxue geming lun"), 216
Chen Peifeng, 202, 330n21
Chen Pingyuan, 189
Cheng, Eileen, 117
Cheng, King (Zhou), 172
China: Japanese imperialism in, 209–13; Korean exiles in, 34, 88–89, 95, 244, 274, 301n49; language reforms in, 102–5; modernized relationship with Japan of, 27–30; modernized relationship with Korea of, 31–32, 33–34; opening to the West of, 25. *See also* Chinese language; Chinese literature; *particular dynasties*
China Discussion (*Qing yi bao*; ed. Liang Qichao), 23–24, 37, 39; cancellation of *Chance Meetings with Beautiful Women* by, 60–61, 65, 305n46; distribution in Korea of, 33; translation of *Chance Meetings with Beautiful Women* in, 37, 44, 46–57, 66, 301n1
Chinese language: in colonial Taiwan, 199, 200–201; creole writing of, in Taiwan, 202, 330n21; dialects of, 104–5, 194; as diplomatic language, 28; imperial suppression of, 202–3, 238, 330n21; and loanword translation, 47, 101, 109; in Manchukuo, 239, 252–53; Mandarin (*guanhua*), 104, 199, 201; of the masses (*dazhongyu*), 113–14; May Fourth-style vernacular, 114, 195, 202, 253; mediating transregional encounters, 27–34; national (*guoyu*), 104, 194, 217; *putonghua/putongyu* (common speech), 104; reforms of, 102–5; use by Japanese imperialism of, 199–202; vernacularization of, 103–4, 195, 252–53. *See also* Chinese script
Chinese literature: as conceptualized by Chen Duxiu, 216; as conceptualized by Hu Shi, 216, 218; as conceptualized by Zhou Zuoren, 215–16, 217–23; Japanese imperial intervention in, 209–10; modern discourse on, 5–7, 107–8, 108–9. *See also particular authors and works*
Chinese script: as aid in loanword translation, 47, 101, 106, 109, 312n8; brush talk in, 28, 201; criticism of, 12–13, 102, 104–5, 105–6, 109, 114, 281–82; and dialects, 104–5; *hanyu pinyin*, 105; as imperial medium, 106, 201–2, 281, 329n12; in Japanese, 42–43, 105–6; in Korean, 12–13, 90, 100–102; as material condition of Chinese literature, 215–17, 219–20, 221–23, 235–36; mythological origin of, 187; reforms of, 104–5, 109, 313n26; regional circulation of, 11, 29, 70, 201–2, 204, 295n41; transcription of, 47, 85, 143; *zhuyin zimu*, 105, 222, 253.
Chinhŭng daeche (Silla), 90
Ch'oe Chaesŏ, as Ishii Kōzō, 337n3
Ch'oe Sŏkha: "The Korean Soul" ("Chosŏn hon"), 69–70
Ch'oe Yŏng/Ch'oe Tot'ong, 81, 310n42
Chosŏn dynasty (Korea), 26, 31–33, 72, 100, 148, 167–75
Christianity, 58, 183. *See also* missionaries

Chu Sigyŏng, 34, 102, 307n14
Chu Yosŏp, 324n12
civil service examinations (China), 119, 199, 216, 217, 258
civilization, concept of: in Chinese modernization, 24–25, 28, 186, 206, 226–27, 232; eclectic engagement in Japanese imperialism with, 198, 206–7; in Japanese modernization, 13–14, 29–30, 106–7, 198, 201, 206, 224, 231, 235, 299n39, 336n96; in Korean modernization, 12, 31–32, 102, 152, 159, 174, 299n39, 300n48; and language reforms, 102, 106–7; in Manchukuo, 205; and modernity, 5, 14, 20, 24, 25–27, 35, 47–48, 118, 198, 205–6, 223, 236, 286–87; in premodern East Asia, 24, 28, 29–30; and Walter Benjamin, 187
Cixi, Empress Dowager (China), 23
class, 96–97, 99, 114, 127, 129, 141, 230, 252, 258, 263, 312n2
Classic in Three Characters (*San zi jing*), 329n10
Classic of Filial Piety (*Xiaojing*), 200, 206
"Clothing, Food, and Housing in Japan" ("Riben de yi shi zhu"). *See* Zhou Zuoren
Cold War, 15, 285–86
Collection of Korean Short Stories (*Chaoxian duanpian xiaoshuo xuan*). *See* Wang He
Collection of Short Stories from Beyond Borders (*Yuwai xiaoshuo ji*; trans. and eds. Lu Xun and Zhou Zuoren), 224
colonial literature, 238, 240, 257, 265, 269, 270, 282; allegorical working of, 240–41; and *Chance Meetings with Beautiful Women*, 303n17; and ellipsis, 249, 250–51, 256–57. *See also* transcoloniality
colonial mimicry, 258, 328n3. *See also* imperial mimicry
Composition (*Munjang*), 271
Comprehensive Meaning of Customs and Mores (*Fengsu tongyi*), 187
Confucianism: abused by power, 250–51; archi- (*yuanshi rujia*), 213–15; Changzhou school of, 4; classics of, 4, 30, 34, 45, 190, 199; doctrine of, 121, 210; education in, 13, 72, 106, 156, 183, 200; great community (*datong*) in, 95, 206, 306n69; in the Han, 4; in historical fiction, 193; *li* as art of life in, 227; Neo-, 34, 226; orthodoxy of (*lijiao*), 119, 227; and Sinocentrism, 82; as symbol of cultural past, 13–14, 44, 106–7, 116, 118, 119, 152, 220–21, 226, 227, 234; used by Japanese imperialism, 199–200, 200–1, 202, 203–5, 205–7, 223; used to criticize Japanese imperialism, 205; virtues of, 13, 55, 62, 116, 118, 147, 152, 174, 204
Confucius, 30, 58, 65, 108, 192–93, 206, 215
Congress of the Writers of the Greater East Asia (daitōa bungakusha taikai), 209–11, 257
contact space, 17, 35
correspondence, 244–48, 271, 282
"Count Q" ("Kyū hakushaku"; Kim Saryang), 246, 271–72, 277–82; and Korean original, 246, 271–72, 277–81. *See also* "Man Whom I Met in a Detention Cell, A"

Cromwell, Oliver, 309n24
cultural capital: of classical letters, 30, 33, 44, 100, 146, 198, 201, 223; imperially sanctioned, 240, 267; of modern intellectuals, 159; of ruling class, 99, 201; transfer of, 107, 201; of the West, 137
cultural past: afterlives of, 5, 8, 10, 11, 18, 20, 25, 35, 71, 93, 98, 118, 153, 181–82, 217, 236, 243, 284; ghosts of, 118, 120, 122, 317n28; historicization of, 6–7, 93, 94; and melancholy, 236–37; modern engagement with, 6–7, 8, 11, 14–15, 18, 45, 97, 110, 111, 117–18, 122, 125, 129, 130, 159, 160, 162, 195, 212, 237, 242, 282, 284–85, 288–89; parody of, 117–18, 124, 126, 129, 1–30, 242; as philosophical resources, 287–89; reactionary revival of, 62, 207, 223; severance from, 5, 6–7, 11, 12–14, 14–15, 19, 71, 111, 143, 198, 207; transregional, 7, 11, 112, 236, 284. *See also* historical fiction
Curtius, Ernst Robert, 15

Daily News (*Maeil sinbo*), 145
"Dancing Girl, The" ("Maihime"). *See* Mori Ōgai
Daodejing, 192–94, 328n104
Daoism/Daoist, 58, 189–93, 249, 255
Daruvala, Susan, 212
De Man, Paul, 7, 63
Deleuze, Gilles, 112
democracy, 47, 77, 285
Denmark, literature of, 131
Derrida, Jacques, 4, 121, 303n12
"Devotee" ("Hŏnsinja"). *See* Yi Kwangsu
dialectic/dialectical, 10, 112, 117, 126, 128, 148, 163, 229–31

dialects, 194, 199; and language reforms, 104–5, 107
dialogic, 20, 244, 246, 248
"Diary of a Madman" ("Kuangren riji"). *See* Lu Xun
Die Philosophie des Als Ob. *See* Vaihinger, Hans
diegesis, 44, 114, 268, 269
diplomacy, 52, 87; and Japanese imperialism, 34, 70, 72, 95; modernization of, 25–27, 28–30, 31, 32, 33, 100, 183; Sinocentric, 82; traditional, 31, 179
Discourse of Change (*Yi yan*). *See* Zheng Guanying
"Discourse on the New People" ("Xin min shuo"). *See* Liang Qichao
Doctrine of the Mean (*Zhongyong*), 200
Don Quixote (Miguel de Cervantes), 112
Dong Bingyue, 210
Dongmyŏng sŏngjo, 90
"Dream Heaven" ("Kkum hanŭl"; Sin Ch'aeho), 71, 89–94; and *mongyurok*, 90–91; and *Ŭlji mundŏk*, 89, 90
Dream in the Jade Chamber (*Ongnumong*), 150
Dream of the Red Chamber (*Honglou meng*), 40, 189–90; and *Old Stories Retold*, 189–90
Du Guangting: "Story of the Guest with Curly Whiskers" ("Qiuranke zhuan"), 135
Duara, Prasenjit, 205
Dutch painting, 228–30

Eagleton, Terry, 8, 63, 322n144
East Asia: in area studies, 15–16; classical letters in, 7, 11, 12, 15, 35, 44, 57, 71, 76, 99, 105, 150, 198, 212,

223, 286; imperial literary field in, 240, 241, 244, 245, 257, 259, 266, 280, 281; Japanese imperialism in, 197–207; as method, 11–16, 284–87; modernization of, 25–27, 99–107; transregional cultural contacts in, 7, 11, 12, 14, 17, 27–34, 35, 39, 53, 61, 75, 76, 77, 112, 198, 227, 233, 237, 282. *See also* Asia; Greater East Asia; *particular languages, literatures, authors, and works*
East Asia Daily (*Tong'a ilbo*), 167
Eastern Miscellany (*Dongfang zazhi*), 126
Edo period, 25–26, 30, 51–52, 132, 175, 182, 232; *ukiyoe* in, 228–30, 231–32; and Zhou Zuoren, 231–32
education: aesthetic, 38, 61–68; affective, 62, 74, 147–48; in colonial Korea, 89, 202–3, 204; in colonial Taiwan, 200–201, 203–4; and colonialism, 145–47, 148, 149, 159, 254, 258, 259, 265, 272, 276; in Japan, 106, 203–5; and language reform, 102, 104, 105–6; in Manchukuo, 206; and modernization, 13, 25–27, 72–73; and narrative, 126, 265, 267; popular, 136–37; traditional, 13, 72, 201
Egypt, 60
eight-legged essay (*ba gu wen*), 216–17, 219–20, 227, 334n45
Elegant Collection from the Emerald Clouds (*Suiun gashū*), 200
Eliot, T. S., 11
ellipsis, 214; and colonial literature, 249, 250–51, 256–57; and politics, 250–51
Ellis, Havelock, 226
Emperor Meiji, 176, 178

Engels, Friedrich, 259
enlightenment, 126, 128–30, 144, 151, 155, 318n48; dialectic of, 128–29
epic, 66, 67
Eulsa Treaty (1905), 72, 75
Eurocentrism, 19, 197, 233. *See also* West, the
Europe, 7, 25–26, 32, 43, 58, 60, 62, 65–66, 76, 80, 103, 133, 136–37, 180, 181, 230, 235; empires of, 198; languages of, 14; literature of, 27, 113, 131, 168, 224; missionaries from, 31; Orientalism in, 14; thought of, 62, 110, 164. *See also* West, the; *particular countries*
Europeanization, 215–16. *See also* Westernization
"Evening Moon" ("Yoizuki"). *See* Long Yingzong
evolution, 34, 116, 165, 195, 218
example/exemplar, 305n63; of literature, 3, 7, 10, 16, 68, 285; of morality, 44, 55, 56, 57, 58, 156, 172, 174, 213, 214, 233–35; of political ideas, 64–65, 67, 77, 79–80, 81, 214, 233–35
excess, 78, 164, 166, 169, 187; melodramatic, 174
exile: of Kang Youwei, 43; of Kim Okkyun, 32; of Kim T'aekyŏng, 34, 301n49; of Koreans in China, 34, 88, 244, 274; of Liang Qichao, 21, 23–24, 33, 37, 65, 80–81; of Sin Ch'aeho, 88–89, 95; stories of, 41, 49, 51, 52, 136, 168, 192–93, 211

Fan Zeng, 57
Fanon, Frantz, 42, 303n17; "On National Culture," 212
Faust. *See* Goethe, Johann Wolfgang von

Index 389

Feng Menglong: *Stories of Love* (*Qingshi*; ed. by), 132, 134–35
Fenollosa, Ernest, 109
Feuerwerker, Yi-tsu Mei, 115
filial piety, 147, 151, 204, 206, 250
First Sino-Japanese War (1894–1895), 24, 31
Fogel, Joshua, 24
folk culture, 114, 130, 255–56, 316n8
folklore, 130
Forum for Building the Culture of Renewed China (kōsei Chūgoku bunka kensetsu zadankai), 211
Foucault, Michel, 9
Four Books, 206
France, 42, 70, 77–79, 135, 225, 286, 302n5; literature of, 131, 132; Revolution in, 163; Shanghai concession of, 89. *See also particular authors and works*
Franz Joseph I, Emperor (Austria), 79
Freedom and People's Rights Movements (Japan), 38
Freud, Sigmund, 144
Frye, Northrop, 8–9, 10
Fukuzawa Yukichi, 13–14, 32, 106–7; "On Leaving Asia Behind" ("Datsu a ron"), 13–14; and Yu Kilchun, 32, 299n39
Future of New China, The (*Xin Zhongguo weilai ji*; Liang Qichao), 38, 65–68, 95, 306n69; ambivalent status of, 67–68; and *Chance Meetings with Beautiful Women*, 66–67
Fuxi, 187

Gao Shi, 150
Gao Yuandong, 186
Gapsin coup (1884), 32
Garibaldi, Giuseppe, 75, 78, 80
gender, 44, 127, 141, 270
Germany, 26, 77, 225, 234; literature of, 131, 132, 136, 145, 146, 163, 245; and Mori Ōgai, 109–10, 113, 132, 142–43; in "The Dancing Girl," 130–36, 179. *See also* Young Germany; *particular authors and works*
ghosts, figure of, 34, 157; and classical letters, 195, 219–20; of cultural past, 118, 120, 122, 317n28; in folk play, 255–56. *See also* haunting
Goethe, Johann Wolfgang von, 163; *Faust*, 131, 145
Gogol, Nikolai, 116, 247
Gongyang school, 4, 21, 292n12, 344n2
Gorchakov, Alexander, 309n24
Gorky, Maxim, 259
Gramsci, Antonio, 311n2
"Grand Battles Between Two Dragons" ("Yong kwa yong ŭi daegyŏkchŏn"). *See* Sin Ch'aeho
Great Learning (*Daxue*), 200, 331n23
Greater East Asia (Japanese imperialism): Congress of the Writers of, 209–10, 211, 257; Co-Prosperity Sphere of, 239–40; literature of, 210, 257, 338
Greece, 96; and Byron, 3, 66; literature of, 114, 131, 168, 209, 211, 225; and Rome compared to China and Japan, 224–25; and Zhou Zuoren, 209, 211, 224–27
Grimm brothers, 142
Gu Ding (Xu Changji): "Bamboo Grove" ("Zhulin"), 249–51; as colonial writer, 247–48, 253–54; conversation with Hayashi Fusao of, 247–48; introduction of Lu Xun to Manchukuo by, 251–53; "Introduction to Lu Xun's Books"

390 *Index*

("Lu Xun zhushu jieti"), 251; on literary language in Manchuria, 252–53; on literature in Manchukuo, 251–53; and Lu Xun, 249–51, 252–53, 255–56; as "Manchuria's Lu Xun," 247–48; *Strenuous Flight* (*Fenfei*), 253–54; "Wasteland" ("Yuanye"), 253–57; Yiwen Publishers by, 248
Gu Hongming, 226–27
Guan Zhong, 172
Guo Tingli, 27
Guo Xiang, 289–90

habitus, 11, 66, 146, 147, 175, 236
Han Myŏnghoe, 170
Han Xin, 57
Han Yu, 57
hangul. See Korean script
happiness, 19, 129, 130, 234, 235, 236, 262, 286, 287, 290
Hartmann, Eduard von, 110. See also *Philosophy of the Beautiful, The*
Hatano Setsuko, 322n128
haunting, 153–54, 180–81, 271, 276, 281; of cultural past, 4, 93, 120–21, 153, 195, 220; and function of documents, 182; and residues of modernization, 118, 154
Hayashi Fusao, 247–48, 249
He Ruzhang, 28
Heartless, The (*Mujŏng*). See Yi Kwangsu
heaven (*tian*; *ten*; *chŏn*): design of, 84; Festival of, 97; in fiction, 55, 57, 59, 78, 79, 87, 91, 93, 96–97, 168, 172, 187–91, 309n32; mandate of, 86, 135, 205; Nüwa's mending of, 187, 189–90; Way of, 55, 59. See also all under heaven
Heavenly Drum (*Ch'ŏn'go*). See Sin Ch'aeho

Hegel, G. W. F.: *Aesthetics*, 163–64, 228–31; discourse on Asia in, 336n97; philosophy of history in, 14, 235, 243
hegemon way (*badao*; *hadō*), 204, 206. See also kingly way
hegemony, cultural, 11, 65, 99, 107, 201–2, 285, 312n2
Heine, Heinrich, 136, 245
Helen of Troy, 58
"Hell of Starving" ("Gakidō"). See Chang Hyŏkchu
hermeneutics: and engagement with classical texts, 17, 83, 86, 88, 94; horizon of, 87; and indeterminability, 71
Herodotus, 58
Hirata Hisashi: *Three Heroes of Italian Nation-Building* (*Itarī kenkoku sanketsu*), 76–79
Hirayama Kenjirō, 30, 299n28
historical fiction/historical novel (*lishi xiaoshuo*; *rekishi shōsetsu*; *yŏksa sosŏl*), 162–96; ambivalent status of, 164–66, 323n2; anachronism in, 163–64, 165, 174, 188; and documents, 165–66, 167, 175–76, 182, 186–87, 191, 194, 327n81; as editing, 182, 185; excess in, 166, 168–73; formal experiments in, 162, 191, 194, 195–96; as generic allegory, 19, 110, 162, 195; and history, 175, 179–82, 186–87, 191, 194; and melodrama, 168–73; and modern literature, 174, 191, 195–96; as theorized by Lukács, 163–64, 174, 323n1. See also *particular works*
historiography: modern, 5–7, 14, 82–83, 122, 195, 295n51; and mythology, 179–82; national, 5–7, 14, 17, 72, 82–83, 88–89, 91, 92, 167, 179–82,

historiography (continued) 186; transregional, 14. See also cultural past; historical fiction; world history

History of Korea (*Chosŏn sa*). See Sin Ch'aeho

History of Korean Antiquity (*Chosŏn sanggo sa*). See Sin Ch'aeho

History of the Fall of Vietnam (*Yuenan wangguo shi*; Phan Bội Châu), 74; Korean response to, 74–75

History of the Jin (*Jin shu*), 249

History of the Sui (*Sui shu*), 84, 85

History of the Three Kingdoms (*Samguk sagi*; Kim Busik), 84, 85, 87, 90, 308n23, 310n53; account of Ŭlji mundŏk in, 84–85; Sin Ch'aeho's engagement with, 85–87, 90

History of Vernacular Literature (*Baihua wenxueshi*). See Hu Shi

Hohendahl, Peter Uwe, 136

homosexuality, 147

Honam Scholarly Journal (*Honam hakpo*), 70

Hong Kong, 219

Hong P'ilju, 70

Hong Yŏngsik, 300n44

Hong Yunsŏng, 170–71

Hongfu, story of, 132, 134–35; and Mori Ōgai, 132, 134–35, 319n63

honor suicide (*junshi*), 176–78

Horkheimer, Max, 128

Hosokawa Tadatoshi, 176–77

How to Read Japanese Writing in Chinese (*Hewen handu fa*), 43, 303n21

Hsia, C. T., 44, 316n16

Hu Feng: *Mountain Soul: A Collection of Korean and Taiwanese Short Stories* (*Shanling: Chaoxian Taiwan duanpian ji*; trans. and ed. by), 240–41, 243–44

Hu Menghua, 327n87

Hu Shi, 122; critiqued by Zhou Zuoren, 217–18; historicizing of vernacular literature by, 195, 218; *History of Vernacular Literature* (*Baihua wenxueshi*), 218; "Some Modest Proposals for the Reform of Literature" ("Wenxue gailiang chuyi"), 216

Huainanzi (*Masters of Huainan*), 187

Huan, Duke of Qi, 172

Huang Zunxian, 28, 33, 103, 226; *Poems on Miscellaneous Aspects of Japan* (*Riben zashi shi*), 226; *Strategies for Korea* (*Chaoxian celüe*), 33

humanism (*rendao zhuyi*), 213–14, 236

Hundred Days' Reform (1898), 4, 21, 23, 25, 43, 70, 103–4

"Hung Woman" ("Nüdiao"). See Lu Xun

Hutcheon, Linda, 111–12

Huters, Theodore, 115, 127

Huxley, Thomas, 34–35

Hwang Hodŏk, 100

Hwarang (Silla), 93–94

Hyŏn Ch'ae, 34, 307n14

Ibsen, Henrik, 168

ideology, 95, 205; of culture, 85, 92, 110, 118, 123, 124, 160, 180, 184, 244, 248–49, 250, 260, 261–62, 274–75, 276, 281, 283, 284; and Japanese imperialism, 175, 206, 239, 240, 244, 248–49, 260, 261–62, 274–75, 276, 281; and modernization, 92, 94, 160, 184, 205, 284; Sinocentric, 82–83, 85, 92

"Imitating the Poems of the Wei Crown Prince's Gathering at Ye" ("Ni Wei taizi Yezhong ji"). See Xie Lingyun

Imjin War (1592–1598), 81
Imperial Capital Gazette (*Hwangsŏng sinmun*), 33, 72, 74, 102
imperial mimicry, 19, 198, 200, 203, 205, 212; and colonial mimicry, 328n3
Imperial Rescript of Education (kyōiku chokugo), 203–5
imperialism: British, 26, 41, 42, 46, 52; French, 42, 286; and Meiji government, 42
imperialism, Japanese: in China, 209–13; and cultural past, 19, 198, 199, 212, 223; and imperial mimicry, 19, 198, 200, 203, 205, 212; in Korea, 72–73, 200, 202–5; literary field in, 240, 241, 244, 245, 257, 259, 266, 280, 281; in Manchukuo, 205–6; and modernization, 13–14, 19, 24, 197–207; in Taiwan, 198–202, 204; and universality, 206–7; and Western imperialism, 197–98, 207
impermanence, 127, 129–30
"Impermanence" ("Wuchang"). *See* Lu Xun
Independent, The (*Tongnip sinmun*), 101
India, 52, 76, 95, 96, 179, 214
Inoue Tetsujirō, 204
Institute for National Language Research (kungmun yŏnguso), 102
intertextuality, 53, 168; and Lu Xun's works, 20, 207, 241–42, 244, 247–48, 249, 256, 258, 261, 271, 276, 282–83; and monologism, 241; transcolonial, 244–48
Into the Light (book; *Hikari no nakani*). *See* Kim Saryang

"Into the Light" (short story; "Hikari no nakani"; Kim Saryang), 245–46, 267–71, 282; discussed in private letter, 245–46, 271, 282
"Introduction to Lu Xun's Books" ("Lu Xun zhushu jieti"). *See* Gu Ding
Ireland, 41, 42, 47, 52–54, 56, 57; literature of, 267
irony, 177, 191, 250, 270; and colonial literature, 251, 255, 256; of *Daodejing*, 192; of Japanese imperialism, 19, 201, 207; and modern literature, 2, 4, 113, 287; and modernization, 29–30, 128; and narrative structure, 115, 117, 123, 124; and parody, 112; in Schiller, 63
Isawa Shūji, 201, 203–4
Ishibashi Ningetsu, 131–32
Italy, 17, 71, 75–81, 94
Itō Hirobumi, 200, 329n8

Jameson, Fredric, 119, 243, 317n24
Japan: Chinese exiles in, 21, 23–24, 33, 37, 43, 65, 80–81; Korean exiles in, 32; language reforms in, 105–7; modernized relationship with China of, 27–30; modernized relationship with Korea of, 32–33; opening to the West of, 25–26. *See also* imperialism, Japanese; Japanese language; Japanese literature; *particular regimes*
Japanese Association for Literature in the Nation's Service (Nihon bungaku hōkoku kai), 210
Japanese language: accented, 271, 272–73, 277–82; adoption by colonial writers of, 146, 238, 240, 244–47, 257–58, 265, 266–67,

Japanese language (*continued*)
267–82; and bilingualism, 267, 271, 280–81; classical style writing (*kanbun kundoku tai*) of, 42–43, 203, 303n18, 304n22; as foreign language, 245; and imperialism, 200–203, 238–41, 329n9; as *kugŏ*, 278–79; in Manchukuo, 253; as *naichigo*, 279–80; national (*kokugo*), 106, 200; reforms of, 105–7; in transcolonial correspondence, 244–47; in transcolonial translations, 240–41; vernacularization of, 105–7. *See also* Japanese script

Japanese literature: and criticism of Mori Ōgai, 109–10; and criticism of Natsume Sōseki, 9, 109; as imperial literature, 240, 257–58, 266–67; modern discourse on, 5–7, 107–8, 109–10; transculturation of, 8, 197–98; Zhou Zuoren's translations of, 224–25. *See also particular authors and works*

Japanese script: and *hangul*, 279, 280–81; *hiragana*, 106; *kana*, 103, 200, 281–82; *katakana*, 271; reforms of, 105–6; in Taiwan, 200

Japanese soul (*yamato damashii*), 70

Japanization, 202–3, 206–7, 238–40

Japan-Korea Treaty (1904), 75

Japan-U.S. Treaty of Peace and Amity (1854), 25

Ji Kang, 249–50

Ji Shao, 57

Jianwen, Emperor (Ming), 172

Jin, ancient state of, 49

Jin dynasty (China; 1115–1234), 184

Jin dynasty, Western and Eastern (China; 265–316, 317–420), 49, 51, 249, 250, 251

Jing Ke, 57

Journal in Japan (*Riben riji*). *See* Luo Sen

journalism, 136; vernacular, 103

Journey to the West (*Xi you ji*), 189

judgment: aesthetic, 8, 9, 10, 64, 81, 165–66; and morality, 130, 166, 173; political, 81

Jurchens, 83

justice, 13, 130, 168, 170, 183–84, 230, 235, 286; against imperialism, 42, 61, 79, 97–98; as *yi/gi/ŭi* (righteousness), 30, 52, 55, 118, 171

Kabo Reforms (1894–1895), 72, 101, 102

Kang Youwei, 4, 21, 23, 25, 43, 206, 292n12, 302n5, 305n46, 344n2

Kanō school, 231

Kant, Immanuel, 8, 305n63

Karatani Kōjin, 165; *Origins of Modern Japanese Literature*, 6, 7, 293n22

Kataoka Teppei, 209–10

Kawabata Yasunari, 338n10

Key, Ellen, 145

Key Technologies of People's Livelihood (*Qimin yaoshu*), 226

Kikuchi Sankei, 30, 299n32

Kim Busik, 84, 85. *See also History of the Three Kingdoms*

Kim Chil, 171

Kim Chongsŏ, 170

Kim Ch'unch'u (Silla), 82

Kim Hongjip, 33

Kim Okkyun, 32, 100

Kim Saryang: as colonial writer, 244–46, 266–67; *Into the Light* (book; *Hikari no nakani*), 271; and Long Yingzong, 244–48, 262, 265, 271, 282; and Lu Xun, 246–47, 271, 272, 276–77, 282; *My Hometown* (book; *Kokyō*), 272; parody in, 276–77; repetition in, 281; self-translation by, 246, 266–67, 271–82; transcolonial correspondence by, 244–48, 262, 271; on translation, 266–67, 281–82. *See also* "Count Q"; "Into the Light" (short story); "Man Whom I Met in a Detention Cell, A"

Kim T'aekyŏng, 34, 35, 200, 300n48, 301n49, 329n8

Kim Tong'in, 144

Kim Yunsik (1835–1922), 31, 100, 299n37

kingly way (*wangdao*; *ōdō*), 204, 205, 206, 251. *See also* hegemon way

Kiyama Hideo, 222

KMT (Kuomintang), 206, 247

Kodama Gentarō, 199–200

Koguryŏ (Korea), 81–88, 89, 90, 91, 310n53

Kōhōsho (bureau of propaganda and censorship; Manchukuo), 239

kōminka, 202–3, 330n21. *See also* Japanization

Korea: Japanese imperialism in, 72–73, 200, 202–5; language reforms in, 100–102; modernized relationship with China of, 31–32, 33–34; modernized relationship with Japan of, 32–33; opening to the West of, 26–27. *See also* Korean language; Korean literature; *particular dynasties and states*

Korea Daily (*Chosŏn ilbo*), 95, 167

Korea Daily News (*Taehan maeil sinbo*), 33, 72, 310n42

Korea-China Commerce Treaty (1899), 31

Korea-Japan Treaty of Amity (1876), 26, 31, 32

Korean Artistic Theater (Chōsen geijutsu za), 245

Korean language: and bilingualism, 267, 271, 280–81; imperial suppression of, 202–3, 238; and loanword translation, 101, 312n8; mixed-style writing (*kuk'anmun honyong ch'e*) of, 33, 100–101, 102, 307n14, 309n42, 312n5, 312n8; national writing (*kungmun*) of, 73–74, 101–2, 152; and nationalism, 280–81; reforms of, 100–102; as represented in Japanese, 271, 272–73, 277–82; vernacularization of, 100–102. *See also* Korean script

Korean literature: colonial, 198, 238–40, 245–48, 266–67, 280–81; as conceptualized by Kim Saryang, 266–67; as conceptualized by Yi Kwangsu, 12–13, 143; modern discourse on, 5–7, 107–8; and transcolonial exchanges, 240–41, 245–47, 248. *See also particular authors and works*

Korean Provisional Government (Shanghai), 94–95

Korean script: and Chinese script, 33, 100–101, 102, 307n14, 309n42, 312n5, 312n8; *hangul*, 33, 90, 101, 152–53, 279, 280; reforms of, 101–2; in translations, 33, 90, 279, 280, 307n14, 310n42.

"Korean Soul, The" ("Chosŏn hon"). *See* Ch'oe Sŏkha

Korea-U.S. Amity and Trade Treaty (1882), 26

Koryŏ, 81, 84, 88, 91

Kossuth, Lajos, 76, 309n24

Kōtoku Shūsui, 95

Kōyama Iwao, 332n4

Index 395

Kropotkin, Peter, 95, 145
Kwon, Nayoung Aimee, 343n110
Kwon Ram, 171–72, 173

language game, 120, 288
language reform, 14, 18, 99–110, 311n2; in China, 102–5; and classical Chinese letters, 99, 100, 103, 105, 106, 107; and cultural hegemony, 99–100; in Japan, 105–7; in Korea, 100–102; and Manchukuo, 252–53; and modern literature, 107–8; and script, 101–2, 104–5, 105–6, 109; and vernacular, 100–101, 103–4, 106–7. *See also* national language
Lao-Zhuang thought, 249
Laozi, 192–94
"Last Testament of Okitsu Yagoemon" ("Okitsu Yagoemon no isho"). *See* Mori Ōgai
League of Leftist Writers, 247
"Leaving the Pass" ("Chu guan"). *See* Lu Xun
Lee, Leo Ou-fan, 117, 323n7
letters: Chinese, 11–12, 13, 19, 25, 30, 42, 44, 57, 103, 106, 132, 133; in East Asia, 7, 11, 12, 15, 35, 44, 57, 71, 76, 99, 105, 150, 198, 212, 223, 286; and ghost, 195, 219–20; Japanese imperialism's recycling of Chinese, 198, 199, 212, 223; as mediating translation, 23, 24, 37–38, 42, 44, 47–54, 57, 59, 61, 64, 66, 71, 75–77, 78–81, 160; vs. modern culture, 99, 100, 103, 105, 106, 107, 108–9, 113; world of Chinese, 107
Li, Lady, 57
Li Bai, 150
Li Hongzhang, 309n24
Li Jing, 134–35

Li Ruoshui, 57
Li Shangyin: "Three Poems on Lady Li" ("Li furen san shou"), 57
Li Shimin, 135
Liang Qichao: and aesthetic education, 63–64; "Discourse on the New People" ("Xin min shuo"), 39; editing of periodicals by, 23–24, 33–34, 39–41; exile of, 21, 23–24, 33, 37, 65, 80–81; and Hundred Days' Reform, 21, 23, 70; on Japanese language, 43; and Japanese materials, 23–24, 24–25, 37–39, 43, 70, 301n1, 306n4; Korean engagement with, 24, 33–34, 69–72, 74–76; *New Fiction* (*Xin xiaoshuo*; ed. by), 39, 40–41, 65; on new fiction, 39–41, 303n12; "On the Relationship between Fiction and the Governance of Society" ("Lun xiaoshuo yu qunzhi zhi guanxi"), 39–40, 73–74; and political fiction, 39–40, 65–68, 95; "Preface to Political Fiction in Translation" ("Yi yin zhengzhi xiaoshuo xu"), 39, 73–74; and Sin Ch'aeho, 34, 71–72, 73–74, 75–81, 94; and translation, 23–24, 33, 37, 39, 42, 45–54, 54–61, 73, 301n1; and Vietnam, 74, 302n5; "Where Is the Chinese Soul?" ("Zhongguo hun an zai hu"), 69–70. *See also Biographies of the Three Heroes of Italian Nation-Building, The* (Liang Qichao); *Chance Meetings with Beautiful Women*; *China Discussion*; *Future of New China, The*; *New People's Journal*
Lin Xie, 103
Literary Capital (*Bungei shuto*), 245

literary field, 240, 241, 244, 245, 257, 259, 266, 280, 281
Literary Mind, The, and the Carving of Dragons (*Wenxin diaolong*). See Liu Xie
literature: comparative, 15–16; historicization of, 5–7, 195; of the masses, 113–14; modernity of, 5–10; redefinition of, 12–13, 107–10; revolution of, 195, 216–17, 253; third-world, 119, 317n24; as translated notion, 7–8, 12–13, 108–9, 110, 113–14, 156, 317n24; of weak nations, 240–41; as *wenxue/bungaku/munhak*, 7–8, 12–13, 108–9, 113–14, 293n25, 314n44. *See also* colonial literature; literary field; modern literature; *literatures of particular countries*
Liu Shan, Emperor (Shu), 308n21
Liu Shipei, 103, 104
Liu Xie: *The Literary Mind and the Carving of Dragons* (*Wenxin diaolong*), 308n23
"Locality and Literature" ("Difang yu wenyi"). *See* Zhou Zuoren
Long Yingzong: "Caricature of Madame Zhao" ("Chō fujin no giga"), 260–61; as colonial writer, 245–46, 257–58; critical realism in, 257, 259–61, 261–62; "Evening Moon" ("Yoizuki"), 246, 262–66; and Kim Saryang, 244–48, 262, 265, 271, 282; and Lu Xun, 247, 259, 261–62, 264–65; as "Taiwan's Lu Xun," 246; transcolonial correspondence by, 244–48, 262, 271; "Village with Papaya Trees, A" ("Papaiya no aru machi"), 245, 247, 258–60, 261–62

Looking Backward: 2000–1887. *See* Bellamy, Edward
Louverture, Toussaint, 42
loyalism/loyalty, 41–42, 49, 51, 52, 54, 56–57, 62, 76, 147, 151, 168, 170, 174, 175, 176–77, 179, 182–83, 204
Lu Xun (Zhou Shuren): "After Death" ("Si hou"), 1–5, 20–21, 287, 291n3, 344n2; "Amateur Talk on Literature" ("Menwai wentan"), 108–9, 113–14; beyond East Asia, 339n26; *Call to Arms* (*Nahan*), 188; "Diary of a Madman" ("Kuangren riji"), 115–18, 120, 124, 126, 153, 247; and *Dream of the Red Chamber*, 189–90; and folk culture, 114, 130, 255–56, 316n8; and Gu Ding, 249–51, 252–53, 255–56; historical fiction by, 163–65, 186–94; "Hung Woman" ("Nüdiao"), 255–56; "Impermanence" ("Wuchang"), 130; in the Japanese empire, 244; and Kim Saryang, 246–47, 271, 272, 276–77, 282; "Leaving the Pass" ("Chu guan"), 191–94; and Long Yingzong, 247, 259, 261–62, 264–65; and "Manchuria's Lu Xun," 247; "Mending Heaven" ("Bu tian"), 187–91; on modern literature, 2–4, 108–9, 113–14; "My Hometown" ("Guxiang"), 247, 252, 259, 262; and myth/mythology, 126, 127–28, 129, 186–87, 190; "New Year's Sacrifice" ("Zhu fu"), 125–30, 264–65; *Old Stories Retold* (*Gushi xinbian*), 164–65, 186–94, 287, 323n7; "On the Power of Mara Poetry" ("Moluo shili shuo"), 2–3; parody in, 117, 118–19, 119–26, 129–30; "Real Story of Ah Q, The" ("A Q zhengzhuan"), 118–25, 126, 246, 247, 259, 261–62, 272, 276;

Index 397

Lu Xun (Zhou Shuren) (*continued*)
and redefining "literature," 108–9, 113–14; repetition in, 125, 129, 130, 189, 190; "Resurrection" ("Qi si"), 287–90; and "Taiwan's Lu Xun," 246; and translation, 113, 224; "Voiceless China" ("Wusheng de Zhongguo"), 109, 252; "Warrior and the Flies" ("Zhanshi he cangying"), 291n3; "Wei-Jin Period's Spirit and Writing and Their Relationship to Drugs and Wine" ("Wei-Jin fengdu ji wenzhang yu yao ji jiu zhi guanxi"), 249–51. See also *Collection of Short Stories from Beyond Borders*

Lukács, Georg: and historical fiction in modern East Asia, 163, 164, 166, 169, 174, 182, 195–96, 323n1; on the historical novel, 163–64; on the novel, 59

Luo Binwang, 57

Luo Sen, 29–30; *Journal in Japan* (*Riben riji*), 29

lyricism/lyrical, 44, 51, 54, 57, 66, 138, 160

Ma Zhiyuan: *Autumn in the Han Palace* (*Han gong qiu*), 57

Macaulay, Thomas Babington, 58

madness, 59, 116–17, 259

Maeda Ai, 42, 303n17

Maejima Hisoka, 105–6

Makers of Modern Italy, The: Mazzini, Cavour, Garibaldi, Three Lectures Delivered at Oxford. See Marriott, John

"Man Whom I Met in a Detention Cell, A" ("Yuch'ijang esŏ mannan sanai"; Kim Saryang), 246, 271–82; Japanese translation of, 246, 271–72, 277–81. See also "Count Q"

Manchukuo (Manchuria; Northeast China), 211; anti-Japanese organizations in, 95; Japanese imperialism in, 197, 205–6, 238–40; and Koguryŏ, 87–88; Korean migration to, 273–74; literature of, 20, 238–40, 247–48, 249–57, 282, 338n10; Lu Xun introduced to, 249, 251–53; Sin Ch'aeho in, 89; writing in, 252–53

Manchurian Incident (1931), 239, 244, 247

"Manifesto of Korean Revolution" ("Chosŏn hyŏngmyŏng sŏn'ŏn"). See Sin Ch'aeho

March First Movement (1919), 95, 167, 175, 204

Marco Polo Bridge Incident (1937), 211

Marriott, John: *Makers of Modern Italy, The: Mazzini, Cavour, Garibaldi, Three Lectures Delivered at Oxford*, 76, 77–79

Maruyama Masao, 205, 331n30

Mary, Queen of Scots, 58

Matsuo Bashō, 335n78

May Fourth Movement (1919), 122, 213, 244; and literary revolution, 195, 216–17, 253; and vernacularization, 114, 202, 253

Mazzini, Giuseppe, 75, 78, 80

medicine: and Lu Xun, 113, 115, 116; and Mori Ōgai, 109, 113, 138, 142–43; and narrative, 115, 116

medium, 211; affective, 74, 75, 76, 94, 160; classical Chinese writing as, 11, 106, 223; and history, 167, 187; Japanese as, 43, 62; Korean as, 101;

literature as, 10, 39, 41, 65, 74, 75, 76, 94, 117, 167, 187, 222, 223, 262, 269, 276, 281, 282, 283; modern print, 5, 38, 73, 100, 103, 106
Mei Ding'e, 248
Meiji Constitution (1889), 38, 39, 78
Meiji Restoration (1868), 26, 28; and civil wars, 41; legitimacy of, 52, 184–85; as model, 100; opponents of, 182–83
melancholy, 89, 93, 144, 147, 185, 243, 244; *jimo* as, 236–37
melodramatic mode: and satire, 260–61; and Yi Kwangsu, 152, 168–69, 174–75, 176, 186, 195, 324n20
Memoir of Zhitang (*Zhitang huixianglu*). See Zhou Zuoren
"Memorial on Sortie" ("Chushi biao"; "Ch'ul sa p'yo"). See Zhuge Liang
Mencius, 30
Mencius, the, 43, 147, 204, 213, 298n26, 321n109, 329n10
"Mending Heaven" ("Bu tian"). See Lu Xun
Mickiewicz, Adam, 3
Middle East, 60
Ming dynasty (China), 2, 4, 31, 231; civil service examinations in, 216–17; criticism in, 215; loyalists to, 42, 52, 56–57; vernacular fiction in, 11, 30, 40, 51, 304n37
Minor Learning (*Sohak*), 156
"Miscellaneous Poems" ("Za shi"). See Cao Zhi
missionaries, 31, 104, 106, 297n7, 314n44
Miyake Setsurei, 329n12
modern literature: as aesthetic concept, 7–10; anachronism of, 2, 4, 5, 7, 8, 115, 131, 220, 221, 286; attempts at defining, 11–14, 108–10; as cross-cultural notion, 71–72, 118, 286; legitimization of, 107–8; and modernization, 11–14, 108–10; openness of, 7–9, 14–15, 87, 220, 284–85; origins of, 4, 5–7, 41, 61–62, 67, 70–71, 94, 217, 227, 237, 248, 282–83; universality of, 16, 65, 284–85; and world, 8, 284–85. *See also* Chinese literature; Japanese literature; Korean literature
modernization: and alienation, 147; and anachronism, 7, 71, 110, 176, 178; aporia of, 148, 151, 154, 186, 207; in China, 25, 102–5; and class, 129, 145, 149; critique of, 33; cultural, 7, 8, 12–15, 102, 110, 112, 117, 146–47, 174, 195, 197, 284–85; cultural rupture caused by, 2, 5, 24, 125, 162, 175, 185, 216, 217, 223, 284; dysfunctional, 256; fictionalized, 65–66; global process of, 10, 13–14, 24, 70, 77, 78, 137–38, 223; grand récit of, in East Asia, 19, 197–98, 243; of historiography, 295n51; institutional, 39, 146; interrelated, in East Asia, 27–34; in Japan, 25–26, 105–7, 176, 183; and Japanese imperialism, 197–98, 207; in Korea, 26–27, 100–102; of language, 100–107; as mystery, 77–81; political, 39, 40; residues of, 113; and self-transformation, 160; and sublime, 159
Mohe, 82, 83
Mongols, 83, 205, 221
mongyurok (dream record), 90–91
Morgan, Lewis H., 259
Mori Arinori, 105

Mori Kainan, 138, 200
Mori Ōgai: "Abe Family, The" ("Abe ichizoku"), 176–78; and aesthetics, 109–10, 165; "As If" ("Kano yōni"), 179–82; and classical Chinese letters, 132; "Dancing Girl, The" ("Maihime"), 130–38, 142; and historical fiction, 165–66, 175–86; "Last Testament of Okitsu Yagoemon" ("Okitsu Yagoemon no isho"), 176; on modern literature, 109–10; parody in, 136–37, 138, 140, 142–43; and *Plum in the Golden Vase*, 138–40; *Principles of Aesthetics* (*Shinbi kōryō*), 315n50; repetition in, 143; "Sahase Jingorō" ("Sahase Jingorō"), 178–79; and translation, 109–10, 113, 131, 135, 142–43, 315n50; "Tsuge Shirōzaemon" ("Tsuge Shirōzaemon"), 182–86; "Wild Geese" ("Gan"), 138–43
Morning Post (*Chenbao*), 118
Motoda Nagazane, 204–5
Mountain Soul: A Collection of Korean and Taiwanese Short Stories (*Shanling: Chaoxian Taiwan duanpian ji*). *See* Hu Feng
mourning, 144, 157–58, 160
"Mulian, the Play of" (folk play; "Mulian xi"), 114–15, 130
Munjong, King (Chosŏn), 167, 173
My Hometown (*Kokyō*). *See* Kim Saryang
"My Hometown" ("Guxiang"). *See* Lu Xun
"My Humble View on Japan III" ("Riben guankui zhi san"). *See* Zhou Zuoren
myth/mythology: and enlightenment, 126, 127–28, 129; and historical fiction in Lu Xun, 186–87, 190; and history, 179–82; and modernization, 71, 81, 129–30

Nagai Kafū, 232; "Appreciation of *Ukiyoe*" ("Ukiyoe no kanshō"), 228–31; and Zhou Zuoren, 229, 231–32
"Nail, The" (Grimm brothers), 141
naisen ittai, 267
Nakae Chōmin, 109
Nakajima Takahiro, 345n6
Nam Hyoon: *Biography of Six Ministers* (*Yuksin chŏn*), 169
Napoleon Bonaparte, 78, 82, 260, 309n24
Napoleon III, 78, 79
narrative, 45, 51, 53, 54, 57, 58, 59, 66, 80, 92, 115, 141, 164, 168, 169, 172, 173, 175, 179, 185, 188, 254, 293n22, 306n66; chasm in, 125, 129; classical form of, 134, 136, 139–40, 186, 189–90; closure in, 114, 117, 124, 125, 126, 129, 270; convoluted/meandering, 64, 144; devices for, 78, 90, 189; dream, 2, 71, 89, 90, 92, 93; as editing, 185; as experience, 157, 158, 160; explanatory, 170, 171, 172, 173; framework for, 116, 136, 256; imperial, 274; of impossibility, 148; insipid, 61; and irony, 115, 117; meta-, 168; of modernization, 32, 77, 78, 218, 243; of national history, 6, 218, 234, 285; nested, 132–33, 137, 276–77; point of view in, 122–23, 124, 125, 164, 168, 261, 268; prolonged/protracted, 64, 67, 158; repetition in, 129; self-conscious, 259–61, 262; of storytelling, 128–29; suspension of, 38, 42, 62, 65; and

400 *Index*

translation, 56; of travel, 33; *zhuan/den/chŏn* as, 76, 94, 120, 121. See also narrator; storytelling
narrator: detached, 129; dramatized, 126, 129, 141–42, 264, 271; in dream state, 129; educated, 126, 265, 267; emotional, 79; inadequate, 117, 126–28, 262–63, 271, 276; and reconstructing totality, 140, 142; regretful, 263–64, 275, 276; reliable, 123; self-reflection of, 120, 265; vulnerable, 126, 130; as witness, 78, 96. See also narrative
national essence (*guocui*; *kokusui*), 214–15, 216, 221, 223
"National Essence and Europeanization" ("Guocui yu ouhua"). See Zhou Zuoren
national language: and assimilation, 107; Chinese, 103–5, 194, 197, 215, 217; and classical Chinese writing, 100–7; as imperial language (i.e., Japanese), 200, 202, 278–79, 329n9; Japanese, 105–6; Korean, 100–102, 281; and language reform, 100–107; and modern literature, 5, 99, 109, 217. See also Chinese language; Japanese language; Korean language; Taiwanese language
nationalism, 69–70, 73, 76, 234, 268, 285–86; Asian, 205–6; and betrayal, 210–12; cultural, 19, 103, 104, 207, 212, 216, 222, 223, 235; and emotion, 54, 76, 94, 150; and history, 5–7, 14, 17, 72, 82–83, 88–89, 91, 92, 167, 179–82, 186; vs. imperialism, 212; and loyalism, 54; and national essence (*kokusui*; *guocui*), 214–15; of oppressed peoples/weak nations, 42, 52, 56, 57, 74, 240–41; and transnational solidarity, 42, 56, 57, 74; and virtue, 52, 54, 55, 150, 206

Nation's Friend (Kokumin no tomo), 131
Natsume Sōseki, 9, 109; *Theory of Literature (Bungaku ron)*, 9
Nelson, Horatio, 82, 310n47
New Accounts of the Tales of the World (Shishuo xinyu), 49, 249
New Citizen's Society (xin min hui), 210
New Dictionary in Shared Script (Dōbun shinjiten), 201
New Discourse on Reading History (Toksa sillon). See Sin Ch'aeho
New East Asian Order, 239–40
New Fiction (Xin xiaoshuo). See Liang Qichao
new fiction (*xin xiaoshuo*; *sin sosŏl*), 148; and aesthetic education, 62, 73–74; as ambivalent genre, 40, 68, 73; and classical aesthetics, 40–41, 73–74; and politics, 39–40, 62, 75; transregional circulation of, 73
New Journal of European Literature (T'aesŏ munye sinbo), 27
New Korea (Sin Taehan). See Sin Ch'aeho
New Magazine of Flowers and the Moon (Kagetsu shinshi), 138
new people, 3, 39, 63–64, 75, 234
New People's Association (sinmin hoe), 73, 88
New People's Journal (Xinmin congbao; ed. Liang Qichao): distribution in Korea of, 33–34
New Records of Fiction (Yuchu xinzhi), 138
New Taiwan People's Paper (Taiwan xinmin bao), 260

"New Year's Sacrifice" ("Zhu fu"). *See* Lu Xun
New Youth (*Xin qingnian*), 115
Nie Zheng, 57
Nietzsche, Friedrich, 2–4; *Thus Spoke Zarathustra*, 2–3, 116, 221
Nishi Amane, 321n110
Nishikawa Mitsuru, 337n3
Nishimura Tei, 107
Nishitani Keiji, 207, 332n37
Nogi Maresuke, 176, 178
Norway, literature of, 131. *See also* Ibsen, Henrik
nothingness, 63, 206–7
Nüwa, 187–91

Observations from a Journey to the West (*Sŏyu kyŏnmun*). *See* Yu Kilchun
Ogata Tsutomu, 178
Okakura Tenshin, 235, 336n96
Old Stories Retold (*Gushi xinbian*). *See* Lu Xun
On Evolution (*Tianyan lun*; Huxley). *See* Yan Fu
On Heroes, Hero-Worship, and the Heroic in History. *See* Carlyle, Thomas
"On Leaving Asia Behind" ("Datsu a ron"). *See* Fukuzawa Yukichi
"On Literary Revolution" ("Wenxue geming lun"). *See* Chen Duxiu
"On National Culture." *See* Fanon, Frantz
On the Aesthetic Education of Man. *See* Schiller, Friedrich
"On the Power of Mara Poetry" ("Moluo shili shuo"). *See* Lu Xun
"On the Relationship between Fiction and the Governance of Society"

("Lun xiaoshuo yu qunzhi zhi guanxi"). *See* Liang Qichao
Opium Wars (1839–1842, 1856–1860), 25, 27–28
Ordinances of Education (Korea), 202
ordinary, the: of language, 10, 117, 289; of life, 141, 232–34, 235, 236; of people, 213, 225, 232–34, 235, 236, 257
Orientalism/Orientalist, 14, 112
origin: anachronistic structure of, 6–7, 94, 217, 242–43; of modern literature, 4, 5–7, 41, 61–62, 67, 70–71, 94, 217, 227, 237, 248, 282–83; as rupture, 5–6; and Walter Benjamin, 242–43
Origins of Modern Japanese Literature. *See* Karatani Kōjin
Osaka Daily (*Ōsaka mainichi shinbun*), 211
Ōuchi Takao, 338n10
"Outline for the Guidance of Art and Literature" ("Geibun shidō yōkō"; Manchukuo), 239, 247
Ouyang Xiu, 298n24
overcoming the modern, 206, 332n37

Paekche (Korea), 82, 90–91
Pak P'aengnyŏn, 169, 170
Pak Ŭnsik, 34, 307n11
Palhae, 91
Pangmun guk (Korean publication bureau), 100
Panofsky, Erwin, 293n22
Parnell, Fanny, 42, 58
parody, 132, 144, 323n7; and cultural past, 97, 112, 117, 118–19, 119–26, 129–30, 136–37, 138, 140, 142–43, 154–55, 157–58, 160, 162, 189–90,

242, 276, 282; definition of, 111–12;
in folk culture, 114; of imperial
literature, 276–77; and repetition,
112, 125, 130, 143
Pasha, Enver, 309n24
Patriotism and Enlightenment
Movement (Korea), 73, 324n7
Peach Blossom Fan (*Taohua shan*), 40
People's Paper (*Minbao*; supplement of
Shenbao), 103
performativity, 18, 53, 85, 87, 118, 121,
165, 187, 191; of colonial identity,
269–70; exclusion by, 271
"Perhaps Love?" ("Ai ka"). *See* Yi
Kwangsu
Perry, Matthew C., 25, 29, 78
Peter the Great, 82
Petőfi, Sándor, 3
Phan Bội Châu, 74. *See also History of
the Fall of Vietnam*
Phan Châu Trinh, 302n5
pharmakon, 40, 74, 303n12
Philosophy of the Beautiful, The (*Die
Philosophie des Schönen*; Eduard
von Hartmann), 110; trans. Mori
Ōgai, 110, 315n50
physiognomy, 170, 268
Plum in the Golden Vase, The (*Jin ping
mei*), 138–40; and Mori Ōgai,
138–40
Plum Tree in the Snow (*Setchūbai*). *See*
Suehiro Tetchō
*Poems on Miscellaneous Aspects of
Japan* (*Riben zashi shi*). *See* Huang
Zunxian
"Poetic Exposition on the Western
Capital" ("Xidu fu"). *See* Ban Gu
poetry, 8, 27, 57, 87, 169, 228, 245, 264;
and anachronism, 163; as art, 8, 156;
ci, 67–68; classical Chinese, 29, 32,
34, 43, 44, 52–54, 64, 66, 84, 86, 138,
149–50, 159, 199, 200, 329n8;
exchanges of, 29, 32–33, 34, 44, 51,
52–54, 58, 66, 199, 200, 299n37,
300n48, 301n49; folk, 114; and
Japanese imperialism, 199–200;
Mara, 2–3; memory of, 50–51;
polysemy in, 86–87; precedents in,
52–54, 65–66; prose, 1–2, 287; of
resistance, 3; Satanic, 3; society for,
201; topos in, 58, 156; and voice of
the heart, 2–3; world, 3; *yuefu*, 159
political fiction/political novel, 17, 23,
37–40, 68, 73, 77, 81, 302n5; and
Liang Qichao, 39–40, 65; in Meiji
Japan, 37–39
Pollock, Sheldon, 15
polyphony, 154, 248
precedents, literary, 37, 42, 43, 44, 45,
49, 53, 54, 55, 56, 57, 58, 59, 60, 62,
64, 84, 101, 136, 156, 195
"Preface to Political Fiction in
Translation" ("Yi yin zhengzhi
xiaoshuo xu"). *See* Liang Qichao
Principles of Aesthetics (*Shinbi kōryō*).
See Mori Ōgai
print culture, 4, 151, 152
prize, literary, 145, 238, 245, 253, 258,
259, 266
"Problem of Chinese Thought, The"
("Zhongguo de sixiang wenti"). *See*
Zhou Zuoren
Public School Regulations (Taiwan),
200–201, 202
Pushkin, Alexander, 3
Puyi, Emperor (Qing; Manchukuo),
206

Qian Liqun, 255
Qin Hui, 184

Qin shihuang/First Emperor of China, 70, 191, 201, 298n24

Qing dynasty (China), 4, 21, 23, 25, 27–28, 31–32, 52, 60, 66, 68, 69–70, 72–73, 96–97, 100, 102–4, 113, 195, 206, 219, 222, 224, 238; civil service examination essays in, 199, 216–17; vernacular fiction in, 11, 30, 40, 51, 189, 304n37

Qiu Tingliang, 103

Qu Qiubai, 114

Qu Shisi, 52

race, 67, 270

racism, 52, 67, 240

Rancière, Jacques, 195

"Real Story of Ah Q, The" ("A Q zhengzhuan"). *See* Lu Xun

realism, 141, 187; colonial, 259, 260, 261, 262; critical, 257, 259–61, 261–62; critique of, 115, 127; fictional, 110, 127, 174; hyper-, 168, 169

Records of the Ancient Matters (*Kojiki*), 225, 233

Records of the Grand Historian (*Shiji*). *See* Sima Qian

Reform (*Kaizō*), 245, 259

Regulation of Schools (China), 104

"Remembering Tokyo" ("Huai Dongjing"). *See* Zhou Zuoren

renaissance (*fuxing*), 226

Renaissance, the, 230, 293n22

repetition, 18, 242; in Kim Saryang, 281; in Lu Xun, 125, 129, 130, 189, 190; in Mori Ōgai, 143; and parody, 112, 125, 130, 143; and translation, 143, 280–81; in Yi Kwangsu, 157–58, 160

Republican Revolution (1911), 104, 105, 119, 123, 217

resemblance, cross-cultural, 43, 80–81, 138, 224–25, 232, 233

"Resurrection" ("Qi si"). *See* Lu Xun

revolution, 77; and late-Qing vernacularization, 104; and Liang Qichao, 65, 306n70; in Manchukuo, 205; and Sin Ch'aeho, 94–97. *See also* America; France; literature; Republican Revolution

Ricci, Ronit, 15

Richard, Timothy, 306n66

Righteous Corps (ŭiyŏrdan), 95

Risorgimento, 77

Roland, Madame, 76

Romance of People's Rights: Swirling Sea of Feelings (*Minken engi: Jyōkai haran*). *See* Toda Gindō

Romance of the Western Bower (*Xixiang ji*), 40

Rome, ancient, 214, 224, 225, 226, 227; literature of, 131. *See also* Greece

Rousseau, Jean Jacques, 145

Ruan Ji, 249–50

Russia, 24, 66, 70, 135; literature of, 27, 113, 114, 116, 131, 224; in Manchukuo, 253. *See also particular authors*

Russo-Japanese War (1904–1905), 24, 201

"Sahase Jingorō" ("Sahase Jingorō"). *See* Mori Ōgai

Saigō Takamori, 309n24

Sasagawa Yūichi, 319n63

satire, 118–19, 124, 125, 145, 186–87, 209, 221, 253, 254, 256, 260, 261, 288, 289; of literature, 120, 193–94, 251–52

Satō Haruo, 132, 259

Saussy, Haun, 320n92

Schiller, Friedrich, 133; *On the Aesthetic Education of Man*, 62–64

scholar and beauty (*caizi jiaren*) romance, 43, 51, 133, 136, 156, 304n37
Schopenhauer, Arthur, 133
Scott, Walter, 163–64, 195
scripts: and civilization, 102; phonetic, 102, 103, 104–5, 105–6, 222, 253, 313n26; reforms of, 101–2, 104–5, 105–6, 109; regional circulation of, 11; shared (*tongwen*; *dōbun*; *tongmun*), 29, 70, 201–2, 204. *See also* Chinese script; Japanese script; Korean script
Second Sino-Japanese War (1937–1945), 19, 206, 224, 238
Second War of Italian Independence (1859), 78–79
Sejo, King (Chosŏn), 167
Seki Kenji, 29
Selection of Refined Writings (*Wen xuan*), 43
self-reflexivity, 9–10, 15, 38, 61–62, 94, 125, 129, 130, 137–38, 142, 154, 160, 195, 258, 260, 277, 282, 284
Self-Strengthening Movement (China), 25; as model, 100
self-transformation, 289; of literature, 7, 10, 144, 220; of the reader, 125, 158, 160, 161
semantic ambiguity, 17–18, 83, 87, 115, 117, 188, 246
semantic instability, 104
semantic openness, 8, 111, 241
Seoul Trimonthly Gazette (*Hansŏng sunbo*), 100
serialization, 23, 37, 39, 60, 65, 88, 95, 118, 138, 145, 146, 167, 260, 306n66, 310n42, 315n50
Seven Sages of the Bamboo Grove, 249–51
Shakespeare, William, 112, 145, 168

Shanghai News (*Shenbao*), 103
shared script/culture (*tongwen*; *dōbun*; *tongmun*). *See* scripts
Shelley, Percy Bysshe, 3
Shengjing Times (*Shengjing shibao*), 253
Shiba Shirō: and Freedom and People's Rights Movements, 38–39; and Liang Qichao, 23–24; and political fiction, 23–24, 38–39; and War of Aizu, 41, 52. *See also Chance Meetings with Beautiful Women*
Shimomura Sakujirō, 340n27
Shinto, 203, 206
Shun (sage king), 172, 174, 183
signification, 4, 87, 117–18, 153, 171, 187, 188, 241, 251, 255, 265–66
Silla (Korea), 82, 90, 92, 93
Sima Qian: *Records of the Grand Historian* (*Shiji*), 191, 192, 308n23
Sima Xiangru, 133–34, 134–35, 150, 156
Sima Zhao, 250
Sin Ch'aeho: "Admonition for the Authors of Recent Fiction in the National Script" ("Kŭn'gŭm kungmun sosŏl chŏja ŭi chuŭi"), 73–74; and affective education, 62, 147; and anarchism, 95–97; and Anarchist Association of Asia, 95; as editor of periodicals, 72–73, 95; exile of, 88–89, 95; "Grand Battles Between Two Dragons" ("Yong kwa yong ŭi daegyŏkchŏn"), 96–98; *Heavenly Drum* (*Ch'ŏn'go*; ed. by), 95; and hero biographies, 81–88; *History of Korea* (*Chosŏn sa*), 89, 95; *History of Korean Antiquity* (*Chosŏn sanggo sa*), 83; and Korean Provisional Government, 94–95; and Liang Qichao, 34, 71–72, 73–74,

Index 405

Sin Ch'aeho (continued)
75–81, 94; "Manifesto of Korean Revolution" ("Chosŏn hyŏngmyŏng sŏn'ŏn"), 95; on national history, 72, 82–83; *New Discourse on Reading History* (*Toksa sillon*), 82–83; and new fiction, 73–74; *New Korea* (*Sin Taehan*; ed. by), 95; and New People's Association (sinmin hoe), 73, 88; parody in, 97–98; and Patriotism and Enlightenment Movement, 73; and Righteous Corps (ŭiyŏrdan), 95; and translation, 71, 75–81. See also *Biographies of the Three Heroes of Italian Nation-Building, The* (Sin Ch'aeho); "Dream Heaven"; *Ŭlji mundŏk*

Sin Kisŏn, 72

Sin Kŏn, 337n3

Singapore, 219

Sinocentrism: and classical culture, 29–30, 70; and Korean historiography, 17, 71, 72, 82–83, 87, 88, 89, 90, 92–93, 94, 97; and modernization, 19, 29–30, 197; parody of, 97

Sino-Japanese Friendship and Trade Treaty (1871), 27

Sŏ Chaep'il, 100

social Darwinism, 32, 34, 61, 91

Society for Elevating Letters (yang wen hui; Taiwan), 199

Society for Unifying National Orthography (kungmun tongsik hoe), 102

Society for Unifying the Chinese Characters (kanji tōitsu kai), 201–2, 330n16

Socrates, 58

"Some Modest Proposals for the Reform of Literature" ("Wenxue gailiang chuyi"). See Hu Shi

"Song of Everlasting Sorrow" ("Chang hen ge"). See Bai Juyi

Sŏng Sammun, 169, 170, 171

Sŏnggyungwan (academy), 72

Songs of the Chu (*Chuci*), 43

Sources of Modern Chinese Literature (*Zhongguo xinwenxue de yuanliu*). See Zhou Zuoren

Spain, 41, 42, 47, 49, 51, 57, 77

Spring and Autumn Annals (*Chunqiu*), 2, 4, 49, 120, 138, 308n23, 344n2; Gongyang commentary to, 2, 4, 21, 292n12, 344n2; Zuo commentary to, 49, 120, 138, 308n23

State Ordinance on Primary School Education (Japan), 106

Stories of Love (*Qingshi*). See Feng Menglong

Story of Ch'unhyang (*Ch'unhyang chŏn*), 150

"Story of the Great Iron Awl" ("Datiezhui zhuan"), 138

"Story of the Guest with Curly Whiskers" ("Qiuranke zhuan"). See Du Guangting

"Story of Xiaoqing" ("Xiaoqing zhuan"), 138

storytelling, 38, 78, 141, 188; classical, 121, 149–50, 154; colonial, 263, 264, 265–66, 276; elliptic, 256; reenchanted, 128–30; story about, 128–29; Walter Benjamin on, 129. See also narrative

strange-tale fiction (*chuanqi*; *denki*), 132, 308n23

Strategies for Korea (*Chaoxian celüe*). See Huang Zunxian

Strenuous Flight (Fenfei). See Gu Ding
structures of feeling, 147, 150
Style (Zuofeng), 241
Su Wu, 211
Subaru (The Pleiades), 138
sublime, the, 3, 144, 158–60, 276, 322n144
Suehiro Tetchō: Plum Tree in the Snow (Setchūbai), 306n66
Suematsu Jirō, 300n44
Sui dynasty (China), 81–88, 134–35
Sun Yat-sen, 205–6, 251, 291n3
supplement, 57–58, 76, 79, 121–22, 189–90, 194, 204
Suyang, Grand Prince, 167, 169–73
Sweden, literature of, 131

Tachibana Shiraki, 205–6
T'aegŭk Scholarly Journal (T'aegŭk hakpo), 69
Tagore, Rabindranath, 145
Taiping Rebellion (1850–1864), 52
Taiwan: anarchists from, 95; and cultural China, 219; Japanese imperialism in, 24, 197, 198–202, 202–3, 203–4; Japanization in, 202–3, 238–39; Sin Ch'aeho in, 95. See also Taiwanese language; Taiwanese literature
Taiwan Daily (Taiwan nichinichi shinpō), 199
Taiwan New People's Journal (Taiwan xinmin bao), 260
Taiwanese language: brush talk in, 199; creole Chinese writing in, 202, 330n21; and Japanization, 238–39; and multilingual writing, 238; and Qing-era Mandarin, 199

Taiwanese literature: colonial, 198, 238–40, 245–48, 257–66; introduction of Lu Xun in, 244; and Japanization, 238–39; multilingual field of, 238; and transcolonial exchanges, 240–41, 245–47, 248. See also particular authors and works
Takeda Katsuyori, 178
Takeuchi Yoshimi, 188, 323n7
"Tale of the Peach Blossom Spring" ("Taohuayuan ji"). See Tao Yuanming
Tanaka, Stefan, 234
Tang, Xiaobing, 77
Tang dynasty (China), 82, 134–35, 146, 150, 159, 218, 226, 227, 308n23
Tanjong, King (Chosŏn), 167–75. See also Yi Kwangsu: Tragic Story of Tanjong, The
Tao Kangde, 211
Tao Yuanming: "Tale of the Peach Blossom Spring" ("Taohuayuan ji"), 51
Tarumoto Teruo, 27, 297n15
Theory of Literature (Bungaku ron). See Natsume Sōseki
Thornber, Karen, 15, 197–98
Three Heroes of Italian Nation-Building (Itarī kenkoku sanketsu). See Hirata Hisashi
"Three Poems on Lady Li" ("Li furen san shou"). See Li Shangyin
Three Principles of the People (Sun Yat-sen), 251
Thus Spoke Zarathustra. See Nietzsche, Friedrich
Toda Gindō: Romance of People's Rights: Swirling Sea of Feelings (Minken engi: Jyōkai haran), 38–39
Tōkai Sanshi. See Shiba Shirō
Tokugawa Ieyasu, 178–79

Index 407

Tokugawa shogunate (Japan), 25–26, 27–28, 29–30, 31, 41, 105, 176, 179, 183, 231; loyalists to, 41, 42, 52, 182–83

Tokutomi Roka: *Black Eyes and Brown Eyes* (*Kuroi me to chairo no me*), 304n23

Tongsŏng, King (Paekche), 90

Toyama Masakazu, 110

Toyotomi Hideyoshi, 31

Tragic Story of Tanjong, The (*Tanjong aesa*). See Yi Kwangsu

transcoloniality, 240–41, 243, 244, 283; and correspondence, 244–48, 262, 271; and intertextuality, 244–48; and railway, 276

transculturation, 8, 155–57, 197

translation: aesthetic, 65; altering original, 56–57, 60–61, 66, 305n46; Chinese as intermediary in, 27–28, 29, 31, 32–33, 34–35, 69–71, 73–81, 297n7, 302n5, 307n18; of Chinese materials into Korean, 33, 71, 75–81, 94; of classical Chinese into Korean, 160, 169; of classical into vernacular Chinese, 103–4; of classical Japanese literature into Chinese, 30, 225; and Gu Ding, 247, 341n44; Japanese as intermediary in, 31, 42–43, 76–79, 101, 113, 214, 240–41, 259, 299n39, 321n110; of Japanese materials into Chinese by Japanese, 30–31, 32, 299n32, 300n44; and Kim Saryang, 246, 266–67, 271–82; and Korean historiography, 90; and Liang Qichao, 23–24, 33, 37, 39, 42, 45–61, 73, 301n1; literal, 145–46, 281–82, 344n129; of "literature," 7–8, 12–13, 108–9, 110, 113–14, 156, 293n25, 317n24; loanword, 47, 101, 106, 108–9, 113, 214, 314n44; and Lu Xun, 113, 224; as mediated by classical letters, 23, 24, 37–38, 42, 44, 47–54, 57, 59, 61, 64, 66, 71, 75–77, 78–81, 160; between metropole and colonies, 200, 238, 239, 247, 267, 281, 337n3, 338n10; of mixed-style writing into *hangul*, 307n14, 309–10n42; and modernization, 25–27, 29, 32–33, 70, 100, 137; and Mori Ōgai, 109–10, 113, 131, 135, 142–43, 315n50; and repetition, 143, 280–81; self-, 246, 266–67, 271–82; and Sin Ch'aeho, 71, 75–81, 94; stiff, 281–82, 344n129; transcolonial, 240–41, 243–44; and transcription, 47, 85, 143, 200, 272, 279, 280, 320n92; of world literature, 27, 113, 297n15, 297n17; and Yan Fu, 34–35, 301n49; and Zhou Zuoren, 209, 211, 224, 225

transregionality: and comparative method, 2, 6, 14, 15, 16, 198, 284; and cultural contacts, 7, 11, 12, 14, 17, 27–34, 35, 39, 53, 61, 75, 76, 77, 112, 198, 227, 233, 237, 282; and world history, 14

travelogues, 29, 30, 31–32, 33

True Records of the Chosŏn Dynasty (*Chosŏn wangjo sillok*), 167

True Treasures of Old-Style Writing (*Komun chinbo*), 156

Tsu, Jing, 16

Tsubouchi Shōyō, 109, 110

Tsuge Masataka, 183–84, 185

"Tsuge Shirōzaemon" ("Tsuge Shirōzaemon"). See Mori Ōgai

Tu, Wei-ming, 219

Twenty-One Demands (1915), 225

U Imköl, 69
Ue Mukō, 138
ukiyoe (Japanese woodblock prints), 228, 231, 232
Ŭlji mundŏk, 17, 81–88, 96; in "Dream Heaven," 89–93
Ŭlji mundŏk (Sin Ch'aeho), 81–88, 89, 90, 94, 309n42, 310n52; engagement with Korean historiography of, 82–88
Ulysses (James Joyce), 112
unequal treaties, 25–26, 42
universality: of classical Chinese letters, 99, 105, 203–5, 212, 222; and Confucianism, 203–6, 223; and humanism, 19, 213–15, 235, 236; of ideas, 8, 15, 64, 66, 93, 220–21, 233; and Japanese imperialism, 203–5, 206–7, 212, 223; of modern literature, 16, 65, 284–85; and modernization, 14, 77; regional, 198. *See also* universalizing
universalizing, 16, 65, 130, 156, 296n56, 344n2
'Urābī Pasha, 42, 60
utopianism, 30, 42, 61, 64, 65, 67, 81, 150, 234, 257, 262; of great community (*datong*), 95, 206, 306n69; and imperial propaganda, 205, 206; and Peach Blossom Spring, 51, 54

Vaihinger, Hans: *Die Philosophie des Als Ob*, 181
Verhaeren, Émile, 229, 230; "Art Flamand," 228
Vernacular Renditions (*Yanyi baihuabao*), 103–4
Vernacular Society (baihua xuehui), 103
Vietnam, 74–75, 95, 286, 302n5, 307n14. See also *History of the Fall of Vietnam*

"Village with Papaya Trees, A" ("Papaiya no aru machi"). *See* Long Yingzong
virtue, 173, 174, 200, 203; and aesthetics, 59, 60, 61, 66, 67; classical, 13, 49, 51, 54, 55, 57, 61, 62, 116, 120, 147, 150, 151, 152, 155, 158, 170, 171, 174, 175, 176, 179, 181, 192, 204, 325n46, 330n23; vs. power, 60, 204; rule by, 204–5
voice: evoking cultural past with, 48–49, 50, 53–54, 86–87, 149–50, 160, 200; of the heart (*xinsheng*), 3; inarticulate, 273, 276, 277–78, 279–80, 281–; internal, 124, 269, 276; and literary medium, 10, 15, 18, 117, 124–25, 129–30, 160–61, 248, 266, 276–77, 281–82, 283, 286; and madness, 117; of the people, 3, 109; poetic, 1, 3, 34, 53–54, 200; prelinguistic, 281; sublimation of, 276; suppressed, 248, 258, 266, 275, 276–77, 283; and voicelessness, 14, 109, 124–25, 129–30, 154, 252–53, 262, 277; weak, 243, 271
"Voiceless China" ("Wusheng de Zhongguo"). *See* Lu Xun

"Wandering" ("Panghwang"). *See* Yi Kwangsu
Wang, David Der-wei (Wang Dewei), 41, 303n12
Wang, Jing, 189
Wang Changling, 150
Wang Dao, 48, 49, 57
Wang He, 244; *Collection of Korean Short Stories* (*Chaoxian duanpian xiaoshuo xuan*; ed. by), 241
Wang Hui, 130, 317n22
Wang Jingwei, 210, 211–12

Index 409

Wang Jingzhi, 327n87
Wang Tao, 28
Wang Yangming, 231, 336n87
Wang Zhaojun, 57
"Warrior and the Flies" ("Zhanshi he cangying"). *See* Lu Xun
Washington, George, 82, 309n24
"Wasteland" ("Yuanye"). *See* Gu Ding
Water Margin (*Shuihu zhuan*), 40, 114, 138, 139, 189, 308n23
Watsuji Tetsurō, 233
Wei dynasty (China), 45, 249, 250, 251, 308n21
"Wei-Jin Period's Spirit and Writing and Their Relationship to Drugs and Wine" ("Wei-Jin fengdu ji wenzhang yu yao ji jiu zhi guanxi"). *See* Lu Xun
Wellek, René, 9
West, the: aesthetics of, 109–10, 229–31; and Asia, 231–32; civilization of, 13–14, 19, 24–25, 35, 39, 102–3, 106, 198, 206, 223, 224, 226; and comparative literature, 15–16, 112, 284–85; competition with, 61, 67; vs. the East, 58, 259; East Asian diplomacy with, 28, 52, 182–83; engagement with East Asia of, 25–27, 35; gender norms in, 44; imperialisms of, 14, 28, 33, 42, 67, 197–98, 206, 207; vs. Japanese imperialism, 206–7, 223, 239–40; medicine from, 143; missionaries from, 104; and modern concept of "literature," 7–8, 12–13, 108–9, 113; political ideas from, 47, 65, 66–67; study in, 32, 89; translation of materials from, 25–27, 28, 31, 42–43, 70, 101, 106. *See also* Europe; Western literatures; Westernization, cultural; *particular countries*

Western literatures, 8, 12, 15–16, 27; authority of, 8, 137, 150–51; transculturation of, 8, 111, 116. *See also* Europe; *literatures of particular countries; particular authors and works*
Westernization, cultural, 91–92, 176; anti-, 214; critique of, 52, 145, 184, 206, 230–31; and transculturation, 155–57. *See also* Europeanization
"What Is Literature?" ("Munhak iran hao?"). *See* Yi Kwangsu
"Where Is the Chinese Soul?" ("Zhongguo hun an zai hu"). *See* Liang Qichao
Whitney, William Dwight, 105
Who's Who of Illustrious Subjects (*Myŏng sin nok*), 170
"Wild Geese" ("Gan"). *See* Mori Ōgai
Williams, Channing Moore, 106
Williams, Samuel, 29–30
Wolf, Christian, 321n110
world history, 14, 24, 32, 137–38, 235, 243
world literature, 15, 16, 284–85; engagement with, 27, 113; and modern literature, 7
world-historical mission (Japanese imperialism), 206, 210, 235, 243
Writings from the Burning Pigweed Studio (*Yŏllyŏsil kisul*), 167
Wu, Emperor (Han), 57, 191
Wuxi Vernacular Paper (*Wuxi baihuabao*), 103

Xianbei, 83
Xie Lingyun, 53; "Imitating the Poems of the Wei Crown Prince's Gathering at Ye" ("Ni Wei taizi Yezhong ji"), 52–53, 54

Xu Fu, 29, 298n24
Xuanzong, Emperor (Tang), 57

Yamada Seizaburō, 338n10
Yan Fu, 34, 300n48, 301n49; *On Evolution* (*Tianyan lun*; Huxley; trans. by), 34, 35
Yang, Emperor (Sui), 82, 83, 84, 90, 91, 134
Yang Guifei, 57
Yang Shoujing, 28
Yang Su, 134
Yano Ryūkei: *The Beautiful Story of Statesmanship* (*Keikoku bidan*; trans. as *Jingguo meitan*), 37, 301n2
Yao (sage king), 172, 174, 183
Yao Wendong, 28
Yi Chaesŏn, 31
Yi Kwangsu: and colonial literature, 337n3; "Devotee" ("Hŏnsinja"), 147; *Heartless, The* (*Mujŏng*), 143–46, 148–60, 161, 174, 322n144; parody in, 154–55, 157–58, 160; "Perhaps Love?" ("Ai ka"), 146, 147; on redefining "literature," 12–13, 108; repetition in, 157–58, 160; *Tragic Story of Tanjong, The* (*Tanjong aesa*), 166, 167–75; "Wandering" ("Panghwang"), 146; "What Is Literature?" ("Munhak iran hao?"), 12–13, 108; "Yun Kwangho" ("Yun Kwangho"), 146–47
Yi Sunsin, 81, 310n42, 310n47
Yin Xi (Wenshi xiansheng), 192–93
Yiwen Publishers. *See* Gu Ding
Yokoi Shōnan, 182–84
Yongle, Emperor (Ming), 172
Yŏp Kŏn'gon, 69
Young Germany, 136
Youth (*Ch'ŏngch'un*), 146

Yu (sage king), 172
Yu Kilchun, 32, 100, 101, 200, 300n48, 330n16; and Japan, 32; and Kim T'aekyŏng, 34; *Observations from a Journey to the West* (*Sŏyu kyŏnmun*), 32, 299n39, 312n8
Yu Ŭngbu, 169
Yu Zhongwen, 84, 86
Yuan, Emperor (Han), 57
Yun Ch'iho, 100
"Yun Kwangho" ("Yun Kwangho"). *See* Yi Kwangsu
Yuwen Shu, 84

Zhang, Xudong, 219
Zhang Jian, 34
Zhang Liang, 172
Zhang Taiyan, 193, 202
Zhang Yang, 172
Zhang Zhidong, 330n16
Zheng Guanying: *Discourse of Change* (*Yi yan*), 32–33
Zhou, Duke of, 172
Zhou dynasty (China), 192
Zhou Enlai, 210
Zhou Zuoren: and aesthetics, 215, 216, 222; apology of, 210; on Asia, 229–33, 235–36; "Clothing, Food, and Housing in Japan" ("Riben de yi shi zhu"), 225–27, 236; critique of Hu Shi by, 217–18; and Japanese imperialism, 209–12, 223; on Japanese language, 303–4n21; "Locality and Literature" ("Difang yu wenyi"), 220–21; *Memoir of Zhitang* (*Zhitang huixianglu*), 210; on modern literature, 217–20, 220–21; "My Humble View on Japan III" ("Riben guankui zhi san"), 236–37; "National Essence and

Zhou Zuoren (*continued*)
   Europeanization" ("Guocui yu ouhua"), 215–16; "Problem of Chinese Thought, The" ("Zhongguo de sixiang wenti"), 209–10, 212, 213; "Remembering Tokyo" ("Huai Dongjing"), 227–28, 229, 232; on Sino-Japanese cultural relationship, 224–30, 231–37; *Sources of Modern Chinese Literature* (*Zhongguo xinwenxue de yuanliu*), 217–20; and translation, 209, 211, 224, 225. See also *Collection of Short Stories from Beyond Borders*

Zhu Xi, 206

zhuan/den/chŏn (biography, story): classical, 83–84, 85, 121, 132, 135, 138, 308n23, 324n7; and history, 78, 79, 121, 308n23; modern adoption of, 71, 76, 77, 81, 94, 119–22, 123, 132; parody of, 119–22, 123; as supplement, 79, 94, 121; transnational circulation of, 76. *See also* biographies

Zhuangzi, the, 43; butterfly dream in, 290; and Lu Xun, 192, 287–90; on making all things equal (*qiwu*), 288–90, 345n6

Zhuge Liang, 172, 308n21; "Memorial on Sortie" ("Chushi biao"; "Ch'ul sa p'yo"), 75–76

Zhuo Wenjun, story of, 132–35; in *Heartless*, 150; and Mori Ōgai, 132–35, 319n63

Zola, Émile, 131–32

STUDIES OF THE WEATHERHEAD EAST ASIAN INSTITUTE
COLUMBIA UNIVERSITY

Selected Titles
(Complete list at: weai.columbia.edu/content/publications)

Building a Republican Nation in Vietnam, 1920–1963, edited by Nu-Anh Tran and Tuong Vu. University of Hawai'i Press, 2022.

China Urbanizing: Impacts and Transitions, edited by Weiping Wu and Qin Gao. University of Pennsylvania Press, 2022.

Common Ground: Tibetan Buddhist Expansion and Qing China's Inner Asia, by Lan Wu. Columbia University Press, 2022.

Narratives of Civic Duty: How National Stories Shape Democracy in Asia, by Aram Hur. Cornell University Press, 2022.

The Concrete Plateau: Urban Tibetans and the Chinese Civilizing Machine, by Andrew Grant. Cornell University Press, 2022.

Confluence and Conflict: Reading Transwar Japanese Literature and Thought, by Brian Hurley. Harvard East Asian Monographs, 2022.

Inglorious, Illegal Bastards: Japan's Self-Defense Force During the Cold War, by Aaron Skabelund. Cornell University Press, 2022.

Madness in the Family: Women Care, and Illness in Japan, by H. Yumi Kim. Oxford University Press, 2022.

Uncertainty in the Empire of Routine: The Administrative Revolution of the Eighteenth-Century Qing State, by Maura Dykstra. Harvard University Press, 2022.

Outsourcing Repression: Everyday State Power in Contemporary China, by Lynette H. Ong. Oxford University Press, 2022.

Diasporic Cold Warriors: Nationalist China, Anticommunism, and the Philippine Chinese, 1930s–1970s, by Chien-Wen Kung. Cornell University Press, 2022.

Dream Super-Express: A Cultural History of the World's First Bullet Train, by Jessamyn Abel. Stanford University Press, 2022.

The Sound of Salvation: Voice, Gender, and the Sufi Mediascape in China, by Guangtian Ha. Columbia University Press, 2022.

Carbon Technocracy: Energy Regimes in Modern East Asia, by Victor Seow. University of Chicago Press, 2022.

Disunion: Anticommunist Nationalism and the Making of the Republic of Vietnam, by Nu-Anh Tran. University of Hawai'i Press, 2022.

Learning to Rule: Court Education and the Remaking of the Qing State, 1861–1912, by Daniel Barish. Columbia University Press, 2022.

Art Across Borders: Japanese Artists in the United States Before World War II, by Ramona Handel-Bajema. Merwin Asia, 2021.

GPSR Authorized Representative: Easy Access System Europe, Mustamäe tee 50, 10621 Tallinn, Estonia, gpsr.requests@easproject.com

www.ingramcontent.com/pod-product-compliance
Lightning Source LLC
Chambersburg PA
CBHW031228290426
44109CB00012B/204